Presence, Prevention, and Persuasion

Presence, Prevention, and Persuasion

*A Historical Analysis of
Military Force and Political Influence*

Edward Rhodes
Jonathan M. DiCicco
Sarah S. Milburn
Thomas C. Walker

LEXINGTON BOOKS
Lanham • Boulder • New York • Toronto • Oxford

LEXINGTON BOOKS

Published in the United States of America
by Lexington Books
An imprint of The Rowman & Littlefield Publishing Group, Inc.
4501 Forbes Boulevard, Suite 200, Lanham, Maryland 20706

PO Box 317
Oxford
OX2 9RU, UK

Copyright © 2004 by Lexington Books

All rights reserved. No part of this publication may be reproduced, stored in a retrieval system, or transmitted in any form or by any means, electronic, mechanical, photocopying, recording, or otherwise, without the prior permission of the publisher.

British Library Cataloguing in Publication Information Available

Library of Congress Cataloging-in-Publication Data

Presence, prevention, and persuasion : a historical analysis of military force and political influence / Edward Rhodes . . . [et al.] . .
    p. cm.
Includes bibliographical references and index.
  ISBN 0-7391-0726-7 (cloth : alk. paper)
  1. Military policy. 2. Armed Forces. 3. International relations. 4. Military history—19th century. 5. Military history—20th century. 6. World politics—19th century. 7. World politics—20th century. I. Rhodes, Edward, 1959–
  UA11. p64 2003
  327.1'17—dc22

                                                                               2003016537

Printed in the United States of America

∞™ The paper used in this publication meets the minimum requirements of American National Standard for Information Sciences—Permanence of Paper for Printed Library Materials, ANSI/NISO Z39.48-1992.

Contents

	List of Tables	vii
	Acknowledgements	ix
	Introduction: Military Power and Peacetime "Shaping" *Edward Rhodes*	1
Chapter 1	A Sword Half Withdrawn from the Scabbard: The Royal Navy and British "Shaping" of the Eastern Mediterranean and the Levant, 1816–1852 *Jonathan M. DiCicco*	13
Chapter 2	Decline, Disengagement, and Shaping the Periphery: Great Britain in the Eastern Mediterranean and the Levant, 1919–1937 *Jonathan M. DiCicco*	65
Chapter 3	A Shadow Cast from Afar: The Royal Navy in South America, 1850–1900 *Thomas C. Walker*	123
Chapter 4	The U.S. Navy in the Caribbean, 1903–1920 *Thomas C. Walker*	157

Chapter 5	*La Chasse Gardée*: Post–World War II French West Africa, 1945–1970 *Sarah S. Milburn*	197
Chapter 6	*Toujours la Chasse Gardée?* French Power and Influence in Late-Twentieth-Century Francophone Central Africa, 1970–1995 *Sarah S. Milburn*	281
Chapter 7	Conclusions *Edward Rhodes*	377
	Appendix: Summary of Cases	407
	Bibliography	421
	Index	437
	About the Authors	449

Tables

Table 1.1	British Relative Sea Power, 1815–1855	18
Table 1.2	Army Sizes of European Powers, in Thousands, 1810–1854	37
Table 2.1	Royal Navy Fleet Strength, 1919–1939	70
Table 2.2	International Crises in the Eastern Mediterranean/Levant, 1919–1939	88
Table 2.3	British Gunboat Diplomacy in the Mediterranean, 1919–1939	89
Table 3.1	Royal Navy Vessels in South America, 1821–1890	126
Table 5.1	African Defense Forces, 1967	210
Table 5.2	French-Trained African Officers, 1961–1973	212
Table 5.3	Arms Transfers to Francophone African Countries, 1960–1969	250
Table 6.1	French Military Advisers in Central Africa, 1980 and 1988	287
Table 6.2	Sizes of Selected African Armed Forces in 1983	288

| Table 6.3 | Relative Magnitude of Armed Forces and Defense Spending, 1994 | 288 |
| Table 6.4 | Arms Transfers to Francophone African Countries, 1970–1989 | 337 |

Acknowledgments

The arguments and conclusions advanced in this volume are the authors' alone. Opinions expressed by the authors should not be attributed to any institution with which any of the authors may now have or may in the past have had any affiliation or association. No institution has exercised editorial control or influence over this volume or the material it contains. The authors had no access to classified documents or materials in the preparation of this study. The authors accept sole responsibility for the contents of this volume and for any errors of fact, interpretation, or judgment it may contain.

The authors do wish, however, to express their gratitude to the individuals and organizations whose support made this study possible. This volume grew out of ongoing discussions between Edward Rhodes and Dr. Mark Montroll of the National Defense University. Dr. Montroll's advice in designing this study was invaluable. All four authors are grateful to Dr. Montroll for his encouragement of this research, for his critical scrutiny of the arguments and evidence presented in this volume, and for his assistance in arranging the support that made this study possible.

The research presented in this volume was conducted under the auspices of Rutgers University's Center for Global Security and Democracy, which was under contract with the Naval Surface Warfare Center Carderock Division. The authors gratefully acknowledge both this direct support and the indirect source of this support: Dr. Andrew Marshall, his staff, and the Department of Defense's Office of Net Assessment. Typesetting costs for this volume were borne by the National Defense University, again thanks to the support of Dr. Marshall and the Office of Net Assessment.

The authors also gratefully acknowledge the support of Rutgers University, the Rutgers University Research Council, Rutgers College, the Rutgers University Department of Political Science, and, of course, the Rutgers University Center for Global Security and Democracy.

Edward Rhodes also wishes to acknowledge the discussions that initially drew the authors' attention to the questions that this volume addresses, and to express appreciation to the individuals in those discussions and to the organizations that made possible his participation in them. As an International Affairs Fellow of the Council of Foreign Relations, Rhodes served on the U.S. Navy Staff in the Strategy and Concepts Branch (N513) of the Office of the Chief of Naval Operations. N513 was at that time commanded by Captain Joseph Bouchard, and included Commanders Richard Kikla, Frank Pandolfe, and David Spain. Their concerns, and those of Captain Edward Smith, Jr. of the Chief of Naval Operations's Executive Panel (N00K), were critical in stimulating this study. This volume also benefited from the authors' opportunity to present and argue their findings in a substantial number of venues, including the National Defense University and the Naval War College.

While the four authors assume joint responsibility for this volume, they acknowledge the division of labor that made its timely completion possible. Edward Rhodes was responsible for the overall research design, the case selection, and the introductory and concluding chapters. Jon DiCicco supervised the editing and production of the volume, prepared the tables, and authored the two chapters on Britain's activities in the Eastern Mediterranean. Tom Walker authored the chapters on British presence in Latin America and American involvement in the Caribbean. Sarah Milburn authored the two chapters on French activity in Africa.

Finally, the authors gratefully acknowledge the assistance of Serena Krombach, Megan Bradley, Robert Carley, and the editorial and production staff of Lexington Books, whose care, commitment, and professionalism made this volume possible.

Introduction

Military Power and Peacetime "Shaping"

EDWARD RHODES

The terrorist attacks of September 11, 2001 produced extraordinary consensus in the American elite and public on the need for U.S. action to destroy the political organizations responsible for these attacks and to create a global environment hostile to terrorism. While much of the United States's attention initially focused on the first of these objectives—the military campaign to destroy the Al-Qaeda network and bring down its protector, the Taliban government of Afghanistan—it is obviously the second of these objectives—creating an international order intolerant of global terrorism and, presumably, supportive of democratic and liberal institutions—that poses the greater challenge.

This second objective plainly goes beyond eliminating immediate threats and closing the books on the past by bringing the guilty to justice. This objective looks beyond the present and the past, to the future. In doing so, it embodies U.S. decision makers' conclusions regarding the prudential and, in some accounts, moral requirement to use American power proactively, to remake domestic and international political systems around the world before unacceptable threats to the security of America, to American values, or to the liberal, democratic international order embraced by the United States emerge, or when opportunities to restore humanity's natural birthright of freedom present themselves. Indeed, some of these potential threats—most obviously those "at the perilous crossroads of radicalism and technology," when tyrants or terrorists appear to be moving toward acquisition of meaningful capabilities to inflict mass destruction—would, American leaders have concluded, be of sufficient magnitude that preventive or preemptive war would be justified. This reasoning was clearly a major factor in the U.S. decision to undertake military action against Iraq in 2003.[1]

More broadly, however, this second objective involves what the American military in the 1990s came to describe as "shaping": using U.S. power, specifically America's overwhelming global military dominance, in an effort to change underlying political, cultural, social, or economic realities in ways consistent with American goals and interests. Even before the events of September 11, 2001, U.S. foreign and national security policy assumed that American security, broadly defined, required not only that the United States remain active on the world stage but that the United States do more than merely respond to crises or dangers as they arose (or, in peacetime, prepare for such crises and dangers), instead using its extraordinary power to shape the international environment. The objective of this "shaping" effort was to create the kind of peaceful, ordered world in which America wanted to live: to prevent crises from arising or spilling over into war and to create institutions or conditions that protected American interests (such as security and economic well-being) and strengthened values embraced by America (such as those embedded in liberal democracy). The effect of the destruction of the World Trade Center was not so much to shift American policy as simultaneously to focus it, to widen it, and dramatically to increase political commitment and resources devoted to it: since September 11, 2001, there has been a focusing of the American policy vision on creating an environment intolerant of terrorism and tyrants (rather than on the more diffuse task of creating an environment conducive to democracy and liberal economic development), a widening of policy vision to embrace the entire globe, and an acceptance of the political and economic costs of using American power—even without widespread international backing and prior to any direct attack on America or its allies. Proclaiming freedom "the birthright of every person—in every civilization,"[2] President George W. Bush has argued that the United States faces both a moral duty and prudential requirement to use its power preemptively, globally, and, if necessary, unilaterally to "defend the peace against threats from terrorists and tyrants" and to "extend the peace by encouraging free and open societies on every continent."[3]

Since the end of the Cold War, and even more explicitly since the events of September 11, 2001, the need to shape political development and influence the evolution of domestic and regional political institutions around the world has thus occupied a central position in U.S. thinking about foreign and security policy. While the greater willingness of President George W. Bush to use military force preventively has been widely noted, it should be clear that post-September 11 policies are broadly consistent with the policies pursued by his predecessors who, though with more reluctance and caution, also saw the need to use American overseas military deployments and interventions to move domestic and international political developments in directions sought by the United States. As the government bluntly explained in the late 1990s in the United States's National Security Strategy (the official statement of American national security policy), "shaping activities enhance U.S. security by promoting regional security and preventing or reducing . . . [a] wide range of diverse threats. . . . These measures adapt and strengthen alliances and friendships, maintain U.S. influence in key regions and encourage adherence to international norms."[4]

Plainly, this task of "shaping" a favorable international environment is not a purely military one, or necessarily even a predominantly military one. It necessarily involves diplomatic and economic carrots and sticks as well. As the National Security Strategy explains, "the United States has a range of tools at its disposal with which to shape the international environment in ways favorable to U.S. interests and global security."[5] Nonetheless, the military component of America's "shaping" efforts has been explicitly acknowledged and is understood as critical:

> The U.S. military plays an essential role in . . . shaping the international environment in ways that protect and promote U.S. interests. Through overseas presence and peacetime engagement activities such as defense cooperation, security assistance, and training and exercises with allies and friends, our armed forces help to deter aggression and coercion, promote regional stability, prevent and reduce conflicts and threats, and serve as role models for militaries in emerging democracies.[6]

Thus, throughout the post–Cold War period, U.S. defense planning has taken as a fundamental premise that the United States needs to act prophylactically, using its military power to shape the peacetime world, encouraging the emergence or preservation of political conditions that reduce the threat of violent challenges to order and that favor peace, prosperity, and democracy. As the U.S. National Military Strategy—the uniformed military's official statement of its objectives, plans, and preparations—explained back in the 1990s, "US Armed Forces help shape the international environment primarily through their inherent deterrent qualities and through peacetime military engagement. The shaping element of our strategy helps foster the institutions and international relationships that constitute a peaceful strategic environment by promoting stability; preventing and reducing conflict and threats; and deterring aggression and coercion."[7]

What has remained unclear, however, are the implications of this peacetime mission for U.S. force posture and defense strategy. What capabilities do U.S. military forces need to possess, and how ought they to be trained and deployed, if they are successfully to meet the challenge of "shaping the international environment in ways that protect and promote U.S. interests?" How can the peacetime presence of American military forces in regions around the world best be tailored to prevent the emergence of dangers to international order and to persuade leaders and societies to embrace the institutions and values integral to this order?

The use of American military forces to overthrow the Taliban government of Afghanistan and the occupation of Iraq by American military forces have given new urgency to these questions. It is apparent that the United States will, for the foreseeable future, be using its ongoing military presence and engagement around the world in an attempt to achieve an extraordinary transformation of global political life.

This study offers an answer to these questions based on a comparative historical investigation of the relationship between forward military presence and success in shaping political order. Examining and contrasting the experience of three democratic great powers—Britain, America, and France—as they attempted to shape outcomes in regions in which they enjoyed military predominance, we explore the particular military capabilities that appear to have given the great powers better (or worse) ability to shape regional political environments consistent with their desires.

Plainly the question posed—what features of military power are desirable if one wishes to use military presence in support of a peacetime political agenda—is a complex, difficult, and controversial one, and this study does not claim to provide conclusive, detailed, or highly nuanced answers. This is not—we hope—the final word on the subject. What we offer is the first cut at an explanation of what works and what does not. Our findings should be understood as a set of inductively derived and empirically grounded, but admittedly still speculative, propositions about what contributes to "shaping," which can be subjected to more rigorous testing.

Military Force and Political Influence

The importance of military power in wartime is self-evident. Winning wars, however, is only one of the functions of military forces. Military forces are also called upon to win the peace, creating or preserving political conditions consistent with national diplomatic, strategic, and economic objectives. Most obviously, in recent American history this peacetime role of military power has been evidenced in the demand that military forces deter potential adversaries from attacking the United States or its allies; during the Cold War, for example, American military forces were designed to dissuade the Soviet Union from even seriously considering aggression against the United States or its allies or a challenge to key U.S. interests. More broadly, however, American military power has been regarded as relevant in a wide range of efforts to influence both friends and enemies—reassuring friends that they can take the risk of embracing political and economic choices that are consistent with their own preferences and American visions, while convincing potential adversaries to rethink the goals or policies that brought them into conflict with the United States or to abandon or fundamentally change their national political or economic institutions in ways that will create a long-term basis for cooperative participation in American-embraced global institutions.

Indeed, in the post–Cold War period American policymakers have increasingly emphasized the relevance of American military power to the achievement of peacetime political goals. As already noted above, both the U.S. national security strategy and the U.S. military strategy have clearly underscored the role of American military power in "shaping" peacetime political environments in regions around the world. Indeed, in the 1990s U.S. military strategy was explicitly defined as one of "Shape, Respond, Prepare Now"—that is, as a strategy of using American military power to shape (the peacetime international political environment in ways favorable to American interests and global security), respond (to crises and wars), and prepare now (for the still uncertain threats of an evolving future).[8]

The clarity of this overarching strategy and of this commitment to use American military power in peacetime to mold a better world, however, masks profound uncertainty about how it is to be done and what specific resources or actions will be necessary. Determining the attributes of military forces that will contribute to a military victory during war, and how best to use these forces during war, is a difficult but conceptually straightforward problem: since war is "won" when the other side sues for peace or it ceases to possess the capacity to harm one's interests, a planner examines the capacities and vulnerabilities of the opposing military forces and political system and determines how best to achieve their collapse while shielding one's own population and political system against harm. Winning the peace, however, is more complicated than winning wars. American planning and peacetime operations proceed despite fundamental uncertainty about what qualities or attributes of military power contribute to the pursuit of peacetime political goals: what military capabilities enhance the ability of a democratic great power like the United States to shape peacetime political conditions?

Resolving this uncertainty and answering this question is important for two reasons. First, in designing military forces it is necessary to make tradeoffs. The ultimately finite size of national budgets means that it is necessary both to choose among military capabilities and to choose between military capabilities and other elements of national power. These tradeoffs, while always present, are particularly salient in a period marked by a sweeping and global conception of U.S. interests.

In the post–Cold War world, U.S. national security strategy has generally enunciated three broad goals of American policy: enhancing American security, bolstering American economic prosperity, and promoting democracy abroad.[9] In this context, the pressing question becomes what military capabilities the United States needs to preserve from the budgetary axe (or enhance despite budgetary pressures to reduce) if it is to shape and guarantee a global political environment consistent with the protection of American lives and property at home and abroad, the diffusion of free markets and economic development, and the spread of democratic values and institutions. Need American forces be designed and deployed to maintain a constant forward presence in critical regions? Need forward deployed American forces be able to offer meaningful military options, or is their peacetime role largely a symbolic one? For peacetime missions, is technological superiority a good investment? Do critical capabilities vary by region and across time? Would "force packages" different from the ones currently envisioned in U.S. strategy be equally (or perhaps even more) effective in the missions envisioned by U.S. planners—that is, in deterring aggression, building alliances and coalitions, supporting international norms, encouraging the spread and strengthening of democratic institutions and values, and stimulating open markets and sustainable economic growth? Understanding what attributes of military power are important in peacetime "shaping" thus becomes essential if the United States is to make wise use of its ultimately finite resources.

Second, however, both in designing current strategy and in preparing now for an uncertain future, it is necessary to have some appreciation of what types and degrees of peacetime "shaping" are plausible, given particular types and levels of military capability. What objectives can realistically be demanded from military forces? To what political outcomes can appropriately designed and employed military forces significantly contribute? How difficult, for example, is it to use military forces to shape a regional environment in which local conflict and outside intervention do not take place? One in which economic growth and the adoption of free-market principles occurs? One in which democracy spreads and human rights are respected? Policymakers need an assessment of the kinds of peacetime "shaping" that the possession of a dominant military force will permit.

Despite the importance of understanding the impact of military posture on peacetime political developments, our knowledge of the relationship remains rudimentary. The present study represents only an initial step in improving this knowledge base, and, as noted, the propositions it derives are simply that—speculative propositions derived from a limited, though careful, examination of a limited number of historic cases.

The relationship between military power and successful "shaping" is obviously complex. Three dimensions of this complexity are worth acknowledging. Each complicates attempts to make predictions about how and when efforts to use military force to shape political environments will work.

First, the interaction between the external, international environment confronting states and domestic political realities is a maze of feedback loops. This means that American "shaping" efforts may have unintended and unpredicted consequences. For example, the presence of a stabilizing American military force in the region may not only directly and immediately influence regional states' foreign policy choices but also transform their domestic political situation, altering the distribution of domestic power, the salience of political issues, and even the construction of political identity. This, in turn, may reshape these states' foreign policy goals and behavior in ways that may not be easily generalizable. An understanding of the impact of military forces on "shaping" efforts thus demands an awareness of the dynamic processes at work in particular nation-states: environmental changes that on first inspection would seem to promote stability, democracy, and economic openness may unleash internal forces or trigger processes of domestic change that lead to entirely unanticipated outcomes. It is not inconceivable, for example, that under certain conditions the presence of "stabilizing" military forces that prevent interstate aggression may result in the emergence of internal political fissures or in political radicalization that ultimately undermines regional stability.

Second, under some conditions, efforts to "shape" peacetime environments may trigger countervailing reactions by other states. The conditions under which other nations tend to "bandwagon" rather than "balance" remain unclear, as are the conditions under which particular visions of the future or sets of values become broadly shared. In the Western world in the wake of World War II, states tended to bandwagon with the United States, accepting (with better or worse grace) American visions of a liberal world order and joining with America in pursuing that order. Historically, however, this sort of bandwagoning and hegemonic ideology appear the exception rather than the rule. When states will welcome, rather than rebel against, a great power's efforts to impose order remains uncertain.

Third, the interrelationship between military tools and influences, on the one hand, and the other resources available to nations, on the other hand, also remains murky. The extent to which military threats and promises need to be linked to economic, diplomatic, and cultural ones, and the fungibility of power resources—the extent to which one kind of power, such as military, can be substituted for another, such as economic—remain critical questions.

We find ourselves, therefore, in a situation in which neither rigorous mathematical modeling, involving comparative analyses of the cost-effectiveness of various inputs and alternative "production" processes in the achievement of various objectives nor gaming efforts and experimentation offer much promise. In this regard the contrast between the wartime uses of military power and the peacetime uses of it stand in sharp contrast. Even in a period of potentially revolutionary change in military technology, our understanding of the dynamics of wartime engagement is sufficiently advanced that calculating the impact of a change in force posture or doctrine is essentially a technical—if admittedly difficult—matter. Relying on computer models, gaming activities, and small-scale field experiments, it is possible for a professional military establishment to determine with a reasonable degree of confidence, although necessarily without absolute certainty, which alternatives will prove cost-effective. This, however, is not the situation when it comes to measuring the effectiveness of military power in peacetime: here, at the present time, we are in the more speculative realm of traditional wisdom and gut hunches when we argue about what works best. The danger, of course, is not simply that this traditional wisdom and these gut hunches will prove to be wrong. It is also that in designing military forces and doctrine we focus solely on those things that are most easily or rigorously measured—their probable efficacy in wartime—and assume that forces and doctrines developed for wartime efficacy will necessarily be cost-effective in the peacetime shaping mission as well. There is, however, no compelling reason to assume that forces optimized for winning a military victory during war will offer the kind of peacetime influence the United States seeks.

Case Selection and Methodology

To begin to develop some working propositions about what attributes of military power and what kinds of military capabilities yield peacetime political leverage, this study examines six historical cases in which great powers have attempted to use their military resources to shape and stabilize the politics of particular regions. In selecting cases, we have looked for historical situations that are in some important respects analogous to the situation facing the United States in the post–Cold War world. First, we have looked for cases in which the great power enjoyed a predominance of military power in the region being studied. Second, we have looked for cases in which the great power was a democracy, subject to whatever constraints on the use of military power that democratic institutions might impose. Third, we have looked for cases in which the great power is acting in a system of sovereign states—that is, we have avoided colonial cases, in which key regional actors lacked formal sovereignty. Fourth, we have looked for cases in which the great power had clearly identified goals. We have also, however, looked for cases involving different great powers and different regions, to permit us to begin to distinguish between idiosyncratic and general findings.

The six cases selected for investigation are:

1. Britain in the Eastern Mediterranean during the Concert of Europe period (1816–1852);
2. Britain in the Eastern Mediterranean during the interwar years (1919–1937);
3. Britain in South America between 1850 and 1890;
4. The United States in the Caribbean between 1903 and 1920;
5. France in West Africa between 1960 and 1970;
6. France in Central Africa between 1970 and 1995.

Using focused-comparison techniques to rigorously compare the cases, in each case we explicitly ask the same set of questions. It should be possible to—literally—lay the answers to particular questions side-by-side, comparing across the six cases. The variables we explore fall into three general categories:

1. What was the great power's military capability—that is, what were the principal attributes of its military power—in the region?
2. What other power resources and what political constraints may have affected the great power's behavior or influence in the region?
3. How successful was the great power in shaping peacetime political environments in ways consistent with its preferences?

From our perspective, the first category represents the relevant explanatory variables, the impact of which we wish to examine. The second category represents control and intervening variables. The third category, the outcome, represents the dependent variable of the study.

The specific questions posed in each of the cases are:

1. What are the great power's military capabilities?
   1a. *Regional military balance*: What is the overall *regional military balance* between great power and regional powers?
   1b. *Technological superiority*: What is the degree of great power's effective *technological superiority* over regional powers (where "effective" implies not merely possession of technology but possession of the training and institutional capacity to maintain and employ it)?
   1c. *Regional presence*: How constant is the great power's *presence* in region, with what kinds and levels of forces?
   1d. *Speed*: What is the *speed* of great power possible response?
   1e. *Range of options*: What military *options* are available to the great power?
   1f. *Political intervention capacity*: Does the great power have the *ability to intervene in domestic political affairs* (e.g., to save or topple governments)?
   1g. *Humanitarian/peace-keeping intervention capacity*: Does the great power have the *ability to conduct humanitarian and peace-keeping operations*?
2. What are the great power's other resources and what constraints on its behavior exist?
   2a. *Economic and political leverage*: What *other power resources* does the great power have?
      —What is the great power's economic leverage?
      —What is the great power's political penetration of regional actors?
   2b. *Domestic political constraints on action*: How much freedom of action does the great power have, given *domestic political constraints*?
   2c. *International leverage and constraints*: What *international regimes and institutions* exist that either support or work against the great power's objectives?
   2d. *Third-state constraints*: Are *other great powers* active or capable of intervening in the region?
   2e. *Reverse leverage*: What realistic options do *regional states* have to put pressure on the great power?
   2f. *Shared agendas*: Do regional states and the great power share *common objectives*?

3. Is the great power able to shape the peacetime environment consistent with its preferences?
   3a. *Ability to deter conflict:* Is the great power able to *deter unwanted conflict* in the region?
   3b. *Ability to determine outcomes:* Is the great power able to *control the outcome of regional conflicts*?
   3c. *Ability to reassure:* Is the great power able to *reassure aligned states* in the region?
   3d. *Ability to protect economic interests:* Is the great power able to *protect its economic interests* in the region?
   3e. *Ability to determine foreign policy choices:* Is the great power able to ensure *regional states pursue foreign policies desired* by the great power?
   3f. *Ability to determine domestic policy choices:* Is the great power able to *further domestic developments* in the region consistent with its values and preferences (e.g., democratic development, economic development, procapitalist economic policies)?

Each of the next six chapters explores a historical case, posing these same nineteen questions. The final chapter summarizes the case findings and, based on these findings, offers some propositions about the attributes of military power that contribute significantly to the ability to conduct peacetime "shaping" and about the kinds of "shaping" that are generally possible. While some of these conclusions are reassuring, others are more troubling. Reassuring or troubling, however, they have important implications for the difficult choices facing the United States in the post–Cold War, post-September 11 world.

Notes

1. For a fuller analysis, see Edward Rhodes, "The Imperial Logic of Bush's Liberal Agenda," *Survival* 45, no. 1 (spring 2003): 131–54.

2. The White House, "The National Security Strategy of the United States of America, September 2002," <http://www.whitehouse.gov/nsc/nss.html> (13 May 2003).

3. George W. Bush, "Remarks by the President at 2002 Graduation Exercise of the United States Military Academy, West Point, New York," 2, <http://www.whitehouse.gov/news/releases/2002/06/20020601-3.html> (13 May 2003).

4. The White House, "A National Security Strategy for a New Century" (National Security Strategy of the United States), October 1998, 8.

5. The White House, "A National Security Strategy for a New Century," 8.

6. The White House, "A National Security Strategy for a New Century," 12.
7. Joint Chiefs of Staff, "Shape, Respond, Prepare Now: A Military Strategy for a New Era" (National Military Strategy of the United States of America), 1997, 12.
8. Joint Chiefs of Staff, "Shape, Respond, Prepare Now," 1.
9. The White House, "A National Security Strategy for a New Century," iii.

CHAPTER ONE

A Sword Half Withdrawn from the Scabbard

The Royal Navy and British "Shaping" of the Eastern Mediterranean and the Levant, 1816–1852

JONATHAN M. DICICCO

Introduction: British Naval Mastery and the Preservation of Peace

As a democratic great power, how has Great Britain used its military resources to shape the international political environment in peripheral areas during peacetime? We begin to answer this question by investigating Great Britain's experiences during the period 1815–1852. Known as part of the *Pax Britannica*, this period was indeed relatively peaceful; from the Congress of Vienna until 1853 the great powers did not fight each other in war. This was a peace that depended in part on British strength in commerce, banking, and diplomacy, but more importantly on naval power. Britain's forces were distributed around the globe in both the formal colonial empire and in peripheral regions pertaining to British interests—and no region was more crucial to British interests than the eastern Mediterranean and the Levant. Here the Royal Navy facilitated and protected trade, and provided the backbone for the clever and sometimes blustery diplomacy of George Canning and Lord Palmerston, deterring other great powers (e.g., Russia and France) and regional powers like Egypt, led by the upstart Ottoman vassal Muhammad Ali. Perhaps most important, the Royal Navy often served these purposes by its sheer presence or even existence. In the words of historian Gerald S. Graham, the "sword of British naval power [was] an instrument of compulsion as well as prestige, although it was rarely withdrawn more than halfway from the scabbard."[1] Limited actions and demonstrations were the order of the day, and these were often sufficient to maintain relatively secure commercial passage, reliable communications, and regional peace. Britain's success in promoting peace, prosperity, and progress in its foreign policies during this period owes a great deal to the Royal Navy and its command of the seas, especially the Mediterranean.

For the purposes of this study, the eastern Mediterranean and the Levant will comprise the area spanning from Greece eastward through Asia Minor (i.e., modern Turkey), the littoral region now known as Syria, Lebanon, and Israel, the Sinai Peninsula, and around to the eastern portion of North Africa, now Egypt and Libya.[2] This region is worthy of investigation because it was relatively free from colonization, yet was of interest to the great powers of the day for strategic and economic reasons. As we will see, the order established in the Levant by the once-strong Ottoman Empire was now jeopardized by the erosion of the Ottomans's power. This is perhaps best reflected in the rebellious and seemingly independent actions by Muhammad Ali's Egypt, technically a part of the Ottoman Empire but in reality a powerful challenger of its master.

The diminishing power of the Ottoman Empire, combined with the varied interests of nearby great powers in the region, set the stage for potential conflict (the issue of the future of the crumbling Ottoman Empire is often referred to herein and elsewhere as "the Eastern Question"). How did Britain respond, or fail to respond, to the Eastern Question and other challenges to British interests in the eastern Mediterranean and the Levant? How did British leaders achieve relative peace, prosperity, and progress in a contentious region sown with the seeds of deadly conflict? In order to answer that question, we investigate Britain's capacity to achieve its goals using military means and nonmilitary means and the various constraints on the employment of military force. We begin characterizing the means available to British leaders by examining British military capabilities relative to regional powers.

Part One: Great Britain's Relative Military Capabilities

The Regional Military Balance

There are many ways to assess the military balance of the powers in the Mediterranean region at this time, from quantitative comparisons of fleets and armies to more stylized assessments of the military balance based upon the impressions of "experts"—statesmen, military and naval officers of the day, and contemporary historians. Our assessment will draw upon these different sources in an effort to characterize the relative military capabilities of the competing powers in the region.

Armies

Though the memories of Wellington's defeat of Napoleon at Waterloo remained fresh through much of the first half of the nineteenth century, the peacetime British army was not a powerful, intimidating force, especially when compared to those of the continental great powers or even regional actors like Egypt. Though the British military was the largest it had ever been during peacetime, it was actually rather small compared to the other great powers that had interests in the Middle East. Moreover, the British army was scattered around the globe for the purpose of maintaining and administering the British Empire. For the purposes of homeland defense, Britain could by most accounts afford a small army, given her natural separation from, and defenses against, the European continent. This small army, however, provided British statesmen with very limited land-based military options in the Middle East.

The British army has been described as a poorly organized and poorly led conglomeration of small, unconnected units that were slow to incorporate new technological innovations.[3] Some historians claim the army was vastly underfunded in comparison to the Royal Navy; whether or not one accepts this opinion, the army was limited in size and quality by the twin governmental impulses of fiscal conservatism and fear that the army would overthrow the government.[4] This period of British military history is frequently characterized as "stagnant."[5]

The British government approved and funded some improvements in the 1830s, following on the Reform Bill of 1832, and in the 1840s, owing to the fear of a French cross-Channel invasion. However, the shortcomings of the British army as a projectable combat force were underscored clearly during the Crimean War, particularly the disastrous Charge of the Light Brigade.

During the waning days of the Napoleonic Wars in 1815, the British army numbered close to 250,000 men. Initial peacetime reductions were modest, as the British sent an occupation force of 35,000 to France while the defeated French remitted reparations to the victorious alliance members (Britain, Russia, Austria, and Prussia). By 1816, the army was still 225,000 strong, including the occupation forces, but more serious peacetime reductions over the next five years brought the total down to 100,000 men. Of these, approximately half were committed to colonial garrisons (20,000 in India, 30,000 elsewhere—totaling about three-quarters of all British infantry) and half for home defense. Reductions included the abolition of the Staff Corps and the Waggon Train, severely hampering the ability to mount foreign military campaigns.[6]

Unlike her continental counterparts, who used conscription to build large armies,[7] Britain relied on a volunteer army. However, there was little incentive for Britons to enlist—the food was terrible, living quarters were smaller than those provided to incarcerated criminals, and the agreement to serve as a soldier in the colonies often ensured a twenty-one-year—or even a life-long—commitment to that task.[8] Given these conditions, it is far from surprising that the recruits were not enthusiastic, able-bodied men anxious to defend their country; Wellington referred to the British soldiers of the time as "the scum of the earth," and the British army as a "filthy receptacle" for society's misfits.[9]

Historians are quick to point out the shortcomings of military elites during *Pax Britannica* as well. Most officers were well-bred, upper-class citizens with little or no military training to speak of. Many acquired their posts through the "Purchase System"—in essence, by buying a commission. The conservative and aging Horse Guards had a great deal of control over army policies, and contributed to the stunting of Britain's military development. Correlli Barnett asserts that "[u]nder their ancient and hallowed hands, the army remained preserved like a garment in a bottom drawer, sentimentally loved but rotted and rendered quaint by the passage of time."[10]

The 1832 Reform Bill and the reorganization of the militia for home defense in 1852 provided some relief to the British rank and file, but did virtually nothing to improve the poorly organized system of regiments which comprised the British army. Units were largely unconnected, and no provisions were in place for the brigading of regiments. Even the improvements introduced by Hardinge in the 1850s were inadequate; "[a]ll the plans for maximising manpower and for reorganising regiments revolved around the demands of home and imperial defence. They did not give any serious consideration to the possibility of a major war overseas."[11] Consequently, the few forces available for deployment on the periphery were not well coordinated.

Under Muhammad Ali, *Egypt* attempted to create and maintain a modern army during the period in question. Aiming for a conscripted army of about 100,000 men, Ali raised an army of approximately 62,000 regulars and 15,000 Bedouin irregulars. Many of the regulars were trained by European instructors, and some of the recruits received special training at Egypt's infantry, cavalry, and artillery schools. While a high-ranking British observer criticized the Egyptian cavalry, he characterized the artillery as excellent and the infantry as "well-armed, well-dressed, well-supplied, in the highest discipline and equal to the best European soldiers except in experience."[12] Indeed, the Egyptians successfully challenged the Ottomans twice, advancing along the Syrian coast toward Asia Minor. However, one analyst warns against inferring too much from these military campaigns against the rather disorganized forces of the Ottoman Empire, asserting that "[i]n any war with a European force the deficiencies of the Egyptians in equipment, training, and logistical support would have been patent."[13]

The *Ottoman Empire's* army is difficult to judge. Optimistic estimates ranged to 300,000 men in the Sultan's army between 1826 and 1853, but such large figures are exceedingly deceptive. Only a fraction of this force, probably about 40,000 men, were trained soldiers; the remainder comprised a collection of unreliable provincial forces.[14] Disciplinary problems abounded as well, making questionable the overall efficacy of the Ottoman forces. While Ottoman Turks did rise to the occasion to defend the core Turkish territorial holdings, the ability of the army to ensure the integrity and internal order of the empire during peacetime was suspect.[15] Reforms in the 1830s and the 1840s helped to some extent, but the Ottoman Turks did not have the capacity for offensive military action on land, especially against great powers like Russia. A great power of Britain's underwhelming army strength might have been at a numerical disadvantage, but Turkey's geographical location would allow the British to bring the Royal Navy's incredible power to bear on the Porte.

Navies

Great Britain was the foremost naval power on the globe. Victory at Trafalgar, the subsequent destruction of large portions of her continental neighbor's fleets in the French Revolutionary Wars and the Napoleonic Wars,[16] and the acquisition of strategically located bases in the Mediterranean and elsewhere contributed to the Royal Navy's reputation. The Britons' ability to cast about the weight of the Royal Navy in the area reflected the image of power and reach conjured up by the British Empire, but the British did not acquire and maintain colonies in the region until the end of the nineteenth century.

The strength of the British position in the Mediterranean, and indeed the backbone of the *Pax Britannica* of the nineteenth century, was based upon the Royal Navy's dominant overall strength and its command of the seas—not only surrounding the European continent but also in the Persian Gulf, the Indian Ocean, and the Atlantic and Pacific Oceans. Castlereagh, the British foreign secretary at the outset of the postwar period, insisted that the British maintain a two-power standard; that is, the Royal Navy ought to be as strong as its two closest competitors combined.[17] Indeed, when measured in displacement, the British Royal Navy did in fact preserve this ratio throughout the period (table 1.1).[18]

In terms of the number of ships, the Royal Navy's peacetime fleet was intended to hover about a level of 100 ships-of-the-line and 160 frigates, sloops, brigs, and other cruiser-type vessels. It took several years to cut wartime naval forces down to size; at the conclusion of hostilities in 1815, the Royal Navy was over 1,000 warships strong, with at least 214 of those ships-of-the-line. This enormous navy clearly outweighed war-torn France's navy of 103 ships-of-the-line and 157 frigates and Russia's 168 warships.[19]

The British drastically reduced the size of the fleet in the two-year period following the end of the French wars. By 1816, 33 ships-of-the-line and 205 other smaller warships were in commission, with 70 ships-of-the-line and 134 others "in ordinary," a sort of reserve status whereby ships were not deployed, but were serviceable enough to be called into action in the event of an emergency.[20] Forces were further reduced to 14 ships-of-the-line and 100 others in commission, and 84 ships-of-the-line and 179 others in ordinary by 1817. Of these, only one ship-of-the-line and five smaller vessels were stationed in the Mediterranean.[21] By 1820, the British Royal Navy comprised 19 ships-of-the-line and 92 smaller vessels in commission, and 98 ships-of-the-line and 145 others in ordinary. This level of warships fluctuated only mildly for the next 25 years or so,[22] though ship deployments in the Mediterranean increased to a more prominent position in the 1830s and 1840s.

Of course, mere displacement figures and ship counts do not reveal the character of the naval balance between these great powers or any others. A

Table 1.1. British Relative Sea Power, 1815–1855

British forces as a percentage of Russian and French naval forces combined, measured in displacement

1815	154
1820	131
1825	110
1830	104
1835	108
1840	106
1845	103
1850	101
1855	121

Source: Adapted from Glete, *Navies and Nations*, 422.

number of important issues are left unresolved, including the technological sophistication of the vessels, the speed and gun-carrying ability of the vessels, the ability of the officers and crews, the deployment or concentration of the vessels, their state of repair, and so forth. Below we assess the relative technological status of the British Royal Navy and the availability and sophistication of the sailors that manned the British warships.

In *Egypt*, Muhammad Ali twice tried to build a powerful navy, and twice that navy was gravely injured by clashes with the European great powers—once directly and once indirectly. The Egyptian navy of the 1820s was the result of Ali's program of rapid modernization and armament. The Egyptians built and operated munitions factories, but Egypt did not have a viable shipbuilding capacity with which to generate a fleet of warships. To compensate for the lack of indigenous production, Ali purchased several European-built warships. Seven super-frigates and several other smaller frigates and corvettes were launched during the 1820s. The Egyptian fleet was not strong enough on its own to confront European ships-of-the-line, but it did make a valuable contribution to the Ottoman navy, which was much larger but of lesser quality.[23]

The Egyptian navy of the 1820s would not last through the decade, however. An Egyptian squadron of some 14–23 vessels, including 4 heavy frigates and at least 3 corvettes, was arrayed with the Turkish fleet at Navarino Bay in 1827.[24] The overall Turko-Egyptian fleet, comprising 3 ships-of-the-line, 15–17 frigates, and 40 or so smaller warships, was destroyed in a point-blank naval engagement with a combined British, French, and Russian naval force consisting of 10 ships-of-the-line, 8–10 frigates, and about a half-dozen smaller vessels.[25] Of the 20 warships in the first line of the Turko-Egyptian formation, 14 were sunk or destroyed; six limped to Alexandria after the engagement, but three of those were discarded.[26] Turkish and Egyptian personnel losses numbered around 3,000.[27] This defeat at the hands of the Europeans dealt a devastating blow to the Egyptian naval program.

Determined to build a bigger and better fleet, Muhammad Ali opened a shipyard at Alexandria and hired French advisers and shipbuilders. By 1832 Ali had two ships-of-the-line, seven frigates, and forty-four smaller warships at the ready; eleven years after the defeat at Navarino Bay, the reconstructed Egyptian fleet included as many as twelve ships-of-the-line.[28] Egypt's battle-fleet at this point measured about 60,000 tons displacement (a 300 percent increase since 1830—and a tenfold increase since 1820), and was fifth largest, smaller only than the navies of Britain, France, Russia, and the Ottoman Empire. This new and improved Egyptian navy was not to endure much longer than its predecessor, however. After the British bombardments of Beirut and Acre and the expulsion of the Egyptians from Syria, the Egyptian armament program was dismantled. Failure to launch new warships to replace older, decaying models resulted in the waning of the Egyptian fleet to only five ships-of-the-line by 1850.[29] Though not beaten in a surface engagement, the Egyptian fleet was indirectly quashed by the Royal Navy.

Reliable data on the *Ottoman* navy are elusive. Readily available data suggest that the Ottoman Empire, including Algiers, Tunis, and Tripoli, had a navy that remained relatively consistent in size throughout the period under investigation. Though it compared favorably to the Russian Black Sea fleet, the Ottoman navy was at its peak only a fourth of the size of the Royal Navy. Making matters worse for the Ottomans, the navy underwent various traumas, including the destruction of much of the fleet at Navarino in 1827, and the mass desertion of naval vessels to Muhammad Ali's Egyptian forces in 1840.[30]

Great Britain's Degree of Effective Technological Superiority in the Region

British naval technology changed very little during this period, remaining essentially the same as the naval technology of the great powers during the French Revolutionary Wars and the Napoleonic Wars. Between 1815 and the early 1840s, changes in warship design were so slight that "basic warship qualities of speed, manœuveurability [sic], weatherliness, seaworthiness, protection and gun platform efficiency" remained at a plateau established in the eighteenth century.[31] While the Americans experimented with larger ships capable of carrying more guns, the British largely maintained their vessels' design well into the nineteenth century. The French began to employ steam-propelled vessels on a regular basis before the British.[32] Even the Egyptians had technology comparable to that of the Royal Navy, many of their ships having been constructed in French and British dockyards, or with the advice of French shipbuilders.[33]

The British tended to have an edge in the training and experience of their seamen and naval officers; this edge would prove decisive in some circumstances.[34] For example, while the Egyptians trained under French supervision and even employed French captains, Ibrahim Pasha's inexperience as a battlefleet commander is often cited as a reason for the mistakes leading to the destruction of the Turko-Egyptian fleet at Navarino Bay.[35]

A more vivid example of superior British training and seamanship is the British action to halt the Egyptians' advance toward Asia Minor in 1840.

Muhammad Ali's army of approximately 70,000 troops had taken much of the Syrian coast and was positioned to threaten Constantinople. The army was supplied via the sea, since the land routes were inhospitable and slow. William Laird Clowes recounts:

> At Alexandria was a large but by no means efficient Egyptian fleet, which, had the sea been open to it, could have accompanied the left wing of the advancing army, protected it, and supplied it. But the sea was not open to it. *The less numerous yet much more efficient fleet under Stopford* not only terrorised the Egyptians into remaining under the forts of Alexandria, or captured such vessels as ventured out, but also struck blow after blow on the flank of Muhammad Ali's communications, landed and supported troops there, and, in less than two months, so imperilled the conquering army of Egypt that the rebellious viceroy was glad to make terms.[36] [emphasis added]

Clowes's report clearly implies that the Royal Navy's superior leadership, seamanship, and prowess gave the British the advantage, even though the Egyptian fleet was numerically superior.

During the period under investigation the British army incorporated some technological advances, namely, the percussion cap, which decreased misfires from approximately 40 percent to four percent, and the Minié rifle, which employed the cylindrical-conoidal bullet.[37] However, the former was not adopted in earnest until 1839, and the Minié rifle (pioneered by the French) did not enter into British use until the Kaffir War of 1851–52.[38] These developments were little more than a palliative for the deeper problems that plagued the British army during this period: poor organization and leadership, inadequate training, and unsanitary living conditions. In this sense, such technological advancements were too little, too late.

In any case, technical superiority of equipment and weaponry played a key role in Britain's colonial wars during this period, but it was far less important in Britain's entanglements in the eastern Mediterranean and the Levant.[39] In this region, the issue was not who had better hardware—the hardware was similar—but rather who had the better training and greater experience. Here the Royal Navy's superiority successfully countered the Egyptians' military prowess on land.

Constancy and Composition of British Regional Presence

Britain maintained naval forces in the Mediterranean Sea on a consistent basis throughout this period; in fact, its regular forces committed to this area increased between the late 1810s and the mid-1830s. The acquisition of the island of Malta at the Congress of Vienna permitted the British to have a centrally located base of operations in the Mediterranean.[40] Malta was complemented by bases at Gibraltar in the western Mediterranean and the Ionian Islands in the eastern Mediterranean, giving the British the strategic capability of controlling the entrance and exit of other naval forces in the Mediterranean.[41]

Reliable figures on exact ship commitments are difficult to come by, since there existed "no general plan for the distribution of the Fleet in peace or war. The size and composition of the squadrons employed were decided by the Admiralty *ad hoc* according to the work to be done and the interests defended,"[42] and deployments changed accordingly. The breadth of British strength in global terms was also Britain's weakness in any one corner of the world, including the Mediterranean. The British needed a navy that transcended the demands of any one particular region; during peacetime, a large navy of large and expensive ships-of-the-line was not terribly appealing to members of Parliament or even the Admiralty. Instead, while the Americans and French built hulking battleships that outgunned the Royal Navy's best, the British focused on maintaining a fleet largely comprised of frigates, brigs, and the smallest ships-of-the-line: "Cheaper to build and maintain, easier to man, and responsive to so many of the needs of the far-flung empire and trade, the existence of such ships is not to be explained solely by the dogged conservatism, the serene indifference to foreign precepts, the obstinate complacency of senile admirals as contemporary critics delighted to declare. What may appear indefensible at a tactical level may wear a rather different guise when viewed strategically."[43] C. J. Bartlett writes "indefensible at the tactical level" because a rival naval power that concentrated its forces in a particular area had a good chance of defeating a British squadron in battle.

Nonetheless, evidence suggests that the Mediterranean became an increasingly important focal point of British naval activity, attributable in large measure to the slow degradation of the Ottoman Empire.[44] The area of the Ottoman Empire was the site of frequent flare-ups, and where there's smoke, one is bound to find fireships—and gunboats, frigates, and even the occasional ships-of-the-line. Indeed, by the early 1840s, the Mediterranean Squadron was "the principal force at the ready disposal of the British government." Presence lapsed on occasion; in 1844, when the French conducted a naval demonstration against Morocco, British political leaders were surprised to learn they had only a single ship-of-the-line in the Mediterranean.[45] However, by 1848 British sea power was firmly entrenched in the Mediterranean, with 31 warships in that station.[46]

Overall, the British maintained a steady naval presence in the region for the better part of the period in question. That presence was not necessarily comprised of ships-of-the-line, and on occasion was even unprepared for an unexpected crisis or engagement.[47] Nonetheless, this relatively consistent presence facilitated rapid response to most crises and problems, and the mere presence of British warships, even if in inadequate concentrations for traditional battle, was often adequate for Britain's purposes.

Britain's Speed of Response

The speed of possible response is contingent on a number of factors, including the communication that a crisis has begun and the decisions of statesmen on the appropriate initiative or response. Communications were very slow; for example, sending instructions from London to Constantinople took at least three weeks, and forwarding them to particular locations in the Levant took another week or so.[48] Keeping this in mind, we can assess the possible response time of the Royal Navy in at least two ways: we could describe the speed of warships and calculate the likely travel times across particular distances to hypothetical trouble spots; or we can take advantage of historical examples and report the response times of forces during actual crises. The former method has many weaknesses, including the poor quality of data on ship speeds, the reliance of wooden sailing ships on the direction of prevailing winds and currents, and the necessity of frequent stops for victuals or repairs. The latter method is also flawed in that it limits our attention to actual events, and says little about dogs that didn't bark—actions that regional powers did not undertake for fear of a swift and forceful response by the British. However, we will employ the latter approach on the assumption that it more accurately reflects the hardships and eventualities of response times that escape the hypothetical approach.

Responses to crises, assuming that instructions already have been transmitted, could take days and even weeks. When at Nauplia, the provisional Greek capital in the 1820s, Admiral Codrington received news of the Treaty of London. His flagship required three days' sail to reach Smyrna, a harbor in western Anatolia, where he could remain in closer contact with the British ambassador at Constantinople.[49] Later, after assembling the British, French, and Russian forces outside of Navarino Bay, the absence of favorable winds delayed the fleet's entrance into the bay for a full day.[50]

From a modern standpoint, the limitations created by sailing ships' reliance on wind are almost farcical. During the Syrian crisis, the Royal Navy was ordered to land ground forces in the vicinity of Beirut. Unaided by wind, the British ships slowly wandered in a southerly direction; so languid was their progress that the Egyptian army was able to keep pace on shore, preventing the ships from depositing the troops on land. Finally a fair wind picked up and rapidly propelled the British ships northward, away from the Egyptians and allowing for a safe landing.[51]

Though British response times clearly depended on factors beyond the control of personnel at the operational level—the winds, currents, and so on—these constraints affected the other powers in the region as well. Not able to eliminate these obstacles (prior to the regular incorporation of steam-powered warships), the British compensated by stationing vessels at strategic points throughout the Mediterranean. By basing ships at Gibraltar, Malta, and the Ionian Islands, the British ensured that they could offer some response—at least a token naval presence—on short notice. Actual responses seem slow by modern standards, but they were rapid at the time.

Available Military Options

Britain compensated for her modest capabilities on land with her impressive strength at sea. As Paul Kennedy notes, European crises that were more amenable to military rather than naval intervention often exceeded the grasp of the British.[52] With constabulary obligations at home well into the 1830s and with colonial commitments abroad, the British army had few soldiers to spare for interstate engagements in the Levant. Even the landing of British troops in Syria in 1840 utilized marines rather than army personnel.

The options available to the Royal Navy included:

1. *Doing nothing*. Sometimes this was the result of a deliberate decision not to respond; on rare occasions it was inevitable for lack of available resources.
2. *"Showing the flag"*: that is, send a warship or squadron of warships to the area, prominently flying the British flag, in a simple display of Britain's as-yet untapped naval power. When used in tandem with threats or ultimata, this option at times was capable of deterring inflammatory action by the enemy.
3. *Blockade*: that is, enforce sanctions by preventing the passage of ships to and from the coastal area of concern. This type of action could also include the boarding and inspection of ships and the detaining or requisitioning of ships. Royal Navy blockades were ubiquitous; consider as examples the blockade of Algiers in 1824, the blockade of the Morea during the Greek War of Independence, and the blockade of Athens during the Don Pacifico affair in 1850.

4. *Offshore bombardment:* usually of fortified positions on land. Examples include Algiers in 1816, Beirut and Acre in 1840.
5. *Deployment of ground forces:* usually marines, as illustrated by the British actions at Beirut and Acre in 1840. On the rare occasion when army units were available, it was also possible to transport these troops into position. An example is the peacekeeping deployment of 4,000 troops in Portugal. A word of caution here: while these operations were plausible they were hardly used in the region, and they were difficult to coordinate. For example, the offshore bombing of Beirut severely weakened the defenses of the city, but the British forces were insufficient to take and occupy the city.[53]
6. *Engagement in battle:* the Royal Navy was capable of sea battle in the Mediterranean, though at times it was numerically inferior to, and thus susceptible to defeat by, great powers like France. Nonetheless, admirals could summon warships from other stations to reinforce existing forces in the event of battle.[54]

The British also exercised some military influence by advising the leaders of other states; for instance, Royal Navy officers assisted the Ottoman Turks in their efforts to maintain a viable navy in the 1830s and 1840s.[55] Still, the most commonly used techniques were showing the flag, blockading enemies, and bombarding coastline cities and installations. Other options such as deploying ground troops were logistically difficult and ultimately unlikely to be used.

British Capacity for Intervention in the Domestic Affairs in Regional Polities

Essentially, Britain had the ability to intervene in the domestic affairs of states proximate to the sea or with rivers accessible by the sea. British armed forces were meager and the availability of troops for interventions was quite limited. In addition, British foreign policymakers publicly acknowledged a policy of nonintervention in the internal affairs of other states, though their intent was somewhat less than genuine. In any case, as Kennedy argues, domestic political events (and armed interventions by continental great powers) often went against British wishes when the states in question were not easily accessible by sea.[56] In the Mediterranean and the Levant, however, where major cities were typically located on or near coastlines, British naval actions could tip the scales in favor of one side or the other in a domestic dispute.

While not in the region of interest, the case of Portugal in the 1820s is instructive here. A Royal Navy presence in the Tagus River allowed the British to shield the recently installed Constitutionalists from internal uprisings; and combined with the dispatch of 4,000 troops to the Tagus, it provided the wherewithal to coerce the Spanish to stop aiding and harboring the Portuguese rebels.[57]

An example that does fall into our area of inquiry is the Greek War of Independence. A Greek rebellion against the Ottoman Empire raged for nearly the entire decade of the 1820s. Initially, under Castlereagh and then Canning, Britain took a noninterventionist, neutral stance. In 1823 Britain recognized the Greeks as belligerents, though this move was designed to enable the British to take legitimate actions against Greek privateers rather than to legitimize the Greek rebellion.[58] By 1825 Britain's status as a neutral had changed, and by 1826 the British were ready to undertake joint action with the Russians against the Turks if necessary. When, along with France, Russia and Britain tried to impose an armistice on the Porte, the Sultan refused and allowed ships in the combined Turko-Egyptian fleet to violate the allied blockade. The allied admirals believed an allied naval presence and blockade would compel the Sultan to accept the armistice, and when it was refused, they utilized their freedom of action to engage belligerent vessels.[59] The results of the Navarino Bay battle are discussed elsewhere in this chapter; the destruction of the Turko-Egyptian fleet left the Ottomans with a disadvantage at sea against the ragtag (but experienced) Greek navy, and helped the Greeks eventually to gain independence from the Turks.[60]

British Ability to Conduct Humanitarian and Peacekeeping Operations
Evidence suggests that humanitarian and peacekeeping operations, at least by contemporary standards, were largely unused at the time in the Levant.[61] Examples of unilateral attempts at peacekeeping do exist. For instance, Admiral Codrington sailed his Royal Navy flagship to Nauplia, the provisional Greek capital during the War of Independence, to suppress a conflict between the provisional government and an upstart faction. In addition, one could argue that the 4,000 troops conveyed to the Tagus to prevent the overthrow of the Portuguese government by Spanish-abetted rebels was a peacekeeping force; however, this would be a bit of a conceptual stretch of our usual definitions of peacekeeping.

Antislave patrols, which were by and large the unique domain of the Royal Navy until the 1840s, could be construed as humanitarian missions, but again, this might be stretching contemporary meanings a bit too far. In terms of late-twentieth-century practice, humanitarian and peacekeeping missions were not undertaken. However, the British did have the capacity to land small numbers of troops at coastal locations in the eastern Mediterranean and the Levant, and British naval presence and mediation appear capable of defusing a potentially escalatory situation between regional powers.

Part Two: Other Sources of or Constraints on British Power and Influence

Economic Leverage

Following the Napoleonic Wars, Great Britain was the commercial and financial leader of Europe and in large measure of peripheral regions as well. While all of the great powers suffered economically to some degree from the long stretch of wartime that had closed the end of the eighteenth century, the Britons' head start in industrialization, and their blossoming interest in pursuing free trade rather than mercantilism, made Britain the logical center of trade and banking.

Even with these advantages, for some years after the wars' end the British economy was gripped by depression. Demobilizing armies created a dearth of demand for agricultural and industrial products. Manufacturing enterprises expanded, based on the mistaken assumption that peacetime would bring prosperity; this exacerbated the lack of demand and led to overproduction. As depression set in, widespread unemployment caused people to tighten their belts, further injuring the home markets for manufactured goods. Disruption of the mining of precious metals generated shortages in financial stores that backed paper currencies, imperiling the financial situation as well.[62]

Britain's financial and commercial problems were dwarfed by those of other European states, however. France, while spared of punitive reparations by Castlereagh and Metternich's judicious construction of the peace, was burdened by an indemnity and the costs of the British postwar occupation. British merchant-bankers eagerly stepped in to bail out the war-torn French economy. Baring Brothers and Company provided a contract for a large loan to assist the French; while Whitehall could not approve of such a measure (France was of course Britain's enemy in war just a few months earlier), Castlereagh made little effort to obstruct the floating of the loan. The loan was a vast success, and it triggered a series of loans to states—including Russia and Austria—suffering from currency crises.[63] Indeed, the states of Europe owed so much to the merchant-banking house that the Duc de Richelieu stated, perhaps only half-jokingly, "There are Six Powers in Europe: Great Britain, France, Russia, Austria, Prussia, and Baring Brothers."[64]

Baring Brothers and Company and the Rothschilds, who floated a £5 million loan for Prussia in 1818 and later came to be known as "the High Treasury of the Holy Alliance," generated deep-seated financial ties among Britons and the states of the European continent.[65] European heads of state recognized their fates were linked to that of the financial houses; when financial panic endangered the solvency of Baring Bros. in late 1818, diplomats arranged for extensions at the Congresses at Aix-la-Chapelle and Paris.[66] Nonetheless, we are enjoined by at least one prominent scholar to avoid the mistake of linking the financial houses too closely with the British state; while the financial interdependence is undeniable, the state neither existed to serve the financial houses nor vice-versa.[67]

British financial houses were active in the eastern Mediterranean, though not to the extent that they were elsewhere in Europe. During the Greek War of Independence (1821–29), British houses floated loans for the Greeks in 1824 and 1825.[68] Unfortunately for the revolutionaries, large portions of these loans did not provide the financial assistance that British philhellenes had intended. Some of the loaned funds were diverted for side payments, and the interest payments due on the loans placed an additional burden on the revolutionaries.

A recession set in around 1825, and combined with the loan defaults of the Greeks, Spain, Portugal, and several South American states, set off a thirty-year state of "financial confusion" and insolvency. As Jenks points out, the decade-long lending spree had generated a reserve of assets in Britain in the form of cash and European securities;[69] however, there appears to be no serious, enduring impact on British foreign policy in the eastern Mediterranean and Levant.

As far as *trade* is concerned, the British had trading relationships with peoples in the Levantine region through the Levant Company, a trade monopolist not unlike the East India Company. In the interest of freer trade, however, the Levant Company was abolished in 1825.[70] The exchange of manufactured products like English cloth for raw materials like cotton and silk and other commodities, including sponges, figs, and honey, became the domain of individual merchants. Through the regularization of trade routes and low tariff levels through the negotiation of commercial treaties, the British established active and nearly barrier-free trade relations with some of the peoples of the eastern Mediterranean and the Levant.

Anglo-Levantine trade was not a one-sided affair; rather, the British came to need certain goods that were available in the Levant and Asia Minor. Britain's agricultural self-sufficiency ended in the 1820s, thus necessitating the import of grains and other foodstuffs; but protectionism on the European continent prompted the British to pressure the Turks to export grain to Britain.[71] Egypt, which competed with British businesses by acquiring British equipment and consultants, by the 1820s had taken a small bite out of Britain's market share for cheap cotton products. The Egyptian state acted as a financial parasite on Anglo-Egyptian trade—state agents acted as middlemen for cotton sales, putting the profits in the treasury. In addition, the Egyptian state tried to monopolize industrial production, for both civilian and military consumption. Nonetheless, even Egypt became increasingly reliant on British goods—including iron, coal, and munitions—during this period.[72]

British ledgers reflected a degree of profitability from the economic interdependence in the Levant. While British imports more than doubled between 1825 and 1853, exports (in £) nearly quadrupled; and the positive trade balance increased from £12 million in 1825 to £110 million in 1852. The Levant—especially Turkey, which became "Britain's third best customer" by the 1840s—contributed heavily to this pattern.[73] Also important was the influx of gold from the Turks, whose reluctance to borrow prior to 1850 resulted in payment of balances using bullion or specie, which pleased British business interests.[74]

Even if the peoples of the Ottoman Empire had had no interest in the goods traded from Britain, Ottoman traders had to rely on British shipping; as James Stokesbury points out (with only the slightest exaggeration), "[A]lmost anyone who went anywhere traveled on a British ship, and anyone who sent goods by water shipped them in a British hull."[75] Many argue that British commercial interest in the Levant was motivated not by the potential benefits of freer trade with the Egyptians and Turks, but rather by the shipping routes to India. While the British went to great lengths to preserve the overseas route to India around the Cape of Good Hope, they also used a mixed sea-land route through the Mediterranean and over the Sinai Peninsula to the Red Sea—construction of the Suez Canal did not begin until 1859—and experimented with a route that used the rivers of Mesopotamia (modern-day Iraq), though these riverine routes later were abandoned.[76] While it took several months to ship cargo around the tip of Africa to India, the same cargo could be shipped via the Mediterranean route in about six weeks.[77] Hence the British had a vested interest in maintaining the viability of the route. During this period, economic leverage played a role in doing just that, by forging commercial links between the British and the Ottomans. Was this the only way to maintain the route to India? Certainly not—as demonstrated by the British colonization of Egypt in the 1880s, there were alternatives to trade relations. The British had economic leverage in the region, but it was limited by British reliance on goods from the region and by an interest in preserving the short route to India.

British Political Penetration of Regional Actors

During this period, British political penetration of the states in the eastern Mediterranean and the Levant was quite limited. The French clearly were entrenched to a greater degree. In Egypt, the French supported Muhammad Ali's attempts to build modern military and naval forces by sending advisers, instructors, and equipment. The British sold warships to the Egyptians but provided little by way of consultation.[78]

D. C. M. Platt argues that the British used commercial and financial ties as indirect mechanisms to penetrate (and essentially prop up) the Ottoman Empire. Rather than attempting to appoint Britons to government positions under the Sultan, British statesmen encouraged the Turks to open their markets and allow free trade and open communications in the hopes that, as Aberdeen put it in 1842, these measures would impart stability to the government of the Sultan. Platt's argument is plausible; however, since the British government was promoting free trade by entrepreneurs and not monopolistic state firms, it is likewise plausible to assert that British *economic* penetration of the Ottoman Empire did not necessarily constitute British *political* penetration of the Ottoman Empire.[79]

Perhaps the most notable exception to this lack of political penetration was the British ambassador to Constantinople for much of the period in question, Stratford Canning (later Viscount Stratford de Redcliffe). Stratford enjoyed a great deal of influence in the Turkish capital and, as an adviser of the Sultan, became something of a kingmaker. His activities discouraged Russian penetration (and potential subjugation) of the Porte and encouraged continued economic relations between the Turks and the Britons. While Stratford encouraged modernization and reform, even he could not convince the Sultan to accept the British offers of military advisers, which were considered interference in the Porte's internal affairs. For instance, the Porte agreed to a naval mission from Britain, but when the officers arrived, they were dismissed.[80]

There was at least one example of Britain's use of temporary political penetrative measures to achieve its ends in the Levant. During the Syrian Crisis in 1840, the British sought to undermine Egyptian control of the coast. Desiring escalation of the general unrest among the Lebanese, British agents disseminated propaganda materials to promote a violent revolt. The Lebanese did indeed revolt, though not as a result of the propaganda campaign, according to historian M. S. Anderson. An effective guerrilla war against the Egyptians did not break out until British forces arrived on the scene, bombarded Beirut, landed British, Austrian, and Turkish forces, and distributed nearly 22,000 muskets to local residents.[81] Therefore, even though political penetration (by way of propaganda) played a part in the stirring of domestic tensions among the Lebanese, the catalyst spurring action in this case was military intervention.

Domestic Political Constraints on British Freedom of Action in the Region

The practice of British foreign policy and the provisions for British action in the Middle East were constrained in at least three ways: by public opinion, by Parliamentary opposition and debate, and by commercial interests. These are not mutually exclusive categories; the positions of parties on various issues were influenced by public opinion, public opinion was shaped and manipulated by Cabinet officials and members of Parliament,[82] and commercial interests overlapped to a large degree with both public opinion and the interests of members of Parliament.

Britain was by 1815 a constitutional democracy, though the royal family reserved some primarily nominal powers. The franchise was limited, but members of Parliament were elected to their posts and were therefore at least somewhat accountable to the citizenry. Parliamentary proceedings were characterized by a three-cornered struggle between two powerful political parties, the Whigs and the Tories, and one minority party, the Radicals. The Whig-Tory dichotomy was mildly evident throughout the government, but prior to 1832 played a prominent, organized role only in Parliament.[83] Reforms brought an expansion of the electorate and changes in the parties: Aristocratic Whigs joined forces with some of the Radicals to form a Liberal party, and the "liberal Tories" of the 1820s gave way to the Conservatives. Prior to and following the reforms, these political parties exerted far greater influence on domestic policy than on foreign policy. Most accounts of British diplomacy and foreign affairs emphasize the role of individual foreign secretaries, especially Lord Palmerston, and the preservation of British ability to use threats and force abroad when needed.[84] Party domination in government may have affected naval and military budgets and the movement toward a freer trade policy, but seems to have had little impact as an immediate constraint on foreign policy action.

Public opinion played a role in foreign policy, but it was the guiding hand neither of the diplomat nor of the general. The "mildly reactionary" public mood was certainly not reflected in the British policies of the day, which were far more liberal than the continental powers that had emerged victorious from the Napoleonic Wars. By and large, leaders were confident that public opinion would follow elite cues; this permitted the British Foreign Office to enjoy a degree of latitude in dealing with crises and disputes on a case-by-case basis.[85]

Further, the influence of public opinion depended in part on the identity of the leaders in government at the time. Viscount Castlereagh, foreign secretary from 1812 through 1822, "attached very little importance to the rather uninstructed public opinion of the time."[86] George Canning, who succeeded Castlereagh after the latter's self-inflicted demise, wooed public opinion to marshal support for his foreign policies. Some assert that Canning actually relied on public opinion; Canning's remark that "public opinion, embodied in a Free Press . . . pervades, and checks, and perhaps, in a last resort, nearly governs the whole constitution" reveals the import he attributed to public attitudes.[87] Castlereagh and Canning represent the extremes; Lord Palmerston, foreign secretary intermittently from 1830 through the 1850s, took a middle course, both employing public opinion to his advantage and manipulating public opinion to fit his views.[88] Though British foreign policy elites reflect a range of attitudes toward public opinion, one consistent theme emerges, according to one analyst who argues, "[w]ithout exception, British ministers were concerned above all with preserving their country's freedom of action."[89]

Only on occasion did the public mood have a direct impact on foreign policy. In 1826, the British negotiated the St. Petersburg Protocol with Russia in the hopes of preventing (or at least delaying) a war between Russia and Turkey. The agreement was suboptimal to the British, but Canning accepted the terms anyway because had a Russo-Turkish war broken out, British public opinion would not have supported British intervention.[90] This example aside, public opinion's impact was for the most part an indirect one—pulling the strings of the government's purse through the members of Parliament. Since public opinion was typically more reactionary than Cabinet members, a minister usually "had to weigh with care the pros and cons of an appeal to Parliament for additional funds with which to execute his desire."[91] This meant that British foreign ministers were often constrained by the immediately available military and naval forces, and they could not bank on generating funding for additional forces. This seems a rather unimportant point, but recall that large portions of the British Royal Navy were laid up "in ordinary" for long periods of time. While in ordinary, these ships were essentially seaworthy and fit for deployment, but they did not have regular crews; thus, their deployment would require an allocation of funds for the recruitment and payment of sailors. Since these requests for funds were largely unpopular during the 1820s and 1830s due to a depressed economy, it was unlikely that such requests would be honored, and the British warships in ordinary would go unused.[92]

Finally we consider the role of commercial interests. In prior eras the connection between the British state and its constituent commercial interests was indeed an intimate one, not because the merchants exerted political influence on the state but rather because the state became wealthy on the basis of (in large part colonial) commerce. During this period the British began to promote free(r) trade. The usual historical signpost marking the free trade movement is the repeal of the protectionist Corn Laws in 1846, but the movement began considerably earlier. In this new, more liberal atmosphere, the state's extraction of monies from commerce diminished. However, the connection between state and trade continued in the form of the Royal Navy's efforts to keep sea lanes open and safe for commerce. Since Great Britain had remarkable advantages in manufacturing capabilities and shipping, freedom of the seas and freer trade were likely to be beneficial. Thus, while merchants and manufacturers benefited from the expansion of the franchise in 1832, the impact of this newfound electoral clout as a constraint on British foreign affairs is hardly paramount. Rather, the virtuous circle of free trade, freedom of the seas, and naval supremacy provided sufficient impetus for the British government to promote commercial interests.[93]

British leaders did prove willing to use British military resources in order to protect British economic interests abroad. The classic example is the Don Pacifico affair in 1850, a rather extreme example that spurred a heated parliamentary debate and a famous speech by Lord Palmerston. Don Pacifico was a Portuguese Jew and, more importantly for our purposes, a British subject via prior residence in Gibraltar. Pacifico had experienced difficulty collecting on debts owed him in Greece. When word of Greek intransigence reached Palmerston, he ordered the Royal Navy to compel the accused parties to repay Pacifico. Over French and Russian objections, Royal Navy warships blockaded Athens until a settlement was reached.[94]

Subsequent commentary in *The Times* and debate in Parliament raised the issue of whether such action was inappropriate or unjust. Richard Cobden objected to using the navy for such a task, asserting that the British action was tantamount to the intervention in another state's internal affairs; Gladstone offered a similar argument, stating that interference in foreign states should be "rare" and "deliberate," unlike Palmerston's overreaction in this case. Palmerston's rousing speech in defense of his actions invoked the image of a subject of the Roman Empire, unmolested by foreign transgressors, stating, "so also a British subject, in whatever land he may be, shall feel confident that the watchful eye and the strong arm of England, will protect him against injustice and wrong."[95] In the end, the government supported Palmerston's initiative.

The Don Pacifico affair is an interesting example for several reasons. First, it demonstrates the relatively unfettered nature of British foreign policy in the international arena. French and Russian disapproval could not stop Palmerston from bullying the small Greek state. Second, it illustrates how domestic influences tended to be responsive rather than "proactive." That is, neither the press nor the political opposition could prevent Palmerston's order to blockade Athens, and their objections were in response to an action that already had been taken, rather than shaping or constraining action. Third, while the controversial action sparked a charged debate, ultimately the government, and the British public, stood behind the chosen action.

The Effects of International Regimes and Institutions

The Concert of Europe

Many scholars attribute the long period of relative peace following the Napoleonic Wars at least in part to the existence of the Concert of Europe.[96] When negotiating the peace after the long and destructive French Wars, representatives of the great powers—led by British foreign secretary Viscount Castlereagh and Austrian minister of foreign affairs Prince Clemens von Metternich—were insistent upon creating a peaceful and just international system based on the principle of the balance of power.[97] Considered crucial to attaining this end was the institutionalization of a system of diplomacy that could defuse crises before they precipitated major wars. To encourage diplomatic exchanges among the great powers, the powers devised a system of periodic conferences, and it was agreed that in the event of a crisis, the great powers would convene a congress to generate discussion among heads of state before any one state took unilateral action.

Unlike the Holy Alliance—"Metternich's masterpiece"—which was built atop a feudal and religious foundation, the Concert of Europe was a less coherent, loosely organized arrangement.[98] How long the Concert worked effectively is a matter of debate; in any case, "in the form in which it was conceived, the system did not last long."[99] The 1820 revolt in Naples, following on the heels of the Spanish revolution, generated anxiety among those great power leaders who had reactionary tendencies and wished to preserve the political status quo in Europe. Austria, Russia, and Prussia coalesced around a position that the great powers ought to intervene in states where the extant government was threatened by revolution. The more liberal British vehemently opposed the call for collective intervention. A conference at Troppau to discuss the Italian problem drew only observers from Britain, and Castlereagh wrote a stinging rebuke of the protocol encouraging collective intervention that emerged from that conference.[100] This disagreement over the imperative for collective intervention in the internal affairs of states intensified, and by 1822 the British withdrew from the Concert.

Kissinger's claim that the Congresses "for half a century came close to constituting the government of Europe" is certainly an overstatement.[101] Congresses did not always elicit appearances from the highest heads of state, and the draw of the Concert as an institution began to peter out by the 1820s. The Concert did not generate permanent institutions, nor did it produce international law or an impartial agency to mediate disputes.[102] A more sensible and apt alternative to Kissinger's statement is Crawley's injunction that the Concert after 1830 failed to act as a supranational body directing European affairs.[103]

Even if the institutional structure of the Concert failed to endure, perhaps its foundation—"a sense of shared values," or a "conceptual norm among the great powers of the proper and permissible aims and methods of international politics"—did manifest itself in great power relations regarding the eastern Mediterranean and the Levant.[104] Existing evidence suggests that an informal variant of Concert diplomacy, along with the "unwritten rules" of the Concert, guided great power reactions to the Belgian Revolution and the Syrian crisis of 1839–41.[105] However, the exclusion of France from great power negotiations regarding the Syrian crisis clearly violated the precepts of the Concert.[106] At least one scholar has noted that the Syrian crisis might not have been necessary at all had the Concert not failed to settle the Eastern Question at least twice during the 1830s.[107]

Any account of the post–Napoleonic Wars period that does not include the Concert of Europe is clearly incomplete, but the Concert hardly dictated great power actions. While Concert principles encouraged restraint and preservation of the status quo, they did not prevent the use of force to pursue desired outcomes, nor did Concert diplomacy decide policy in the eastern Mediterranean and the Levant. The Concert arguably moderated British military action in the region, but it did not infirm such action; it encouraged British elites to accept the status quo, but British interests centered around the preservation of the status quo anyway.

The Trucial System in the Persian Gulf

The Persian Gulf, though treated only intermittently in this essay, is another piece of the puzzle of the British experience in the Levant. Primarily the domain of the British East India Company, which had its own collection of cruisers (called the "Indian Navy" after 1830), the Gulf served as a link in the Mesopotamian route to India. Of the eight rival sheikdoms with maritime access, six had piratical operations in the Gulf, a source of consistent irritation to British traders and disruption of British communications. In 1835 the British negotiated a truce among the sheikdoms that created a neutral "highway" through the Gulf that would not be interrupted by war dhows. The truce was formalized in 1843 and encoded into a treaty in 1853. The Trucial System was policed by the Indian navy and later by the Royal Navy, and provided relatively safe passage through the Persian Gulf through the end of this period, and indeed well into the twentieth century. An effective regime allowing for maritime commerce and relative tranquility in the Gulf, the Trucial System had little or no effect on the eastern Mediterranean, except by way of not requiring Royal Navy vessels for its enforcement until 1859.[108]

Antislave Patrols

One other international regime in existence during the later portion of this period was based upon maritime antislave trade patrols. Britain had outlawed slavery in the empire by 1807, and under diplomatic pressure other European states agreed to do the same.[109] However, extensive smuggling still occurred, and the United States was still very active in slave trade. Although France, Portugal, and Spain announced their support of Britain, the Royal Navy was practically alone in maintaining antislave patrols. During the 1830s, the British deployed as many as 104 antislaving cruisers.[110] While most of these were patrolling the Atlantic Ocean, there were twenty-three antislaving cruisers in the Mediterranean. Despite the efforts of the British patrols, naval officers acknowledged that it was virtually impossible to suppress the slave trade effectively, and Rear-Admiral Patrick Campbell of the African station asserted that slave traffic actually increased during the mid-1830s.[111]

International cooperation began in earnest only in the 1840s. Atlantic slave patrols came to include French, Portuguese, and American vessels, but Royal Navy cruisers still comprised the lion's share of the patrols.[112] Nonetheless, international cooperation was essential, and the real blow to maritime slave trade came with the signing of the Quintuple Treaty in 1841, which encoded the great powers' agreement to the right of antislavers to visit upon and search suspicious vessels.[113] The deployment of cruisers around the world for the purpose of suppressing the slave trade certainly hurt the ability of the Royal Navy to concentrate many vessels in one place in times of crisis. However, the antislave trade regime also provided the Royal Navy with a valuable tool—the legitimacy of stopping and searching other states' vessels, a capability the Americans condemned as permitting

Britain to "mask her ambition under the guise of humanity."[114] Thus in terms of its impact on British action abroad, the antislave regime was something of a wash; it both helped and hindered British freedom of action in the Mediterranean.

Other Great Powers Capable of Intervening in the Region

Britain's potential great power opponents in the eastern Mediterranean and the Levant had to consider the possibility of a major continental war. Russia, France, Austria, and Prussia all built and trained large military forces during this period (see table 1.2).[115] Simply counting soldiers does not necessarily give us an accurate assessment of comparative army strength, but these numbers provide a convenient starting point. Note that the first five-year period coincides with the last years of the Napoleonic Wars.

Britain's enemy-cum-tentative ally *France* was capable of both military and naval action in the eastern Mediterranean and the Levant, though most French actions during the period focused on the coast of North Africa. The French capture of Algiers in 1830 both illustrated the capacity for unilateral military action and provided the French with a military base in the Mediterranean, expanding France's regional presence.[116] Even with this greater military presence, the French did not taken unilateral action in other parts of the Ottoman Empire. Rather, in Egypt, the French tried to weaken the Porte through military assistance to the revisionist Muhammad Ali.

France's navy was in the fortunate position of having a base at Toulon, which facilitated French naval activity in the Mediterranean despite the consistent British presence there. The composition of the French navy, vastly underfunded

Table 1.2. Army Sizes of European Powers, in Thousands, 1810–1854

Years	France	Britain	Austria	Prussia/Germany	Russia
1810–14	811	227	359	153	645
1815–19	75	125	360	136	800
1820–24	400	115	333	145	749
1825–29	331	107	307	153	860
1830–34	262	107	280	162	553
1835–39	352	117	305	200	677
1840–44	259	133	330	200	800
1845–49	366	139	417	200	790
1850–54	478	154	445	273	996*

Source: Rasler & Thompson, *The Great Powers and the Global Struggle.*
*Bartlett, *Great Britain and Sea Power, 1815–1853*, 101.

immediately following the peace settlement at Vienna, slowly changed from a capital ship navy to "something of a cruiser navy" with only a few large ships-of-the-line.[117] The French, however, did build large super-frigates that were capable of wielding more guns than the largest British frigates. The French had a history of exercising naval power in the Mediterranean and, though almost always overshadowed by British sea power in the region, did maintain a presence there through much of this period. For fleeting moments, the French even enjoyed numerical parity with—and even superiority over—the Royal Navy in the Mediterranean; however, this was the exception rather than the rule. Even as late as 1830, France's navy could hardly match the Royal Navy. For example, the fleet that participated in the seizure of Algiers was "hastily gathered and manned, and was more of a convoy of transports than an effective war-fleet."[118] Since the French fleet in the region was usually weaker than the Royal Navy— "*le tyran de la mer*," as the French called it—French action generally took the form of *guerre de course*, the disruption of maritime commerce, to irritate and intimidate the British.[119]

Like the British, the French kept powerful contingents of warships in commission in the Mediterranean toward the end of the period under investigation. In 1840, during the development of the Syrian crisis, the French built up their Mediterranean fleet to nineteen ships-of-the-line—roughly even with the British, and with greater firepower. The failure of this force to achieve France's desired ends in that crisis spurred an even greater commitment to the navy; the response in kind by the British set the stage for an Anglo-French naval race during the 1840s and beyond.[120]

Technological change played a role in the Anglo-French naval dynamic, though closer to home than in the Mediterranean. The incorporation of paddle-steam frigates into the French navy in the early 1840s caused quite a stir; British elites speculated about the possibility of the French mounting a cross-Channel attack, a heretofore unlikely event. While an invasion of England might have exceeded French ambitions, one author notes that French naval policy had a compelling rationale: "By maintaining a strong French navy and by keeping technology in a state of turmoil, France might deter Britain from going to war over minor questions or using its naval power with arrogance and total confidence in success. . . . Such insecurity in London might create greater latitude of action for France . . . as long as Britain was not provoked."[121] In any case, while the French navy was never a peer of the Royal Navy during this period, France strengthened both its army and navy, particularly during the 1830s and 1840s. Indeed, France appeared capable of challenging the British in the region during these decades, and was on the brink of doing so during the Syrian crisis.[122]

Russia, which enjoyed the largest army in Europe and the benefit of geographic proximity to Asia Minor and the Levant, certainly was capable of intervening in the region and did so several times during the period in question. Russia appeared to have an intimidating and dangerous military presence; though cracks in the foundation are evident in hindsight, at the time the Russian army elicited a fearful wariness from the leaders of the other great powers. In retrospect we note that while large, the Russian army's ability to mount extended campaigns far from home was questionable. Russia's campaigns in the 1827–1829 Russo-Turkish War demonstrated the difficulties the Russians had with maintaining a force beyond Russian borders—the Russians' method of supply via requisition (plunder) was insufficient and resulted in "much suffering" of Russian soldiers.[123] Other examples of Russian intervention in the region are the Russian naval action at Navarino Bay (alongside the British and French); military intervention in the Greek War of Independence, which prompted the Russo-Turkish War of 1827–1829; and the dispatch of warships and 30–40,000 troops to the Asiatic side of the Bosphorus in 1833.

Russia's pattern of ship construction during this period tended to move in tandem with Britain's, though the overall strength of the Russian navy in terms of displacement and ship counts was probably never more than about half of British naval strength. The Russian navy was divided into two major fleets, one in the Baltic Sea and one in the Black Sea; both were predominantly capital ship forces, but they were supplemented by oar-powered gunboat flotillas as well.[124] The Black Sea fleet had to pass through the Bosphorus and the Dardanelles to gain entry to the Mediterranean. The 1809 Anglo-Turkish Treaty codified the old rule that disallowed the passage of warships through the Straits during peacetime; the 1833 Treaty of Unkiar-Skelessi between the Russians and the Turks reiterated this injunction, but a secret article arranged for the closure of the Dardanelles to foreign warships at Russia's behest, while permitting Russian warships to pass.[125] The ability to act without fear of reprisal in the form of a Royal Navy contingent sailing into the Black Sea and attacking the Russian fleet bolstered Russian freedom of action in Asia Minor and the Levant.

Naval forces in the Baltic Sea were stronger than they probably needed to be for home defenses, and they were available for deployment elsewhere in Europe. However, since the Russian bases and dockyards in the Baltic were frozen-in for months during the winter, movement of this fleet at certain times of the year had to be planned well in advance. Even when not frozen in port, in order to sail to the Mediterranean the fleet would have to circumnavigate western Europe, which would make warship response time much slower than British or French vessels, and even of the smaller Austrian navy's vessels. Moreover, most scholars agree that the notion of a Baltic fleet action against Britain was highly unlikely, as the Baltic fleet was used primarily to intimidate smaller states in the immediate area.[126]

Austria, with its modest navy, could exercise some limited naval power in the region, but probably more so in and around the Peloponnesians and the Morea in Greece than in Syria or North Africa. The Austrian army, vying for second in manpower (with the French) among the great powers, had vast potential, but most of this was limited to Europe. Mobilization and transport of large numbers of troops to the Levant would present a difficult challenge to the Austrian navy at the time. In the Syrian crisis, Austrian troops were landed via British vessels. Like the Prussian military, the Austrian army was, for the most part, better suited for defense and actions in central Europe than for use in the periphery.[127]

While *Prussia* was developing the roots of a professionalized, modern army, it was probably the least capable of the great powers to intervene directly in the Levant. Rather, the impact of Prussia was more indirect. For instance, if France went to war in 1840 or thereafter in support of Egypt against the Porte and the British, Prussia could seize the opportunity to attack France. We should be wary of asserting that such an action would be likely without France provoking Prussia in some way. However, the great power relations of the day hinged in large measure on the Eastern Question. Prussia, along with Austria, was aligned with Russia, and all three were linked with the British via the 1840 London Treaty. Should France have sought to undermine actively the Ottoman Empire's hold in Syria and Asia Minor, the Russians and British were likely to react quickly, and could request the Prussians to engage the French in Europe, thus distracting French military efforts and reducing the potency of French action in the Levant. This would probably be the most likely scenario for Prussian action regarding the region—direct intervention was unlikely and, with an army of fewer than 200,000 for much of this period, probably less effective than Russian or Austrian intervention.

Though the *United States* impressed British observers with its large warships and capable crews during the War of 1812, the extent of the Americans' naval influence was primarily limited to the Western Hemisphere. Jan Glete describes the American navy as "predominantly a cruiser force with world-wide commitments," but in fact these commitments were geographically limited. The Americans did have a squadron in the Mediterranean, but it was quite modest, and really of secondary priority to naval home defenses and the ships they cruised in the area of Latin America and the Pacific.[128] The reader should note that the Americans did maintain a naval presence in the eastern Mediterranean, stationed for part of the period with Spanish permission at Port Mahon on Minorca. The American naval forces primarily protected American citizens (especially missionaries) and property, and helped ensure the maintenance and expansion of American commerce with the Turks and others.[129]

Regional States' Options for Pressuring Great Britain

Regional states could put pressure on Britain by using faits accomplis on land, especially in inland areas out of range of the guns aboard British warships. In addition, regional states could interfere with commercial objectives by raising tariffs or internal levies on goods being shipped through the area. The Ottoman Empire, however, did not put many restrictions on British trade, and agreed to commercial treaties that enabled the British to promote relatively free trade in the area. Egypt, under Muhammad Ali, had less favorable conditions for British trade, since Ali encouraged indigenous monopolies in certain key sectors, but eventually (after the failed attempt at northward expansion) Egypt relaxed the restrictions and commercial intercourse with Britain increased. The major avenue by which regional states could, and did, put pressure on Britain was by playing Russia and France against the British state. Both the Sultan of the Ottoman Empire and Muhammad Ali of Egypt used this tactic frequently, though occasionally it may have backfired.

Congruence of British Objectives with Regional Actors' Objectives

Britain and the states of the eastern Mediterranean and the Levant did have some common objectives, and the pursuit of these objectives no doubt helped the British shape regional interactions to their liking. For instance, both the Turkish leadership (the Sublime Porte) and the British wanted to maintain a viable Ottoman Empire, and the pursuit of that goal led the British to improve their financial and trading relationship with the Turks during this period. Likewise, British trade with Egypt increased significantly especially toward the end of this period—trade which was not forced on the Egyptians by the British but rather was mutually beneficial to both states.

Of course, British interests did not overlap completely with those of state leaders in the region. Muhammad Ali's vision of Egyptian expansion (with French assistance in the background) certainly clashed with the British interest in maintaining a short route to India for commerce and communications. Further, while Egyptian autonomy was nearly inevitable due to the weak Ottoman state structure, the severance of ties between the Porte and Egypt would also be to Britain's detriment. Additionally, the Porte's use of the Straits (the Dardanelles and the Bosphorus) as a political tool to balance the great powers was occasionally unsettling to British leaders—namely, when the Porte granted the Russians passage through one or both waterways.

Part Three: Great Britain's Ability to Shape the Peacetime Environment in the Region

To best address this rather vague idea of "shaping," we ask to what extent were the British able to achieve their preferred political and economic conditions in the eastern Mediterranean. Lord Palmerston encapsulated Britain's preferences, in the most general sense, when he asserted that the British sought prosperity, progress, and peace with honor.

1. *Peace (with Honor)*: Essentially, British statesmen sought to employ the mechanism of the balance of power in Europe to both maintain the status quo and to maintain peace, which would facilitate continued communications with India and presumably foster free trade (see below). In barest terms, this required that Britain prevent gains by France and Russia in the Levant without going to war with either, and that Britain prevent, or at least delay, the disintegration of the Ottoman Empire. Peace "with honor" meant that peace ought to be upheld without making unilateral concessions or otherwise sacrificing prestige.
2. *Prosperity*: The British were experimenting with free trade, a novel idea for Europeans, who had advocated a mercantilist approach for such a long period. Along with free trade, the British saw the potential for investment and insurance in the area, and while the primary trade route to India still wrapped around the Cape of Good Hope, communications with India and the possibility of a short commercial route to India were motivating factors for British leaders when making policy in the eastern Mediterranean. Creation of new colonies was less of a priority at this time.
3. *Progress*: The British had an enterprising attitude, morally as well as economically, manifested perhaps most prominently through the attempts to eradicate the slave trade. Britons also had visions of bringing civilization and economic progress to barbaric peoples, primarily by encouraging liberalism (from afar). A tangential but important motivating factor for the British was the continuing imperative to navigate the seas, which would facilitate the pursuit of both the scientific progress of humankind and the development and maintenance of reliable trade routes, which in turn would contribute to peace. Curiously, the British

did *not* try in earnest to spread the tenets of constitutional democracy in the Levantine region during this period.

Deterring Regional Conflict

The Royal Navy, omnipresent and able to respond quickly to crisis situations, deterred both regional powers and great powers from taking aggressive action in the eastern Mediterranean and the littoral areas of the Levant. While difficult to find examples clearly demonstrating successful deterrence, we highlight a few instances suggesting that Britain's naval capacity was an effective deterrent in the region.

Royal Navy presence in the Mediterranean, for example, deterred Muhammad Ali from attempting to invade Asia Minor in the early 1830s. Had the Porte been on its own against Egypt, Ali would have been willing to send his armies toward Turkey.[130] However, the viceroy of Egypt recognized the dangers posed by Britain and her warships in the eastern Mediterranean to any military efforts that Egypt might mount against the Turks. Ali is reported to have said in 1830, "The hostility of the British Government paralyzes all my efforts . . . with the English for my friends, I can do everything; without their friendship I can do nothing . . . wherever I turn she is there to baffle me."[131] The mainstay of this hostility and deterrent effect was the Royal Navy's ability to disrupt sea-based communications and supply lines between Alexandria and the Syrian coast.[132] Less than two years later the Egyptians sent their army to occupy Syria, but went no further; Ali was reluctant to generate the suspicion that Egypt was endangering the existence of the Porte, since that would almost certainly provoke the British.[133] When war broke out, it was the result of a Turkish attack on the Egyptians, not the reverse.

The example of the Egyptians is significant because Egypt was probably the most expansionist and revisionist regional power during this period. If Britain was capable of (at least temporarily) deterring Egypt, Britain was capable of deterring most attempts at regional expansion.

Great Britain also engaged in deterrence of other great powers during the period in question, though rarely unilaterally. An example illustrating such deterrence came in 1839. The outbreak of the Turko-Egyptian war meant that the Ottoman Empire was in grave jeopardy, owing both to the imminent military threat of Muhammad Ali's army and the potential threat posed by Russia, should she jump through the opening window of opportunity. To deter the Russians, Britain and France conducted joint naval exercises in the eastern Mediterranean and positioned their naval forces in a manner favorable to forced passage of the Straits, should the Russians attempt an attack on Constantinople. No such attack materialized.[134]

Naval historian Andrew Lambert attributes the failure of the French to intervene on Muhammad Ali's behalf during the Syrian crisis of 1839–1840 on the deterrent effect of the British naval reserve fleet. Lambert asserts that "French interest in the campaign collapsed when their naval mobilization failed to keep pace with Britain . . . King Louis Philippe opted for peace . . . France had been deterred by the superior reserves of the Royal Navy."[135] While the Royal Navy's reserves certainly played a role in the French decision, the reader should bear in mind that the other great powers had sided with Britain's position, and the French were incapable of standing alone against all of Europe.

Controlling Regional Conflict Outcomes
British actions could have, and did have, an impact on the outcome of regional conflicts in the Levant. However, the action was often collaborative. In the Greek War of Independence, British forces together with French and Russian forces destroyed the Turko-Egyptian fleet. In Syria in 1839–1840, British naval power, combined with British, Austrian, and Turkish complements on the ground, had a decisive impact on the direction of the fighting. Unilateral intervention by Britain was infrequent during this period. We can speculate that, in the vicinity of the coastline, Britain would be able to deploy a substantial naval contingent, and in so doing, play a decisive role in an ongoing conflict among regional actors. However, military action inland was hardly likely to be as effective, and was in fact hardly as likely to be undertaken at all.

Reassuring Aligned States in the Region
Especially in the mid-1830s and later, as the Ottoman Empire's integrity began to diminish rather momentously, the British reassured the Porte promptly and effectively. In 1834, "[Palmerston] strengthened the Mediterranean squadron and ordered the Levant fleet to act upon the authorization of the British ambassador at the Porte should the Sultan need assistance against Russia." Accordingly, the Mediterranean squadron "was to be kept as a unit at Malta, ready for immediate action" in the Straits or anywhere else in the Levant.[136] This blank-check approach did provide the Porte a certain peace of mind, and the Turks came to rely on the British offer of naval intervention as a cornerstone of their defense policy.[137]

However, this ability to reassure aligned states was only so solid in the last decade and a half of the period under investigation because of the dismal failure to reassure the Porte in 1832 and 1833. The Turks, threatened by an advancing Egyptian army, requested British naval assistance. The British ambassador at Constantinople joined in the call:

Stratford Canning begged the Cabinet to send the fleet to Constantinople, where the Russian fleet was anchored. This would reassure the Sultan, for Ibrahim [Pasha, commander of Egyptian forces] would never dare attack Constantinople or Smyrna if British flags or ships were in these ports. Also, Russia could be deprived of a chance for single-handed intervention. Metternich pressed this plan and Palmerston favored it, but his more timid colleagues opposed and there were simply no ships to send, owing to Palmerston's foreign policy. The largest British fleet was coercing the Dutch over the Antwerp affair and another squadron was in the Tagus. So he refused to aid the Sultan and Russia did.[138]

The Sultan's turn to Russia for help backfired. The Russians used the opportunity to extort previously denied privileges of passage through the Straits, encoded in the Treaty of Unkiar-Skelessi.[139] The British and the French were upset by this unseemly turn of events, and we gather that the blank check given the British ambassador in Constantinople after Unkiar-Skelessi was granted—at least in part—to avoid such embarrassment in the future.

Protecting Regional Economic Interests

The British had both direct economic interests in the Levant and indirect economic interests in India, by way of the Levant. That is, the British needed to develop and maintain short routes to India for economic as well as strategic purposes. British military and political capabilities were equal to these tasks. Though great power rivalries generated competition for trade with the Ottomans, the Britons used commercial treaties to keep a foothold and even gain an edge over the more geographically proximate Russia.[140] The Anglo-Turkish economic relationship, in conjunction with the military protection (though short of alliance) Britain offered the Sublime Porte, helped to promote both Britain's direct and indirect economic interests in the region. Of course, the military dimension required a nearby presence, which was maintained by the Royal Navy's warships stationed at Malta.

The consistent presence of the Royal Navy also facilitated the freedom of the seas for trade, and the safety of the seas from pirates. Chasing and apprehending pirate vessels was a major function of British warships. At times, antipiratical operations were combined with more general threats to use force. For example, during the Greek War of Independence, Greek privateers were detaining and plundering nonbelligerent British and French merchant vessels under the pretense of a blockade against the Turks. The British and French commanders, Codrington and de Rigny, anchored off the Greek coast and sent letters to Greek authorities demanding that the piratical operations cease. They then wrote a joint letter to the legislature, invoking the recent decimation of the Turko-Egyptian fleet at Navarino Bay: "There remains for you no pretext. The armistice by sea exists on the part of the Turks *de facto*. Their fleet exists no more. Take care of yours, for we will also destroy it, if need be, to put a stop to a system of robbery on the high seas, which would end in your expulsion from the law of nations."[141] This threat had an impact on the Greek leadership, who neither wanted their ships sunk nor their chances of statehood imperiled, and the piracy dwindled rapidly. Commerce resumed with far less molestation.

Ensuring Regional States Pursued Desirable Foreign Policies

During the period under investigation, Great Britain was in a better position to react to the activities and policies of regional powers than to shape them. While a consistent British naval presence certainly affected the decisions of regional leaders, British officials hardly had the ability to dictate the policies of those leaders. During the War of Greek Independence, it took the British years to decide which side to support in the fray. In 1833, the British leadership certainly did not want the Turks to look to the tsar of Russia for assistance, but indeed that is precisely what the Sultan did. An even clearer illustration is the "foreign" policy of Muhammad Ali's Egypt, which engaged in two major campaigns against the Turks. The British, jealously protective of the integrity of the Ottoman Empire, were decidedly opposed to Egyptian aggression but could do little to dissuade Ali short of military threats and intervention.

Encouraging Desirable Domestic Developments in Regional Polities

Great Britain, especially under Whig leadership but also when governed by the Tories, generally encouraged liberalism and constitutionalism in Europe and the immediate periphery. While the British actively promoted the dissolution of monopolistic practices and encouraged freer trade, especially after the 1820s, they did far less to actively promote constitutional government. While the British alignment with France on some issues revolved around a generally liberal tendency, British foreign policies toward domestic political developments in Levantine states tended to be hands-off.

In Turkey, the heart of the weakening Ottoman Empire, Palmerston's predecessors did not seek to bolster the state, nor did they try to build up British influence at Constantinople. Rather, the aim of the foreign policies of Viscount Castlereagh and George Canning seems to be the delaying of the collapse of the Porte.[142] With the accession of Palmerston to the foreign office in the 1830s and the crisis of 1833, however, British policy was reoriented toward the reform of the Turkish state apparatus. The primary aims were to improve the deteriorating Ottoman military and naval forces and to rebuild the finances of the Turkish state after the strains of the War of Greek Independence and the Russo-Turkish War.[143]

As for the nature of the political system in Turkey, the British did not encourage constitutional government as they had in several European states. Palmerston and other British elites, including Brian Urquhart, favored enlightened despotism and a revamped state apparatus in Turkey, but not parliamentary government.[144] British aid contributed to military reform and improvement in Turkey, but most military and naval advisers sent to Turkey were refused; the Turks looked upon such advisers as interference in the internal affairs of the Ottoman Empire.[145]

Conclusion

A number of factors influenced Britain's ability to shape the regional political environment in the eastern Mediterranean and the Levant during the period between 1816 and 1852. Britain's expanding financial and commercial influence gave British leaders some leverage in dealing with peoples in foreign lands. Defeat in the Napoleonic Wars, and the consequences thereof, prevented the French from challenging the British for preeminence in the region; other great powers were constrained by limited capabilities. The Concert of Europe purportedly promoted diplomatic solutions to crises involving the great powers. Yet most striking in its impact was the Royal Navy. Operating on the two-power standard, it was an omnipresent fixture in the Mediterranean, a consistent source and symbol of British power in the region.

British leaders pursued—and for the most part achieved—three goals in the region: peace with honor, prosperity, and progress. Success depended in large measure on naval capabilities and presence. A weak and debilitated army, scattered across the globe for home and imperial defense, was for the most part unavailable for deployment in the region. The strength of the Royal Navy compensated for weakness of the army, acting as the cornerstone of British influence over political developments in the region. Other powers' navies were far weaker in overall capabilities, and they could not maintain as consistent a presence in the region.

The Royal Navy was an effective instrument of policy even though it was relatively stagnant in terms of technological advances. Slow to incorporate new innovations, it failed to keep pace with the technological progress of other regional powers. Rather than emphasize a fully modernized battle fleet in the Mediterranean, Britain employed a force primarily comprised of cruiser-type vessels, which were outsized and outgunned by the most recent capital ship designs, but permitted distribution over a larger area.[146] In addition to coverage, Britain's comparative advantage centered on training and seamanship rather than a technological edge. Outmaneuvering the enemy proved a useful approach when engaging less experienced adversaries.

Consistent forward presence and access to local bases facilitated rapid response to problems and crises. It is hard to say (based on the research to date) whether the impact of this forward presence was symbolic, or whether potential adversaries felt the locally stationed forces could themselves deliver a swift and deadly blow. Nonetheless, this consistent presence minimized the occurrence of dangerous crises by deterring possible challengers to the status quo. An important exception is aggressors' use of inland military faits accomplis, which essentially hamstrung Britain's response because she could not configure and deploy ground forces in the region in a speedy manner.

Britain's ability to achieve its goals in the eastern Mediterranean was also facilitated, conditioned, and constrained by a number of nonmilitary factors. Britons were the world's leaders in terms of international trade and finance, though this distinction did not supplant the need for military forces in the region. Naval forces were in fact integral to the protection of commerce from raids, and to the coercion of those who defaulted on financial obligations. In addition, neither Britain nor the local powers were particularly vulnerable, since financial ties were limited and trade was mutually beneficial but in most cases not crucial. Thus, few asymmetries with the possibility of generating political influence for either side existed.

With few exceptions, British political penetration of regional powers was quite limited and contributed little to the achievement of British objectives in the region. Diplomacy in conjunction with military demonstrations was more efficacious than political influence exercised from within regional states.

At home, British defense spending was constrained for much of this period by political leaders' and citizens' concerns about the economy. Yet domestic political factors such as the electorate, party interplay in Parliament, and special interests played minimal roles in constraining British actions abroad. Foreign secretaries were occasionally mindful of public opinion, but more often they led or even manipulated it to their advantage; interparty debate tended to focus more on domestic issues, while converging to some degree on foreign affairs; and commercial interests had a symbiotic relationship with British leadership.

International regimes and institutions affected great power interactions during this period, encouraging the preservation of peace and the status quo. Yet their immediate impact on Britain's ability to achieve its regional aims was actually quite minimal. The Concert of Europe neither dictated British foreign policy in the eastern Mediterranean nor prevented Britain from using force in the region. By promoting the peace and the status quo, the Concert served mostly to reinforce British aims. The international antislavery regime, promulgated and implemented primarily by Britain, was a double-edged sword. Its implementation required that Britain's cruiser forces be scattered around the world, thus preventing them from being concentrated in a particular region like the Mediterranean. However, the accompanying ability to stop and search suspicious vessels provided a subtle, but hardly inconsequential, advantage to British captains in the Mediterranean.

Other great powers had the ability to use force in the region, with France and Russia the most likely, and most capable, candidates. Yet Russia's ability to project force abroad in massive concentrations was suspect; the Russians' difficulties in sustaining land campaigns against Turkey were duly noted. France only became militarily competitive with Britain toward the end of the period, and then the French threat was thought to be to the British Isles, not to British interests in the periphery. Austria and Prussia had little impact on the area, and the United States was not yet up to the task of competing for markets and influence in a region halfway around the world.

The leadership of the Ottoman Empire generally had aims consonant with British objectives, though occasionally the Sublime Porte played the Russians and Britons against each other. Revisionist Egypt posed a continual challenge to British aims, but the Egyptians were forced to rely upon the military fait accompli, conducted sufficiently inland so as to be out of the Royal Navy's reach. Rapid inland military action was the only viable military option for pressuring the Britons; naval engagements reinforced notions of British superiority at sea.

For the most part, Britain achieved its overarching goals in the region—peace with honor, prosperity, and progress. Realization of peace (with honor) is reflected in the characterization of this period as part of the *Pax Britannica*. Britain deterred revisionist Egypt from taking aggressive action on several occasions, and Britain's participation in some multilateral actions promoted peace or the rapid conclusion of ongoing conflicts. In addition, Britain reassured the leaders of the crumbling Ottoman Empire, prolonging the life span of that state (and perhaps forestalling the violence that accompanied its ultimate demise). Promotion of prosperity is evident in Britain's effective protection of its economic interests abroad, from both piracy and default. More importantly Britain successfully protected its communications, and its future short trading route, with India. British cruisers also helped to keep sea lanes open for increasingly freer trade. Britain's actions in the region resulted in some progress, in a nineteenth-century British sense of enlightenment, which comprises rejection of slavery, embracement of liberalism, and the navigation of the seas. While British success in promoting these causes is evident, Britain did not encourage the peoples in the eastern Mediterranean and Levant to adopt constitutional democracy.

A number of intriguing issues emerge from this study that bear further inquiry. First, why did events at the end of this period of relative peace spiral downward into the Crimean War? Here our concern is a bit more specific than the underlying causes of the war. Rather, we might consider Russia's prodding of the Ottoman Empire to reflect a deterrence failure on Britain's part. Did the manner in which the British configured and utilized military force in the eastern Mediterranean and the Levant encourage or permit the Russians to antagonize the Turks in a way that eventually precipitated great power war? How might the British have employed force differently in the decades following the Napoleonic Wars so that great power war would have been avoidable?

Second, how did the potential targets of British deterrence perceive the Royal Navy and other instruments of force available to British policymakers? During a Parliamentary debate in 1821, the Marquis of Titchfield asserted, "The strength of England consists in the reputation she enjoys of being able to undertake war."[147] Was the Royal Navy's reputation, symbolized in a token appearance of British warships, enough to deter or halt aggressive action? Or did the British have to maintain an operational capacity capable of inflicting heavy costs on a potential aggressor near at hand in order to neutralize possible threats to the status quo? The evidence consulted for this study suggests that the latter was more important. C. J. Bartlett's observation that British influence hinged in part on Britain's ability "to concentrate sufficient ships at a particular point" is vague but nonetheless contains a kernel of truth.[148] Bartlett implies that operational capacity is necessary for deterring or containing potential adversaries; the preceding case study supports that implication, insofar as a conspicuous lack of operationally capable British presence resulted in setbacks to British aims in the eastern Mediterranean. These findings are more suggestive than definitive, however, and further research into the dynamics of conventional deterrence and military presence is warranted.

Notes

1. Gerald S. Graham, *The Politics of Naval Supremacy* (Cambridge: Cambridge University Press, 1965), 110.

2. Although not treated herein, other portions of the modern Middle East and southwestern Asia such as Persia (Iran) and Afghanistan are also of potential interest. Future investigations would do well to include these areas.

3. Correlli Barnett, *Britain and Her Army, 1509–1970* (New York: William Morrow and Co., 1970), chapter 12; Richard L. Blanco, "Reform and Wellington's Post Waterloo Army, 1815–1854," *Military Affairs* 24, no. 3 (fall 1965), 123–31; Hew Strachan, *Wellington's Legacy: The Reform of the British Army, 1830–54* (Manchester: Manchester University Press, 1984).

4. The basis for the claim that the army was underfunded is not necessarily self-evident. Blanco quotes Sidney Herbert on the reluctance of the House of Commons to allot more funding to the army: "it is easier to get £1,000 in the House of Commons for the Navy, than it is to get £100 for the Army" ("Reform," 125, fn. 18). Blanco also points out that the amount of money spent annually on the army was largely unchanged from 1820 through 1853 ("Reform," 125, fn. 11). This is indeed borne out in the statistical record as presented in Brian R. Mitchell, *British Historical Statistics* (Cambridge: Cambridge University Press, 1988), 587–88. The annual expenditures on the army fluctuated between £11.1m and £7.6m during the 1818–52 period (1816–17 were higher due to the occupation of France and gradual demobilization). The statistical evidence also reveals that naval expenditures, despite any favoritism in the House of Commons, also remained fairly constant throughout that period. Annual naval expenditures fell within a range of £7.5m and £4.1m, with the higher figures primarily coming in the 1840s, an unsurprising pattern, given the invasion scares of that decade and the transition to steam-powered warships. This decade is also the only time at which gross naval expenditures ever approached parity with army expenditures; however, at no time during the entire nineteenth century did annual naval expenditures exceed army expenditures except during the late 1890s.

5. Military historians frequently attribute this stagnation to the absence of continental wars requiring British involvement; see for example, D. H. Cole and E. C. Priestley, *An Outline of British Military History, 1660–1937* (London: Sifton Praed, 1937), 170.

6. Eric William Sheppard, *A Short History of the British Army*, 4th ed. (London: Constable and Company, 1950), esp. 206; Barnett, *Britain and Her Army*, 273.

7. Article ii of the Constitutional Charter of 1814 in France forbade conscription, but the practice was revived de facto in 1818; M. S. Anderson, *The Ascendancy of Europe, 1815–1914* (New York: Longman, 1985), 294.

8. Barnett, *Britain and Her Army*, 280–83, describes the plight of the British soldier in some detail. For example, he points out that an imprisoned convict had living quarters that encompassed a modest 1,000 cubic feet of air, but a British soldier's space in the barracks amounted to only 400 cubic feet of air. See also Edward M. Spiers, *The Army and Society, 1815–1914* (New York: Longman, 1980), chapter 2; Blanco, "Reform," *passim*; and John Fortescue, "The Army," in *Early Victorian England, 1830–1865* (New York: Oxford University Press, 1934), 350–52, who

complains that Parliament's meager funding for the army was "criminally imbecile," and that Parliament "grumbled at the cost of recruits and did its best to kill them off as rapidly as possible."

9. Quoted in Blanco, "Reform," 126.
10. Barnett, *Britain and Her Army*, 282.
11. Strachan, *Wellington's Legacy*, 220.
12. John Marlowe, *Perfidious Albion: The Origins of the Anglo-French Rivalry in the Levant* (London: Elek Books, 1971), 169. Rudolf von Albertini asserts that by 1830, the Egyptian army had grown to 100,000 men, but it is unclear whether this is a reliable statistic or based on Ali's aims rather than what he actually accomplished. Rudolf von Albertini, with Albert Wirz, *European Colonial Rule, 1880–1940: The Impact of the West on India, Southeast Asia, and Africa*, trans. John G. Williamson (Westport, Conn.: Greenwood Press, 1992), 228.
13. David B. Ralston, *Importing the European Army: The Introduction of European Military Techniques and Institutions into the Extra-European World, 1600–1914* (Chicago: University of Chicago Press, 1990), 89–90.
14. Estimates based on M. S. Anderson, *The Ascendancy of Europe*, 297; Frank Edgar Bailey, *British Policy and the Turkish Reform Movement: A Study in Anglo-Turkish Relations, 1826–1853* (New York: Howard Fertig, 1970), 15–16; and Stanford J. Shaw and Ezel Kural Shaw, *History of the Ottoman Empire and Modern Turkey, Volume II* (New York: Cambridge University Press, 1977), chapter 1.
15. Bailey, *British Policy and the Turkish Reform Movement*, 15–16.
16. D. K. Brown, *Before the Ironclad: Development of Ship Design, Propulsion and Armament in the Royal Navy, 1815–60* (London: Conway Maritime Press, 1990), 8–9.
17. C. J. Bartlett, *Great Britain and Sea Power, 1815–1853* (Oxford: Clarendon, 1963), 21.
18. Jan Glete, *Navies and Nations: Warships, Navies, and State-Building in Europe and America, 1500–1860*, 2 vols. (Stockholm: Almqvist and Wiksell International, 1993), 422.
19. Paul M. Kennedy, *The Rise and Fall of British Naval Mastery* (Atlantic Highlands, N.J.: Ashfield Press, 1983), 156; C. C. Lloyd, "Navies," in *The New Cambridge Modern History, Vol. IX*, ed. C. W. Crawley (Cambridge: Cambridge University Press, 1965), 76–90, esp. 90; Glete, *Navies and Nations*, 422. Counting rules differ from author to author, so settling on a single authoritative number can be difficult. The figure in George Modelski and William R. Thompson, *Seapower in Global Politics, 1494–1993* (Seattle: University of Washington Press, 1988), 71–72, is much lower, as we would expect from their counting rules, which discount many "surplus vessels" (but see also their reference to Walker 1860 on p. 208). While many assessments of sea power are impressionistic, Glete and Modelski and Thompson are commendable for their rigor and transparency in the compilation of their data.
20. C. J. Bartlett's reproduction of some instructions sent from the Admiralty to the Navy board in 1815 illuminates the concept of "in ordinary" to a limited degree. The Admiralty prescribes a force of 100 (fully constructed) ships-of-the-line, 14 of which should be kept in commission, while "the others should be laid up in ordi-

nary in such a state of repair and equipment as will admit of their being on any emergency brought forward for immediate service." Bartlett, *Great Britain and Sea Power*, 23–24. Bartlett later writes that during the 1830s, "despite frequent efforts to keep abreast of repairs to ships in ordinary, considerable alarm prevailed at the Admiralty concerning the true state of many of the ships of the line in reserve. [M. P. Charles] Wood believed that no one 'knows much of the *real* state of our ships in ordinary'" (emphasis in original); Bartlett, *Great Britain and Sea Power*, 126.

21. Fred T. Jane, *The British Battle-Fleet: Its Inception and Growth throughout the Centuries* (London: Conway Maritime Press, 1997), 150; Brown, *Before the Ironclad*, 26; Bartlett, *Great Britain and Sea Power*, 60–61.

22. Brown, *Before the Ironclad*, 26; Glete, *Navies and Nations*, 422.

23. Glete, *Navies and Nations*, 431.

24. R. C. Anderson, whose work excels regarding ship counts and detailed naval information, attributes the smaller number to P. Richards and the larger number to Muhammad Ali's correspondence. R. C. Anderson, *Naval Wars in the Levant 1559–1853* (Princeton, N.J.: Princeton University Press, 1952), 524 and 525, respectively. Anderson favors the latter, though he notes that the difference is due to small vessels.

25. These figures are based on several sources: R. C. Anderson, *Naval Wars in the Levant*; C. M. Woodhouse, *The Battle of Navarino* (London: Hodder and Stoughton, 1965); and Jane, *The British Battle-Fleet*. "Smaller vessels" is a catchall category referring to corvettes, brigs, schooners, fireships, and cutters. Though the Turko-Egyptian fleet outnumbered the Europeans in warships, the opposing sides were rather evenly matched in number of guns. R. C. Anderson, *Naval Wars in the Levant*, 526.

26. R. C. Anderson, *Naval Wars in the Levant*, 532.

27. J. David Singer, and Melvin Small, *The Wages of War 1816–1965: A Statistical Handbook* (New York: John Wiley and Sons, 1972) assert a high level of confidence in this estimate. R. C. Anderson, *Naval Wars in the Levant*, (the source of Singer and Small's estimate!) is a bit more circumspect, but offers a range of 3,000–4,000. These figures are certainly more widely accepted than Codrington's inflated estimates of 6,000 enemy dead and 4,000 wounded; Woodhouse, *The Battle of Navarino*, 141.

28. For the 1832 figure see Marlowe, *Perfidious Albion*, chapter 7, and for the 1838 figure see Glete, *Navies and Nations*, 431. The number of ships afloat and under construction in 1832, according to Marlowe, lead the author to be a bit surprised at Glete's figure, though Glete's data are thoroughly documented.

29. Glete, *Navies and Nations*, 431.

30. Glete, *Navies and Nations*, 430–33.

31. See Glete, *Navies and Nations*, 450. Those who are familiar with the history of ship design will likely dispute this claim on the grounds that Sir Robert Seppings made significant contributions to warship design in the early part of this period (ca. 1815–32). Indeed, Seppings's improvements, especially in hull design and the strength of the supporting structure of wooden sailing ships-of-the-line, facilitated increases in the length and weight of vessels. However, these improvements were, in the opinion of the author, more evolutionary than revolutionary. The essence of the

warship did not radically change as a result of Seppings's advances; rather, it was refined. On Seppings's contributions, see Andrew Lambert, *The Last Sailing Battlefleet: Maintaining Naval Mastery 1815–1850* (London: Conway Maritime Press, 1991), 59–67, and Brown, *Before the Ironclad*, 16–19.

32. By the middle of the nineteenth century, British officers and heads of state acknowledged the enduring importance of technological advances—particularly steam, screw-type propulsion, rifled guns, and heavy armor for warships—and allowed the conversion of the British Royal Navy from wooden ships to iron. At first, steam-powered warships were considered vulnerable in battle and expensive to operate, and demanded seamen with special training, which were not in abundance. The Royal Navy's begrudging use of them prior to the 1850s primarily was in support of sail-powered ships-of-the-line. The effects of these developments on the events in the eastern Mediterranean and the Levant during the period in question were, in any event, quite limited. The British and French enjoyed slight advantages in technology when developing steam warships, but such advantages were fleeting, as knowledge of the next wave in warship technology diffused rather quickly. Prior to steam's popularity, Britain's chief advantage probably lay in superior warship maintenance and seamanship rather than in superior technology. American and French ships-of-the-line outweighed and outgunned similar British vessels, but the British emphasis on cruisers gave British captains the option of averting direct engagement and speeding off to regroup or retreat to safe haven.

33. Muhammad Ali (often referred to as Mehemet Ali in older histories) hired also European officers to command and man his best warships. These were mostly French, but Ali succeeded in recruiting the occasional Briton as well. Marlowe, *Perfidious Albion*, 168. Results of confrontations with European navies, however, indicated that a handful of disaffected or money-hungry European naval officers does not a navy make.

34. Kennedy, *Rise and Fall*, 172.

35. For example, see Woodhouse, *The Battle of Navarino*, 88.

36. William Laird Clowes, *The Royal Navy: A History from the Earliest Times to the Present, Volume VI* (London: Chatham Publishing, 1997), 311.

37. On the impact of the percussion cap, which allowed the firearm to discharge properly even in wet conditions, see Cole and Priestley, *An Outline of British Military History*, 170–71.

38. J. F. C. Fuller, *Armament and History: A Study of the Influence of Armament on History from the Dawn of Classical Warfare to the Second World War* (New York: Charles Scribner's Sons, 1945), 109–10. On these developments see also M. S. Anderson, *The Ascendancy of Europe*, chapter 6, and especially Trevor N. Dupuy, *The Evolution of Weapons and Warfare* (Fairfax, Va.: Hero Books, 1984), chapter 19. As for why development of the British Army lagged behind that of its European competitors, conventional wisdom seems to suggest that Britain's involvement in colonial wars—where superiority came easily and there was no impetus for further development—are largely to blame. See Byron Farwell, *Queen Victoria's Little Wars*

(New York: Harper and Row, 1972), and Philip J. Haythornwaite, *The Colonial Wars Sourcebook* (New York: Arms and Armour, 1995) for more on these conflicts. Hew Strachan, "The British Army and 'Modern War': The Experience of the Peninsula and the Crimea," in *Tools of War: Instruments, Ideas, and Institutions of Warfare, 1445–1871*, ed. John A. Lynn (Urbana, Ill.: University of Illinois Press, 1990) offers an alternative explanation, blaming not only colonial responsibilities but the added pressures of an overwhelming wave of technological innovations in the 1830s and the British domestic reform bill of 1832.

39. A good place to start for inquiries into the British use of technological superiority in the colonies is Daniel R. Headrick, *The Tools of Empire: Technology and European Imperialism in the Nineteenth Century* (New York: Oxford University Press, 1981), especially chapters 1, 2, and 4.

40. Many naval historians consider Malta to be a crucial part of the British naval presence in the Mediterranean during this period; but see the dissent by Williams who argues that Malta was "an island entrepôt of great importance in war, [but] . . . very limited usefulness in peacetime." Judith Blow Williams, *British Commercial Policy and Trade Expansion, 1750–1850* (London: Oxford University Press, 1972), 88–89.

41. The Ionian Islands were, under a cloud of debate, relinquished in 1863. See Walter Frewen Lord, *England and France in the Mediterranean 1660–1830* (Port Washington, N.Y.: Kennikat Press, 1970), 61–62. Of course, the Treaty of Unkiar Skelessi allowed Russia's Black Sea fleet entry to the Mediterranean; but the Ionian Islands provided a convenient base of operations close enough to the Straits to give the British an opportunity to challenge such an entry.

42. John B. Hattendorf et al., eds., *British Naval Documents, 1204–1960* (Brookfield, Vt.: Scholar Press, 1993), 567.

43. Bartlett, *Great Britain and Sea Power*, 34.

44. W. C. B. Tunstall, "Imperial Defence, 1815–1870," in *The Cambridge History of the British Empire, Vol. II: The Growth of the New Empire, 1783–1870* (Cambridge: Cambridge University Press, 1961), 806–41.

45. Hattendorf et al., *British Naval Documents*, 567.

46. Kennedy, *Rise and Fall*, 170–71; note that the two African stations combined for 37 warships, the Western Hemisphere merited 36, the East Indies and China 25, and home waters 35. By this count, only 19 percent of British warships in commission were stationed in the Mediterranean. As Kennedy notes, the number of ships in home waters is deceiving, since a spurt of fortification-building and militia-raising in England gave enough peace of mind to allow the overseas deployment of the larger warships typically earmarked for home defense; *Rise and Fall*, 172–73.

47. One might argue that this ability to let battle-readiness dwindle at times in the Mediterranean was facilitated by the norms of the Concert of Europe, which emphasized joint consultation of great powers prior to taking revisionist actions. There is a kernel of truth to this claim, though note that the 1844 incident occurred when the Concert already had lost much of its currency with the great powers. Moreover, one might expect the French action to go unchallenged by other Concert powers, as

Russia, Prussia, and Austria were eager to encourage distrust between the more liberal-leaning Britain-France combination. Gordon A. Craig and Alexander L. George, *Force and Statecraft: Diplomatic Problems of Our Time*, 3rd ed. (New York: Oxford University Press, 1995).

48. Woodhouse, *The Battle of Navarino*, 57–58.

49. The London Treaty was signed on 6 July 1827; Codrington was told of the treaty on or about 19 July, and did not receive additional instructions until 7 August. See Woodhouse, *The Battle of Navarino*, 51; R. C. Anderson, *Naval Wars in the Levant*, 515.

50. R. C. Anderson, *Naval Wars in the Levant*, 526.

51. Clowes Vol. VI (1997: 314). What makes this story even more interesting is that the troops were transported in steamers, which ostensibly were not subject to the whims of Mother Nature. However, the warships that provided covering fire and bombarded the fortifications of the coastal cities were powered by sail, and thus restricted the movement of the fleet.

52. Kennedy, *Rise and Fall*, 168–69.

53. Clowes, *The Royal Navy*, 314.

54. Unlike the seventeenth and eighteenth centuries, which featured large reserve fleets called into service only in wartime, most modern ships were kept in commission by the mid-nineteenth century. The British did have a substantial number of vessels in ordinary, but increasingly rapid communications (and quicker crisis escalation) toward the end of this period required increased readiness on the part of British naval forces. Glete, *Navies and Nations*, 421.

55. Glete, *Navies and Nations*, 421.

56. Kennedy, *Rise and Fall*, 168–69. Kennedy mentions the Austrian armed intervention against rebels in Piedmont in 1823 and the French intervention in Spain that returned King Ferdinand to power as examples of this phenomenon.

57. Bartlett, *Great Britain and Sea Power*, 75–77. The Royal Navy's practice of keeping 2 to 3 ships-of-the-line and 2 to 3 frigates in the Tagus cut both ways for the Portuguese government, however; while offering needed protection (the king literally sought refuge in the *Windsor Castle*, a British ship-of-the-line) the British contingent also ensured a peaceful, though reluctant, severance of colonial ties between Portugal and Brazil.

58. G. D. Clayton, *Britain and the Eastern Question: Missolonghi to Gallipoli* (London: University of London Press, 1971), 46; cf. Douglas Dakin, *The Greek Struggle for Independence, 1821–1833* (Berkeley: University of California Press, 1973), 152.

59. Clayton, *Britain and the Eastern Question*, 53, argues that there "is little doubt that the allied commanders intended to force a battle" with the Turks and Egyptians. The orders from the allied governments apparently were ambiguous, and Codrington, de Rigny, and Heyden took the initiative to challenge the Ottoman combined fleet.

60. However, this is not the only contributing factor to Greek independence. As Clayton notes, the immediate cause of peace in 1829 and the consequent granting of

independence to Greece was Russian military action, independent of the other great powers (*Britain and the Eastern Question*, 55–56). Nonetheless, other scholars attribute enormous significance to the destruction of the Ottoman fleet. See, for example, C. I. Hamilton, *Anglo-French Naval Rivalry, 1840–1870* (New York: Oxford University Press, 1993), 3.

61. Although such operations arguably would be in the spirit of the Concert of Europe; in fact, several prominent Britons advocated a policy of humanitarian intervention in Turkey, but it never came to pass. On the argument for collective intervention for humanitarian purposes, see the discussion of Stratford de Redcliffe and John Stuart Mill in Carsten Holbraad, *The Concert of Europe: A Study in German and British International Theory, 1815–1914* (New York: Barnes and Noble, 1970), 162–65. Their arguments, which Holbraad links to progressive thought, began to take shape in the 1830s and 1840s. Multinational peacekeeping efforts like those arranged by the United Nations were possible, if exercised by the great powers, but would require some very delicate diplomacy, since the Concert was roughly divided along ideological lines, with the British and French having liberal tendencies and Austria, Prussia, and Russia being more conservatively inclined. In addition (and partly as a consequence of this ideological division) the British had taken a public stand against collective intervention in other states' internal affairs.

62. Bailey, *British Policy and the Turkish Reform Movement*, 68; Leland Hamilton Jenks, *The Migration of British Capital to 1875* (New York: Alfred A. Knopf, 1927), chapter 2.

63. These currency crises largely took the form of runaway inflation. States needed loans as a means to secure increasingly scarce bullion to retire paper money, which would in turn deflate the currency.

64. Quoted in Jenks, *The Migration of British Capital*, 36.

65. The Holy Alliance included Prussia, Russia, and Austria. In addition to the £5m. loan floated for Prussia, the Rothschilds arranged for loans of 100m. florins to Austria for military purposes, 40m. rubles to Russia for the retirement of inflated currency, and 40m. thalers to Prussia for armaments; see Jenks, *The Migration of British Capital*, 41ff.

66. Jenks, *The Migration of British Capital*, 39.

67. D. C. M. Platt, *Finance, Trade, and Politics in British Foreign Policy, 1815–1914* (New York: Oxford University Press, 1968).

68. See Dakin's detailed work on the British philhellene movement and the first loan and on the second loan; Dakin, *The Greek Struggle for Independence*, 107–20 and 166–72, respectively.

69. Jenks, *The Migration of British Capital*, 61–62.

70. For a discussion of the Levant Company's role in Anglo-Levantine trade see Patricia Crimmin, "The Royal Navy and the Levant Trade, c.1795–c.1805," in *The British Navy and the Use of Naval Power in the Eighteenth Century*, eds. Jeremy Black and Philip Woodfine (Leicester, U.K.: Leicester University Press, 1988). for a discussion of why the British dissolved the company, see Vernon John Puryear, *France and*

the Levant: From the Bourbon Restoration to the Peace of Kutiah (Hamden, Conn.: Archon Books, 1968), 37–39.

71. P. J. Cain and A. G. Hopkins, "The Political Economy of British Expansion Overseas, 1750–1914," *The Economic History Review*, second series, 33, no. 4 (November 1980), 463–90, on 476; John Gallagher and Ronald Robinson, "The Imperialism of Free Trade," *The Economic History Review*, second series, 6, no. 1 (1953): 1–15, esp. 11–12.

72. von Albertini with Wirz, *European Colonial Rule, 1880–1940*, 230; Williams, *British Commercial Policy and Trade Expansion*, 299. For more on Egypt's modernization and economic development during this period, see the opening part of chapter 7 in von Albertini with Wirz, *European Colonial Rule, 1880–1940*.

73. Bailey, *British Policy and the Turkish Reform Movement*, 70; Clayton, *Britain and the Eastern Question*, 90.

74. Interestingly, the British continued to accept payments in gold from the Turks, even though it forced the Turks to devalue their currency, driving prices up and weakening the financial health of the Ottoman Empire, which the British expended so much diplomatic and military energy trying to strengthen. See Bailey, *British Policy and the Turkish Reform Movement*, 77.

75. James L. Stokesbury, *Navy and Empire* (New York: William Morrow and Co., 1983), 238. Note however that the law requiring that Turkish goods be imported only in British hulls was abolished in 1822; Bailey, *British Policy and the Turkish Reform Movement*, 119.

76. The maintenance of colonies in South Africa required several instances of armed conflict, including the Kaffir Wars and later in the century, the Boer Wars. For a list and brief descriptions of these conflicts see R. Ernest Dupuy and Trevor N. Dupuy, *The Encyclopedia of Military History from 3500 B.C. to the Present*, 2nd rev. ed. (New York: Harper and Row, 1986), 783–84; Micheal Clodfelter, *Warfare and Armed Conflicts: A Statistical Reference to Casualty and Other Figures, 1618–1991*, Vol. I (Jefferson, N.C.: McFarland and Company, 1992); and Farwell, *Queen Victoria's Little Wars*. The Cape was the middle link in a string of bases along the traditional route to India (the others were Ascension, St. Helena, Mauritius, and Ceylon); see Lloyd, "Navies," 90.

77. Graham, *The Politics of Naval Supremacy*, 66. These estimates are based on steam-powered vessels.

78. This would change much later when the British colonized Egypt in the 1880s.

79. Platt, *Finance, Trade, and Politics*, 185. This is not to understate Bailey's observation that communications between the British government and the ports of the Ottoman Empire increased after the Levant Company (which previously had undertaken those communications) was disbanded (Bailey, *British Policy and the Turkish Reform Movement*, 118–19). However, Bailey suggests that this improved the flow of information to Britain regarding conditions in Turkey; it does not necessarily imply that the Britons had any political influence.

80. Clayton, *Britain and the Eastern Question*, 92–94; Bailey, *British Policy and the Turkish Reform Movement*, 146–49.

81. R. C. Anderson, *Naval Wars in the Levant*, 559–60; M.S. Anderson, *The Eastern Question, 1774–1923: A Study in International Relations* (New York: St. Martin's Press, 1966), 102–3; Paul W. Schroeder, *The Transformation of European Politics, 1763–1848* (New York: Oxford University Press, 1994), 744; Clayton, *Britain and the Eastern Question*, 83.

82. Jack L. Snyder, *Myths of Empire: Domestic Politics and International Ambition* (Ithaca, N.Y.: Cornell University Press, 1991), chapter 5.

83. Derek Beales, *From Castlereagh to Gladstone, 1815–1885* (London: Thomas Nelson and Sons, 1969), 77.

84. See for example Beales, *From Castlereagh to Gladstone*, 166–67.

85. Stokesbury, *Navy and Empire*, 214; Henry Kissinger, *Diplomacy* (New York: Simon and Schuster, 1994), 96.

86. Ian C. Hannah, *A History of British Foreign Policy* (London: Nicholson and Watson, 1938), 100.

87. Quoted in Beales, *From Castlereagh to Gladstone*, 75–76; see also Goldwyn Smith, *A History of England*, 2nd ed. (New York: Charles Scribner's Sons, 1957), 568. Schroeder implicitly suggests that Canning played to the British public when he notes that Metternich was wary of France and Britain in late 1822 and early 1823. The Austrian diplomat felt threatened because he "viewed Chateaubriand [Montmorency's successor in France in late 1822] and Canning as equally dangerous, both of them being capable of setting Europe aflame for the sake of personal popularity and power." Schroeder, *The Transformation of European Politics*, 626.

88. Snyder, *Myths of Empire*, chapter 5.

89. Kissinger, *Diplomacy*, 97.

90. Kenneth Bourne, *The Foreign Policy of Victorian England, 1830–1902* (London: Oxford University Press, 1970), 20–21.

91. C. J. Bartlett, "Statecraft, Power and Influence," in *Britain Pre-eminent: Studies of British World Influence in the Nineteenth Century*, ed. C. J. Bartlett (New York: St. Martin's Press, 1969), 173.

92. In addition, the impact of demobilization after the Napoleonic Wars had a backlash effect in that merchant marine crews, who would typically serve as recruits for the Royal Navy in times of need, were largely unwilling to come to H. Majesty's service.

93. Graham, *The Politics of Naval Supremacy*, 118–19.

94. Hannah, *A History of British Foreign Policy*, 121. There is some question as to why this particular case merited a house call from British men-of-war, while several such incidents of failure to remit payments occurred in South America and drew no response.

95. Quoted at length in Bourne, *The Foreign Policy of Victorian England*, 301–9, along with Gladstone's statement.

96. Richard Elrod makes the stronger claim that the absence of great power war from 1815 through 1854 is a consequence of the adherence to the Concert "as a conscious and generally effective attempt by European statesmen to maintain peaceful

relations between sovereign states." Richard B. Elrod, "The Concert of Europe: A Fresh Look at an International System," *World Politics* 28, no. 2 (January 1976), 159–74. Paul Schroeder offers an argument similar in spirit but a bit more circumscribed, arguing that the Concert of Europe combined with the "fencing off" of the European system from the extra-European world and the establishment of "intermediary bodies"—primarily buffer states—to yield a peaceful four decades. Paul W. Schroeder, "The 19th Century International System: Changes in the Structure," *World Politics* 39, no. 1 (October 1986), 1–26. See also Kalevi J. Holsti, *Peace and War: Armed Conflicts and International Order 1648–1989* (New York: Cambridge University Press, 1991), chapter 7, esp. 164–69; for a more pessimistic assessment of the Concert of Europe's impact on great power behavior in the eastern Mediterranean during this period, see Korina Kagan, "The Myth of the European Concert: The Realist-Institutionalist Debate and Great Power Behavior in the Eastern Question, 1821–41," *Security Studies* 7, no. 2 (winter 1997/98), 1–57.

97. Henry Kissinger, *A World Restored: Metternich, Castlereagh, and the Problems of Peace, 1812–1822* (Boston: Houghton Mifflin, 1973).

98. Karl Polanyi, *The Great Transformation: The Political and Economic Origins of Our Time* (Boston: Beacon Press, 1957), 9.

99. Craig and George, *Force and Statecraft*, 28.

100. C. W. Crawley, "International Relations, 1815–1830," in *The New Cambridge Modern History*, Vol. IX, ed. C. W. Crawley (Cambridge: Cambridge University Press, 1965), 668–90, on 670.

101. Kissinger, *Diplomacy*, 82.

102. Inis L Claude, Jr. *Swords into Plowshares: The Problems and Progress of International Organization*, 4th ed. (New York: Random House, 1984), 28.

103. Crawley, "International Relations, 1815–1830," 690.

104. Quotations from Kissinger, *Diplomacy*, 78–79, and Elrod, "The Concert of Europe," 163, respectively. The principles of the Concert were seemingly evident in the great powers' handling of the Belgian Revolution and the 1839–41 crisis in the Levant (see Crawley, "International Relations, 1815–1830," 690), but the actual machinery of the Concert was not a key to the settlement of these issues, and even the spirit of the Concert was fading by this time. For instance, in the latter case, France (a member of the Concert) was isolated by the other four great powers, who secretly agreed to quietly stand behind British action against Egypt, France's protégé in the eastern Mediterranean.

105. Elrod, "The Concert of Europe," 164–66, lists the unwritten rules as responding to crises with conference diplomacy, avoiding territorial changes without consent of all great powers, protecting certain key states in the system, and avoiding actions that would tarnish the prestige of any great power. At times, it can be difficult to sort evidence that suggests these principles were observed by the great powers from evidence that suggests the great powers tried to preserve the status quo.

106. James L. Richardson, *Crisis Diplomacy: The Great Powers since the Mid-Nineteenth Century* (New York: Cambridge University Press, 1994), 50 ff., 229. In

chapters 4 and 5 Richardson argues that the adherence to some of the principles of the Concert allowed the great powers to avert war in the Syrian Crisis, while the deterioration of Concert diplomacy permitted the crisis in the early 1850s to escalate into the Crimean War. Nonetheless, Richardson acknowledges that Britain, France, and Russia all violated some of the Concert's 'restraints' during the Syrian (or "Eastern") Crisis.

107. Charles Webster, *The Foreign Policy of Palmerston, 1830–1841: Britain, the Liberal Movement and the Eastern Question*, 2 vols. (New York: Humanities Press, 1969), chapters 4 and 7.

108. This section is based largely upon Clark G. Reynolds, *Command of the Sea: The History and Strategy of Maritime Empires* (New York: William Morrow and Co., 1974), 341–42.

109. David Thomson, *England in the Nineteenth Century (1815–1914)*, (Baltimore, Md.: Penguin Books, 1959), chapter 4.

110. Reynolds, *Command of the Sea*, 343–45. Commitments were heaviest on the shipping and receiving ends of the cross-Atlantic route. Reynolds offers the following distribution of vessels for the 1830s: 26 in North America, 14 along West Africa and the Cape, 23 in the Mediterranean, 15 in Lisbon, 16 in South America, and 10 in the East Indies.

111. In Hattendorf et al., eds., *British Naval Documents, 1204–1960*, 626–28.

112. Reynolds, *Command of the Sea*.

113. William Law Mathieson, *Great Britain and the Slave Trade, 1839–1865* (New York: Octagon Books, 1967), chapter 2. American outrage at the Britons' asserted right to search vessels at sea spilled over to the continent, as the Americans persuaded the French to disassociate themselves from the Quintuple Treaty. French refusal to ratify the treaty was not particularly surprising, given that the French had just suffered a diplomatic defeat in the Syrian Crisis/ Turko-Egyptian War at the hands of the British (71–73).

114. Quoted in Mathieson, *Great Britain and the Slave Trade*, 68.

115. Karen A. Rasler and William R. Thompson, *The Great Powers and the Global Struggle, 1490–1990* (Lexington: University Press of Kentucky, 1994), present in appendix A a large, rigorously collected data set on army sizes of great powers from 1490–1990. They also provide an extensive list of sources of data for each state (see 195–99) though unfortunately these are not annotated. The five states identified herein as great powers match Jack Levy's well-known classification of the great powers, which accurately reflects much of the historical literature. Jack S. Levy, *War in the Modern Great Power System, 1495–1975* (Lexington: University Press of Kentucky, 1983), chapter 2. I also examine the United States, though technically it was not yet a great power.

116. Hamilton, *Anglo-French Naval Rivalry*, 9. Schroeder asserts that 37,000 French troops initially were stationed in Algiers; Schroeder, *The Transformation of European Politics*, 668–69. As an aside, it appears that having a base at Algiers served as an impetus for committing more resources to the French navy.

117. Glete, *Navies and Nations*, 450.

118. Hamilton, *Anglo-French Naval Rivalry*, 7.

119. On *le tyran* and other nicknames for Great Britain and her navy, see Hamilton, *Anglo-French Naval Rivalry*, 1. On the French reliance on *guerre de course*, see Lambert, *The Last Sailing Battlefleet*, 9, and Glete, *Navies and Nations*, 428.

120. Hamilton, *Anglo-French Naval Rivalry*, 10–11; this book assesses the Anglo-French naval rivalry with an eye to the role of technological innovation. For the earlier portion of the period, see e.g. Lambert, *The Last Sailing Battlefleet*.

121. Glete, *Navies and Nations*, 429.

122. See Clowes, *The Royal Navy*, 308–23.

123. Martin van Creveld, *Supplying War: Logistics from Wallenstein to Patton* (New York: Cambridge University Press, 1977), 76–77. Note that the Russians used requisition as the primary method of supplying their armies throughout the period in question, in accordance with the Russian Administrative Regulations of 1812. "Ambulent magazines" were introduced into Russian armies in 1846, but proved largely ineffective in the Crimean War.

124. On Russian naval forces see Glete, *Navies and Nations*, 429, 447. Russian shipbuilding also affected its naval strength relative to Britain's. Russian use of inferior wood (fir) in ship construction meant that the Russian warships decayed and lost their shape more quickly than the superior British vessels, and as such the Russians had to try even harder just to keep pace with the British; Bartlett, *Great Britain and Sea Power*, 103.

125. Harold W.V. Temperley, *England and the Near East: The Crimea* (New York: Longmans, Green and Co., 1936), 48, 70–74, and Clayton, *Britain and the Eastern Question*, 67. Clayton accuses both Temperley and M. S. Anderson of unjustifiably downplaying the importance of the secret article, which he implies was crucial to Russia's security at the time.

126. Glete, *Navies and Nations*, 429; in addition, the Baltic fleet was poorly equipped and crewed by inexperienced sailors; Bartlett, *Great Britain and Sea Power*, 104. With the benefit of hindsight we can say that the probability of a Russian invasion of Britain using the Baltic fleet was slim; however, during the 1830s, British policymakers considered this a potential threat and accordingly voiced their concerns about home defenses. Bartlett, *Great Britain and Sea Power*, 103–4.

127. Crawley, "International Relations, 1815–1830," 671–72.

128. Glete, *Navies and Nations*, 439. After the War of 1812 the United States was in the process of building several large, powerful ships-of-the-line. The British were wary of this potential challenge, but building proceeded very slowly, and a thaw in Anglo-American relations mitigated British fears of a challenge to the Royal Navy's predominance—except as an unlikely participant in an American-Franco-Russian alliance. Hamilton, *Anglo-French Naval Rivalry*, chapter 1; Bartlett, "Statecraft, Power and Influence," 182–83. In any case, American naval capabilities were not particularly strong, even in the Western Hemisphere; many historians assert that the real teeth of the Monroe Doctrine were the ships of the Royal Navy, not the U.S.

Navy. See for example Brown, *Before the Ironclad*, 29; Stokesbury, *Navy and Empire*, 216.

129. Thomas A. Bryson, *Tars, Turks, and Tankers: The Role of the United States Navy in the Middle East, 1800–1979* (Metuchen, N.J.: Scarecrow Press, 1980), 20–27.

130. Temperley, *England and the Near East*, 91.

131. Quoted in Temperley, *England and the Near East*, 91.

132. Comments by Wellington indicate that the British naval squadron presented an ever-present threat to communications and supply lines from Alexandria to Syria via the Mediterranean; he asserted, "No army can march forward into the heart of Asia Minor when its sea communications are interrupted" (quoted in Temperley, *England and the Near East*, 91).

133. Ibrahim Pasha, Muhammad Ali's son, had grander designs and wished to continue northward, but Ali refused to sanction such a move; Schroeder, *The Transformation of European Politics*, 727. While French diplomacy also strongly discouraged an Egyptian attempt to depose the Sultan, Muhammad Ali was arguably more concerned about swift retribution by Britain, and possibly Russia, than any consequences of failing to heed French advice. On French diplomatic efforts see Puryear, *France and the Levant*, Chapter V, esp. 170–72.

134. Richardson, *Crisis Diplomacy*, 45–46; Vernon John Puryear, *International Economics and Diplomacy in the Near East: A Study of British Commercial Policy in the Levant, 1834–1853* (Hamden, Conn.: Archon Books, 1969), 152–54.

135. Andrew Lambert, "The Shield of Empire, 1815–1895," in *The Oxford Illustrated History of the Royal Navy*, eds. J. R. Hill and Bryan Ranft (New York: Oxford University Press, 1995), 161–99, on 171.

136. Quotations from Bailey, *British Policy and the Turkish Reform Movement*, 134–35, and Puryear *International Economics and Diplomacy in the Near East*, 16, respectively.

137. Glete, *Navies and Nations*, 426.

138. John William McCleary, "Anglo-French Naval Rivalry, 1815–1848," Ph.D. diss., Johns Hopkins University, 1947, 74–75.

139. The implications of the Treaty of Unkiar-Skelessi (1833–1841) are widely debated. Bailey, *British Policy and the Turkish Reform Movement*, 50–51, summarizes the fray to some extent. Essentially, part of the debate turns on the treaty's reaffirmation of all existing Russo-Turkish treaties. Article 7 of the Russo-Turkish Treaty of 1805 allowed the Russians to send warships through the Straits into the Mediterranean at will. But, argues Bailey, that treaty was formally denounced by the Turks a year later in 1806 and hence was not reaffirmed by the Treaty of Unkiar-Skelessi. Cf. Clayton, *Britain and the Eastern Question*, Part III, *passim*; also Temperley, *England and the Near East*, 413–14, n.109, who argues that the treaty opened the Bosphorus to the Russians, but not the Dardanelles (which permit access to the Mediterranean).

140. Bailey, *British Policy and the Turkish Reform Movement*, 115–28, *passim*.

141. Quoted in C. G. Pitcairn Jones, ed., *Piracy in the Levant, 1827–28*, Vol. 72 (London: Navy Records Society, 1934), 225–29.

142. Bailey, *British Policy and the Turkish Reform Movement*, 131.

143. See for example M. S. Anderson, *The Eastern Question*, 92–93.

144. Bailey, *British Policy and the Turkish Reform Movement*, 154. Urquhart's agreement with Palmerston's sentiment is significant not only because the two were frequently at odds but more importantly because Urquhart, for a time the ambassador to Constantinople, publicly argued that the Turks displayed "the strongest desire of instruction and respect for [British] customs and institutions;" quoted in Allan Cunningham, *Eastern Questions in the Nineteenth Century: Collected Essays by Allan Cunningham*. Vol. 2. Ed. Edward Ingram (London: Frank Cass, 1993), 73. Likewise, Stratford Canning, whose "high faith in the material and spiritual benefits of British civilization" drove his efforts to bring British "progress" to the Turks, "saw no justification for transferring political power to the Sultan's subjects." Cunningham, *Eastern Questions*, 39–40.

145. Bailey, *British Policy and the Turkish Reform Movement*, 146–48.

146. First and foremost for the purpose of commerce protection; my thanks to Jan Breemer for emphasizing this point.

147. Quoted in Bartlett, *Great Britain and Sea Power*, 19.

148. Bartlett, *Great Britain and Sea Power*, 101.

CHAPTER TWO

Decline, Disengagement, and Shaping the Periphery

Great Britain in the Eastern Mediterranean and the Levant, 1919–1937

JONATHAN M. DICICCO

Introduction

The unprecedented devastation of World Wars I and II was briefly interrupted by a period of relative peace, lasting roughly from 1918 to 1938. The British were instrumental in constructing the peace in 1918, and the weakness of Britain's continental rivals provided an opportunity to improve the foundations of British influence in the historically disputed region comprising the eastern Mediterranean and the Levant. Though Britain and France shared the spoils of World War I, Britain clearly was the more prominent great power with a political, economic, and military foothold in that region.

However, Britain was also a global power in relative decline. The costs of total war, the burden of empire maintenance and defense, and the rise of the geographically insulated United States combined to produce a set of foreign policy challenges that made it difficult for British leaders to focus their efforts on any one region of the world. Yet, British leaders could ill-afford to neglect the eastern Mediterranean. The strategic importance of the Suez Canal, the increasing importance of oil as an energy source, and the wish to preserve peace in a region which had precipitated various great power disputes led British leaders to make the eastern Mediterranean a priority in their foreign policy calculus.

How then did Britain, a democratic great power with vested interests in the eastern Mediterranean but waning global influence, employ its military resources to shape the regional environment during the interwar period? We investigate Britain's pursuit of national aims in the eastern Mediterranean in an effort to illuminate the somewhat shadowy world of the use of military resources abroad during peacetime. We are less interested in the also-important issue of Britain's preparations (or lack thereof) for the next great power war than in efforts to retain and reinforce Britain's influence in the Levant while peace prevailed. The old dictum requiring leaders to prepare for war in order to ensure peace might, or might not, have empirical relevance in this case.

Of course, the entire Middle East—not just the eastern Mediterranean and the Levant—is worth studying. However, this study is limited to the region cradling the eastern Mediterranean, from Greece, eastward through Turkey, around through what are now Iraq, Lebanon, Syria, Jordan, Israel, and Egypt. After World War I, Egypt was a British "protectorate," more or less a British colonial ward. Iraq and Palestine were League of Nations mandates under British supervision (the Palestine mandate included both Palestine and Transjordan); Syria and Lebanon were French mandates. Greece was an internationally recognized state, and Turkey was the independent state carved from the core remnants of the Ottoman Empire, though the great powers sought to exercise control of the strategically important straits connecting the Mediterranean Sea to the Black Sea.

Temporally speaking, this study confines its focus to the period between 1919 and 1937. Prior to 1919, diplomats were still negotiating the terms of the peace, and postwar demobilization had not yet begun in earnest. After 1937, signs of Hitler's impending aggression began to take shape, and though clinging to hopes that conciliation and concession could preserve peace, British leaders did begin to prepare for war. Therefore the period of 1919–1937 seems an appropriate span of time for our investigation.

We will examine Britain's relative military capabilities in the eastern Mediterranean and the Levant; we will discuss the impact of domestic political factors, nonmilitary avenues of influence, and international constraints on British action; and finally we will assess Britain's ability to realize the aims of peace, political primacy, and preservation of the status quo in the region. Each section has a specific focus, but occasional cross-references are provided to assist the reader in finding items presented only once to prevent redundancy. We begin by looking at the military situation in the Levantine region.

Part One: Great Britain's Relative Military Capabilities

Regional Military Balance
Upon the signing of the armistice to end World War I, Lord Curzon announced that the British Empire was at its strongest in history, and that "the

power of Britain to shape the destinies of the world had never been so great."[1] At the time such a statement appeared boastful but grounded in a kernel of truth; in retrospect, the statement conveys hubris and a seemingly myopic vision of Britain's future. The British indeed did have the world's strongest navy,[2] the largest Regular Army they had ever assembled, and a newly developed Royal Air Force, but would soon find that they did not have the financial and economic foundation to support the war-inflated armed forces.[3]

Nonetheless, even after postwar demobilization, draconian defense cuts, and naval arms limitations imposed through the Washington Treaty, the British armed forces were far superior to those of any one of the states of the eastern Mediterranean and Levant, where individual states of military consequence were scarce. Consider the following:

Egypt, which was still under British control for a large part of the interwar period, had a modest police force and "a small and inefficient army"[4]—hardly the modern, powerful force that Muhammad Ali had aspired to construct in the early nineteenth century. The interwar years were characterized by British domination of Egyptian politics and policy, even after nominal independence was granted in 1922. This position allowed the British to keep the Egyptian military "in a state of dependency and starved of instructors and equipment" for much of the period, though by the late 1930s this hold was loosening.[5]

Turkey was wracked by internal conflict, not to mention war with the Greeks, early in the interwar period. Nonetheless, under the Young Turks the military gained a dominant position in Turkish society, reflected in the army's claim to 40 percent of the budget. This was reduced to 28 percent by the early 1930s, but the Turks were still able to maintain an army of approximately 80,000 troops during the period between the wars.[6] One contemporary observer, on the other hand, described Turkish naval power in 1927 as "continually eclipsing" and only of remote concern to British policymakers.[7] He noted that the Turks had plans for a new fleet—indeed, in the late 1920s and 1930s the Turks purchased several vessels from European states—but by no means were they capable of a substantial, prolonged challenge to the British during this period.

Iraq had a very modest army during the interwar period. Some indigenous Arabs were incorporated into the levies, which were completely British-controlled and operated military organizations; this precluded them from participating in the Iraqi army, which numbered approximately 9,000 troops. Even this army was under considerable British control prior to Iraq's independence in 1932. After 1932, Iraq undertook a substantial effort to create a more powerful military, but as we will see below, delays on British shipments of weapons prolonged the weakness of the Iraqi forces.

Great Britain

Army. The decade after the close of World War I reflected a reaction against the horrors of war and the dawning realization that demobilization might have to be paired with strategic adjustment to overextended overseas commitments. Nonetheless, the latter came only very slowly, and British garrisons abroad drew heavily on the diminished military forces available in the 1920s and early 1930s. Some 60,000 troops, comprising nearly a third of the entire British army, were committed to the peacetime defense of India alone.[8] These colonial and overseas commitments left few soldiers available for emergencies, though ostensibly some units were earmarked precisely for that purpose. As Clayton notes, "In theory there were four regular infantry divisions and one cavalry division stationed in Britain available for service overseas; in practice the units in these divisions were generally far below the necessary strengths, or even in some cases entirely non-existent except as a paper project. It was accepted that *only one division and one cavalry brigade could be deployed at short notice*; the rest of the force would only be available after six months" [emphasis added].[9]

British service chiefs were hardly happy with this situation; General Sir George Milne "complained that the army was fully stretched to meet routine commitments and could not cope with an emergency."[10] Nonetheless, the army was only to diminish further in size through the late 1920s and well into the 1930s, though a core of about 200,000 troops was maintained. When rearmament began in the mid-to-late 1930s, the army was the lowest priority of the three service arms, and remained "in limbo" while the RAF and the Royal Navy received increased funding, waiting until 1939 before a substantial rearmament program was undertaken.[11]

Air force. Like the other service arms, British air power deteriorated during peacetime, though less dramatically than the army and navy. Though some policymakers envisioned strategic bombing as the cornerstone of a new defense policy vis-à-vis the continent, a large portion of British aircraft were committed to overseas positions, for colonial defense or the maintenance of internal order in British mandates. In 1924, of a total of forty-three squadrons of aircraft, eight were in Iraq, six in India, and four in Palestine and Egypt. In a confrontation with the French in 1923, the British could only muster twenty-four serviceable front-line warplanes to challenge the 2,400 planes in French airfields.[12] By 1933, the RAF had grown to eighty-seven squadrons, but colonial/mandatory commitments increased as well; additional squadrons were stationed in Iraq, India, Palestine, and Egypt, as well as Aden, Malta, and Singapore.[13] These overseas RAF commitments turned out to be a relatively cheap and effective tool for the maintenance of British influence in the eastern Mediterranean region.

The aircraft of the 1920s were not terribly difficult to operate, and policymakers believed that a proportion of squadrons could be effectively manned by reservists. Approximately 25 percent of squadrons were assigned to reservists in the late 1920s; but by the mid–1930s increasingly sophisticated aircraft designs generated a demand for fully-trained pilots that could not be met right away.[14] This is not to suggest that the RAF was a pillar of technological advancement during the interwar period. In 1926, of 660 first-line aircraft some 36 percent were of pre–1917 design types. Even the prioritization of the RAF over its older sister services in rearmament, which began around 1934, did not completely solve this quandary; in early 1938, of 666 fighter planes available, fewer than 100 were considered "modern."[15] Nonetheless, the RAF provided Britain with a military dimension as yet out of reach of the peoples of the eastern Mediterranean and the Levant.

Navy. Great Britain emerged from World War I with a remarkable navy. Impressive battle fleets left afloat, combined with the scuttling of the German fleet at Scapa Flow, a French emphasis on land power, and unfinished shipbuilding programs in the United States and Japan, Britain's relative naval superiority was unquestioned. Corelli Barnett describes 1919 as the "apogee of English naval supremacy at sea," adding, "[n]ot since 1815 . . . had England been able to survey the world with such assurance of safety and power."[16] There are discrepancies among naval histories of the period, but the Royal Navy appears to have consisted of at least forty-two capital ships (battleships and battlecruisers), over 100 cruisers and light cruisers, a dozen aircraft carriers, over 450 destroyers and flotilla leaders, and over 120 submarines (see table 2.1).[17] The Royal Navy in 1919 was stronger than all of the navies of Europe combined, having more than double the number of cruisers of the French and American navies combined, and more than triple the number of destroyers in the Italian and Japanese navies combined.[18]

The wartime economy reverted back to a peacetime economy, however, and funding of the Royal Navy was slashed over 50 percent from 1919 to 1920.[19] While the impact of the Treasury's parsimony during the 1920s is a matter of scholarly debate, there is no question that these cuts reduced the Royal Navy's overall efficacy to some degree. Changes in relative naval capability among the great powers compounded these changes in absolute capability. Attempts to limit naval armaments in the 1920s, along with American and Japanese shipbuilding programs, further reduced British naval superiority in both a quantitative and a qualitative sense.

By 1926, the Royal Navy consisted of about twenty capital ships, forty-one cruisers, six aircraft carriers, 162 destroyers, and fifty-eight submarines, less than half of the force levels of 1919; in addition, most of

Table 2.1. Royal Navy Fleet Strength, 1919–1939

Year	Capital Ships	Cruisers	Aircraft Carriers	Destroyers	Submarines
1919	58	103	12	456	72
1920	42	72	5	359	92
1921	36	50	4	190	86
1922	29	49	4	188	84
1923	22	44	4	188	58
1924	22	44	4	188	58
1925	22	43	8	192	61
1926	22	41	8	175	56
1927	18	42	8	160	55
1928	20	42	8	151	53
1929	20	45	7	142	50
1930	20	48	6	142	51
1931	18	47	6	140	57
1932	15	46	6	140	52
1933	15	46	6	148	55
1934	15	44	6	137	52
1935	15	44	6	147	51
1936	15	46	6	156	51
1937	15	45	6	144	51
1938	15	53	6	151	52
1939	15	55	7	149	54

Source: Adapted from Higham, *Armed Forces in Peacetime*, 135.

these warships were aging and becoming obsolete when compared to the newer vessels being constructed by other great powers.[20] Nonetheless, even the obsolescing ships of the fleet provided the British with a technological advantage over the peoples of the eastern Mediterranean and the Levant.

The early to mid-1930s provide a vivid contrast with 1919 in terms of British naval capabilities. Government-imposed pay cuts induced the Invergordon Mutiny in September 1931; officials met the demands of the mutinous sailors, but it is unlikely that morale rebounded as quickly as pay levels. The Royal Navy, which had claimed about 25 percent of British government expenditure prior to World War I, by 1932 received just six percent of government expenditure.[21] Having accepted the condition of naval parity with the United States, the British kept only 15 capital ships in commission during the 1930s,[22] and capital shipbuilding was virtually moribund for most of the interwar period. The Admiralty instead devoted the greater part of their limited budgets to light cruisers and smaller surface ships, primarily for the protection of commercial vessels.

Great Britain's Relative Technological Efficacy in the Region

Great Britain, progenitor of the Industrial Revolution and generator of technological advancement in peace and in war, enjoyed myriad advantages over its mandates and the other states in the eastern Mediterranean region. From aircraft to warships, armored cars to tanks, the British possessed weapons platforms and expertise that, by and large, easily surpassed the actors in the region. Though the British failed to keep in lockstep with the naval innovations of the Japanese and the Americans—British warships could not quite match the firepower of the main rivals' newest warships—they did enjoy some notable technological innovations during the interwar period.[23] However, of the notable technical developments, which included carrier aviation and antisubmarine warfare, perhaps the only one that was truly meaningful to the British experience in the Levant was land-based air power. Aircraft based in Iraq in particular enabled the British to maintain order, deter challenges to the British client government, and nip internal conflicts in the bud. Air power was an effective tool for these tasks for at least three reasons: it was cheaper than heavily manned garrisons, it allowed for a rapid response to problems,[24] and it facilitated the coverage of a large area with a small commitment of resources.

The Trenchard system of air policing, as it came to be called, operated on the principle that an investment in punishment now would yield dividends via deterrence later. "Air route marches" of RAF planes flying over tracts of sparsely populated land served to both scout for trouble and as a visual reminder of British omnipresence. If the visual deterrent of British planes failed, as it did occasionally, the British employed coercive bombing. Upon learning of a disturbance in the countryside, the British would warn the villagers of the risk of an impending attack in hopes that the villagers would surrender the guilty parties; if cooperation were not forthcoming, RAF planes would engage in limited bombing of the village. If a single punitive raid was ineffective, the British used a method called "blockading out," whereby regular bombing of the immediate vicinity of a village forced the villagers from their homes and their means of sustenance until the accused parties were surrendered.[25] The coercive use of air power allowed the British to maintain order and authority in the sparsely populated Iraqi countryside; however, this strategy (made possible in part by British technological superiority) was implausible in the densely packed urban areas of the Levant like Palestine, Cairo, and Baghdad.[26]

Occasionally, the British technological advantage was impractical or ineffective for particular tasks. Frequent challenges to British aims in the Levant came in the form of violent demonstrations and rioting, particularly in Egypt and Palestine. Similar rioting elsewhere in the Empire taught British officers a valuable lesson about how a technological advantage can become a disadvantage, and consequently how to downplay the technological superiority of their forces in such situations. According to one account, "Captain Smith found during riots in Bombay that if his men carried rifles there were two dangers: that an accidental discharge would bring on general firing . . . and that apart from the fact that [the rifles] were awkward weapons as clubs, the crowd tried to seize them. The solution, he found, was to sling the rifles and arm men with pick-axe handles which they could flourish like truncheons without a feeling of restraint and which the crowd understood in a hurry."[27]

The slow pace of improvements in British naval vessels during the interwar period seems to have had little or no effect on the ability of the British to achieve their objectives in the eastern Mediterranean. While the British lagged behind their rivals in warship firepower, and managed to launch only two new capital ships in the 1920s, the aging fleet was adequate for British purposes in the region. Even British technology that was over a decade old was impressive to the comparably underequipped peoples in the Levant. Consider, for example, the British military demonstration in response to the assassination of Sir Lee Stack, British governor-general of the Sudan and Sirdar of the Egyptian army, by Egyptian dissidents. A detailed description of the demonstration, recorded by a Briton on the scene, is worth quoting at length.

> A battle squadron from Malta anchored off Alexandria and several regiments from the same station were temporarily ordered to Egypt . . . it was remarkable to witness the instantaneous effect of the measures taken. In Alexandria detachments of the Royal Marines marched through the city with their machine-guns shining like silver in the bright sunlight, while the big guns of the *Iron Duke*, *Valiant*, and *Benbow* stimulated in the population a sense of wholesome respect for the British Navy. In Cairo the garrison marched along streets lined with gaping Egyptians, who turned out in great numbers to watch the imposing spectacle. The regiments were in review order, and marched at attention the whole time, the men with bayonets fixed, the officers with drawn swords. Batteries of artillery were included in the columns, and the streets re-echoed with the music of regimental bands, the rumble of field guns and the heavy tramp of the ammunition boot.
>
> I watched the onlookers with great curiosity, and the most common expression on the face of the average Egyptian was that of utter astonishment . . . the people gazed on the troops with almost surprised admiration. In a few days the whole Egyptian attitude had changed, and whereas just previously the demeanor of Egyptian officials towards British subjects was distinctly off-hand, if

not actually insulting, these same individuals could not now do enough to show their respect for the British ... so anxious were the Egyptians to regain British good-will that for some considerable time the Customs officers merely glanced at one's closed baggage as a matter of form, and the Englishman was attended to first on every occasion.[28]

Relative to the ships and military weapons of other great powers, the British instruments of war were obsolescing. Yet relative to the Egyptians, the British military enjoyed a substantial technological advantage, and the visual impact of these aging ships and guns was not degraded by their outdated design.

For the decade of the 1920s and the better part of the 1930s, Britain maintained a qualitative technological advantage over the states and mandates in the eastern Mediterranean region. There were notable exceptions to this condition of technological superiority. For example, the Turks, in rebuilding a navy, acquired capital ships built in the United States and Italy. During the 1930s the British supplied the Iraqis with the very same armaments allocated to British units, along with instruction on the use and maintenance of these armaments; some Iraqi officers and soldiers even trained at British military institutions.[29] Nonetheless, the British level of technological sophistication was head-and-shoulders above regional powers. In some situations (namely, urban settings) the technological advantage was superfluous, but in most cases it served to promote the achievement of British aims.

British Military Presence in the Region

The Royal Navy maintained a consistently impressive presence in the Mediterranean between the world wars. In fact, the Mediterranean was "the navy's strategic center of gravity," meriting nearly half of the Royal Navy's effective capacity during the interwar period.[30] By the early 1920s, the Mediterranean Fleet comprised six battleships, six light cruisers, 16 destroyers, a submarine flotilla, and an aircraft carrier.[31] Peacetime reductions continued; in January 1921 the British withdrew two battleships from the Mediterranean, and in April 1921 the crews of many Mediterranean vessels were reduced to three-fifths complement and maintained at Malta in a reserve capacity. Events in the area of Greece and Turkey required the reinforcement of the Mediterranean fleet in 1923–1924; while these reinforcements were temporary, perhaps these events underscored the perceived need for a strong(er) naval presence in the Mediterranean. In 1924 and 1925, the Mediterranean Fleet traded up for several new destroyers, and benefited from a redistribution of the fleets resulting in eight battleships' assignment to the station.[32] Although additional reductions in the mid-1920s brought overall naval force levels down considerably, the Mediterranean Fleet remained a priority. In early 1928, just before the last round of categorical reductions, the British kept six battleships, an aircraft carrier, eleven cruisers, thirty-eight destroyers, and seven submarines in the Mediterranean.[33]

At the close of the 1920s the British found themselves with a glut of warships in the Mediterranean, clogging the harbors at Malta when the entire fleet was stationed at the base. To remedy this situation the Admiralty redistributed the fleets, gradually transferring *Queen Elizabeth*-class battleships from the Mediterranean to the Atlantic during the early 1930s.[34]

Immediately following World War I, Britain maintained a military presence in several of the Levantine "states," including Turkey, Palestine, Mesopotamia (Iraq), and Egypt. In early 1920, these commitments amounted to over 30,000 British soldiers and were supplemented by over 90,000 Indian troops.[35] These force levels would be reduced, however, and by the late 1920s the British army was less heavily represented in the region.[36] These were not wholesale reductions; actual troop commitments depended on the particular site. For example, consider the contrasting examples of Turkey and Egypt. While the British left Turkey promptly after the Treaty of Lausanne had cemented the postwar map of southwestern Asia, the British army lingered in Egypt well after the Egyptians were granted nominal independence in 1922. In fact, the British garrison in Egypt was the largest of its kind in the region; in 1928 it still included two infantry brigades, three cavalry brigades, two RAF bomber squadrons, and an RAF fighter squadron.[37]

The turn toward the Trenchard system of air policing permitted the British to reduce military personnel on the ground throughout the Levant, and as a result RAF contingents in the region increased. These were typically stationed at local bases that were guarded by a token garrison of soldiers. While air policing was partially effective, the British were required to step up troop commitments in some instances involving urban unrest, most notably the deployment of some 50,000 troops in Palestine between 1936 and 1938.[38]

Speed of British Response

British responses to crises and challenges to authority in the eastern Mediterranean were typically swift. Improvements in warship technology prior to World War I enabled the Royal Navy to float a faster fleet than it had in centuries past. Detachments of British troops, though typically modest in size, were stationed in Egypt, and later Palestine. Finally, RAF squadrons were based at several locations in the Middle East, providing a forward position for the deployment of British aircraft in times of need. Naval bases at Malta and Alexandria, and air bases in Iraq provided vantage points for speedy projections of force.[39]

Even when they had to scramble to assemble an adequate force to address a problem or crisis, in most parts of the region the British were able to at least make their presence known nearly immediately. Consider the case of Palestine in 1929, in which a violent Arab-Jew confrontation precipitated a rebellion. British forces were spread rather thinly at the time; the commitment of only two armored car companies and a single RAF squadron for the defense of the mandate of Palestine (including Transjordan, the unfortunately inconvenient location of the armored cars when the insurrection in Palestine began) was later the subject of censure by the Permanent Mandates Commission of the League of Nations.[40] As Brian Bond notes, these insufficient units, however, were quickly reinforced:

> Even when due allowance is made for the fact that at this stage the disturbances were entirely inter-communal and not directed at British forces or property, British response to the 1929 crisis was remarkably prompt and effective. Within hours of the emergency being proclaimed a small advance party of troops had been ferried from Egypt to Jerusalem by air while the body of three battalions and an armoured car squadron promptly followed by rail and within a few days were reinforced by nearly a thousand sailors.[41]

Bond adds that this incident reveals British political control of Palestine to be predicated on little more than a bluff; but it also demonstrates that the British had the capability to redeploy troops and equipment from neighboring states in a swift manner.[42]

Britain was hardly omnipotent, however. British response to crisis was more likely to be rapid if the trouble was occurring along a coastline; the British had considerably greater difficulties mounting an efficient response to problems in an inland area. For example, when spontaneous revolts broke out in Iraq in 1920, mounted Arab guerrillas attacked British outposts deep in Iraq, slaying the British and Indian troops manning those locations. Overland communications outside Baghdad were so poor that it literally took weeks to send supplies and reinforcements to the besieged area.[43] The revolts began in June 1920; reinforcement in July and August contributed to the total reinforcements of 25,000 Indian and 5,000 British troops, and an RAF squadron, in place by the end of September. Thus, while additional British deployments allowed them to reestablish authority in southeastern Iraq by early 1921 and engage in punitive actions against suspected rebels, it took over two months to deploy the forces necessary to do so.

The sluggishness of communication and reinforcement, and consequently the long period of time required to establish control on the ground, exemplifies difficulties the British faced in taking inland action. The relative ease and quickness of establishing a littoral military presence were not reflected in less accessible inland areas, and as a result British military reach declined the further one moved from the sea.

Available Military Options
Britain's military options in the Mediterranean region expanded during the century that passed between the Concert of Europe and the interwar period. With the exception of the close blockade, most of the old staples remained, and several new operational options became available. First, technological advancement rendered the close blockade practically impossible, though blockade at a distance remained an option.[44] However, Britain was capable of employing warships in offshore bombardments of positions on land, using warships to land marines and sailors in littoral regions, and simply cruising the seas, showing the Union Jack. Even after peacetime cutbacks, Britain's naval forces were capable of fighting sea battles—though such clashes with regional powers were extremely unlikely, as the only regional states with any semblance of sea power were the relatively weak Greece and Turkey.

In addition, the British military could occupy stretches of territory, though large tracts were better suited for patrols by the RAF. The Trenchard system of air policing (viz., coercive bombing) became a popular alternative to occupation by land forces, and the maintenance of air bases in Iraq and elsewhere made this strategy plausible.[45] The continuing commission of at least one aircraft carrier in the Mediterranean also allowed the British to have at least one mobile source of air power.

Recognition that fixed bases were vulnerable to air attack—Malta, for example, had inadequate antiaircraft capabilities—led to the development of the Mobile Naval Base Defence Organisation (MNBDO) and the assignment of its defense to the Royal Marines in 1929. The MNBDO was intended to permit the British the confidence of being able to establish a littoral base of operations within forty-eight hours of the fleet's arrival in the chosen harbor, to prepare moderate defenses against sea or air attack within a week, and finally to erect complete defenses within a month. In 1935, the Italo-Abyssinian Crisis and the resulting threat of war prompted the first use of the MNBDO. Not yet given a harbor destination ("Port X"), the MNBDO was to report to Alexandria. From initial mobilization on 25 August, to the voyage from England to Alexandria (16–26 September), and the concentration and organization of the MNBDO at Alexandria (completed 15 October), the MNBDO's total mobilization and deployment time of fifty-one days was a disappointment. The MNBDO did not set up a viable base during the crisis, and in fact did not do so until 1941.[46]

British Ability to Intervene in Regional Actors' Domestic Affairs

Britain's ability to conduct an intervention in the domestic politics of the Levantine states varied on a case-by-case basis. In most cases, a combination of a British bureaucratic and military presence in-country allowed the Britons to push and pull domestic political actors in desired directions. Consider the illustrative cases of Iraq, Egypt, Greece, and Turkey:

In *Iraq*, the British were unable to enjoy the fruits of military victory for long. Britons had established military rule in Iraq immediately after World War I, with Iraq's administration overseen by the War Office. Arabs were poorly represented in the largely British political administration, and became increasingly intolerant of British rule, with its prompt collection of taxes and military enforcement of law. Assassinations of British officers in 1919 were perhaps warning signs of the trouble to come in 1920. Widespread but uncoordinated uprisings that emerged in June 1920 perhaps were facilitated by General Haldane's reduction of available mobile forces to 3,500 troops (for an area comprising 170,000 square miles).[47] British military occupation of Baghdad appears to have stanched potential urban unrest, but in the Iraqi countryside sparse forces and the inability to promptly reinforce weak garrisons led to the deaths of over 400 British troops and approximately 2,000 missing or wounded.[48] When British forces in Iraq were properly reinforced, the Britons were able to reestablish authority, though they discontinued military rule and began to restructure the governing apparatus to incorporate native leaders, civil servants, and even a local militia.[49]

Though the British relinquished the trappings of governance to the indigenous population, they still played a kingmaking role in the Iraqi political arena. In spite of the fact that the majority of Iraq's population was either Shi'ite Muslim or Kurdish, the British favored Feisal—a Sunni Muslim—as ruler of Iraq. Though nominally affirmed by an election, Feisal was handselected by the British, who also quieted opposition to Feisal: "When Saïd Talib Pasha and the *naqib* expressed their reservations about an alien Hejazi ruler in a Persian Gulf nation, [Sir Percy] Cox had Saïd arrested forthwith and deported to Ceylon. The *naqib* and others immediately hastened to affirm their support of Feisal."[50] The British may have retreated from strict military rule of Iraq, but the continued presence of a small British contingent enabled the British administrators of the mandate to intervene in Iraq's domestic political scene.

The withdrawal of British troops in the 1920s eroded the security of Britain's position in Iraq, and this increasing insecurity contributed to British leaders' decision to end the mandate early and grant Iraq independence in 1932. Subsequently, British ability to intervene in domestic affairs began to crumble. In

1933, the British could not prevent the Iraqis from massacring the Assyrians, who had assisted the British loyally for years, and in 1936, the British were unable to prevent the hostile General Bakr Sidqi from ousting British-friendly prime minister Yasin al-Hashimi.[51]

In *Egypt*, Britain had the ability to intervene in the Palace's rule, and did so with some frequency, but most scholars question the decisiveness of this capacity. Essentially, the challenge of the Wafd, the nationalist party, created a three-cornered fight for political control. Palace leadership did not appreciate British administrators in the Egyptian government, and British administrators were often frustrated with the Palace's obstinacy; but the British High Commissioner and the Palace needed each other to counterbalance the Wafd. To use Sir Miles Lampson's metaphor, should one of the three legs disappear, the triangle would collapse in on itself, yielding a straight line.[52] Though the British needed the Palace, the High Commissioner was not above threatening the king's right to rule. An illustrative incident occurred in 1935, when Lampson bullied King Fu'ad with precisely such a threat, which was perceived as credible on the basis of the British ousting of Abbas II in 1914. After that, "no Egyptian king dared assume that, if he incurred their displeasure, the British might not remove him altogether." The threat to King Fu'ad might have also derived credibility from a more recent source; in 1934, when Premier Yehia Pasha rejected British administrative advice, he promptly "fell from power."[53] The British might have been constrained by the need to keep a three-cornered fight in Egypt, to prevent either the Palace or the Wafd from consolidating Egyptian popular opinion, but they did not hesitate to intervene as they saw fit.

In fully independent states, the British capacity to intervene domestically was suspect. In *Greece*, the British did not try to reverse the fall of Venizelos from power, though he was pro-British and his successor was pro-German. In *Turkey*, the nationalist movement led by Mustafa Kemal was able to assume political control, despite British military intervention.

British Capacity for Humanitarian and Peacekeeping Operations

Great Britain was capable of conducting—and in fact did conduct—peacekeeping and humanitarian operations in the eastern Mediterranean region during the interwar years. As an analyst writing for *Brassey's Naval Annual* in 1933 observed, "the phrase 'A British warship has been sent' has become so commonplace that the nation hardly realises the value of the influence for order and tranquillity, for succour in distress, and for humanitarian purposes generally exerted by [Royal Navy] officers and men."[54]

Many smaller operations are not heavily documented, but the evacuation of Smyrna—perhaps the most famous (or infamous) example of British humanitarian intervention—is well documented, and bears mention. Smyrna is a particularly interesting case because it reflects British failure in a peacekeeping role and British success in a humanitarian relief operation.[55]

In the early 1920s the war between the Greeks and the Turks took a chilling turn after the Turks thwarted the Greeks' expansionist campaigns and drove the Greek troops out of Anatolia. As they hastily retreated, wounded in tow, the Greeks amassed in the coastal city of Smyrna, which was also inhabited by local residents, noncombatants in the war. British naval officers initially persuaded the Turks to enter the city in an orderly manner so that innocent people could be removed from harm's way. A multilateral force of warships,[56] coordinated by the British commander in chief of the Mediterranean, landed marines and sailors at Smyrna and, with the assistance of commandeered merchant vessels, began to evacuate thousands of mostly Greek refugees. The atmosphere of an organized evacuation diminished quickly however when fires were set, violence broke out and "fear-crazed, hysterical refugees fought for places in ships and lighters against an appalling backcloth of flames, smoke, pillage, and machine-gun fire."[57] Perhaps invoking the symbolic power of the British uniform rather than relying on the Turkish soldiers' sense of humanity, one naval officer stood in front of Turkish machine gun muzzles so that Greek and Armenian refugees could safely board evacuation vessels.[58]

Personal acts of heroism and sacrifice aside, it is clear that the British were unable to fulfill their role as a peacekeeping force in the port city of Smyrna. British naval vessels were in the harbor and uniformed British forces appeared onshore, yet the peace was preserved for only a few days before chaos triumphed. Some 30,000 people—mostly Greeks and Armenians—were massacred, though some attribute the outbreak of hostilities to atrocities committed against well-disciplined Turkish soldiers.[59] Regardless of the initiator of the veritable holocaust that ensued, the British were unable to prevent the horrible scene. However, the British forces were able to successfully evacuate approximately a quarter of a million refugees. While this may seem like a "is the glass half-empty or half-full?" type of assessment, consider that nearly 200,000 people were removed prior to the conflagration that destroyed the Christian quarters of this ethnically and religiously mixed city.

The British did conduct other peacekeeping missions, though their capability to do so was limited due to the taxing nature of such operations. A prominent example is the deployment of British troops in Palestine. Note that Palestine was a British mandate, so this is an example of intrastate (and arguably even colonial) action rather than an interstate peacekeeping operation. Disputes between Arabs and Jews, beginning in 1929 and coming to a head in 1936–1938, were a constant source of instability within Palestine. The initial British commitment of one RAF squadron and two armored car companies for the internal and external defense of Palestine proved terribly insufficient. British leaders learned that the Trenchard system of air policing simply would not work in urban, densely populated settings. As Field Marshal Lord Carver observed, "bombing villages to keep the people in order could clearly not be applied to Palestine, and the army had to take over."[60] The armored cars and aircraft gave way to a much larger commitment of some 50,000 ground troops.

Smaller peacekeeping and humanitarian functions of the British military are likely to be overlooked in the historical record, partly as a function of their size and partly due to the roles played by "men-on-the-spot." Often, these men-on-the-spot handled local affairs without direct orders from the British government. Rear-Admiral Sir Henry Pelly of the Egypt-Red Sea station, for example, responded to a minor crisis in Jeddah. His prompt response helped to ensure the protection of 10,000 Muslims and British subjects from an imminent local military threat. Successful, he reported "all-quiet" to the Admiralty; two weeks later he received an urgent message ordering him to begin the very operation he had conducted two weeks earlier. The Admiralty "blushingly cancelled the operation" when Pelly reported the mission had already been completed.[61]

Part Two: Nonmilitary Sources of, and Constraints on, British Power and Influence

Economic Leverage

The economic situation in interwar Great Britain was a precarious one. After a brief boom following World War I, many sectors descended into a deep slump. The stock market crash in the United States in 1929 set off a wave of financial uncertainty and ruin worldwide, and Britain was one of the victims. The Great Depression exacerbated economic problems of the mid-1920s like unemployment and declining exports. Even though domestic consumption levels remained relatively constant, Britain was unable to export goods at the prewar rate. The governments of European states reacted to the depression by raising tariffs and other barriers, making international trade prohibitively costly.

Erection of trade barriers and the drop in demand outside the British Isles contributed to the poor performance of the industries that had propelled Britain to its preeminent status: revenues from textiles were down two-thirds and coal one-fifth: steel and pig iron were down about 45 percent and

53 percent, respectively, in the crucial years 1929–1932. Shipbuilding (partially but not entirely due to the naval disarmament regime) was down to a level of 7 percent of what it had been prior to World War I, and 62 percent of those who had worked in the dockyards were unemployed. Prior to the war, about one-quarter of British-produced goods were exported; by 1939, the proportion had shrunk to one-eight Even British shipping, at one time the dominant method of transporting goods overseas, shrank by over 50 percent in a single decade (1924–1933).[62]

The decline of exports wreaked havoc on Britain's balance of payments.[63] Combined with the incredible debt burden assumed during wartime—the national debt increased eleven times over during World War I—the British nation and state were in dire economic straits. Unemployment was rampant, ranging between 9.7 percent and 22.1 percent between 1921 and 1934, with the worst levels during the period 1931–1933.[64]

While the economic downturn damaged the budgets of the armed services,[65] it did not destroy British economic advantages in the eastern Mediterranean and the Levant. British businesses conducted a relatively small but brisk trade in the region, trading carpets, grains, minerals and fruit with the Greeks and the Turks. While the grain trade was important, neither Greece nor Turkey's trade was necessary for British sustenance, nor was British trade in the region crucial to local economies.

An obvious source of leverage against the British was oil, the increasingly important energy source which geologists began to realize existed in large quantities in the Middle East. However, Turkey was unable to prevent the presumably oil-rich Mosul province from being incorporated into Iraq, where British interests had access to it. Moreover, the British received a large portion of their needed oil from Persia (Iran), thus obviating any potential dependency on Iraq or other oil-bearing territories.

Lastly, finance was a potential source of economic leverage for the British in the region. "Subsidies" that looked suspiciously like bribes provided local officials with needed resources, and they provided the British with political allies who were loyal more often than not. In fact, in 1919 the British actually provided financial assistance to Emir Feisal to support the activities of his Arab anti-French campaign in Syria.[66] Britain also provided financial assistance to Egypt, Palestine, and Transjordan, since financial solvency was seen as a cornerstone of political order.[67]

Political Penetration of Regional Actors
British political penetration of regional actors varied in degree and form, but its essence comprised "a complex system of controls which depended partly

on military force, partly upon British prestige built up over several generations, and partly upon subsidies and other support to native rulers who looked to British diplomats and other officials for guidance."[68] The challenge facing the British was how to maintain this complex network in an era of parsimony and reduction of external commitments. John Gallagher's list of British techniques for lessening imperial commitments neatly characterizes the different versions of British political penetration during the interwar period:[69]

1. *Pull out of local government and focus on the center.* The prototype of this technique is Canada; it was not used in the Mediterranean/ Levantine region.
2. *Abandon detailed administration, focus only upon essential British interests.* For example, Britain granted nominal independence to Egypt in 1922, but there was a catch. Egyptian authorities were encouraged to deal with most domestic problems, though British military forces remained to help retain order. British authorities reserved the right to ensure the security of the Suez Canal, to defend Egypt from external threats, to protect foreigners, and to maintain the integrity of the Sudan. As Elizabeth Monroe put it, "the independence [the Egyptians] were given amounted to independence to do right, but not independence to do wrong, in situations in which the sole arbiter of right and wrong was Great Britain."[70] Though the military presence in Transjordan was far smaller, the British used the technique there as well. While still under the British Palestine mandate, Transjordan was granted independence in 1923, though a British officer assumed command of the Transjordanian military.[71] A 1928 treaty with Transjordan provided that a British Resident, chosen by British authorities, would "guide the Emir Abdullah on foreign relations, jurisdiction over foreigners, finance and related matters."[72] When in 1937 the British urged the splitting of Palestine into separate Arab and Jewish territories, Arab outrage was nearly universal. Not surprisingly, the rather conspicuous exception was Emir Abdullah, who voiced his support and encouragement of the plan.[73]
3. *"Pull out and prop up,"* or retrench from a sphere of influence and tolerate or encourage a leader who is capable of maintaining a stable regime. Gallagher lists as examples the accession of the Amanullah in Afghanistan, the Resa Khan in Persia (Iran), and Mustafa Kemal (Atatürk) in Turkey. Like Ambassador Stratford Canning in the 1830s and 1840s, Ambassador Sir Percy Loraine befriended the leader of

Turkey; he both influenced Atatürk's decisions and provided Whitehall with a window into Atatürk's thinking. Loraine's diplomacy in Ankara fostered an increasingly close political relationship between Britain and Turkey during the 1930s.[74] However, British diplomacy vis-à-vis the Turks was not all smoking hookahs and drinking strong coffee; rather, since the Turks saw the Soviets as a threat, the British military was a diplomatic factor as well. As one historian notes, "It was to a large extent symbolic that the first major step in the rapprochement between Turkey and Britain in 1929 was the official visit to Istanbul of a British naval squadron."[75] In the 1930s, as relations warmed, Atatürk sent military officers to Britain for training, and the British sent RAF instructors and British aircraft to Turkey.[76]

4. *Stay in country and rely on collaborators.* British officials would recruit "collaborators," local authorities or residents who worked with British authorities to govern and maintain order. In this manner, the British attempted to promote both indigenous governance and acceptance of British presence and the promotion of British interests. The method of collaboration worked moderately well in Iraq for the fifteen years or so between World War I and Iraqi independence. On the other hand, this method failed miserably in Palestine, where the Britons never gained the trust of the Arabs, and perhaps promised more than they could deliver to the Jews. Rather than peaceful governance by a combination of British and local authorities, the history of the Palestine mandate is one of rioting and unrest, the quelling of which required deployments of British troops.

"Collaborators" rarely came cheap, and this technique fell out of favor in an era when Britain was financially strapped. Though the British gladly emptied their pockets to collaborators during wartime, by the early 1920s "British officials could pay only small subsidies to local tribes and rulers," and perhaps equally important, "no longer had liaison officers of the caliber of H. St. John Philby and T. E. Lawrence to cultivate relations with them."[77] Though the British continued to give arms, money, and tax breaks to certain shaykhs,[78] it was nearly impossible to ensure order in the sprawling Iraqi countryside through collaboration alone. The British instead came to rely on cheaper and easier (but also more forceful) methods, such as air policing.

Domestic Political Constraints on British Involvement in the Region
The interwar period was characterized by economizing measures and substantial antiwar sentiment combined with optimism regarding the League of

Nations' prospects for maintaining the peace. Under these conditions it is hardly surprising that domestic political factors constrained the ability of Great Britain to act on the world stage. We will train our attention to the usual suspects: institutional constraints, domestic political coalitions, the press, and the electorate.

A voluminous literature asserts that one part of the institutional structure of the British state—the *Treasury*—had an appreciable impact on the ability of Great Britain to conduct foreign and defense policy during the interwar period.[79] Scholars have marshaled substantial evidence to support this argument, which typically goes hand-in-hand with a discussion of the so-called Ten Year Rule.[80] The Ten Year Rule refers to the often-repeated conventional wisdom that British defense planning should proceed as if no war will occur for at least ten years. After 1929, the Ten Year Rule is alleged to have had a particularly pernicious effect because the rule became "automatically self-perpetuating—that is to say that *on any given date* it was to be assumed for the purposes of preparing the service estimates that no major war would take place for ten years." The Ten Year Rule was formally abandoned in 1933.[81]

Historian John Ferris contends that the Ten Year Rule only began to affect the armed services in 1925. Implementation of the rule allowed the Treasury to assert control over the funding of the armed forces. By slashing the budgets of the armed services time and again, the Treasury reduced the acquisition of new equipment, the modernization of existing forces, the training of officers, and the payment of servicemen. The Treasury's budgetary control was not unconditional, however; rather, it was linked to government oversight. Ferris's words bring us to the next piece in the domestic political puzzle: "[The Treasury] was formally entitled to question any department's spending and to delay or refuse authorisation for specific expenditures even after estimates had been approved. These financial means of control would be formidable if the Cabinet backed the Treasury, but not without that help. *The Treasury could only control the services only if the Cabinet let it do so.*"[82]

When we think about domestic constraints on action abroad, we frequently turn to the effects of *political parties and coalitions*. The most notable change in British party government was the remarkable growth in the power of the Labor Party (a development intimately connected to the expansion of the British electorate—see below). Not surprisingly, unemployment fueled support for Labor, which claimed many urban and industrial seats in Parliament, to the detriment of the Liberal Party.[83] The Liberals' political mistakes in the 1918 reform bill and the division between the supporters of Asquith and Lloyd George made Liberal Party decline the complement to the growth of Labor. By 1932, calls for protectionism took away the core of the Liberals' platform, free trade, and the Liberals more or less fell off the political map.

The power shift between parties is vastly important for Britain's domestic political and social history; yet its impact on foreign policy is far less. Both the Liberals and Labor supported disarmament and the promotion of international peace; even the newspapers of the Conservatives, who were traditional benefactors of the military, supported these pacific initiatives.[84] Though some foreign policy decisions spurred debates tinged with party politics, party competition rarely had an acute effect on Great Britain's ability to act abroad. As historian John Gallagher notes,

> [T]he rivalries inside [political] parties and between parties was not sharp enough to cause sudden changes in policies toward world issues. In foreign policy their difference lay chiefly in rhetoric. In essentials there is little to distinguish between the diplomacy of MacDonald, Austen Chamberlain and Henderson. All of them saw that peace was the great British interest, that war would be the great British disaster; "the aim of every statesman in the British Empire," said Chamberlain, "is, and must be to preserve peace."[85]

In addition, Martin Pugh asserts that during the interwar period, none of the general elections (from 1922 on) were decided by foreign or defense policy issues.[86]

The *press* in most cases reflected the public's general aversion to war and its concerns about domestic well-being. Traditionally Conservative papers like the *Daily Telegraph* and the *Morning Post* criticized plans to reduce Royal Navy cruiser fleets and the proposal to abandon Remembrance Day, but even these news sources shared an aversion to the use of military force.[87] When the British appeared to be on the brink of hostilities with the Turks at Chanak in 1922, the *Daily Mail* attacked the British government for its allegedly belligerent stance and provoking another Gallipoli.[88] The British forces did not stand down; nor, however, did the British issue an ultimatum to the Turks. Charles Mowat hardly attributes this to the impact of a hostile press, however; the Cabinet *did* order an ultimatum (over the objections of major government figures) but the British commander purposely delayed its delivery until the crisis took a turn toward peaceful resolution.[89]

Paul Kennedy's assessment of the impact of newspapers at the turn of the century applies as well to the interwar period: "While the press occasionally *did* influence governmental policy, historians should not assume that it was of overwhelming import . . . it was rarely the case that statesmen and permanent officials became the helpless puppets of the press."[90] The press promoted a variety of critical views running against government policy, but newspapers largely responded to governmental initiatives rather than provoking action, and they generally did not have an instantaneous impact on decision making during crisis situations.

Though the newly enlarged electorate might not have voted officials in or out of office on the basis of foreign policy, *public opinion* was a notable, consistent constraint on British behavior in the international arena during the interwar period. The extension of the franchise marked the beginning of a new era, when aristocratic influence would be swept aside by the public attitudes of the majority. In the years following the end of World War I, British leaders could not ignore the public outcry for peace and restraint: "With almost unanimous fervour and emotion, the British people revolted against the idea of war and all that contemporary sources of wisdom—politicians, historians, publicists—claimed could cause it: arms races, military *ententes*, imperialism."[91] The public pressured the government to use open diplomacy, and public support for the League of Nations ran high. The Peace Ballot, though more of a propaganda tool and political pressure tactic than a reliable measure of public opinion, suggested that the British people wanted peace, and that they supported disarmament and the notion of collective security espoused by League supporters.[92]

The public also cried out for a "return to normalcy"— that is, the end of high taxes, the relaxation of government controls, and a renewed focus on domestic rather than international problems. The popular "antiwaste" campaign of 1920 alarmed Conservative leaders, leading them to form the Geddes Committee, which reviewed government expenditures and recommended a number of economizing measures. Known to military historians as the "Geddes Axe," the budget cuts recommended by this committee imposed stringent limitations on defense spending.[93] They also contributed to British willingness to negotiate and comply with naval disarmament agreements. Military historians often react with some trepidation to the domestic political impetus for these naval conferences; Robin Higham, for example, bitterly notes that such conferences "appealed to the momentary, fickle, pacific consciences and the pocket-books of politicians and voters."[94] Cost-cutting measures blocked cost-of-living increases in wages for British soldiers and sailors, reportedly damaging morale and prompting the Invergordon Mutiny.

Changes in the military administration in the Levant, including withdrawal of troops and the use of the RAF for imperial policing in Near Eastern mandates, owe something to public opinion and the impulse of parsimony, but public opinion usually did not act as an immediate constraint on British use of force abroad. For example, the maintenance of political influence in Iraq was a priority for British statesmen in the early 1920s. In the general election of 1922, public opinion was largely opposed to the holding of the Iraqi mandate. Despite this opposition, British leaders preserved the mandate for another ten years (though for appearances' sake the Anglo-Iraqi treaty was signed, changing little in Iraq but obviating the need to use the term "mandate").[95]

Symptoms of the domestic-political variety were typically general rather than acute. Public opinion certainly had a noticeable impact, particularly on defense spending; but it hardly directed British foreign policy. Likewise, institutional constraints limited the acquisition and deployment of military hardware and personnel, but could be bypassed to some degree in times of crisis.[96] Political parties and the press, which reflected partisan leanings, had little impact on the substance or conduct of British foreign policy in the eastern Mediterranean.

The Impact of International Regimes and Institutions

The League of Nations

The formation of the League of Nations would on first blush seem to generate a sea change in the way international affairs were handled by member states, including Great Britain. However, if we examine the record of disputes and crises in the Levant during the interwar period, we find that the League was not very active in these disputes. On many occasions, the British chose to provide aid or munitions to one side, or even intervene forcefully, without formally consulting the League. For example, in Brecher and Wilkenfeld's study of interstate crises, the British were involved in only one interstate crisis in the region (the Mosul crisis in 1926) that was arbitrated by League of Nations instruments (see table 2.2). When we contrast this paucity of League action with a list of illustrative cases of British gunboat diplomacy in the region (table 2.3), it becomes apparent that, even though British officials were very supportive of the League of Nations in spirit, they did not hesitate to dispatch a cruiser or even a fully armed capital ship in times of crisis.

In those instances when the League of Nations was called upon to arbitrate a dispute, the British were supportive and usually willing to contribute to the physical enforcement of a League decision. This is hardly surprising, however, since the decisions of the Council of the League of Nations, as well as the British government, typically favored the status quo. In the Mosul land dispute between Turkey and Iraq (a British mandate at the time), the Council and the Permanent Court of International Justice basically supported the status quo, following the established precedent by awarding almost the entire

Table 2.2. International Crises in the Eastern Mediterranean/Levant, 1919–1939

Crisis	Dates (D/M/Y)	Crisis Actors, Trigger (T)	British Involvement	League of Nations Involvement
Smyrna	3/1919–29/4/1919	Greece, Italy (T)	Heavily involved (no details provided)	Not yet in operation
Cilician War	11/1919–20/10/1921	Turkey, France (T)	Landed troops on Anatolian coast	None
Greece-Turkey War I	22/6/1920– 9/7/1920	Turkey [T: Greece]*	Gave military aid to Greece	None
Greece-Turkey War II	6/1/1921–12/9/1921	Turkey [T: Greece]	Gave political support to Greece	None
Greece-Turkey War III	26/8/1922–15/9/1922	Greece [T: Turkey]	None	None
Chanak	23/9/1922–11/10/1922	Turkey, U.K. (T)	Armistice offer triggered crisis; troops put on alert	None
Hijaz-Najd War	7/3/1924–19/12/1925	Najd, Hidjaz	Had controlled conflict in past, but not involved	None
Mosul Land Dispute	29/9/1924–15/11/1924	Turkey, U.K. (T)	Frontier skirmishes, ultimata threatening force	Arbitration
Sa'udi-Yemen War	18/12/1933–20/5/1934	Sa'udi Arabia, Yemen (T)	Warships sent to pressure Sa'udis to halt advance	None
Alexandretta	9/9/1936–23/6/1939	Turkey, France (T)	Pressured France to yield to Turkey	Arbitration

Source: Adapted from Brecher and Wilkenfeld, *A Study of Crisis.*
*Triggers in brackets (e.g., [T: Greece]) not coded as crisis actors.

Table 2.3. British Gunboat Diplomacy in the Mediterranean, 1919–1939

Assailants	Targets	Date
Great Britain	Russia	1919
Great Britain	Greece	November 1920
Great Britain	Soviet Union	February 1921
Great Britain	Austria-Hungary	November 1921
GB/US/France/Italy	Turkey	Sept., Nov. 1922
Great Britain	Turkey	November 1922
Great Britain	Egypt	May 1927
Great Britain	Egypt	April 1928
Great Britain	Egypt	July 1930
Great Britain	Greece	March 1935
Great Britain	Italy	September 1935
Great Britain	Italy	May 1936
GB/France/Germany/Italy	Spain	March 1937
Great Britain/France	Italy	September 1937
Great Britain	Italy	February 1938
Great Britain	Spain/Germany/Italy	February 1939

Source: Adapted from Cable, *Gunboat Diplomacy*, 175 ff. Included here are those cases in the vicinity of the Mediterranean in which Britain was coded as the assailant state.

tract to Iraq.[97] When Greece invaded Bulgaria in 1925, both Britain and the League called for the cessation of hostilities and the removal of Greek forces. While the League contemplated sanctions, the British Cabinet was ready to contribute British vessels to a multilateral show of force aimed at persuading the Greeks to cease firing and withdraw their troops.[98]

As Salvador de Madariaga, Spain's representative to the League of Nations, is reputed to have said, "When Great Britain stops, the League stops; when Great Britain goes forward, the League goes forward, too."[99] British leaders appeared to have a genuine interest in promoting the League and its causes; they also found the League's "interests" to be in line with their own. Even when this was not the case, however, Britain often used or displayed force without fear of reprisal from the ultimately doomed League of Nations.

Naval Arms Limitation and Disarmament

British participation in the 1921–1922 Washington Conference and acceptance of the resulting Washington Naval Limitations Treaties marked the first time in British history that force levels of the Royal Navy were regulated externally. The agreement also marked the first time since Britain had become a maritime superpower that the British accepted naval parity with another state (the United States).

Scholars have spared no effort in the study of naval disarmament during the interwar period, especially the Washington Conference. It was at this conference that the British accepted the ratio of capital ships that allowed the Americans to match the number of battleships floated by the storied Royal Navy.[100] This had little effect on the immediate future of Anglo-American relations in the eastern Mediterranean, since the United States rarely projected a naval presence in that region. However, the capital ships ratio also affected France and Italy, both of which did keep notable naval contingents in Mediterranean waters. Anglo-French relations were tarnished by British willingness to allow the Italians to maintain an equivalent number of capital ships as the French.

Yet the Washington Conference really had little impact on the management of British affairs in the eastern Mediterranean during the interwar period. The key was that cruisers remained unregulated by international agreements, so the British—whose resources were more efficiently distributed through smaller vessels anyway, given their world wide commitments—were able to focus their efforts on maintaining and upgrading their cruiser fleets. Though originally deployed for the protection of maritime commerce, cruisers played an additional role as instruments of British power projection in peripheral regions. Additional evidence that the British (perhaps begrudgingly) accepted smaller vessels as adequate is the program of building small sloops expressly for the purpose of "showing the flag," even though they preferred majestic warships that maximized "visual prestige impact."[101]

A subsequent arms limitation conference at Geneva in 1927 failed to generate a new agreement primarily because the British were unwilling to impose limitations on cruiser forces. Just three years later, however, the increasing pressure of a backsliding economy and the accession of a Labor government markedly diminished British unwillingness to restrict naval forces. At the London Conference of 1930, which Paul Kennedy has characterized "the high point in Britain's policy of naval disarmament,"[102] the British accepted a five-year extension of the moratorium on capital ship construction and moreover agreed to restrictions on cruisers.[103] These restrictions required the reduction of Britain's cruisers from seventy to fifty, much to the chagrin of the Admiralty but to the relief of Treasury officials.

The assets and liabilities of naval disarmament during the interwar period can, and have been, debated. We can summarize the impact of this short-lived regime in the following manner. First—for several reasons but notably to avert a naval race with the United States, to prevent the expansion of the Japanese navy, and to conserve scarce resources—British officials took naval arms limitation talks and the resulting restrictions seriously. Salvageable warships were scrapped, and new ship construction was carefully regulated to reflect Washington and London quotas. Second, while the French and Italians had soured on naval arms limitation by the late 1920s, the British continued to observe the rules of the regime for the better part of the interwar period. This asymmetry in naval arms reduction had a significant but primarily indirect impact on British naval presence in the region. Arms reductions did not change the priority status afforded to the Mediterranean Fleet, but the vacuum created by the reductions elsewhere in the world generated heavier demands on that Mediterranean Fleet. For example, the fleets were redistributed so that ships could be dispatched from the Mediterranean to Singapore should British interests be threatened there.[104]

Other Great Powers Active or Capable of Intervening in the Region
France was an important actor in the Mediterranean, and despite the devastation wreaked by World War I, did maintain the capability to conduct an active, interventionist foreign policy in the Levant. Initial Anglo-French disagreements over spheres of influence in that region were reconciled when Syria and Lebanon were placed under French mandate. French naval presence was noteworthy, but not overpowering, centered around a force of five to seven battleships in the Mediterranean during the interwar years. Counting all capital ships, France enjoyed approximately 10 to 13 percent of global power sea power during the period between 1922 and 1940.[105] While France's calculated relative sea power never amounted to more than half of interwar Britain's sea power share, a large proportion of France's ships were stationed in the Mediterranean, while the British fleets were distributed far more widely. In addition, France's building program turned out the largest number of warships (163) of any power in the period 1922–1934,[106] and the French were adamant about preventing restrictions on submarines at multilateral disarmament conferences.

Even during peacetime, France's military strength reflected its vulnerable geographical location on the European continent. Maintaining an army of approximately 600,000 men during the period between 1920 and 1934, the French had a clear numerical superiority over the British forces.[107] Even so, one analyst describes the peacetime French military as "nothing more than a skeleton," the flesh of which would be the conscripted recruits mobilized in wartime.[108] Despite this detraction, the French had the ability to take naval and military action, with air support, in the region; an example is the stiff repulsion of Feisal's defiant uprising in Syria in 1920, in which French tanks and planes proved too much for the ill-equipped rebels.[109] While the British regarded the French presence with caution, the typically friendly (or at least accommodative) relations between these states hardly warranted alarm, and the French appeared to be more preoccupied with the potential German threat than the British one.

Italy also played a major role in Mediterranean affairs during the interwar period. Italian military effectiveness seemed to improve substantially from the 1920s to the 1930s, though one analyst suggests that the increased success of the Italians in the mid to late 1930s owed more to British (and to some degree, French) lack of resolve than military superiority. Nonetheless, during the first decade of this period the Italians seemed militarily weak in the face of opposition:

> [W]hen Italian goals conflicted with the interests of a major military power willing to defend them by force, Italian forces proved incapable of gaining national objectives. This was shown by Italy's failure to gain Fiume and Dalmatia in 1919–20 in the face of French resistance, Mussolini's retreat from confrontation with Britain during the Corfu Crisis, his inability to undermine Yugoslavia in 1926–34 while it was backed by France, and his failure to gain French Somaliland by threats of force in 1938–39.[110]

Despite these failures, the Italians maintained a consistent presence in the eastern Mediterranean, and strengthened their forces as the years went on. In 1935 the Italo-Abyssinian Crisis found the British navy at a lower level of readiness than the Italian navy, which by mid-September of that year was fully deployed in the eastern Mediterranean and the Red Sea. Moreover, the Regia Aeronautica, the Italian air force, was capable of controlling the skies of the Mediterranean by the mid-1930s.[111] Prominent naval historian Stephen Roskill asserts that an Italian challenge against the British for control of these waters "would certainly not have been a walk-over for Britain,"[112] and indeed the British could not prevent the Italians from achieving their aims in that crisis of 1935–1936. The Italians had rearmed before the other European great powers, and consequently enjoyed a temporary edge; like the French, the Italians were able to focus their efforts in the Mediterranean region. As Brian Sullivan notes, "[b]etween 1934 and 1937 Italian military strength was at its apogee."[113] Less than a decade earlier, a contemporary observer commented that Italy posed a growing threat to the French position in the Mediterranean.[114] By the mid-1930s, Italy had become a cause for concern for British policymakers as well—even if Admiral Chatfield thought their reaction a bit tardy, saying of the Abyssinian Crisis, "It is a disaster that our statesmen have got us into a quarrel with Italy, who ought to be our best friend because her position in the Mediterranean is a dominant one."[115]

The *United States*, in its bid to become a global naval power, continued to build modern warships through the interwar period, and via the Washington Conference got the British to accede to codified parity in capital ships. Boasting naval force levels on a plane with the Royal Navy and controlling the Panama Canal, the United States certainly was the primary challenger to Great Britain in terms of global naval capacity. However, most of American naval power was focused in the Caribbean, Latin America, and the Pacific Ocean—that is, in regions other than the Mediterranean. The U.S. naval presence in the Mediterranean was extremely modest.

Prior to 1919, the United States maintained a few warships in the Mediterranean, but it did not participate in, for example, the British defeat of Turkey. In November 1918, the U.S. Naval Detachment in Turkish Waters was established, with all of the awe-inspiring strength of three converted yachts. Within a year this contingent grew to include four subchasers and eight destroyers, which served a variety of purposes, including communications, transportation of citizens and diplomats, relief operations, and so on in the area of Turkey, Syria, Lebanon, and Palestine. At its peak—during the conflict within and around Turkey in the early 1920s—the detachment grew to include twenty destroyers. After the signing of the Treaty of Lausanne in 1923, however, nearly all of these ships were recalled, and the United States kept only one or two warships in the region for the remainder of the interwar period. British admirals considered the United States a competitor for global naval supremacy, but this threat was hardly manifested in the Mediterranean.[116]

Germany, defeated in World War I, and the *Soviet Union*, wracked by revolution and burdened by the costs of World War I, were not in a position to be terribly enterprising in the eastern Mediterranean and the Levant. The Germans scuttled their fleet at Scapa Flow to prevent the British from requisitioning the vessels, and while they did engage in rearmament through the 1930s, did so relatively quietly. German military action in the eastern Mediterranean region was inconsequential, though Hitler's anti-Semitic policies and the resulting emigration of Jews from Germany contributed to the increasingly volatile situation in Palestine. The Soviets were subjected to military intervention by British forces during the revolution, and for the most part were not considered a major threat to the region under investigation.[117] Hector Bywater wrote in 1927 that the only potential naval threat emanating from the Black Sea and the Turkish Straits would be a combination of a renovated Turkish fleet, which was slow in materializing, and a revitalized Russian Black Sea fleet, which at the time he characterized as "a negligible quantity."[118]

Lawrence Pratt assesses the overall British position in the Middle East during the interwar years as paramount: the British were stronger in the region than the Germans and even the Italians, the Americans and Russians had little influence in the area during the 1920s and 1930s, and the French, while clearly influential, had a modus vivendi with the British and were far more preoccupied with the German threat in the 1930s than with antagonizing the British. Elizabeth Monroe suggests that it was precisely this freedom from great power interference that allowed the British to exercise a great deal of influence in the Levant during the interwar years.[119] We will revisit this issue in a more general context in part three.

Regional States' Options for Pressuring Britain
For the most part, regional states had few options for putting effective pressure on the British. The states in which Britain had notable interests, including Egypt, Iraq, and Palestine, were riven by internal disagreement and factions. Egypt was divided between those supporting the monarchy, which usually complied with British wishes, and the Wafd, the nationalist party. Moreover, British officials essentially ran Egypt's foreign policy. Iraq was populated by Shi'ite Muslims, Sunni Muslims, and Kurds; though the Sunnis were fewer in number than the Shi'ites, the Sunnis retained power. Palestine was sharply divided between Arabs and Jews, and like its sister mandate Transjordan, was financially weak. Internal division, British control of foreign policies, and lack of resources made it exceedingly difficult for these states to pressure Britain.

Presumably the British-supervised mandates' right to file complaints with the League of Nations against Great Britain for failure to adequately fulfill its obligations as mandatory gave these states some leverage, but it was far more symbolic than substantive. The League could do little to Great Britain, and the British hardly took the mandatories' rights seriously. Consider Foreign Secretary Lord Curzon's remarks in 1920: "It is quite a mistake to suppose . . . that under the Covenant of the League or any other instrument, the gift of the mandate rests with the League of Nations. It does not do so. It rests with the Powers who have conquered the territories." Thus these partially dependent entities had little recourse against the British.

Independent states presumably had a wider range of options—consider Turkey, for example. Turkey, like its Ottoman predecessor, had the ability to play the Britons and Russians against each other. Though the Bolshevik-led Soviet Union was weakened by war and revolution, the Turks knew that the British feared great power incursion upon the routes to India. To make the British shift uncomfortably in their chairs, the Turks would simply reach out to the Soviets. Turkish nationalists did just that during the 1920s, including the signing of the Turkish-Soviet Treaty of Friendship in 1921, which made the Soviet Union the first great power to break the moratorium on recognition of the Ankara government.[120]

In addition, Turkey had the military wherewithal to pressure the British, at least for a short time, as illustrated by the Chanak crisis. At Chanak, a British force of 4,700 troops maintained a four-mile perimeter that was vulnerable to a Turkish position. British intelligence estimated that the Turks could challenge the British perimeter with a force of 36,000 infantrymen and over 100 artillery guns. While backed by Royal Navy warships off the coast, the meager British ground force could not count on an outnumbered and partly ill-equipped RAF force to establish air superiority. Ferris asserts that

> Had war occurred, Britain's forces could not have maintained Britain's political aims [keeping the Dardanelles open, and preventing the fall of Constantinople] and might even have failed to defend themselves. Yet this strength—a large fleet, 6½ RAF squadrons and one division—was the entire force Britain had available short of mobilisation. The maximum reinforcements it could have provided 25–48 days *after* mobilisation would have been another 10–12 RAF squadrons, one cavalry brigade and 2½ infantry divisions.[121]

While a mobilized Britain could defeat the Turks with ease, the time required to mobilize would have allowed the Turks, who were also capable of effectively closing down the Dardanelles with artillery fire, to defeat the insufficient British forces.

We might suspect that oil was a potential source of political leverage against the British, but Britain enjoyed a relatively secure source of much of its needed oil in Persia (Iran). After oil was discovered in Iraq in 1927, the potential advantage for Iraq was neutralized to some extent by British influence. Iraq granted oil-drilling rights to the Turkish Petroleum Company, a multinational corporation chaired by a Briton and, by extension, assumed to be heavily influenced by British interests.

Congruence of British Objectives and Regional Actors' Objectives

Though the record is mixed, regional states by and large did not share common objectives with Britain. Rather than provide a lengthy, detailed examination of the objectives of the different states in the region as compared with British objectives, this study will offer a summary presentation that will admittedly obscure some subtle differences among states. Examples will provide a small window into some aspects of particular cases.

The mandates wanted independence and the ability to govern themselves. By contrast, the British wanted to maintain a controlling influence in the region, and London sought to prolong the mandates as necessary for this purpose. While under the mandate, Iraq's leaders shared common objectives with the British—some by force, others voluntarily[122]—save the aim of Iraqi independence. When such independence became a reality in 1932, the pursuit of objectives contrary to British interests followed. In 1933, Iraqi forces massacred some 550 Assyrians, who had been friends and servants of the British during the mandate. The Iraqis anticipated British military intervention on behalf of the Assyrians, but such an intervention never came. The Iraqis were willing to risk a confrontation with the British, but British strategic interest in maintaining a viable relationship with the Baghdad government precluded an armed response to the pogrom. Sadly, the British were even obligated (under the Anglo-Iraqi treaty of 1930) to provide the Iraqis with bombs for use against the Assyrians. While the British delivered these bombs, increased demands during the 1930s caused a backlog in British arms production. The Iraqis, unable to obtain weapons promptly, made arrangements to purchase armaments from Germany and Italy in 1937, disrupting the previously firm British grasp on Iraqi arms supply and angering the British leadership, which regarded the Germans and Italians with suspicion. While the question of independence prevented the British and Iraqis from seeing eye-to-eye during the 1920s, the granting of independence only exacerbated the obstacles to the achievement of British objectives in the region.

In Egypt, independence also loomed as an important source of disagreement. However, for political reasons, the British and the Palace had a common interest in each other's survival in the face of the nationalist challenge from the Wafd. In addition, Elizabeth Monroe points out that the British and Egyptians had at least "one common interest: to establish a parliamentary government," an objective that was realized in 1924.[123] During the 1920s in general, the dual imperatives of modernization and secularization—hardly objectionable to the British authorities—received widespread support and proceeded at a brisk pace. However, British mishandling of the Palestine question and increasing local opposition to British rule in Egypt eroded support for these initiatives in the 1930s. Even when "real" independence was granted to Egypt in a 1936 treaty, the Society of the Muslim Brothers (a traditionalist Islamic faction) described the agreement as "an iron around Egypt's neck."[124]

Looking to those states not under British administration, Turkey provides an interesting example. Kemalist Turkey sought revision of the Treaty of Sèvres, which the British helped negotiate, and the rights to Mosul, which

Britain retained after World War I and again after League of Nations arbitration. After settling these disputes, however, Britain and Turkey were able to reach a modus vivendi. This relationship was based on some common interests, including the (new) territorial status quo and, coincidentally, the integrity of Turkey.[125] Turkish and British business interests coincided, allowing for a mutually beneficial trade relationship. These common objectives were counterbalanced by Turkey's defense policy, which included the admission of German military advisers (to the exclusion of most British advisers) and Atatürk's continued relations with the Soviet Union. Though clashing on these issues, Britain and Turkey did share enough aims to establish a working relationship during the 1930s.

Part Three: Great Britain's Ability to Shape the Peacetime Environment

Britain's general preferences regarding the eastern Mediterranean and the Levant might be summarized as preserving the postwar status quo, maintaining peace, and preventing the encroachment of other great powers into the strategically important region. British leaders sought all of these while entering an era of relative decline in economic and military terms, and achieved varying degrees of success.

Preserving the Status Quo

According to most historians, British national objectives included the preservation of the existing political and territorial arrangements in Europe and elsewhere in the British Empire. British involvement in the Levant had expanded during World War I, and the Britons wished to retain this area as a sphere of influence after the war. Postwar settlements awarded the British political control of much of the region in the form of mandates, including Iraq and Palestine. Britain had no reason to "rock the boat." An excerpt from a 1926 Foreign Office memorandum summarizes this preference and provides a segue into the next one as well: "We have no territorial ambitions nor desire for aggrandizement. We have got all that we want—perhaps more. Our sole object is to keep what we want and live in peace . . . so manifold and ubiquitous are British trade and British finance that, whatever else may be the outcome of a disturbance of the peace, we shall be the losers."[126]

Maintaining Peace

As discussed earlier, Britons were disillusioned with the trappings of war. Peace was of paramount interest to Britons regardless of station in life; British society at large was exhausted by the war effort and desperate for quieter times. Moreover, Britons wished for a peace they did not have to enforce. Domestic imperatives and constraints, and the hope to conduct uninterrupted business abroad contributed to the move toward arms limitations and collective security mechanisms.

Primacy of Britain in the Near East

Finally, for strategic and economic reasons, British leaders sought to retain Britain's position as the most prominent great power influence in the Near East. Though it clearly overlaps with the preservation of the status quo, this preference is a bit more specific. The Near East held strategic importance as the gateway from the Mediterranean to the Persian Gulf and Indian Ocean via the Suez Canal. Despite the backlash from the 1919 Amritsar massacre and Gandhi's nonviolent protest movement, British interests in India remained a concern, and the Suez was the key to South Asia. Concerns about control of the Suez Canal were particularly acute because the protection of British interests in Asia and the Pacific required the ability to project British sea power into South and Southeast Asia. Since no significant fleet was assembled at Singapore, British warships from the Mediterranean squadron had to have access to the Suez Canal to ensure as rapid as possible a response to threats from potential enemies (e.g., Japan).

Oil was also becoming an increasingly important resource. While the British had a fairly reliable source in Persia (Iran), Britain's prominence in the Near East put Britons in a position to benefit from the future discovery of oil. Retention of the formerly Ottoman province of Mosul within the boundaries of Iraq, for example, was a priority, since experts suspected the province was a rich source of oil.

For these reasons, British leaders tried to prevent the encroachment of other great powers—France, the United States, the Soviet Union, for example—into the region. Some scholars have gone so far as to assert that the establishment of British hegemony in the Middle East became a priority. Moreover, the British leadership wanted to do this with as small a commitment as possible. That is, the British wanted to exercise control of the Near East without having to impose direct political control in regional states, and with as small a military presence as possible.[127]

Deterring Regional Conflict

Although few interstate conflicts occurred in the eastern Mediterranean during the interwar period, it is difficult to know how much of this we can attribute to British military presence and ability to project military force in the region. British presence in Iraq probably helped prevent great power incursions, but the historical record is hardly replete with "smoking guns" that convince us this is the case. On the other hand, there are notable deterrence failures, probably the most notorious of which is the Italo-Abyssinian Crisis of 1935–1936.

In 1934, the Italians began to provoke Abyssinia, which sought help from the League of Nations. As early as January 1935 the Italians began to assemble their forces in Somaliland, and by August appeared fully prepared for war. The League resolved to impose economic sanctions; the British stepped up the supply process to forces in the Mediterranean, preparing to uphold their collective security duties under the League of Nations. However, even the threat of retaliation from the Royal Navy failed to dissuade Mussolini from attacking Abyssinia. As for ground forces, the Italians amassed around 56,000 troops in Libya, while the British had 15,500 in Egypt. The Admiralty sent the Home Fleet to Gibraltar and and the Mediterranean Fleet to Alexandria.[128] Italy proceeded despite the sanctions and the reinforced British naval presence, and by May 1936 entered Addis Ababa, victorious in its aggressive action. The British spent the interwar period trying to muddle through with the smallest military possible; the failure to deter Italy exposed the erosion of the Royal Navy, that it "had been whittled down to its basic skeletal structure and vital arteries [and] was physically quite unfit for hostilities."[129]

Controlling Regional Conflict Outcomes

Speaking strictly in terms of physical capabilities, Britain probably had the wherewithal to intervene decisively on behalf of any one state in the eastern Mediterranean and Levant, bringing a regional conflict to a conclusion satisfactory to British elites. However, there are two problems with this assertion. First, these capabilities were not always available in proportions large enough to take control of a regional conflict at a moment's notice. If a token presence or limited action was not enough to influence the course of events, British impact on a major regional conflict would have to wait for mobilization. Second, finding a clear-cut example of a concerted British effort to control the outcome of a regional interstate conflict is difficult, so we will try to learn what we can from available information.

Consider as an example the fighting between the Greeks and the Turks after World War I. Preparing to impose a harsh treaty on the Turks, British forces intervened, first helping evacuate Greek communities in Turkey, then confronting the Turks. When the Royal Navy's occupation of Constantinople provoked a surge of support for Mustafa Kemal's nationalist movement, the Turks advanced and forced the withdrawal of a British garrison. Mediterranean Fleet Commander in Chief Admiral Sir John de Robeck ordered a naval bombardment of the Turks, followed by a seaplane bombing of retreating Turkish forces. The British forces also staged a landing to divert the Turks' attention and allow the Greeks to land at a different location.[130] British actions temporarily boosted the Greek effort, but ultimately the Greeks were expelled from Anatolia. Though suggestive, this example hardly tells the whole story, since the British backed away from supporting the Greeks after the ousting of the Venizelos regime. We can infer that limited British military action had a marked influence on the course of the conflict, but it is difficult to speculate what would have happened had the Anglo-Greek alignment remained intact.

To supplement the above example, consider the nationalist Turks' rejection of the Treaty of Sèvres, an extension of the Peace of Paris that imposed territorial losses on the Turks. After driving the Greeks out of Anatolia, the Turks turned toward Constantinople and the Dardanelles, carefully guarded by British forces. Vigilance, however, can prove insufficient against forces superior in number, and the nationalist Turks were able to establish a temporary numerical superiority over the British. Short of mobilization, even a reinforced British presence was inadequate to halt Atatürk's advance. Though the crisis was resolved without resort to war, the nationalists did move into Constantinople, and regained previously ceded territory via the more favorable Treaty of Lausanne. Here we see that, without resort to mobilization, the British were unable to resolve the conflict to their satisfaction.[131]

Reassuring Aligned States in the Region
Great power encroachment in the British sphere of influence in the eastern Mediterranean was minimal during the interwar period, though there is very little doubt that the British would hasten to defend their mandates and allies in the region against external threats.[132] As mentioned earlier, the reception of British delegates as accompanied by warships of the Royal Navy in 1930 had a symbolic effect for the Turks; it suggested that the British were capable of sending military help in the event of a Russian threat from the north.

Against *internal* threats, however, the British were not always willing to reassure the leaders of aligned states. Three years after Iraq became independent, Iraqi leaders were forced to repulse a Shi'ite tribal uprising on their own when repeated appeals to the British RAF for assistance fell on deaf ears. In 1936, the repulsion of another Shi'ite uprising was impeded by a lack of guns, the consequence of delays in the delivery of British military equipment.

These delays hindered British leaders' attempts to promote a trusting relationship with Iraqi leaders after independence by providing armaments. The inability of British factories to meet the production levels required to fill all extant orders for armaments during the mid-1930s damaged Anglo-Iraqi relations; the angry Iraqis sought arms from other suppliers, which irked the British. Even though the British continued to supply arms and instruction regarding their use to Iraq throughout the 1930s, the failure to adequately reassure the Iraqis led to an expanding rift between the two states.

Protecting Regional Economic Interests
Unlike nineteenth-century commerce, British economic interests in the eastern Mediterranean and the Levant were not threatened by pirates; rather, they were threatened by the competition of other interested powers. Though Britain had promoted free(r) trade for nearly a century, British leaders were somewhat possessive of economic advantages in the region, and were loath to share. For example, the British expressed concern over the Americans' attempts to promote their economic interests in the British sphere of influence. To the dismay of British leaders, Admiral Gough-Calthorpe reported in 1919 that representatives of Standard Oil and the National City Bank of New York arrived in Turkey accompanied by the senior American naval officer in the Mediterranean.[133]

Though oil was an important economic and strategic resource, one historian asserts that the story of oil in Iraq can be told with very few references to governments, since private firms conducted much of the business. The British government had no agent or representative that could effectively protect British oil interests. The Anglo-Persian Oil Company owned only 23.75 percent of the Turkish Petroleum Company (TPC), the first firm contracted to drill for oil in Iraq.[134] The remainder of the corporation was owned by French, Dutch, and much to the irritation of the British, American business interests. Another major contract was awarded in 1932 to the British Oil Development Company. Despite the auspicious-sounding title, Italians owned a controlling interest in the firm.[135] The TPC changed its name in 1929 to the Iraq Petroleum Company (IPC), and the British were able to take some solace in the IPC's successful bid to control the British Oil Development Company in 1937.

While it might be true that oil was largely the domain of private investors, Britain clearly made an investment in oil acquisition as well. British airbases in Iraq facilitated the protection of British oil interests. Many viewed these airbases, particularly the Mosul airbase, as a deterrent against potential foreign transgressors seeking to undercut British access to oil in both Iraq and

Persia (Iran).[136] In addition, the levies—British-trained and -led military organizations composed of indigenous peoples— provided a measure of defense for the economically important oil-bearing region.

In addition to military measures, the British used political pressure to combat the competitive practices of other states' firms and multinational corporations. For example, in Turkey the British pressured the Turks into signing treaties to generate exclusive opportunities for British commercial interests. Overall, favorable financial and trading relationships between Britons and regional actors were well served by the combination of consistent British military presence and political backing, and were rarely in jeopardy during this period.

Ensuring Favorable Foreign Policies in Regional States
The degree to which Britain could ensure that regional states pursued agreeable foreign policies varied widely from state to state. *Egypt, Transjordan,* and *Palestine,* for example, had no choice in the matter—the British retained control of foreign policy making, regardless of the preferences of local administrators. Even after nominal independence was granted to Egypt, British authorities managed Egyptian foreign policy. For example, following the Stack assassination in 1924, Lord Allenby presented the Egyptian government with a list of seven demands, whose fulfillment would serve as compensation for the failure to prevent Stack's murder. The Egyptians agreed to apologize, investigate the crime, and pay an indemnity, but refused to withdraw Egyptian forces from the Sudan and to increase Sudanese water rights. Allenby's response strongly suggested that the Egyptians had no choice in the matter. The Egyptian forces were to be removed at once, the Sudanese were informed of their now unlimited rights to irrigation in the Gezira, and British troops occupied the Alexandria Customs House until these measures were carried out.[137] Transjordan's subservience to British foreign policy initiatives was perhaps more subtle, but hardly less complete, as illustrated by the Emir Abdullah's advocacy of the Britons' proposed division of Palestine in the face of united Arab opposition.

Iraq, especially after independence in 1932, had more autonomy in foreign policy than the states mentioned above. In the 1920s, though, Britain played hardball with the newly formed state. In treaty negotiations with the British in 1921, the Iraqi leadership asked for the moon but settled for far less: "Initially, Iraqi leaders refused to conclude a treaty with Britain unless it would replace the mandate and guarantee them complete independence. Ultimately, however, they yielded because Britain had superior force and, by arresting some of the leading opponents of the treaty, demonstrated a willingness to use it if necessary."[138] The resulting treaty, signed in 1922 and expected to be in force for twenty years, provided for British advice to the Iraqi king on all international and financial matters. The treaty also paved the way for further agreements guaranteeing extensive military rights to the British,[139] and more embarrassing, the employment of British officials in Iraq at the expense of Iraqi citizens.

As time passed, however, the British eased their grip on Iraq. Believing that friendship with Iraq would become increasingly important to the British position in the region, the British accommodated Iraq by terminating the mandate early, granting Iraq independence in 1932; by closing strategic airbases in Iraq; and by supplying armaments and credit to the Iraqis. Initially successful, Britain later saw the Iraqis become less hospitable to British interests. Iraq purchased arms from Germany and Italy, considered potential enemies of Britain, and conducted a propaganda campaign against the British-friendly shaykh of Kuwait.[140] While Britain's essential interests were not jeopardized, Iraqi foreign policy clearly diverged from the British path after the British administrators and soldiers withdrew.

British leadership hoped *Greece* would be a bastion of British influence in the eastern Mediterranean after World War I, but this collapsed when Greece underwent a government transition and became too eager to revise the regional status quo. The fall of Venizelos's pro-British government from power allowed the accession of Constantine, whose known association with Germany caused Britons to recoil in disgust. In British leaders' eyes, Greece went from being a potential guard of the Dardanelles to a revisionist power seeking territorial gains at the expense of Turkey.[141] Britain could not stop the Greeks from campaigning against the Turks, short of intervening militarily, but both Britain and France damaged the Greek war effort by canceling financial credit to Greece.[142] The British could not dictate Greek foreign policy, but they did manage to cripple a crucial part of it.

Turkey probably had the greatest freedom from British influence in foreign policy, though toward the end of the interwar period an Anglo-Turkish relationship was blossoming. Relations during the 1920s were marred by trials and tribulation. Britain and Turkey nearly went to war at Chanak in 1922, had to submit the Mosul land dispute to the League of Nations Council for arbitration in 1926, and could rarely come to terms in treaty-making sessions. Once these disputes subsided, however, Turkish foreign policy seemed more agreeable to the Britons. Atatürk professed to be concerned only with Turkey's independence, sovereignty, territorial integrity, and defense. If these basic needs were met, Turkey would accept the status quo and peace—a stance certainly reconcilable with British interests. Less acceptable to British leaders was Germany's prominent position in Turkish markets and Turkey's close relationship with the Soviet Union, but the Turks signed commercial treaties with Britain and established a diplomatic relationship. British influence grew in Turkey, but the British never exercised control over Turkish foreign policy—nor, for the most part, did they have to.

Promoting Favorable Domestic Developments in the Region
Britain's ability to foster domestic developments consistent with its own preferences has a spotty record during the interwar years, but in general can be described as diminishing. Early in the period, Britons exercised a great deal of influence over the development of domestic structures in regional states. In Egypt, for example, British administrators forced the Palace to accept a parliamentary political system, despite the king's contrary wishes, which were based in part on the desire to keep the nationalist Wafd out of power circles. However, as time passed, British administrators began to feel that their efforts were increasingly futile.[143] By 1936, the British agreed to a treaty of alliance with the Egyptians that recognized the latter's independence in a more genuine fashion. Likewise, free-trade liberalism begun in Egypt by Lord Cromer yielded to increasing nationalization of the economy in the 1930s.[144]

Britons' ability to achieve domestic and economic aims within their dependencies seemed to hinge at least in part on the presence of British soldiers and administrators. This pattern is reflected in the British experiences in Iraq and Palestine, where the ability to promote domestic developments consonant with its own preferences existed only while the means to pressure local residents and enforce such developments were in place. As these states and mandates became independent and increasingly free of British presence in-country, British capacity to influence domestic development declined.

Fully independent states like Turkey were largely immune from British attempts to promote domestic development. For example, the Turks turned to the Soviet five-year plan as an economic model, much to the disappointment of British leaders (though the British had some influence on plan design).[145]

Conclusion

During the relatively peaceful period between World Wars I and II, Britain enjoyed regional prominence in the eastern Mediterranean and Levant, but it was experiencing relative global decline. British leaders used a variety of means in an attempt to maintain the status quo established after World War I, maintain peace, and preserve British primacy in this crucial region. Sometimes their efforts were successful; other times they were not, and these accumulating failures foreshadowed the British loss of dominance in the region that was to occur in the decades following World War II. One of the most frequently used instruments of British policy in the region during the interwar years—though certainly not the only one—was the Britons' already overextended military.

British army personnel based on-site in the Levant (though in modest numbers due to other imperial defense and administration obligations) were important for maintaining internal order in British dependencies. However, they were less appropriate for deployment as a concentrated force abroad, and probably gave little pause to other regional powers. The Royal Air Force (RAF) represented a new military dimension inaccessible to the peoples of the region, and provided a cheap, effective method of policing large expanses of sparsely populated land, thus compensating for the inability to deploy larger numbers of ground troops. The Royal Navy emerged from World War I quite strong but was reduced time and again because of domestic pressure for budget cuts and compliance with international naval arms limitation agreements. By the second decade of the interwar years, British naval preeminence was at best regional.

The British did not consistently employ the latest military technology, and when they did it cut both ways. Neglect of the navy contributed to the Royal Navy's relative decline, but naval capacity still clearly exceeded that of small regional powers, and it was capable of making remarkable visual impact on the right audience. The RAF proved an invaluable asset for maintaining internal order in British dependencies via the Trenchard system of air policing. However, this system was not feasible in urban settings, where the presence of lightly armed troops and the creation of networks of bribed informants were critical (though not always effective).

Local presence and the ability to respond rapidly to problems or crises were mainstays of the British military configuration in the region. In fact, the active presence of British soldiers and administrators, in combination, within regional states was integral in the (re)direction of regional states' policies to minimize clashes with British aims. One problem with these methods, however, was that they possibly provoked a nationalist response, or exacerbated violent nationalist movements. Still, occasional lapses in presence, inability to appear on-site due to difficulties projecting forces into rugged inland areas, and, most important, the withdrawal of British military and bureaucratic personnel are associated with a diminishment of British political influence in the region.

Britain's ability to achieve its goals in the eastern Mediterranean was also facilitated, conditioned, and constrained by a number of nonmilitary factors, including Britain's economic situation relative to regional actors, domestic political pressures, participation in the League of Nations and the naval disarmament regime, and other great powers with interests in the region.

Britain's economic slumps and relative decline globally were not reflected in a degradation of economic leverage in the region. The British economy was mildly sensitive to changes in trade, but this took little away from British influence in the region, often exercised through "subsidies" to local leaders. Oil was an important strategic resource, but Britain's supply at the time came primarily from Persia, thus preventing Levantine states from holding Britain hostage to a well-controlled oil supply.

British political penetration of regional states and dependencies varied widely, but in the most dramatic cases gave British leadership control over these actors' foreign and defense policies. British administrators were typically inclined to allow local leaders to address domestic issues if they did not impact upon Britain's strategic interests. In politics at home, domestic political actors and institutions constrained British action abroad to a much greater degree than in earlier periods. The increased constraints owe much to the dramatic expansion of the franchise to peace-minded voters calling for inward-looking governance. Also important was the institutionalized drive for parsimony (partially motivated by voter sentiment), reflected in the influence of the Treasury over defense spending. These factors tended to have a general impact, conditioning Britain's capabilities rather than creating immediate constraints on British action in crisis situations.

International regimes and institutions played integral but uneven roles in the history of the interwar period in the eastern Mediterranean. The League of Nations, though involved in arbitration of some regional disputes, put few real constraints on British ability to use force. Moreover, it tended to reinforce the status quo, much to the satisfaction of the Britons. The naval armament limitations regime, reflected in the Washington Conference of 1921–1922 and subsequent conferences that generated several written agreements, had an impact on British relative capacity. The impact is sometimes difficult to separate from the impetus of defense budget cuts, but clearly British compliance with these agreements affected the naval forces available for overseas commitments. Nonetheless, for much of the period the cornerstone of the scattered Royal Navy's peacetime forces—cruisers—were unregulated, leaving the British a great deal of freedom.

Leaders of regional states, especially dependencies, were often interested in pursuing goals at odds with British aims, but they had few options for pressuring the British. British military presence and/or internal dissension within these states often stood in the way of a concerted nationalist attempt to expel British agents, presumably the first step toward real independence. States that were already independent like Turkey had modest military means, and typically relied on the diplomatic ability to appeal to other great powers capable of pressuring the British. In particular, France and later, Italy, were competitors of the British in the Mediterranean. France and Britain's policies were more accommodative than combative, but Italy's aggression against Abyssinia was not deterred by British presence in the eastern Mediterranean, nor was it reversed in response to Britain's expressed disapproval of the act.

To characterize the period in its entirety, we note that British leaders concerned with preserving the regional status quo, maintaining peace, and promoting British primacy in the region had a record of early successes but that become increasingly spotty over time. In the effort to maintain peace, Britain sought to deter potential aggressors and curtail regional conflicts at an early stage. Clear examples of deterrence success are hard to come by and perhaps not so meaningful, since British control of its dependencies' foreign policies from within would presumably preclude some conflicts. However, we cannot dismiss the British failure to deter Italy from attacking Abyssinia as being at odds with British aims. In the interest of preserving the status quo, Britain sought to maintain internal order within dependencies and to prolong direct British influence on policy. Several bloody uprisings show that British presence was insufficient to deter internal conflict in urban settings, though British armed forces were usually capable of quelling such conflicts quickly and effectively once they broke out. The pressure brought upon Britain within these dependencies sometimes precipitated early withdrawal of British agents, and allowed for these dependencies to become independent states, thus disrupting the carefully constructed post–World War I status quo.

Britain's reasons for trying to maintain its status as the primary great power in the region were largely strategic, including access to the Suez Canal for passage to India and Singapore and access to oil to fill future energy needs. Keeping other great powers out of the region was a priority, but despite Britain's influence in the region and continued access to the Suez, American and Italian economic interests made inroads into the oil-producing areas, and challenges to British primacy appeared on the horizon. By the end of the interwar period, the erosion of Britain's effective capacity to shape political outcomes in the eastern Mediterranean and the Levant had begun, an erosion associated in part with overcommitted and continually shrinking British military resources.

Britain's Experiences in the Mediterranean: Comparing the Two Cases

Britain faced many challenges around the world during the interwar years. The challenge of maintaining peace, primacy, and the status quo in the eastern

Mediterranean and the Levant, while one among many, did constitute a major part of the British foreign policy agenda. The importance of this corner of the world is no surprise from an historical standpoint; indeed, the companion case study of Britain in the early nineteenth century clearly notes the importance of the Levantine region. However, both the context and the specific challenges the British faced in the region were somewhat different between the two cases.

One major difference in context was the level of great power involvement in the region. In the early nineteenth century, the Eastern Question became a priority issue for nearly all European great power rulers. Britain had to compete and cooperate with France, Russia, and Austria-Hungary in an effort to realize British aims in the region loosely controlled by the waning Ottoman Empire. In the interwar period, Britain's battered but victorious emergence from World War I permitted British leaders a chance to consolidate the influence built up during wartime in the region. While France wanted—and got—a piece of the action, the Levant (and much of the Middle East) became a British sphere of influence, largely free from molestation by other great powers.

A second major difference was the nature of the challenges within the region. In 1815, the entire region was under the nominal rule of a storied empire. While this nominal rule concealed the de facto independence of Egypt, the challenge facing British leaders concerned the problem of maintaining a coherent and defensible political entity in the region that would resist great power domination and allow for the passage of British military, merchants, and mail from the Mediterranean to the Indian subcontinent. The challenge largely required external military action in support of this weak political entity against its enemies, including breakaway Egypt. By way of contrast, in 1919 new states and mandates were formed under institutionalized British tutelage. The challenges to British influence primarily came from within these territories (though Greece and Turkey's clash presents a notable exception) and often were characterized by nationalist or religious animosity among local groups. Here, British leaders and officers found themselves responsible for the maintenance of internal order via political and bureaucratic assistance and military policing.

A third major difference was the available level of technology. British military commanders in the early nineteenth century had to concern themselves with two dimensions of operations—land and the surface of the sea. By the time of the interwar period, technological advances allowed military power to be exercised not only on, but also below the surface of the sea, and perhaps more dramatically above the surface of both sea and land with the advent of military air power. Additionally, during the early nineteenth century, the political entities within the region typically had access to technologies very similar to those of their great power suitors; during the interwar period, this was hardly the case. The rapidity of military-technical advances provided the British with a substantial advantage which diffusion had not yet diminished.

Keeping these differences in mind, let us now assess the findings of the cases in comparative perspective. First, let us consider Britain's military capacity in the region. In both cases we find that Britain's military capabilities, not surprisingly, are strongest in the naval realm. Not coincidentally, situations requiring British military action typically resulted in different political outcomes depending on geographical location. In littoral areas, British military action tended to be particularly effective. British leaders could feel confident in both shows of force and seaborne attacks against littoral targets during both the nineteenth and twentieth century cases. The visual impact of Royal Navy warships, the firepower of these warships, and the ability to respond quickly to a particular trouble spot contributed heavily to the British ability to deter and control conflict in the region. The employment of cruisers and other smaller vessels in large numbers facilitated the openness of sea lanes and protection of merchants from piracy, thus protecting economic interests. The ability to blockade (though more so in the earlier case) provided British leaders with another tool for exercising influence over offending states, though this technique was slow to make an impact.

Maintaining a consistent forward military presence thus is important for at least two reasons: to be able to respond promptly to crises and calls for help, and to remind local residents and political elites that they were within the reach of British military power. However, the efficacy of British naval presence vis-à-vis littoral regions did not automatically extend British influence inland. Here, the British navy had little impact, short of the long-term effects of blockade. During the Syrian Crisis in 1840, British warships successfully destroyed the defenses of the city of Acre; but ground troops were necessary to aid in the establishment of control of inland areas. Likewise, the maintenance of order in Iraq, which is hardly accessible by water, required a non-naval presence as well. However, ground troops were not the only solution. Effective uses of new technology allowed the British to maintain order cheaply and efficiently using a system of air policing. Existing aircraft stationed at a few lightly guarded local bases provided a viable tool for coercing local residents.

The technological edge was far less decisive in urban inland areas, however. In densely populated inland areas, neither sea power nor air power provided a substantial advantage for the realization of British aims. Here, there was little recourse to a heavily entrenched political presence complemented by the presence of British troops. Since the British hardly had sufficient military resources to fulfill their worldwide commitments, operations such as these, which were so costly in terms of both money and manpower, were problematic.

Nonetheless, the British were generally successful at achieving their minimal aims. This may reflect the supposition that if you set your sights low enough, you are unlikely to fail. British aims in both cases were quite similar. The preservation of peace, the protection of economic interests, and the maintenance of access to strategically important areas occupied British statesmen in both the early nineteenth century and the interwar period. For the most part, Britain was able to realize these goals in both periods. Greater ambitions, such as the establishment of political hegemony in the region, were not fully achieved.

Notes

1. Raymond Sontag, *A Broken World, 1919–1939* (New York: Harper and Row, 1971), 90. Sontag apparently paraphrases Curzon; the verbatim quotation is not supplied.

2. Geoffrey Till, "Retrenchment, Rethinking, Revival," in *The Oxford Illustrated History of the Royal Navy*, eds. J. R. Hill and Bryan Ranft (New York: Oxford University Press, 1995), 319–47; see also Arthur J. Marder, *From the Dreadnought to Scapa Flow* (New York: Oxford University Press, 1970), 224.

3. The British army reached a peak size of over 2 million in World War I; after demobilization, army size stabilized between 200,000 and 250,000 for the better part of the interwar period. Karen A. Rasler and William R. Thompson, *The Great Powers and the Global Struggle, 1490–1990* (Lexington: The University Press of Kentucky, 1994), 198; Brian Bond and Williamson Murray, "The British Armed Forces, 1918–39," in *Military Effectiveness, Volume II: The Interwar Period*, eds. Allan R. Millett and Williamson Murray (Boston: Unwin Hyman, 1988), 98–130, on 107.

4. Anthony Clayton, *The British Empire as a Superpower, 1919–1939* (London: Macmillan, 1986).

5. Lawrence Pratt, "The Strategic Context: British Policy in the Mediterranean and the Middle East, 1936–1939," in *The Great Powers in the Middle East, 1919–1939*, ed. Uriel Dann (New York: Holmes and Meier, 1988), 12–26, on 20). Pratt notes that part of the reasoning behind British reluctance to promote an Egyptian military is that they suspected potential recruits of being nationalists who would turn on their British masters.

6. M. E. Yapp, *The Near East since the First World War* (New York: Longman, 1991), 150. Under the republic, the role of the army in politics was nominally de-

emphasized—for example, serving officers were excluded from the Assembly, but even under the republic, the army played a prominent role (at least in a budgetary sense).

7. In the early 1920s this was hardly surprising, since the original peace settlement prohibited the rebuilding of a Turkish navy. Bywater asserted that the Turkish navy would only be a threat if combined with a rebuilt and revitalized Russian (Soviet) Black Sea squadron. Hector Charles Bywater, *Navies and Nations: A Review of Naval Developments since the Great War* (New York: Houghton, 1927), 252.

8. Correlli Barnett, *The Collapse of British Power* (Phoenix Mill, UK: Alan Sutton, 1972). These forces included nearly seventy artillery batteries, eight armored car companies, five cavalry regiments, and forty-five infantry battalions. Anthony Clayton, *The British Empire as a Superpower, 1919–1939* (London: Macmillan, 1986), 27–28 and 35.

9. Clayton, *British Empire*, 27–29. Technically this force was available for overseas deployment because the defense of the British Isles could be (perhaps begrudgingly) entrusted to the reserves, a combination of time-expired regulars and the part-time Territorial Army. Though the latter was described as "under-equipped, under-trained and under-manned," it did include fourteen divisions, two cavalry brigades, ten cavalry regiments, twenty-eight artillery brigades, three anti-aircraft artillery brigades, nineteen coastal defense brigades, and five armored car companies.

10. Bond and Murray, "The British Armed Forces," 107.

11. Bond and Murray attribute the low priority of the army in British rearmament to the purpose of rearmament in general, which "increased military strength to *deter* potential enemies rather than as a practical preparation for war" [emphasis in original], "The British Armed Forces," 99–104. See also Barnett, *Collapse*, 496–505. Once rearmament began, the army approximately tripled in size. Rasler and Thompson, *Great Powers*, 198.

12. Within a few months the twenty-four serviceable planes for British home defense dropped to sixteen.

See Edward Ranson, *British Defence Policy and Appeasement between the Wars, 1919–1939* (London: The Historical Association, 1993), 24, though Ranson fails to illuminate the reader as to how many of the 2,400 French planes were considered "front-line". See also Robin Higham, *Armed Forces in Peacetime: Britain, 1918–1940, a Case Study* (Hamden, Conn.: Archon Books, 1962), 154–55.

13. Clayton, *British Empire*, 25–26.

14. Clayton, *British Empire*, 26; also Higham, *Armed Forces in Peacetime*, chapter 5, *passim*, who notes (p. 186) that even by 1938, of 2,500 reservists designated to fly RAF aircraft, only 200 had adequate training.

15. Higham, *Armed Forces in Peacetime*, 186.

16. Correlli Barnett, *Collapse*, 249–50.

17. These figures err on the side of conservative estimates. Marder's *From the Dreadnought to Scapa Flow* and Paul M. Kennedy's *The Rise and Fall of British Naval Mastery* (Atlantic Highlands, N.J.: Ashfield Press, 1983), both of which are cited

very frequently, disagree on the specific ship counts. The two authors' figures are given below:

	Marder (1970: 224)	Kennedy (1983: 268)
Capital ships	42	58
Cruisers	109	103
Aircraft carriers	13	12
Destroyers	527*	45
Submarines	137	122

*includes torpedo boats

While Marder does not document the source of these figures, Bywater's *Navies and Nations* supplies precisely the same numbers, though Bywater claims forty-two Dreadnought-type battleships, while Marder counts forty-two total capital ships, of which thirty-three were Dreadnoughts, and nine were battle cruisers; Marder, *From the Dreadnought to Scapa Flow*, 248. Modelski and Thompson number the battleships at forty-four in 1918 and 1919; George Modelski and William R. Thompson, *Seapower in Global Politics, 1494–1993* (Seattle: University of Washington Press, 1988), 78, 230. See also table 2.1.

18. Bywater, *Navies and Nations*, 22; Barnett, *Collapse*, 249.

19. Modelski and Thompson, *Seapower*, 82. The annual naval expenditures went from over £62 million in 1919 to just under £29 million in 1920 (in constant 1913 British £).

20. Bywater, *Navies and Nations*, 84; compare to table 2.1. For First Sea Lord Sir Frederick Field's summary assessment of the weaknesses of the Royal Navy in April 1931, see Barnett, *Collapse*, 296–97.

21. Kennedy, *Rise and Fall*, 272.

22. Modelski and Thompson, *Seapower*.

23. For a partial discussion, see Stephen Peter Rosen, *Winning the Next War: Innovation and the Modern Military* (Ithaca, N.Y.: Cornell University Press, 1991); on the British attempt to develop an antisubmarine warfare capability (known as "asdic"—essentially, sonar), see Willem. Hackmann's at times unsparingly technical *Seek and Strike: Sonar, Anti-Submarine Warfare and the Royal Navy, 1914–54* (London: Her Majesty's Stationery Office, 1984). The often-maligned British asdic system was actually quite effective at detecting submarines—as long as they were submerged. The Achilles' heel of the ill-fated asdic system was that German submariners in World War II adjusted to the use of underwater submarine detection and, under cover of night, would bring the submarines to the surface—largely undetected—and attack Allied ships.

24. As Higham notes, the RAF commanders enjoyed a considerable degree of latitude in responding to disturbances in the Iraqi countryside. Indubitably this arrangement contributed to the ability of the British to act promptly. Higham, *Armed Forces in Peacetime*, 65–66.

25. Army brass accused the RAF of violating the principle of minimum force, since women and children were endangered by the bombings, but RAF officers de-

fended the practice, emphasizing the role of explicit prior warnings to villagers using leaflets. Thomas R. Mockaitis, *British Counterinsurgency, 1919–60* (New York: St. Martin's Press, 1990), 27–32.

26. Higham, *Armed Forces in Peacetime*, 65–66. See also Daniel Silverfarb, *Britain's Informal Empire in the Middle East: A Case Study of Iraq, 1929–1941* (New York: Oxford University Press, 1986), chapter 3, *passim*, which discusses the functions of the British airbases in Iraq in some detail. For example, the base at Mosul primarily served to deter external transgression, while the location of the base at Hinaidi was convenient for deterring internal disorder (25–27). While the policy of air policing caused some consternation among the British people back home who associated it with large-scale bombing of cities, it was not enough to discontinue the policy. Other powers expressed little concern over air policing capabilities because the aircraft used were not very threatening to major powers, and the 100-pound bombs used in the attacks were very modest in destructive power. Higham, *Armed Forces in Peacetime*, 66.

27. Higham, *Armed Forces in Peacetime*, 42–43.

28. E. W. Polson Newman, *The Mediterranean and Its Problems* (London: George Allen and Unwin, 1927), 287–88.

29. The British provided Iraq with artillery, machine guns, and even airplanes. In addition, an average of 25 Iraqi officers received training in Britain each year from 1932 to 1936. Silverfarb, *Britain's Informal Empire in the Middle East*, 85.

30. Till, "Retrenchment, Rethinking, Revival," 328. Clayton also notes that the Mediterranean was a strategically convenient center of operations, since the British had no Far East fleet and could use the Mediterranean Fleet as a source of power to project eastward. Clayton, *British Empire*, 9.

31. Bywater, *Navies and Nations*, 23; *Brassey's Naval Annual 1920–21*.

32. Compare to the Atlantic Fleet, which included five battleships. *Brassey's Naval and Shipping Annual*, various years.

33. Clayton, *British Empire*, 9–10. Bywater's failure to include aircraft carriers and submarines in his ship counts might indicate a lack of those warships in the Mediterranean, or it might reflect the continuing reluctance to admit that airplanes and submarines were important parts of sea power; Bywater, *Navies and Nations*.

34. The notable exception being the eponymous *Queen Elizabeth*, which remained as the flagship of the Mediterranean Fleet.

35. Clayton, *British Empire*, 45.

36. As was the Indian army, whose commitments were also drastically reduced through the 1920s, partly due to increased Indian domestic reluctance to support such deployments. See, e.g., Clayton, *British Empire*, 34 ff.

37. The British garrison in Egypt also included six artillery batteries, sixteen armored cars, and six tanks. Clayton, *British Empire*, 40–41.

38. Yapp, *Near East*, 381.

39. Yapp notes, "Alexandria's utility [as a base] was reduced because of Britain's dubious position in Egypt." The British would have preferred to employ the port city

Haifa as a base, but its use was restricted by the terms of the Palestine mandate. Yapp, *Near East*, 380.

40. As an interesting aside, Monroe asserts that the British attributed the rebellion to an insufficient presence of British troops, apparently overlooking or failing to emphasize the more deeply rooted disagreements between Arabs and Jews that were becoming more acute, and would further worsen during the 1930s regardless of the British military presence. Elizabeth Monroe, *Britain's Moment in the Middle East, 1914–1971*, 2nd ed. (Baltimore: The Johns Hopkins University Press, 1981), 81.

41. Brian Bond, *British Military Policy between the Two World Wars* (New York: Oxford University Press, 1980), 87–88.

42. Further, it shows the double-edged nature of British air power in the region. While the Trenchard system of RAF control (which was relatively successful in Iraq) completely failed in urban areas of Palestine, the use of airplanes to transport troops increased the mobility of British forces in emergency situations. Monroe and Bond note the former but choose not to emphasize the latter. Monroe, *Britain's Moment*, 81, and Bond, *British Military Policy*, 87–88.

43. Howard M. Sachar, *The Emergence of the Modern Middle East: 1914–1924* (New York: Alfred A. Knopf, 1969), 372.

44. Essentially, the close blockade consisted of warships literally cutting off important harbors from the open sea. Steam-powered ships required frequent refueling, and hence were not as adept at maintaining blockade position for long stretches of time as the old wooden sailing ships. However, the close blockade remained plausible until the advent of long-range coastal gun batteries, the torpedo-launching capabilities of small vessels and submarines, and the mine. These capabilities made it virtually impossible to maintain a blockade without suffering heavy losses. Bernard Brodie, *Sea Power in the Machine Age* (Princeton, N.J.: Princeton University Press, 1941), 98–102, 361–62, and 436–37.

45. Bond, *British Military Policy*, 85ff., discusses the army brass' reaction to air policing at length. To summarize briefly, the success and economy of air policing in Iraq led the British government to assign the Air Ministry to oversee the defense of Palestine, Transjordan, and Aden as well, much to the chagrin of army officials, who protested the decision regarding Aden. When Trenchard further proposed that the RAF assume responsibility for defending Sudan, British holdings in East and West Africa, the Red Sea, the Persian Gulf, and coastal defense for the entire empire, the Royal Navy joined in the army's vigorous outrage. One Royal Navy officer remarked "with almost apoplectic contempt: 'Aircraft! Good God—Aircraft! I'd rather have *one gun* at Famagusta [Cyprus] than all the aircraft you could produce.'" Quoted in Bond, *British Military Policy*, 86 (emphasis in original).

46. Stephen Roskill, *Naval Policy between the Wars, Volume II: The Period of Reluctant Rearmament, 1930–1939* (London: William Collins Sons and Company, 1976), 258–60.

47. Sachar, *Emergence*, 371.

48. David Fromkin, *A Peace to End All Peace: Creating the Modern Middle East 1914–1922* (New York: Henry Holt, 1989), chapter 51, 449–54; Sachar, *Emergence*, 373.

49. Silverfarb points out that the decision to encourage Arab governance predated the anti-British uprising, so the 1920 revolts did not cause the Britons to bring the Arabs into the political fold. However, he acknowledges that the revolts might have hastened the implementation of this decision. Silverfarb, *Britain's Informal Empire in the Middle East*, 8.

50. Sachar, *Emergence*, 379.

51. Silverfarb, *Britain's Informal Empire in the Middle East*, 142–43.

52. On the British practice of playing the Wafd and the Palace off each other, see inter alia John W. Young, *Britain and the World in the Twentieth Century* (New York: Arnold, 1997), 83, and John Darwin, "Imperialism in Decline? Tendencies in British Imperial Policy between the Wars," *The Historical Journal* 23, no. 3 (September 1980), 657–79.

53. Both quotations from Darwin, "Imperialism in Decline?" 671–72.

54. *Brassey's Naval Annual* (1933), 29.

55. The reader should note that, since the Kemalist Turks considered themselves to be at war with the British (because Mustafa Kemal did not accept the Treaty of Sèvres—see Alan Palmer, *Kemal Atatürk* (London: Macdonald, 1991), 65—the operations at Smyrna probably do not fit into contemporary understandings of peacekeeping made popular by the United Nations.

56. Three British battleships, a British cruiser and several destroyers, joined by a squadron of French warships, an Italian cruiser, and two American destroyers. Clayton, *British Empire*, 68; Thomas A. Bryson, *Tars, Turks, and Tankers: The Role of the United States Navy in the Middle East, 1800–1979* (Metuchen, N.J.: Scarecrow Press, 1980), 58–59.

57. Clayton, *British Empire*, 68. Clayton and C. L. Mowat use neutral language regarding the outbreak of fires that ravaged the city, although Richard Clogg asserts that the Turks set the fires, and points out that the Turkish quarter of Smyrna survived the blazes intact. Charles Loch Mowat, *Britain between the Wars, 1918–1940* (Chicago: University of Chicago Press, 1955), 117; Richard Clogg, *A Concise History of Greece* (Cambridge: Cambridge University Press, 1992), 97–98. Palmer discusses the issue at some length, noting that each side blamed the other for the fires, the Turks arguing that the Greeks were continuing their scorched-earth tactics as they retreated; Palmer, *Kemal Atatürk*, 65–66. Shaw and Shaw describe the situation as one in which the Turks were trying desperately to maintain order; when the fires broke out, the Turks tried to extinguish the blaze but found that the city's fire hoses and cisterns had been sabotaged, rendered useless. As they note, culpability for the arson (buildings were soaked in gasoline prior to the blaze) was never proved. Stanford J. Shaw and Ezel Kural Shaw, *History of the Ottoman Empire and Modern Turkey, Volume II* (New York: Cambridge University Press, 1977), 363.

58. Clayton, *British Empire*, 68. Despite the records of heroic British acts during the evacuation, some 30,000 people were killed at Smyrna (Clogg, *A Concise History of Greece*, 97–98), "butchered" by Turkish troops (Bryson, *Tars, Turks, and Tankers*, 58).

59. Palmer, *Kemal Atatürk*, 65–66.

60. Lord Carver, *The Seven Ages of the British Army* (New York: Beaufort Books, 1984), 202; also noted in, inter alia, Monroe, *Britain's Moment*, 81, and Bond, *British Military Policy*, 87. Incidentally, Carver also notes that Bernard Montgomery, who commanded the 8th Division in Palestine, bemoaned the absence of "any clear-cut statement defining the situation and what is to be done about it."

61. Higham, *Armed Forces in Peacetime*, 57.

62. Kennedy, *Rise and Fall*, 268–69.

63. Britain ran a balance of payments deficit every year from 1927 to 1931, with the marginal exception of 1928. See Barry Eichengreen, *Golden Fetters: The Gold Standard and the Great Depression, 1919–1939* (New York: Oxford University Press, 1992), 178.

64. Kennedy, *Rise and Fall*, 270, notes that the servicing of the war debt was extremely taxing; approximately 40 percent of the total budget was earmarked for annual interest payments. Nonetheless, the British governments consistently strove to eke it out with a balanced budget, which promoted the fiscal standing of the state (possibly) at the expense of the working and middle classes, who suffered from high levels of unemployment. Keith Laybourn, *Britain on the Breadline: A Social and Political History of Britain between the Wars* (Gloucester, U.K.: Alan Sutton, 1990), 125.

65. As Clayton notes, "OUNE" (Owing to an Urgent Need for Economy) became a familiar acronym in military circles. Clayton, *British Empire*, 18.

66. Richard Meinertzhagen, *Middle East Diary, 1917–1956* (London: Cresset Press, 1959), 27.

67. John Darwin, *Britain, Egypt and the Middle East: Imperial Policy in the Aftermath of War, 1918–1922* (London: Macmillan, 1981), 54.

68. Harold Sprout and Margaret Sprout, *Foundations of National Power*, 2d ed. (New York: D. Van Nostrand, 1951), 712.

69. Much of the following section is based on John Gallagher, "The Decline, Revival and Fall of the British Empire," in *The Decline, Revival and Fall of the British Empire: The Ford Lectures and Other Essays*, ed. Anil Seal (Cambridge: Cambridge University Press, 1982), 73–152, esp. 109–114.

70. Monroe, *Britain's Moment*, 72.

71. Peter Mansfield, *A History of the Middle East* (New York: Penguin Books, 1991), 208.

72. Ritchie Ovendale, *The Middle East since 1914* (New York: Longman, 1992), 14. In addition, a British subsidy provided nearly 40 percent of the annual state budget for Transjordan in the early going (ca. 1925); Mansfield, *A History of the Middle East*, 206–9.

73. Mansfield, *A History of the Middle East*, 206.

74. Palmer, *Kemal Atatürk*, 104–5.

75. Aryeh Shmuelevitz, "Atatürk's Policy toward the Great Powers: Principles and Guidelines," in *The Great Powers in the Middle East, 1919–1939*, ed. Uriel Dann (New York: Holmes and Meier, 1988), 311–16.

76. Sir Reader Bullard, *Britain and the Middle East: From the Earliest Times to 1950* (London: Hutchinson's University Library, 1951), 91–93.

77. Joseph Kostiner, "Britain and the Northern Frontier of the Saudi State, 1922–1925," in *The Great Powers in the Middle East, 1919–1939*, ed. Uriel Dann (New York: Holmes and Meier, 1988), 29–48, esp. 30–31).

78. Silverfarb, *Britain's Informal Empire in the Middle East*, 14.

79. See for example G. C. Peden, *British Rearmament and the Treasury: 1932–1939* (Edinburgh: Scottish Academic Press, 1979), and Higham, *Armed Forces in Peacetime*, 278–83. In contrast, G. A. H. Gordon asserts that the Treasury was actually the Royal Navy's "greatest . . . ally." G. A. H. Gordon, "The British Navy, 1918–1945," in *Navies and Global Defense: Theories and Strategy*, ed. Keith Neilson and Elizabeth Jane Errington (Westport, Conn.: Praeger, 1995), 161–80, esp. 168.

80. On the Ten Year Rule, see for example the debate in the *Journal of the Royal United Services Institute* among Silverman, Booth, and Roskill; Peter Silverman, "The Ten Year Rule," *Journal of the Royal United Services Institution*, 661 (1971), 42–45; Ken Booth, "The Ten-Year Rule—An Unfinished Debate," *Journal of the Royal United Services Institute* 116, no. 663 (1971), 58–63; Stephen Roskill, "The Ten Year Rule—The Historical Facts." *Journal of the Royal United Services Institution*, 117 (March 1972), 69–71. For a more recent corrective, see John Robert Ferris, "Treasury Control, the Ten Year Rule and British Service Policies, 1919–1924," *The Historical Journal* 30, no. 4 (1987), 859–83.

81. Stephen Roskill, *Naval Policy between the Wars, Volume I: The Period of Anglo-American Antagonism, 1919–1929* (London: William Collins Sons, 1968), 215 (emphasis in original); Roskill, "The Ten Year Rule," 70.

82. John Robert Ferris, *Men, Money and Diplomacy: The Evolution of British Strategic Policy, 1919–1926* (Ithaca, N.Y.: Cornell University Press, 1989), 17 (emphasis added).

83. It is common to assert that the combination of the expansion of the franchise and the suffering of the working classes due to the poor economic conditions (especially high levels of unemployment) propelled the Labor Party into the position of chief alternative to the Conservative Party. See for example Laybourn, *Britain on the Breadline*, 210.

84. Paul M. Kennedy, *The Realities behind Diplomacy: Background Influences on British External Policy, 1865–1980* (London: George Allen and Unwin, 1981), 242.

85. Gallagher, "Decline, Revival and Fall," 106.

86. Martin Pugh, *State and Society: British Political and Social History, 1870–1992* (London: Edward Arnold, 1994), 208.

87. Kennedy, *Realities*, 242.

88. Gallipoli, of course, being the site of a military disaster for the British during World War I. Roger Adelson, *London and the Invention of the Middle East: Money, Power, and War, 1902–1922* (New Haven, Conn.: Yale University Press, 1995), 208.

89. Mowat, *Britain between the Wars*, 118–19.

90. Kennedy, *Realities*, 56 (emphasis in original).

91. Kennedy, *Realities*, 241.

92. We should note with caution that those who wanted peace were not all pacifists. Some were clearly against war and advocated disarmament; others supported the idea of collective security. The "peace debate" was a politically charged issue in the 1930s, and Michael Pugh warns, "the argument that the peace movement was a point of consensus can only be valid at a superficial level." However, to assert that a "middle opinion" preferring peace to war emerged during the interwar period would not be inaccurate. Michael Pugh, "Pacifism and Politics in Britain, 1931–1935," *The Historical Journal* 23, no. 3 (September 1980), 641–56, quotation on 641.

As for the Peace Ballot, Pugh notes that it was used to rally support for the League of Nations Union, a pressure group whose support was waning due to the League of Nations' failures and the challenge of pacifists who did not favor collective security; Pugh, "Pacifism and Politics," 652–53.

93. Although Higham (*Armed Forces in Peacetime*, 103) notes that by the time the Geddes Axe fell, the army had reached a peacetime equilibrium, and where the estimates fell short, grants-in-aid were awarded to make up some of the difference. These grants-in-aid did not become a part of the estimates, yet were used for military purposes; ergo I urge caution to those who infer too much from the published Estimates from this period. For example, in 1922 the estimates dropped from £69 million to £40 million, but an additional £19.7 million appropriation-in-aid was awarded for activities in the Middle East. Higham, *Armed Forces in Peacetime*, 85.

94. Higham, *Armed Forces in Peacetime*, 145.

95. Monroe, *Britain's Moment*, 78.

96. Gordon's account of the actions of the Treasury Emergency Expenditure Committee (TEEC) in 1935 demonstrates this; but Gordon also hints that the emergency appropriations in this case were too little, too late. G. A. H. Gordon, *British Seapower and Procurement between the Wars: A Reappraisal of Rearmament* (London: Macmillan, 1988), chapter 15.

97. George Scott, *The Rise and Fall of the League of Nations* (New York: Macmillan, 1973), 131–35.

98. James Barros, *The League of Nations and the Great Powers: The Greek-Bulgarian Incident, 1925* (Oxford: Oxford University Press, 1970), 80–81.

99. Quoted in Scott, *Rise and Fall*, 179.

100. For example, see Till, "Retrenchment, Rethinking, Revival;" Roskill, *Naval Policy between the Wars, Volume I*, chapter 8; Higham *Armed Forces in Peacetime*, chapter 4; Harold Sprout and Margaret Sprout, *Toward a New Order of Sea Power: American Naval Policy and the World Scene, 1918–1922* (Princeton, N.J.: Princeton University Press, 1940). The ratio was roughly 5 (Britain, United States) : 3 (Japan):

1.75 (France, Italy). Additional restrictions on ship size and gun caliber size were also included in the arms limitation treaty; see Sprout and Sprout, *New Order*, appendix B). A capital ship was defined as a warship (excluding aircraft carriers) exceeding 10,000 tons standard displacement or carrying guns of caliber greater than eight inches.

101. Clayton, *British Empire*, 29–30.

102. Kennedy, *Rise and Fall*, 278.

103. The bulk of the London Treaty was acceptable to the five naval powers—Britain, the United States, Japan, France, and Italy—though the latter two rejected the part restricting cruisers. However, the signatories included an "escalator clause," which allowed signatories to build over the limit if nonsignatories "engaged in significant naval construction." See Richard W. Fanning, *Peace and Disarmament: Naval Rivalry and Arms Control 1922–1933* (Lexington: University Press of Kentucky, 1995), 128–29. The escalator clause was in the preface to the restrictions on cruisers, which set a ratio of approximately 10 (Britain): 10 (United States): 7 (Japan). See e.g. Clark G. Reynolds, *Command of the Sea: The History and Strategy of Maritime Empires* (New York: William Morrow, 1974), 481; Roskill, *Naval Policy between the Wars*, Volume II, chapter 2.

104. Admiral Jellicoe's plan for a British fleet in the Far East centered at Singapore had to be scuttled as a result of the Washington treaties; see Kennedy, *Rise and Fall*, 275–76). The British haltingly engaged in the construction and improvement of a controversial base at Singapore, but they never had the resources and vessels to maintain a daunting presence in the Far East; see James Neidpath, *The Singapore Naval Base and the Defence of Britain's Eastern Empire, 1919–1941* (New York: Oxford University Press, 1981), especially chapter 4. As the years went by, it became apparent that the British could not possibly defend their interests in the Far East against a Japanese naval challenge (Reynolds, *Command of the Sea*, 487), and many had their doubts about the plans to send warships from the Mediterranean to Singapore. Anthony Clayton minces few words, noting, "the much-repeated assertion that Britain could send a fleet to Singapore within seventy days, later optimistically reduced to forty-two and then to twenty-eight, only added self-delusion to the reality of weakness." Clayton, *British Empire*, 23.

105. Modelski and Thompson, *Seapower*, 124, table 5.9. Note that the other "global powers" used in the pool of states calculated in the relative sea power scores were Great Britain, Russia/USSR, the United States, Germany, and Japan. Distribution of Dreadnought-type battleships is provided in Modelski and Thompson, *Seapower*, 78, table 4.3.

106. Robert A. Doughty, "The French Armed Forces, 1918–1940," in *Military Effectiveness, Volume II: The Interwar Period*, eds. Allan R. Millett and Williamson Murray (Boston: Unwin Hyman, 1988), 39–69, on 48.

107. Rasler and Thompson, *Great Powers*, appendix A, esp. 198.

108. Doughty, "The French Armed Forces," 43.

109. Mansfield, *A History of the Middle East*, 181–82.

110. Brian R. Sullivan, "The Italian Armed Forces, 1918–40," in *Military Effectiveness, Volume II: The Interwar Period*, eds. Allan R. Millett and Williamson Murray (Boston: Unwin Hyman, 1988), 169-217, esp. 181–82.

111. Sontag, *A Broken World*, 290; see also Kennedy, *Rise and Fall*, 292–93.

112. Roskill, *Naval Policy between the Wars, Volume II*, 254.

113. Sullivan, "The Italian Armed Forces," 182.

114. Bywater, *Navies and Nations*, 248–49.

115. Quoted in Till, "Retrenchment, Rethinking, Revival," 334.

116. The section on the United States is based in large part on Bryson, *Tars, Turks, and Tankers*, 52–61.

117. Monroe, *Britain's Moment*, 85. The Soviets did have an active interest in Anglo-Persian relations, but that falls beyond the scope of this study.

118. Bywater, *Navies and Nations*, 252.

119. Pratt, "The Strategic Context," 25. Monroe (*Britain's Moment*, 74) notes that the extent of Russian political influence in the Arab world was a single diplomat in Saudi Arabia from 1924 to 1938.

120. Shaw and Shaw, *History of the Ottoman Empire*, 358–59.

121. Ferris, *Men, Money, and Diplomacy*, 118–21; quoted portion on 121 (emphasis added).

122. Elizabeth Monroe suggests that Iraq was neighbored by stronger states and might well have looked to Great Britain as a protector even if Iraq was not a British mandate. Monroe, *Britain's Moment*, 76.

123. Monroe, *Britain's Moment*, 75.

124. Israel Gershoni, "Rejecting the West: The Image of the West in the Teachings of the Muslim Brotherhood, 1928–1939," in *The Great Powers in the Middle East, 1919–1939*, ed. Uriel Dann (New York: Holmes and Meier, 1988), 370–90. Also notable is the Brothers' assertion that the only language the British could understand was force.

125. Shmuelevitz, "Atatürk's Policy."

126. Quoted in Kennedy. *Realities*, 256; see note 15.

127. On not wanting to assume direct control, see Ann Williams, *Britain and France in the Middle East and North Africa, 1914–1967* (New York: St. Martin's Press, 1968), 38; on minimizing the military commitment, see Higham, *Armed Forces in Peacetime*, 77, who asserts, "As British policy was traditionally defensive, her postwar policy needed to provide for forces sufficiently strong to deter any power from molesting her interests, which essentially meant from disturbing the peace, and powerful enough, nonetheless, to prevent a bellicose opponent from compelling her to concede the point in dispute either by diplomatic pressure or by war."

128. Arthur J. Marder, *From the Dardanelles to Oran: Studies of the Royal Navy in War and Peace, 1915–1940* (New York: Oxford University Press, 1974), 74. The movement of the Mediterranean Fleet to Alexandria came not because Alexandria provided a superior vantage point but rather because the British had little confidence in the inadequate air defenses of the main base at Malta. See, for example, Gordon,

British Seapower and Procurement, 136–37; and Till, "Retrenchment, Rethinking, Revival," 332.

129. Gordon, *British Seapower and Procurement*, 140. Gordon also discusses the extraordinary measures taken under the Treasury Emergency Expenditure Committee. The committee approved vast increases in procurement in response to the crisis, but Gordon takes the need to do so as further evidence of the unpreparedness of the Royal Navy for a major confrontation in the Mediterranean.

130. These actions are inventoried in Clayton, *British Empire*, 63–71.

131. France, Italy, and Greece had to forgo territorial cessions; the British retained Mosul, which they included in the new state of Iraq, but they did suffer a bruise to British prestige. Young, *Britain and the World*, 85.

132. A more detailed investigation of this issue might suggest that it was this ability to reassure aligned states that contributed heavily to the absence of great power encroachment in the first place.

133. Roskill, *Naval Policy between the Wars, Volume I*, 23.

134. Gallagher, "Decline, Revival and Fall," 125.

135. Silverfarb, *Britain's Informal Empire in the Middle East*, 96.

136. Silverfarb, *Britain's Informal Empire in the Middle East*, 25–26.

137. Newman, *The Mediterranean and Its Problems*, 286–87.

138. Silverfarb, *Britain's Informal Empire in the Middle East*, 9.

139. Britain "acquired the right to station its military forces in Iraq, raise and command a local military force in Iraq, use Iraqi roads, railways, rivers, and ports to move British troops across Iraq, inspect the Iraqi army at will, control the movements of the Iraqi army, control any joint Anglo-Iraqi military force which was placed in the field, and compel the king of Iraq to declare martial law and entrust its administration to a British officer." Silverfarb, *Britain's Informal Empire in the Middle East*, 9.

140. Silverfarb, *Britain's Informal Empire in the Middle East*, 142–43.

141. Prime Minister Lloyd George and some of his supporters hoped that Greece could expand into Anatolia and become a British client state that could assist Britain in dominating the eastern Mediterranean; Clayton, *British Empire*, 64. But when a greater Greece suddenly had a chance to become the handmaiden of Germany, the British leadership reversed course and opposed Greek expansion.

142. Erik Goldstein, "Great Britain and Greater Greece, 1917–1920," *The Historical Journal* 32, no. 2 (June 1989), 339–56.

143. Consider British High Commissioner Lord Lloyd's frustration: "our present position is impossible.... We cannot carry on much longer as we are. We have magnitude without position; power without authority; responsibility without control. I must insure that no foreign power intervenes in education, aviation, wireless communications, railways or army (where all seek to do so), and I must achieve this without upsetting the parliamentary regime which we forced upon the country against the king's wishes." Quoted in Mansfield, *A History of the Middle East*, 189.

144. Mansfield, *A History of the Middle East*, 190–91.

145. Shaw and Shaw, *History of the Ottoman Empire*, 393.

CHAPTER THREE

A Shadow Cast from Afar
The Royal Navy in South America, 1850–1900

Thomas C. Walker

Introduction

The second half of the nineteenth century found Britain at the height of empire. By the end of the century Great Britain ruled nearly one-quarter of the world. The Royal Navy was unrivaled. And with the introduction of steam power, British naval presence was easily extended around the globe. British preeminence was buttressed further by London's leading role in international finance. Finally, Britain also led in the realm of ideas. Liberalism, especially its stress on open markets and free trade that had preoccupied British thinkers for centuries, was emerging as the guiding force toward progress and development.[1] This recognition facilitated British efforts to promote and protect free trade around the world. With all of these factors converging, Great Britain's influence has been rarely matched in world history.

Compared to other regions, Britain had relatively few interests in South America in the latter half of the nineteenth century. The Middle East, the Indian subcontinent, and Africa were far more important to British security and economic interests. While trade and investment with South America amounted to nearly 10 percent of British totals, this consisted of private loans, investment, and trade.[2] With few strategic concerns and no important colonies, the Foreign Office and the Royal Navy paid relatively little attention to regional developments. For instance, up until 1872 the Foreign Office maintained "legations (second-rank missions headed by a minister)" only in Brazil and Argentina.³ The Foreign Office persistently advocated policies of neutrality and nonintervention. Lord Clarendon characterized this as a policy of "perfect indifference." One historian described the behavior of the Foreign Office in South America as "masterful inactivity." Instead of extensive efforts to shape the peacetime environment, Britain pursued rather limited goals of deterring any imperial ambitions from other great powers and promoting free trade in South America. With these limited goals, British policy can be characterized as one of caution, if not neglect.⁴

As the leading global power, however, Britain still sought to maintain some presence in South America. This presence took the form of limited naval presence. The warships of the Royal Navy's South American Squadron were always outnumbered and often obsolete when compared to those sailed by Brazil, Argentina, and Chile. Yet the scant resources London dispatched to the region did not stop Britain from achieving its limited foreign policy objectives. How much the token naval presence contributed toward these goals remains open to question.

The latter half of the nineteenth century is considered the heyday of gunboat diplomacy. However, British naval activity in South America bears only a slight resemblance to gunboat diplomacy—those efforts to further a state's political aims by the use of warships in peacetime. According to Paul Kennedy these powerfully armed, shallow draught gunboats were developed after the Crimean War and were widely used "for the expansion of western influence up rivers in the British habit." Kennedy also notes: "The occasional punitive measures by gunboats in support of British interests in Africa and China were far less important than the existence of the main battle-fleets in waters of international interest." The distant battle fleets served as a "reminder to other powers of the need to accord due weight to London's opinion. A fleet of warships, to use Nelson's quip, were always the best negotiators."⁵ The effectiveness of smaller vessels dispatched to South America should not be considered independently from the main battle fleets cruising distant waters. The mere presence of obsolete ships may have served as a reminder of British power. This may help explain how an outgunned, token British naval presence in South America still commanded respect from regional powers. While the obsolete vessels dispatched to South America were important reminders of British power, the shadow cast by the distant state-of-the-art battle fleet loomed large in British efforts to shape the peacetime environment in South America from 1850 to 1900.

Naval presence, of course, is only one aspect of British policy in South America. In this chapter we will explore many aspects of British influence and how successful this influence was wielded in South America at the height of the British Empire. In addition to naval power, British influence was enhanced by several other factors. These factors include Britain's historic role as protectorate of the nascent states in South America shortly after independence and a certain affinity between British liberalism and elite ideology in the capitol cities throughout the region. London's role as the center of global finance also played a role in British efforts to shape the peacetime environment. All of these factors contributed in limited ways to the limited British ambition to keep free trade flowing through the region.

Part One: Great Britain's Relative Military Capabilities

Regional Military Balance

The second half of the nineteenth century has been considered the golden age for the British naval power and the role it played in diplomacy.[6] Although the exact degree of naval superiority fluctuated, British naval mastery was unchallenged throughout the period. The Royal Navy sought to adhere to a two-navy standard, which meant Britain should maintain a navy that is at least as large as any two other naval powers combined. This margin was exceeded in 1883 when "Britain's battleship total was larger than that of the next three European navies—those of France, Russia and the new German empire—put together at 41 to 33."[7] Although the Royal Navy was by far the most powerful in the world in the second half of the nineteenth century, in South America its preeminence was less than impressive.

In the waters immediately off South America, British naval might was far from overwhelming. Due to the fact that interests and presence was limited in the region, few scholars have devoted much attention to it. Rory Miller, in the most recent and comprehensive study of British foreign policy in South America, noted that the "final, though under-researched, factor in the equation [of British influence in Latin America during the nineteenth century] is the naval presence."[8] Few have looked at this question because strategic interests in the region—especially those concerning the Royal Navy—were so limited.

With the signing of the Clayton-Bulwer Treaty in 1850, the United States and Britain acknowledged a condominium of sorts and finally put to rest any notions of serious rivalry in the region. With this agreement, Britain was fairly confident that its commercial interests in South America would not be challenged. The United States was equally confident that its leadership role in the hemisphere would not face British opposition.

With little threat to its commercial interests and of little strategic importance, the South American Squadron of the Royal Navy received limited resources. On occasion there were even calls from within the Admiralty itself to reduce naval expenditures by abolishing the South American station altogether.[9] When arguments were put forward in favor of naval expansion, they tended to emphasize smaller vessels to be deployed in the waters immediately off the coast of Britain.[10] With the exception of some merchants with particular economic interests in the region, there was very little support for naval forces in regions like South America where there were no outposts of empire.[11] The declining importance of South America is represented in the notable decline of Royal Naval deployments in table 3.1.

British naval forces in the region reached its peak in the 1840s, when the South American Station maintained twenty ships. The Station included two 50-gun-ships, two 44-gun-ships, three 26-gun-ships, one 20-gun-ship, seven 16-gun-ships, and six 10-gun-ships.[12] The smaller ships were particularly useful in traveling up the shallow rivers of the region. But following the 1840s, and the unsuccessful attempt to blockade the River Plata, the Royal Navy drastically reduced its presence in South America. By the 1880s and 1890s, there were only four aging British war ships in the region.

Table 3.1, however, tells only half the story. As developed in the next section, the British ships dispatched to South American waters were typically

Table 3.1. Royal Navy Vessels in South America, 1821–1890*

	Fighting Vessels			Nonfighting Vessels		
Year	Entire Royal Navy	South American Station	Percentage	Entire Royal Navy	South American Station	Percentage
1821	70	12	17	32	0	0
1826	84	12	14	28	0	0
1830	95	14	15	17	1	6
1835	99	14	14	28	1	4
1840	120	20	16	42	3	7
1845	112	9	8	47	5	10
1850	114	8	7	50	2	4
1856	149	8	5	30	2	7
1860	133	8	6	25	2	8
1865	145	11	8	44	3	7
1871	100	8	8	18	1	6
1876	98	4	4	16	0	0
1881	101	5	5	22	0	0
1886	101	4	4	23	0	0
1890	91	4	4	1	0	0

Source: Beeler (1997).
*After 1890, ships cruising South American waters were based in the Pacific Station or the Atlantic Station.

the most obsolete in service. While many regional powers purchased relatively advanced ships mainly from Britain, ships flying the British flag in South America were, in relative terms, not as advanced.

By looking specifically at the year 1894, we are offered a snapshot of the naval balance between Britain and the regional powers. While Britain maintained four warships on active duty in the region, Argentina maintained a naval force of more than forty ships. The flagship of the Argentine fleet was the *Admirante Brown*, launched in 1880 and carrying eight 8-inch-guns, displacing 4,200 tons and capable of just under fourteen knots. In addition to scores of gun boats and torpedo boats, Argentina also had a recently constructed cruiser from 1890 which was capable of a speed of twenty knots.[13] In 1894, Chile had four armored ships in its navy. The most modern was the *Capitan Prat*, launched in 1890. This "barbette ship" was capable of nineteen knots and carried four 24-c.m. guns and eight 12-c.m. guns. Other Chilean ships older but still effective.

The Brazilian navy, the strongest in the region, championed fourteen armored warships in 1894, including several modern cruisers launched after 1890. Two additional third-class cruisers were being constructed by Armstrong's in Britain. Of any state in the region, Brazil was the most capable of challenging British presence in the region. In spite of these advantages, few states challenged British presence. Some of the reasons why Brazil did not challenge British interests in the region will be developed in future sections.

When we look to the number of British military personnel stationed in South America, again we see low deployment and general neglect. British personnel amounted to very few in comparison to the land forces of regional powers. For most years explored in this case, there were less than 1,000 British military personnel in the region. Not only was the quantity low, but so too was the quality of the British forces. Discipline was poor and desertion rates were so high that one flagship captain was forced to relax "drill and disciplinary rules." The routine demands of discipline were frequently met with intransigence and desertion. He complained to his superiors that this situation required him to accept "a general level of maintenance that would not have been tolerated in British or Mediterranean waters."[14] While the evidence is fairly sketchy, it generally indicates that the region was an outlet for malcontents and misfits from the British military and the Foreign Office alike.

Turning to the question of total land forces, the number of men under arms, and annual military expenditures, we see that the regional powers were far less powerful than Britain's overall force levels. For instance, Britain had more than 300,000 men under arms in 1860. Brazil's army, the largest in

South America, had a force of roughly 21,000. British military spending throughout the period overshadowed all of the regional powers combined.[15] However, these resources were devoted to British forces around the world. If we turn exclusively to personnel and resources in the region, Britain again lags far behind. If instead we turn to total global force, Britain is overwhelmingly more powerful than all the regional states combined.

To conclude this section, on the regional level the British had absolutely no advantage in naval forces and in terms of military personnel in general. On the global level, however, Britain was the unrivaled leader in naval power and possessed a great advantage in numbers of military personnel. Simply put, within the region at any given time, the British did not enjoy a favorable position in terms of military capabilities. However, the prestige of British power based on its global military capabilities put the British at a decided advantage.

Great Britain's Relative Technological Efficacy in the Region

While Britain boasted the largest and most technologically advanced navy in the world during the second half of the nineteenth century, the most technologically advanced British naval forces were never stationed in South American waters. Most of these vessels were in distant regions of the world, where vital imperial interests were to be defended.[16] When state-of-the-art British vessels did pass through the Western Hemisphere, they were typically in the waters from Bermuda to Halifax. When compared to the pride of the Royal Navy, British vessels stationed in South American waters can be characterized as second-rate at best. Their purpose was not a serious fighting fleet but rather one of a "marine constabulary" composed of many types of leftovers from an earlier age—ranging from "tiny gunboats to corvettes almost 300 feet in length."[17] Their purpose was to show the flag on occasion and reassure British merchants by "countenancing and protection of English trade."[18] In the 1870s, one historian noted, "it was generally admitted that many of the vessels were so obsolescent that they could do little else than conduct such patrols along a distant and relatively peaceful coast [of South America]."[19]

While the Royal Navy plied the waters with obsolete and mostly wooden vessels, some of the regional powers had recently introduced powerful ironclads to their navies. For example, throughout the period Brazil's navy surpassed British forces in the region in terms of both quantity and quality. In the late 1870s the Chilean navy had two powerful, British-built ironclads: the *Almirante Cochrane* and the *Blanco Encalada*. Both ships mounted heavy rifled armaments.[20] Peru had one two-hundred foot British-made ironclad as well as several smaller ironclads.²¹ The vast majority of British ships were wooden and outgunned.

Although the regional powers possessed a technological edge in naval hardware, this did not necessarily translate into superiority over the Royal Navy. In those rare instances where there were militarized disputes between Britain and a regional force, the Royal Navy typically prevailed, even when it had technologically inferior equipment. In 1877, the Admiralty replaced an armored cruiser with an unarmored and fairly obsolete wooden frigate, the Shah. The Admiralty was well aware of the difficulties the Shah might face if matched up against the "small but potent ironclads" in the region. Later in 1877, an exchange of fire between the Peruvian ironclad and two British unarmored and undergunned warships, the Shaw and Amethyst. The Amethyst was an old wooden corvette and the Shah was faster but little more advanced. Neither British ship was armored. The Peruvian Huascar, on the other hand, was a British-built, low-freeboard turreted ironclad displacing 1,130 tons and known for its great maneuverability at sea. The conflict started after the Huascar's interference with the passage of two British merchant vessels. The Huascar was under the command of renegade Peruvian naval officers. A week later, the Shah and the Amethyst engaged the Huascar in battle. After several hours, the Huascar was unable to strike the older, wooden British ships and slipped away under the darkness of night. Shortly after its engagement with British forces, the Huascar surrendered to Peruvian authorities. Thus, even in cases where the regional forces enjoyed a technological advantage, the advantage was by no means decisive. The incident, however, prompted the Admiralty to reassign two ironclads to the Pacific station, but these assignments lasted for only two years.²² The Huascar, on the other hand, remained one of the regions most technologically advanced warships into the 1890s. The fact that the Huascar remained the qualitative benchmark for nearly three decades is a strong indication of how slowly naval technology advanced in the region.

The low level of troop training and discipline as well as poor use of technology became apparent during the War of the Pacific and the Chilean Civil War. William Laird Clowes offered an extensive report on the naval engagements in the Chilean Civil War during 1891. While both factions had ironclads in their naval forces, Clowes noted that the shells were not filled with modern explosives but rather "brown prismatic powder." As a result, the damage done by these shells was far less severe. But most noteworthy to Clowes was how "the waste of projectiles was conspicuous in the engagements. Much of it was, no doubt, due to the men's lack of training."²³

While the Royal Navy enjoyed superior training and a greater institutional capacity than the regional forces, there was no intrinsic technological edge enjoyed by British naval vessels dispatched to the region. However, the prestige and reputation of the Royal Navy seemed to stand behind every showing of the flag, regardless of the ship's actual speed and firepower. There is little evidence that any regional actors disregarded or disparaged British naval presence because of the obsolete nature of the vessels. The lack of technological sophistication wielded by British forces does not seem to have mattered much to the regional targets. Similarly, British commanders in the field demonstrated little concern with the fact that they were technologically upstaged by most regional actors. From what evidence we have, British officers were primarily concerned with provisions, personnel, and maintenance than with the actual type of vessels deployed. This may well be a result of the commanders' recognition that they were indeed relegated to the backwaters—literally and figuratively—of the empire. Consequently, they held out little hope that their obsolete ships would be replaced by anything more advanced.[24] One of the most surprising aspects of British presence in South America is how little technologically advanced weapons seemed to matter in British efforts to shape the peacetime environment.

British Military Presence in the Region
The relatively small and obsolete British squadron assigned to cruise South America indicates how little the British were concerned with maintaining constant presence throughout the region. The waning commitment to South America is evident by the transfer of the Pacific Fleet Headquarters, from Valparaiso to Vancouver Island in 1859. Still, the Admiralty thought it prudent to maintain some presence in the region from three small bases: Callao, Valparaiso, and Rio de Janeiro. Additional naval support could be sent from the more established bases on St. Helena, Ascension, Kingston, and Bermuda.[25]

However, it should be noted that these so-called bases were rudimentary and were very limited. In most cases, the British did not maintain control of coastline in the harbor—as it did in Bermuda and Kingston. For the most part, they relied on foreign facilities and providers. In Callao, for instance, the Royal Navy used an iron floating dock built jointly by private British and Peruvian interests and operated by Peruvian officials. In Valparaiso, the Royal Navy relied on two wooden floating docks. Further complicating the use of the "Chilean base" was "the Chilean port regulation that prohibited the storage afloat of gun powder, which had to be kept ashore under the general supervision of the local authorities and, therefore unavailable except during local working hours."[26]

Although there were always British ships somewhere in the vast waters surrounding South America, their presence at any one locale was sporadic at best. Even in the so-called bases, there were times when no British ship was present. After the shift of Naval Headquarters to Vancouver in 1859, the senior naval officer "required a ship to remain in Callao to watch over British interests in Peru." But the demand for constant presence at Callao "could not always be met." This was due in part to the scarcity of ships and to the fear instilled by frequent yellow fever epidemics in Peru.[27] With a few aging and slow vessels to patrol a vast coastline, the presence of British naval vessels may have been on a fairly regular basis, but it appears to have been hardly reliable and certainly not constant.

Speed of British Response
Given the limited nature of British interests in South America, there were few cases in which the Foreign Office or the Royal Navy demonstrated a sense of urgency. Most actions were measured with caution and rarely were they carried out in haste. It is therefore difficult to gauge with any precision how rapidly the Royal Navy could respond versus how rapidly it actually did respond.

Even when events appeared urgent, the Royal Navy was rather slow to move. For example, slow response can be seen in the crisis involving intervention in Mexico by Britain and France in the early 1860s. When the flagship *Nile*, under the command of Sir Alexander Milne, was ordered to Vera Cruz from Halifax in November 1861, Milne saw fit to delay his departure for thirty-eight days. Milne waited for the arrival of the H. M. S. *Emerald* from Plymouth, which carried with it new long-range Armstrong guns to be installed on his flagship. The new weapons on the *Emerald* never arrived because storms forced her return to England.[28] This account not only demonstrates the uncertainties and difficulties posed by long passages during the period, it also shows the slow response of the flagship to one of the more important British naval operations in the hemisphere during the period under study.

As noted, the ships assigned to the South American waters were not the most technologically advanced of the British fleet. While there were some steam-driven ironclads, the force was mainly composed of obsolete ships that relied primarily on sail. Even those ships with auxiliary steam power would rarely use it. This reluctance was based on the cost-cutting efforts of the Admiralty, which issued a standing order "to rely on canvas instead of steam whenever possible." Many ships went into storms under canvas, choosing to risk ruin rather than burn expensive coal.[29] Bach estimated that on average in 1875 the Royal Navy operating off the coast of South America would be traveling under sail twenty times more often than under steam.[30] The Royal Navy's reliance on sail rather than steam certainly limited its coverage and slowed the possible speed of response.

Available Military Options
With the low force levels deployed in South America, the immediate military options open to the British were severely limited. With four or five obsolete ships and a few hundred marines spread across the shoreline of a vast continent, there were few options immediately available to British commanders. Backed up by distant military forces, the British still managed to carry on the options of brief bombardment, naval blockade, and the show of naval force.

Of these options, naval bombardment may have been the easiest to carry out, but it was not very plausible given the high degree of interdependence between British interests and the potential targets. When gunboats were summoned, they were typically summoned by the interests of British merchants with the goal of gently swaying local authorities. Compared to shows of naval force, explicit threats to actually deploy that force appear very rare. Since British merchants would be the most likely to face local reaction and retribution, they often tried to discourage excessively coercive actions, especially that of bombardment.[31]

A second naval option would be the imposition of a blockade. The level of British naval forces, however, did not very often permit such an action. As one historian of the period noted: "the Royal Navy often did not have the resources [in South America] to mount a full blockade."[32] Efforts to mount blockades were unlikely for several reasons. First, any blockade with existing forces would have to be very limited in scope—which defeats its purpose. Second, to succeed, a blockade would require the deployment of additional naval forces to the region—which would not be supported in London. Third, a blockade might be conducted with assistance of another power, but as a result of the dramatic failure of the British-French attempt to blockade the River Plate in 1847, there was little likelihood of this option garnering support in London. Fourth, given the primacy of its commercial interests, British efforts to impose "blockades and interventions, by depressing trade and inflaming nationalism, probably did bondholders, as well as merchants, more harm than good."[33] Another historian noted how the effort on the Plate was "unpopular with the British merchants at Buenos Aires and in Parliament [back in London]."[34] So blockades could not be deployed effectively to secure British interests in free trade throughout the region.

A third military option was the display of naval force. Shows of naval force may have been the most important tool of British diplomacy in South America. While navalists like Lord Brassey were severely critical of these demonstrations especially when carried out by inferior vessels,[35] showing both force and flag appeared to play an effective role in demonstrating British commitment regardless of the obsolete nature of the craft deployed. These demonstrations carried out by obsolete vessels—like the unarmored frigate *Shah*—may have been perceived by the target as the level of a British commitment as well as a symbol of the global naval might that could be brought to bear on any given situation. The distant threat of the Royal Navy in all its greatness may have contributed to the effect rather than the regional British forces. As Miller concluded, even though British naval forces were relatively small in the region, "To a Latin American minister . . . the [British] consuls' power to summon cannons appeared a reality."[36] Any show of British naval force surely served as a keen reminder of the power of the Royal Navy, even if the show was carried out by an aging, wooden corvette.

British Ability to Intervene in Regional Actors' Domestic Affairs
Britain's ability to intervene in the domestic political affairs in South America was severely restricted. The most obvious restriction was imposed by the relatively small military force maintained by the British throughout the region. But this small military force was largely a result of the longstanding British policy of nonintervention in the region. This policy of nonintervention was informed and reified by two early failures of the British to intervene in the domestic affairs. In light of these failures, Britain not only pursued a policy of nonintervention, the Royal Navy also sought to deter any other European power from intervening.

D. C. M. Platt's (1968) study of trade and politics in the region has been celebrated as "the one attempt of any length to generalise about the British government's role in Latin America between 1815 and 1914."[37] Platt convincingly argued that British foreign policy since Canning has been one of nonintervention: "British statesmen resolutely refused to intervene, or to become entangled, in the internal political affairs of the Continent."[38] From Argentina's infamous default on the Baring's loan in 1824 to the twilight of British power in 1914, British foreign policy—with only a few sporadic exceptions that failed—was one of nonintervention. Britain's role in the region was to encourage open markets and free trade, since it was in the best position to benefit from such policies. Using military intervention to achieve these ends were often thought to be counterproductive.

Britain established its policy of nonintervention amidst the revolutionary movements early in the nineteenth century. Bolivar noted the importance of the Royal Navy to the independence movements: "Only England, Mistress of the Seas, can protect us against the united force of European reaction."[39] Britain sought to apply this policy nonintervention to all European powers in the region. Paul Kennedy referred to British commitment to nonintervention as among the "most readily remembered in its history books . . . the famous policy of preventing European powers from interfering in the revolutions of Latin America."[40] Throughout the second half of the nineteenth century, this policy was the source of regional goodwill toward Britain, and one from which Britain rarely strayed.

These policies of nonintervention were reinforced by two failed efforts in the 1840s. These failures strengthened those who advocated the policy of nonintervention. Palmerston was quick to point out how the British chargé in Brazil used Secret Service funds in the 1840s to "finance informants, bribe officials and subsidize newspapers" and how these efforts failed.[41] A more noted failure was the Anglo-French effort to topple the Rosas regime in Argentina. The Anglo-French blockade served only to generate popular defiance against the great powers, resulting in a rally-around-the-flag effect that increased the popularity of Rosas.[42] The failure of the intervention led London to question both the manner in which the affair was conducted and wisdom of its undertaking. There were cases of ships run aground and scuttled while achieving very little compliance by the Rosas regime. While the intervention was by far the most ambitious British effort to wield influence in South America, it remained a peripheral issue for London. As one historian of the intervention noted, the "affair is a small and relatively insignificant incident in British imperial history . . . it was driven by absent-minded British half a world away."[43] William Laird Clowes, perhaps the most prolific historian of the Royal Navy, referred to the operations as a "spirited little action."[44] Spirited or not, it was one met by failure at a time when the Royal Navy maintained twenty warships in the region, more than at any time in the century.

These two British failures helped ensure that few others would be undertaken. The second half of the century witnessed very little intervention in South American domestic politics. Palmerston, somewhat ironically, voiced the most opposition to the naval actions against Argentina. In the end it was Palmerston, the champion of gunboat diplomacy, who initiated British withdrawal from the Plate in July of 1846 and who advocated more faithful adherence to Canning's policy of nonintervention.[45] And it was this policy of nonintervention that would serve as an enduring guide to ships of the Royal

Navy operating off the shores of South America for the second half of the nineteenth century.

British Capacity for Humanitarian and Peacekeeping Operations

Britain had the ability to conduct successful peacekeeping operations in the region. This ability, however, was based on its reputation and good standing in the region, rather than on the military forces deployed in the region. Britain gained its good standing by its assistance to many of the independence movements in the early part of the century. It maintained its standing by refraining from territorial acquisitions in the region, even when annexation was proposed by the regional actor.[46] This placed Britain in a position to offer its good offices and mediate conflicts. As Cady noted, "England alone of the nations of Europe was trusted in Spanish America."[47] It did not, however, have the naval or military forces available to dictate peace in the region, and there was very little evidence to indicate any sustained interest or ability to conduct any such humanitarian operations.

There were, however, a few examples where mere naval presence by the British was able to keep peace, at least for the short term. In October of 1848, Venezuelan president Monagos sent thirteen of his vessels to Maracaibo and threatened to destroy the city for its part in staging a rebellion against his rule. "Suddenly," noted one historian, "the British warship *Electra* appeared off Maracaibo to protect British interests there. The Monagras squadron slunk back . . . to take on additional armament and consult with the capital."[48] In the end, the presence of the British force succeeded in keeping the peace.

The British capability to keep peace, however, did not always translate to keeping peace. The most notorious example of British failure to keep peace took place prior to the Spanish bombardment of Valparaiso in 1866. American naval officers commanding a small force made repeated efforts to discourage the Spanish action. Many Chilean officials believed that the presence of a strong British and American naval force would certainly be used to deter the Spanish bombardment. One Chilean minister stated how "Two powerful maritime nations, the United States and Great Britain had in Valparaiso very considerable naval forces, sent to our waters according to all appearances, on account of the existing war, and for the protection of the interests of their respective citizens. It was natural to believe that although the Spanish squadron might attempt the bombardment, the naval forces of the United States and Great Britain would prevent the consummation of an act of such useless barbarity, which would involve the ruin of many British subjects and North American citizens."[49]

The American officials at the scene appealed to the British, who had a superior force present, to offer a joint statement that might deter the Spanish. While the Americans had the monitor *Monadnoc* present, the Royal Navy had the frigates *Sutlej* and *Leander* present as well as the gunboat *Nereus*. But the British did not veer from their policy of neutrality and they refused to intervene. The American commander pointed out how British interests were "much more extensive" than American and how the British merchants would suffer more from the bombardment. The American commander recorded how "The English Admiral finally determined to throw the responsibility upon the Prime Minister, who did not choose to act in the premises ... English cooperation having failed, no separate action on my part was taken, as none had been proposed. I have used such measures as I could to bring about an accommodation, but without success."[50]

On the eve of the bombardment, the British diplomatic officials secretly departed and the Royal Navy sailed its warships out of the harbor. The Americans, with little force to prevent the Spanish bombardment, observed the Spanish attack. In Valparaiso, British policy of neutrality triumphed, however injurious it proved to be for peacekeeping and humanitarian interests.

Part Two: Nonmilitary Sources of, and Constraints on, British Power and Influence

Economic Leverage

Turning to nonmilitary sources of British influence in South America, again we see an enormous potential for influence. This is especially true in the realm of economic power. While the vast economic holdings of British citizens might appear to provide Britain with a great deal of economic leverage, this leverage was rarely applied. The second half of the nineteenth century was the height of British faith in economic liberalism, guided as it was by principles forbidding governmental meddling in markets and other economic practices. In the minds of British officials, these principles led to a clear divide between private and public. Indeed, the Foreign Office was never enthusiastic about protecting private property and in many cases simply refused to do so. The ability of the British government to employ the leverage of private investments to advance foreign policy goals is therefore very questionable.

Although British citizens and private interests yielded financial might, this was rarely translated into political influence available to the Foreign Office. Britain's brand of free trade liberalism combined with the policy of neutrality and nonintervention ensured a separation between the private realm of economics and the public realm of politics and diplomacy. From Canning's advocacy of nonintervention early in the nineteenth century to Salisbury's late in the century, British decision makers sought to distinguish between the interests of private capital in South America and the interests of British foreign policy in the region. As a result, there was very little effort to leverage Britain's economic power to achieve political outcomes.

Throughout the nineteenth century London served as the financial capital of the world. Through London commodities were traded, currencies were converted, and large international loans were floated. However, it does not follow that these British financial interests formed an easy alliance with the British Foreign Office and the Royal Navy, as some have asserted. While Gallagher and Robinson's speculations about informal empire may apply to some regions, there is little evidence to support the thesis for South America.[51] Platt noted: "Of the areas where questions need to be asked about the relationship of trade, finance and politics in British foreign policy—Egypt, Turkey, Persia, Africa, China—Latin America alone was unquestionably a-political."[52] Without empire or strategic interest, the bond between economics and politics for the British in South America was very weak indeed.

British foreign policy toward South America was founded by Canning in the 1820s. While the Royal Navy would protect the young republics from foreign intervention, Canning refused any government sanctioning of loans to these republics. In Platt's view, Canning was well aware of how financial ties between governments would bring a host of political complications to relationships best left to economic forces. One British diplomat was "disowned and recalled from his post in Mexico in 1824 for proposing a British guaranteed loan."[53] As British private investments grew throughout South America, the Foreign Office did its best not to be saddled with any special responsibility to British merchants who exposed themselves to the risky markets of Latin America.

Throughout the century successive British governments divorced themselves from intervening to support private investments in the region. In 1848, the Foreign Office published the following advice to "discourage hazardous loans for foreign Governments." The government found it "undesirable that British subjects should invest their capital in loans to foreign Governments instead of employing it in profitable undertakings at home . . . for the British Govt. has considered that the loses of imprudent men who have placed mistaken confidence in the good faith of foreign governments would prove a salutary warning to others."[54] In 1880, more than thirty years after these warnings of the Foreign Office, the *Economist* referred to ill-advised investments in South America as "a thorn in the flesh of British investors."[55]

There is perhaps no better statement of the relationship between British private capital and foreign policy than the one presented by Rear Admiral Kingcome in 1871. When an impending war between Peru and Ecuador threatened many British loans and investments, Kingcome proffered the following advice to the senior officer of the Southern Division of the Pacific Station: "As British Subjects, those creditors are entitled to the good offices of the H.M.G., but those who prefer the hazards of South American Loans to the moderate interest of the English Funds, cannot and must not expect to derive from British Squadrons and British influence, the security of the 3 per cents in addition to the high interests of South American Republics."[56] Since the British merchants in South America were motivated by a narrow and particular interests, many in the Foreign Office and the Royal Navy persistently refused to offer their support.

As a result of the efforts of the Foreign Office to avoid active military support for private investment in the region, British economic investment rarely translated to political influence. Fermandois noted that in the case of Chile, tight financial and commercial ties "did not give Britain any coercive leverage over Chilean domestic or foreign policy."[57] Smith stressed how Latin America was unique in this regard. British "investment was not accompanied by political involvement [in Latin America] as it was in Asia and Africa."[58] Most of the evidence from the second half of the nineteenth century points to a British policy that promoted free trade with a minimal interest in wielding influence within the domestic realm.

Political Penetration of Regional Actors

A more substantial source of British influence resulted from its historic role as protector of the young republics just after their revolutions in the 1820s. The reputation of protector of national self-determination endowed Britain with a special status in the region that no other great power could approach. Perhaps the most important source of British influence rested in what has been termed "soft power" or "political penetrative power."[59] This source of influence is based on a shared ideology or a shared attraction to a similar way of viewing the world. This appears to be the case of British liberalism, which promoted self-determination, open markets, and a general faith in progress. Many South American élite looked to Britain as a model of progress. The exact impact of this soft power, however, is extremely difficult to evaluate with certainty. There are, however, many anecdotes highlighting the British soft power. For instance, one member of the nineteenth-century Brazilian Parliament confessed how his liberal credentials were rooted in British liberalism: "When I enter the Chamber I am entirely under the influence of English liberalism, as if I were working under the orders of Gladstone. . . . I am an English liberal . . . in the Brazilian Parliament."[60] While the prevalence of this thinking is difficult to measure with certainty, British policy in the region was facilitated by even the smallest of measures.

The British also gleaned some influence in the region through immigration. By the late 1820s there were already as many as four thousand British subjects residing in Buenos Aires.[61] Nearly all of the major cities in South America had sizable British populations. These large British communities surely promoted a sense of economic liberalism among the South American elite. However, not all elite groups in Brazil during the nineteenth century were guided by notions of British liberalism. Ridings has recently demonstrated that there was a wide variety of loosely organized interest groups in Brazil, many of which were not liberal-minded.[62] Nonetheless, among many of the elite there was a certain adherence, if not begrudging respect, for British liberalism. This presence of large British immigrant communities surely contributed to a degree of soft power and facilitated Britain's ability to encourage free trade policies from which Britain stood to benefit a great deal.

Domestic Political Constraints on British Involvement in the Region
Given the limited nature of British foreign policy ambitions in South America, domestic political constraints are difficult to detect. The wide domestic support for free trade reinforced efforts to promote economic liberalism in the region. Domestic consensus over liberalism, then, provided the government with the freedom to pursue limited policy objectives concerning free trade. On the other hand, Parliament and the British public would have certainly opposed efforts to engage in more ambitious policies that might include deployments of large military forces. The result is a British policy in which free trade was joined with a certain indifference toward other political questions. This joint policy appears to have been an accurate reflection of popular British sentiments at the time. In sum, British policy in the region sought limited goals with limited means, both of which seemed to reflect a consensus in the British political arena.

One of the most striking features of the early years of the period under study is the sheer neglect of foreign policy matters, especially those in distant lands like South America that were not a part of the empire. Beeler pointed out that "Naval affairs, even defense policy in general, were not issues of central importance to the mid-Victorians."[63] Kennedy noted that in the wake of the Crimean War "the mid Victorians lapsed into a state of complacency about their navy and their world politics."[64]

In spite of this general indifference toward foreign policy, the British maintained their belief in the virtues of free trade. The repeal of the Corn Laws in 1846 marked the end of any serious opposition to free trade in Britain. What followed was the widespread support for foreign policies that promoted open markets around the world. Domestic consensus on free trade fit neatly with the Foreign Office's interest in its promotion in South America.

Support for military and naval policy during this period, however, was more idiosyncratic. Broad domestic support for a global naval presence emerged due in part to a curious coalition composed of high-minded liberals and Palmerstonian Conservatives.[65] The two often agreed in supporting an active fleet, yet their motives for doing so were sometimes at odds. Many liberals envisioned the Royal Navy as an agent for progress. Just as the Royal Navy had effectively ended the slave trade, the fleet would now work to promote free trade, thereby bringing civilization to the unenlightened. According to Semmel, British radicals, liberals, and conservatives of the mid-Victorian period shared two interconnected foreign policy goals: "first, to destroy the slave trade, and, this accomplished, to open Africa to a civilizing commerce."[66] Both policies, most acknowledged, would require a large and effective naval force. For some, the task of fostering free trade in the world's remotest regions was more than the British version of *la mission civilisatrice*, it was following the will of Providence. Toward the end of his life, Canning reflected upon how Britain was acting "in obedience to the Creator in promoting and protecting the salutary process of international trade; commerce was the source of blessings to our race, the bond of nations, and the first born of peace."[67] Lord Granville, who replaced Palmerston in 1851, saw a clear connection between maintaining open trade routes—with the help of the Royal Navy—and the march of civilization. Although the government should not sacrifice "all considerations of a higher character in pushing our manufactures by any means into every corner of the world," Granville pointed out that the government must recognize "the great natural advantages of our Foreign Commerce, and the powerful means of civilization it affords, one of the first duties of a British Government must always be to obtain for our Foreign Trade that security which is essential to its success."[68] A large and active Royal Navy that could reach around the world was needed to protect British interests and promote free trade. The two were neatly intertwined and support for the Royal Navy therefore garnered some support not only from conservative navalists but also from many of the fervent, free-trade liberals.

The Royal Navy thus found domestic support from both strategic-minded militarists like Palmerston and more high-minded liberals. Most of the British populace supported the Royal Navy for a combination of reasons that fall along this wide spectrum. While there were frequent discussions of the Admiralty's efficient use of resources, there was little popular opposition to its policies.

Although the prevailing attitude was one of support for the Royal Navy, there were recurring complaints of the Admiralty's inefficiency. Complaints of mismanagement were most pronounced in the wake of war scares. The first of these war scares occurred in 1844 and was followed by several others.[69] They were typically based on an improbable French coastal attack. These scares were usually followed by appeals for more attention to coastal defense—a brick-and-mortar defense rather than a blue-water navy. Even Lord Brassey, far from an opponent of naval interests, argued in 1871 that "by suspending construction on the large ironclad *Devastation* and reallocating the sums, the Admiralty could provide 36 vessels of a type admirably adapted for coast defense."[70] Placed in relative terms, the efficiency of the British military establishment in the nineteenth century was remarkable. Paul Kennedy noted how Britain was able to maintain *Pax Britannica* "at a cost to the nation of £1 or less per annum per head of population in defense expenditure—equivalent to somewhere between 2 and 3 percent of the national income. Rarely has such a position in the world been purchased so cheaply."[71] The fact that the military drew relatively little from state coffers may be one additional reason for the widespread support of naval funding.

However unwarranted, these war scares and concerns with coastal defense resulted in limiting resources devoted to distant operations. In a speech to the House of Lords in 1888, Lord Brassey criticized the Foreign Office and the Royal Navy for building inferior vessels "to satisfy demands pertinaciously pressed upon the Admiralty for the display of the flag in every quarter of the globe where we had commercial interests to protect and consuls to represent us, no matter how inferior the vessel upon which it was borne."[72] While the Foreign Office and the Admiralty might justify resources devoted to foreign stations defending the empire, it was more difficult to justify large deployments of ships and marines to regions like South America.

The Impact of International Regimes and Institutions

Although the second half of the nineteenth century can be characterized as an evolving international society among European states, the interactions between the great powers of Europe and smaller states in the periphery certainly cannot be so characterized. International regimes and institutions played very little apparent role in constraining British policy in South America. Instead, certain norms and ideas based on liberalism provided an enabling role for the British in South America.

Britain's foreign policy in South America was certainly guided by the dictates of liberalism. First, Britain, along with the United States, supported the norm of national self-determination throughout South America. Britain recognized and supported the Monroe Doctrine of 1823 and deployed naval forces as a means of deterring outside powers from any colonization in the region. By preventing the encroachment of other European powers, Britain could keep the region free of colonial trade agreements like those enforced when Spain and Portugal dominated the region. This relates to the second norm of liberalism that Britain pursued in the region: free trade. Britain encouraged the norm of free trade throughout the region. By helping enforce norms of free trade, Britain was uniquely situated to benefit.[73] As the world industrial leader, free trade in the region translated to an increase in British trade in the region.

The international norm against the act of blockade may have acted as a secondary constraint on British actions. As noted in the previous section, the primary reason that Britain did not impose blockades was due to a lack of naval forces in the region. Even in the event that Britain deployed additional forces, it is unlikely that blockades would have been undertaken. In 1856 Britain bowed to international pressure and promised to abandon the practice of blockades. By signing on to the Declaration of Paris of 1856 Britain pledged to allow passage of contraband goods by neutral ships during times of war. According to Paul Kennedy, "This was an incredible gesture by the world's strongest sea power in favour of the continental states' view that the nationality of any merchant vessel should cover its cargo: at one stroke the weapon of the blockade had been neutered."[74] After 1856, Britain recognized explicitly the international norm against the act of blockade.

Finally, the attitudes of paternalism and civilizing mission can be considered an international norm that was widely recognized by the European powers of the period. As a result, this norm granted Britain wide-ranging freedom of action in South America. While Britain did not exercise its full range of options in the region, its decision had little to do with the constraints imposed by international norms and regimes.

Other Great Powers Active or Capable of Intervening in the Region

Britain was not the only great power who sought influence in South America. The United States, although not typically considered a great power until the end of the nineteenth century, maintained a very small and sporadic naval presence in the region. France and Spain, primarily in the 1860s, also attempted to wield influence in the region. But the efforts of other great powers rarely clashed with the British interest in maintaining free trade in the region. As demonstrated in the Spanish bombardment of Valparaiso, British policy was one of indifference unless the encroaching major power was bent on territorial occupation. Since none appeared to be intent on territorial occupation, the British never sought to discourage the activities of other great powers.

In the 1840s–1850s, France was Britain's chief competitor for markets and influence in South America. By the end of 1865, the United States had replaced France as the chief rival to Britain in the region.[75] It is important to acknowledge that the competition between Britain and the United States was played out in the economic realm, not in the political. If there was a rivalry, it was an economic rivalry rather than a military rivalry. In political and strategic concerns, a sense of condominium evolved between the United States and Britain. Smith noted how the "Anglo-American economic rivalry in Latin America was a reality, but on the diplomatic level British policy toward Latin America stressed conciliation and cooperation with the United States."[76] The standard historical interpretation maintains that the Monroe Doctrine would be enforced by the Royal Navy so long as the British had access to Latin American markets. When the United States wanted to act in the region, as in efforts to prevent Spain's bombardment of Valparaiso in 1866, it often looked to Britain for cooperation and support. When denied that support, the United States did not typically intervene. This understanding between Britain and the United States remained until the emergence of the United States as a naval power in the 1890s.

Perhaps the best explanation for infrequent American intervention in South America was the lack of naval forces. While there was a great deal of fluctuation, generally speaking, there was a very small and obsolete American naval force cruising South American waters during the second half of the nineteenth century. In the late 1840s, the United States devoted four ships to South American waters, three 18-gun sloops and one aging 44-gun frigate. The British, for comparison, maintained a fleet of twenty-one warships including two 50-gun ships, two 44-gun ships, and three 26-gun ships.[77] In 1860 there were seven American warships in the Pacific Station, with the one old side-wheel steamer *Saranac* responsible for cruising the west coast of South America.[78] During the Civil War all the ships were recalled. During the 1870s, Congress limited naval spending to the point that "As old ships grew older they were taken out of commission until by 1875, in the opinion of one specialist, the South Pacific Squadron had become almost non-existent."[79] By the late 1870s the United States Pacific Squadron, nominally responsible for cruising the west coast of Mexico and South America, consisted of only three ships: its flagship the *Pensacola* lying idle at Mare Island without boilers, the *Adams* cruising the shores of Samoa, and the *Onward*, "a hulk which served as the United States Navy's supply ship at Callao, Peru."[80] What exactly the *Onward* was supplying has been difficult to ascertain. Not until the mid-1890s did the United States begin to demonstrate a more determined presence in South America.

While the United States was not terribly active in the region, Spain and France still occasionally sought influence. According to one historian, this resurgence of this "new imperialism" by France and Spain in the 1860s "was generally unopposed by Great Britain, preoccupied as she was with her own imperial interests in Africa and Asia . . . and the United States was either in the midst of its civil war or still reeling from its effects."[81] The Spanish efforts to reassert influence in the region concluded with the bombardment of Valparaiso in 1866. But in the end—and it was the end—Spain's naval action against Chile served as the swan song marking the final demise of Spanish influence in South America. In the wake of the bombardment, there were formal protests by nearly all the states in South America. In some cities, anti-Spanish sentiment swelled into violence and shouts of "Death to all Spaniards" could be heard.[82]

Toward the end of the nineteenth century, British naval presence was superseded by the American New Navy. But for the vast majority of the second half of the century, the most significant great power presence in the region was that of the Royal Navy.

Regional States' Options for Pressuring Britain

States in the region had very few options open to them that would put effective pressure on Britain. One obvious option would be to interrupt trade with Britain. This, however, does not appear to be a serious option. Since the British economy was widely noted for producing the best manufactured goods at the cheapest prices, seeking other trading partners or imposing tariffs specifically on British goods would have proven costly. Business interest groups would have surely objected to any policy that would have deprived them of easy access to British goods. As a result, there is very little evidence of regional powers attempting to curtail trade with Britain.

Since Britain never posed serious security threats to regional powers, alliances countering Britain also seemed unlikely. In the absence of threats from outside the region, efforts to form alliances in the region frequently met with failure. From the first conferences headed by Simon Bolivar in Panama in 1826 to the Second Lima Conference in 1864, the South American republics could not overcome mutual distrust and enter into meaningful alliances as a way of potentially checking the influence of outside powers.[83] Several have noted how "Unsettled and unmarked boundaries still plagued the relations of the Latin American nations with each other."[84] In an environment of unresolved territorial disputes and high degrees of political disturbances, decisionmakers would rarely look to form any regional agreements.

Alliances with major powers from outside the region also appeared unlikely. Any such alliance would be perceived as major power meddling or expansion. This would surely ruffle the British-American condominium in the region. Throughout the period the United States sought to maintain the Monroe Doctrine and curb the influence of powers outside the hemisphere. And with Britain intent on enforcing the doctrine, any alliance with an outside power could prove costly. With the inability to form alliances with other great powers, their chronic distrust of one another, and their dependence on relatively inexpensive British goods, there were few realistic options that would exert pressure on Britain.

Congruence of British Objectives and Regional Actors' Objectives
Britain and the states of South America shared, to varying degrees, those common objectives that are associated with liberalism: free trade and self-determination.

Beginning in the 1820s, with the early revolutionary movements in South America, Britain envisioned their interests in the region to be linked to the independence of the regional states. Canning, in one of his most famous remarks, proclaimed that "Spanish America is free and if we do not mismanage our affairs sadly, she is English." In the 1820s, Canning set out to protect the independence of these states by use of the Royal Navy. For Britain, sovereign states in South America meant open markets for British goods. For the states of South America, Britain's commitment to their self-determination allowed them the opportunity to be free of other foreign powers' intimidations and threats. In addition to ensuring self-determination, Canning also established most-favored nation status and entered into robust trade with the young republics.[85] These were the first in a series of mutually beneficial treaties for both Britain and the new republics. For the fledgling South American states, such recognition by Britain legitimized their status independent states in the international system. For Britain, this meant a large, new market for British goods. This policy of Canning's, expressed in the Treaty of Friendship, Commerce, and Navigation (1825), according to Ferns, "was simple, mature, and in many ways, the earliest and best instance of new liberalism in economics and politics."[86]

Free trade was especially valued by the new states in South America. After a long history of paying the inflated prices imposed by the Spanish and Portuguese monopolies, free trade with Britain was highly prized throughout the region. For Britain, free trade meant not only profits, but in the words of Lord Granville, it also pushed "the powerful means of civilization" that would have otherwise been missed.[87] For the Victorians, free trade to South America allowed them to *do well* and *do good* simultaneously. For the states in South America, free trade gave them access to the best and least expensive goods in the world, something they had been denied under colonial rule.

In order to safeguard these markets Britain had to keep other powers from reasserting colonial rule in the region. Encouraged by the Monroe Doctrine, the Royal Navy sought to prevent outside states from challenging the principle of self-determination. This suited both British commercial interests, American strategic interests, and the security of states throughout South America.

Part Three: Great Britain's Ability to Shape the Peacetime Environment

Any evaluation of British foreign policy success in shaping the peacetime environment has to be understood in the context of the severely limited nature of British goals in South America. This is clearly a case where the British aimed low and achieved their goals. The South American states opened their markets to British goods and trade grew rapidly. By 1865, 10 percent of British investment abroad was in Latin America. From 1865 to 1875 British investment grew from £80 million to £175 million. By 1913, British investment grew to nearly 1 billion pounds.[88] By opening South America to British investment and commerce, Canning's policy was undeniably successful.

This goal was achieved with a very small and obsolete naval force in the South American Squadron. The pride of the Royal Navy was deployed far from the shores of South America. By keeping the most destructive forces at a distance, like a trump card that is never played, the Royal Navy's larger forces may have contributed from a distance to British efforts to shape the peacetime environment. However, if a major battle fleet had been deployed, regional opposition to British interests may have hardened. In 1842, one British diplomat in South America depicted the complex relationship between influence and force: "consuls without cannons had little impact, yet the use of warships had often inflamed local feelings and been counter productive."[89] In South America, British consuls had cannon, and even from a distance, these cannon appeared salient to the regional actors in South America.

However, the goal of shaping the peacetime environment by "bringing civilization to the backward parts of the world," ideas embedded in the thinking of Canning, Granville, and many other free-trade liberals in the Victorian period, went largely unmet. Many free traders in the Victorian era like Cobden and Bright argued that "free trade was the panacea for all ills: it brought prosperity to all, it ensured international goodwill, it prevented war."[90] Clearly free trade failed to bring about these benefits in South America. Instead, the period from 1850 to 1900 was one full of conflict and war in South America. Throughout these conflicts Britain maintained its "perfect indifference" and refused to intervene. Business was business. Internal matters were something altogether different and they need not be meddled with. The only goal Britain sought was to promote free trade. And this goal was achieved in a very parsimonious, if not Victorian, manner.

Deterring Regional Conflict
Given the deliberate policy of neutrality and nonintervention in the region, Britain by design did not do a very good job of discouraging conflict within the region. Although there were some isolated episodes where the presence of a British ship could deter an isolated exchange—like that in 1848 in Maracaibo and discussed in an earlier section—there were four international wars in South America from 1850 to 1900. The most destructive was the Lopez War in which nearly 2 million perished.[91] Throughout the war British policy was simply to assist in avoiding the destruction of British property.[92] But interstate wars were only a small fraction of the conflict in the region.

Civil wars were extremely frequent throughout the period. There were eighteen civil wars in the second half of the nineteenth century, beginning with the Chilean Civil War of 1851 to the Colombian Civil War beginning in 1899. At the very least, each of these wars resulted in a minimum of one thousand battle deaths. Each involved sustained fighting between state sanctioned armies and organized opposition forces. In sum, there were a total of twenty-two wars—both civil and interstate—fought in South America over the fifty-year period.[93]

While conflicts in South America were both frequent and harmful to British interests, British resolve to mediate these conflicts was lacking. In 1897, Salisbury restated the British policy of neutrality and nonintervention in fairly religious terms: "We have no intention of constituting ourselves a

Providence in any South American quarrel. We have been pressed, earnestly pressed, to undertake the part of arbitrator, of compulsory arbitrator in quarrels in the west of South America. . . . [Her Majesty's Government is not] in the least degree disposed to encroach on the function of Providence."[94]

Controlling the Outcomes of Regional Conflicts

Britain certainly had the global power to control the outcome of any regional conflict, but it demonstrated little interest in doing so. Instead, the British government and the Royal Navy appeared to care little as to which faction or "association of individuals" should rise to power, so long as this association of individuals pursued policies that did not directly harm the cherished principles of free trade.[95] During the War of the Pacific, where the interests of British merchants were at stake and there was strong public support for Chile—both in England and among the British in South America—there is very little evidence to indicate any digressions away from the long-established policy of neutrality and nonintervention. One historian concluded that the Foreign Office was "always calm and correct, usually alert, and sometimes notably good at masterly inactivity."[96] Another described it as a "perfect indifference."[97]

Reassuring Aligned States in the Region

Supported by the Royal Navy, Britain successfully reassured the South American states that they would not be invaded by any European power. This was especially important in the early part of the century when Bolivar made his famous claim that "Only England, Mistress of the Seas, can protect us against the united force of European reaction."[98] But as the young republics became more stable, the likelihood of a European invasion dissipated, and so too did the relevance of British reassurances.[99] So far as policies of free trade go, there was little need to reassure the regional actors.

Protecting Regional Economic Interests

The Foreign Office and the Admiralty sought to avoid the role of protector of British-owned assets in South America. As Rear Admiral Kingcome noted in 1871, "those who prefer the hazards of South American Loans to the moderate interest of the English Funds, cannot and must not expect to derive from British Squadrons and British influence, the security of the 3 per cents in addition to the high interests of South American Republics."[100] As a result, the Foreign Office and Royal Navy were reluctant to intervene to support any particular merchant or business interest. There were several cases in which the Royal Navy could have acted to protect particular interests but failed to do so. This often led to complaints by British merchants. As Smith noted, the "destruction of a large amount of their [British] property in Valparaiso by the Spanish bombardment of 1866 provoked British merchants to criticize bitterly the inaction of the local British naval force. The Foreign Office disagreed . . . the British captain had been right to advising British residents to remove their property" from the designated area of hostilities.[101] Another historian noted how even in those rare cases in which the Royal Navy made efforts to protect property those efforts were "looked upon by the investors themselves as highly inadequate."[102] Rather than acting to protect private British investments, Britain defined its economic interests very neatly and narrowly in terms of bolstering free trade.

Surprisingly, in spite of the limited naval presence in the region and a general reluctance on the part of the Foreign Office to support the interests of British merchants, there was a perception that the British would indeed act to protect all their economic interests. Manchester argued that throughout the century there was still a widely held perception that British merchants in Brazil could look to "their government to protect them . . . and the British navy was the right arm of the merchants."[103] Yet this perception never seems to have been reflected in reality. Manchester pointed out that by 1850 British capabilities and willingness to intervene had come to an end.[104] Just as Miller noted, "To a Latin American minister . . . the [British] consuls' power to summon cannons appeared a reality,"[105] these perceptions of British naval might and of a British commitment to protect British interests might have been more important than the reality. In other words, the perceptions of British capability and willingness to intervene seemed to be more important than the reality that intervention rarely took place.

Ensuring Favorable Foreign Policies in the Region

The British succeeded in their efforts to encourage free trade throughout the region. As Canning predicted, free trade reigned in South American and the lion share of this trade was with Britain. British trade with Latin America measured around £20 million sterling per year during the second half of the century. No other power approached this level of trade.[106]

Another British concern with the regional states' foreign policies—but one that was hardly relevant by 1850—was the influence of the United States. Early in the century Canning also sought to prevent American predominance in South America. In his famous directive in 1826 Canning warned that "any project for putting the United States of North America at the head of an American confederacy . . . would be highly displeasing to your government."[107] Yet by mid century, there was very little likelihood of such a confederation. And there is little evidence to support the claim that the United States was even interested in such an alliance or confederation early in the century.[108] But by the end of the century Britain demonstrated little fear of America's ascendance in the hemisphere. By this point in time, Britain had achieved its primary goal of ensuring that the regional states pursue policies of free trade. And British interests in other parts of the world were considered far more important than those in South America.

Promoting Favorable Domestic Developments in the Region
Britain's primary goal in terms of domestic developments was based on the premise that free trade provided "the powerful means of civilization," as Granville claimed.[109] In the Victorian mind-set, ensuring free trade between Britain and South America amounted to much more than a boost to the home economy; it was part and parcel of Britain's "civilizing mission." Once the notion of a free market gained prominence in the economic sector, some liberals reasoned, a free market would emerge in the political sector and democracy would ultimately emerge.[110] While Britain succeeded in promoting pro-capitalist economic policies, the secondary goals of democratic development and economic progress were hardly furthered by British policy.

It is important to note that Britain did not actively pursue goals of democratic and economic development. Instead, it was assumed that progress and civilization would be the natural outgrowth of free trade. Such optimism is a leitmotif of all the Manchester liberals and is especially apparent in the works of Cobden and Bright.[111] Free trade, however, failed to accomplish these secondary goals. While the British accomplished their goal of free trade throughout the region, these secondary democratic and economic development did not progress as easily as prophesied by so many in the Victorian Age.

Conclusion

While Britain remained influential in the region, the sources of that influence are varied. The level of military force deployed in the region was so low that it had little material effect. The overall distribution of naval forces in the region favored the regional powers. From 1850 to 1894 there was a relative decline in British naval force in South America compared to those of regional powers. However, the Royal Navy still maintained a naval presence in the region that commanded respect by the regional powers. This respect may have been the result of the once formidable Royal Naval force plying South American waters before 1850. Or the respect may have been the result of British global naval strength of the period, which of course was unrivaled.

Other sources of British influence were distinctly nonmilitary in nature. British influence may have been based on Britain's vast economic resources and the recognition of the central role played by London in all international economic transactions. Or it may have been the widely shared allure of liberalism and the common interests that emerged with liberal trade policies. Or, finally, the British success in wielding influence in South America may have been a result of limited goals in the region. Britain, after all, only asked what was clearly in the regional states' best interest: free trade.

A combination of all these factors led to British success in promoting free trade in the region. The military dimensions of influence rested upon the global power of the Royal Navy, while its South American Squadron was more of a reminder than a representative of that power. The economic dimensions of the influence rested not on direct leverage of economic interests but rather on the recognition of London's central role in all international economic transactions of the age. Finally, the ideological dimensions of influence rested on the widely shared recognition that the British variation of liberalism would provide the best guide to progress and economic development.

In the end, British foreign policy in South America is a tale of a liberalism informed by Victorian optimism. In this tale economic concerns play the most prominent role. It was simply and optimistically assumed that if economic forces were allowed to operate freely, progress would naturally follow. After 1850, most deployments of naval force consisted of merely showing the flag. There were no Big Stick policies because there were no big sticks in the region. Instead, there were only occasional and slight reminders of British power. Demonstrations and appeals to the mutual benefits to be gained by free trade were far more frequent, and given Britain's primary objectives, these were also the most effective.

Notes

1. Douglas Irwin, *Against the Tide: An Intellectual History of Free Trade* (Princeton, N.J.: Princeton University Press, 1996).

2. Joseph Smith, *Illusions of Conflict: The Anglo-American Diplomacy toward Latin America, 1865–189* (Pittsburgh: University of Pittsburgh Press, 1979), chapter 1.

3. Rory Miller, *Britain and Latin America in the Nineteenth and Twentieth Centuries*(New York: Longman, 1993), 49.

4. On Clarendon see D. C. M. Platt, *Finance, Trade, and Politics in British Foreign Policy, 1815–1914* (Oxford: Clarendon Press, 1968), 324. For the general neglect by

the British, see Smith, *Illusions of Conflict*, chapter 1. The claim of "masterful inactivity" was cited in Miller, *Britain and Latin America*, 64.

5. Paul M. Kennedy, *The Rise and Fall of British Naval Mastery* (London: Ashfield Press, 1983), 166–67.

6. Anthony Preston and John Major, *Send a Gunboat! A Study of the Gunboat and Its Role in British Foreign Policy, 1854–1904* (London: Longmans, 1967), 13.

7. John Keegan, *The Price of Admiralty: The Evolution of Naval Warfare* (New York: Penguin Books, 1988), 111.

8. Miller, *Britain and Latin America*, 59.

9. Admiral Paget in Palmerston's second government in 1859 favored a reduction in naval spending by abolishing the South American Station. C. J. Bartlett, "The Mid-Victorian Re-appraisal of Naval Policy." Pp. 189–208 in *Studies in International History: Essays Presented to W. Norton Medlicott*, ed. K. Bourne and D. C. Watts (London: Longman, 1967), 196.

10. See Kennedy, *Rise and Fall of British Naval Mastery*, for detailed discussions of the movement supporting a reliance on a brick-and-mortar defense rather than the deployments of a large blue-water navy or squadrons plying distant waters.

11. Several provide compelling evidence of the Foreign Office's reluctance to intervene on behalf of particular economic interests. Smith, *Illusions of Conflict*, 12; John F. Beeler, *British Naval Policy in the Gladstone-Disraeli Era, 1866–1890* (Stanford, Calif. Stanford University Press, 1997), 23; D. C. M. Platt (1976), "Further Objections to an 'Imperialism of Free Trade,' 1830–1860." Pp. 153–61 in *Imperialism: The Robinson and Gallagher Controversy*, ed. William Roger Louis (New York: Franklin Watts, 1976), 159.

12. Donald Griffin, "The American Navy at Work on the Brazil Station, 1827–1960," *American Neptune* 19, no. 2 (March 1959): 24.

13. Thomas Brassey, *The Naval Annual* (Portsmouth, N.J.: Griffin and Company, 1892) 194.

14. John Bach, "The Maintenance of Royal Navy Vessels in the Pacific Ocean, 1825–1875," *Mariners Mirror* (August 1970): 271.

15. Brassey's *Naval Annual* (1892) and Correlates of War Project material capabilities data (http://cow2.la.psu.edu/)

16. See Bartlett, *The Mid-Victorian Re-Appraisal*, 190, for the role that suspicions of the French and Russian naval forces had of British naval deployments.

17. Beeler, *British Naval Policy*, 6.

18. Bach, *The Maintenance of Royal Navy*, 259.

19. Bach, *The Maintenance of Royal Navy*, 261.

20. Kenneth J. Hagan, *American Gunboat Diplomacy and the Old Navy, 1877–1889* (Westport, Conn.: Greenwood Press, 1973), 131.

21. The *Huascar* was ultimately seized by Chile and incorporated into the Chilean navy during the War of the Pacific. Robert Burr, *By Reason or Force: Chile and the Balance of Power in South America, 1830–1905* (Berkeley: University of California Press, 1967).

22. Beeler, *British Naval Policy*, 24–25.
23. Noted in Brassey, *The Naval Annual, 1892*, 133; 152.
24. Bach, *Maintenance of the Royal Navy*, noted the various concerns of the commanders in the Pacific from 1825–1875.
25. Preston and Major, *Send a Gunboat*, 83; 5.
26. Bach, *Maintenance of the Royal Navy*, 263.
27. Preston and Major, *Send a Gunboat*, 85.
28. Regis Courtemanche, *No Need of Glory: The British Navy in American Waters, 1860–1864* (Annapolis, Md.: Naval Institute Press, 1977), 68–69.
29. Preston and Major, *Send a Gunboat*, 6.
30. Bach, *Maintenance of the Royal Navy*, 261.
31. John Cady, *Foreign Intervention in the Rio de la Plata 1838–1850* (New York: AMS Press 1969), 35.
32. Miller, *Britain and Latin America*, 59.
33. Miller, *Britain and Latin America*, 58.
34. Platt, *Finance, Trade, and Politics*, 323.
35. Brassey, Thomas Lord, *Papers and Addresses: Naval and Maritime, 1872–1893*, ed. by S. Eardley Wilmot (London: Longmans, Green, and Company, 1894), 185.
36. Miller, *Britain and Latin America*, 59.
37. Miller, *Britain and Latin America*, 47.
38. Platt, *Finance, Trade, and Politics*, 312.
39. Kennedy, *Rise and Fall*, 168.
40. Kennedy, *Rise and Fall*, 167.
41. Miller, *Britain and Latin America*, 54.
42. H. E. Davis, J. Finan, and F. T. Peck, *Latin American Diplomatic History* (Baton Rouge: Louisiana State University Press, 1977), 84.
43. Peter Riviere, *Absent-Minded Imperialism: Britain and the Expansion of Empire in Nineteenth Century Brazil* (New York: Tauris Academic Studies, 1995), 177.
44. E. A. M. Laing, "The Royal Navy on the River Parana during the Allied Intervention, 1845–1846," *American Neptune* (1976), 143. Also, Clowes, William, *The Royal Navy: A History from the Earliest Times to the Present* (London: Low Marsten and Company, 1913) vi: 336.
45. Laing, *The Royal Navy*, 142.
46. Uruguay was one case in which there was a proposed protectorate or annexation by Britain. Palmerston responded tersely and would not even entertain the possibility. See Platt's *Finance, Trade, and Politics*.
47. Cady, *Foreign Intervention*, 17.
48. Francis James Dallett, "The Creation of the Venezuelan Naval Squadron, 1848–1860," *American Neptune* (1970): 266.
49. William Davis, *The Last Conquistadores: The Spanish Intervention in Peru and Chile, 1863–1866* (Athens: University of Georgia Press, 1950), 295.
50. Davis, *The Last Conquistadores*, 298–99.

51. Gallagher and Robinson's "The Imperialism of Free Trade" (*Economic History Review*, 1953) introduced the concept of informal empire. This work has acted as a central theme for those who equate commercial interests of British private citizens with British foreign policy. While this thesis gained wide acceptance for its explanation of British policy in Africa, it has not been convincingly applied to South America. For strained efforts to apply the informal empire thesis to the region see Peter Winn's "British Informal Empire in Uruguay in the Nineteenth Century" (*Past and Present* 1976) and Richard Graham's "Robinson and Gallagher in Latin America: The Meaning of Informal Empire" in *Imperialism: The Robinson and Gallagher Controversy*, edited by W. R. Lewis (New York: Franklin Watts, 1976). Platt's extensive work in *Finance, Trade, and Politics*, and his short critique, *Further Objections*, present the most compelling evidence that the informal empire thesis does not apply to South America. Much of the above analysis of the nature of British influence in the region has been informed by Platt's work.

52. Platt, *Finance, Trade, and Politics*, 312.

53. Platt, *Finance, Trade, and Politics*, 316.

54. J. Fred Rippy, *British Investments in Latin America, 1822–1949* (Minneapolis: University of Minnesota Press, 1959), 199.

55. Rippy, *British Investment*, 197–200.

56. Preston and Major, *Send a Gunboat*, 86.

57. Fermandois, *Chile and the Great Powers*, 77.

58. Smith, *Illusions of Conflict*, 4.

59. Joseph Nye, *Bound to Lead: The Changing Nature of American Power* (New York: Basic Books, 1990), 188.

60. Graham, *Robinson and Gallagher in Latin America*, 220. Graham, it should be noted, used this statement as evidence to demonstrate how informal empire fits nicely with South America. Graham, however, does not demonstrate a compelling connection between a common ideology and a common pursuit of the British national interest. The latter is essential to the thesis of informal empire.

61. Leslie Bethel, "Britain and Latin America in Historical Perspective" in *Britain and Latin America: A Changing Relationship*, ed. by Victor Bulmer-Thomas (Cambridge: Cambridge University Press, 1989), 4.

62. For an extensive analysis of interest groups see Eugene Ridings' *Business Interest Groups in Nineteenth Century Brazil* (New York: Cambridge University Press, 1994).

63. Beeler, *British Naval Policy*, 237.

64. Kennedy, *Rise and Fall*, 178.

65. Kennedy, *Rise and Fall*, 178, noted how the public outcries for a stronger navy was unleashed during the war scares of the mid-1880s. See also Cynthia F. Behrman, *Victorian Myths of the Sea* (Athens: Ohio University Press, 1977), 144.

66. Bernard Semmel, *Liberalism and Naval Strategy: Ideology, Interest, and Sea Power during the* Pax Britannica (Boston: Unwin Allen, 1986), 41.

67. In Platt, *Finance, Trade, and Politics*, xvi.

68. Platt, *Finance, Trade, and Politics*, xv.

69. Kennedy, *Rise and Fall*, 171.
70. In Beeler, *British Naval Policy*, 20.
71. Kennedy, *Rise and Fall*, 150.
72. Brassey, *Papers and Addresses*, 185.
73. See Clark Reynolds, *Command of the Sea: The History and Strategy of Maritime Empires* (Malabar, Fla.: Kreiger Publishing, 1983), 361.
74. Kennedy, *Rise and Fall*, 175.
75. Harry Ferns, *Britain and Argentina in the Nineteenth Century* (New York: Arno Press. 1977), 429.
76. Smith, *Illusions of Conflict*, 14.
77. Griffin, *The American Navy at Work*, 241.
78. Mitchell Goldberg, "Naval Operations of the United States Pacific Squadron in 1861," *American Neptune* (1973): 42.
79. Kenneth Hagan, *American Gunboat Diplomacy and the Old Navy, 1877–1889* (Westport, Conn.: Greenwood Press, 1973), 127.
80. Hagan, *American Gunboat Diplomacy*, 128.
81. Davis, Finan, and Peck, *Latin American Diplomatic History*, 108.
82. Davis, *The Last Conquistadores*, 306–7.
83. Samuel Inman, *Inter-American Conferences 1826–1954: History and Problems* (Washington, D.C.: University Press, 1965), 21.
84. Davis, Finan, and Peck, *Latin American Diplomatic History*, 105.
85. Bethel, *Britain and Latin America*, 4.
86. Ferns, *Britain and Argentina*, 113.
87. In Platt, *Finance, Trade, and Politics*, xv.
88. Bethel, *Britain and Latin America*, 6–7.
89. Miller, *Britain and Latin America*, 54.
90. Kennedy, *Rise and Fall*, 152.
91. Dupuy, R. Ernest and Trevor N. Dupuy, *The Encyclopedia of Military History: From 3500 B.C. to the Present* (New York: Harper and Row, 1977), 911.
92. Platt, *Finance, Trade, and Politics*, 320.
93. This is drawn from Singer and Small's compilation of data on both interstate and civil wars. See J. David Singer and Melvin Small, *Resort to Arms* (Beverly Hills, Calif.: Sage, 1982). An recently updated list is available at www.cow2.la.psu.edu/.
94. Platt, *Finance, Trade, and Politics*, 319.
95. The language of "perfect indifference" as to which "association of individuals" should come to rule in Latin America was used to explain British policy in Central America. However, as Platt argues in *Finance, Trade, and Politics*, p. 324, this policy characterizes British policy throughout Latin America.
96. In Miller's *Britain and Latin America*, 65.
97. Platt, *Finance, Trade, and Politics*, 324.
98. In Kennedy's *Rise and Fall*, 168.
99. For the case of Brazil, this point was made by Alan Manchester's *British Pre-eminence in Brazil: Its Rise and Decline* (Chapel Hill: University of North Carolina

Press, 1933), 284. Platt, in *Finance, Trade, and Politics* (p. 310) also noted the declining importance of British reassurances as regional states stabilized.

100. Preston and Major, *Send a Gunboat*, 86.

101. Smith, *Illusion of Conflict*, 12.

102. Norman Bailey, *Latin America in World Politics* (New York: Walker and Company, 1967), 43.

103. Manchester, *British Preeminence*, 275.

104. Manchester, *British Preeminence*, 284.

105. Miller, *Britain and Latin America*, 59.

106. Smith, *The Illusion of Conflict*, 4.

107. Bailey, *Latin America in World Politics*, 41.

108. The United States failed to even send a delegate to several of the early Pan American Conferences at which discussions of a federation were first explored. See Inman, *Inter-American Conferences*.

109. Platt, *Finance, Trade, and Politics*, xv.

110. This was clearly the view of many liberals and is often hinted at by the likes of Granville and Canning. See Semmel's *Liberalism and Naval Strategy* for the evolving relationship between liberalism and the Royal Navy.

111. See Kennedy, *Rise and Fall*, 152, for a brief introduction to Cobden and Bright.

CHAPTER FOUR

The U.S. Navy in the Caribbean, 1903–1920

THOMAS C. WALKER

Introduction

By most measures, the United States rose to the status of a great power just before 1900. Nowhere was this ascent more dramatic than in terms of its relative naval power. From the late 1880s to 1903, the United States Navy rose from the twelfth to the third most powerful navy in the world. This rise to naval prominence was matched with an increased dependence on the navy to pursue foreign policy objectives. The Caribbean was the first region where the United States would rely on military force to pursue its interests and shape the peacetime environment as a democratic great power.

Once the United States committed to building the Panama Canal, its interests in the Caribbean expanded significantly. The primary strategic objective became protection of the Caribbean entrance to the Canal. While Great Britain maintained some naval presence, American decision makers were primarily concerned with German expansion in the region. Drawing lessons from the Venezuelan crisis of 1902–1903 (where the naval forces of Britain, Germany, and Italy were deployed to force the Venezuelan government to pay its international debts), many American decision makers concluded that the only justification for European expansion into the region would involve regional indebtedness or political instability. These decisionmakers reasoned that if a Caribbean state fell into debt to a European power, this would justify seizing ports and customs houses. Indebtedness might also lead a regional power to lease or sell base rights to a European great power like Germany. Also, if political instability threatened the property of European powers, they would be justified in intervening. This justification was reinforced by a Hague ruling on the Venezuelan case in 1904. One way for Washington to counter these threats would be to encourage political stability, economic growth, and good government throughout the Caribbean. If these objectives were achieved, European powers would have little opportunity to expand in the region.

American foreign policy in the Caribbean during the Progressive Era was the first time that national security interests were directly linked to economic and political stability in other states. With increased political and economic stability in the Caribbean, no European power could meddle in the region. As a result, American foreign policy toward regional actors evolved into a complicated mixture of military-strategic issues, economic development issues, good governance, and humanitarian issues. The confluence of these issues makes any study of American policy in the Caribbean in the early part of the twentieth century difficult. According to one historian, this policy was "actuated by a number of motives the exact weight of which it is impossible to determine. Among them were the desire for national security and zeal to promote political and economic profit."[1] Another historian notes how this complexity was intensified by the ambitions of the reform-minded Progressives who had risen to prominence in Washington during this period.[2]

To help achieve this goal of shaping the peacetime environment, decision-makers in Washington looked to the U.S. Navy. With a large naval presence in the region and the use of the new wireless telegraph, the United States could rapidly respond to crises and act as arbiter and peacekeeper. The United States sought to use its overwhelming naval forces to shape the peacetime environment in the region and maintain its hegemonic control to the eastern entrance of the Panama Canal.

In this case, the United States enjoyed optimal conditions and resources to successfully shape the peacetime environment. The United States possessed not only overwhelming military capabilities but faced no serious opposition from other great powers. The United States also enjoyed enormous economic leverage to wield throughout the Caribbean. Another factor facilitating American influence was the international convention that permitted great power intervention. Finally, there was strong domestic political support for active interventionism in the region. This support grew out of the Progressive movement's emphasis on action, charity, and good governance by expanding democracy. In spite of all these advantages, the record of American efforts to shape is mixed. While the United States successfully protected the Caribbean from any European great power ambitions, it failed to meaningfully transform the domestic political institutions or contribute to good governance within the regional powers.

Part One: Relative Capabilities of the United States

Regional Military Balance

American military power was overwhelming throughout the Caribbean in the early years of the twentieth century. This is especially true in terms of its naval power. The United States maintained a large naval base at Guantánamo, with lesser facilities at San Juan and Culebra.[3] Perhaps more important, throughout the period under study American naval power was in the midst of unprecedented peacetime increases. In 1889, some estimated the U.S. Navy to be the 12th most powerful in the world, trailing the likes of Sweden, Turkey, China, and the Netherlands.[4] Fifteen years later Brassey's *Naval Annual* estimated that the "United States will shortly become the second naval power of the world."[5] From 1897 to 1910, the U.S. Navy increased from 141 vessels to 371.[6] While a significant proportion of this force was based in the Pacific, the United States could assemble an overwhelming naval force in the Caribbean. The display of American naval might during the Venezuelan Crisis of 1902–1903 served as a sharp reminder to both regional and global powers of American naval supremacy in the region.[7] Simply put, no regional naval force could mount a challenge to the American navy in the Caribbean.

The Caribbean Squadron was officially formed in 1902. Its mission, according to the secretary of the navy, was "to provide at all times a force in Caribbean waters which can proceed quickly, whenever needed, to such points as may demand protection for American interests."[8] Initially, the squadron consisted of eight warships—either cruisers (second or third class) or gunboats. Ships in the Caribbean would often be joined by and rotated with ships from the European and South Atlantic Squadrons.[9] In the winter months naval presence increased dramatically because ships from the North Atlantic Fleet would sail to the Caribbean for fleet maneuvers and training.[10] However, most routine patrols would still be conducted by gunboats. Cruisers would be typically summoned to trouble spots. Unlike the British naval presence discussed in the previous chapter, the Caribbean Squadron routinely maintained American presence in Caribbean waters throughout the period.

American naval presence was magnified by the ineffective naval forces maintained by Caribbean powers. The Caribbean powers could neither build nor purchase modern naval vessels. While there was a vibrant naval arms trade between some of the larger South American states and the European powers in the early years of the century—even the delivery of Dreadnought Class battleships to Brazil and Argentina—these vessels rarely strayed into Caribbean waters. Even if these ships had been dispatched to the Caribbean, their numbers were few and many have questioned their effectiveness due to lack of training.[11] Little threat emerged from the South American states bordering Caribbean waters.

When the financially strapped and unstable Caribbean states could afford to purchase a naval vessel, they typically purchased the most obsolete gunboats from other powers. As a result, regional navies were small, poorly maintained, and obsolete. Arguably, Haiti was the leading naval power in the region behind the United States. In the 1913 *Naval Annual*, Haiti had one steel gunboat, 260 tons and armed with three 9-inch guns; an iron corvette; two sloops; and a small gun vessel. The *Annual* also reported that the previous year the Haitian gunboat *Liberté* was blown up and destroyed. Cuba, in 1913, had one aging cruiser and a gunboat. In 1913, Colombia had a light cruiser, 1,200 tons, built in 1892 and purchased from Morocco. Ecuador has a small torpedo cruiser, 812 tons, and two small gunboats. The Dominican Republic had a couple of small British built gunboats in 1913. One was built in 1894 and carrying seven Hotchkiss quick firing light guns and the other was built in 1896. Another was being "reconstructed" after being removed from service.[12]

Even after obtaining these obsolete craft, the regional powers were often incapable of operating them. In spite of their efforts to maintain a strong navy, Haitian naval forces were persistently ineffective. For example, in January of 1915 the Haitian president announced a blockade of rebel held ports. But the two Haitian gunboats that constituted the core of the Haitian navy could not move for lack of coal. While an American schooner was full of coal near the gunboats, the Haitian government had no money to buy the coal and the American captain would not accept credit. So the gunboats sat dead in the water. Once the ships had coal, they became only marginally more functional. During another crisis, the *Nord Alexis* was used to transport 766 Haitian soldiers from Cap Haïtien to Port-au-Prince, which was typically a day journey at most. It took four days due to repeated engine failure. In that period, the soldiers had no provisions. Once the *Nord Alexis* arrived, the crew of the U.S.S. *Washington*—already on the scene of the crisis—donated their entire breakfast for 1,100 to the 700 hungry Haitians.[13]

In yet another example of inept seamanship by the Haitian navy, when a storm passed through Port-au-Prince in late summer of 1915 the pride of the

Haitian fleet, the gunboat *Pacifique* found itself on the beach. The next day an American seaman "broke his leg when a hauser (sic) snapped in an effort to pull her off." Eventually, the U.S.S. *Osceolo* kedged the *Pacifique* off the beach, but it suffered a damaged hull and machinery.[14] The aid offered by the Americans to assist the Haitian ship is a sound indication of how little threat the Haitian navy posed to the United States.

The Haitian navy represents the leading regional naval power. In terms of both training and equipment, it cannot compare to the United States naval forces in the region. In every aspect of naval power, the United States maintained an overwhelming advantage over the other regional powers.

In addition to its naval supremacy, the United States also enjoyed superior ground forces. Although the U.S. Army decreased its personnel from 1900 to 1910, both the navy and marine corps witnessed significant increases in manpower during the same period. Naval personnel more than doubled from 1900 to 1910, rising from 18,000 to more than 48,000. The marine corps nearly doubled in size during the same period.[15] This rapid growth in naval power, in terms of both ships and personnel, facilitated naval operations in the region during the period under study.

Relying on material capability data from the Correlates of War Project, regional forces were very small compared to the United States. From 1900 to 1913, the U.S. military personnel ranged from 112,000 to 155,000. Haitian military personnel, the second largest force in the region behind the United States, ranged in size from 7,000 to 12,000. The Dominican Republic had approximately 1,000 men under arms over the period. Nicaragua ranged from 2,000 to 4,000 and Guatemala had a force of 7,000.[16]

While these figures may reflect the actual number of men reported to be in the armed forces, they overestimate the actual fighting capabilities. Regional militaries were notorious for their poor training, inadequate provisions, and questionable loyalties. When faced with battle, the small military forces would dissipate rapidly and often switch loyalties. As a result of the limited control that military leaders had over the rank and file, it is extremely difficult to accurately measure the capabilities of regional land forces. The difficulties of a reliable estimate of regional forces is evident in Dupuy and Baumer's effort to measure the forces led by Benoit Batraville, a leader of the anti-American forces in Haiti in 1919: "Benoit's own forces numbered some 2,500 but he exercised a vague control over many more cacos, *it seemed*" (emphasis added). But when Benoit actually wanted to mobilize for an attack on Port-au-Prince, he could muster only 300 men. The attack was easily repulsed, leaving 150 insurgents dead, wounded, or captured while two American marines were wounded.[17]

Most regional forces were relatively small and unreliable. This was especially true of cacos and caudillos. These peasant mercenary-bandits were often the kingmakers in Haiti and the Dominican Republic. The forces were unreliable, poorly trained, and often switched loyalties at the drop of a hat. Sometimes this lack of loyalty served U.S. interests. Soldiers in Haiti and the Dominican Republic would gladly sell their guns and go home. During the American intervention in Haiti beginning in 1915, Admiral Caperton sought to disarm the rebel soldiers by offering each ten gourdes—two dollars—for surrendering their guns. Their leaders would receive 100 gourdes for simply returning home with the promise not to engage in further hostilities. This policy worked sporadically. The greatest success came in St. Marc where in one day 512 rifles were turned in for cash. While Haitian military bands were widely known for their bribery and desertion, the two never came as a packaged deal until the Americans offered them ten gourdes in exchange for their weapons and the promise to return home.[18]

American military capabilities in the region were far superior not only to any regional power but to any combination of regional powers. The predominance of American power may be one reason why U.S. foreign policy was different in the Caribbean than in other regions. Hans Smidt argued that because the states in the region were so small and underdeveloped, American decisionmakers did not advocate an "open door" policy in the Caribbean because it was capable of exercising "sufficient military power to enforce its own absolute hegemony."[19] The unrivaled military superiority held by the United States in the Caribbean may well be the best example of absolute hegemony in recent international politics.

Technological Superiority of the United States in the Caribbean
Although the technological superiority of the U.S. military is most ostentatious in naval forces, the regional ground forces were no better than their foundering navies. Neither could compare with the military forces of the United States in terms of technology and training. Like the navies of regional powers, the armies had little discipline and very few modern weapons. One American observed that the Haitian forces were "simply a conglomerate lot of poor ignorant half clothed men and boys, who are forced into the army."[20] In all the regional states there was very little in terms of a professional regular army. Most of the military training was geared toward maintaining domestic calm and protecting the current regime from domestic threats. As a result of their small numbers and lack of training, small American forces were able to land and bring order and domestic calm to highly unstable if not volatile situations. For instance, riots in Port-au-Prince in 1915

that witnessed mobs dismembering President Guillaume Sam was calmed by the arrival U.S.S. *Washington* and the landing of "three companies of bluejackets and two of marines."²¹ A mere five companies on shore and the presence of the *Washington* successfully brought calm to the city.

When the Haitian and Dominican forces began to fight the U.S. interventions, they suffered immensely due to the superiority of U.S. training and technology. They were poorly armed and a "minority of them carried old-model black-powder rifles; the majority went into battle with swords, machetes, and pikes."²² The obsolete weapons as well as the lack of training and institutional control over the regional armed forces ensured American military preeminence in the region. The American edge in training and equipment often resulted in one-sided military successes. Dupuy and Baumer noted how a "handful of marines" succeeded in defeating a much larger cacos force: "Some seventy-two cacos were killed, including seven known bandit chiefs. The attacking marines suffered only a few slight wounds."²³ While clashes were rare, when they did occur, superior tactics, training, and weaponry by American forces repeatedly prevailed against poorly trained regional forces.

The U.S. Marines, especially in the latter part of the interventions, began to use radios and aircraft against the guerrilla fighters. Graham Cosmos, for instance, argued that battling guerrilla fighters in the Dominican Republic afforded the U.S. Marine Corps their first opportunity to test methods of counterinsurgency. By using radios to rapidly deploy air and artillery support, the marines were able to defeat large and mobile forces while sustaining few casualties. These technologies proved useful in marine actions in Nicaragua as well.²⁴

In terms of sheer numbers, training, equipment, no regional power could challenge U.S. military supremacy in the Caribbean. Naval power was beyond challenge. Indeed, there is no account of an American vessel being attacked or even threatened by regional forces throughout the period being studied. When U.S. forces were challenged by the smaller regional forces it was manifested in occasional sniping and other forms of low-intensity conflict. Even these seemed to be extremely rare.

American Military Presence in the Caribbean

The United States maintained constant naval presence in the region. Rather than maintaining fleet formations, vessels were often dispersed on individual missions that consisted of cruising the region and showing the flag. These were the most common uses of naval vessels in the Caribbean.²⁵ Naval forces were also used to protect American property and bring calm to domestic crises. These practices led Admiral Bradley Fiske, then in charge of naval operations, to complain that the constant dispersion of ships in the Caribbean—due in large part by State Department requests—had drawn away from the fleet's combat readiness by denying adequate time for training and fleet maneuvers.[26]

The State Department's typical response to any instability in the region was to cable a request for the presence of a warship. "In most instances the Navy detailed single ships of the gunboat or small cruiser classes, though occasionally numerous warships of many types, including battleships, were sent. Once on station, the warship(s) usually produced a calming effect on the indigenous factions."[27] In many cases, however, some level of American naval force was already present at the scene.

While the Caribbean Squadron initially had eight warships in full time patrols around the region, the number tended to fluctuate, ultimately being reduced to five.[28] This number, however, is misleading. The presence of American ships in the Caribbean increased drastically in the winter months since training maneuvers would typically take place involving ships from other regions. Judging from secondary sources and an extensive evaluation of messages between Washington and ships in the Caribbean during the period, there were no cases in which the United States failed to have a ship available at one of the trouble spots in the Caribbean.[29]

While it would be a very tedious task indeed to document the degree of presence of the U.S. Navy, a glimpse at the log of the U.S.S. *Marietta*—a ship with a long history of service in the Caribbean Squadron—provides a good snapshot of the wide-ranging activities of an American naval vessel at the time. The *Marietta* was a 1,000-ton displacement gunboat launched in 1896. It was 174 feet in length with six four-inch inch guns, and capable of 13.2 knots. January 1907 found the *Marietta* spending two weeks in Santo Domingo. On January 18th she set off for Guantánamo for three days before returning to Dominican waters. On February 5 the *Marietta* passed through Guantánamo before sailing to Greytown, Nicaragua. From February 10 to 20 she sailed from Greytown to Bluefields and Corn Island. Then on the 21st, she arrived in Costa Rica. In early March she visited more ports in Nicaragua and Port Cortez in Honduras.[30] In the first three months of 1907, the *Marietta* made its presence known widely across the Caribbean.

The presence of the *Marietta* in the waters off Nicaragua is particularly important to American efforts to shape. At the time, American decision makers became alarmed by the rise of Nicaraguan dictator José Santos Zeyala. Zeyala wanted to unite the long-bickering states of Central America in order to ward off U.S. influence in the region. Zeyala also envisioned possible control of the Panama Canal, which was then under construction. U.S. naval presence was important not only for its ability to react to trouble spots but also to monitor the developments within states that might escalate.[31] This presence helped foil Zeyala from ever mounting a direct challenge to American interests in Central America.

In addition to warships like the *Marietta*, there was an assortment of vessels in the Caribbean Squadron performing a wide variety of tasks. For instance, the *Eagle*, a converted yacht, was used to survey and chart the waters as well as the political climate of Hispaniola.[32] The presence of larger warships along with these small support vessels ensured a near vigilant American presence throughout the region.

Speed of Response

By the early twentieth century, several factors combined to ensure rapid responses by American naval forces throughout the Caribbean. First, there were fairly large numbers of American consuls and embassies monitoring domestic developments around the region. Second, there were a number of dispersed ships routinely patrolling the region. Third, and most important, by 1904 consuls and ships were easily contacted through telegraph and radio telegraph. The large and dispersed U.S. squadron combined with the use of new technologies permitted the United States to respond rapidly to any crisis in the region.

The U.S. Navy rapidly incorporated Marconi's technology. In 1903, seven U.S. naval vessels were already equipped with radio. By 1904, however, the U.S. Navy established a training school devoted exclusively to training radio operators and communications specialists. Also in 1904, the navy maintained eighteen shore stations which communicated with radios on thirty-three ships.[33] The development of long-range radio telegraph reduced naval response times to regional crises considerably. Ships could be alerted by State Department consuls to impending crises and promptly dispatched. This technology proved very helpful in ensuring a rapid U.S. response to regional crises.

Perhaps the most dramatic example of response time took place in 1907 in Central America. After the *Marietta* had been cruising the coasts of Nicaragua and Honduras in March of 1907, Washington received several reports that Nicaraguan forces led by José Santos Zelaya threatened to bombard Amapala. Washington cabled the U.S.S. *Princeton* and U.S.S. *Chicago* with the following orders: "Proceed at once to Amapala. Department informed the Nicaraguan forces propose to bombard Amapala in violation [of the] customs [of] modern warfare among civilized nations. You will prevent such bombardment by use of such force as may be necessary."³⁴ The *Princeton*, steaming from Corinto, was at the location in less than twelve hours. The *Chicago* arrived shortly thereafter. The timely arrival of the two ships dissuaded the Nicaraguan forces from bombarding the town.

There are several other examples of prompt responses to regional crises by American naval vessels. When an insurrection erupted in Puerto Plata, Dominican Republic, in 1904 the U.S.S. *Detroit* arrived within forty-eight hours, but was preceded in port by the H.M.S. *Pallas*. A month later the *Detroit* was relieved by the U.S.S. *Newark*—a third class cruiser—and *Columbia*—a second class cruiser. Both were faster ships that would further reduce response time.

When domestic strife in Haiti escalated in 1915, news of the uprisings were reported by Roscoe C. Moody, commander of the gunboat *Wheeling* that was already anchored in Port-au-Prince. A day after receiving the news, Admiral Caperton sailed the 15,000-ton armored cruiser *Washington* into Port-au-Prince. The *Washington* happened to be en route to Santo Domingo at the time. In addition to the *Washington*, the *Machias*-class gunboat *Castine* arrived within a day as well. One day after Moody's radio report of problems in Port-au-Prince, the navy had three ships in the harbor.³⁵

While the presence of American naval power quieted the mobs, it was too late for President Guillaume Sam, who was dragged from the French embassy in Port-au-Prince, killed, torn to pieces, then paraded through the streets, and, by one account, ringleaders of the mob consumed his heart. This anarchy led to American intervention in Haiti in July of 1915. The intervention would least for nearly two decades.³⁶

Both radio communications as well as a large and dispersed fleet helped ensure a rapid response. The United States could respond promptly to any regional crises in the Caribbean during the period being studied. However, even extremely rapid responses could not always deter the spasms of violent unrest like the one that ended Guillaume Sam's presidency in Haiti.

Available Military Options

The United States enjoyed a wide variety of military options for two reasons. First, the United States had overwhelming military power in the region without any other major power to keep this American power in check. Second, the international norms of the time allowed great powers great latitude in their relationships with smaller powers. Appeals to sovereignty and self-rule were few in the international community in the early twentieth century. As a result, there was very little to limit the military options of the United States. These options included everything from simply showing the flag to outright military occupation of the troubled small states.

The most frequent use of military force was showing the flag as a reminder of American power and interest in the region. Often the mere presence of a U.S. naval vessel—whether it had four-inch guns or twelve-inch guns—was enough to convey a credible threat and bring domestic calm.[37] One State Department official in Haiti claimed that the mere presence of a U.S. warship "would suppress the excited state of feeling."[38] These shows of force were by far the most prevalent use of force throughout the period. It was relatively inexpensive and often an effective way to convey support for a friend or threaten an enemy.

The second military option was the selective shelling to bring calm or compliance. In 1904, shelling from the U.S.S. *Columbia* and the U.S.S. *Newark* brought calm to Santo Domingo. A decade later, twelve four-inch shots from the U.S.S. *Machias* rid Puerto Plata of an insurgency.[39] These acts of shelling were not an infrequent options used to shape the peacetime environment.

A third military option was seizing the customs houses—and thereby seizing the primary source of revenue to the regime. Backed with naval support, these seizures were conducted on several occasions and often lasted for many years. The first seizure appears to have been prompted by Captain Dillingham of the U.S.S. *Detroit*. On 17 March 1904, Dillingham sent the following message to Washington from the *Detroit*: "The Minister advises that the Italian Minister to Cuba will arrive Santo Domingo on 5/17, to insist upon immediate payment of claims. If not fulfilled, there is more or less possibility of the Italian forces taking customs. With authority of Navy I can possession(sic) of Customs."[40]

Secretary Moody's response to Dillingham was unequivocal. First, he ordered: "Do not take possession of custom duties nor any action of the kind." Then he ordered the U.S.S. *Glouchester* to "proceed immediately to S. Domingo City" to assist Dillingham in not seizing the customs house.[41] A year after Dillingham's request, the United States actually seized the customs houses in the Dominican Republic. The United States also seized and operated the customs houses in Haiti and Nicaragua. These seizures were typically done with a small number of marines—usually a few companies—and the presence of at least one warship. They incurred no casualties.

A fourth option was to deploy ground forces—usually a combination of marines and sailors for more thorough control over an area. This could range from a temporary occupation of coastal cities to outright occupation or annexation. In a review of the American press, Blassingame argued that the big question was not whether to use military force to intervene, but the question was whether the United States should merely intervene or annex the troubled island states. Brands (1998: 52) demonstrated how many leading American intellectuals like Herbert Croly supported annexation. When yet another revolution broke out in the Dominican Republic in 1904, the *Baltimore American* reported that annexation was "the only remedy" and ought to be applied immediately. Similar views regarding annexation were shared by influential Progressives like Albert Beveridge, as well as realpolitik strategists like Richard Olney.[42] On the domestic front, few questioned whether or not the United States should intervene. If questions were raised, they were often framed around the question of annexation.

This range of options enjoyed by the United States in the Caribbean may have been historically unique. Few historical periods afforded a major power so many options with neither external nor domestic constraints.

American Ability to Intervene in Regional Actor's Domestic Affairs

The range of options enjoyed by the United States included relatively easy intervention in the domestic political affairs of all the states in the region. While the United States could topple some governments by merely withholding customs revenues, the more frequent mode of toppling or supporting governments was through well-timed threats and strategic deployment of naval vessels.

On several occasions, naval guns were used to impose a peace and support the ruling government. In 1904, Captain Dillingham reported to Washington that insurgents in Santo Domingo "agreed to armistice . . . after the *Columbia* and *Newark* have shelled insurgents. Have landed force for protection from *Columbia* and *Newark* gave chase to insurgents."[43] In March 1914, with "twelve four inch shells from the *U.S.S. Machias* resulted in the resumption of silence [and peace in the city]."[44] But most times the mere threat of a salvo from naval guns or the deployment of ground forces would bring about a temporary truce and deter further rebellion. A year after the *Machias* shelling another insurrection threatened the Jimenez regime. Sumner Welles attributed the peaceful resolution to American military presence. "While the threatened insurrection in Puerto Plata was peacefully settled . . . it was not settled without the practical intervention of the United States . . . the *U.S.S. Castine* with a large body of American marines undoubtedly hastened the conclusions of the agreement reached."[45]

In most cases, the United States naval forces would work to bolster the ruling government. The U.S. not only had interests in maintaining the status quo regime, it promised not to recognize a regime that rose to power through armed revolt. In an effort to foster democratic transitions, the United States joined the Central American Treaty Convention of 1907. Signatories agreed not to recognize a Central American government that rose to power "by coup d'état or revolution until the country had been constitutionally re-organized by a free election."[46] Munro noted that in "general practice the United States was in accord with it [in the early part of the twentieth century]."[47] This treaty, however, failed to stop the United States from recognizing authoritarian regimes throughout the Caribbean.

When naval forces were perceived to be in favor of the revolutionary forces, the standing government would often appeal directly to Washington for either neutrality or support. Washington would then give the fitting directives to its ships in the region. In January 1908, the following message was sent from Washington to the U.S.S. *Eagle*, operating off the coast of Haiti: "The Haytien Government seems to consider your vessel in a friendly attitude with the revolutionists. Take no part in the troubles in Hayti further than to protect American interests. It is considered important that revolution must not be successful."[48] Since American interests would be best served by limiting violent revolution, naval forces typically sided with the status quo regime and worked to repress revolution, regardless of democratic merit.

However, there were cases when American naval forces lent assistance to the revolutionary forces. In Nicaragua in 1910, U.S. naval forces prevented José Madriz from seizing a rebel base at Bluefields. Madriz, who was the crony-successor to the dictator Zelaya, shared a similar anti-American rhetoric. With U.S. protection, rebel forces were able to withstand Madriz's attack. Later, again with American assistance, the rebels succeeded in defeating Madriz. The rebels created a government that promised policies more in line with American interests.[49] With occasional U.S. support, the new government remained in power until 1917.

Given the overwhelming material superiority of the United States, saving or toppling governments was the easy part. The difficult part was discerning which rival faction—for there were always some rival factions—would most likely succeed in bringing domestic calm; would most likely pursue policies of free trade and democracy; and would look most favorably upon U.S. interests in the region. The latter was not an easy task, as Captain Dillingham reported to Washington because revolution in the Caribbean is "not one of principle, but between factions."[50]

American Capacity for Humanitarian and Peacekeeping Operations

While the United States played many creative roles as peacekeeper in the region, instances of humanitarian assistance are very rare. One of the few examples of providing humanitarian assistance took place in Haiti beginning in 1915. Combined with the domestic upheavals, the war in Europe further interrupted trade and commerce in Haiti. Disease and starvation were widespread. Admiral Caperton reported that many towns were "invaded by beggars suffering from leprosy, jaws, elephantiasis, and open sores. . . . If our government is not prepared to undertake [assistance], representations should be made to the Red Cross."[51] Yet the secretary of the navy denied Caperton's appeals for humanitarian aid. After several denials, Caperton did appeal to the American Red Cross to provide relief. Even without official sanction, Caperton took many measures to deliver humanitarian assistance. One of his most effective was to order all "unused food" from the *Washington* be collected after each meal and sent ashore for humanitarian efforts. These leftovers, when coupled with rice from the Red Cross, fed thousands of starving Haitians each week.[52]

Munro pointed out how American military occupation of the Dominican Republic had several beneficial consequences. Besides bringing peace to all but the most remote areas, the American military helped construct a network of roads. The American occupation also devoted much more attention to education. Under American occupation the number of Dominican children attending school rose from 12,000 to more than 100,000.[53] It is important to note that these humanitarian efforts were as novel as they were rare in world politics of the early twentieth century.

In most cases, American forces were concerned with brokering peace agreements between embattled domestic rivals, rather than providing humanitarian assistance. In April 1902, the United States landed forces in Bocas del Toro in Colombia to protect American residents and property from an impending attack by Liberal forces. The American commander, Henry McCrea, held a conference on the U.S.S. *Machias* and convinced the National officers to give up the town peacefully since they were clearly an inferior force compared to the Liberals. The Nationalists agreed to turn the town over peacefully to the Americans, who would in turn surrender it to the Liberals. After this peaceful transition was complete, a very large Nationalist force arrived two days later. "The military situation on shore reversed," Offutt noted, "the Liberals agreed to capitulate."

Not all the American peacekeeping efforts were met with such temporary truces. When the U.S.S. *Princeton* and U.S.S. *Chicago* arrived in Amapala Honduras in April of 1907, they successfully deterred Nicaraguan forces from bombarding the city. The captain of the *Chicago*, noted that the Nicaraguan commander "shows obstinate determination . . . notwithstanding all efforts to dissuade him. Informed them I should not permit bombardment."[54] In the end, the Nicaraguan delegation returned for consultation and ultimately accepted the American offer to mediate the dispute on board the *Chicago*.

In Haiti, Admiral Caperton took a different approach to peacekeeping. Caperton used U.S. naval presence to reassure insurgents that a general amnesty offered them would indeed be respected by the governing party. The Haitian government's promises of amnesty to rebels, Caperton sadly acknowledged, were only promises and "served their purposes only while the printer's ink was damp." The government promised not only amnesty but some monetary reward to those insurgents who turned in their weapons and returned to peaceful pursuits in their home villages. But Caperton was well aware that the insurgents "would accept the Government's proposition relative to disarmament [and amnesty], if the money involved would be handled and paid to them by the Americans." So Caperton had the money transferred to the commanding officers of the *Connecticut* and the *Castine* and he instructed them to "publish and broadcast" the specifics of the amnesty program. Finally, to quell any lingering doubts, Caperton directed his officers to "inform the Caco chiefs [the insurgents] that the proclamation of general amnesty made by [the Haitian] president would be insisted upon by the United States Forces."[55] In the short term, the amnesty worked. But eventually the Cacos returned to their prime occupation of trying to overturn the current government for that faction that promised the richest payoff.

In other cases, naval actions were intended not so much to enforce the peace as they were to limit damage to the infrastructure and protect noncombatants, especially Americans. One such case occurred in Puerto Plata in January 1904. Commander A. C. Dillingham of the U.S.S. *Detroit* was sent to Dominican waters to bring about peace between warring factions. Upon arriving in Puerto Plata, he went ashore with the British commander of the H.M.S. *Pallas* to inform both factions that no armed conflicts would be permitted within the city limits. To clearly define the city limits, the British and the Americans placed a line of flags around the city. Dillingham also eased the *Detroit* into a position where her guns could effectively stop an oncoming force from entering the city. After a few days of this enforced peace, the troops under General Deschamps, who had held the city, "marched out of Puerto Plata to meet the Cespedes forces and fought them outside the cordon of flags. They were quickly defeated and retreated through the cordon of flags, throwing down their arms as they reached the line of flags." The town quickly surrendered to the rebel forces.[56] Dillingham kept the *Detroit*—now joined by the U.S.S. *Newark* and U.S.S. *Columbia* in Dominican waters. In June, Dillingham offered his diplomatic services to the warring factions. The conference was held on board the *Detroit* and proved successful, according to Dillingham, given "the moral influence toward peace exerted by naval vessels."[57]

The Caribbean in the early twentieth century provided some of the earliest peacekeeping operations by the United States. While its success rates varied considerably, this variance was not due to a lack of creative efforts by naval personnel in the field. In Haiti, Caperton's use of American military power to ensure that promises of amnesty would be kept is one notable effort. Another is his attempt to disarm a heavily armed society with monetary inducements. Another creative but more limited form of peacekeeping was Dillingham's efforts to shift the field of battle away from civilian centers. All the complexity surrounding peacekeeping efforts are reflected in the diverse approaches taken by the United States in the Caribbean early in the twentieth century.

Part Two: Nonmilitary Sources of, and Constraints on, American Power and Influence

In this section we explore the nonmilitary sources of American influence. We will also examine any ways in which American influence may have been constrained by nonmilitary factors. American economic power played a large role in wielding influence in the Caribbean. Perhaps the most surprising feature of the American experience in the Caribbean during the Progressive Era was the complete lack of any constraints whatsoever on American efforts in the region. Not only did the United States enjoy military preeminence relative to the regional states, no other great power attempted to check or balance American influence in the region. Both Great Britain and Germany turned their attention to Europe, giving the United States free rein in the Caribbean.

On the level of global society and international law, American intervention in the Caribbean was permissible. Through the decision of the Hague Court of Arbitration of the Venezuelan Crisis of 1903, the court ruled that states had the right to intervene to protect the property of their nationals. This was interpreted by Theodore Roosevelt and other leading American internationalists as a carte blanche for intervention. On the domestic front, the United States also enjoyed a great deal of popular support for interventions in the Caribbean. Much of this support can be traced to the ideology of the Progressive Movement at the domestic level.

Economic Leverage

The United States exercised an enormous amount of economic leverage throughout the Caribbean during this period. The term "dollar diplomacy" was coined as a result of the tight relationship between the American State

Department and private capital. Noting this relationship, Rippy noted that private banks "were the agents through whom American dollars were sent into Caribbean states. At times the government at Washington used them [banks], and at times they practically used the government. It was this intimate connection that caused the term dollar diplomacy to become in the popular mind a term of reproach."[58] In perhaps the most egregious example, the National City Bank of New York came to gain full control over the National Bank of Haiti. Not only would National City manage the currency, its subsidiary would negotiate U.S.-backed loans to the National Bank, drawing high commissions at both ends of the deal.

In addition to bonds and guaranteed loans that often hinged on adherence to the Washington line,[59] there was also a great deal of private investment in more tangible enterprises. Starting in 1900, American investment in transportation, mining, petroleum, sugar, and fruit production rose drastically. From 1900 to 1912, these investments are estimated to have risen three times.[60]

The official role of the United States in the Caribbean economies was not limited to guaranteeing bonds and loans. In what constitutes an astounding display of political and economic leverage, the United States took over the customs houses in several Caribbean states to help manage their international finance. The primary purpose was to curb corruption and ensure that creditors—primarily American but also some European—were paid in a timely fashion. By doing this, the United States was certain that the other great powers would be denied any justification for intervening in the Caribbean. Creditors who were paid would stay out of the region and the replay of the Venezuelan crisis could be averted and no European power would attempt an intervention in the Caribbean.

The first control of customs houses took place in the Dominican Republic in 1905. Through a coerced treaty, the Dominican government agreed to hand over administration of customs to the Americans. In the Dominican case, the Americans took 55 percent of the revenues to pay foreign debts—many of which were made through American banks for European interests—and 45 percent was given to the Dominican government for administration.[61] Similar programs were deployed in several other Caribbean states. Munro noted how the success of customs collection in the Dominican Republic prompted President Taft to consider it "a panacea for the ills of disorderly Caribbean countries."[62]

With the power of the purse, the United States could exercise a great deal of influence over policy. There are many examples where American administrators simply withheld monies to run the government if the government was acting out. Even salaries of the highest leadership would be withheld. With little money to give to its cronies, even the most popular regime would be threatened.[63] By 1912, Sumner Welles pointed out that the "ultimate decision regarding the domestic policies of the Dominican Government [rested] in the hands of representatives of the United States."[64] While decisions in other states might be made independently of the United States, they would rarely challenge, either directly or indirectly, American interests in the region.

Political Penetration of Regional Actors
The United States wielded several different means of influence in the region besides sheer military force. Of all the sources of influence the United States enjoyed, political penetrative power, or soft power, was probably the least effective. There was little ideological affinity between Americans and most of the rulers in the region. This was a consistent complaint of Admiral Caperton during his time in Haiti. One description of the relationship between the American occupying forces and the Haitian elite maintained how "The [Haitian] elites looked down on the occupying *blancs* as uncouth, unschooled clods; most of them did not even speak *francais!* The marines seethed at the mulattos' pretensions and demands for privileged positions."[65] Haiti, with its heavy French influence, may have been the most difficult arena for Americans to exercise soft power.

In other states, a few Caribbean elites tended to identify more with American values than with those of their own people. There are several cases where elites invited American intervention and even annexation. Of the latter, the most famous case is when Dominican president Buenaventura Baez was negotiating American annexation of the Dominican Republic following the American Civil War.[66] Elite faith in American beneficence combined with American economic and strategic advantages granted the United States some influence within the domestic political arena. But this influence was terribly limited, and perhaps undermined by excessive use of American military force. This was a persistent theme in many of the criticisms of American interventions in the Caribbean published in the United States after World War I.[67]

Domestic Political Constraints on American Policy
Turning to the American domestic arena, remarkably few constraints were placed on an active American policy in the Caribbean during the Progressive period. In Congress, there was often bipartisan support for an interventionist foreign policy in the region. Even the limited congressional constraints on

action such as the Teller Amendment, which denied any intention to annex Cuba in the wake of the Spanish-American War, were rare. Like Congress, the media often encouraged an active foreign policy in this hemisphere. Finally, with some notable exceptions, public opinion also tended to support interventionist policies in the Caribbean.[68]

The widespread support for intervention can be explained by examining the Progressive Era in American history. At the height of the Progressive Era, the first fifteen years of the twentieth century, most Americans considered interventionist foreign policy in the Caribbean as charitable acts informed by Christian principles.[69] Interventionism also fit nicely with the "activism" that was one hallmark of the Progressive Era. Activism, Richard Hofstadter argued, was the foundation of Progressivism and was premised on the assumption "that social evils will not remedy themselves, and that it is wrong to sit by passively and wait for time to take care of them."[70] Intervening to expand democratic rule in the Caribbean can also be equated to reforms that Progressives sought in the domestic realm, such as nominations by direct primary, direct elections of senators, the right to recall elected officials, and breaking up huge trusts and corrupt political machines. "Having applied their reform notions to America's cities, then to the states, and most recently to the nation as a whole," another historian noted, "the progressives now intended to go global."[71] In this period, military interventionism had not yet been labeled as an illiberal abuse of power. Instead it was the moral responsibility to exercise power on behalf of those who were unable to do so on their own.

Underlying Progressive notions of service and order were assumptions of paternalism and racism. In the Progressive mind, inferiority largely resulted from disorder, graft, and denial of democracy. It would be morally unconscionable to sit idle and permit these evils to fester and grow within any society, even the most inferior society. These ideas of racial superiority guided American decision making throughout the period. Healy noted how the main tenets of Progressivism influenced American officers working in the Caribbean. "Career officers in all three services valued order, good government, and progress. They shared the spirit of the Progressive Era, believed in social and racial inequality."[72] Most domestic political support for active interventionism in the Caribbean, while well-meaning, was rife with racism and simply assumed American superiority over these "retarded peoples," as one historian of the 1940s referred to Caribbean peoples.[73]

Since we are dealing with democratic great powers, the press is a good place to conclude our evaluation of how Progressive Era principles contributed to the free-hand the United States enjoyed in the Caribbean. In a systematic study of the American media, Blassingame demonstrated that

"The vast majority of American periodicals supported intervention in Haiti and the Dominican Republic from 1904 until 1919." While American security interests were frequently noted, the call to service and humanitarian interests received more space in the newspapers of the day. For instance, Walter Hines Page's popular periodical, *World's Work*, consistently stressed how intervention was founded on the Progressive idea of Christian charity. "We are simply going in there . . . to help our black brother put his disorderly house in order." The *New York Times* envisioned the policy of intervention as essential to keep the Latin Americans "harmless against the ultimate consequences of their own misbehavior."[74] On the domestic front, few opposed intervention. A few even supported annexation, as noted above. The majority of American society supported an active and interventionist American foreign policy in the Caribbean.

After World War I, however, the optimism about what could be attained through ardent internationalism had long dissipated. Starting in 1919, *The Nation* began publishing critiques of American policies in the Caribbean. By this time, all the battling optimism of the Progressive was gone from both American domestic and foreign policies. The only question facing the Harding administration was how to scale down American involvement in the Caribbean. In the 1920s, disillusionment with international crusades had proven particularly acute and spelled an end to domestic political support for interventionism in the Caribbean.

The Impact of International Regimes and Institutions

Since the United States justified its interventionism in terms of promoting domestic calm and protecting life and property of Americans and other foreigners, many American interventions could be supported by principles of international law. Milton Offutt noted how the "right to protect its citizens abroad" can be traced back to Vattel's *Law of Nations*, published in 1773. In the early twentieth century, it was simply assumed that if a great power was capable of intervening to protect its citizens and their property, they must do so. Offutt chronicled more than one hundred military interventions by American forces to protect American life and property abroad between the years 1813 and 1928.[75] During the Progressive Era American interventions were justified in terms of protecting property of nationals. Dana Munro noted how "The idea that the government had an obligation to protect American citizens and their lives and property rights" abroad was a principle never lost on the Roosevelt and Taft administrations.[76] International right in this period was thought to be more important than individual state sovereignty, especially when the offending state was small and with a relatively weak military.

The right to intervene to safeguard investment and coerce payment of debts was codified to a certain degree by the Hague Arbitration over the Venezuelan crisis of 1902–1903. After Washington brokered the agreement to submit the claims against Venezuela to the Hague Court of Arbitration, the court ruled that states not only had the right to engage in violent and coercive acts to secure repayment of loans—as Britain, Germany, and Italy had done—but the court went on to give preference to those states that actually exercised military force in the crisis. Although debts were owed to many foreign states, the Hague ruled that Venezuela must repay Britain, Germany, and Italy first. After repaying the states whose militaries attacked their coastline, Venezuela could consider paying debts to other creditor states like Spain and Belgium.[77]

By favoring the debts owed to states that intervened militarily, the Hague ruling sent a signal that military intervention may be the best way to ensure repayments. This interpretation was not lost on the American State Department. The department's leading solicitor reported back to Washington how the Hague's decision was "a notable event in its relation to the law of nations. It was . . . an impressive assertion of the right of intervention for the protection of subjects of intervening states."[78]

Shortly after the Hague's decision, President Roosevelt offered his famous corollary to the Monroe Doctrine, which called for the United States to play the role of "international police power" with the right to intervene throughout the hemisphere. One of the primary motives behind Roosevelt's corollary was to inform the European powers that if intervention were to take place in the Western Hemisphere, the United States would be the one to intervene. While the corollary may have been a bold assertion of American power in the region, it was an assertion buttressed by the Hague ruling in 1903. The commitment to serve as an international police force in "flagrant cases of wrongdoing" also played well with the Progressive spirit of activism. If American life and property were threatened, one must act to protect them. International institutions like the Hague justified the interventionist policies pursued by the United States.

The practice of deploying naval force to pursue political ends against lesser powers—gunboat diplomacy—was so prevalent in the late nineteenth and earlier twentieth centuries that it can be considered an international norm of the period. By the beginning of the twentieth century the United States routinely sought to further its political position by deploying its warships in peacetime. Gunboat diplomacy was so widely practiced by all major powers in the period that no international institution at the time opposed the practice. Later in the twentieth century, this practice became less acceptable in international society. However, during the Progressive Era, the efforts to shape the peacetime environment were facilitated by the easy deployments of naval power.

Other Great Powers Active or Capable of Intervening in the Region
The obvious candidate for leading maritime rival in the Caribbean during the Progressive Era was Great Britain. Yet there is little evidence to support the presence of any serious British challenge to American naval supremacy in the Caribbean. As noted in the previous chapter, the American-British relationship in Latin America can be characterized as one of condominium. By the turn of the century—and the escalation of the Anglo-German naval race—Great Britain turned much of its attention away from the Caribbean and toward the Continent. Faced with a rising German navy in Europe, British naval strategists were quick to shy away from challenging American naval supremacy in the hemisphere. In 1906, Sir John Fisher directly addressed the question of American naval prominence in the Caribbean. "The U.S. Navy will soon be beyond rivalry *in its own waters* unless we are in a position to divide our battle fleet on this side, which we shall never be able to do."[79]

British politicians were also unwilling to challenge U.S. hegemony in the region. In 1902, British prime minister Arthur Balfour noted how Latin American republics "are in a great trouble, and I wish the U.S.A. would take them in hand." A dozen years later when the American navy and marines did intervene in Mexico, then British prime minister Sir Edward Grey had a similar reaction. "These small Republics," Grey argued, "will never establish decent govt. themselves—they must succumb to some greater and better influence and it can only be that of the U.S.A."[80] The British leaders simply assumed that their own interests overlapped with the those of the United States. The two leading interests were to foster free trade and keep other major powers from gaining influence in the region. With only brief and infrequent exceptions, the British thought that few of their vital interests would be threatened by American power in the Caribbean. In many cases, British and American officials saw their interests as tightly intertwined. The special condominium is evident from several cooperative endeavors between the Royal Navy and the U.S. Navy. One example is the joint peacekeeping efforts in Puerto Plata in 1904, previously discussed. Another indication is the cable sent in 1906 by Secretary of the Navy Newberry to the U.S.S. *Marietta* in Cienfuegos: "Use force under your command at your discretion to protect American and British interests where possible."[81] There is no mention of German or French interests, although their investments in the region were still significant.

The United States was always more suspicious of German intentions than of British or French. If there was a great power that at least nominally sought to limit American hegemony in the region, it was Germany. Tirpitz had long coveted an island in the West Indies for a naval base. This was thought to be the surest way to protect German interests in the region. These interests, it should be added, were not insignificant in terms of both German immigration and German investment in the region.

American policymakers and naval planners took a very suspicious if not paranoid view of German intentions in the Caribbean. First, Germany was completely unwilling to recognize the Monroe Doctrine. As a way of reiterating their opposition to the doctrine, the German Foreign Service officially referred to the United States as the "United States of North America."[82] This moniker remained in place until around 1902. The German reluctance to acknowledge the Monroe Doctrine cast an ominous shadow over all their actions in the hemisphere.

German naval activity in the region also proved troubling to Americans. On 6 December 1897, a German naval vessel shelled Port-au-Prince after a German citizen was arrested by Haitian officials. In September 1902, the German gunboat *Panther* intervened against Haitian naval forces during Haitian civil unrest. While this force was used with some justification, for most American policymakers they reflected a German determination to act independently and deploy their naval forces throughout the Caribbean and South America.

Deployments of the German navy in the Caribbean grew more threatening to the United States when combined with German rhetoric and war plans. Near the turn of the century, Wilhelm II, never one known for diplomatic understatement, charged that "We will do whatever is necessary for our navy, even if it displeases the Yankees." On another occasion he admitted that the "German naval construction is directed not against England but America."[83] German captain Lt. Von Veltheim, in an address to the German Navy League in 1901, stressed the importance of a German fleet plying the waters of the Caribbean. "If the German population is to remain in those countries (Central America and the Caribbean), the German fleet must be able to say to the Americans *Hands Off!*"[84] By 1901, the German military had a series of war plans involving naval attacks on all the major American cities on the Atlantic.[85] None of this was lost on American alarmists or those advocating naval expansion.[86]

In the end, German reluctance to recognize the Monroe Doctrine, the naval shellings, the bravado of Wilhelm, and the not-so-well-hidden war plans[87] all served notice to American policymakers of Germany's intentions in the hemisphere. Chief Officer of Naval Intelligence Charles Sigsbee demonstrated a fear of Germany that bordered on the paranoid. He remarked on nearly every aspect of German naval growth. The Germans, Sigsbee pointed out, "have 504 (Naval Cadets) and we but 388. . . . We should be twice as strong. Double Germany in [each and every aspect] of sea power."[88] Sigsbee grew fearful of German infiltration of the American navy. He recommended that the Navy conduct background checks on all U.S. naval personnel with German surnames to ascertain whether or not they were native-born or naturalized American citizens. In Sigsbee's view, the latter might become tools of German treachery in the event of war between Washington and Berlin.[89] While the legitimacy of the German threat remains an open question to historians, there is little doubt that most American policymakers in the early twentieth century took it rather seriously.

Nothing speaks more directly to the American naval superiority in the region than the show of naval force during the Venezuelan crisis. Of the small European force of fourteen ships, Great Britain floated a force estimated around 28,750 tons. The Italian contingent amounted to approximately half of the British force. The German forces weighed in at around 11,147 tons. By comparison, Dewey brought together an American fleet of fifty-four warships with an estimated tonnage of 129,822. Through the Venezuelan crisis, according to one historian, Dewey "accomplished his primary objective of flaunting American naval might."[90] Upon returning to Washington, Dewey specifically referred to Germany by publicly proclaiming that the exercises served "as an object lesson to the Kaiser more than any other person. . . . Think of it, fifty-four warships including colliers and all. Germans could not possibly get a fleet over here that could fight such a fleet."[91]

Before the crisis Roosevelt noted how "the Monroe Doctrine does not touch England . . . the only power that needs to be reminded of its existence is Germany." A few years following the crisis Roosevelt claimed that he had "succeeded in impressing on the Kaiser . . . that the violation of the Monroe Doctrine by territorial aggrandizement on his part around the Caribbean meant war, not ultimately, but immediately, and without delay."[92] Roosevelt's claim may have been somewhat accurate. In the wake of the American response to the Venezuelan blockade, George Baer noted, "the Royal Navy called back its West Indies Squadron."[93] The German withdrawal from the region was less dramatic. But it is important to note that after 1903, Germany's war operations plans for the Caribbean and North America were "reduced to a mere theoretical exercise."[94]

Following the adoption of the Schlieffen Plan in 1905, German strategists largely turned away from plans that would divert a war effort away from Europe. In 1906, after largely abandoning the Caribbean, Admiral Büchsel informed the Foreign Office that the Admiralty had "virtually no interests in German ships visiting ports on the eastern coast of South America."[95] The Admiralty then redeployed the two cruisers that composed the core of the South American Squadron. Then in 1909 the Admiralty abandoned all pretense of a naval presence in the hemisphere.[96]

After 1903, Britain and Germany made no serious efforts to limit American influence in the Caribbean. By this time, Great Britain had all but passed the torch representing naval prominence in the region to the United States. Germany, recognizing its inability to bring enough force to the region, rather reluctantly retreated from challenging American hegemony in the region. As Bradford Perkins noted, "The American flag waved unchallenged over American water for the first time in history."[97]

Regional States' Options for Pressuring the United States

The regional states had very few realistic options to put pressure on the United States. The United States had successfully deterred any other major power from effectively seeking influence in the region. By doing so, the United States succeeded in denying smaller states the option of seeking powerful allies and tempering American hegemony in the region.

As previously noted, Tirpitz had long coveted a naval base in the West Indies for Germany.[98] In 1912, the State Department was informed of a possible German loan to Haiti of $2,000,000. This supposed loan was to be secured by port rights, control of customs, as well as a coaling station and naval base at Mole St. Nicholas.[99] To deter such a deal, the United States began playing a more intense role in Haitian affairs that ended with seizure of the gold assets of the Haitian National Bank and wrestling control of the customs houses in 1914.[100] Military intervention took place 28 July 1915. Finally, in November 1915, the American supported government signed a treaty with the United States agreeing not to surrender any territory or enter into agreement with any other power. The case of Haiti made it clear that the United States would not allow any type of alliance that might bring a potential rival into the Caribbean.

An earlier episode sent a similar message. José Santos Zelaya, Nicaraguan dictator, sought to challenge American hegemony in Central America. Zelaya had ambitions to unify—by force if necessary—Nicaragua with Honduras, El Salvador, and Panama. In 1907, Zelaya assisted armed rebellions in Honduras and El Salvador. Zelaya threatened bombardment of Amapala, but was dissuaded by American naval presence. There were rumors of Zelaya negotiating another canal treaty with Japan and Britain.[101] Zelaya's adventurism prompted President Taft's reference to the dictator as "a blot on the history" of the region.[102] After two American citizens were executed for serving in an anti-Zelaya revolutionary force, the United States hastened Zelaya's resignation. Zelaya's movement came to an end after the United States failed to recognize his successor, José Madriz. American policy of nonrecognition was followed by open assistance to rebels fighting Madriz. In the end, Madriz and his supporters were routed, and Zelaya's efforts to challenge American influence proved to be futile, as discussed in the previous section. The fate of Zelaya served as an example of the likely fate awaiting any leader who challenged the United States.

In cases in which the United States directly intervened with military force, regional actors had the option of leading guerrilla activity against the intervention and fostering nationalist movements. Unlike more recent anti-imperialist movements, however, elites were reluctant to look to guerrilla movements as legitimate nationalist forces.[103] Instead of inspiring uprisings against the Americans, regional elites often looked to the United States to provide stability and guidance. As Caperton noted, "The better class of Haitians were convinced that only permanent intervention by the United States would save their country."[104] In many cases, the elite saw more commonality with the Americans than they did with other groups in their own society.

Without the possibility of alliances with major powers, nor the ability to form regional alliances, there was little that these small regional powers could do to put pressure on the United States.

Congruence of American Objectives and Regional Actors' Objectives
One common interest between the regional states and the United States would be the maintenance of international peace throughout the region. Outbreaks of international hostilities, like those threatened by Zelaya in Nicaragua, would further strain unstable regimes. Wars would also threaten foreign interests and could lead to an American intervention, which would be an unfavorable outcome for both the United States and the ruling elite within the regional power.[105]

Since the overarching objectives of decision makers in the regional states revolved around remaining in power, maintaining the status quo in domestic politics would be another shared interest between the United States and the regional powers. The United States agreed to this by promising to refuse to recognize those governments that seized power through the use of force, as discussed earlier. While this was often impossible to carry out in practice since so many governments seized power violently, it still signaled an American interest in maintaining a modicum of domestic stability.

In many cases, regimes changed so quickly it would have been difficult for the United States to identify any shared interests with the ruling government before that government was overturned. The extremely frequent change in regimes in Haiti prompted Admiral Caperton to sarcasm: "During the preceding year [1914–1915] the country had been blessed with two presidents, while since 1911 six chief executives had been given the opportunity of making a name for themselves in the history of the country."[106] With such rapid changes in governments and so many different states in the region, identifying the emergence of common and sustained interests over the period being studied is difficult.

Part Three: The United States's Ability to Shape the Peacetime Environment

While the United States succeeded in achieving its primary objective, secondary objectives were not so easily achieved. The primary objective was to keep other great powers from gaining influence in the region. Although the probability of this occurring was low, several possible scenarios, if played out, might have led to German expansion into the region. The most likely of these scenarios would have involved political instability and heavy indebtedness followed by military intervention by a European power like Germany, which would then negotiate base rights with the indebted small power. Fears of this scenario explain why the deployment of British, German, and Italian naval forces in the Venezuelan debt crisis of 1902–1903 brought forth such a strong showing of American naval force. Another remote possibility of this surfaced prior to World War I when Haiti was supposedly entertaining the idea of leasing Mole St. Nicolas to Germany for a naval base. While the plausibility of this remains open to question, the United States responded in a determined manner.[107] First, the United States began by wielding economic leverage in terms of loans. This was followed by taking control of Haitian customs houses and finally with a full-fledged military occupation of Haiti. With all the advantages the United States enjoyed relative to regional powers, achieving its primary objectives of keeping European powers out of the region and safeguarding access to the Panama Canal were easily accomplished.

Achieving many secondary goals in the region proved more difficult. Political instability and conflict within states were quick to surface in spite of American efforts at peacekeeping. However, throughout these periods of instability naval presence played a key role in protecting American interests and property. Finally, efforts to shape the regional peacetime environment along the lines of good Progressive principles failed. The limited efforts to nurture good government and democratic institutions ended in failure. Sometimes these failures were blamed on the lack of American resolve and commitment. For instance, Munro claimed that American efforts to reform and train the local constabularies in the Dominican Republic were destined to fail because of the lack of resources.[108] Other historians claim that American occupation of Haiti was a period of unparalleled progress in terms of the construction of roads, bridges, irrigation canals, and hospitals.[109] Somewhat ironically, those states in which the United States made the greatest efforts to foster political stability by direct intervention—Haiti, the Dominican Republic, and Nicaragua—over time came to be ruled by the most oppressive dictators. Turning to specific efforts to shape the peacetime environment, we see a mixed degree of success.

Deterring Regional Conflict
When exploring the question of conflict in the region we must distinguish between interstate conflict and intrastate or domestic political conflict. Over the past two centuries, the Caribbean has experienced relatively little interstate conflict.[110] Violent domestic conflict and political instability, however, have been endemic throughout the region. The United States was more successful in shaping the regional environment than it was in shaping the domestic political environments within the states.

The ability of the United States to maintain a peaceful status quo between states in the region is noteworthy. There were only two short clashes in Central America in 1906 and 1907. The success in deterring Zelaya's forces in Amapala in April of 1907 and ultimately putting an end to the conflict has been noted in two previous sections. Like any claim of successful deterrence, some caveats must be noted. First, given the high levels of political instability, the most pronounced challenges facing most decision makers were domestic—how to remain in power—rather than foreign. So it is doubtful how much international conflict would have taken place had the United States not been present.

The United States, however, was far less successful at deterring conflict on the domestic level. There were sporadic and short-lived examples of successful peacekeeping at the domestic level. But most of these efforts involved the United States brokering short-lived agreements between rival factions. The promises were rarely kept and conflicts typically reemerged. Caperton noted that in Haiti the government's promises were "only promises and served their purposes only while the printer's ink was damp."[111] While Dillingham celebrated the "moral influence toward peace exerted by naval vessels" in the Dominican Republic in 1904, the agreement he helped forge was followed by decades of political instability and violence. American military presence in the region was capable of imposing truces on the battling factions. But military presence—or even outright occupation—failed to bring peace and stability in the long run.

American presence and policy still had a dampening effect on the levels of violence. For instance, the American policy of disarmament by purchasing weapons from insurgents certainly reduced the intensity of the violence that engulfed Haiti in subsequent years. And the sporadic successes of naval peacekeeping certainly did reduce bloodshed and destruction in many instances. One can safely conclude that a heavy American presence in the region reduced the level of domestic political violence and deterred violence between states. But the American presence did not eradicate political violence.

Controlling Regional Conflict Outcomes

The United States could intervene decisively and determine the outcome of all conflicts in the region. Ensuring that a favorite faction prevailed was the easy part. But given the opportunistic nature of factions, it was always unclear whether a specific faction would ultimately pursue policies agreeable to American interests and therefore warrant American support. As a result, the United States often remained neutral in regard to domestic political strife, so long as American property and lives were spared in the conflict. While capable of acting in a decisive way, the United States usually chose to not act at all.

Typically, American neutrality tended to lean in favor of the status quo. This is evident in Washington's carefully worded directive to the *Eagle*: "Take no part in the troubles in Hayti further than to protect American interests. It is considered important that revolution must not be successful."[112] This is an accurate reflection of American response to most of the conflicts in the region. In other words, try to remain neutral, but also try to deter revolutionary movements that will wreak instability and threaten American interests.

While remaining neutral, American presence in the region allowed a close monitoring of domestic political struggles. Once the outcome of a struggle was obvious, American naval officers in the field would try to broker relatively peaceful transitions. By brokering transitions, loss of life and property could be minimized. One example of this, previously noted, was Henry McCrea's efforts to broker a peaceful transfer of Bocas del Toro, Colombia, in 1902. More generally, State Department officials would try to discourage violent transitions by agreeing not to recognize those governments that seized power through the use of force by signing agreements like the Central American Convention of 1907, also noted above.

In the few cases in which the United States clearly took sides, such as Nicaragua in 1909, the outcome was certain to be the one sought by Washington. This, however, does not mean the outcome will be stable and enduring. Short-term outcomes could be easily determined by the United States; long-term stability could not be enforced so easily. As a result of this uncertainty, the United States often sought neutrality so long as faction did not threaten American interests.

Reassuring Aligned States in the Region

With its awesome material capabilities the United States could reassure aligned states of just about anything. Perhaps as a result of the preponderance of American power in the region, these states could turn a blind eye on international politics and the threats to security that sometimes characterize the international system. Simply put, regional states seemed to pay little attention to external threats. In terms of external threats, the United States could most certainly provide security and reassurance to aligned states.

Serious challenges facing the regional states, however, were internal, not external. As a result, most of a regime's attention and resources were devoted to reducing internal threats. In regard to internal threats, the policy of neutrality sometimes limited American ability to reassure even those aligned states. But the record of support and neutrality is a mixed one throughout the period. In most instances, the United States remained neutral in domestic struggles. However, when the United States took sides, the American-backed side typically prevailed.

Protecting Regional Economic Interests

The United States was both able and willing to protect its economic interests. One of the major concerns of Washington was to maintain naval presence in order to protect American economic interests. It may well have been the prospects of a forceful response by the American navy and marines that led many Caribbean insurgents to avoid harming American interests. One of the more remarkable features of the period of study is the frequent calls for naval presence to safeguard American property—presumably being threatened—and sheer dearth of cases where American property was actually damaged.

J. Fred Rippy argued that American investment in the Caribbean was not only protected but augmented as a result of U.S. military activity in the region. During the early part of the century there was at least a threefold increase in American investment and trade in the Caribbean.[113] Investors, according to Rippy, knew that there was a high probability of protection—typically by American naval forces—in the case of domestic upheavals. During this period, "the persons and property of citizens of the United States in the Caribbean region received rather vigorous support, and under the Roosevelt Corollary of the Monroe Doctrine the United States often took care of the interests of European nationals in order to limit the action of European governments in their behalf."[114] In other words, the United was not only capable of protecting the economic interests of its own nationals, but also those of all foreign investors in the region.

Ensuring Regional Foreign Policies in Regional States
Regional states rarely pursued foreign policies that defied the United States. This, however, may have more to do with the low salience of foreign policy issues than with American effort to influence those policies. In the Caribbean during the early part of the twentieth century, there was no primacy of foreign policy. Instead, domestic politics were the primary, if not exclusive, concern of decisionmakers in the region.

In those rare instances when regional decisionmakers did so, they were typically short-lived. Zelaya sought to challenge American hegemony in Central America by unifying Nicaragua with Honduras, El Salvador, and Panama.[115] In the end, the United State instigated the removal of Zelaya from office and supported the armed ouster of his crony successor. Zelaya, ironically, retired in exile in New York City.

In other cases in which foreign policies might diverge from American interests, the United States usually reacted promptly and vigorously. When rumors emerged that Haiti was discussing a possible coaling station with Germany in exchange for a large loan, the Americans stepped in and ultimately seized the customs houses and intervened militarily. But in the vast majority of cases the United States did not have to wield any influence over a regional state's foreign policy simply because these states tended to pursue policies that did not diverge from American interests.

Most Caribbean states, however, devoted few resources to foreign policy. Their primary concern rested with domestic policy matters. When issues of foreign policy or finance did arise—such as treaties over custom houses and trade policies—they tended to be directly negotiated with the United States and ultimately they reflected the interests of the United States.[116]

Promoting Favorable Domestic Developments in the Region
Many historians exploring the American role in the Caribbean during the Progressive Era note the varied motives that were driving interventionism.[117]

Many Americans looked to improve living conditions by fostering economic development and good government in the region. The goals of shaping the domestic political institutions or generating economic growth, however, were not achieved.

If there is an obvious failure in American presence in the Caribbean, it rests in the failure to promote and shape favorable domestic developments in the region. While any data that measures economic growth for the period is very unreliable, it would appear that economic development was sluggish at best.[118] The increased American investment in the region did not typically translate into higher standards of living. One possible exception is Haiti and the Dominican Republic. During the American occupation of Haiti, a small occupying force mobilized with the population to build 1,000 miles of road, 210 bridges, 9 air fields, 1,200 miles of telephone lines, 82 miles of irrigation canals, 11 modern hospitals, and 147 rural clinics. The Dominican occupation also achieved progress, though more modest, in education, literacy rates, and infrastructure.[119] These developments, however, did not foster development in the long run.

The promise of better government and democratic development, among the primary goals for many Progressives, also failed. These failures were most striking in those cases in which the United States made the most sustained efforts toward order, good government, and possibly democratic institutions by active intervention. The fact that lengthy American interventions in Nicaragua, Haiti, and the Dominican Republic were all followed by brutal dictatorships may not be coincidental. While speculative, the rise of these dictators may have been part of a backlash against American intervention. In all of these interventions, the United States ultimately engaged in press censorship and other strong-armed policies that often drew criticism from some American officials.[120] These strong-armed policies sparked popular resentment of the American intervention. Based on the notion of a common foreign enemy and the rally-around-the-flag phenomenon, a more militant, nationalist opposition to the American presence may have emerged.[121] With this intensified nationalism, a hard-line nationalist leader would be sought out to lead opposition against the American intervention. In other words, American intervention may have inadvertently helped to create environments conducive to the rise of dictatorship. In the three Caribbean cases in which the United States intervened most substantially, Haiti, the Dominican Republic, and Nicaragua, brutal dictatorships subsequently rose to power.

Conclusion

The years between the dramatic show of American naval power during the Venezuelan debt crisis of 1903 and the reconsiderations of American global presence in 1920 constitute an exceptional effort to shape the peacetime environment in the Caribbean. Over these seventeen years the United States enjoyed optimal conditions for successfully shaping the environment. On the military front, the United States enjoyed unchallenged military power and presence throughout the Caribbean. No regional or global power challenged American influence in the region. The United States also enjoyed enormous domestic support for an active, interventionist foreign policy in the region. This domestic support was hardened by certain Progressive Era principles advocating charitable action and democratization. Finally, international norms at the time permitted great power intervention to protect property and promote stability.

Even with these highly optimal conditions for shaping regional affairs, the historical records reflect both successes and failures. The United States succeeded in maintaining its leadership in the region and deterred any encroachment from rival powers. As a result, the strategic objective of maintaining easy access to the Panama Canal was achieved. American naval presence also worked to maintain international peace and stability between regional states. Regional peacekeeping efforts within states, however, were less successful. Although naval forces frequently brokered truces between warring factions, few of these truces endured. Naval forces also sought to limit the death and destruction resulting from civil unrest. In this regard, success was sporadic. American interests and property were rarely damaged, but violent upheavals still wreaked severe damage to regional actors, especially in Haiti and the Dominican Republic.

The greatest failure of American efforts to shape the peacetime environment was the inability to introduce Progressive principles of good government anywhere in the region. This Progressive objective was one of the reasons so many Americans supported an active, interventionist foreign policy in the region. In spite of sustained and creative efforts in Haiti and the Dominican Republic, these ambitious efforts ended in failure. After nearly two decades in Haiti, there was little appreciable improvement toward democratic governance, or even responsible governance.

American experiences in the Caribbean highlight the differences between shaping a regional-strategic environment and shaping domestic environments. Efforts to protect strategic interests through an active presence proved easier than those efforts to bring democracy, political stability, and economic development to the region. With the end of the Cold War, the United States is now more frequently faced with what Barry Blechman referred to as "the intervention dilemma."[122] As the United States is increasingly faced with complex questions of intervention, peacekeeping, and democratization, much can be learned from the U.S. efforts in the Caribbean. The American experience in the Caribbean during the Progressive Era should serve as a reminder of the difficulties inherent in a policy of fostering democracy abroad. Even when the United States possessed overwhelming military capabilities, enormous economic leverage, little international opposition, and strong domestic support, it was unable to meaningfully alter the political institutions of its neighbors in the Caribbean.

Notes

1. Fred Rippy, *The Caribbean Danger Zone* (New York: Putnam, 1940), 150.

2. Walter LeFeber, *The American Age: United States Foreign Policy at Home and Abroad since 1750* (New York: W. W. Norton, 1989), 261.

3. Donald Yerxa, *Admirals and Empire: The United States Navy and the Caribbean, 1898–1945* (Columbia: University of South Carolina Press, 1991), 27.

4. Several note how the United States had the option of building many other bases but chose not to due the expense and to the recent success enjoyed by colliers in refueling at sea. See David Healy, *Drive to Hegemony: The United States in the Caribbean, 1989–1917* (Madison: University of Wisconsin Press, 1988), 28.

5. *Brassey's Naval Annual* (London: W. Clowes and Sons, 1904), 17.

6. Charles Paullin, *Paullin's History of Naval Administration, 1775–1911* (Annapolis, Md.: United States Naval Institute, 1968), 473.

7. Given the length of time being studied, obtaining a reliable measure for naval force in the Atlantic—and more specifically the Caribbean—is difficult. Less problematic is the fact that the United States could quickly assemble an awesome array of naval power in the Caribbean in short notice. This is evidenced in the Venezuelan crisis of 1902–1903. The exact role of American naval might during the crisis is better developed in a latter section of this chapter.

8. Yerxa, *Admirals and Empire*, 33.

9. Yerxa, *Admirals and Empire*, 33.

10. The number of ships that would ply Caribbean waters during the winter months is most dramatically evident during the 1902–1903 Venezuelan crisis when Dewey assembled a fleet of fifty-four warships. This was accomplished by limited redeployment of ships. See Holger Herwig, *The Politics of Frustration: The United States in German Naval Planning, 1889–1941* (Boston: Little, Brown, 1976), 81. Also Ronald Spector, *Admiral of the New Empire* (Baton Rouge: Louisiana State University Press, 1974), 145.

11. Several technologically advanced battleships were sold to South American states in this period—mainly Brazil, Argentina, and Chile. See Richard Hough's *Dreadnought: The History of the Modern Battleship* (New York: MacMillan, 1964), chapter 1. Hough also notes the inability of these navies to fully utilize these technologically advanced ships.

12. Viscount Hythe, *The Naval Annual, 1913* (New York: Arco Publications, 1970) 282–83.

13. David Healy, *Gunboat Diplomacy in the Wilson Era: The U.S. Navy in Haiti, 1915–1916.* (Madison: University of Wisconsin Press, 1976), 114–27.

14. Log Book of the U.S.S. *Washington* (8/13–14/1915), Ship Log Books of the United States Navy, Record Group 41, General Records, National Archives, Washington D.C. (Hereafter, Ship Log Books).

15. See Allan Millett and Peter Maslowski. *For the Common Defense: A Military History of the United States of America* (New York: The Free Press, 1994) 655.

16. These figures are from the Material Capabilities Data Set (Vol 2.1) collected by the Correlates of War Project, www.cow2.la.psu.edu/>.

17. Ernest Dupuy and William H. Baumer, *The Little Wars of the United States* (New York: Hawthorne Publishers, 1968), 152.

18. Reported in William B. Caperton, "History of U.S. Naval Operations under Command of Rear Admiral W. B. Caperton, January 1915 to March 1919" 400 pages of the Naval Records Collection of the Office of Naval Records and Library, Subject File ZN (Personnel) 1911–1927, Record Group 45, National Archives, Washington D.C. (Hereafter known as Caperton Papers), 97.

19. Hans Schmidt, *The United States Occupation of Haiti, 1915–1934* (New Brunswick, N.J.: Rutgers University Press, 1995), 5–8.

20. Healy, *Gunboat Diplomacy*, 118.

21. Dupuy and Baumer, *Little Wars*, 146.

22. Graham Cosmas, "Cacos and Caudillos: Marines and Counterinsurgency in Hispaniola, 1915–1924," in *New Interpretations in Naval History*, ed. William Roberts and Jack Sweetman (Annapolis, Md.: Naval Institute Press, 1991), 294–305.

23. Dupuy and Baumer, *Little Wars*, 150.

24. Cosmas, *Cacos and Caudillos*, 305.

25. John Williams, "U.S. Navy Missions and Force Structure: A Critical Appraisal," *Armed Forces and Society* (1981), 501.

26. Bradley Fiske, *From Midshipmen to Rear Admiral* (New York: The Century Company, 1919), 550–51.

27. Yerxa, *Admirals and Empire*, 31.

28. Yerxa, *Admirals and Empire*, 33.

29. Evidence of American presense and ability to respond was drawn from the following primary sources: *Translations of Messages Sent in Cipher* (10 vols.) Record Group 45, General Records, 1798–1910. National Archives, Washington D.C. These records consist of loosely bound collection of messages sent from Washington to various naval vessels. The majority of the ten volumes represent the years from 1895 to 1910 (hereafter known as Messages Sent) and *Translations of Messages Received in Cipher* (6 vols.) Record Group 45, General Records, 1798–1910. National Archives, Washington D.C. These consist of the messages sent to the Navy Department in Washington primarily from ships on missions abroad (hereafter known as Messages Received).

30. From Ship Log of the U.S.S. *Marietta* (1907/vol. 1).

31. Thomas G. Walker, *Nicaragua: The Land of Sandino* (Boulder, Colo.: Westview Press, 1981), 17.

32. Messages Sent 1/22/1908. For a firsthand account of the varied tasks performed by the *Eagle*, see F. L. Oliver's "Havana Episode," *United States Naval Institute Proceedings* (October 1952).

33. Robert Bigelow, "The Wireless in Warfare, 1885–1914," *United States Naval Institute Proceedings* 77, no. 2 (1951), 117–20.

34. Messages Sent 4/1/1907. This discussion of Amapala—in Salvador—is pertinent to the Caribbean since stability throughout Central America was deemed essential to American Caribbean policy of the period.

35. Healy, *Gunboat Diplomacy*, 25. Also see the report of January 27, 1915, in the Caperton Papers.

36. For accounts of the anarchy and murder of Guillaume Sam, see Dupuy and Baumer, *Little Wars*, 145, and Healy, *Gunboat Diplomacy*, chapter 1.

37. For one account of how previous shelling made the current threat to resume shelling much more credible, see Sumner Wells, *Naboth's Vinyard: The Dominican Republic, 1844–1924* (New York: Arno Press, 1972), 750.

38. Yerxa, *Admirals and Empire*, 33.

39. Wilfred Callcott, *The Caribbean Policy of the United States* (New York: Octagon, 1966), 400. Welles, *Naboth's Vinyard*, 750.

40. Messages Received, 3/17/1904.

41. Messages Sent, 4/18/1904.

42. John Blassingame, "The Press and American Intervention in Haiti and the Dominican Republic, 1904–1920," *Caribbean Studies* 9 (1969); H. W. Brands, *What America Owes the World: The Struggle for the Soul of Foreign Policy* (New York: Cambridge University Press, 1998), 52. For Olney's and Beveridge's views on annexation see Albert Weinberg, *Manifest Destiny: A Study of Nationalist Expansion in American History* (Chicago: Quadrangle Books, 1963), 438.

43. Messages Received 2/12/1904.

44. Wilfred Callcott, *The Caribbean Policy of the United States*, 400.

45. Welles, *Naboth's Vinyard*, 745–750.

46. Dana Munro, *The United States and the Caribbean Republics, 1921–1933* (Princeton, N.J.: Princeton University Press, 1974), 125.

47. Munro, *Intervention*, 125.

48. Messages Sent, 1/22/1908.

49. Walker, *Nicaragua*, 18.

50. Messages Received 1/5/1904.

51. Caperton Papers, p. 413 (10/6/1915).

52. Healy, *Gunboat Diplomacy*, 107.

53. Munro, *The United States and the Caribbean*, 44.

54. Messages Received, 4 April 1904.

55. Caperton Papers, 153–55; 87.

56. Milton Offutt, "The Protection of Citizens Abroad by the Armed Forces of the United States," *Johns Hopkins University Studies in Historical and Political Science* (1928), 99–100.
57. In Offutt, *Protection of Citizens*, 101.
58. Rippy, *The Caribbean Danger Zone*, 229.
59. Munro, *The United States and the Caribbean*, 51–53.
60. Rippy, *The Caribbean Danger Zone*, 25.
61. Bruce Calder, *The Impact of Intervention: The Dominican Republic during the U.S. Occupation of 1916–1924* (Austin: University of Texas Press, 1984), 4.
62. Munro, *The United States and the Caribbean*, 162.
63. See Healy, *Gunboat Diplomacy*, 144, for examples in Haiti. Blassingame, *The Press*, 41, noted how *The Nation* began reporting on this practice in its series on U.S. policy in the Caribbean from 1919 to 1920. For two early critical accounts see Ernest Gruening, "Conquest of Haiti and Santo Domingo," *Current History* (1922) and Henrik Shipstead, "Dollar Diplomacy in Latin America," *Current History* (1927).
64. Welles, *Naboth's Vinyard*, 748.
65. Max Boot, *The Savage Wars of Peace* (New York: Basic Books, 2002), 166. Also, Caperton Papers, *passim*.
66. This case is discussed in Robert Ferrell's *American Diplomacy: A History* (New York: W. W. Norton, 1975), 288–90. There are several other cases in which government officials believing that only the United States could bring order to their troubled states invited U.S. intervention. See Healy, *Gunboat Diplomacy*.
67. The most famous of these criticisms appeared in many iterations in *The Nation* beginning in 1919.
68. Perhaps the most sustained critique of American interventionist foreign policies was leveled by the Anti-Imperialist League. The league's most poignant criticism, however, targeted American policy in the Philippines. American intervention and imperialism in the Caribbean was less open to criticism. This may be due in part to national security concerns with the region and lingering beliefs in Manifest Destiny.
69. For the Protestant origins of Progressive internationalism, see Eldon Eisenach, "Progressive Internationalism," in *Progressivism and the New Democracy*, ed. Sidney Milkis and Jerome Mileur (Amherst: University of Massachusetts Press, 1999), 226–58.
70. Richard Hofstadter, *The Progressive Movement, 1900–1915* (Englewood Cliffs, N.J.: Prentice Hall, 1963), 4.
71. Brands, *What America Owes the World*, 49; LaFeber, *The American Age*, 117.
72. Healy, *Drive to Hegemony*, 219.
73. Rippy, *The Caribbean*, 139.
74. Blassingame, *The Press*, 29–37.
75. Offutt, *The Protection of Citizens*.
76. Dana Munro, *Intervention and Dollar Diplomacy in the Caribbean, 1900–1921* (Princeton N.J.: Princeton University Press, 1964), 162.

77. For arbitration rulings see A. M. Stuyt's *Survey of International Arbitrations, 1794–1970* (Dobbs Ferry, N.Y.: Oceana Publications, 1972). Robert Ferrell's *American Diplomacy* offers a concise interpretation of the ruling.

78. Miriam Hood, *Gunboat Diplomacy, 1895–1905: Great Power Pressure in Venezuela* (London: Allen and Unwin, 1983), 183.

79. Authur Marder, *From Dreadnought to Scapa Flow* (London: Oxford University Press, 1961), 125.

80. Bradford Perkins, *The Great Rapprochement: England and the United States, 1895–1914* (New York: Atheneum, 1968), 161.

81. Messages Sent, 9/23/1906 (vol. 5).

82. Herwig, *Politics of Frustration*, 70.

83. Herwig, *Politics of Frustration*, 69–71.

84. Alfred Vagts, "Hopes and Fears of an American-German War, 1870–1915," *Political Science Quarterly* (1939), 525.

85. Healy, *Rise to Hegemony*, 74–75.

86. For a contemporary document on American reaction to German war plans see Homer Lea's *Valor of Ignorance* (New York: Harper, 1909).

87. Lea, *Valor of Ignorance*, 134.

88. Vaghts, *Hopes and Fears*, 526.

89. Vaghts, *Hopes and Fears*, 527.

90. Herwig, *Politics of Frustration*, 81.

91. Spector, *Admirals of the New Empire*, 145.

92. Healy, *Gunboat Diplomacy*, 72.

93. George Baer, *One Hundred Years of Sea Power: The U.S. Navy, 1890–1990* (Stanford, Calif.: Stanford University Press, 1994), 36.

94. Baer, *One Hundred Years of Sea Power*, 75.

95. Yerxa, *Admirals and Empire*, 14.

96. Yerxa, *Admirals and Empire*, 14.

97. Perkins, *The Great Rapprochement*, 158.

98. Herwig, *The Politics of Frustration*, 70.

99. Carl Kelsey, "The American Intervention in Haiti and the Dominican Republic," *Annals of the American Academy of Political and Social Science* (1922), 134.

100. Healy, *Gunboat Diplomacy*, 1976.

101. Walker, *Nicaragua*, 18.

102. Walker, *Nicaragua*, 16.

103. Calder, *The Impact of Intervention*, develops this thesis for the Dominican Republic.

104. Caperton Papers, 9.

105. This assumes that the United States was typically reluctant to intervene in the region. This reluctance is noted repeated by Caperton in Haiti in 1915.

106. Caperton Papers, 2.

107. On the plausibility of a German base, see Kelsey, "The American Intervention," 134.

108. Munro, *The United States and the Caribbean*, 51.
109. Max Boot, *The Savage Wars of Peace*, 180.
110. Singer and Small, *Resort to Arms*.
111. Caperton Papers, 155.
112. Messages Sent, 1/22/1908.
113. Rippy, *The Caribbean*, 224; Chester Jones, *Caribbean Interests of the United States* (New York: D. Appleton and Company, 1916), 338.
114. Rippy, *The Caribbean*, 224–27.
115. Walker, *Nicaragua*, 18.
116. Healy, in *Gunboat Dipomacy*, examines the negotiations between the United States and Haiti over Customs Receivership. Although many Haitians objected to the treaty, the American position prevailed due to the overwhelming American military and financial capabilities.
117. See, for instance, John Milton Cooper, *The Warrior and the Priest: Woodrow Wilson and Theodore Roosevelt* (Cambridge, Mass.: Harvard University Press, 1983); Brands, *What America Owes the World*; Rippy, *The Caribbean*.
118. Rippy, *The Caribbean*, is perhaps one of the best sources. Jones, *Caribbean Interests*, also presents some rudimentary data on the growth of trade, which does not really tap economic growth.
119. Boot, *The Savage Wars*, 180; also, Munro, *Intervention and Dollar Diplomacy*.
120. Munro (1974: 44) notes some criticism from the Department of State. Admiral Caperton made several efforts to refrain from any undemocratic practices, Healy, *Gunboat Diplomacy*. Also see Gruenig, "Conquest of Haiti," for a more general critique.
121. For a discussion of relationships between external conflict and domestic cohesion (i.e., and rally around the flag) see Jack S. Levy, "Domestic Politics and War," *Journal of Interdisciplinary History* 18, no. 3 (1988).
122. See Barry Blechman, "The Intervention Dilemma" in *Order and Disorder after the Cold War*, ed. Brad Roberts (Cambridge, Mass.: MIT Press, 1995).

CHAPTER FIVE

La Chasse Gardée

Post–World War II French West Africa, 1945–1970

Sarah S. Milburn

Introduction

France's manipulation of events in its former African colonies is integrally linked to the French leadership's perception of France itself as a major global player during the second half of the twentieth century. French leaders used the sub-Saharan African colonies in order to regain, and then preserve, the political prestige, economic strength, and military capability that had distinguished France on the world stage before World War II. In spite of changes in leadership over time (from the Fourth Republic to the Fifth, from President de Gaulle through the post-Gaullists to the Socialists), postwar French interaction in sub-Saharan Africa reflected, for the most part, a coherent, consistent, carefully managed and largely bipartisan policy designed to retain and shape these countries as sources of strategically important materials, and as an important component of France's military, economic, and cultural sphere of influence.

This chapter, and the next, examine France's behavior as a great power in West and Central Africa along several dimensions, which include France's military capability and security policy, other resources and constraints which have affected France's influence in Africa over time, and France's consequent capacity to preserve a stable peacetime political and economic environment in these former colonies. To put this in the current doctrinal framework of "Shape, Respond, Prepare," most of the research so far has examined how

France shaped the postindependence peacetime environment in West and Central Africa in order to obtain the desired resources, strategic flexibility, and global prestige and power in the region. The shape intended for its former colonies, here called *"la chasse gardée,"* determined in large part how France responded to conflict or the threat of conflict, why and when she was most likely to respond, and how well prepared France was for the larger-scale, more regionalized conflicts during the period following the independence of its African possessions.

The three main challenges to France in achieving its goals during the second half of the twentieth century were: *first*, the traditional and ancient challenge of preserving and extending French power and influence against the encroachments of the English-speaking world, often broadly termed *"les Anglo-Saxons"*[1] but personified by members of the Atlantic Alliance, particularly the United States; *second*, staving off determined attempts at influence in the developing world on the part of the Soviet Union and its allies; and *third*, the need to manage impulses toward nationalism in its colonies and offer a form of "independence" which maintained their dependency within the French sphere of influence (what might be seem as a policy of deflecting revolution in favor of cooperative evolution).

Seventeen modern sub-Saharan African countries have developed the special military, economic, juridical, and cultural relationships with France that include them in what is generally meant by "francophone" or French-speaking Africa. Three of these, Rwanda, Burundi, and the former Zaïre (originally and once again the Democratic Republic of Congo or DRC), use the French language as their lingua franca because they were Belgian colonies. Rwanda and Burundi became independent in 1962, and the DRC in 1960. France's former West and Central African colonies had also become fourteen independent countries by that time, thirteen of them en masse in 1960. The fourteenth, Sekou Touré's Guinea, broke away in 1958 from President Charles de Gaulle's offer of a French Community partnership and preceded the others to independence by two years.

Most of the fourteen had been French possessions throughout the twentieth century. French Congo was lost to Germany in 1911 and retrieved in 1914. Togo and Cameroon were in German hands until they became French mandate territories at the end of World War I. At independence, the former French West Africa of the early twentieth century (*Afrique Occidentale Française* or AOF) became the nine West African countries of Senegal, Guinea, Mauritania, Mali (formerly "French Soudan"), Upper Volta (now Burkina Faso), Dahomey (now Benin), Côte d'Ivoire, Togo, and Niger. The former French Equatorial Africa (*Afrique Équatoriale Française* or AEF) became the five Central African countries of Chad (the northern part of which had been a part of AOF), Cameroon (incorporating the formerly British and anglophone north), the Central African Republic (formerly "Oubangui-Chari" and briefly, the "Central African Empire"), the Republic of Congo (formerly, and more familiarly, "Middle Congo," "French Congo" or "Congo-Brazzaville" to distinguish it from the DRC, which is also known as "Congo-Kinshasa"), and Gabon. I will offer an occasional example from these countries as illustrations, although the stories of French military, intelligence, economic, and cultural interventions and influences in the sub-Saharan region are legion, and the literature is extensive.

Shaping the *Chasse Gardée*

To describe the shape of France's desired peacetime environment, I use a phrase often seen in the literature on French colonialism, "*la chasse gardée.*" A *chasse gardée* is a hunting preserve, or what we might think of as a private game park.[2] The epithet is essentially pejorative, although French sources often use it purely for descriptive purposes. In this way, the colonial and even postcolonial relationship between France and francophone Africa is presented as one in which the responsible lord of the manor cares devotedly for his parks and creatures, in order to preserve their health and security for his own use and pleasures.[3] A well-run *chasse gardée*, in these terms, contains human inhabitants who remain convinced enough of the advantages of their living arrangement, and the benevolence of their overlord, that they have little inclination to leap the fence, go into the deer business for themselves as sole proprietors, contract hunting rights out to a competing "*patron,*" or even evict or kill their protector. The economic advantages of living in the park, security and a stable economy, outweigh the loss of autonomy, the risk of punishment, and the additional chores required in the lord's service.

This feudal metaphor, and the dilemma it poses, are not peculiarly French. However, the French have distinguished themselves by retaining and exploiting a relationship with their former colonial preserves of which no other European power can boast. The relationship is by no means perfectly harmonious, but it remains a political and economic force to be reckoned with nearly four decades after the political independence of the African colonies. An efficient *chasse gardée* relies not only on force, fences, and the economic neediness of the inhabitants. It also requires what we might now call ecological or situational awareness: the ability to sense troublesome conditions which will destabilize a region or destroy the ability of the rangers to control the park. The rangers themselves are a key element. They must be both faithful and knowledgeable, answering to France and yet understanding African nuances, languages, and lore. Long-distance management was no substitute for a constant and watchful French *presence*.

Since its arrival in the previous century, France has never left Africa. The 1881 diary of the French explorer Pierre Savorgnan de Brazza says that he offered Congolese a choice, "White men have two hands. The strong hand is the hand of war. The other hand is the hand of trade," and records that they chose the weaker hand.[4] In reality, these two French hands have reinforced one another, the one heavier at times than the other, but always operating in tandem. The military hand has been the more egregious of the two, although the economic hand has been just as pervasive. French rule in the colonies was established by force, and elements of the French military have been found actively engaged in Africa from 1830 until the present day.

Brazza's optimistic economic opening gave way quickly to the cruelties of colonial resource extraction techniques: forced labor, head taxes, beatings, and executions. Colonial authority in the territories was essentially arbitrary, and maintained by the *indigénat* code. Crucial to the *indigénat* was the capacity for summary punishment, including execution, for any act or word deemed disrespectful of French authority.[5] Africa's main contributions to France's own military security and prestige were material resources and manpower. African subjects served France as soldiers, military porters, and servants, both as forced conscripts and as volunteers.

The colonial French perceived this form of exploitation as morally acceptable because such a partnership "added to the dignity" and advancement of indigenous peoples. The apparent support to the overlord metropole demonstrated by the service of African soldiers was also thought to lend legitimacy to France's authority over the region as a whole. In theory, the democratic patriotism of French citizens was supposed to be demonstrated by France's practice of universal conscription, which was intended to insure an egalitarian "nation in arms." Colonial-era politicians hoped that a rhetorical stretch of the "nation in arms" concept to cover African colonies-in-arms might convince the French public, and other nations competing with France for Africa, that France belonged there as a redemptive and constructive presence. African military service to France was therefore an integral part of what the French called their civilizing mission, the *"mission civilisatrice."*

Whatever the rhetorical justifications, however, French colonial rule was comfortable with being hated so long as it was feared. Marshal Lyautey, who formulated and executed much of the French colonial policy in North Africa, believed that *"Il faut manifester la force pour en éviter l'emploi*"—force should be demonstrated in order to avoid having to use it.⁶ Lyautey himself demonstrated what Clayton calls the colonial self-confidence that led at times to "gaps of self-delusion" between political ideals and real behavior.⁷

As Anthony Clayton notes, French empire-building bore particularly striking philosophical and practical similarities to classic Roman imperialism both as a centralized authority and in its capacity for assimilating indigenous colonials into the lower military ranks. French "direct rule" also mandated a large number of French civil servants in proportion to the population in order to administer the territories. The possessions of France, as befitted those of a centralized imperial power on the Roman model should, "within the limits of their resources and quality of their manpower, provide soldiers for regiments of indigenous men under officers from the metropole, as part of the concept of these territories paying for themselves"⁸ Colonial subjects used as soldiers were cheaper in the short run, and were believed to survive and fight better under those adverse conditions where the loss of too many French citizens was politically unacceptable.⁹ France was trying to be, at once, a modern European democracy and the imperial governor of a vast colonial domain. The strains of maintaining this dual identity are manifest in the political rhetoric of the postindependence decade; the duality persists to this day.

De Gaulle, the Franco-African Military, and the Transition to Independence

At independence in 1960, the African colonial contingents of the French military *became* the militaries of their own new nations, but they continued to receive large amounts of military aid, training, and troop contingents in the form of "cooperative" assistance from France. "*Coopération*" of this kind provided France with the most useful and significant continuing opportunities to maintain her influence as the preponderant great power in its former colonies, and to continue to preserve and shape the environment of the *chasse gardée*.

The original nine countries of *Afrique Occidentale Française* (Senegal, Guinea, Mauritania, Mali, Upper Volta, Dahomey, Côte d'Ivoire, Togo, and Niger) are the focal points of chapter 5. Their history illustrates the earliest techniques of French military penetration in the region, a presence which persists to this day. Their contribution from the late 1950s through their first independent decade to French military power and security also parallels the service to France of its most influential twentieth-century president, Charles de Gaulle. De Gaulle's ideals for France, and the practical uses of Africa in the service of French prestige, were a significant influence on African political development. The assumptions upon which France's African security policy has been based since de Gaulle's Brazzaville Conference of 1944 are still discernible in France's African affairs in the 1990s.

The Brazzaville Conference was organized by deGaulle's *Comité Français de Libération Nationale*, established in 1943 by the Free French in Algiers to promote French unity in exile. De Gaulle's appeal to the francophone Africans to cut off Vichy gave renewed importance to the French colonies, and suggested that salvation could come from francophone unity in the empire while France itself was divided in two.[10] The colonies became the base of operations for the Free French government in exile.[11] During World War II, Francophone Africans remained convinced (or coerced) for a number of military, economic, and political reasons of the continued necessity of contact with one of the French governments. While most began the war loyal to Pétain and Vichy, many of the sub-Saharan governors and military leaders of Central Africa soon switched their allegiance to de Gaulle. Chad[12] joined de Gaulle in June 1940, followed by Cameroon, Congo (Brazzaville), and Oubangui-Chari. The governor of Gabon chose Vichy but committed suicide in November 1940 after the Free French troops arrived. The West Africans joined much later, Senegal waiting until Allied forces had landed in North Africa in November 1942. Côte d'Ivoire supported Vichy until midway through the war. However, by the time Tunisia was recovered in 1943, most of French Africa was aligned with the Free French.[13]

Although Gaullist histories record the 1944 conference of French colonial governors in Brazzaville as the first step toward decolonization, its purpose was not to promote self-government. Africa, to de Gaulle, was a vital extension of territory which supported France's claim to imperial greatness. The purpose of the Brazzaville conference was to maintain Africa's dependency in such a way as to renew the grandeur and power of France, and not to begin the process whereby Africa could regain power over itself. In fact, the Africans who participated at Brazzaville were laying the groundwork for reshaping their own relationship with their colonial overlord. The Indochina war began soon after Brazzaville, and provided an object lesson concerning the risks to France of other, less peaceful paths to independence.[14]

The heightened political consciousness and sense of entitlement of returning African veterans was a catalyst to a number of emerging political movements in West Africa. Both French and African politicians competed for the loyalties of recently demobilized veterans.[15] After World War II,

France could no longer rely completely on the old colonial relationships of patronage and fear to maintain the *chasse gardée* as a source of manpower and wealth. Africans at all social levels had lost limbs, lives, wealth, family, and self-respect in the course of liberating France from German occupation. Many no longer regarded these losses as an imperial tribute but rather, as a repayable debt. If France wanted to keep its army in Africa, and Africans as a part of the French security sphere, something had to be given back in return.

In 1945, the French colonial minister argued that "During the war that has just ended it was in the Empire that French liberty survived, it is by the Empire that France constantly persevered in the struggle, it is from the Empire that the French forces of liberation were launched."[16] Part of France's post–World War II claim, in spite of Vichy, to belong once again among the great powers of Europe was based on de Gaulle's insistence that a power which had maintained its empire was a great power whether or not it had been conquered by another. To continue to make this claim, it was necessary for France to continue as an empire in spite of its African colonies' increasing assertiveness. De Gaulle maintained to the colonies themselves that it was their status as colonies (and, postindependence, as allies) of France *in particular* that made them especially fortunate, because France was grand, powerful, and—importantly—independent of the increasingly bipolar power groupings of the postwar era. France presented itself as able to retain *its* culture and its independence within the international system of states, and tried to demonstrate its supposed sensitivity to other states desiring the same level of enlightened culture and political independence, if only as French appendages.[17]

This argument, accepted and promoted in various forms throughout the colonial and postcolonial administrations, demonstrates what is perhaps France's greatest strength where its former colonies are concerned: the ability to adapt the necessary ideological justifications for the French presence in Africa to the historical circumstances at hand. The goal that France set for the African states aligned with France, therefore, was to mirror France's own resolute nonalignment, and to support the choices made on their behalf by France. Before independence, France's continuing control over its colonies and its general discouragement of their national independence movements was justified on the basis of containing Soviet expansionism (as expressed in Soviet support of those movements) and providing a defense of the West's flank and rear in Africa and the Mediterranean.[18] Even the French socialist left agreed with, and participated in promoting, this political strategy formulation.[19]

Part One: France's Military Capabilities vis-à-vis Its Former Colonies in French West Africa

The Regional Military Balance

French military capability in West Africa during the two and a half decades following World War II grew out of the military history of France in Africa during the previous century. France became a nuclear power, an achievement that made it once again a great power after its embarrassing conquest by Germany during World War II. France needed not only to convince its own people of its renewed greatness, but its fellow great powers as well. France obtained its nuclear capability, the *force de frappe*, concurrently with the official independence of France's African colonies. However, the overwhelming military superiority which France has possessed in comparison with all African countries and even with the larger regional powers in West Africa (Nigeria and Libya) is as much a function of the consistently maintained historical relationship between France and francophone Africa as it is a function of France's impressive technological superiority.

To understand why and how France has maintained its power in Africa during the post–World War II period requires a historically informed examination of how three distinct facets of French military power have penetrated the region:

- *France's physical presence* (composed of troops, military command structures, French officers, and well-maintained bases),
- *France's intelligence and diplomatic presence* (both formal and informal military advisory connections and personal friendships formed between French and African leaders), and
- *France's ongoing military aid transfers and sales* to its former possessions (sales and donations of arms, trainers, and joint exercises).

These three military manifestations of French power are interwoven with French diplomatic initiatives and with another equally significant form of penetration: French economic support. For example, the preferential treatment that French companies generally receive in African markets and investment opportunities is mirrored by the continuing preference shown by the most faithful francophone African allies for purchasing most of their arms and police equipment from French companies. This is so even though many francophone nations also purchased arms from elsewhere, including the Soviet bloc countries, the United States, and China.

Of these three expressions of French military power, the first (physical presence) was the earliest, and it formed the historical basis of the two latter facets as they grew in importance during the post–World War II period. As its own history has always been an important part of France's justification of its continued presence in Africa, and the basis of many of its publicly expressed goals, it is necessary to offer a brief history of the Franco-African armies.

The History of the *Armée Coloniale*

The colonial army, as a unit, was separate from the army of the metropole.[20] There were multiple French armies in Africa, with no single commander in chief or permanent officer corps.[21] Crawford Young[22] characterizes France's "science of hegemony" as the opposite of British (Lugardian) indirect rule, calling it "prefectoral, hierarchical, centralizing and Cartesian." The French military system was empowered completely from the metropole; every military policy focused outward from the political control center, and was subject to the center's political currents.

Three distinct military groupings formed the French armed forces in Africa: the *Armée Métropolitaine*, the *Armée d'Afrique*, and the *Armée Coloniale*. The *Armée Métropolitaine* consisted mostly of French conscripts, France's "nation in arms," who could only be ordered to serve off of French soil if they so chose, or if the legislature approved. The two other armies of France were created in order to do what the homegrown draftees of the *Métropolitaine* could not. As Clayton explains, "In no other way could the paradox of France's wish as a great power to assert a global presence be squared with the French electorate's wish that conscript soldiers remain linked to their native soil."[23] The *Armée d'Afrique*, initially an army for maintaining the conquest of northwest Africa, included North Africans, and was created in the 1830s to replace white French metropolitan forces serving in North Africa. It should not be confused with *La Coloniale*; sub-Saharans were not included in this force.[24]

It is the third army that forms the historical basis for French military power in sub-Saharan Africa. Before 1900 and also after 1957 (with independence on the horizon), the *Armée Coloniale* was known as the *Troupes de Marine*.[25] *La Coloniale*'s history begins with the colonization process itself. Regular infantry and artillery garrisons were installed in the French African and Caribbean colonies during the seventeenth and eighteenth centuries, and they became a permanent part of the navy's command structure as the *Régiments d'Infanterie de Marine* and *Régiments d'Artillerie de Marine*. Local recruits were used increasingly as these regiments grew in size during the nineteenth century, becoming the forerunners of the now-famous African troops who served France during two world wars and the final part of the colonial period as the *Tirailleurs Sénégalais*.[26] They served not only in African military operations and pacification campaigns but as far away as Europe, the Middle East, and Indochina.

It had become politically costly to use French soldiers in regions where they succumbed rapidly to diseases in dramatic numbers. France was expanding its influence in West Africa at a pace too rapid for French manpower sources to supply. Once established and systematized, Africa's manpower contribution to France's military power and prestige was as significant, if not more so, as Africa's natural resource contributions to the French economy. By the 1920s, there were 48,000 *Tirailleurs Sénégalais* augmenting France's European and North African units all over the world.[27] Often, although not always, forcibly conscripted, they continued to be equipped below the levels of French troops, however, and were not even given machine guns in the European theater in 1914.[28]

The history of the *Tirailleurs* demonstrates the early and complete French military penetration of the regions that became Afrique Occidentale Française and Afrique Équatoriale Française. The first phase (1857–1905) began with the establishment of the *Tirailleurs* garrisons in Senegal. From 1905 to 1919, French sub-Saharan possessions were more secure, and the *Tirailleurs* served farther from home. An estimated quarter of a million sub-Saharans fought for France in World War I.[29] African troops numbered disproportionately among the dead,[30] mainly since racialist French military and political authorities believed that Africans were the best front-line troops for all-out assaults because they had different nervous systems, experienced less pain and fear, and were naturally more inclined to violence.[31]

During World War II, Africans made up almost 9 percent of the French army in France, whereas they had constituted roughly 3 percent of French forces during all of World War I. At least 100,000 sub-Saharan Africans were mobilized at the outbreak of the World War II; by the armistice of June 1940, between 24,000 and 48,000 of these were declared missing, and at least 15,000 of these were prisoners of war. After June 1940, most French forces were removed from combat. From June 1940 until France's liberation in 1944, sub-Saharans and North Africans made up a significant part of de Gaulle's Free French armies, constituting approximately 20 percent of Jean de Lattre's forces as late as September 1944. The Free French recruited roughly 100,000 sub-Saharans by various means between 1943 and 1945 to fight at the front. Meanwhile, inside of what Vichy still held of French West Africa, the Vichy government increased the size of *its* standing army of Africans to 100,000 men in order to hold on to what it could of the West African colonies.[32]

France did its best to control the numbers of Africans who attained leadership roles during this period. A few more African officers emerged during the interwar period, but most of these remained in the lower ranks, and most troops continued to be commanded by Frenchmen.[33] The only other route to a commission was to achieve the nearly impossible feat of qualifying for entry at one of France's own military schools. This occurred, but only rarely, producing a scattering of North Africans, and a few sub-Saharans, at the rank of second lieutenant and above. The special military school for North Africans and sub-Saharans, the École Spéciale des Sous-Officiers established at Fréjus, closed temporarily in 1939, but re-opened after World War II. Although only 5 percent of its 1931 graduates were from sub-Saharan Africa, many of these graduates achieved considerable political and military importance during the transition to independence. Fréjus graduates started at the rank of sergeant major, with promotion to second lieutenant only after lengthy service. Some subaltern officers were graduates of the Écoles des Enfants de Troupe, which offered a limited primary-level education, tied to a five-year military service contract, to the children of veterans. Only a tiny number of the École graduates were ever promoted beyond the rank of sergeant.[34] Because of their general lack of French language skills, the training given to most African soldiers continued to be very simple, with little or no vocational or trade content; most *Tirailleurs* remained infantrymen.[35]

The postwar phase of *La Coloniale* ended just prior to independence when the *Armée Coloniale* became once again the *Troupes de Marine*. In spite of the name change and a lukewarm commitment to professionalizing the African armies with better training and officer cadre development, the change in command structures was a gradual one, only in part because of the paucity of African officers. African bourgeois "*evolués*" tended to be underrepresented in the officer corps, because it was more prudent to staff the officer corps with French citizens or with less well-informed, educated, and independent Africans who could be more easily controlled. The glacial speed of professionalization of African armies preserved (or at least greatly slowed the loss of) one of the main advantages that France maintained in its African sphere of influence: the continuing presence of French officers in command of their African "marines." At independence, the armies of the new African nations were no longer French in name, but remained French in concept, used mostly French arms and were commanded by French or French-trained officers. This condition was critical to the maintenance of good intelligence networks in France's former colonies, the "ecological watchfulness" of the *chasse gardée*, greatly enhancing the solidity of France's sphere of influence.

The Overall Military Balance between France and Other Powers in the West African Region

The overall military balance between France and the other European powers in the West African region during the postindependence decade demonstrated clear French preponderance, but *only* in those countries which had been a part of its colonial empire. De Gaulle maintained this preponderance in French West Africa in spite of France's largely subordinate role in the NATO alliance, and despite efforts by the Soviet Union to encroach on the *chasse gardée*. The French military's physical presence in francophone West Africa during the 1960s, along with its intelligence and diplomatic presence, and its ongoing military training, transfers, and sales, was more consistent, more numerous, and more reliable than that of any other great power.

Indeed, France's determined and persistent presence in its former colonies made it quite difficult for the Soviet Union to establish itself as a military or diplomatic presence, except in those countries (like Guinea and, at first, Mali) which had rejected French cooperation, or those (like Congo-Brazzaville) which declared a preference for communist government and flirted with the USSR while continuing to cultivate France as their foremost ally. The active attempts on the part of the Soviet Union to exploit these ideological ties, however, made France aware that other nations were ready to fill any gaps left by French inattention to its sub-Saharan interests. The Franco-African defense cooperation agreements, signed at independence, were essential to its ability to keep the sub-Saharan military balance favorable toward France. During the bipolar Cold War time frame, France viewed herself as a third "pole," and often as an "equidistant" intermediary between East and West,[36] preserving and enhancing its prestige as an entity independent of, and yet diplomatically linked to both. Relationships with particular African leaders were judged first, according to their loyalty to France and only secondarily according to whether the leader displayed pro-United States or pro-USSR tendencies.

The French military had two sorts of missions in the late 1950s and 1960s: participation in the Western European security alliance which was dominated by the United States, and keeping the peace in the *chasse gardée*. The latter actions took immediate precedence during the decolonization period just prior to independence. In 1956, most of the NATO-related French mission forces had to be sent to fight in Algeria.[37] The Allies resisted using the Atlantic Treaty framework to commit Allied forces outside the area encompassed by the treaty, in particular in the overseas territories of the alliance, and French leaders concluded that France's own independence within that alliance needed to be underscored. North Africa was considered vital to the defense of NATO interests in the Mediterranean, the Unied States was allowed by France to place five air bases in Morocco, and Algeria became the focus of concerted Allied attention. The West, including France, maintained a watchful military policy in North Africa, aware that the USSR was attempting to establish bases there as well. After the loss of Algeria as a colony, France managed to renegotiate its military relationship with Algeria, signing a military assistance agreement when they evacuated their former port facility at Mers-el Kebir; however, France was no longer Algeria's sole potential patron. Morocco and Tunisia also maintained close relationships with other Western powers after independence, and France found itself in increasing competition with the other great powers in North Africa. Its position in North Africa fading already by the early 1960s, France concentrated on maintaining power in the place where little or no Western competition was evident: sub-Saharan Africa.[38]

De Gaulle had observed how dependency on Britain had weakened France between the wars, and he was not pleased that the Allied victory in World War II resulted in a similar French military dependence on the United States. Having to clothe and feed the Free French armies by begging the Allies for funds had been humiliating enough. De Gaulle's return to France came after it became clear that the Fourth Republic would be unable to avoid war at any time in any part of its territories. The Indochina war began just after World War II, and lasted for nine years, after which Algérie Française began to deteriorate. Peace was necessary, and a respite from financial and military drain of the colonial wars in order for de Gaulle and the Fifth Republic to achieve the Fourth Republic's desired goals of (1) renewed French greatness, (2) a recovered French military presence in Europe itself, and (3) independence from the Atlantic Alliance.[39] Since French forces in France had not reached a point where they represented a strong contribution to the defense of Europe, Gordon suggests that "rather than saying de Gaulle tore down the French pillar from the NATO temple, it might be more accurate to say he refused to erect one that had never been there in the first place." On March 7, 1966, de Gaulle told U.S. president Johnson that he would terminate all French participation in NATO command structures. France did not withdraw from NATO, precisely, but it now had no formal obligations to them other than consultation.[40]

France's physical presence was much larger, of course, than any of the African forces during the period of study. The overall size of the French forces demonstrated large increases and decreases over time, falling from 1,200,000 men in 1945 (a figure which includes all North African and sub-Saharan colonial troops as a part of the French army), to 470,000 in 1947, rising to 1,153,000 in 1957, and dropping to 675,439 in 1964 after decolonization, when France's sub-Saharan troops became the armed forces of their own nations.[41]

Table 5.1. African Defense Forces, 1967

Country	Army Size	African Officers	Expatriate Officers	Air Force Size	Navy Size
West Africa					
Dahomey (Benin)	1,750	30	9	18	—
Guinea	5,000	150	—	60	—
Côte d'Ivoire	3,500	120	90	130	110
Mali	3,000	150	—	20	—
Mauritania	1,400	30	12	21	20
Niger	2,000	30	2	30	—
Senegal	5,000	185	35	170	150
Togo	700	17	—	10	—
Upper Volta	1,700	58	8	15	—
Central Africa					
Cameroon	3,800	120	16	150	110
Central African Republic	1,000	45	15	40	35
Chad	1,500	20	25	50	—
Congo-Brazzaville	1,900	60	2	75	—
Gabon	450	18	7	50	25
Former Belgian Colonies					
Burundi	2,000	60	30	—	—
Rwanda	1,500	60	10	—	—
DRCongo (Zaïre)	35,000	1,500	70	2,000	—
Nigeria[a]	12,000[b]	600	—	1,000	1,500

Source: Adapted from J. M. Lee (1969: 5).[42]
[a] Former British colony; included for comparative purposes.
[b] Before the Nigerian Civil War. Wartime army estimates are 50,000 for Nigeria (possibly even 80,000 in some estimates according to Lee), and 14,000 for Biafra.

The small size of the African armies in 1967 is shown in the table above, which represents only minuscule gains on their part since independence in 1960. In contrast to two countries experiencing major conflicts during the 1960s (Nigeria and Zaïre are included on the table for comparative purposes), the former French colonies' armies remained tiny, and not much increase in size was evident during the following decades.

France's physical presence, intelligence presence, diplomatic presence, and military trainers and arms sales have been maintained in the independent West African countries through the military cooperation agreements, even during African changes in government. This reflects the built-in flexibility with which France has been able to interpret the substance of the agreements, which were signed at independence with most of the former colonies. She is still the more powerful partner in any given agreement. Decisions concerning military or political support for particular African leaders continued to be weighed against the loyalty of those leaders to France, the most important criterion of in any particular country. (These decisions have been facilitated by France's consistently watchful and locally experienced intelligence capacity.) The military cooperation agreements are considered at greater length in later sections, but it should be noted here that armed troops were not the only sort of park rangers or, more properly, "coopérants," to be found in the *chasse gardée*. Johnson describes *coopérants* as the primary agents of the technical cooperation agreements:

> The *cooperant* provides a continuing governmental presence for the French in a way unique to Black Africa. To be sure, Israel, South Korea, Japan, Poland, the United States (AID and Peace Corps) and other countries have provided technical assistance through specialized missions or projects, but the *cooperation* accords signed between France and most of its ex-colonies have provided a continuity interpreted by some critics as the very heart of neo-colonialism. Critics admit that many of these agents offer valuable services, especially in the technical sphere, which developing countries could never pay for on their own; on the other hand, the criticism is leveled that the *cooperants* breed a continued dependence upon things French, whether in supplies, parts, or techniques. Breaking this condition of independence would, according to the argument, go a long way in helping establish real independence.[43]

The number of official French military technical advisers in Africa was close to three thousand in the years just following independence, plunging steadily throughout the 1960s to a low of 1,272 in 1969. It had risen again to 1,591 in 1971 but continued to fall throughout the 1970s to it lowest point of 1,010 in 1977. However, in the following year a steady rise in military *coopérants* was once again evident,[44] reflecting changes in military and political strategy during the Mitterand years that are described in the next case, which also offers more data on Soviet technical advisers during the 1970s. These figures cover only the official military advisers, and not the base troops, or even the large number of teachers, economic advisers, or other French personnel that were stationed in Africa for various purposes. The broader definition of "*coopérant*" is that given by Johnson, and covers a number of missions and which may be military, diplomatic, intelligence-related, or completely nonmilitary in nature. Most of the *coopérants* discussed here are military advisers, but there were also many teachers, economic experts, and administrators who went by that title too.[45] *Coopérants* in the intelligence networks could be both military and civilian to some degree.[46]

In addition, France continued to educate the officer corps of Africa on French soil. Chaigneau[47] notes that African officers and troops trained in

France numbered under 1,000 per year until the mid-1970s, but that number had doubled by 1982. During the twelve postindependence years between 1961 and 1973, the number of African junior and senior officers given French training was as follows from each of the West and Central African countries:

Table 5.2. French-Trained African Officers, 1961–1973

West Africa	
Senegal	1,904
Côte d'Ivoire	1,296
Upper Volta	846
Dahomey	636
Mauritania	618
Niger	516
Togo	429
Mali	88*
Central Africa	
Cameroon	1,222
Congo (Brazzaville)	920
Gabon	742
Chad	574
Central African Republic	550
Former Belgian Colonies	
Zaïre	202*
Burundi	21*
Rwanda	15

Source: Adapted from Chaigneau (1984).
*Between 1970 and 1973 only.

French aid also took the form of substantial arms transfers. A comparison of French arms transfers with those of other powers is provided in part two of this chapter.

France's Effective Technological Superiority over the Regional Powers

France's technological capacity remained quite superior to that of francophone Africa during this period. Under the cooperation agreements, the French maintained francophone Africa's armies during the 1960s at a low level of technical sophistication commensurate with France's own needs in the region for interoperative forces. The aspirations of its clients toward higher levels of military development only began to be answered during later decades. French training missions and military aid stressed interoperability by insuring that African client states were able to work with the French troops based in Africa. "Effective" implies not merely possession of technology but the training and institutional capacity to maintain and employ it. As the arms aid given elsewhere shows, most of what France provided to its clients was infantry weapons, rocket launchers, and light artillery, and the training that went with these. The weapons were good ones, and not cheaper versions dumped as foreign aid, because France still regarded its African alliances as an integral part of its own security. However, African clients during the 1960s generally did not receive as aid any of the more sophisticated weapons being developed by the French electronics and aerospace industries.

France's own forces in Europe were less modern compared to the other members of the Atlantic Alliance, and de Gaulle gave first priority, in terms of technical sophistication, to improving the army, navy, and air forces composed of Frenchmen who were to fight in Europe. The precolonial conflicts had required a large infantry investment with little concern for technical superiority. Even in Indochina and Algeria, the army had been the primary force, and the navy and air force had purely logistical roles and were used primarily for surveillance and transportation. Propeller-powered aircraft, a pre–World War II invention which could land on short airstrips and perform low-speed surveillance, were the most technologically advanced aircraft required for the Algerian operations. The equipment of armored and motorized units sent to Algeria had to be taken apart before being packed, and often ended up unused.

The need to modernize those French forces that were destined for service in Africa was not really perceived until well into the 1960s. Michel Martin makes the case that this lack of technological inventiveness, and the continuing French dependence on colonial manpower to solve strategic problems, left an enduring negative legacy on the armies of France that may have been usefully ruptured by the independence of the colonies in 1960. The Fourth Republic's military establishment remained dominated by its land forces, causing interservice tension with the naval and air service branches which felt technologically deprived. Between 1950 and 1960, the average percentage of the military budget allocated to the French air force was seldom more than 23 percent, a figure incommensurate with the advancing technology in this area during that decade, and lower than the air force allocation between 1936 and 1939. By contrast, the United States and United Kingdom, during the 1950s, allocated at least a third of their military budgets to air force expenditure.[48] Technological expansion occurred only *after* 1960, when francophone Africa took command of its own armies, and de Gaulle realized that the European commitment (and French prestige in the Atlantic Alliance) required a serious French commitment to modern military research and development.

Later in the 1960s, once it was established that defending the *chasse gardée* would occasionally require airborne weapons, ground vehicles, communications systems and artillery more sophisticated those used in Algeria, more sophisticated weapons began to appear. However, since France's own Africa-based troops would be available to fly planes and operate the more complex weapons systems, the superior technology remained in French hands even when it was used in Africa. The institutional capacity for maintaining the more sophisticated airplanes and electronic communication systems also remained under the control of French *coopérants*, and missions that used these were generally under French command.

France's technological superiority over all African states was quite significant, although the most obvious evidence of that superiority was based, not in Africa, but in Europe. The missile platforms were in Europe or at sea, tanks were sent infrequently because they were not always the best way to fight on African terrain, and the larger field artillery only arrived when needed. Air bases were the most visible manifestation of France's modern technology in Africa. The development of the nuclear *force de frappe* consumed much of the French arms budget during the 1960s, which made cheap African troops all the more attractive as a way to augment French power in regions were they would not be likely to use nuclear weapons in any case.

The most serious technological gap between France and Africa was perhaps at the most basic level. African educational capacity was far below that of France. Although too much technical capability on the part of African clients would have made them more independent, too little was also a potential security threat. During the postwar period, it became necessary to gradually increase the competence of African armies first, in order to serve France better, and then, in order to narrow the gap between the African and French armies during the transition to independence. French technical superiority remained overwhelming, but Africans became better trained, and better able to work with the more specialized equipment which had become necessary in the 1950s, even in the infantry, for Africans fighting France's anticolonial wars.

The modernization of African armed forces was also slowed by a lack of what Arlinghaus calls "military microcompetence," that is, the lack of an adequate educational and industrial base, especially with literacy rates of under 50 percent in many places, from which to create a versatile, technically trainable, or even competent pool of military personnel. While this condition is slowly being remedied, it remained a problem in many parts of Africa in the 1990s as it did in the 1960s.[49] Although France managed to transplant African versions of French systems of primary, secondary, and university education, access to anything above the primary levels remained limited by financial resources and by the extremely competitive nature of the *lycée* system. As military equipment became more varied and more complex, it became more difficult to find recruits who could be trained to use it, drive it, fix it, fly it, or use it to communicate in the manner required. Distributed weapons systems caused particular problems in technical training. As Arlinghaus says, recipients of arms aid sometimes failed to understand that they were not receiving just a weapon, but an interrelated complex of subsystemic components. A plane was not simply a single weapon that could be flown through the air, but rather an airframe, engine, electronic fire control and navigation components, and the necessary ground support facilities and equipment. Specialists (pilots, mechanics, air traffic controllers) were required to deal with distributed systems. Those countries that received arms transfers from multiple sources exacerbated the problem by multiplying the types of systems for which they would need training, also creating interoperability problems. Filling the gaps with French personnel was the only solution in many cases, even though it was a solution that was sometimes resented by African militaries.[50]

France's effective technical superiority was therefore less of an issue than African technical inferiority. Methods of improving African forces existed, but they were implemented only gradually. The African version of the competitive French school system in no way guaranteed universal literacy, but at least provided the most talented with some technical training and the cultural background deemed necessary to a citizen of *La Francophonie*. The military officer corps was also improved and augmented through an educational process referred to since the colonial period as "*Promotion Africaine*." Africans could become officers in the following ways: four years at Saint-Cyr or another of the French officer-cadet candidate schools, two years at one of the Écoles Spéciales Militaires Interarmés located in France (for senior NCOs desiring a commission), promotion from the ranks for meritorious service,[51] or two years of special training at Fréjus, which had become by 1959 the École de Formation des Officiers Ressortisants des Territoires d'Outre-Mer (EFORTOM, or the Officers' Training School for Those from the Overseas Territories). The EFORTOM program, which trained 174 African officers between 1958 and 1965, was the most successful of the programs created to train African officers, but its students tended to remain at much lower educational levels than French officers, and very few graduated from Fréjus with the equivalent of the first part of the *baccalauréat* (roughly a twelfth grade education). Most of these officers came from West Africa, rather than Central Africa, with the larger numbers from Senegal, Upper Volta, Dahomey, and Mali.[52] The curriculum continued to be focussed on the defense of the French metropole, and featured courses on French defense issues and French civilization. In spite of this educational disadvantage and the small number of officers produced at Fréjus,

EFORTOM did increase the number of African officers, if not the quality, and also presented the French military with a convenient group of African military men in the territories who shared much of their ideological outlook and were accustomed to operating within a French-dominated system of military operations. EFORTOM therefore eased the transition of the African armed forces to nominal African control at independence, and it also provided opportunities for a number of African officers to become powerful actors within the new postcolonial system.[53]

In spite of these improvements, the higher levels of military technology remained in French hands in francophone Africa during the 1960s, even on those occasions when more sophisticated noninfantry weapons were used there. Although some level of technical education was provided to Africans in order to facilitate their ability to work with their French patrons, the technological gap perpetuated a relationship of dependency, which in large part maintained France's position as the major great power influence on its West African clients.

The Constancy of French Presence in the Region: Types and Levels of Forces

There is considerable evidence that France maintained a constant troop, intelligence, and military assistance presence in West Africa, although troop levels were lowered during the decade following independence. Lessened troop "presence," however, was compensated for by increasing the potential for interventionary reactions which could provide an augmented "presence" when necessary. Arms transfers were reliable, although largely constrained to infantry weapons and light artillery. The military cooperation agreements, even as altered occasionally by France's African clients, provided France with a legitimized framework for maintaining the constancy and pervasiveness of its influence in the *chasse gardée*.

Before independence, French-paid garrisons composed of former *Tirailleurs* continued to be stationed in Cameroon, Gabon, Côte d'Ivoire, and Senegal, with smaller units stationed in Mauritania, Niger, Chad, and Oubangui-Chari (CAR). The last four of these French-paid African garrisons were withdrawn during the 1960s.[54]

Throughout the 1960s, France divided its non-European strategic commitments and military commands into three zones: the Pacific, the Indian Ocean (headquartered in Madagascar with a significant military base at Djibouti), and the Central and West African countries. This last zone was subdivided into three Zones d'Outre-Mer, headquartered at their historic locations in Dakar in Senegal, Abidjan in Côte d'Ivoire, and Brazzaville in the former French Congo. Five categories of African military facilities existed at the time of independence, which included over one hundred French garrisons:

- *principal bases*, which stationed elements of all three branches of France's armed forces [at various times Djibouti, Diego-Suarez (Madagascar), Dakar (Senegal), and N'Djamena (Chad), Port Bouet (Côte d'Ivoire), Libreville (Gabon) and Bangui (Central African Republic)],
- *intermediate bases*, which allowed the convenient shifting of French troops and armaments around the continent,
- *replacement bases*, which could be built up in the event of losing a principal base,
- *ad hoc security garrisons*, as needed,
- *locations where staging rights had been established* by the cooperation agreements.

Indeed, sub-Saharan Africa and Madagascar were as militarized in 1960 as they had been throughout the colonial period, although this heavy French military presence began to abate somewhat soon after decolonization, assisted by the technical improvement and Africanization of African army commands. One lingering effect of the colonial period was the heavy military involvement in policing duties. *Tirailleurs* had often been used as reinforcements for the African and French police forces, and this led to a general neglect of training specific to police duty, which persisted after independence.[55] By the mid-1980s, there were only six French bases in sub-Saharan Africa, although these maintained a significant military capacity for active intervention.

Pascal Chaigneau identifies two "axes" in the French strategy with regard to its former colonies: *la Presence* and *l'Intervention*.[56] *Presence* has two facets: technical and economic, and local military bases and apparatus. The military bases provided France with: first, a "dissuasive" presence by their very existence; second, an immediate local intervention capacity; and third, a formal symbolic indication of France's global presence.[57]

According to Chipman, French base troop levels in Africa numbered approximately 58,000 in 1962, had been lowered to 21,300 by 1964, and dropped to about 6,400 between 1965 and 1970.[58] IISS gives a total French troop strength in Africa of 12,500 in 1970, which includes paramilitary gendarmes and troops in North Africa and Madagascar. In West Africa, these included:[59]

In Côte d'Ivoire: 1 "mixed regiment" (about 600 army troops), including an armored car squadron on detachment in Niger,

In Senegal: 1,450 army troops (including two mixed regiments), 550 navy (with two coastal escorts and 1 tank landing craft), 200 airforce (with 6 Noratlas transports and 1 light aircraft flight).

Part of the troop withdrawal was supposed to be mitigated by de Gaulle's creation in 1962 of the Force d'Intervention Interarmées, which was to be based in France and capable of speedy intervention in the event of an increased need for troops in Africa. France's fellow Western nations, and French domestic opinion, agreed that a large number of Frenchman based overseas was undesirable for a number of reasons. After independence, the remaining Frenchmen who had served in La Coloniale (now the Troupes de Marine), plus those units of the Légion Étrangère who had survived the Algerian campaign, were reorganized as the nucleus of this *Force d'Intervention*. The original 1963 intervention force was composed of a single brigade of marines, additions after 1964 brought it up to division strength (two airborne brigades, 1 motorized brigade) as the 11th Division d'Intervention.[60] Most of the smaller-scale interventions of the 1960s were accomplished, however, using France's Africa-based troops.

The new system after 1962 made three levels of military power available to France:[61]

- The immediate defense of African territory by the national armies of African countries which had benefitted from increased French training and technical support.
- The Africa-based French Overseas Forces (Forces d'Outre-Mer), stationed according to the defense and cooperation agreements with African countries, largely on those bases established in 1960 and 1961. These were deemed "Forces de Présence."
- The Force d'Intervention Interarmées, stationed in the south of France which was to provide the Forces d'Outre-Mer with land, sea, and air reinforcements as needed.

The levels of France's presence in the region were preserved, determined, and occasionally altered by the cooperation agreements, of which there were two types: defence agreements (giving African states the ability to ask France for security assistance) and military cooperation agreements (which provided African states with technical advisers, military equipment transfers, and the continued opportunity to train African officers in France). France retained in this way not only base rights and strategic materials control but the right *not* to send more French forces to Africa, or use the ones based there, if this were deemed inadvisable for any reason. Thirteen sub-Saharan states signed defence agreements in 1960 and 1961: Senegal, Madagascar, Côte d'Ivoire, Mali, Dahomey, Niger, Mauritania, Togo, the Central African Republic, Chad, Congo-Brazzaville, Gabon, and Cameroon. Mali abrogated its signed military agreement (which had been made with the Mali Federation, including French Soudan and Senegal) shortly after independence, and refused to sign another military agreement until 1977, although it made other agreements with France. (Foltz suggests that symbolic issues like Algeria's fate and Senegalese acquiescence to the Saharan atom bomb tests may have been a factor in the disintegration of the Mali Federation.[62]) Upper Volta told France to dismantle its existing bases, probably because French soldiers had intervened there on behalf of the Mossi Emperor in an attempt to overthrow the Voltaic government in October 1959. France was able to retain its garrisons at Bobo-Dioulasso and Ouagadougou, but Upper Volta distrusted further direct collaboration between its troops and French soldiers. France was granted only overflight, staging, and transit rights in Upper Volta. Mauritania and Cameroon signed much more limited military assistance agreements than the others.[63]

Training and arms assistance were coordinated by the establishment of a military aid mission or office in each of the countries that had signed co-operation agreements with France. The military cooperation offices were directed in Paris by the French Ministry of Cooperation, established in 1961 entirely for this purpose. (The defense agreements were directed by the Ministry of Defense, which only in 1998 acquired the military assistance programs under its administration.) In addition, the Council of African and Malagasy Affairs was established in 1961 to ensure the participation of France's highest officials (the president, the prime minister, the foreign minister and the minister of cooperation) in African regional policy. This council has since ceased to exist; however, high officials continue to have immediate and direct influence over Africa policy in a manner unique to France. The Elysée Palace maintained an adviser with a continuing responsibility for African affairs who often met weekly with high-level officials.[64]

The defense accords signed between France and several key francophone nations, including Senegal and Gabon, instituted the following military administrative structures. At the individual state level, defense matters were referred to a "mixed Committee" assisted by the Bureau of Defense. The committee contained the French ambassador assigned to the country, the French commander of that particular overseas zone, and the African head of state. The Defense Bureau contained a French superior officer, the African country's superior military officer, and one or more *fonctionnaires* (bureaucrats) from the French embassy. At the regional level, if multiparty defense agreements were to be considered, there was another defense council, including once again the relevant African heads of state, the prime minister of France (or his representative), and a general of the French army delegated for this purpose in each African state. According to Pascal Chaigneau, France had a twofold objective in maintaining its advisory presence in African armies: to preserve the free maneuverability and ready networks indispensable to the conduct of military operations and to guarantee the internal security of each of the participating states.[65]

Military assistance agreements included financial support, logistical (arms and equipment, and maintenance) support, and the training of military personnel both locally and in France.[66] A typical "AMT" mission (Assistance Militaire Technique)[67] was composed of military and diplomatic personnel from France and the cooperating African nation, and frequently included French *coopérants* whose purpose was intelligence, even if their ostensible function was administrative, diplomatic, or advisory in a technical, or even economic, capacity.

Military cooperation agreements are not necessarily directly linked to the defense agreements. The decision to intervene in the event of internal threats to African presidents was reserved to the French president in most of the defense agreements. French response was not automatic, therefore, but greatly assisted by the opportunities for regular consultation offered by organizational structure like that given above.[68] However, the informal friendships maintained between African and French presidents, and their high-level representatives, dated from the colonial period, and they were maintained with remarkable closeness during the 1960s and even thereafter. For "preferential allies," Senegal, Côte d'Ivoire, Gabon, and later Cameroon and the Central African Republic, the AMT agreements were an additional guarantee and indication of security and stability. For the other countries, the lesser though still substantial levels of support guaranteed France a continuing presence.[69]

The Speed of France's Possible Response

The Force d'Intervention was composed of the airborne and motorized brigades of the 11th Division d'Intervention. It could be mobilized and deployed by air within days. It became a parachute division in 1971. In particular, the elite 2^e Etranger de Parachutistes trained for, and maintained, a reputation for effective commando intervention on short notice, and (in Zaïre in 1978) on very little sleep.[70] Most of the smaller-scale interventions of the 1960s were accomplished, however, using France's Africa-based troops, which could be transferred within twenty-four hours from the country in which they were based to wherever they were required.

The creation of the Force d'Intervention Interarmées in 1962 was intended to preserve the immediacy of military response that France had maintained by continued militarization of the colonies throughout the 1940s and 1950s. Communication between the intervention forces in the south of France and the overseas forces based in Africa was to be closely coordinated enough to serve as a deterrent to both external aggression and internal disorder which would threaten French interests. Between 1956 and 1964, the creation of these external forces of intervention served to cement the transition of local command of African forces to the new African nations and also to "disengage," or at least place in an external location, many of the French forces previously located in Africa. France promised to continue to maintain peace and equilibrium in Africa, but Paris also needed to pay attention during this period to its European troop commitments and to its intervention capacity on its own continent.[71]

Before 1962, there had been a number of local interventions in African countries by French soldiers based there. The creators of the Force d'Intervention argued that reposting the French troops outside of Africa, with the capacity to intervene in Africa in a crisis, meant that unstable conditions could still be dealt with effectively with appropriate force without the necessity of basing large numbers of Frenchmen in the region. The deterrent capability was to be met with better organization, modern communications, and a reputation for reliable action rather than by an egregious French presence of overwhelming numbers of troops.

French forces were active in the 1960s in a number of countries in Central and West Africa in spite of the waning troop presence. The French sent at least 300 officers and NCOs to assist government forces in Cameroon which were fighting the Soviet-assisted Union des Populations du Cameroon. Mauritania was the site of interventions between 1956 and 1963 to restore order in the Western Sahara and keep the peace until a cooperation agreement had been signed. More limited interventions occurred in Gabon, Congo, Chad, and Niger in the early 1960s to end internal conflicts. The most public intervention in accordance with a defense agreement took place not in West Africa, but in Gabon in 1964, when French forces put down an uprising by opposition leaders. The defense agreement with Gabon had contained an implicit provision for the personal protection of Gabonese president Mba. This intervention came as a surprise to those not involved in French Africa policy because France had exercised its option *not* to intervene following the assassination of President Olympio of Togo in 1963, probably because of Olympio's ambivalence to the wishes of his own military leaders and to the constraints posed by continuing French influence,[72] and had also not sent troops to Congo-Brazzaville that year in response to continuing internal conflict. The defense of Mba had the effect of speeding the deployment of the new intervention forces outside of Africa, accompanied by political rhetoric concerning the advisability of external deterrence threats and increases in economic aid that might forestall the need for military action.[73]

In addition, although Gabon's defense agreement stipulated that the president was required to ask for French assistance in order to receive it, it is possible that Mba made no such request. With the help of de Gaulle's Africa adviser, Jacques Foccart, and his French intelligence network in Gabon (see the next chapter for more on Foccart), which was somehow "activated" by a meeting of the Foccart network, Mba was surrounded by French advisors and troops during all of the ensuing unrest, and he remained president of Gabon until his death from cancer later in the year, at which point the Foccart network managed to replace him with a hand-picked successor, Omar Bongo.[74] The overall speed of France's response was determined by the nature of each military cooperation agreement with a given country, and the resulting consistency and strength of the French presence in that country. In Gabon, that presence was clearly sufficient to maintain good intelligence and a careful guiding hand to restrain local conflict and influence local politics in directions advantageous to France.

Military Options Available to France

France's military options during the 1960s were closely related to the ways in which the West African nations' cooperation agreements structured the French presence in each country. These agreements gave France a number of options if its help was needed (assisting or preventing a coup, fighting insurgency) to defuse or prevent African threats to French or African security, or if an African client became embarrassing or opposed French objectives to an untenable degree. France used all of the resources enshrined in the cooperation agreements for insuring that her preferences were served in the *chasse gardée*. The following options could be used separately, sequentially, or combined as part of a coordinated plan. These options, broadly, included both "carrots" (inducements to behave, only some of which were military) and "sticks" (punitive measures). The "carrots" were:

- Nonmilitary economic, infrastructural, and educational assistance, using civilian *coopérants*;
- Maintenance of the Franc Zone, and a stable African currency pegged to the French franc;
- Financial aid and investment;
- Diplomatic contacts and mutual friendships between French and African officials, including personal contacts between presidents;
- Franco-African solidarity and mutual political support at the annual Francophone Summit meetings and the United Nations;
- Arms transfers;
- *Gendarmerie* and officer-cadet training, in Africa and in France;
- Military logistical and technical assistance, using French intelligence networks and military *coopérants*;
- Military intervention with base troops and/or Intervention forces to protect an African president from internal security risks;
- Military intervention with base troops and/or Intervention forces to protect an African country from external security risks.

Since the cooperation agreements left intervention decisions in the hands of the French presidency and the French were not obliged in all cases to intervene or to continue aid in the event of an uncooperative client, the punitive "sticks" included:

- Withdrawal, or the threat to withdraw, any and all of the "carrots" listed above;
- Covert operations, making use of the French Intelligence networks, including paramilitary, mercenary, and other unofficial French operatives;
- Military intervention, using the Africa-based French troops;
- Military intervention, flying in the France-based Force d'Intervention.

The substance and structure of these cooperation agreements is described more fully below.

The Cooperation Agreements: Independence Protracted becomes Independence Contracted

Paramount to maintaining the colonial empire was the ability to maintain the ability to use force in a form that could be justified with some semblance of legitimacy both to France's fellow independent states, and to its colonial subjects. The political and military advantages of this became evident just before independence when the example of Guinea demonstrated that a total French withdrawal would mean a substantial reduction in security, order, and access to resources for states that chose independence over French guidance and cooperation.

Cooperation agreements offering *"maintien de l'ordre," "assistance militaire technique," and "soutien logistique"* (keeping order, technical military assistance, and logistical support), were signed at independence with most countries, including in West Africa: Senegal (in 1960), Côte d'Ivoire (1961), Niger (1961), Dahomey (1961), and Togo (1963). Mali signed a more limited agreement in 1960 which had lapsed by 1970, and refused to sign a military agreement until 1977. Guinea refused to sign one of these agreements as well, of course, and much of its military aid came from the Soviet Union. To this day, Guinea maintains a more independent and autonomous military structure, although relations with France have become much friendlier. Mauritania had signed an agreement by 1970, at which time Mali's agreement had lapsed.[75]

The linchpin of the cooperation agreements lay in the relationship that France maintained with its former colonial army. In 1950, French sub-Saharan Africa had only 66 African officers, 90 percent of whom were lieutenants or sub-lieutenants. This figure and rank distribution remained substantially the same at independence a decade later.[76] During the post–World War II period, some attempts were made by the French to slowly Africanize the officer corps of the colonial armies but, as Claude Welch suggests,[77] there was a limited budget for professionalizing African armies, and France preferred to continue the practice of providing its own officers directly to the colonial armies. This practice continued after independence, in spite of the increasing availability of comparably trained African officers. France after 1960 continued to bear many of the equipment and training costs of its former colonies' armed forces, and in spite of several educational and training programs intended to educate an elite African officer corps, continued to assign a number of its own officers to command positions in francophone African armies. This practice, although partly a function of France's own institutional constraints and low expectations of African ability, also had the useful effect of placing French citizens strategically within African military structures, and cemented into place military intelligence networks and African habits of institutional dependency on military aid and training that were vital to continuing French influence in the region.

Almost all of the francophone African states which became independent in 1960 signed "cooperation" agreements, with some doing so only after UN recognition. In each case, however, it was clear that France was to be a donor and protector of independence only in return for *continued* cooperation. As a contractee in these agreements, France remained in control of many of the internal developmental processes of the new states, not only their military development, but economic, legal, and cultural development as well. A unified economic zone with a common African franc currency value pegged to the French franc, the continuing use of the French (Napoleonic) legal code in spite of its numerous conflicts with persisting traditional legal practices, and African educational systems mirroring those of France and using the French language as the standard for all civilized communication, all served to support and enhance continued French military power in West and Central Africa.

Although pressure was certainly exerted by de Gaulle on African leaders at independence to accept these cooperation agreements, which had contractual force, France continued to claim that they were freely chosen at independence by the contracting parties. The obligations were mutual and France's own contributions were seen as substantial. Most of the world audience was willing to accept that these forms of cooperation were *desired* (and therefore seen as legitimate) by their African partners. In return for developmental aid, and the promise to maintain the internal and external military and economic security of the new states, France was guaranteed the continuing strategic, economic, linguistic, and cultural hegemony that had been its goal since the Scramble. It had lost Algeria and Guinea, but maintained a sizable, powerful, and internationally acceptable form of *grandeur* that no longer appeared to require apologies for lingering imperialism, while retaining many of the practical advantages that had been inherent in colonial expansion.

The cooperation agreements resembled both treaties and contracts in form. They included provisions for defense and the use of strategic minerals, foreign policy agreements, technical assistance arrangements including personnel, training and equipment, and financial and legal cooperation. Some of the agreements were bilateral (as with Senegal) and some were regional (Côte d'Ivoire, Dahomey, and Niger had a multilateral agreement with France). As the African nations began to deal as sovereign states with states other than France, some of the agreements of the 1960s were revised or even canceled. The renegotiated agreements of the 1970s continued to give France significant power and influence, however, particularly the military accords. French presence in the form of French officers and base rights, technical military assistance and control, and France's promise to defend African governments from both external danger and internal disorder were the centerpieces of the military agreements. In return, France received prior notice and approval rights for any decisions involving military development, political changes, and the transfer or sale of strategic materials.[78] Just as trade within the CFA (African Franc) Zone remained mutually preferential, so did military decisions, and even UN voting bloc arrangements. The African leaders who negotiated these agreements did so in the knowledge that the visible results they would achieve would secure their own power bases at home. In time, the very mutuality of these agreements, the continuing need of France for African bases, markets, and influence, and the close relations perpetuated by these contracts made African leaders into an influential lobbying group in Paris as well. Their voices in French foreign policy formation continued to be a salient presence.[79]

In addition to the agreements, which were bilateral, the French sponsored a multilateral military agreement, the Union Africaine et Malgache de Défense (UAMD), was arranged to include Madagascar and most of the sub-Saharan states (except for Guinea, of course, as well as Mali and Upper Volta). In contrast, Britain made only bilateral agreements with its former colonies; none were multilateral. France agreed to come to the defense of any member of the UAMD that was threatened, and Paris set up a headquarters that maintained consultative contact with UAMD members.[80]

"Assistance Militaire Techniques (AMT)" allowed the French authorities to respond to African defense requests in three major ways: training of military personnel (locally and in France), financial support, and logistical support (providing arms, tools and vehicles, and aid in their maintenance). Two types of defense conventions were available, including conventions covering external defense, and conventions that covered internal *"intérieure"* defense, which is what is meant above by *"maintien de l'ordre."* Under these defense agreements, African partners were responsible in general terms for their own external and internal defense, but might ask for aid from France.[81]

The demand that France provide personal protection to African leaders from internal opposition has not always placed France in an advantageous political position vis-à-vis its fellow great powers, but France has continued to value its African partnerships with authoritarian African leaders above its historic reputation as a defender of democratic governance. What Africa added to French power proved to be too important to give up easily or quickly. France's military "hand" (in Brazza's phrase) has been reinforced by the reproduction of French military and police organizational structures within African countries, which not only used French methods but also retained French personnel in command positions. France's intelligence and power has only been as strong as its ongoing ability to remain an active part of the military and diplomatic structures of its African partners. French *coopérants* and technical advisers, French arms, weapons platforms, bases, marines, intelligence officers, and every other concrete manifestation of France's political and strategic concerns were almost as much a part of francophone African life in the 1990s as they were at independence.

France's Ability to Intervene in Domestic Political Affairs (e.g., to Save or Topple Governments)

France maintained its ability to intervene, and used all of the "carrot" and "stick" options at its disposal to maintain and insure cooperative alliances with the francophone African states, replacing or improving leaderships as necessary, and fending off challenges to its most reliable long-term friends. After independence, the ability to intervene militarily was enhanced (at least in theory), and made more politically acceptable in France, by the creation of the Force d'Intervention, and the continuing insurance provided by the Africa-based presence of the Forces d'Outre-Mer. There were a number of occasions in which France exercised its ability to intervene militarily, and also some occasions in which French intervention took more subtle forms. Occasionally, France would exercise its option to *refrain* from intervening, usually in the event of a coup d'état in which France supported the outcome or believed that the situation could be manipulated to its advantage. Toward the end of the decade, however, it became clear that France was more effective at deterring internal security threats in African states, and manipulating coup outcomes, than it was at controlling conflicts that were either intractably lengthy or involved countries outside the francophone sphere.

Chipman[82] lists the following French military interventions in the early 1960s, which do not include more "discrete" actions (e.g., preemptive aid increases and garrison reinforcements) that are less documentable, but as often effective, as the obvious shows of force:

> Cameroon in 1959–1960 (Action against insurgents of the Union des Populations du Cameroon)
> Mauritania in 1961 (Suppression of revolts)
> Senegal in 1959–1960 (Support to President Senghor during collapse of the Mali Federation)
> Congo-Brazzaville in 1960–1962 (Suppression of riots)
> Gabon in 1960 and 1962 (Suppression of opposition riots)
> Gabon in 1964 (Prevention of a military coup against President Mba)
> Chad in 1960–1963 (Suppression of minor uprisings)

In addition, French troops repressed a military revolt in Niger in 1963 and unrest in the Central African Republic (CAR) in 1967. The 1964 intervention in Gabon used the local French garrison supplemented by reinforcements from the base in Senegal and French parachutists based in Brazzaville.[83] The 1960 intervention in Cameroon used the local French garrison to put down a Bamileke uprising.[84] The Senegal intervention was primarily caused by the disintegration of the Mali Federation, which involved both peasant uprisings and independent actions by the gendarmerie. French participation was limited to protection of President Senghor, and diplomatic activity aimed at minimizing damage to the military cooperation agreements with the now-separate states of Mali and Senegal.[85]

France regarded military coups d'état as crises which, although potentially dangerous, could offer useful opportunities for securing French power and influence. French military presence was not necessarily a coup deterrent; there were many successful military coups d'état in the francophone African states during the first ten years of independence, including:[86]

Upper Volta (1966)
Mali (1968)
Togo (1963 and again in 1967)
Dahomey/Benin (1963, twice in 1965, 1967, and again in 1969, although Welch concedes that this count for Dahomey includes shows of force that showed no evidence of a plan to overthrow civilian government)
Central African Republic (1966)
Congo-Brazzaville (1963, and again in August and September 1968)
Congo-Léopoldville (1960, and again in 1965 as Zaïre)
Burundi (twice in 1966)

Upper Volta, Mali, Togo, and Dahomey are all in West Africa, and all of their precoup leaders had less trouble-free relationships with France than did France's most reliable supporters in the region, Côte d'Ivoire and Senegal. Since many of the coup leaders showed promise of being able to work with France, they were not interfered with significantly, except where local unrest in the wake of a coup was a danger to French interests or to strongly francophile leaders like President Senghor or President Mba. This is in line with some of the more established theory on coups d'état and African military governments, including the now-classic statement by Aristide Zolberg[87] that such coups do not represent a political rupture, or a derailment of progress, so much as "an institutionalized pattern of African politics" that does not necessarily change the basic character of a society or its political structure. Since the structural character was largely unchanged by these coups, and France had played a long-term role in establishing that structure, military coups represented changes of personnel. These changes did not necessarily require the total reconstruction of France's entire relationship with each country, which had been largely of a military nature from the beginning.

Coups d'état, and the postindependence phenomenon of a number of military governments in the former colonies, did not generally constrain French power in the region during this period, but seemed, rather, to offer France the option of working closely with government leaders who had been steeped in French military culture, and held wartime ties with France. Military governments offered, in addition, less need for France to deal with or penetrate internal political parties in the new nations, and a consequently greater opportunity to concentrate on using military aid as a form of diplomacy. If one assumes, as Zolberg did, that military governments have the ability to moderate the potential decision-making capabilities (and resulting conflicts) of political parties by taking over as a nonpolitical guarantor of internal stability,[88] then it is not difficult to see why de Gaulle and later French presidents found them as agreeable to work with, if not more so, than those states in which political factionalism was less restrained. Factional disputes within African militaries remained a problem, however (as 1963 Niger shows), particularly during the decades covered by the next chapter, as a generation of military leaders emerged who had not shared the World War II experience with de Gaulle.

In one notable case, however,[89] the presence of a strong president who maintained his close historical ties to Paris also staved off the possibility of a military coup. Military nonengagement in Côte d'Ivoire can be clearly tied to the enduring legitimacy of its head of state in the eyes of both Ivorian and French leaders. President Houphouët-Boigny, furthermore, was adept at constraining the political factionalism of his own colony (and then country) by nonmilitary methods, particularly by the careful maintenance of networks that linked key Ivorian business and political elites to French investments and other opportunities available through Paris's political and economic patronage. As Bratton and van de Walle note, the use of state resources as patronage for elite clients was often an important factor in an African government's political legitimation. Government, parastatal and diplomatic positions increased vastly in number in Côte d'Ivoire after independence, increasing access by loyal elites to power and wealth, as well as to official houses, cars, assistants, and pensions.[90] Close civil and military relations in Côte d'Ivoire, combined with one of the healthiest economies in West Africa, maintained Houphouët's power and, with the exception of a small and unsuccessful military revolt in Gagnoa in 1970 (at which the presence of French troops remains a persistent rumor), the Ivorian military stayed in its barracks until after Houphouët's death. The army did participate in a few joint maneuvers with the French troops based in Port Bouet near the Abidjan airport. Domestic peacekeeping in Côte d'Ivoire was in the hands of the gendarmerie, and the Ivorian military was reputed to be the least politically active in Africa.[91] After Houphouët's death, however, this relative inactivity was shattered by political factionalism and civil conflict.

In spite of the implicit protection of some African presidents embodied in the defense agreements, France's military presence inside and outside of the region was not in itself a deterrent to coups d'état. While France had no military interventions between 1964 and 1968, this four-year period included coups d'état in Dahomey, the Central African Republic, Upper Volta, Algeria, Burundi, and Congo-Léopoldville (later Zaïre). Although France did not intervene directly in these cases, French policymakers were concerned about the effects that these disruptions of their carefully cultivated relationships with heads of state would have on the French reputation and French interests. President de Gaulle warned shortly after the coups in CAR and Upper Volta that the new military heads of state in these two countries would need to rule with fairness and apparent legitimacy or risk the loss of what French aid their countries were due from the cooperation agreements. Both military and economic deterrence were threatened, and cooperation funding was held back for a short time until it was established that France would be able to work with the new governments.[92] The fairness and legitimacy of either Colonel Bokassa or Lieutenant Colonel Lamizana as rulers turned out ultimately to be less important to the French than their loyalty to France, and their willingness to cooperate with de Gaulle. Bokassa ousted President Dacko on 1 January 1966 and established his anticommunist credentials, at least temporarily, by ordering all communists and Chinese nationals to leave the Central African Republic (the Chinese were invited back later, bringing economic assistance), and dismissing a number of military officers for collaborating with a "Peoples Army" of the CAR.[93] It has been noted that Dacko may have brought the coup on himself, in part, by encouraging the CAR gendarmerie to act as his personal presidential guard in order to balance the growing power of Bokassa within the army.[94] Bokassa proved to be an obliging partner for France in the beginning, however. In 1967, France airlifted troops to Bangui upon Bokassa's request for protection when he asserted that his austerity program, which included restraints on corruption and civil service salaries, was causing internal hostility.⁹⁵ The Togolese coup of 1963 also represented an instance in which the coup produced a result desired by France in terms of new leaders who were approved by, if not welcomed by, Paris.⁹⁶

Where French Intervention Was Less Effective
The 1963 Niger insurrection is interesting in that it is a case in which the demonstration of French power actually worked *against* France's ability to maintain that power at the same level over the long run. The army mutiny may even have been caused in part by what Decalo calls the paternalism of *Nigerien* leadership, the heavy French administrative presence, and the lack of power given to the indigenous military, many of whom had been educated in France, but who continued to be commanded by French officers. The French commanders had more direct access to President Diori and were clearly monitoring the *Nigerien* army for evidence of subversion. The "direct" French presence in Niger ended in 1965, although as of 1974 there were still 250 French officers and NCOs serving in the *Nigerien* army and gendarmerie, and 1,000 troops from the Forces d'Intervention. In 1974, Kountché's takeover expelled the head of the resident French military mission, and evacuated most of the French military presence.⁹⁷ Niger continued, however, to be enormously dependent on France economically, particularly for the extraction and marketing of strategic minerals.

The hope which accompanied de Gaulle's creation of the Force d'Intervention was that an obvious display of France's willingness to intervene, combined with the continued cultivation of privileged and fruitful relationships between the French *patron* and African client states would forestall as much as possible the need for actual military intervention. As the next chapter will demonstrate, however, several of the client states in Central Africa required military actions during the following decades, and these actions demonstrated a number of the limitations inherent in France's intervention capacity when it came to larger-scale conflicts that had ramifications beyond the francophone nations themselves. Two of these were Chad, engaged in almost two decades of civil war and including interventions not only by France but Libya and other African nations, and the Nigerian Civil War, which demonstrated that French influence was not enough to prevent the largest anglophone nation in the West African region from becoming a regional power in its own right.

The Chad intervention in 1968, which had its roots in the "minor uprisings" of 1963, was the final French intervention in Africa before the death of President de Gaulle. It marked the beginning of France's most serious, long-term, and significant series of military actions in a francophone African state until the recent policy disaster represented by Operation Turquoise in the wake of the Rwandan genocide of 1994.[98] This occurred when the territorial integrity of Chad was breached in 1968 by a revolt in the north. Not intervening in such an instance would have been a blow to the credibility of the Franco-African defense agreements with several countries: the neighboring governments of Niger and the Central African Republic were also concerned about the spread of violence throughout the region. In addition, CAR, Chad, and particularly Niger all held significant uranium deposits[99] which remained of importance to France, although it defended Chad on the principle of "territorial integrity" rather than strategic interest. The Chadian intervention is more fully described in the next chapter because 1968 represented the start of an ongoing problem for France in containing insecurity in Chad and honoring its security agreements with successive victors in the Chadian conflicts.

In the same year, with unintended irony, de Gaulle apparently contradicted the "territorial integrity" principle stated at the outset of the Chad action, and he recommended to the francophone governments of West Africa that they support the secession of Biafra from Nigeria. France never officially recognized the Ojukwu government, but Paris made increased arms transfers to Côte d'Ivoire and Gabon which were intended for further transfer to the government of Biafra. De Gaulle's interest in this conflict lay in his early recognition that anglophone Nigeria was not only a cultural and linguistic rival to French grandeur in West Africa but a potentially strong regional power which would soon be able to compete effectively with France in West Africa as a military and economic rival. In spite of considerable French investment and oil drilling concessions that remained under the control of the Nigerian government, de Gaulle continued his support of Ojukwu. The costs to de Gaulle and France of this intervention were soon evident: diplomatic relations were broken, French oil concessions were suspended, and the francophone states of West Africa were divided concerning the wisdom of the choice that de Gaulle had compelled them to make. Francophone African leaders, and their sympathetic connections within the French government, persuaded de Gaulle to reconsider. Only in the 1980s, with the sale of French military equipment to Nigeria, has some of the lingering resentment between Nigeria and France been repaired.[100] The divisive memory of Côte d'Ivoire's support of Biafra has persisted in inter-African state relations in the form of occasionally strained relationships between the anglophone and francophone states of the Economic Community of West African States (ECOWAS).[101]

France's Ability to Conduct Humanitarian and Peacekeeping Operations

During the 1960s, humanitarian operations and peacekeeping interventions were well within France's capacity for the most part, and France's ongoing military, diplomatic, and intelligence presence facilitated the speed and effectiveness of delivery. Short-term military interventions were preferred, however, as was a consistent level of military and economic aid that forestalled the need for any intervention forces at all. Longer-term interventions during the 1960s were avoided as politically and financially costly (except in Chad), largely because the recent colonial pacification operations in Indochina and Algeria were remembered as expensive, exhausting, and ultimately ineffective.

France had the capacity to offer humanitarian aid to the francophone African countries, but preferred to maintain the internal security and economies of these countries at such a level that large-scale humanitarian disaster aid (e.g., in the not-infrequent event of a drought in the Sahel) was not frequently necessary. French economic and infrastructural aid was defined as humanitarian, but usually occurred in the context of the cooperation agreements, rather than as a reaction to unforeseen events. France was well aware of the politically destabilizing effects of economic hardship, and considered Sahelian droughts and commodity price fluctuations to be enough of a continuing security risk to institute careful financial controls in the Franc Zone and a constant level of various types of assistance.[102] Although France could and would certainly provide humanitarian aid in emergencies, it preferred preventive, rather than reactive measures. The types of aid that current Western governments often refer to as "capacity building" were evident in the areas of agriculture, health, education, business, banking, road construction, and sanitation, and most of it fell within the ongoing contractual arrangements of the cooperation agreements.

The same was somewhat true of France's capacity for military peacekeeping, continuing Lyautey's philosophy of "*Il faut manifester la force pour en éviter l'emploi.*" Preventing the need for too-frequent policing of warring parties was built into the very notion of French presence. During the 1960s, France conducted a number of successful small-scale operations which it defined as peacekeeping, including most of the interventions listed earlier, because these largely involved riot suppression and the containment of internal disturbances. The operations which the French called "peacekeeping" were more accurately pacification operations which preserved French power in the region by maintaining leaders in power who acted in the French interest most of the time. Any humanitarian aid delivered in the context of such operations was secondary to the overall military peacekeeping objectives.

However, large-scale peacekeeping operations requiring thousands of intervention troops over the long term continued to be unpopular in Paris during this decade and after. In Chad, starting late in the 1960s, the internally warring parties had enough external support to make France's peacekeeping operation into a long-term campaign with sporadic increases and decreases in troops and equipment. France tried to minimize her presence in Chad, using only as many troops and as much equipment as was politically tolerable at home at any given time. Although France maintained some control over Chad, and slowed the progress of the various warring parties, it was unable to stop the Chadian rebellion completely.

Part Two: Other Resources and Constraints That Affected French Power in Postindependence Francophone West Africa

France's Nonmilitary Power Resources

After African independence in 1960, France not only preserved its preponderant military power in the former sub-Saharan colonies but its economic power and political power as well. This economic and political influence also contained an element of cultural exportation, which facilitated the African assimilation (at least on the part of elites) of some useful and powerful French preferences in business, education, and governance. Economic and political leverage was combined with military power in such a way as to reinforce continuing dependence on France. France's economic leverage in francophone Africa during the final fifteen years of the colonial period had been overwhelming, and what Foltz calls "the usual signs of colonial economic dependence" was visible as late as 1956, a condition which improved very little during the 1960s. Foreign trade remained the export of raw materials for manufactured items, and domestic capital accumulation was minimal. Imports dominated exports, with France making up the cash deficit.[103]

Economic Leverage

The new francophone African economies were all the more completely dependent on France because of the Franc Zone, an arrangement put in place after World War II that bound the African and French economies almost inextricably to one another. The zone was a monetary transaction association under French fiscal control which included most of France's former colonies after World War II. The African nations that remained in association with France stayed in the zone after independence and continued to use its currency as their national currency. African leaders accepted this arrangement in order to insure the benefits that their financial stability as members of the zone brought to their national economies. The zone would not necessarily make them rich, but it was a certain hedge against total impoverishment. Many of the francophone African economies were heavily dependent on cash crop production, and membership in the zone lessened the severity of agricultural crises while also providing a secure environment for foreign investors and (largely French) multinational corporations.

The zone included the Communauté Financière Africaine or CFA. The CFA Franc (CFAF) was pegged to the French Franc (FF), freely convertible into other hard currencies and transferable throughout the zone. The CFAF was issued in two forms, one by the monetary union of the West African states and one by the monetary union of the Equatorial (Central) African States. During the first two decades after independence, more of the francophone states achieved limited but steady growth rates, comparatively low inflation rates and more open economies than the nonfrancophone states. They also remained heavily dependent on the French economy and banking system, and continued French investment. The occasional threat posed by France (occasionally a real need) to devalue the CFAF offered France a significant bargaining chip in its relationships with these countries, although any decision to devalue the CFAF was fraught with consequences for France as well.[104]

African leaders were given access to investment opportunities in Europe that allowed them the proper lifestyles to maintain presidential prestige, augmented by easy private access to foreign aid money. These resources were also useful for patronage of loyal elites, and they established the domestic power bases of a number of francophone African presidents.

Political Penetration of African States

After independence, the ongoing development neediness and endemic debt of the African nations, combined with France's participation in African parastatal companies, agricultural concerns, manufacturing, banking, mining, petroleum extraction, telecommunications, transportation, and other economic concerns, ensured an interlocking network of obligation and investment that was as necessary to French political interests as it was to the functioning of francophone African economies and governments. Diplomatic and economic *coopérants* were also, frequently enough, operatives in the intelligence network, and, because they were placed in situations in which they had a considerable policy-making voice in African governments, the intelligence presence was never solely a military one, although it certainly enhanced France's strategic position. Within the cooperation agreements, economic demands could be met in return for military concessions. In those countries without military bases or full-scale defense agreements, the cooperative Assistance Militaire Technique agreements left room to insure opportunities for intelligence, strategic placement of various kinds of military and nonmilitary *coopérants*, an early warning system for potential conflicts or leadership changes, and numerous ways for France to use development aid, the economic interests of African leaders, arms transfers, and other incentives as political leverage.

This situation was one of the more pervasive historical vestiges of France's political penetration of African leadership and parties during the final colonial period, which was no less significant than its economic penetration. During the period just before independence, what Foltz calls "patron parties" with more traditional power bases such as local chiefs, wealthy traders, religious leaders, or members of the colonial administration, were preferred by French administrators, and they received privileged access to French resources. "Mass parties," those based on common political ideologies with a universalistic (principle-based) rather than exclusive (patronage-based) membership, were considered more potentially divisive and often a security risk, and they were discouraged by France. Nonetheless, mass parties had a significant influence on the preindependence nationalist movements, partly because they still needed a territorial power base in order to have any influence on Paris. The patron parties, in turn, often found that they needed to deemphasize their local particularistic ties in order to achieve the larger support required to hold territorial or even interterritorial offices.[105] As the distinctions between the two party types became blurred, France became adept at manipulating the local, regional, and territorial power bases and interests of African leaders in order to exploit political divisions like those between future presidents Senghor of Senegal and Houphouët-Boigny of Côte d'Ivoire.

Throughout the 1950s, France was able to control local elections in the colonies well enough to discourage the more radical nationalists from achieving any real power base.[106] France managed to prevent a pan-Africanist strategy for independence from taking precedence over the eventual, more manageable plan which left France in its leadership role over a group of relatively small, weak new states whose only unifying force was the need for French support. In fact, there could have been a solid bloc of African swing votes in the French National Assembly if the Africans had been able to organize without risk to their own positions. There was said to be an "unwritten rule" during the colonial period parliaments, however, that overseas deputies should "behave like good Frenchmen" by not interfering in the affairs of the metropole, and they should always vote with the metropolitan party to which they were affiliated. African party members did so even when they privately disagreed with their party's position, as many did regarding Algeria. Senghor and Houphouët both knew that, although they had an occasional voice in the Council of Ministers attached to the National Assembly, Africa policy was made primarily and finally in the French Overseas Ministry. Senghor concentrated on maintaining his influence at this ministry, by consulting with them on education matters.[107] Since these two most influential West African leaders had both achieved power (in spite of their disagreements) as participating members of the French political system, and they were not the only African leaders whose power bases included influential members of the French parliament and successive cabinets, French "penetration" of political leaders may be said to have been achieved partly by allowing Africans to penetrate, in the limited fashion allowed by *assimilation*, the French domestic political scene.

France was able not only to discourage Senegal from participating at the first Bamako conference (by having the minister for Overseas France pressure his fellow Socialists Guèye and Senghor not to attend[108]) but also some other African political groups as well. In addition, members of the French Socialist Party were appointed to the Governorship of Côte d'Ivoire and also to the Governor-Generalship of the West African Federation in order to strengthen more moderate ties to Houphouet, and discourage the affiliation which Houphouet's RDA had made with the French Communist Party. By mid-1950, Houphouet had been convinced to cut off the French Communist Party in order to cement his position as the future president of his country. This was done by none other than François Mitterand, whose presidency of France is discussed in the next chapter, and who was at that time minister of Overseas France.[109] This incident not only cemented a connection which remained valuable to both future presidents of France and Côte d'Ivoire in later years but also helped France politically with anticommunists in the U.S. government whom it wished at the time to impress. Houphouët's strategy of independence for individual colonies as political units won out over Senghor's desire for a more regional power structure. The preindependence Loi Cadre, which divided French West Africa into many small, relatively weak proto-states ("balkanizing" them in Senghor's phrase[110]), perpetuated their dependency on France and made such political manipulation (via the threat of withdrawal of political influence in Paris, and of economic assistance) much more effective.

The Political Advantages of Exporting French Preferences: Cultural Assimilation

Francophone Africa provided ample evidence that French culture could be exported as profitably as French arms. There was even a cultural argument in favor of retaining Africa within France's sphere of influence, which, although no longer framed as France's *mission civilisatrice*, remained an important component in the maintenance of French power in Africa. French political independence was often conjoined rhetorically with France's own cultural distinctiveness, with each aspect justifying and supporting the other. As Chipman[111] puts it: "While evidence of an ability to control others or to impose conditions on their behaviour would always be necessary to prove that power had been wielded, the fact of French civilization was often put forward, during the nineteenth century, as itself evidence of the existence of power. If French civilization was influential, so was the French state." In the nineteenth century, when cultural influences were becoming rapidly globalized, the French already believed that a culture that was not exported would stagnate. The *mission civilisatrice*, and the continued promotion of French culture after independence, were not simply the export of the products of French culture, but of the organizational structures (in the military, law, religion, education, business and politics) that would transform colonial subjects into first, consumers, and then reproducers of this culture.[112]

This "*assimilation*" of Africans into France[113] started out as an intentional colonial security policy against the total loss of its imperial possessions. "Assimilation," however, was and remains limited by how much real assimilation of Africans France itself can tolerate and still remain in control of (or feel superior to) its dependent peoples. During the postwar era, if what was assimilated made French power insecure (e.g., the ideals of French communists, or even the political power aspirations of educated African *evolués*), assimilation was limited or discouraged altogether. West African *evolués*, in turn, learned that, the more "French" their behavior appeared, the more individual benefits came their way, that is, unless they asked for too much at once, or on behalf of too many of their fellow Africans. African colonial politicians, like Senghor and Houphouët-Boigny, who learned how to manipulate such a system of double standards, did well for themselves over the long run, and managed to accomplish a great deal for their new nations as well.

An especially selective limit was placed on the cultural absorption process in the realm of political leadership. French democracy in full measure remained an ideal to be delayed in the colonies so that the French could maintain control for as long as possible over the political process. Under French rule, a tiny number of Africans were allowed to participate in politics by adding their minority voice to the politics of the metropole in the French National Assembly, as Léopold Senghor and Félix Houphouët-Boigny did, both becoming heads of state. After independence, authoritarian forms of government (like Houphouet's) were both tolerated and supported by the French in most of the countries of their former empire. This gradualist delay was woven into the *mission civilisatrice*: The early colonial policy of *assimilation*, defined as the indoctrination of non-French peoples into French culture and the political body of France itself,[114] gave way quickly to *association*, on the basis of fraternity but not equality,[115] and a relationship of continued patronage and dependency. Francophone Africans were apparently French enough to fight for France in Indochina, consume French wine, write French literature, and contribute to French political campaigns,[116] but not yet considered quite French enough to govern themselves as democrats, even after independence, in part because the authoritarian leaders of Africa were such useful and reliable partners in France's global policy. In return, if France wished to remain a global power, it needed the *cooperation* of those same leaders.

France also provided some of the more attractive visual trappings of power to its African clients, not only to make them happy with French patronage but also to demonstrate the benefits of French friendship to those African nations whose loyalties might be slipping, or to those who had not experienced French rule but might benefit from French patronage. Uniforms for the gendarmerie, joint Franco-African troop exercises with much ceremony, presidential jets, and other visual perquisites of official power often arrived accompanied by some of the less visible manifestations of French power, such as the Foccart intelligence network, and the continued French administrative presence that came with Assistance Militaire Technique. Each of the capitals generally had an "Avenue Charles de Gaulle" and streets named for other French presidents.

Ironically, the form taken by French democracy during the Fifth Republic may have had a powerfully "assimilative" influence on the forms of presidential authority which have appeared in its former colonies. De Gaulle's firm belief in the need to centralize the executive power of the French presidency, protecting it from partisan factionalism and political interference, has been mirrored or distorted by numerous francophone African presidencies whose commitment to that other French political ideal, multiple-party democracy, has been either cosmetic or nonexistent. Authoritarian presidencies like those of Houphouët-Boigny of Côte-d'Ivoire, Omar Bongo of Gabon, and Jean-Bédel Bokassa of the Central African Republic have not only been tolerated but actively supported by France, with little pretense of encouraging evolution toward the French model of parliamentary participation in democratic government.

The French presidency itself has, within a democratic structure, incorporating popular participation, maintained a significant measure of independence and autonomous authority compared with the presidencies of other democratic states. This independence is particularly striking with regard to French policy first toward the African colonies and then toward the new African francophone nations. France's Africa policy has remained until the mid-1990s centralized in the Elysée in a ministry with immediate and often intimate ties to the French presidency. Personal relationships between Charles de Gaulle, François Mitterand, other members of the French military and political elite, and francophone African leaders like Houphouët-Boigny, Senghor of Senegal, and Mba and Bongo of Gabon, began during the period between the world wars, were cemented during the Free French period and continued to be cultivated after independence because they were a useful feature of the Franco-African relationship which gave some leverage to all parties.

Jean-François Bayart describes an interesting aspect of this phenomenon: the relationships which were cemented into place by Africans who attended non-military schools in France. Houphouët-Boigny sent 150 such scholars from Côte d'Ivoire to France in 1946, one of whom was Thérèse Brou, his future wife. She studied in Villeneuve-sur-Lot, the mayor of which was later appointed French ambassador to Côte d'Ivoire, remaining in that post for fifteen years. In addition, a number of French citizens have been appointed to positions in the Ivorian government, including Raphaël Saller, who was a colonial senator in Guinea and became Houphouët's minister of the economy, finance and planning at independence. Senegal, Niger, Chad, the Central African Republic, and Gabon have all employed French citizens in government posts.[117] Beginning in 1945, the French had seven-year *lycées* (high schools) in every colony, as well as four-year *collèges*. Examinations were administered by the University of Bordeaux and the diplomas were valid in France as well as in Africa. Standards were much higher in these secondary schools than in the primary schools, however, and admission was extremely restrictive and competitive. By 1946, the French government was also granting scholarships to Africans for higher education in France. By the end of the Fourth Republic, there were at least 400 such scholarship holders in French schools, along with a number of other Africans who were there without scholarships.[118] The small group of often influential Africans educated in this manner frequently maintained their French school friendships and business connections, and they used them to increase their own political or economic influence at home. There were reciprocal benefits to France from streamlined political connections with this cadre of sympathetic elites in the new African nations.

France's Freedom of Action, Given Domestic Political Constraints
France's Africa policy was directed almost entirely by the executive branch of government, and it was influenced very little by any ministry other than the Ministry of Cooperation, by domestic parliamentary debate, or by the

French public's opinion of various interventions. In general, de Gaulle did not need parliamentary approval to conduct the interventions of the 1960s. There remained one significant military limitation, however, in that both public opinion and French law did restrain the president from sending French conscripts onto non-French soil except under extraordinary circumstances, and then only with the blessing of the legislature. This placed significant logistical and manpower constraints on France's ability to conduct large-scale military interventions. It also required the military to actively encourage volunteer enlistment, and also to maintain, train, and improve the all-volunteer Foreign Legion at a highly functional level as professional intervention specialists.

French domestic political constraints on Africa policy after 1960 also included competition for parts of the military budget from government arms research and development (building up France's naval, air, ground, and nuclear capabilities in Europe), and the continuing attempts on the part of the French president and parliament to place restraints on one another's ability to make policy. Once France made the decision to become a nuclear power, nuclear expenditures received priority. (France needed to do much of this work from the ground up, reinventing the wheel — or rather the bomb, because of the United States's nonproliferation concerns.)

The various military program laws after 1960 represented successive plans for modernizing all levels of French forces from the nuclear weapons to the infantry. However, early concentration on the *force de frappe* constrained some of the budget which might have been offered to the other parts of the armed services.[119] These decisions affected the military cooperation assistance offered to African governments as well, and made their promises to assist France in whatever way possible to secure their own region and support France's international policies all the more important. Also, because modernization of the ground forces to be deployed in the former colonies was delayed by the nuclear budget commitments, the missions which these forces carried out were still performed during the 1960s much as they had been in the 1950s, and they were unintegrated with the Europe-focused nuclear deterrence policy.[120]

International Regimes and Institutions That Either Supported or Worked against France's Objectives

France needed to reshape its strategic policies in the years after the 1960s in order to take into account the increasing number of regional and international regimes and institutions that might offer either opportunities or threats to French interests in the African region. The Organization of African Unity, founded in 1963, and the United Nations, were relatively ineffective during the period of this case study, although they became more important during the period of the second case study. International human rights organizations began to be active during the period, including Amnesty International, founded in 1961 to promote the goals of the International Declaration of Human Rights, but they had only just begun during this period to have an influence on the way human rights questions were framed in African politics. While intergovernmental (IGO) and nongovernmental (NGO) organizations provided new fora in which to raise issues related to governance in the new nations, these were not yet powerful enough to have a substantial influence on French policy in the region. The OAU's participation in Chad in the 1970s was limited, and it was influenced substantially by the interests of the wealthier and more powerful countries in the region (particularly Nigeria and Libya).

The increasing number of regular summit conferences by francophone heads of state has been an important regional institution. It was established by Pompidou's first invitation to African heads of state, and it was welcomed by African governments, which found the summits a useful venue for putting pressure on France as well as for presenting their positions. Social links among these heads of state include shared military experiences, relationships formed in those universities and schools which were open to Africans (like the École William Ponty near Dakar which educated a large number of the Africans in the colonial civil service who achieved political power before and during independence[121]), and French freemasonry, which has many members among African elites and heads of state, including President Omar Bongo of Gabon.[122]

Francophone Influence in a Regional Intergovernmental Organization: The Case of Liberia

The time frame of this chapter has not provided numerous examples of effective regional organizations which have had a major impact on strategic policy in West Africa. However, one regional organization has provided an interesting forum that tests the ability of francophone and anglophone nations of West Africa to work together. This forum, the Economic Community of West African States (ECOWAS), was created out of the political resources and rivalries visible in West Africa in the 1960s and early 1970s, but its first major military test arrived a decade and a half later in Liberia. Since this case concerns West Africa, however, and since the Liberian war was in many ways a *continuation* of conflicts which had been an inherent part of the regional atmosphere since the colonial period, a brief examination of the Liberia case highlighting French and francophone security interests is useful here, even though these events occurred well after the immediate post-independence period. Note that francophone linguistic unity, and pressure from France, could not guarantee that all francophone countries would make the same political decisions.

ECOWAS, founded in 1975 and containing as members both French and English-speaking West African countries, has been a testing ground for Nigeria and Côte d'Ivoire's ambitions as regional powers. ECOWAS members signed a Non-Aggression Treaty which was to form the moral platform for the ECOMOG peacekeeping force in Liberia.[123] ECOWAS was a fairly low-profile economic organization until its Liberian intervention in the early 1990s, which gave it a higher profile as a regional actor, in spite of the anglophone/francophone divisions.

Charles Taylor's insurgent armies in Liberia not only included Liberians but also Burkinabés (from Burkina Faso) and Ivorians, as well as some rebel Gambians, Ghanaians, and Sierra Leonians whose home countries were concerned about their Libyan training and their possible return home to be destabilizing elements in their own countries. ECOWAS's proposed intervention force, the ECOWAS Monitoring Group (ECOMOG), was to be three-quarters Nigerian in 1993,[124] and it later included armed forces members from Ghana, Guinea, Gambia, and Sierra Leone. To insure regional balance among the ECOWAS countries, ECOMOG was monitored by a committee with members from Togo, Gambia, Senegal, Guinea-Bissau, and Côte d'Ivoire. It was originally a mediating and peacekeeping force, and not intended for offensive action, although offensive air attacks by ECOMOG against Taylor's forces were observed early on.[125]

The first ECOMOG contingent landed at Monrovia in August 1990. Taylor opened fire, calling them a "Nigerian invasion force." The impartiality of ECOMOG was questioned by a number of the francophone members of ECOWAS, and Togo, Côte d'Ivoire, and Burkina Faso refused to contribute troops, although Mali and Senegal did. Initial troop strength was about 4,000, growing to 12,000 by 1993. The impartial mission of ECOMOG was questioned by a number of the francophone members of ECOWAS, several of whom (including Togo, and Taylor's Ivorian and Burkinabé allies) refused to contribute troops. When it became clear to those outside of West Africa that ECOMOG had never been an impartial monitor, the United Nations established the United Nations Observer Mission in Liberia (UNOMIL), composed of 303 military observers with administrative and medical support[126] Côte d'Ivoire initially opposed UN involvement but later welcomed it when it was clear that ECOWAS as a regional body was unable to play any real peacekeeping role, or even balance Nigeria's influence. In 1994, ECOMOG was expanded to almost

19,000 with the addition of battalions from Tanzania, Uganda, and Zimbabwe, the first non-ECOWAS African countries to contribute to ECOMOG. At this time, the first official troop strengths for the Liberian groups were reported as 60,000 for Taylor's NPFL, 8,000 for the interim government's armed forces, and 12,000 for the group of warlords allied to the interim government, and opposing Taylor.[127] By fall of 1995, however, ECOMOG's troop strength was down again to 7,200 and ECOWAS was requesting an increase.

Opposing concerns of the francophone and anglophone blocs in the ECOWAS nations, and the shifting relationship between the United States and Libya, led to alliances and levels of military support that enabled Charles Taylor to invade at a time when Doe's outside support was on the wane. Zartman suggests that civil conflicts like Liberia's are under "constant pressure to internationalize."[128] The relationship changed when the internal conflict between Doe's government and Taylor's NPFL became internationalized with the addition of Côte d'Ivoire and Burkina Faso, and the later addition of ECOWAS and Nigeria. Conflicting coalition possibilities appeared, interstate relations were affected, and the conflict became more intractable. Since Côte d'Ivoire and Burkina Faso were in opposition to Doe's regime before the NPFL was in existence, the external conflict may have existed alongside of the original internal one during the same time period.[129] Libya originally supported Samuel Doe, but it disliked Doe's subsequent overtures to the United States in search of hard currency. Libya, Côte d'Ivoire, and Burkina Faso encouraged dissidents within Doe's junta, and then supported Taylor himself, whose forces went to Tripoli for training, returning to Burkina Faso to prepare their attack.[130] Houphouët-Boigny of Côte d'Ivoire also never forgave Doe for executing not only President Tolbert but Tolbert's son, who was Houphouët's son-in-law. This daughter, after the death of Tolbert's son, became a close friend of another Libyan ally, President Blaise Compaoré of Burkina Faso.[131]

Nigeria's strength in West Africa balanced that of Côte d'Ivoire aided by Libya, causing conflict even in a corner of Africa where the United States and France were assumed to be the guarantors of regional peace (although neither the United States or France offered any support other than financial assistance). These regional rivalries exacerbated what started out as a civil war, while client-patron relationships on the part of several of the Liberian factions with the more powerful regional actors (Babangida of Nigeria, Houphouët of Côte d'Ivoire, and Qaddafi of Libya) allowed these internal rivalries to be used by outsiders as proxies to promote their own international interests. The United States assisted ECOMOG financially in order to balance the ambitions of Libya (and thereby the Soviet bloc) in the region, including the prevention of further Libyan meddling in conflicts in the Middle East as well as Africa.

The continuing presence of France as regional guarantor of the West African francophone economies was a threat to Nigeria's desire, as the richest and most populous state in the region, to promote a *Pax Nigeriana*.

Therefore, in spite of the presence of international organizations such as ECOWAS and the OAU, West Africa in the early 1990s remained a regional system defined by lingering aspects of the Cold War, and by linguistic rivalries and national boundaries dating from the colonial past which continued to determine regional polarities. Although the anglophone-francophone rivalry allowed other countries in the region to coalesce around the two most powerful, populous, and resource-rich countries (Nigeria and Côte d'Ivoire), the simmering conflict between the United States and Libya provided a competing polarity. Houphouët's Côte d'Ivoire, as a bastion of capitalism supported by France and driven by foreign investment, makes a very odd ally indeed for Qaddafi's *Jamahirya*, especially given what had happened in the 1980s in Chad. Yet these strange bedfellows landed temporarily on the same side, as each of them supported Taylor's effort for broadly dissimilar reasons. Also, even with the francophone-anglophone polarity in evidence, the looseness of these linguistic bonds allowed Senegal and Mali to join ECOMOG, and considerable shifting around within ECOWAS in terms of alliances and political maneuvering. It remains to be see what kind of influence a regional organization like ECOWAS will have in the future, given this initial military outing, but there are indications from the Liberian war that francophone unity may no longer be the primary determinant of regional alliance patterns.

Other Great Powers Active and Capable of Intervening in the Region

Other great powers were active in francophone Africa, providing arms, training, and financial assistance, but they were not really inclined to intervene militarily or to try to replace France as the most influential political and economic power in any part of the *chasse gardée* during the 1960s. The exception is perhaps Zaïre, which was not yet truly within France's sphere of influence. (The U.S. Central Intelligence Agency and Belgium's interventions there are examined in chapter 6.) Throughout the first ten years of independence, the dependency of these countries on France was truly striking. Although Guinea went its own way, taking help from the Soviet Union and rejecting France, it served more as an object lesson than as a role model, and even Dahomey and Mali, which had left-leaning tendencies, never entirely rejected French assistance and the obligations which came with it. Therefore, although other great powers would certainly have been capable of intervening in the region by force of arms had there been a compelling reason of state to do so (as was argued in Zaïre), their influence would have lacked the historical advantages accruing to the French from over a hundred years of military, political, economic, and cultural patronage and cliency. Consequently, the other great powers paid relatively little attention to those countries which, in their eyes, were still under France's influence or outright protection.

The Regional Military Presence of European States
Many of the British West African states achieved independence during the same period, and independence in those colonies was also largely a matter of transferring command of the local armed forces to the newly independent states. As in francophone Africa, British officers remained in many of the command positions, however, this condition did not persist nearly as long as it did in the former French colonies, nor were their former colonies' economic and political ties with London as strong or persistent as those of the francophone states with Paris. While Britain has maintained diplomatic and arms trade links with her former African colonies, notably through the Commonwealth, its agreements with these nations have not been nearly as all-encompassing a political factor in their postindependence development as have the links maintained by France with the francophone nations. The French military cooperation agreements are clearly a factor in the maintenance of these ties.[132]

Regional power politics and global politics can be factors in interpreting the cooperation agreements as well. The British-French rivalry of the early colonial period has persisted, but it has been transformed into a set of linguistically-based alliances. The public rivalry between anglophone and francophone influences in Africa continues to this day in spite of the independent status of Britain and France's former colonies on the continent. "Proxy" relationships were evident, where the United States, the USSR, and European nations provided diplomatic, intelligence, training, and financial and arms aid to friendly African counterparts, without contributing actual troops. The Nigerian civil war of the Biafran secession in the 1960s was one example of francophone-anglophone rivalry, as Côte d'Ivoire and other francophone nations in West Africa supported Biafran independence at France's request, at times channeling French support to Biafra. The lingering resentment that this support caused between the anglophone and francophone West African nations translated decades later into francophone (and particularly Ivorian) support for Liberia's insurgent Charles Taylor, when Taylor's main regional opposition was coming from the ECOMOG forces led by Nigeria.[133]

By the end of the first postindependence decade in 1970,[134] only three Western European countries were listed by IISS as having a significant troop strength on the African continent. France had a total of 12,500 troops stationed in various parts of its former colonies. Spain had 27,000 troops, all of which were in Spanish Sahara, or Ceuta and Melilla. Portugal had 125,000 troops, all in Angola, Mozambique, and Portuguese Guinea. Spain and Portugal maintained a very large military presence in Africa in order to retain their colonies, which were not to achieve independence until 1975. Of the three, France was the only one with a significant troop presence based in nations that had been politically independent for ten years.

The Regional Military Presence of the Soviet Union and Other Communist States

Soviet military aid in francophone Africa, as in the rest of Africa, was tied closely to the USSR's foreign policy goals of supporting independence movements and linking ideology and policy with the nationalism of emerging states. Communist doctrine largely took a back seat to pragmatic concerns, such as gaining a foothold for Soviet interests, hence Soviet willingness to support a monarchy like Ethiopia with economic aid, and pro-Western Nigeria with military aid, during the postindependence period. Sub-Saharan Africa remained a fairly low priority to the USSR, however, with a few exceptions where potentially powerful states like Ethiopia and Nigeria were concerned, or where influence could be tied directly to ideological commonality. The francophone states, with the exception of those with leftward-leaning regimes, were more difficult to penetrate during this period because of the comprehensiveness of the military cooperation agreements that most of the francophone colonies had signed with France. Even where leftist governments provided openings for the USSR (as in Congo-Brazzaville or Mali), French influence predominated, and France's tolerance toward socialism allowed it to maneuver pragmatically and often successfully among its socialist former colonies.[135]

Guinea, having rejected the French Community, was the first, and really the only, francophone West African nation to give the USSR, along with other Eastern bloc allies, a real opportunity for military, and economic penetration. When de Gaulle withdrew all military, technical, and economic cooperation, President Sekou Touré first asked the United States for aid, was refused, and accepted an offer of arms and military advisers from Czechoslovakia early in 1959. Russian advisers and technicians followed in 1960, as did a sizeable loan (at least $3 million, not including some arms already received from the USSR).[136]

A number of francophone African military personnel were also trained in the USSR and Eastern Europe. Between 1955 and 1979, 505 Congolese, 30

Dahomeyans, 75 Burundians, 885 Guineans, and 360 Malians were trained in the USSR, and 85 Congolese, 60 Guineans, and 10 Malians trained in Eastern Europe, mostly in East Germany. The number of Soviet trainees was far higher, of course, from more strategically important states like Libya (1,310), Ethiopia (1,290), and Somalia (2,395), and more in line with the numbers of African allies that France was training during the period.[137] The Chinese during the same period trained the following francophone African military personnel in China: 125 Cameroonians, 415 Congolese, 360 Guineans, 50 Malians, 55 Togolese, and 175 Zaïrians.[138] Given that this represents a significant number of Communist trainees for these countries, it is particularly interesting that France was able to remain the primary military guarantor in most cases, and the Eastern bloc and Chinese influence remained a peripheral irritant in the *chasse gardée*.

The Regional Military Presence of the United States

The United States trained a number of sub-Saharan Africans in its IMET and FMS programs during the 1960s and 1970s, but very few from the francophone nations, with the notable exception of Zaïre, which had 160 trainees in 1971, and sent between 50–100 yearly throughout the 1970s.[139] In spite of its earlier refusal of Touré, estimated United States military aid to Guinea during the period 1956–1967 was about $1 million. U.S. aid went during this period to potential political opponents, as well as to politically friendly governments, in order to counter Soviet influence. The United States also sent the following amounts of aid during the 1956–1967 period to francophone African governments:

Dahomey (later Benin)	$0.1 million
Côte d'Ivoire	$0.1 million
Mali	$2.8 million
Niger	$0.1 million
Senegal	$2.6 million
Upper Volta (later Burkina Faso)	$0.1 million
Cameroon:	$0.2 million
Congo-Kinshasa (later Zaïre)	$16.1 million

The aid given to Congo-Kinshasa reflects the fact that the United States was very much involved there both militarily and politically during the conflicts that attended the independence of this former Belgian colony, which was not yet as much under French influence as it became later under Mobutu Sese Seko. However, the Congo intervention was the last major U.S. military intervention in sub-Saharan Africa until the Soviets became active in Angola, and the United States entered that conflict in 1975.[140] The military aid figures to the other countries, all former French colonies, is extremely small compared to both aid from France to these countries during the period and to aid given outside of sub-Saharan Africa by both the United States and the USSR. Compare, for the same period, the aid given to Thailand ($600 million) or Ecuador ($29 million). Africa during this period received 2 percent of the U.S. military aid budget, and 1 percent of the Soviet military aid budget. (The Middle East received 48 percent of both the United States and the USSR's military aid budgets, and Latin America—the African continent's closest competitor—got 14 percent of the United States and 13 percent of the Soviet military aid budgets respectively.)[141]

Sub-Saharan Africa was not, during the 1960s, a scene of intense United States versus USSR military aid competition, except for Ethiopia and Somalia. Most francophone recipients relied on one of the two but not both, and then only to supplement aid from France. Those former French colonies receiving U.S. aid generally got no Soviet aid, except for Mali and Guinea, which received aid from both.[142] Congo-Brazzaville received Soviet aid, but it remained under significant enough French economic influence to make the Soviets peripheral players there by the 1990s.

Arms Transfers to Francophone Africa by France and Other Nations

France's arms transfers to the *chasse gardée* during the 1960s concentrated noticeably on infantry weapons and the lighter artillery, but France also sent weapons to many more of the francophone countries than its nearest competitors, remaining their primary source of supply during the period. The scale of the transfers was modest in scope, but France maintained a near-monopoly on transfers to her former colonies. After 1978, French arms transfers increased in both quantities and level of sophistication.[143] Here are some data on arms sales to francophone Africa by the principal armorer nations during the decade just after independence. For comparative purposes, look at the change in the character and number of arms sales to the region by the same sellers (and a few others) during the 1970s and 1980s, which is provided in this same section of the next chapter. Note also that the character of the arms transferred by China and the USSR tended to be heavier (e.g., more antiaircraft and antitank weapons).

These figures make clear that, although some items were sent to these countries by the United States and the USSR, the most consistent supplier

Table 5.3. Arms Transfers to Francophone African Countries, 1960–1969

France, to
Dahomey	Infantry weapons, mortars, and a few 105mm howitzers
Upper Volta	Infantry weapons and mortars
Cameroon	Infantry weapons including mortars and field howitzers
Cent. African Rep.	Infantry weapons and mortars
Chad	Infantry weapons and mortars
Congo-Brazzaville	Infantry weapons (at independence) and a few guns
Gabon	Infantry weapons and mortars
Côte d'Ivoire	Infantry weapons and mortars
Madagascar	Infantry weapons, mortars, and some light artillery
Niger	Infantry weapons, mortars, and rocket launchers
Senegal	Infantry weapons, mortars, and rocket launchers
Togo	Infantry weapons, mortars, and rocket launchers

Great Britain,* to
Upper Volta	A few scout cars
Cent. African Rep.	A few armored cars

Belgium, to
Burundi	
Cameroon	} A few antitank rocket launchers
Rwanda	
Zaïre	Infantry weapons

USSR, to
Guinea	45 medium tanks, 35 armored vehicles, 40–60 armored personnel carriers, small numbers of artillery pieces and anti-tank guns, infantry weapons, and 7 surface-to-air missiles
(some	weapons may be Chinese or Czech in origin)
Mali	45 medium tanks, 40 armored personnel carriers, light artillery pieces, and infantry weapons

China, to
Cameroon	Light antiaircraft guns, rocket launchers and light antitank guns

Czechoslovakia, to
Guinea	Infantry weapons (these were sent after 1960, in addition to more substantial transfers after Guinean independence in 1959)

United States, to
Upper Volta	A few armored cars
Cameroon	A few armored cars and armored personnel carriers
Madagascar	A few armored personnel carriers
Niger	A few armored vehicles
Senegal	A few field guns
Togo	10 armored cars
Zaïre	Infantry weapons

Sources: Bayrham (1986: 228–49) and Joshua & Gibert (1969: 34).[144]
*Most British arms transfers were to anglophone Africa.

of the former French African colonies was France, and infantry arms and training remained the highest priority for French security purposes in the region. Arms transfers by the United States and USSR continued to favor clients chosen for their strategic value, rather than for their historic relationship to their patron. For France, however, history and strategy were still inextricably intertwined.

France also, for the most part, was willing to teach Africans how to operate what it sent, and how to fix it, even if *what* was sent was not of the greatest complexity. In contrast, in spite of the large amounts of Soviet military "training" and the generally greater sophistication of the arms sent, the USSR remained reluctant to transfer much of the technical knowledge that would have helped African recipients maintain their equipment by themselves. The USSR's preference was to send Soviet repairmen (and often Soviet pilots to fly the MIGs themselves), and to use spare parts and repairs as a means to control the actions of their aid recipients. This kind of diplomatic manipulation alienated a number of the USSR's African clients, notably Guinea.[145]

As demonstrated by large numbers of Soviet and Cuban "technicians" (who were often troops), arms transfers and the opportunities offered to Africans for military training in the USSR, China and East Germany mentioned earlier, other powers did offer economic and military aid in a number of ways, but less than they might have had France not been in the picture. They also provided teachers, agricultural specialists, and other infrastructural support, but again, not on the scale of France. France's own tolerance of socialism remained much greater than that of the Atlantic allies. This tolerance proved to be a political advantage in holding on to states which might otherwise have gone completely into the Soviet sphere of influence. The clearest illustration of this phenomenon comes from Central, and not West Africa: the former People's Republic of Congo.

Samuel Decalo says of Marxist (often more Maoist) Congo-Brazzaville that it provided a fascinating early contrast in rhetoric and pragmatic alliances: "Nowhere in Africa is international capitalism more roundly and consistently vilified at home, and at the same time so assiduously courted abroad."[146] Congo declared itself Marxist in 1963 under the moderate socialist Massemba-Debat, who toppled Fulbert Youlou's government largely because the small Congolese army, mostly commanded by French officers, refused to help Youlou. (Youlou resigned on de Gaulle's command, reportedly telephoning him to say, *"J'ai signé, mon général."*) The Congolese army helped preside over the transition. In spite of early assistance from Cuba, China, and the USSR, most of Congo-Brazzaville's leadership throughout the 1960s and 1970s "proceeded with the same deferential attitude to France and foreign-capital markets as Youlou's ministers." Congolese leaders did play off the various Soviet-bloc and Chinese aid sources against one another, but nearly always in accord with France's wishes.[147]

Cuba, China, and the USSR continued to provide significant military aid (weapons and advisers) to various factions within the Congolese military and also to sympathetic political and ideological cliques among Congolese politicians (some of whom had their own paramilitary militias), but, although these clashed occasionally, and the Massemba-Debat government's continued maintenance of French ties was strongly criticized in Brazzaville, France, never lost its foothold in Congo. Indeed, when the far less moderate Marien Ngouabi took over from Massemba-Debat in 1969, and declared Congo a People's Republic, nationalizing several French enterprises, the economy remained effectively under French control in spite of the rhetoric. Ngouabi continued to juggle the factions with their various leftist aid donors, but his attempts to control the state made Congo effectively more militarized than Marxist. Many powerful figures in his government remained pro-French, including Colonel Jacques-Joachim Yhombi-Opango, who succeeded Africa's (arguably) most preeminent Marxist martyr as president when Ngouabi was assassinated in 1977. Yhombi's successor, Denis Sassou-Nguesso, billed himself as a hard-line Marxist, but made good use of Yhombi's pro-Western initiatives and French aid.

Congo-Brazzaville was one of the francophone nations most assiduously and continuously courted by the Soviet Union during the postindependence years. However, in 1988, Sassou-Nguesso's Republic of Congo held a gala celebration of the hundredth anniversary of French colonization with a ceremony that ranked the USSR only 16th in the protocol arrangements after France, the United States, and a number of African nations.[148]

Regional States' Options to Put Pressure on France
What small amount of African influence existed tended to be exercised on a personal level at the highest levels of government. Léopold Senghor, who became the first president of Senegal, considered that many of his political projects before independence had failed because French policy was determined to divide African energies and prevent Africans from achieving strength through unified political efforts. In spite of his service, and that of other Africans in the French Assembly, France refused a true political integration with her former colonies and held steadfastly to the French political doctrine of administrative centralization. Senghor believed that his single most powerful influence on French policy had come through his lifelong

friendships with Georges Pompidou and other French leaders, whom he had been able to sensitize to African cultural and political developments.[149] Pompidou, de Gaulle's closest adviser for a long period, and his chosen successor as president, had held Senghor in high regard since they attended *lycée* together in Paris as young men.[150]

The options available to the leaders of francophone Africa are rooted firmly in the history of the pursuit of independence from France. The postcolonial relationship was one of continuing dependency, with relatively few opportunities for the African states to put pressure on their French patron for any favors outside of the cooperation agreements. The agreements themselves were clearly subject to French discretion, and the relationship continued to leave France the first among putative equals in *la Francophonie*. Those African leaders with the strongest ability to pressure France remained those whose loyalty had remained firm over many years, and especially those who had cemented their relatively powerful positions in this patronage structure during the years just prior to independence. They knew French politics well, often as insiders, and understood how to play the game of cooperative nationalism.

After independence, the French presence in African domestic politics remained pervasive. Increasingly, independent African leaders made the discovery that France itself had strategic, economic, and political needs that could be manipulated. The West African states did not have a large influence over French policy in their region, but the military cooperation agreements provided some room for maneuver, and the ambiguous nature of France's continuing cultural and linguistic relationship with the former colonies provided some of the same anti-colonial rhetoric of democracy which leaders like Senghor, Houphouët, and Touré used to their advantage during the decolonization period. Especially after the first decade of independence, renegotiating the cooperation agreements provided a significant opportunity for putting pressure on France. Since these agreements, as Welch states,[151] carried "a strong odor of neocolonialism," there was always the opportunity to threaten to renegotiate them, or even to reject them altogether, as Congo-Brazzaville, Mauritania, and Madagascar did in the early 1970s. Indeed, after the death of de Gaulle, many of the agreements were revised or dropped in favor of less all-encompassing forms of aid agreements.

African governments became more adept at exploiting these needs, in spite of their relative weakness. They gained more leverage over the relationship as the twentieth century came to a close. However, France's freedom of action during this period remained nearly absolute within the flexible interpretations allowable in the cooperation agreements. To illustrate why this was so, what follows is an abbreviated history of France and francophone West Africa's interpenetration of one another's political spheres.

How Independence "Balkanized" Francophone Africa

Sub-Saharan nationalism in West Africa centered largely in Senegal and Côte d'Ivoire. Félix Houphouët-Boigny's Parti Démocratique du Côte d'Ivoire (PDCI) formed in 1946 the political base for Houphouët's subsequent election to the first French Constituent Assembly, and his participation in the Fourth Republic's constitutional debates. Léopold Senghor established his own party, the Bloc Démocratique Sénégalaise (BDS) in 1948. Both of these parties had regional connections to parties and political elites in the other West African colonies. Both Houphouët and Senghor, from their different power bases, worked from Paris within the French system for colonial reform. Both were deputies in France's parliament and believed in working from within the metropolitan political structure, even if they disagreed ultimately on the final form that independence should take. Armed revolution was not an option for either Senghor or Houphouët, given the overwhelming strength which French military force represented, and also given West Africa's continuing economic dependency.[152]

The most significant reform during the period between World War II and independence was the 1956 enabling law or "Loi Cadre." Houphouët at this time served in a convenient location for policy influence: in the French cabinet as minister of health.[153] The Loi Cadre decentralized the colonial administration somewhat, and it also granted governing councils to organize public services and universal suffrage in the territories. The French Union was still regarded as a single entity for certain purposes, however: sovereign power remained with France on matters of defense, foreign policy, and currency regulation.[154] Senghor argued for a unified independent territory in West Africa, but Houphouët-Boigny's plan prevailed. Each individual colony was given a council, and each developed its own leadership as a single unit. Having thus divided the larger territories into small potentially independent units, France further weakened the interterritorial political groups and virtually insured continuing dependency on the part of the weak states that were to result from this initial division. The debates in the French parliament and territorial assemblies began to center on federation and independence rather than on territorial autonomy.[155]

It is perhaps the most significant indicator of French power at this point that decolonization continued to be a matter of managed collaboration rather than revolution. Federation of some sort was still the model defended by most participants, even Guinea's Sekou Touré. For Houphouët, whose political fate was tied to the Loi Cadre and his Ivorian power base, federation could be tolerated only if there were to be full equality for African states within a France-centered federal structure. As the leader of one of the two wealthiest colonies (the other was Gabon), it was clearly in Houphouët's interest to promote Côte d'Ivoire as an autonomous unit. A federal government based in Dakar would be a drain on the comparatively rich Ivorian economy, which would be asked effectively to subsidize the rest of the region.[156] Touré and others continued to argue for greater pan-African unity in order to strengthen the African position vis-à-vis France, but France was able to use its considerable political leverage on the African parties in order to prevent this from happening.[157]

Riots in Algiers in May 1958 and the ensuing crisis produced two important results: first, a clear message to France concerning the continued risks and costs in delaying decolonization, and, second, the return of Charles de Gaulle to solve the Algerian problem and establish the Fifth Republic of France. French constitutional reform again presented an opportunity to African politicians, now far more well-connected and better organized than they had been at Brazzaville in 1944, to push for independence. "Cooperation," in contrast to what Algeria was doing, made an attractive alternative to war. *"L'Homme de Brazzaville"* was formally voted into power in France, on 1 June 1958, and given the independent executive powers as president that he had always asserted were necessary to French destiny and glory. Recommended constitutional reforms were to include a federal system incorporating France and its territories, according to a committee of French ministers, one of whom was Félix Houphouët-Boigny. De Gaulle's plan for a federated French state was then presented to an African consultative committee including Gabriel Lisette of the RDA (Houphouët's representative), Senghor and Lamine Guèye of Senegal representing the Parti de Regroupment Africain, and Philibert Tsiranana, the future president of Madagascar.[158] Senghor argued at that time that any colony's disagreement with de Gaulle's proposed form of federation should not necessarily constitute an automatic decision for secession. Tsiranana proposed successfully that the word "federation" should be dropped and changed to "French Community," meaning a "free association of states." This "community" would still be led by France, and the result could not yet be called full independence. The purpose remained evolution toward independence by all member states except France (apparently presumed to have already evolved enough to be fully free).

A referendum on the constitutional draft for the French Community was set for 28 September 1958. De Gaulle began a promotional tour of Africa in order to strengthen old ties, establish new ones, and impress forcefully on every African capital's political elites and their supporters that a lack of support for the referendum would probably entail a total loss of French military, technical, economic, and even diplomatic support. All African leaders except for Touré preferred French support to an impoverished destiny (however free), at least for the time being.[159] The total French withdrawal from Guinea in 1958 created a local object lesson to the other states and demonstrated what valuable benefits they had purchased with their freedom by choosing de Gaulle's formula for security within the protective *chasse gardée*. For some time after Touré's vote of "*non*," Guinea was left bereft of military and economic support, arms, teachers, and technical advisers, a state disorganized, solitary, poor, and powerless. All French troops were withdrawn by November of 1958, and the French also repatriated Guineans serving in the French army.[160] Later Soviet bloc support picked up some of its expenses, but Guinea has only recently become once again a regional military power.

The new constitution stated that the matters formerly controlled by France (defense policy, finance, foreign policy, law, higher education, strategic raw materials, transport, and telecommunications), would now be controlled by the French Community. This "change" meant effectively, however, that France still held these powers, although they were now administered through the Community's institutions: a president, senate, and court under French control. When Algeria rejected a similarly ambiguous relationship with France, and when members of the "French Community" in Mali, Upper Volta, and Dahomey began plans for the Mali Federation (which failed but resulted in Mali's decision to seek independence) de Gaulle began in December 1959 the negotiations with Mali, and then with Madagascar and the rest of French Africa that led to full political sovereignty for all of the sub-Saharan colonies as independent states.[161]

As of 1960, the French Community was no longer an official constitutional entity; however, the collaborative links with France were still a necessity for most of the new states. Each of the states which decolonized manageably and cooperatively in 1960 retained significant benefits in return for continued contractual agreements and promises to follow France's leadership and direction in numerous ways.

There was some reciprocal influence involved in France's continuing control over the strategic mineral and other natural resources of West African nations. For example, France discovered uranium in Niger in 1958 and maintained most of the market for it for decades, even purchasing it at well above the market price during price depressions as an indirect subsidy to the *Nigerien* economy. Niger was the fifth largest uranium producer and contained up to 10 percent of the world's known reserves. As late as 1979–1981, France was the principal purchaser of Niger's uranium, buying twice as much in 1981 as its nearest competitor, Japan. Interestingly, given what happened later in neighboring Chad, one of the other buyers was Libya, although in much lower amounts. Libya was an economic competitor in northern Central Africa as well as a military competitor.[162]

France remained the political tutor, the financial backer, the sponsor of UN membership, the armorer, and the military guarantor for these cooperative francophone African nations, and often for their individual leaders as well. The *chasse gardée* was still maintained by force, but that force was now embodied in the threat of French withdrawal of privileges rather than the old threat of punishment under the *indigénat*. French military force was still based in Africa, but it was now combined with the new African armed forces in such a fashion as to blur the distinction between the legitimate monopoly on military and police action held by the new governments, and the use of French arms and armed personnel at the *request* of African governments. African armies now served African governments, but they were often still commanded or organized by French military and technical *coopérants*. French army bases, arms, and personnel remained by contractual agreement in Africa as much to control internal disorder in African states (and so were at least nominally in service to the leaders if not the people of those states) as they did to display the continuing French influence and global reach of France as a great power. Given the shared, "cooperative" nature of this security structure, and even though France was by far the more powerful partner, there was room for the new African states to learn *why* it was that France continued to desire their cooperation and, apparently, their friendship. They were able, to varying degrees, to manipulate France's needs to use Africa as an extension of France's historic power base, and to maintain France, in both appearance and fact, as a great power with an intercontinental reach.

Common Objectives Shared By the Regional States and France

Throughout this chapter, it has been necessary to distinguish between African states and their individual leaders, just as it has been necessary to distinguish France's presidents from France herself. Where the interests and objectives of states have been mentioned, it is with the understanding that it is the leadership of these states that is meant. Since democracy has not been the type of government common to the African states during this period, one cannot say that all Ivorians held objectives in common with their state, or with the French. It is certainly possible, however, to detect instances in which African government policy and goals (territorial integrity, the personal security of the president and high officials, access to loans and development aid, the ability to conduct business and distribute patronage in such a way as to guarantee a stable leadership by rewarding loyalty with opportunities for enrichment), were furthered by the French government's policies and goals (access to strategic military locations and strategic minerals, the continued political loyalty of African leaders, access to markets and opportunities to sell French products and spread French culture). If the goals and preferences were not identical, they were at least complementary, and the basis in large part for profitable political, economic, and military relationships.[163]

As Savorgnan de Brazza hoped, the colonial "hand" of trade has been reinforced by the development of francophone cultural preferences in the African marketplaces of goods and ideas. African governments are now somewhat more able to restrict and manipulate market access according to what they want France to give in return. French language and culture, French legal and pedagogical methods, French banking and investment concerns, and French religion have also become integral structural parts of the daily life of every "francophone" African, even for those who cannot speak or read French. A francophone African's level of ability in French continues to define his or her access to power and economic resources. Conversely, this widening of "la Francophonie," the cultural expression of what it means for a non-Frenchman to speak the French language and participate in the French political sphere of influence, has proven to be not only a boost to French prestige but also a challenge to French identity. This challenge to what it means to be French has not always been welcome to the French themselves. Nonetheless, the resulting internationalization of French society has arguably enriched francophone culture and preserved French influence in countries which provide France with a continuing claim to global great power "*grandeur*."

As Chipman states, "French military co-operation with francophone African countries has created a dependency which is in the service of French political interests but not always to the long-term benefit of African countries."[164] France was never as liberal concerning the political rights of its African subjects during the colonial period as it was with its own citizens, establishing a pattern of political repression that proved to be convenient for African presidents at independence. During the colonial period, correspondence between Africa and other countries was intercepted and censored (as was still true in Bokassa's Central African Empire in 1978 when this author was there as a Peace Corps volunteer), and African newspapers were subjected to continuing surveillance and interference, particularly if they had leftist sympathies. Such newspapers were legal in France, where leftist parties held considerable power within the organizational structures of French democracy, but were seized as "revolutionary propaganda" in Africa because they might be (and often were) anti-French.[165] Repression of journalists and censorship of the mail persists to this day in most francophone African countries, and it may well be in the best interests of both French and African *leaders* that this is so, even if French citizens would not allow either of these tactics on the scale that they are practiced in Africa, and African human rights groups have protested against them.

Some of the African states had clearer common objectives with France than others. Those states, like Senegal and Côte d'Ivoire, whose presidents had brought their countries to independence by working within the French political system, had a common interest in perpetuating a system profitable to both France and its colonies in terms of political stability, territorial integrity and the mutual enrichment of French and African political elites. Where interests diverged massively, as with Guinea, commonality of objectives was lost with the rupture of the historic relationship. With those states that remained in the *middle* of these two extremes (accepting French bases or allowing no French presence at all), such as Mali, Dahomey, and Togo, the African state's objective became to see how much security and support could be obtained from France without sacrificing the apparent independence of one's nation to French control. As has been noted, some of these shifting conditions left room for indigenous military coups. France, in turn, would try to get as much political support as possible from these states, pulling the strings attached to military cooperation agreements, and preventing as much Soviet or anglophone encroachment as possible, without getting pushed away too often for looking like an overlord instead of a partner.

Interestingly, as Welch notes,[166] Gabon, Senegal, and Côte d'Ivoire, at one end of the continuum, having continually accepted French garrisons on their soil since independence, have not yet experienced a *successful* intervention in government by their own military. Gabon's attempted coup in 1964 was reversed immediately by the action of French paratroopers.[167] Although the presence of these French garrisons was perceived by the other francophone nations as a sacrifice of Gabonese, Senegalese, and Ivorian sovereignty, the leaders of these three nations found it to be a sacrifice which paid considerable dividends toward their internal security and personal power. Decalo is even stronger in emphasizing the role that the French base garrisons in the Central African Republic, Côte d'Ivoire, Senegal, and Gabon have played in discouraging coups. He includes CAR (even with Bokassa and Kolingba's coups) because France accepted and even assisted both coups, the implication being that French permission was a factor in removing regimes which had become costly or embarrassing to French interests.[168]

Part Three: France's Ability to Shape the Peacetime Environment in Its Former Colonies according to its Preferences during the First Decade after Independence

An efficient, productive, and secure *chasse gardée* could not simply be enclosed and left to its own devices. Constant and systematic internal maintenance was required on the part of the French in order to shape the peacetime environment in its former colonial preserve. No other European colonial power was able to retain as much influence in a former colonial empire. France's patronage relationship with its African client states was not always harmonious; however, four decades after independence, it is still the major guarantor of peace and security in many of its former sub-Saharan colonies, and often a port of first resort for the others in the event of a crisis. Economic and military dependency on France during the postindependence decade remained stable and guaranteed France a continuing source of carrots and sticks with which to keep order. The French troop and *coopérant* presence remained relatively constant over the course of the decade, and African elites continued to learn and use French as the primary language of government and business affairs. Maintaining the elites' preference for French insured that French economic, intelligence, health, education, and other technical advisers remained just as "interoperable" with Africans working in these areas as their military counterparts.

External vigilance was also required to preserve the *chasse gardée*. As suggested, preserving French power and influence in Africa against any attempt at cultural, economic, or military encroachment by the English-speaking world (whether this was a great power like the United States or a regional hegemon like Nigeria), or by the Soviet Union, was as important as preventing the newly independent nations from becoming too independent. The types of internal maintenance suggested above, however, lessened some of the need for external protection by giving the United States, the USSR, and other powers less of an incentive to encroach when there were more attractive targets available (like Ethiopia).

France's interests generally prevailed, although numerous ways were found to make them prevail which coincided with the interests of African leaders or ambitious elites. France's main advantage was that, throughout the Fourth and Fifth Republics, there had been remarkable clarity and consistency of vision concerning what France wanted from its African possessions. De Gaulle's return to power in France brought back a leader who was able to imagine, promote, and explain France to itself and to the rest of the world as a reemerging great power with a universal cultural message, an independent policy voice, a global (or at least bi-continental) alliance structure, and the military power to support its aspirations.

Whether or not all of these things were actually true of France during the entire period covered here, this vision was the motive force behind French military and foreign policy throughout the decades after World War II, and the emerging African countries caught in its wake could do little until quite late in the century except take advantage of what France offered for their cooperation, learning the rules of the game well enough to begin to manipulate them to their own advantage. De Gaulle was only the most modern and articulate proponent of this visionary model of France which, in fact, owes as much to Napoleon as it does to de Gaulle.

France's preference in West Africa during the period since 1945 was clearly to slow down the decolonization process as much as possible without causing violent revolution (as in Indochina or Algeria) and without causing a colony to reject France, once it was an independent nation (as did Guinea). Having learned the lessons taught by Algeria simultaneously with the process of decolonizing West and Central Africa, France was perhaps fortunate only to have lost one sub-Saharan colony completely, and then only until the death of Sekou Touré in 1984. Many of the difficulties of this process were caused by the contradictions inherent in France's self-image: France was a colonizer and civilizer, by force if necessary, of those who were deemed not quite ready to govern themselves as the French did. France was a democracy ruling an empire, run by an autonomous president who discouraged parliamentary interference, but who believed nonetheless that it was France's duty to bring its particular political, social, and economic virtues (including democratic participation, if only as a part of France) to as much of the world as possible.

Not surprisingly, those who were ruled by this paradoxical hegemon learned as much as they could about the opportunities and ideologies which France presented to them, particularly while they helped France fight its wars, and applied their knowledge to setting themselves free while getting what they could out of their *patron* in the process. As Michel Martin states, "The fundamental objective contradictions that colonization bears in the germs of its own essence and that are ultimately detrimental to its existence had already given birth to the ideology of nationalism. The participation of diverse members of the colonial empire in a combat aimed at the defense of democracy, racial and religious equality, civil liberties, and self-determination, further nourished the indigenous peoples' conviction, at least that of their leaders, of the righteousness of their desire to be freed from alien domination."[169] France could not grant independence without leaving a few chains, but some of these were as firmly fastened to the jailer as they were to the prisoners.

De Gaulle began to recognize by 1955 that the complete preservation of the colonies that he so desired was beginning to work against another of his goals: renewing and maintaining the prestige of France. De Gaulle opposed liberalization in the colonies between 1945 and 1955, but Algeria changed his mind when it became clear that France's prestige would be far more greatly enhanced by managing a careful transition to self-determination among its colonies than it would by losing them altogether.[170] The certainty of their eventual loss due to nationalism, compared with the prestige to be gained (among them and in the rest of the Third World) by letting them go, dictated the plans which were set in motion by the Loi Cadre. Pan-Africanism was discouraged and the new states were weak enough to be easily led. The new nations would be independent in name and dependent in fact, sovereign and yet filled with Frenchmen, and the *chasse gardée* would remain available as an instrument of French policy and an extension of France's wealth, security, and *grandeur*.

France's advantages were its continuing consistency and clarity of vision concerning what it wanted from its former colonies, greatly aided by de Gaulle's articulate formulation of the goals of French great power *grandeur*, a patience born of preponderant power, historical presence and experience, and a deep understanding of the people and cultures it had ruled. Unlike other great powers which tended to prefer immediate results from their African initiatives, France understood that the *longue durée* of colonial history generally worked to its advantage, because a reliable and predictable (if forceful and parental) overlord was generally preferred to other patrons with short-term goals, less shared history, and less of their wealth and effort invested in the region.

France's Ability to Deter Unwanted Conflict in the Region

France's ability to deter domestic-level conflicts and civil wars within the regional states after independence remained excellent once its willingness to use force during the postcolonial period had been demonstrated a few times; again these were cases of *"Il faut manifester la force pour en éviter l'emploi."*[171] Occasional conflicts did occur which required France's immediate attention. However, the historically entrenched military and economic dependence and the personal relationships developed between French and African military and political figures during the colonial period and thereafter, gave France a number of useful options (carrots and sticks) and considerable flexibility in the event of the usually purely internal postcolonial conflicts. Often, conflict was deterred by means other than a show of preponderant force.

In at least one case, Côte d'Ivoire, it is probable that the presence of French bases as well as an internal defense agreement mandating France's long-term loyalty to President Houphouët-Boigny prevented Houphouët-era opposition members or movements from using armed force to remove the government or begin a civil war. Indeed, preemptive military aid increases and garrison reinforcements often made more dramatic measures (like the use of the Force d'Intervention) unnecessary in other countries as well.

An obvious show of French force was necessary in Senegal in 1959–1960 to support President Senghor during disturbances accompanying the collapse of the Mali Federation, but rarely thereafter. Most of the armed revolts suppressed in West Africa by the French during the 1960s were dispatched quickly and efficiently, using the base troops, which enhanced the reputation of these troops as a dissuasive presence and a deterrent threat against further conflict. Base troops in Central Africa were also used to suppress revolts in West Africa and vice versa. The countries in which French troops were based preferred that "their" garrisons not be used elsewhere, but their leaders recognized that France could and would do so if the need arose. France, as the preponderant partner, was allowed considerable flexibility in interpreting what it would be allowed to do in each circumstance.[172] The 1964 intervention in Gabon used the local French garrison supplemented by reinforcements from the base in Senegal and French parachutists based in Brazzaville.[173]

In spite of France's undoubted military superiority within its *chasse gardée*, a number of serious conflicts took place that affected West and Central Africa during this period of study, although only one conflict was within her boundaries, and that occurred in one of the two countries which were given to France as mandate territories when Germany lost World War II. Although Cameroon was a crossroads of German, British, and French influence, due to careful and consistent French attention it is now one of the most loyal of France's African allies. Sivard records that the insurrections surrounding Cameroon's independence process between 1955 and 1960 resulted in a total of 32,000 civilian and military casualties in the fighting between Cameroonian, French, and British troops. Cameroon required no major armed interventions, however, after the French garrison was used to suppress the Bamileke in 1960.[174]

France was unable to deter internal conflict during the 1960s in the former Belgian colonies. Interethnic conflict in Rwanda between 1956 and 1965 resulted in totals of 3,000 military deaths and 102,000 civilian deaths. The Shaba insurrection in Zaïre was responsible for approximately 100,000 total deaths. France's indirect participation in Nigeria's Civil War (1967–1970), during which several francophone nations transferred French aid to Biafra, in no way prevented the loss there of 2,000,000 military and civilian lives. France's participation in these conflicts was limited by the cooperation agreements within the African Community. France's priority in these engagements was to protect the lives of French citizens and French economic and strategic interests in these countries, and its participation does not seem to have mitigated the severity of these engagements in terms of African lives lost.[175]

De Gaulle's withdrawal of France's forces from many of its overseas commitments during the 1960s may well have lessened its ability to intervene in major wars in parts of Africa which bordered on its former colonies. However, this withdrawal needs to be seen in the context of de Gaulle's policy choice to concentrate on preserving the economic and political alliances with sub-Saharan nations, while guaranteeing the safety of particular leaders and of the overall territorial integrity of the many small nations which France had once conquered and subsequently divided into states. The small interventions were the most successful during the 1960s, in that they offered large political advantages in return for relatively small troop commitments. Major participation in regional wars was avoided during the first ten years of the Fifth Republic by fulfilling the terms of the cooperation agreements and by solidifying France's relationships with the new African governments.

France's Ability to Control the Outcome of Regional Conflicts
During the various incidents of armed revolt or civil uprising in francophone Africa during the 1960s, the following countries required armed intervention on the part of France: Cameroon in 1959–1960, Mauritania in 1961, Senegal in 1959–1960, Congo-Brazzaville in 1960–1962, Gabon in 1960, 1962, and 1964, Central African Republic (CAR) in 1967, and Chad in 1960–1963.[176] The fighting that occurred in these incidents was suppressed, and France remained the paramount influence in all of these countries for the remainder of the decade, with the exception of Chad, where the initial conflict died down only temporarily, leaving antagonisms which surfaced later in the 1960s as a full-scale civil war lasting a couple of decades, and which France was only partly able to control.

France was generally able to ride out each domestic conflict, civil riot or armed revolt, finding sufficient strings to pull among its clients to remain an influential voice, leaving old friends in power or facilitating the installation of new ones, and more often than not controlling the outcome in its favor. Occasionally, a conflict occurred that France was not able to control or manipulate completely. Niger, as stated, proved to be an interesting exception to this rule. As described previously, the French presence was partially removed at the request of Niger after the 1965 insurrection, and 1974's military coup expelled the French military mission. However, even in Niger, France's economic power, particularly over the extraction and marketing of uranium, remained strong enough to retain significant influence for France even with the loss of some of its military presence. [177]

However, France's ability to control the outcomes of interstate conflicts involving both francophone and nonfrancophone countries was much more limited. This was demonstrated by France's unsuccessful attempt to support the secession of Biafra during the Nigerian Civil War, and also by France's inability to prevent Chad's neighbors (Libya and Sudan) from giving aid to the various internally warring parties, thereby escalating and continuing that civil war over the long term.

France's Ability to Reassure Aligned States in the Region

During the 1960s, France was able to reassure its francophone African allies that they would be protected from both external threats and internal destabilization. The visible consistency and constancy of France's economic and military presence, combined with its willingness (except in cases of disloyalty or uncooperative leadership) to live up to the provisions of the cooperation agreements, provided African leaders with reassurance that their interests would be protected as long as they supported the interests of France.

The confidence that African leaders placed in Charles de Gaulle was, for the most part, absolute. Presidents Senghor of Senegal and Mba of Gabon knew with certainty that de Gaulle would protect their interests on the basis of a phone call to de Gaulle or to Jacques Foccart, or any signs of unrest detected by their local French intelligence *coopérants*. (After the death of de Gaulle in 1970, this confidence was less obvious, but remained relatively strong.) The defense agreements were signed, revised, and resigned by enough of the most faithful allies (Gabon, Senegal, and Côte d'Ivoire in particular), to continue a strong and visible troop base in the region. Even if not every state had a French garrison, their leaders were aware from past experience that the French would consider using any or all of the garrisons to protect states without them. France's refusal to intervene in Togo in 1963 when President Olympio was assassinated provided another kind of reassurance, this time an object lesson to African leaders of what could happen in the event that their support of France wavered or was withdrawn. This lesson was clearly that consistent compliance on their part would insure continuing support from France.

However, even those states which fell from grace occasionally (like Togo), or who held France at arms length or lapsed in their support, were continually invited back in to the community, and were reminded in a number of ways of the potential advantages of doing so. French arms sales and training were still offered as "carrots." The relative economic stability of the nations of the *chasse gardée* provided a constant object lesson to those who did not belong, and an incentive for those who did to stay put. The establishment of the Franc Zone was perhaps the most concrete daily reminder, with CFAF in everyone's pocket, that France was their financial guarantor, and the ultimate arbiter of patronage opportunities for the faithful. Enough of the elites in each country profited visibly from this system, as demonstrated most cogently in the case of Côte d'Ivoire, to make it appear possible for all to do so as long as they cooperated, and the system was not disrupted. The continuing willingness of French companies, and those of other nations, to invest in francophone Africa was primarily based on the stability provided by the Franc Zone. Even the poorer nations of the zone remained convinced that French influence was a sure hedge against total economic collapse.

France's Ability to Protect Its Economic Interests in the Region

France's ability to protect its economic interests was consistently excellent, occasionally even more so than its considerable ability to protect its military interests. A centrally directed, coordinated, and pervasive intelligence presence provided on-the-ground insurance that the *chasse gardée* continued in every country except Guinea to be a potential, if not always extremely profitable, extension of France's economic empire. During this decade, the former colonies remained almost as dependent on France as they had been during the colonial period. Francophone Africa continued to offer France the most favorable access to raw materials and strategic resources. The development of an African industrial base was slow, perpetuating dependence on French imports for arms, manufactured products, luxury goods, and even food and clothing. This dependency was strengthened considerably by the cultural assimilation of French consumer preferences.

Where strategic resources were concerned, as in Niger (uranium) and Congo-Brazzaville (oil), French access, influence, and profit continued even though the former country dismissed the French military presence and the latter was flirting with socialism. Not even in Congo were all French companies nationalized, although the threat to do so was often used by the Congolese government to get France's attention. Even when French companies engaged in resource extraction *were* nationalized, enough French employees often remained in them to provide leadership, technical expertise, and business connections. Socialist governments in the French sphere did not tend to reorganize agriculture and local markets in as systemic a fashion as, say, Tanzania, and even when such reorganization occurred it tended to be mitigated by what was usually an authoritarian or military government structure. Franc Zone membership, with its capitalist rules and regulations, generally prevented socialist economic practices from rooting themselves too firmly even if socialist experiments were attempted.

In those states that remained utterly loyal to France in all respects, such as Côte d'Ivoire and Senegal, France's access to materials and markets remained completely secure. While the institutions of the Franc Zone insured a secure basis for French and other Western investments in the region, membership in this zone was predicated on each country's entire relationship with France, and its willingness to follow French directives in return for the privileges of Franc Zone membership. Trade and defense (Brazza's two "hands") relied on one another's strength to some degree in each country to maintain the continuing relationship. While financial corruption did persist in the patronage structure of these governments, France and its allied African presidents controlled elite access to patronage well enough to make corruption a manipulable, predictable, and occasionally profitable, if distasteful, part of the system.

The neediness of the inhabitants of the *chasse gardée*, and France's preponderant power (both financial and military), provided the best possible insurance for France's economic interests. The French economic presence required a French military presence of some type, overt or not, and the French military presence could be enhanced using economic leverage. French financial support, and the strategic placement of *coopérant* employees in parastatal industries and businesses run by African elites, insured an interlocking network of aid, debt, investment, and intelligence. Jacques Foccart's network of carefully placed intelligence *coopérants* were located where they could have considerable access to information on both government industries, enhancing France's strategic position with early warning of potential problems in either the diplomatic or economic sphere. The structure put in place by each cooperation agreements facilitated as much as possible ways in which pressure could be put on African countries and industries to put France's interest first. Military pressure was available to back up economic incentives. In those countries without military bases or internal defense agreements, the arms and training assistance offered as cooperative Assistance Militaire Technique provided similar opportunities and early warning capability.

France's Ability to Ensure That Regional States Pursued Foreign Policies Desired by France

France was successful most of the time in manipulating the foreign policies of its francophone African allies during the 1960s. Most significantly, they tended in large part to mirror France's own independence and nonalignment during the Cold War, except where France itself was concerned. They might dally with the United States and USSR, expel or invite the Chinese, and collect what aid they could from other great powers, but ultimately, France's goal was their complete loyalty to France, and their willingness to follow its lead and cooperate with whatever global or regional goals which France might have.

Francophone African nations during the postindependence period offered France some voting bloc strength in the United Nations (although this also gave them some small leverage occasionally with which to influence France). It is not clear, however, how necessary this voting bloc was to France, although de Gaulle made an effort to stand as UN sponsor for the new African nations, and this was an issue at independence for all parties. The most concrete evidence of France's ability to ensure congruence of foreign policy lay in the continuing willingness of some of the francophone nations to support French policy, and even to act as proxies for it, as several of them did in conducting French aid to Biafra during the Nigerian Civil War. Francophone African nations have also contributed troops to French intervention efforts, although this has actually occurred more frequently in the period encompassed by the next chapter. France's continuing policy influence was evident in some of the failures of the OAU to reach agreements on important issues such as a pan-African defense force. The disagreements within this organization often occurred along "linguistic" lines, as the francophone nations would occasionally be in opposition to perceived attempts at Nigerian hegemony. However, the language spoken may have been less of a factor than Nigeria's burgeoning ability to throw around its considerable weight in terms of population, oil wealth, and military power.

The best evidence of French control over African foreign policy is the fact that, in spite of continuing and persistent attempts on the part of the Soviet Union, China, Libya, and Cuba to penetrate francophone countries, the communist countries made only temporary gains in the *chasse gardée*. These temporary gains were made possible by these countries' opportunistic support of opposition factions and nationalist movements that either espoused marxism, or did so on an occasional basis in order to attract aid from as many sources as possible. Even in the People's Republic of Congo under Marien Ngouabi, the French maintained contacts with government factions and remained in charge of various economic concerns. Wherever these countries gained a foothold in the region (usually by supplying military aid and arms), France had enough economic or military leverage to balance them, and often enough to nudge them out eventually or marginalize their influence.[178]

Where domestic-level conflict resulted in a change in government, such as a military coup, France was frequently able to remain in control of the policies of the African state even if the coup had taken place without the participation of French troops. In a number of these cases, of course, French troops or French intelligence personnel did play a role in the transition to a new government, whether publicly or "deniably." A public show of arms, or even the presence of a base, was often enough to keep whichever African faction rose to power in line with French preferences. While not all of the new nations fell into line, only one was lost to French influence completely, and even Guinea was edging back into the French sphere of influence by the early 1980s. Even those that resisted complete French control, like Mauritania, Upper Volta, and Dahomey (whose cooperation agreements were much less extensive in scope than, e.g., Côte d'Ivoire's), were indebted and francophile enough to continue receiving considerable French training, aid, and arms during the 1960s and thereafter, and more often than not rejected any policy initiatives on the part of either the United States or USSR which conflicted with French preferences.

France's Ability to Promote Domestic Developments Consistent with its Values and Preferences (Democratic Development, Economic Development and Capitalist Policies, Support for French Interventions Elsewhere, Preserving the *Chasse Gardée*)

During the 1960s, the French were successful in developing the domestic political, economic, and military capacities of the *chasse gardée* insofar as such development was consistent with French values and preferences. Any domestic military, political, or economic development occurred in a controlled fashion that allowed France itself to stay well ahead of its clients in these areas.

Local democratic development was not really necessary for pursuing France's goals in Africa, and neither were nationalized resource extraction capacities or industrial growth and development, as these would have increased these nations' actual independence from France politically and economically.

France was successful in preventing excessively rapid growth in democratization, resource nationalization, and industry. However, some controlled development of pro-capitalist economic policies, preferential import and export relationships, and francophile cultural preferences *was* important to preserving the region as an opportunity zone for French profit and prestige enhancement, and so the maintenance of the Franc Zone and continuing infrastructural assistance was a necessary feature of French policy.

African support for French military security initiatives was key to the perpetuation of the French sphere of influence, and African militaries were only developed, armed, and trained to the basic level needed in any given year for them to remain interoperable, compliant, and generally satisfied clients of France. Although France itself had democracy, an industrial growth economy, and excellent educational, health, and technical expertise, and therefore the potential for assisting the African nations in developing in these directions, the desired postcolonial relationship between France and francophone Africa was intended to be one of vigilant and thorough maintenance and controlled evolution, rather than nurturance of rapid growth.

Conclusion: Preferences, Goals, Benefits, and Costs That Shaped the *Chasse Gardée*

France's values and preferences, considered historically, are nearly identical to what they were at the end of World War II. William Foltz lists five general strategic roles and uses for Africa[179] during the colonial period and beyond, all of which are facets of the *chasse gardée* that France wished to develop, and which have been borrowed and expanded upon here:

> *First*, Africa has historically been either an obstacle or, more positively, a buffer against potential interference from the Middle and Far East. It has served France well as a place to demonstrate the limits of Soviet power. France developed only those types of governance which were in its interest, providing little support to grassroots democracy and managing generally to co-opt any impulses toward socialism. The varieties of socialism which developed in the chasse gardée were ultimately as manipulable and containable as those which developed in France itself.
>
> *Second*, Africa has also been a necessary component of the sea-lanes; West African coastal nations, their defenses and resources are a part of the strategic trade and supply pattern. France's relationships with the oil-producing countries on the West African coast are now a part of this ancient pattern, and the coastal cities of francophone West Africa remain key sites of French influence.

Third, Africa has been a potential launching pad for military efforts directed at other continents. France has not used it in this way since its African soldiers returned from Indochina, with the exception of the base at Djibouti, but parts of French Africa have certainly served during this period as launch sites for actions against *other* parts of Africa, a pattern that was established as early as the founding of the *Tirailleurs Africains*.

Fourth, Africa is a source of strategic resources, which France continued to exploit effectively during the 1960s.

Fifth, Africa is also a source of "surrogate terrain," used particularly effectively by France in its continuing attempts to prove that a culture must be exported in order to remain great.

All five of these features of Africa described by Foltz were a part of France's overall goals during the postindependence period, which was to maintain French power in such a way as to preserve the francophone African states as military and economic extensions of France itself, and to make its African subjects as loyally French as possible, without encouraging them to be as independent globally as France itself. After the loss of Indochina and Algeria, France needed to find ways to retain the benefits of the *chasse gardée* without its feudal overtones. It allowed the colonies to become independent, but their new relationship was framed by cooperation agreements, which offered secure and extensive military and economic benefits in return for African agreements which gave priority to French military, economic, and diplomatic interests.

The terms of this relationship required France to hold firm to its priorities in Africa, to insure the consistency and clarity of approach that had characterized de Gaulle's vision of the French Community, where France and the new African nations would interact as independent states, but where France continued to be the first among equals. By the 1960s, a pattern had developed which was to characterize French interaction and intervention in Africa for the next three decades. France would intervene militarily to guarantee the safety of French citizens, to protect the territorial integrity of its former colonies and cooperative allies, to defend strategic natural resources and commercial routes, to fulfill France's obligations under its military cooperation agreements, and to participate in unilateral and multilateral peacekeeping missions. These goals were clarified and restated under the Mitterand government, but they did not differ from the intentions of previous French governments, and closely resembled the reasons which France had kept such a tight rein on its colonies during the post–World War II period.

France's goals in its African colonies during the post-war period and the first post-independence decade were largely met. It maintained its military presence, its ability to intervene effectively, and its economic strength there, and lost very little of its influence in West and Central Africa, especially when compared to its setbacks in Algeria, its need to share the rest of North Africa with its NATO allies, and its complete loss of Indochina.

The military cost was considerable, as was the cost of maintaining the Franc Zone, but many of the costs were spread out over a period of decades, during which time France retracted most of her soldiers from Africa, leaving just enough for effective *Presence*, and placing enough others in specially-targeted forces to convince African clients and other great powers that she was still capable of immediate and reliable *Intervention*. Ultimately, the cost of preserving the *chasse gardée* has been, over the long run, at least as great as the cost of the *force de frappe*. The returns on de Gaulle's nuclear investment are far less concrete, however, than the benefits to French wealth, military reach, diplomatic influence, anti-Soviet insurance, and general prestige brought by de Gaulle's African initiatives. The cost of maintaining a sub-Saharan sphere of influence was returned in a number of ways by exploiting control of African resources, particularly petroleum and uranium, by creating markets for French goods and French investments, and by preventing Soviet influence from establishing enough of a foothold to cause major wars of independence in France's backyard.

France did not manage, however, to remove the lingering taint of neocolonialism that attended its efforts. French gains in prestige as a preponderant great power must be weighed ultimately against the potential loss in *grandeur* from appearing to hang on too tightly to a highly militarized region where it had led Africans to sacrifice much of their own sovereignty, autonomy, and pride as independent nations in order to preserve their economic and military security. The costs of French neocolonialism, and of its persistent and pervasive pull on the strings of its African marionettes, are examined in the next chapter. It becomes increasingly evident that the relationship, while still one of preponderant power, was no longer as easily manipulated. While the weaker partners in the cooperation agreements, the puppets nonetheless found their strings, and began to pull back.

Notes

1. Indeed, the ancient, persistent, and still perceived rivalry with anglophone influences in the *chasse gardée* apparently inhabits French Africa policy to this day in a form that Gérard Prunier refers to risibly but quite seriously as "Fashoda Syndrome,"

meaning that "the whole world is a cultural, political and economic battlefield between France and the 'Anglo-Saxons.'" Gérard Prunier, *The Rwanda Crisis: History of a Genocide* (New York: Columbia University Press, 1995), 105.

2. See, for example, John Chipman, *French Power in Africa* (Oxford, U.K.: Basil Blackwell Ltd., 1989), 126. See also Douglas A. Yates, *The Rentier State in Africa: Oil Rent Dependency and Neocolonialism in the Republic of Gabon* (Trenton, N.J.: Africa World Press, 1996), 111.

3. Another more modern nickname for Africa current among French policymakers is *"le pré carré,"* idiomatically translatable as "our own backyard." Prunier, *The Rwanda Crisis*, 103. The difference in interpreting these metaphorical references to Africa may be that game parks contain animals to be managed, and backyards often contain children to be educated. This distinction may be borne in mind as one compares the rhetoric of the colonial period with more modern rhetorical defenses of French interests in Africa.

4. Thomas Pakenham, *The Scramble for Africa: White Man's Conquest of the Dark Continent from 1876 to 1912* (New York: Avon Books, 1991), 143.

5. Crawford Young, *The African Colonial State in Comparative Perspective* (New Haven, Conn.: Yale University Press, 1994), 116.

6. Quoted in Anthony Clayton, *France, Soldiers and Africa* (London: Brassey's Defence Publishers, 1988), 5.

7. Clayton, *France, Soldiers and Africa*, 12.

8. Clayton, *France, Soldiers and Africa*, 4.

9. By no means, however, did this translate into a relationship of equality in arms among the French. When victory became a possibility, the order was given by de Gaulle to "whiten" the Free French army and allow young Frenchmen to participate in the final assaults. Because his troops were supplied essentially by American charity, DeGaulle was limited by the Allied budget to supplying a maximum of 250,000 troops in the Free French armies. De Gaulle was also concerned that young Frenchmen were too much attracted to the communist partisans; he hoped to separate them from the far left by getting them into military service at a critical moment. He believed that the humiliation of Vichy could be remedied if the next generation of young Frenchmen were to liberate France, and renew France's commitment to its destiny. By the time of the planned invasion in the fall of 1944, there were over 20,000 experienced African combat veterans fighting with Jean de Lattre in France, all of whom had expected to participate in the final victorious assault on German forces. On de Gaulle's command, these troops were relieved of their uniforms, their supplies, their opportunity to share in their army's triumph, and much of their honor, and sent to the south of France with the liberated African POWs during the brutal winter of 1944. See Myron Echenberg, *Colonial Conscripts: The Tirailleurs Sénégalais in French West Africa, 1857–1960* (Portsmouth, N.H.: Heinemann Educational Books, 1991), 98–99.

10. Chipman, *French Power in Africa*, 88.

11. Serving as a possible precedent for dissident "governments in exile" formed by emigrés from modern francophone African regimes, most recently that of post-Lissouba Congo-Brazzaville.

12. Samuel Decalo, *Historical Dictionary of Chad*, 2nd ed., African Historical Dictionaries no. 13 (Metuchen, N.J.: Scarecrow Press, 1987), 124.

13. Chipman, *French Power in Africa*, 90.

14. Yates, *The Rentier State*, 97.

15. Echenberg, *Colonial Conscripts*, 102, 127, 146–48.

16. Quoted in Chipman, *French Power in Africa*, 76–77.

17. Chipman, *French Power in Africa*, 7, 17. See also William J. Foltz, *From French West Africa to the Mali Federation* (New Haven, Conn.: Yale University Press, 1965), 22.

18. Edward A. Kolodziej and Bokanga Lokulutu, "Security Interests and French Arms-Transfer Policy in Sub-Saharan Africa," in *Arms for Africa: Military Assistance and Foreign Policy in the Developing World*, ed. Bruce E. Arlinghaus (Lexington, Mass.: D.C. Heath and Company, 1983), 126–27.

19. French socialists were able not only to discourage Senegal from participating at the first Bamako conference by having the minister for overseas France pressure his fellow Socialists Lamine Guèye and Léopold Senghor not to attend but also some other African political groups as well (Foltz, *From French West Africa to the Mali Federation*, 54; also Echenberg, *Colonial Conscripts*, 148). In addition, members of the French Socialist Party were appointed to the Governorship of Côte d'Ivoire and also to the Governor-Generalship of the West African Federation in order to strengthen more moderate ties to future Côte d'Ivoire president Félix Houphouet-Boigny, and discourage the affiliation which Houphouet's RDA had made with the French Communist Party. By mid-1950, Houphouet had been convinced to cut off the French Communist Party. This was done by none other than François Mitterand, who was at that time minister of overseas France. See Chipman, *French Power in Africa*, 97; also Foltz, *From French West Africa to the Mali Federation*, 58. See also George E. Moose, "French Military Policy in Africa," in *Arms and the African*, ed. William J. Foltz and Henry S. Bienen (New Haven, Conn.: Yale University Press, 1985), 87. This incident not only cemented a connection which remained valuable to both the future presidents of France and Côte d'Ivoire in later years but also helped France politically with anticommunists in the U.S. government whom she wished at the time to impress.

20. Richard D. Challener, *The French Theory of the Nation in Arms 1866–1939* (New York: Russell and Russell, 1965), 176.

21. Clayton, *France, Soldiers and Africa*, 6.

22. Young, *The African Colonial State*, 150.

23. Clayton, *France, Soldiers and Africa*, 6.

24. Echenberg, *Colonial Conscripts*, xvi.

25. Clayton, *France, Soldiers and Africa*, 6.

26. Clayton, *France, Soldiers and Africa*, 7.

27. Echenberg, *Colonial Conscripts*, 7.

28. Charles Balesi, "West African Influence on the French Army of World War I," in *Double Impact: France and Africa in the Age of Imperialism*, ed. G. Wesley John-

son (Westport, Conn.: Greenwood Press, 1985), 96.

29. Balesi, "West African Influence," in Johnson, *Double Impact*, 99.

30. Echenberg, *Colonial Conscripts*, 80–83. Challener, *The French Theory of the Nation in Arms*, 81, 108.

31. Clayton, *France, Soldiers and Africa*, 338. Echenberg, *Colonial Conscripts*, 29.

32. Echenberg, *Colonial Conscripts*, 88.

33. Echenberg, *Colonial Conscripts*, 5–6.

34. Echenberg, *Colonial Conscripts*, 66.

35. Echenberg, *Colonial Conscripts*, 63.

36. John Chipman, Veme *République et défense de l'Afrique*, trans. R. Manicacci, (Paris: Éditions Bosquet, 1986), 125.

37. Michel L. Martin, *Warriors to Managers: The French Military Establishment since 1945.* (Chapel Hill: University of North Carolina Press, 1981), 34–35.

38. Chipman, *French Power in Africa*, 114–15.

39. A glance at hundreds of years of French history indicates that the Fifth Republic represented a new start on these three rather traditional French projects.

40. Philip H. Gordon, *A Certain Idea of France: French Security Policy and the Gaullist Legacy* (Princeton, N.J.: Princeton University Press, 1993), 29. See also Martin, *Warriors to Managers*, 22–24.

41. Martin, *Warriors to Managers*, 93–94.

42. J. M. Lee, *African Armies and Civil Order* (New York: Frederick A. Praeger, Publishers, 1969), 5.

43. G. Wesley Johnson, in Johnson, ed., *Double Impact*, 384.

44. Pascal Chaigneau, *La Politique Militaire de la France en Afrique* (Paris: Le Centre des Hautes Études sur l'Afrique et l'Asie Modernes, 1984), 118.

45. Chipman, *French Power in Africa*, 197.

46. U.S. Peace Corps volunteers (author Milburn included) serving in francophone Africa were also referred to locally as *coopérants* by both French and African colleagues.

47. Chaigneau's source here is Robin Luckham, "Le militarisme français en Afrique," *Politique Africaine* 5 (February 1982). For the trainee numbers, he cites Jacques Guillemin's doctoral thesis, "Coopération et intervention, la politique militaire de la France en Afrique Noire francophone et à Madagascar," Université de Nice, 1979.

48. Martin, *Warriors to Managers*, 36–38, 61–62.

49. Bruce E. Arlinghaus, *Military Development in Africa: The Political and Economic Risks of Arms Transfers* (Boulder, Colo.: Westview Press, 1984), 71.

50. Arlinghaus, *Military Development in Africa*, 73–74.

51. The French officer-candidate schools and the NCO programs were nearly inaccessible because Africans were at an educational disadvantage in the entrance exam. Meritorious service, the oldest and least well-documented route to promotion through the ranks available to African officer candidates, produced two (very different) African military presidents: Sangoulé Lamizana of Upper Volta and Jean-Bédel Bokassa of the Central African Republic, both of whom came to power by coups d'état. See Samuel Decalo, "Military Rule in Africa: Etiology and Morphology," in

Military Power and Politics in Black Africa, ed. Simon Baynham (New York: St. Martin's Press, 1986), 48. See also Pierre Kalck, *Historical Dictionary of the Central Africa Republic*, 2nd ed., translated by Thomas O'Toole, African Historical Dictionaries no. 51 (Metuchen, N.J.: Scarecrow Press, 1992), 27–28.

52. Clayton, *France, Soldiers and Africa*, 360.

53. Graduates of EFORTOM during the late 1950s and early 1960s included a number of military presidents and presidential aspirants, including Seyni Kountché (president of Niger), Mathieu Kérékou (president of Benin), Moussa Traoré (president of Mali), and Seye Zerbo (president of Upper Volta). Many of these were second-generation soldiers educated at the African military academies established by France for the sons of veterans. Echenberg, *Colonial Conscripts*, 122–26. See also Samuel Decalo, *Historical Dictionary of Niger*, 2nd ed., African Historical Dictionaries no. 20 (Metuchen, N.J.: Scarecrow Press, 1989), 138.

54. Clayton, *France, Soldiers and Africa*, 382.

55. Clayton, *France, Soldiers and Africa*, 382.

56. Chaigneau, *La Politique Militaire*, 41. Also Martin, *Warriors to Managers*, 42.

57. Chaigneau, *La Politique Militaire*, 49.

58. Chipman, *French Power in Africa*, 121–22.

59. International Institute for Strategic Studies (IISS), *The Military Balance 1970–1971* (London: Brassey's Publishers), 54.

60. Clayton, *France, Soldiers and Africa*, 436, 382–84. Also IISS, *The Military Balance 1975–1976*, 21–22.

61. Chipman, *French Power in Africa*, 120–22. Martin, *Warriors to Managers*, 355.

62. Foltz, *From French West Africa to the Mali Federation*, 173.

63. Pascal Chaigneau, *La Politique Militaire*, 22. Also Chipman, *French Power in Africa*, 117. Clayton, *France, Soldiers and Africa*, 382.

64. Chipman, *French Power in Africa*, 121.

65. Chaigneau, *La Politique Militaire*, 29.

66. Chaigneau, *La Politique Militaire*, 24.

67. Chaigneau, *La Politique Militaire*, 120.

68. Chipman, *French Power in Africa*, 117–19.

69. Chaigneau, *La Politique Militaire*, 33.

70. Clayton, *France, Soldiers and Africa*, 436, 382–84. Also IISS, *The Military Balance 1975–1976*, 21–22.

71. Chaigneau, *La Politique Militaire*, 69, 75.

72. Claude E. Welch, Jr., ed., *Soldier and State in Africa: A Comparative Analysis of Military Intervention and Political Change* (Evanston, Ill.: Northwestern University Press, 1970), 15–17.

73. Chipman, *French Power in Africa*, 123–25.

74. Yates, *The Rentier State*, 112–14.

75. Chaigneau, *La Politique Militaire*, 22, 111, and Chipman, *French Power in Africa*, 117. See also Wynfred Joshua and Stephen P. Gibert. *Arms for the Third World: Soviet Military Aid Diplomacy* (Baltimore, Md.: The Johns Hopkins University Press, 1969), 34.

76. Claude E. Welch, Jr., *No Farewell to Arms? Military Disengagement from Politics in Africa and Latin America* (Boulder, Colo.: Westview Press, 1987), 33. Also Lee, *African Armies*, 39.

77. Welch, *Soldier and State*, 10.

78. Chipman, *French Power in Africa*, 110.

79. Chipman, *French Power in Africa*, 111.

80. Welch, *Soldier and State*, 11.

81. Chaigneau, *La Politique Militaire*, 25–27.

82. Chipman, *French Power in Africa*, 124.

83. Chaigneau, *La Politique Militaire*, 94.

84. Clayton, *France, Soldiers and Africa*, 383.

85. Foltz, *From French West Africa to the Mali Federation*, 182–83.

86. Claude E. Welch, Jr., "Military Disengagement from Politics: Incentives and Obstacles in Political Change," in Baynham, ed., *Military Power and Politics*, 89–90.

87. Aristide R. Zolberg, "The Structure of Political Conflict in the New States of Tropical Africa," *American Political Science Review* 62, no. 1 (March 1968), 77–78. Also Welch, *No Farewell to Arms?*, 14.

88. Zolberg, "The Structure of Political Conflict," 77–78. Also Welch, *No Farewell to Arms?* 14–15.

89. Welch, *No Farewell to Arms?* 172–73.

90. Michael Bratton and Nicolas van de Walle, *Democratic Experiments in Africa: Regime Transitions in Comparative Perspective* (Cambridge, U.K.: Cambridge University Press, 1997), 66.

91. Welch, *No Farewell to Arms?* 179–81.

92. Chipman, *French Power in Africa*, 125–26.

93. Kalck, *Historical Dictionary of the Central Africa Republic*, 37.

94. Lee, *African Armies*, 79.

95. Welch, *Soldier and State*, 273.

96. Samuel Decalo, *Coups and Army Rule in Africa: Motivations and Constraints*, 2nd ed. (New Haven, Conn.: Yale University Press, 1990), 214.

97. Decalo, *Coups and Army Rule*, 265, 330.

98. For a full account of the political and military aspects of *Operation Turquoise*, read Prunier, *The Rwanda Crisis*, 1995. Gérard Prunier accompanied *Turquoise* as a policy adviser.

99. Decalo, *Historical Dictionary of Niger*, 227.

100. Chipman, *French Power in Africa*, 126.

101. Stephen Ellis, "Liberia 1989–1994. A Study of Ethnic and Spiritual Violence," *African Affairs* 94 (1995), 168.

102. Chipman, *French Power in Africa*, 171.

103. Foltz, *From French West Africa to the Mali Federation*, 33.

104. Decalo, *Historical Dictionary of Niger*, 100. See also John F. Clark and David E. Gardinier, eds., *Political Reform in Francophone Africa* (Boulder, Colo.: Westview Press, 1997), 15–16.

105. Foltz, *From French West Africa to the Mali Federation*, 49–51.
106. Chipman, *French Power in Africa*, 258.
107. Janet G. Vaillant, "African Deputies in Paris: The Political Role of Léopold Senghor in the Fourth Republic," in Johnson, *Double Impact*, 145–46.
108. Foltz, *From French West Africa to the Mali Federation*, 54. Also Echenberg, *Colonial Conscripts*, 148.
109. Chipman, *French Power in Africa*, 97. Foltz, *From French West Africa to the Mali Federation*, 58. See also Moose, "French Military Policy in Africa," in Foltz and Bienen, *Arms and the African*, 87.
110. Foltz, *From French West Africa to the Mali Federation*, 76. Chipman, *French Power in Africa*, 100. Also Echenberg, *Colonial Conscripts*, 162.
111. Chipman, *French Power in Africa*, 18.
112. Foltz, *From French West Africa to the Mali Federation*, 143.
113. Chipman, *French Power in Africa*, 56–57.
114. Yates, *The Rentier State*, 95.
115. Chipman, *French Power in Africa*, 57–58.
116. Prunier, *The Rwanda Crisis*, 318.
117. Jean-François Bayart, *The State in Africa: The Politics of the Belly*, trans. Mary Harper and Christopher and Elizabeth Harrison (New York: Addison Wesley Longman Publishing, 1993), 197. See also Vaillant, "African Deputies," in Johnson, *Double Impact*, 142.
118. David E. Gardinier, "The French Impact on Education in Africa, 1817–1960," in Johnson, *Double Impact*, 341.
119. Martin, *Warriors to Managers*, 66–67.
120. Martin, *Warriors to Managers*, 84–85.
121. Foltz, *From French West Africa to the Mali Federation*, 21. Bayart, *The State in Africa*, 159. See also Peggy Sabatier, "Did Africans Really Learn to Be French? The Francophone Elite of the École William Ponty," in Johnson, *Double Impact*, 179ff.
122. Yates, *The Rentier State*, 122.
123. ECOWAS Protocol on Non-Aggression, 22 April 1978, in *Regional Peace-Keeping and International Enforcement: The Liberian Crisis*, ed. M. Weller, Cambridge International Documents Series, vol. 6 (Cambridge, U.K.: Cambridge University Press, 1994), 18–19.
124. Agence France Press report of 29 September 1993, in Weller, *Regional Peace-Keeping*, 416.
125. BBC Monitoring Report, 17 September 1990, in Weller, *Regional Peace-Keeping*, 99.
126. United Nations Secretary-General, Report on Liberia, 9 September 1993, in Weller, *Regional Peace-Keeping*, 374.
127. Agence France Press, 24 December 1993, in Weller, *Regional Peace-Keeping*, 450.
128. I. William Zartman, "Internationalization of Communal Strife: Temptations and Opportunities of Triangulation," in *The Internationalization of Communal Strife*, ed. Manus I. Midlarsky (New York: Routledge, 1993), 27, 29.

129. Zartman, "Internationalization of Communal Strife," 39.
130. Ellis, "Liberia 1989–1994," 178–81.
131. Ellis, "Liberia 1989–1994," 180–81.
132. Welch, *No Farewell to Arms?* 37.
133. Chipman, *French Power in Africa*, 126. See also Ellis, "Liberia 1989–1994," 168.
134. IISS, *The Military Balance 1970–1971*, 54–55.
135. Joshua and Gibert, *Arms for the Third World*, 31–34.
136. Joshua and Gibert, *Arms for the Third World*, 34.
137. Roger E. Kanet, "Military Relations between Eastern Europe and Africa," in Arlinghaus, *Arms for Africa*, 87.
138. George T. Yu, "Chinese Arms Transfers to Africa," in Arlinghaus, *Arms for Africa*, 111.
139. Joseph P. Smaldone, "U.S. Arms Transfers and Security-Assistance Programs in Africa: A Review and Policy Perspective," in Arlinghaus, *Arms for Africa*, 194.
140. Moose, "French Military Policy in Africa," in Foltz and Bienen, *Arms and the African*, 60.
141. The data in this section was taken from Joshua and Gibert, *Arms for the Third World*, 130–31, which was compiled from U.S. Department of Defense *Military Assistance Facts*, and from figures in the *New York Times*.
142. Joshua and Gibert, *Arms for the Third World*, 137.
143. Moose, "French Military Policy in Africa," in Foltz and Bienen, *Arms and the African*, 62–63.
144. Data taken from Anthony Clayton, "Foreign Intervention in Africa," in Baynham, ed., *Military Power and Politics*, 228–49. Also Joshua and Gibert, *Arms for the Third World*, 34.
145. Arlinghaus, *Arms for Africa*, 223–24.
146. Decalo, *Coups and Army Rule*, 39.
147. Decalo, *Coups and Army Rule*, 39–88.
148. Decalo, *Coups and Army Rule*, 80.
149. Vaillant, "African Deputies," in Johnson, *Double Impact*, 149.
150. G. Wesley Johnson, in Johnson, ed., *Double Impact*, 382.
151. Welch, *No Farewell to Arms?* 197.
152. Chipman, *French Power in Africa*, 97–99. Foltz, *From French West Africa to the Mali Federation*, 55–58.
153. Foltz, *From French West Africa to the Mali Federation*, 69. Also Vaillant, "African Deputies," in Johnson, *Double Impact*, 147.
154. Chipman, *French Power in Africa*, 100.
155. Chipman, *French Power in Africa*, 100–1.
156. Chipman, *French Power in Africa*, 103. Foltz, *From French West Africa to the Mali Federation*, 73–75.
157. Foltz, *From French West Africa to the Mali Federation*, 87.
158. Foltz, *From French West Africa to the Mali Federation*, 91.

159. Chipman, *French Power in Africa*, 104–6. Foltz, *From French West Africa to the Mali Federation*, 92, 106.

160. Welch, *Soldier and State*, 12.

161. Chipman, *French Power in Africa*, 107. See Foltz's *From French West Africa to the Mali Federation* for much greater detail.

162. Decalo, *Historical Dictionary of Niger*, xxv, 227–28.

163. Chipman, *French Power in Africa*, 153.

164. Chipman, *French Power in Africa*, 152.

165. Charles H. Cutter, "The Genesis of a Nationalist Elite: The Role of the Popular Front in the French Soudan (1936–1939)," in Johnson, *Double Impact*, 115.

166. Welch, *No Farewell to Arms?* 188.

167. Welch, *No Farewell to Arms?* 188, 193.

168. Decalo, *Coups and Army Rule*, 14.

169. Martin, *Warriors to Managers*, 16.

170. Martin, *Warriors to Managers*, 21.

171. Quoted in Clayton, *France, Soldiers and Africa*, 5.

172. Chipman, *French Power in Africa*, 152.

173. Chaigneau, *La Politique Militaire*, 94.

174. Clayton, *France, Soldiers and Africa*, 383.

175. Ruth Leger Sivard, *World Military and Social Expenditures*, 16th ed. (Washington, D.C.: World Priorities, 1996), 19.

176. Foltz, *From French West Africa to the Mali Federation*, 182–83.

177. Decalo, *Coups and Army Rule*, 265, 330.

178. The most egregious example of this comes, unsurprisingly, from President Bokassa, who at one point named an avenue in the Central African Republic's capital for Muammar Qaddafi, and espoused Islam in return for Libyan aid and diplomatic support. Within a year of this decision, the now "Emperor" Bokassa had decided that Napoleon was a better role model and Giscard a more profitable patron. He reaffirmed his French Catholicism.

179. Foltz and Bienen, *Arms and the African*, 2–10.

CHAPTER SIX

Toujours la Chasse Gardée?

French Power and Influence in Late-Twentieth-Century Francophone Central Africa, 1970–1995

Sarah S. Milburn

Introduction

The original five countries of *Afrique Équatoriale Française* (Chad, Cameroon, Central African Republic, Gabon, and Congo-Brazzaville) are the focal points of this chapter, because their relationships with France have presented a number of useful examples of the penetration and persistence of French power and influence during the period of this study. Their contribution to French military power and security has been maintained and developed over the long term as a coherent series of policies persisting throughout the administrations of every French president from Charles de Gaulle to Jacques Chirac. The assumptions upon which France's African security policy have been based since the Brazzaville Conference of 1944 are still discernible in France's African affairs in the 1990s. The sources of this continuity of French influence are not simply expressed in military aid. The economic, cultural, and juridical factors that support and enhance France's military power in Central Africa need to be considered as an integral part of its ability to shape the peacetime environment in its former colonies.

France's relationships during this period with Central African Republic, Gabon, Cameroon, Congo-Brazzaville, and (especially) Chad will be discussed in this chapter, and those with the former Belgian colonies of Rwanda, Burundi and Zaïre will be mentioned. Examples from West Africa will also be raised briefly, because Central and West African nations share a number of borders, security issues, and economic structures. There were interventions in West Africa by France that made use of French troops based in Central Africa, and vice versa.

The three main challenges to France in achieving its goals during the second half of the twentieth century remained in this period much as they were in the immediate postcolonial phase: *first*, preserving and extending French power and influence against the anglophone world, especially the other Western members of the Atlantic alliance, particularly the United States; *second*, staving off attempts at influence in the developing world on the part of the Soviet Union and its allies, and *third*, managing, not nationalism exactly, but its sequelae: the growing independence of the francophone African states from French influence, and their increasing willingness to play off the French against other nations who could strengthen them against internal and external security threats.

France continued to follow the pattern established during the colonial period of mounting its efforts in sub-Saharan Africa with as few French troops as possible: "the profile would always be African troops surrounded by French cadres and officers."[1] National security bargains were made by the leaders of African states with a number of external and internal actors, but mainly with the French via the postindependence cooperations agreements. As shown in the previous chapter, France's African military bases, added to its economic clout, were used as carrots or as sticks as the need arose.

Interestingly, while France's own definition of national security continued to include the maintenance of its clout in Africa, recent events in *la Francophonie* (particularly in Zaïre) have lessened that clout considerably. Consider the comment of Daniel Simpson, former U.S. ambassador to Zaïre, that "France is no longer capable of imposing itself in Africa. . . . Neo-colonialism is no longer tolerated. The French attitude no longer reflects the reality of the situation." While there was Africa-wide agreement with Simpson, the French were furious with this assessment.[2] In the long run, the French neocolonial militarization of its African clients may in fact have increased not only their dependency but also their fragility as states.[3]

France's interest in manipulating events in its former African colonies remained integrally linked to the French government's perception of France itself as a major global player. The bitter and quite public rivalry between anglophone and francophone influences in Africa continued in spite of the independent status of Britain and France's former colonies on the continent. This rivalry has been evident in the competition between France and the United States for influence in Zaïre, and France's growing influence in the two other former Belgian colonies of Burundi and Rwanda. As Paul Kagame's Rwandan Patriotic Front and its ally, Laurent Kabila's Congolese AFDL demonstrated, however, Rwanda and Zaïre's ties to France were by no means tight enough to prevent insurgent groups with anglophone allies (Uganda, South Africa, and others) from trying to cut France out of the picture. Indeed, the ancient, persistent, and still-perceived rivalry with anglophone influences in the *chasse gardée* apparently inhabits French Africa policy to this day in a form that Gérard Prunier refers to risibly but quite seriously as "Fashoda Syndrome," meaning that "the whole world is a cultural, political and economic battlefield between France and the 'Anglo-Saxons.'"[4] Fashoda Syndrome may simply be the insecure "other face" of France's confident public expression of its own great contribution to world civilization. The negative part of possessing prestige is the knowledge of how much one has to lose, which France had gained firsthand during the German occupation and did not wish to experience again. The attraction of Gaullism lay precisely in de Gaulle's ability to inspire France to reclaim its own independent destiny, and his articulation of the idea that glory given to France was justly deserved.

Part One: France's Military Capabilities vis-à-vis Its Former Colonies in French Central Africa

France remains the most influential great power in francophone central Africa, although its power is tempered by regional and local politics and the growing influence of the United States as a competing source of aid and investment. Although France outguns by far even the strongest regional actor in the *chasse gardée* (Libya), her military power in Africa is by no means based entirely on hardware. The overwhelming military superiority which France has possessed in comparison with all African states is as much a function of the consistently maintained historical relationship between France and francophone Africa as it is a function of France's impressive technological superiority.

Three distinct facets of military power continued to characterize France's penetration of the Central African region:

- *France's physical presence* (composed of troops, military command structures, French officers and well-maintained bases),
- *France's intelligence and diplomatic presence* (both formal and informal military advisory connections and personal friendships formed between French and African leaders), and

- *France's ongoing military aid transfers and sales* to its former possessions (sales and donations of arms, trainers, and joint exercises).

These continued to be interwoven with French diplomatic initiatives and economic support. France's most faithful francophone African allies still preferred to purchase most of their arms and police equipment from French companies, even though many also purchased arms from the Soviet bloc countries, the United States, and China.

One of France's strongest assets in Africa is the use it has made of the infrastructural and administrative support provided to its former colonies over the years since the Brazzaville Conference. This support includes the education of African military and administrative elites which replaced most, if not all, of the French bureaucrats in the colonies with "assimilated" African trainees (as explained in the preceding chapter), as well as roads, banking facilities, and communications networks, all of which form important aspects of France's military aid agreements to the former colonies. France's preponderant power in the Central African region is deeply rooted in the colonial years, during which France cemented a relationship of dependency on the part of its African partners, aspects of which remain to this day.

The limits to this power lie largely in the African leaders' growing knowledge that France still has need of them for a number of reasons. The depth of their understanding of French culture allows them to manipulate the relationship with their former colonial overlord and make the most of what little reciprocal power is available to them. Their greatest advantage remains that France continues to need its African *chasse gardée*. France's need for strategic resources like petroleum and uranium were only part of the picture, and perhaps not even the most salient part. While the loss of *Algérie Française* meant that one could no longer say, in the words of General Raoul Salan,[5] that "The Mediterranean runs through France as the Seine runs through Paris," it remains true that France continues to view its former sub-Saharan possessions as a vital extension of its own power and prestige. By integrating its interests closely with those of its African "partners" in a relationship of fraternity (if not complete liberty and equality), France has continued to preserve itself as an African regional power.

The Overall Military Balance between France and Other Powers in the Central African Region

Despite the global superpower rivalry, French power in Africa remained a significant and reliable balancing force of *"equidistance"*[6] between the poles, preventing U.S. or USSR influence from gaining much of a foothold in the francophone nations until only recently. In francophone Central Africa (with the exception of Zaïre, where the United States assisted Mobutu in order to balance the USSR and Cuba's influence in Angola), France remained the preponderant and most influential great power for much of the 1970s and 1980s.

In 1980, France's total armed forces numbered 509,300, of which a little over half were conscripts. In 1987, this number was 546,900, again, over half conscripts, and there were 391,000 in the reserves.[7] By 1994, France's armed forces numbered 409,600, although IISS puts the potential mobilization including reserves at 1,353,700.[8] By African standards, these numbers are overwhelming. While clearly not in the league of the United States or even the former Soviet state by the end of this period, France's army and military spending in 1994 dwarfed that of the sub-Saharan African nations, all of whom *together* managed to field an armed forces total of 943,000 on a combined military expenditure of $3,891 million. Some of this total reflects the considerable aid given to sub-Saharan nations by the West and the Soviet bloc, much of which subsidized the Africans' ability to purchase weapons and field troops. France's aid, as well as the participation in and out of African uniforms by French military *coopérants*, provided a significant enhancement of francophone African military power.[9]

By the time of de Gaulle's resignation in 1969, his goal of renewing the sovereignty and confidence of France had been largely met, but he left his successor with a number of economic and diplomatic problems. President Pompidou, while publicly faithful both to de Gaulle, and to Gaullism, made a number of changes in the composition of the French forces and military capacity.[10] Pompidou continued de Gaulle's policy of lessening French troop commitments in francophone Africa as part of a policy aimed at maintaining the consistency of the French commitment, while attempting to make it less obvious. He concentrated like his predecessor on reminding the rest of the world that there was still a link between the French commitment in Africa, and France's image as a global power, and he found the Force d'Intervention useful more as a general deterrent to the Soviet threat in Europe, even though it could still be used as needed in other theaters of operation. France's interventions in Africa were presented to the other Western powers as one of its contributions to containment of the USSR's global ambitions.

While de Gaulle and Pompidou's terms in office had diminished the land army in Europe in favor of the *force de frappe*, President Giscard d'Estaing, elected in 1974, increased military spending by 16 percent, along with the defense-related portions of the French economy. The conventional forces in Europe were strengthened, tactical nuclear weapons received new types of training programs, and the need for overseas intervention, in Africa in particular, increased in importance. The ambitious reforms and expectations of Giscard's military program were not all met, however, because of economic constraints. The result, though, was not incompatible in any way with the Gaullist principle of a more prominent military role for France in Europe,[11] and the resulting increase in flexibility of response was useful in several African interventions.

Giscard's "centrist" presidency represented a rupture in the Gaullist policy of decreasing France's African military presence. *Displaying* French power became once again an important way to show just how well France could preserve Western influence in Africa, and how much more able it was to do so than any of the other Western powers. In 1977, French military aid to Africa went from 414 million FF to 644 million FF, and began a steady climb, although it was still a small portion of the overall French defense budget. An increased number of Africans began to be trained in French military schools and Giscard increased the weapons capacity and troop strength of the existing Force d'Intervention.[12]

A key element in maintaining French military power has been its intelligence capacity. The largest of France's intelligence services in 1986 was the 2,000-member, seven-department SDECE (Service de Documentation Extérieure et de Contre Espionage), which has an entire department devoted to intelligence and military intervention in Africa. The SDECE and the Service d'Action Civique have paid particular attention, during the Cold War period and after, to the activities of the other major powers in Africa, including the United States and the USSR, so that France could shore up its interests where necessary in the face of other superpower activities in its *chasse gardée*.[13]

French policy since independence was to improve, modernize, and "Africanize" the francophone African armies, building upon the small improvements described in chapter 5 during the last part of the colonial period, when African troops were still members of the armies of France. The French government saw France's military interests and its African clients' interests as coextensive (whether or not this was actually the case), and maintained a corps of French officers and NCOs within African armies as a convenient way to streamline interoperability of technical support, and also as a way to emphasize the continuation of these shared interests and French influence.[14]

Table 6.1. French Military Advisers in Central Africa, 1980 and 1988

	1980[15]	1988[16]
Gabon	132	111
Cameroon	75	69
Central African Republic	32	76
Chad	81	41
Congo-Brazzaville	8	13
Burundi	17	28
Rwanda	8	20
Zaïre	128	105
Other Francophone Africa	510	448
Totals	991	911

Source: Adapted from Chaigneau (1984: 45) and Chipman (1989: 147).

Chaigneau notes that the number of French military advisers in Africa fell constantly from 1960 to 1977, but tended to rise after that date. As the above table demonstrates, the numbers of military *coopérants* remained at a fairly high level throughout the 1980s.

The numbers of advisers fluctuated between 900 and 1,000 throughout the 1980s, reflecting other policy changes on the part of France and these countries, but also because of a variety of trainings, maneuvers, and other features of the various agreements that might vary the numbers of advisers needed in a given year. Chad's decreased number of "advisers" between 1980 and 1988 may actually reflect fluctuations in troop presence: France's temporary withdrawals in 1980 and 1984 were each followed by renewed operations by troops, many of whom would not be classified as *coopérants*. These figures for military advisers do not include the numerous other categories of advisers sent by France (teachers, economic representatives), nor do they include French base troops in the total, and so represent only a portion of the French presence. Arlinghaus gives a *coopérants* total of 22,000 in all of Africa for 1982, stating that although French troops and technical advisers in Africa were outnumbered in general by the Soviets and Cubans, they were better organized and distributed throughout the region, and they had more potential for effective intervention.[17]

Chaigneau notes that the number of African junior and senior officers trained in France rose steadily since 1970, and even saw a significant jump after 1979. African officers and troops trained in France numbered under 1,000 per year until the mid-1970s, but that number had doubled by 1982.

Clayton places the number of African officers trained in France at 1,734 in 1979 and 2,226 in 1983, remaining roughly at this level for at least a decade.[18]

African Military Forces

In 1983, the following sizes were recorded for the francophone Central African armed forces (many though not all of which still number under 10,000, as shown in the 1994 table below), and a few of the regional powers for comparison (Angola, Nigeria, and Libya). These figures do not include paramilitary forces, reserves, or gendarmerie:[19]

Table 6.2. Sizes of Selected African Armed Forces in 1983

Number of Personnel	Countries
Under 5,000	Central African Republic, Chad, Gabon
5,000–10,000	Cameroon, Congo-Brazzaville, Rwanda, Burundi
10,000–25,000	Zaïre
25,000–50,000	Angola
50,000–100,000	Libya
Over 100,000	Nigeria

Source: Adapted from Brayton, "Arms Control in Africa," in Baynham (1986: 272).

Charles P. Snyder gives the following brief impressions of some of the francophone African ground forces in 1984:[20] Zaïre's army was 22,000 in 1984, enormous by francophone standards, but not nearly as well equipped (and nowhere near as disciplined) as other neighbors with comparable forces (e.g., Angola). Gabon's forces were small, but well trained to provide enough internal security in a crisis until French help arrived. The Congo-Brazzaville army in 1984 was 8,000, and well equipped with artillery and armored vehicles, but suffered from politicized ethnic divisions in its ranks. Cameroon had a more modernized army than many of its neighbors, and was said to be well disciplined and capable of both internal defense and external engagement. Chad's armies in 1984 were riven by war and factionalism. The Central African Republic's army of 5,000 was unable to control its porous borders; smuggling was a significant problem. Rwanda and Burundi were in the process of modernizing with French help. On balance, however, these armies' capabilities were dwarfed by those of France, as well as by the forces of several neighbors: Angola, Libya, and Nigeria. A comparison in 1994 illustrates the relative magnitude of armed forces and defense spending in the region:[21]

Table 6.3. Relative Magnitude of Armed Forces and Defense Spending, 1994

	Armed Forces (in thousands)	Military Expenditures (in millions of US$)
Cameroon	15	139
Central African Republic	3	23
Chad	25	31
Congo-Brazzaville	10	45
Gabon	3	85
Rwanda	5	125
Burundi	11	33
Zaïre	49	91
Angola	82	498
Libya	70	927
Nigeria	77	195
France	410	34,442
United States	1,650	230,896
Former Soviet Union	2,587	32,740

Sources: Sivard (1996: 28, 45–47) and IISS, The Military Balance (1994–1995: 22, 111).

For those states whose military spending is available for comparison from 1960, it is evident that their military budgets did increase at least a little since independence. The factors that are difficult to reconcile or determine from these figures are (a) the degree of militarization of each of these economies (many have military governments), and (b) the levels of aid received from France and the other great powers which have subsidized the military budgets both directly within the budgets and indirectly in the form of training exercises and other forms of cooperation. Thus, the percentages of military spending in each country's budget are not always directly comparable. Richer states, like Gabon and Cameroon, appear to have higher military expenditures, although again, these figures do not show the subsidizing effects of foreign aid on any country's total expenditures. Rwanda, not a wealthy country, was at war in 1994 with the insurgent Rwandan Patriotic Front, and receiving considerable military aid and training from the French government; its expenditures here reflect the ongoing state of civil war. Highly militarized states, like Congo-Brazzaville, Zaïre, and Burundi, have higher totals of troops and military spending relative to their populations.[22]

Chad's armed forces total is higher than most, reflecting the frequent state of either civil war or external aggression in that country, and the continuing presence of a military government with ongoing concerns about internal security, although its expenditure is now in line with that of many other more peaceful states. Libya, France's primary external opponent in the Chad conflict (and a frequent diplomatic and military factor in central African regional politics to this day) had a total of 70,000 in its armed forces in 1994, with a military budget of $927 million. Libya's military expenditures have been enormous, buoyed by the nation's oil resources, and its arms purchases between 1973 and 1983 were estimated at $17,260 million. Although it has the physical capacity to be a preponderant power in the region, the military itself is increasingly less involved in political decisions, and Qaddafi's own variety of ideologically-based diplomacy has made Libya's use of its power somewhat erratic in effect. Nonetheless, it was a power to be reckoned with during the period covered by this chapter, and particularly during the period from 1973 to 1987 when it was operating in Chad.[23,24]

In spite of their relative weaknesses, sub-Saharan African armies began to acquire force projection capabilities that were better equipped and more versatile than their colonial incarnations. African armies were no longer solely composed of infantry. Many had acquired some limited air strike and paratrooper capacity. African air forces, however, were not always capable of making the most of their more advanced aircraft. The topmost leaders tended to be well-educated and good flyers; however, the aviation ability in the ranks immediately below the top tended to vary widely in quality. Also, in most African armies, the air force took its orders from the ground army command, which often lacked a full understanding of air potential. Air force capacity was largely used only for support of ground troops.

Libya's air force presented a vast contrast in preponderance to the other African air contingents in the 1980s, although it was less extensive than that of France. Where Libya had 479 fighters, 30 COIN aircraft, 7 bombers, assorted other aircraft and 8,500 air force personnel, the nearest sub-Saharan francophone African competitor to Libya in 1984 was Guinea, with 6 fighters and an air force of 800 men. Gabon had 7 fighters, but only 500 air personnel, and Chad had no fighters, only helicopters and trainers, and an air force of 200 men. In contrast, Nigeria—ECOWAS's military hegemon and the most substantial power in West Africa, had an air force of 9,000 men, 30 fighters, and a number of other helicopters, trainers, reconnaissance planes, and transports.[25]

Francophone African nations with rivers and coastlines had tiny naval capacities as well, largely in the form of a couple of small patrol boats. However, as of 1986, Cameroon, Congo-Brazzaville, Gabon, Guinea, Côte d'Ivoire, and Zaïre all had slightly larger navies with more numerous, larger, and better-armed patrol craft. None are in the same naval league, however, with the two African competitors most frequently mentioned here. Libya's navy by 1986 had at least eight (Soviet and Yugoslav) submarines, a frigate, four minesweepers, and numerous well-armed (with missiles) corvettes and patrol boats. Nigeria's navy at this time had no submarines but was similarly well-endowed with surface warships.[26]

In addition to their technical cooperation agreements with France, Francophone African states signed agreements among themselves for transnational training of their militaries. Some non-Francophones offered these training opportunities as well, particularly if their regional interests are concerned. For example, following the mercenary raid in Benin in 1977, Nigeria and Benin signed an agreement to train Beninois officer cadets at military school in Nigeria.[27]

While not in itself an explicit empirical measure of the force projection strength of African armies, numerous incidents of intervention by African nations demonstrate that the African theater cannot be defined solely in terms of French preponderance and superpower rivalry. Hughes and May conclude that, of forty-three independent states in sub-Saharan Africa, a surprising total of thirty-one have, for various foreign policy reasons, either provided or received deployments of military forces from *other* sub-Saharan African states during the period of study. This total represents regular armed forces contributions alone, in support of three types of objectives: regime-supportive and regime-opposing foreign policy, and state-supporting objectives (when a state is in danger of collapse). Regime-supportive interventions by African nations closely resemble those of France in support of French client regimes; most of these were by Guinea, Tanzania, Zaïre, Senegal, and Nigeria. Guinea intervened on five separate occasions on behalf of other endangered regimes. Zaïre intervened in Burundi in 1972, and in the Central African Empire in 1979 out of President Mobutu's personal friendship for President Bokassa in order to reinforce Bokassa's attacks on protesting schoolchildren. Mobutu also stationed a small air-liaison unit in Chad under Tombalbaye, and he later contributed fighter aircraft and 2,000 ground troops to assist President Habré against the Libyan-backed opposition army of Goukouni Oueddai. Zaïre also joined the OAU-sponsored inter-African force in Chad in 1981.[28]

Senegal's regime-supportive interventions were often accused domestically of being proxy forces for French security interests. Senegal participated with Morocco and other francophone African countries in the inter-African force which replaced French and Belgian troops in Zaïre's Shaba Province in 1978. Senegal has also intervened twice in the Gambia in 1980 and 1981. Nigeria's largest external intervention with ECOMOG in Liberia was discussed in chapter 5. In addition, Nigeria was also involved in Chad, and perhaps on both sides of the conflict. Nigeria has sent forces twice to Chad as peacekeeping troops, and it also probably supported the opposition FROL-INAT's Third Army.[29]

Regime-opposing interventions are fewer, although not few enough to discount as evidence of the growing military power of some sub-Saharan states. The mid-1990s have given numerous other examples of inter-African and also unilateral intervention on the part of Angola (most recently in Congo-Brazzaville against President Lissouba, and in Democratic Republic of Congo/former Zaïre against Mobutu), and also Uganda (in Rwanda against the Habyarimana regime, and also in DRC/Zaïre against Mobutu). Earlier interventions of this type by francophone nations include, by some definitions, long-term Zaïrean support for the insurgent movements of Holden Roberto and Jonas Savimbi in Angola (gaining in return Angolan support for anti-Mobutu insurgency), and a 1977 attack on the government of Benin by mercenaries possibly backed by the French with the help of Morocco and Gabon, but this (along with accusations of help by Senegal, Togo, and Côte d'Ivoire) was never proved. The Tanzanian intervention in Uganda which overthrew President Idi Amin was the clearest, most provable case of regime-opposing intervention during this time period.[30]

One of the earliest state-supportive contributions by African armed forces was the large inter-African force that served from 1960 to 1964 in Congo-Léopoldville (Zaïre). Such interventions, as was true of the OAU-backed intervention in Chad twenty years later, were expensive, logistically complex, and difficult to maintain for long periods.[31]

France's Effective Technological Superiority over the Regional Powers
France's technical potential was clearly superior to that of every other power in the Central African region in hardware and capacity for rapid response, except for the United States and the Soviet Union. However, even the United States and USSR could not match France's political and economic penetration capability, which resulted in a greater strategic flexibility and better cooperation with the much smaller, and technically inferior, forces of the francophone African armies. The armed forces of francophone Central African states continued to depend on France for training, arms purchases, infrastructural support, and cooperative liaison.[32-34]

France's technological edge gave it the capacity for rapid intervention, improved under President Mitterand. The new 7,000-man Force d'Action Rapide (FAR) created in 1983, was intended to demonstrate France's commitment to European defense while maintaining France's continued autonomy and independence of action. In theory, the five-division (parachute, alpine, marine, aeromobile, and light armored) FAR was to be flexibly deployable (although focused on central Europe), immediately mobilizable, and technically well-endowed, with enough *Milan* antitank missiles, armored vehicles and helicopters, for modern front-line ground warfare.[35]

The reality was less impressive. In 1991, France's limited participation in the multilateral force sent to Iraq during the Gulf War was delayed for three weeks by transport and logistical problems. France's globally oriented rhetoric during this period, as Gordon demonstrates, could not always be matched by its force projection capabilities for larger operations. In addition, much of the Force d'Action Rapide was made up of conscripts, nonprofessionals who could not be sent overseas by French law unless they agreed to this type of service. This meant that France made smaller troop contributions to multilateral forces. The French military was being redesigned yet again in the mid-1990s in order to increase the numbers of trained professionals for overseas service, and also to increase the number of conscripts who agreed to overseas service.[36]

As will be demonstrated later, France's intervention capacity remained constrained by its mobility and transport problems, personnel constraints (particularly the still-high ratio of conscripts to professional personnel in these forces, which Mitterand tried to remedy in the 1980s), and technical contingencies having to do with preparing French forces for dealing with guerrilla-style warfare and Africa's exigent climate conditions. Its previous near monopoly of the air began to be seriously eroded by improved African access to antiaircraft weapons.[37]

The Constancy of French Presence in the Region: Types and Levels of Forces

French presence in Central Africa remained quite constant during this period in terms of the three distinct facets of military power described at the beginning of this chapter, which continued to characterize France's penetration of the Central African region: physical presence, intelligence and diplomatic presence, and arms aid (transfers and sales).

Physical Presence

The loss of faith in pure deterrence doctrine placed renewed emphasis on improving the capacity of French forces to respond to nonnuclear crises. Giscard d'Estaing's policy of flexibility included the reorganization of French forces. Of greatest importance to Africa, the distinctions between de Gaulle's three France-based forces—the Forces d'Intervention, the home defense Forces du Territoire, and the mechanized First Army or Forces de Manoeuvre—were eliminated. Their specialization was preventing the army from adapting to rapid change, and limiting its capabilities. The Forces du Territoire were reintegrated into the Forces de Manoeuvre, and all units were given the same level of equipment to fight in a conventional war: nonnuclear artillery, HOT and Milan antitank weapons, and Roland antiaircraft weapons.[38]

The formal defense agreements, supplemented by informal defense understandings, continued to exist during the period after the death of de Gaulle with many if not all of the countries of France's former colonial empire. These agreements offered weapons as deemed appropriate for African needs and French interests, infrastructural creation and maintenance, training, and the promise of protection against external attack. Some of these agreements still included the implied promise to defend the head of state and his government against internal oppositional attacks as well, as demonstrated in the cases of the Central African Republic and Gabon. French military readiness and response capability varied during the period, according to the terms of each of the defense and military cooperation agreements.

The two types of military agreements, defense agreements (allowing for direct military intervention in African countries at the discretion of the French president) and military cooperation agreements (providing for training, technical assistance and equipment transfers) continued to insure France's continuity in the region, although these were occasionally renegotiated. Central African Republic and Gabon (both of which maintained large French bases on their soil) had maintained their defense agreements without much alteration since signing their accords in the early 1960s. As of 1989, defense agreements existed between France and Cameroon (signed in 1974), Central African Republic (in 1960), and Gabon (in 1960). Military cooperation agreements were signed by a much larger number of former colonies, as well as several that were not formerly French. These included Cameroon (1974), Central African Republic (1960), Chad (1976), Congo-Brazzaville (1974), and Gabon (1960), and the former Belgian colonies: Burundi (1969), Rwanda (1975), and Zaire (1974). Libya signed a military cooperation agreement with France in 1978.[39]

By the mid-1970s, only a few of the cooperation agreements were on the same comprehensive scale as those signed in the 1960s. Of the twelve agreements in existence in 1960 and 1961, only Côte d'Ivoire, Central African Republic, Gabon, Togo, and Cameroon kept their agreements largely as they had been drawn up at independence.[40] Cameroon did not sign a new agreement, but its relations with France remained in accordance with the former agreement. From the mid-1970s on, French forces remained officially only in Senegal, Côte d'Ivoire, Gabon, and the Central African Republic, with additional support from the base in Djibouti.[41] Chad, as will be described in a later section, received a significant military commitment from France throughout a period of nearly continuous internal strife and external insecurity, although this commitment varied according to the ability of each successive French president to offer aid to various Chadian leaders.[42,43]

During the 1970s, France renegotiated military cooperation agreements which provide training assistance and joint exercises, as well as military equipment, with Cameroon, Central African Republic, and Gabon. In the former Belgian colonies, Zaïre's agreement placed French officers in command of Zaïrean troops, as had occurred in all of the French African colonies since the colonial-era creation of the *Tirailleurs Sénégalais*. The same was true in Rwanda and Burundi.[44]

French garrison troops in 1986 at the largest French bases numbered 450 marines in Côte d'Ivoire, 1,200 in Senegal, and 650 in Gabon. Gabon also rotated in occasional metropolitan cavalry and engineers. Spahi or Marine regiments usually served in the Central African Republic.[45] Details on the varied uses of the garrison troops, or "Forces de Présence," will be given in the next few sections concerning France's speed of response and intervention capability. As supported by the military *coopérant* data given earlier, Chaigneau notes that the number of military advisers in Africa fell constantly from 1960 to 1977, but tended to rise after that date.

Intelligence Presence

The French intelligence presence is perhaps the least quantifiable aspect of French presence, although as constantly maintained as the other facets. Most of the Central African militaries were commanded by French officers until independence, and even in 1995 there were French citizens in African uniforms among the officer corps of the Central African militaries. The ambiguity of the allegiances of these officers was a strong factor in preserving the personal relationships between African heads of state and the French president and military that have characterized France's penetrative diplomacy in its former colonies, a form of diplomacy which continues to be called "*coopération*."

Most of the defense agreements provided opportunities for Africans to serve in the French army, and for Frenchmen to wear African uniforms and serve as military support in African armies. In a fascinating extension of the always ambiguously defined sense of Franco-African solidarity developed during the two World Wars, African and French interests continued to be blurred by the frequent occurrence of Africans continuing to serve France and Frenchmen continuing to command African troops.[46]

The more covert French intelligence presence in francophone Central African countries is harder to determine, in part (as Anthony Clayton emphasizes) because successful covert operations remain so, and also because some of these operations, when made public, are explained away by the authorities as cases in which the local French operatives have overstepped their authority. Clayton suggests that, in 1960–1962 during Congo-Léopoldville's unrest, French personnel tried to attach part of northern Congo-Léopoldville (later Zaïre) to their own sphere of influence, and make it part of Congo-Brazzaville.[47] Algerian parachute veterans and other French forces served under Tshombe in Katanga "on local contract but with covert Paris approval." Covert French intelligence support played a role in the aftermath of its more overt military Operation Barracuda, which replaced Emperor Bokassa with David Dacko in the Central African Republic (CAR), allowing the French to acquiesce in the subsequent overthrow of Dacko by General André Kolingba in his 1981 coup d'état. France maintained a constant and consistent influence in the CAR, probably delivering some limited military support to Kolingba.[48]

Other examples of French intelligence involvement center on the activities of Jacques Foccart, de Gaulle's African affairs adviser, and an influential figure in Franco-African affairs throughout the time frame of both this and the previous chapter. In addition to the regular intelligence service, the SDECE, there is the Service d'Action Civique, also called the "Foccart Machine" after its long-time director. This agency used diplomats, business, and aid personnel in order to extend the reach of the intelligence and security services, and kept the Elysée well informed of the initiatives of other great powers (primarily the United States and USSR) in the domestic politics and military operations of nations within France's sphere of influence.[49] Foccart was probably the prime mover in the decision to supply Biafra with arms via Gabon and Côte d'Ivoire, as described in the previous chapter.

Gabon makes a particularly interesting case study in constancy of French presence because it is one of the few former French colonies on the continent which not only maintained the more politically penetrative form of cooperation agreement (for internal as well as external security), but also kept its agreement largely as it had been drawn up at independence. Jean-François Bayart tells one of the famous Foccart stories concerning the rise to power of Omar Bongo in Gabon, demonstrating the very ordinariness of "foreign interference" via some of the intelligence and/or advisory relationships maintained with France, and the often astute use made of these relationships by Africans who could manipulate them:

> Inasmuch as it is quite open, the interference does not involve any conspiracy. A former French ambassador in Libreville, for example, quite calmly told the story of how in 1966 the vice-president of the Gabonese government, who was "almost illiterate," asked him "whether or not he could sign some documents"

in the absence of the head of state who was ill, how he himself "regularly took instructions from Jacques Foccart who was following the situation very closely" and how, in the end, he obtained from the dying Léon Mba a draft constitutional reform in favour of Bongo.[50]

The French could not afford to lose Gabon (in particular, its large military base and effective control over its considerable oil resources) after the death of the loyal francophile President Mba, and groomed his successor, Omar Bongo, while Mba was dying of cancer in a French hospital. Omar Bongo, like most francophone heads of state, had a French military background. He was from a younger generation of African leaders, and had joined the French Army Air Corps in 1958, becoming a second lieutenant, and stationed at Brazzaville (Congo), Bangui (CAR), and finally at N'Djamena in Chad. He left the army with the rank of lieutenant, and firm credentials as a Gaullist. He worked in Gabon first in the Ministry of Foreign Affairs, and then in Mba's cabinet. After the attempted coup, Bongo began to receive funds from France via Foccart, and he picked up one cabinet portfolio after another during Mba's illness until he became vice president of Gabon, and effectively, Mba's successor. Mba was pressed to agree to all of this on his deathbed, according to the personal memoirs of then-French ambassador Delauney. Bongo remains, as of this writing, President of Gabon.[51,52]

Chad is another country which has maintained a constant French presence in both the physical presence and intelligence dimensions. France has frequently subsidized the African security services by providing its own expert personnel as advisers and as operatives. Clayton cites the example of the French captain of Chad's security service in the 1960s, who was paid by France to serve President Tombalbaye until 1968, when he "retired" from the French military, and was reemployed and paid by Tombalbaye himself. This captain was responsible for the arrest of 100 Chadian opposition members after the failure of the 1963 coup.[53,54]

French security doctrine has been supported by France's position as francophone Africa's primary arms merchant through most of the decades since independence. Arms transfers and sales, and the repair, maintenance, and training in the use of these arms, remains a source of political leverage even though some nations now purchase arms from elsewhere to supplement France's contribution.[55,56] Data on the types and sources of these arms transfers during the two decades following the death of de Gaulle are given in part 2.

The Speed of France's Possible Response

France has developed a substantial and variably mobile force projection capability in Africa over the decades. In terms of actual speed of response, those actions which were able to use French troops based already in Africa (like the Togo and Central African Republic interventions described above) could act with all necessary speed. Those interventions, like Zaïre and Chad, which required larger-scale troop transport, occasionally ran into logistical difficulties, and actions which required massive deliveries of troops and armament (like France's participation in the Gulf War) ran into real political and logistical constraints at home and overseas. By the spring of 1978, with simultaneous interventions needed in Chad and Mauritania/Western Sahara, it had become evident that France's ability to fulfill its commitments under the cooperation agreements was seriously limited by the nature of the French army as primarily a conscript force. Since the 1964 intervention in Gabon, draftees could not be sent overseas or even into foreign countries at all without the permission of the Assemblée Nationale. The whole intervention capacity of France was composed of enlisted personnel, all of whom would be sent overseas in the event of action on two fronts, leaving the draftees to defend the homeland. Prolonged interventions would cause even more severe problems in terms of service and in further unbalancing the composition of France's forces at home and abroad.[57]

In spite of his continuing anticolonialist rhetoric, the government of President François Mitterand (1981–1995) improved France's military capacity for intervention in Africa and offered an even higher level of security aid to African governments than did the administration under Giscard. Mitterand demonstrated a remarkable ability to present himself as, first, the modern version of France's distinguished socialist past, harkening back to Léon Blum and Jean Jaurès, while simultaneously developing the presidentialist centralism and opportunities to personalize presidential power that were bequeathed to his office by de Gaulle. While this dual orientation, both to socialism and to Gaullist presidentialism, gave the Mitterand presidency an air of ambiguous integrity at times, it also offered maximum flexibility where francophone African affairs were concerned. Mitterand was adept at exploiting the historical ties of the past and simultaneously making good use of the structure of the French state and the political opportunities and constraints it presented to him.

Mitterand's main innovations came from the 1984–1988 Military Program Law. These innovations were deepened and perpetuated during a four-year plan from 1988 to 1992. The Force d'Action Rapide (FAR) which came out of the Military Program Law, was intended to provide the capacity for intervention in Europe required by France's allies, along with the flexibility to intervene in the Middle East or Africa as required. Which of these needs was given priority in the FAR's organization was unclear to the Allies, as this force's purpose was very similar to de Gaulle's and Giscard's Forces d'Intervention. The French insisted that the FAR was capable of intervention in both theaters (Europe and the Third World) and would provide, as Charles Hernu said,[58] "independence and solidarity." France would continue to defend its friends while remaining, as little as possible, dependent on its allies for policy direction. French loyalty without subservience was as important a symbolic message in the Mitterand years as it was for de Gaulle and his followers.

In actuality, this restructuring was of greater importance to the overseas theatres than to Europe, although some of the units, like the anti-tank division, were clearly designed for Soviet containment operations in central Europe, and would need NATO air and logistical support in order to make a viable contribution there. Mitterand was considerably more responsive than his predecessors to the practical need on the part of NATO to consider France's defense as vital to Europe's overall security. However, since France was still seeing action with relative frequency overseas, but not in Europe, it was fairly clear where the bulk of the FAR's operations would be. During the Mitterand presidency, there was little change in the substance of the African cooperation agreements, and those commitments remained important factors in the Elysée's overall security deliberations.[59]

Mitterand's new Force d'Action Rapide was roughly twice the size of Giscard's Force d'Intervention, and included five divisions totalling 47,000 troops and logistical personnel:

- *The 9th Marine Infantry* (2 motorized regiments, 2 light-armed regiments with an anti-tank squadron, 1 artillery regiment, 1 engineer regiment, 1 command and support regiment).
- *The 11th Parachute* (6 infantry regiments, 1 light armed regiment, 1 artillery regiment, 1 engineer regiment, 1 command and support regiment, and 1 support battalion).
- *The 6th Light Armored* (2 light-armed regiments, 2 infantry regiments with armored personnel carriers, 1 artillery regiment, 1 engineer regiment, 1 command and support regiment).
- *The 27th Alpine* (6 mountain infantry regiments with *Milan* anti-tank weapons, 1 light-armed regiment with anti-tank squadron, 1 artillery regiment, 1 engineer regiment, 1 command and support regiment).
- *The 4th Aeromobile* (3 combat helicopter (*Gazelle, Puma, HOT*) regiments, 1 infantry regiment with *Milan* anti-tank weapons, 1 command and support regiment, 1 super-Puma support regiment).

The 9th and 11th Divisions were mostly *Troupes de Marine* and used to action overseas. The 6th Light Armored had some *Legionnaires*. The other two divisions were new additions to France's intervention forces. The FAR divisions were given a single commander but not necessarily intended to fight as a unit or even participate in joint exercises. As the FAR was improved, however, the divisions began to operate together more frequently, and to participate as well in joint exercises with the Marines and the Legionnaires, regular forces which continued to have the potentiality of overseas action both by tradition and by continued training. However, the FAR itself remained largely a command structure and forces which were available in France for crisis intervention rather than long-term action. This was because, in wartime, there was need of considerable logistics support which was not built in to the FAR.[60]

The five FAR divisions were highly mobile. The Aeromobile and 27th Alpine were primarily for European operations involving helicopter use, mountain experience, and antitank warfare. As was characteristic of France's operations in Africa, the other divisions were more lightly equipped. The possible European missions remained dependent on NATO support, and were consequently defined in terms of France's current relationships with the Atlantic allies. The overseas missions were far clearer; there were five *conditions under which France would intervene*:

- To guarantee the safety of French citizens overseas.
- To protect the territorial integrity of overseas territories.
- To defend energy and strategic materials supplies and commercial transport routes.
- To fulfill France's obligations under its military cooperation agreements with allied nations.
- To participate in international peacekeeping missions.

Since nearly all of the FAR was composed of nonconscripts who were able to serve overseas, this increased the force's flexibility considerably. Conscripts still could not, under French law, be sent overseas without their own permission and that of the French parliament. Filling the FAR with professional soldiers shortened the decision-making process considerably in a crisis by bypassing the need for a political debate of the various aspects of any given crisis. Intervention in Africa, de facto, was a decision granted to the French president by virtue of this feature of the internal structure of the FAR, enhanced considerably by the immediacy of the relationship between the Ministry of Cooperation and the French presidency. It was the Cooperation Ministry that managed the military cooperation agreements, and not the Defense Ministry, and so the decision-making process for military interventions often began there as well.[61]

At one point, the contribution of France's elected representatives to the intervention process became so scanty that the soldiers' organizations themselves protested their own use for what they saw as undemocratically driven purposes. Chipman quotes a 1984 statement from the Mouvement Information pour les Droits du Soldat, which complains that "with the professionalization of a quarter of our armed forces . . . the government has given itself an intervention capability of a colonial type—without the parliamentary debate considered a democratic minimum."[62] This is an excellent example of the (nominally) socialist government of France making full use of the potential power inherent in Gaullist *presidentialisme*. It is also an indication that the conscription problem of the early twentieth century, described in the historical introduction to these cases, continued to contribute to the paradoxical duality of France as a democratic "nation in arms" which had nonetheless retained much of the imperial intervention capacity of a colonial military organization.

This institutionalized duality was not merely political, but translated into concrete logistical problems in troop deployment. There were continuing difficulties with those interventions that required something more than the logistics support necessary for the simple in-and-out operations envisioned by those who designed the FAR. Operation Manta in Chad required a refuelling detachment that could not be sent immediately (when needed) because all of the technicians were conscripts. This problem has been corrected by forming the technician corps entirely of enlisted volunteers.

Military Options Available to France

France's military options during the 1970s and 1980s were closely related to the ways in which the Central African nations' cooperation agreements structured the French presence in each country. These agreements gave France a number of options if its help was needed (assisting or preventing a coup, fighting insurgency) to defuse or prevent African threats to French or African security, or if an African client became embarrassing or opposed French objectives to an untenable degree. These options were described as "carrots" (inducements to behave, only some of which were military) and "sticks" (punitive measures) in the analogous section of the previous chapter, and remained substantially the same during this time period. The "carrots" were, once again:

- Nonmilitary economic, infrastructural, and educational assistance, using civilian *coopérants*.
- Maintenance of the Franc Zone, and a stable African currency pegged to the French franc.

- Financial aid and investment.
- Diplomatic contacts and mutual friendships between French and African officials, including personal contacts between presidents.
- Franco-African solidarity and mutual political support at the annual Francophone summit meetings and the United Nations.
- Arms transfers.
- Gendarmerie and officer-cadet training, in Africa and in France.
- Military logistical and technical assistance, using French intelligence networks and military *coopérants*.
- Military intervention with base troops and/or Intervention forces to protect an African president from internal security risks.
- Military intervention with base troops and/or Intervention forces to protect an African country from external security risks.

Since the cooperation agreements continued to leave intervention decisions in the hands of the French president, who was not obliged in all cases to intervene or to continue aid in the event of an uncooperative client, the punitive "sticks" included:

- Withdrawal, or the threat to withdraw, any and all of the "carrots" listed above.
- Covert operations, making use of the French Intelligence networks, including paramilitary, mercenary, and other unofficial French operatives.
- Military intervention, using the Africa-based French troops.
- Military intervention, flying in the France-based Force d'Intervention.

The French options during this period can still be characterized as Chaigneau does, in terms of *"intervention"* (whether by the Forces d'Intervention or the later *FAR*) or *"presence"* (as in the Africa-based Forces de Présence). For instance, as stated in chapter 5, defense accords offering *"maintien de l'ordre," "assistance militaire technique,"* and *"soutien logistique"* (preserving internal order, technical military assistance and logistical support), were signed at independence with Congo-Brazzaville (1960), Gabon (1960), Central African Republic (1960), and Chad (1960). Cameroon did not sign one of these agreements at independence, but had done so by 1970.[63] Assistance Militaire Technique (AMT) allowed the French authorities to respond to African defense requests in three major ways: training military personnel (locally and in France), financial support, and logistical support (providing arms, tools and vehicles, and aid in their maintenance). Two types of conventions were available: conventions covering external defense, and conventions covering internal "*intérieure*" defense, which is what is meant above by "*maintien de l'ordre.*" African partners were responsible in general terms for their own external and internal defense, but they could ask for aid from France.[64]

As of 1984, only Cameroon, Central African Republic, and Gabon in Central Africa (and Senegal and Côte d'Ivoire in West Africa) continued to have the most comprehensive defense accords. These five also continued to have AMT agreements, as did Congo-Brazzaville, Zaïre, Rwanda, and Burundi.[65,66]

As the previous section outlines, Mitterand's Force d'Action Rapide, as with the Force d'Intervention of de Gaulle and Giscard, remained effective as a force of first resort on some long-term peacekeeping missions where troop commitments and logistical needs were carefully limited, but they were unable to prosecute a full-scale African war far from home, or any long-term war against insurgents with sophisticated training and significant resources. The mobility and flexibility which helped the FAR on short-duration operations that made use of the base troops also made it unsuitable for some larger-scale overseas operations. Ground forces remained the bedrock of the intervention force, but air transport and "marine" specialists were critical components as well.[67]

Air and Sea Transport Options and Limitations
There were limits in the 1980s on the types of overseas action that could be mounted with the available air transport. Troop transport capacity with the *Transall* aircraft remained problematic even in 1984 when the twenty-five second-generation air-refuellable *Transalls* were added to the 48 older ones originally put into service in 1967. The *Transalls* of whatever age still required the use of staging bases for interventions in Africa. France bought U.S. Hercules cargo planes in 1987, but not the larger American C-141 Starlifters, and relied primarily on national civil aviation to provide mission transport on short notice. An agreement between the French government, Air France, and UTA stipulated a twelve-hour notice for providing air transport to the French armed forces. France has continued to augment its military air transport in the 1990s, and it set long-term goals for a fully military transport system by the year 2000. However, air transport was a considerable problem throughout the 1970–1980 interventions in Africa covered here.[68]

Sea transport was slower but less fraught with logistical problems and the need for support from civilian transport agents. The Military Program Law also augmented France's sea transport with three new landing ships (10,000 tons displacement) ordered for the 1990s, primarily for material not deliverable by air (e.g., tanks). Most of France's defense agreements were with landlocked states, so the naval enhancements to its security presence were important primarily for maintaining its relationship with four of its most important and loyal allies in Africa, all of which were accessible by sea: Côte d'Ivoire, Senegal, Gabon, and Cameroon.[69] Maintaining a flexible response capability on the Atlantic side of Africa continued to be warranted. These states experienced a number of internal security difficulties in the 1990s. Houphouët-Boigny's death in Côte d'Ivoire and the tensions surrounding his successors' inheritance of a presidency geared to the personalism and patronage networks of Houphouët's regime, the tension surrounding Gabon's elections and the likely disarray of Gabon following the eventual loss of long-term president Omar Bongo, as well as electoral and social unrest in Cameroon, mean that France cannot assume that its influence will continue seamlessly in these three countries into the next century.

In addition, the ability to intervene from the sea may well be of value if France needs to protect its offshore oil interests in Cameroon, Côte d'Ivoire, Gabon, or Congo-Brazzaville, but this capacity will be limited by how much the show of force will be a political advantage in an era in which France's "neo-colonialist" interventions are more frequently criticized. If democratization occurs with more frequency, and becomes less cosmetic (less a show of procedure without democratic substance), African presidents may well decide that French intervention would be a liability. France will probably, therefore, continue its hitherto useful policy of using the smaller, subtler interventions which employ quiet enhancements of troop capacity, arms sales and transfers, and economic aid to preserve its influence among African governments. Warships and other oceangoing troop transports will continue to be available, enhancing France's flexibility of response, but held in reserve.

There have, nonetheless, been a few instances in which seaports were useful. The 1983 Chad intervention equipment was brought in by sea to Cameroon and taken overland to Chad. However, air transport remains a necessity for most operations, and it has been a weak link in the crisis intervention process. Getting a large force to Chad, which was France's biggest troop commitment overseas since Algeria in the 1950s, was exceedingly difficult. Defined as a "peacekeeping mission" rather than an overseas war, it required, even so, a total of about 10,000 Frenchmen, over thirteen months from all three branches of its armed services. The initial deployments and most others were by air, and, arguably, France could not have deployed many more than this for a longer period without considerable cooperation—both logistical and political—from neighboring African governments as well as from Paris.[70]

Military Capacity Building

Both the long-term "peacekeeping" actions and the short-term interventions envisioned for the FAR were constrained by the local conditions and infrastructure of the states in which it intervened. This was the primary reason for the concentration of Assistance Militaire Technique on infrastructure and capacity-building aid. With airstrips large enough to receive civilian transport, troop transport was considerably simplified. During the 1983 Chad "peacekeeping" operation, French engineers rebuilt the N'Djamena and Faya-Largeau airstrips to handle the civilian transport that was used to ferry French troops into Chad via Dakar and other African bases.

Other infrastructural improvements in Chad, needed because of the relative sophistication of Libya's forces, included the installation of a *Centaure* radar system and the deployment of Hawk missile installations in N'Djamena, which allowed the French and Chadians in 1987 to bring down a Libyan *Tupolev 22* that was bombing the capital. Chad was indeed the first place where France was willing to bring its most modern equipment into the operation and supply Africans with it as well. This choice vastly improved interoperability with the Chadian forces, and the upgrading of African armaments that took place since 1987 made similar improvements in the ability of French and francophone African armies to operate together.[71] *Milan* antitank missiles, for instance, were supplied to the Chadians in 1987, and also to the Rwandan government for use against the insurgent Rwandan Patriotic Front.[72] As the opponents of France's African allies have acquired more modern military capacities, France has tried to match these developments with capacity-building aid to its allies. This aid, in turn, should have upgraded France's own capacity to intervene.

There is enormous irony, however, in France's need to upgrade forces in Chad to balance Libya. As late as 1981, France was still supplying Libya with aircraft and arms in return for concessions having to do with the Chadian conflict, as well as with the preservation of French oil interests in Libya. Mitterand ceased the transfers, but only after a number of bargains had been struck. His predecessors in office had been no less conciliatory with Libya, in spite of continued irritation from that source. Giscard had imposed an arms embargo on Libya because of Qaddafi's interventions in Chad, but this was lifted in order to allow previously ordered French arms to be delivered (*Mirage* F-1 fighters, helicopters, and patrol boats). By 1982, the USSR was Libya's main supplier in any case, and France had lost even this ineffective form of leverage on Chad's northern aggressor.[73]

Specialist Troops
Since all of the 11th Division troops in the FAR had parachute training, they could clear an airfield of opponents and ready it for the landing of ground troops. Every regiment of the 11th Parachute also contained an intelligence-gathering unit of specialists (a traditional and useful feature of

French paracommando units that dates from Foccart's time in the Free French paras) that was trained to operate in hostile territory, concentrated in the Détachements d'Assistance Opérationelle (DAO). There were only 200–400 of these specialists in peacetime, too small a number for all-out war, but nonetheless key to securing an area in the midst of a domestic uprising or insurgency. The *most* specialized of the DAO units was at the direct disposal of the French president (the 1st Régiment Parachutistes d'Infanterie de Marine). This particular unit was used for rescues or special intelligence operations and is not a part of the FAR. It was used a number of times in Africa, for example, supported by *Jaguar* aircraft and followed by ground troops in Shaba. It has been argued that this type of small-scale specialist intervention capacity is better suited to the dispersed and decentralized nature of African guerrilla armies and therefore more useful to France in Africa than large numbers of nonspecialist ground troops.[74]

Use of Africa-Based Troops (the "Forces de Présence")

Positioning stocks and supplies at the bases simplified intervention in Africa by making use of the bases' ongoing connections with local suppliers. The Africa-based troops were not part of the Force d'Action Rapide, but were needed and used for interventions as logistical and manpower support.[75] They could be used to intervene by themselves, of course, wherever only a small number of Frenchmen in uniform were needed to make a force projection statement, to add protection or provide training to a president's own security forces, or to remind local clients of the potential power of their French *patron*.

As of 1977, the Forces de Présence were a consistent presence. The 10th Battalion d'Infanterie de Marine or Marine Infantry Battalion (BIMa) was stationed in Senegal, the 4th BIMa in Côte d'Ivoire, and the 6th BIMa in Gabon. The Djibouti contingent was far more extensive, including the 13th Foreign Legion Armored Division, the 5th Interarmed Overseas Regiment, the 6th Marines Artillery Regiment, the 6th Command and Support Battalion, and army aviation.[76] Mitterand renamed them the Forces d'Assistance, in order to make their "presence" more palatable.[77] As of 1989, the 23rd BIMa was stationed in Senegal, the 43rd BIMa in Côte d'Ivoire, and the 6th BIMa was still in Gabon. The Djibouti base continued to provide further marine infantry that could be called upon for support. There were also some FAR troops rotated semi-permanently through the bases in the Central African Republic. All could interact with the FAR in spite of the cooperation agreements with Senegal, CAR, Côte d'Ivoire, and Gabon, which stipulated that the territories of these countries could not be used for direct interventions in other countries, but only as staging posts. This staging capacity, however, has been vital. For instance, the Libreville (Gabon), Bangui, and Bouar (both in CAR) bases were used to stage the 1983 Chad intervention. The 1986 Togo intervention (in West Africa) used French troops based in Central Africa.

Host governments disapproved of external use of these battalions, often citing the OAU Charter's African sovereignty (i.e., nonintervention) principle, but they have not refused France the use of French troops when France has formally asked their permission. Since these French forces were primarily intended as a local deterrent against domestic unrest, this official reluctance is understandable. President Bongo of Gabon found French troops to be of immediate use to him domestically on several occasions, and he has been particularly *exigent* about their return to Gabon after any use elsewhere.[78] These Forces de Présence insured a continuing capacity to deter internal conflict, and acted as an early warning system, providing immediate intelligence on events with a larger potential for conflict. The host countries' armies rarely went on maneuvers without including French troops.[79]

In addition to the occasional maneuvers which combined the armies of host countries and the French troops based in them, the French organized annual maneuvers that included the host country armies (particularly those from Senegal, Gabon, Côte d'Ivoire, and Central African Republic), the base troops of the Forces de Présence, and the FAR. The first-ever of these exercises took place in Senegal in 1967, and included counterinsurgency and antiguerrilla training. Bilateral exercises also took place occasionally in those countries in which France had defense agreements, but no bases. These exercises continued to provide a concrete demonstration of political solidarity between these countries and France, and also a place where each partner's force projection potential was displayed. Representatives from other francophone African countries often observed these exercises.[80]

It is now less frequent, however, that bilateral training exercises with one francophone country will be attended by officials from another. Many of France's ex-colonies, especially those without French bases, have a competing interest in not revealing whatever closeness remains in their ongoing relationship with France.[81] While the varieties of "carrot" and "stick" remained identical to those of the first ten years of postindependence, France's ability to exercise them, particularly over the course of longer-term military interventions, became more and more subject to accusations of neocolonialism, not only from its fellow great powers but also from its African clients. This did not mean that France did not continue to intervene, only that more subtlety was required in order to preserve the appearance of benevolent overlordship.

France's Ability to Intervene in Domestic Political Affairs (e.g., to Save or Topple Governments)

President Giscard was as politically active in Central Africa as he was militarily active, although his Africa policy, like most other parts of his military policy, became more restrained toward the end of his tenure in office. It was Giscardian interventionism, however, that earned France a title it holds to this day, "the *gendarme* of Africa." To stretch this concept a bit, however, France is both the *gendarmerie* on the beat, managing the chronic day-to-day problems ("Présence") and preventing most of them from becoming national histoires, and the riot police, who are deployed in the event of an acute crisis ("Intervention").

However, interventions, to be popular in France, needed to be timely, limited, and short-term. This could reasonably be said of the 1978–1979 Zaïre intervention, but was far less so in the case of the Central African Republic and particularly untrue in Chad.[82]

Sometimes, *présence* was enough. Samuel Decalo suggests that the pattern of military interventions is such that:

> probably all that really prevents the overthrow of many 'stable' civilian regimes (e.g. Senegal, Ivory Coast, Gabon) may be nothing more than the physical presence of French troops in these countries and/or the known commitment of France to the preservation in office of the existing civilian hierarchies.[83]

In spite of the French presence, there were quite a few additional and successful military coups d'état in a number of the francophone states during the period 1970–1984, including:

Benin/Dahomey (1972)
Rwanda (1973)
Upper Volta (1974, 1980, 1982, and twice in 1983)
Niger (1974)
Chad (1975)
Burundi (1976)
Congo-Brazzaville (1977 and 1979)
Mauritania (1978, 1979, 1980, and 1984)
Central African Empire/Republic (1979 and 1981)

This list does not include unsuccessful or abortive coups d'état, which included one in Congo-Brazzaville in 1972 and another attempt in the CAR in 1982.[84] As in the first decade after independence, coup leaders who were willing to work with France were generally not prevented from taking power, provided that local unrest was kept under control and no French interests or personnel were threatened. For purposes of comparison, and in apparent congruence with Decalo's conclusion above, those francophone states which maintained civilian control from independence through late 1980 included Cameroon, Côte d'Ivoire, Gabon, and Senegal, and also Guinea (which had a military coup in 1984 after the death of Sekou Touré). In all of these cases, it might be said that the heavy presence of French troops (or the Soviets in the case of Guinea) guaranteed the continuing presence of certain civilian leaders (Ahidjo, Houphouët-Boigny, Mba and Bongo, Senghor, and Touré).[85]

The ability to intervene, as described in the previous case, was preserved in the form of the Force d'Intervention, combined with the continuing presence on African bases of the Forces d'Outre-Mer. Chipman lists the following French military interventions in Central Africa since decolonization in 1969, which (again) do not include the more "discrete" actions (e.g., preemptive aid increases and garrison reinforcements) that are less documentable but as frequently effective as obvious shows of force:[86,87]

> Chad in 1969–1975 (Intervention in the war against FROLINAT)
> Zaïre in 1977–1978 (Suppression of rebellion in Shaba province)
> Chad in 1978–1980 (More war against FROLINAT)
> Central African Empire in 1979 (Operation *Barracuda* supporting Dacko and deposing Bokassa)
> Chad in 1983–1988 (Various operations supporting President Habré)

In 1981, one of Mitterand's foreign policy priorities was to adapt France's Africa policy to changing global conditions and to changes in France's relationship with the Atlantic allies. There would not just be military changes but political, economic, and cultural adaptations. Mitterand promised, as well, that the historical links between France and Africa would no longer be used to support the private interests of particular African leaders, but rather, the interests of African citizens. One of the keys to improving the lives and governments of African people was to be the renegotiation of the cooperation agreements on a case-by-case basis. In addition, France would also try to reinforce the ability of the Organization of African Unity to solve African security problems so that there would be less need of outside (French) military assistance. These promises were applauded, and then largely ignored by African leaders who generally had no desire to renegotiate their defense and military cooperation agreements in ways that would in fact lessen their ability to call for French help if their own security were threatened. (Almost immediately, Mitterand found himself providing internal security aid to the Cameroonian president.)[88] It soon became clear that Mitterand's Africa policy was going to resemble more closely his pragmatic political mediation as a minister of Overseas France in the 1950s than his socialist campaign rhetoric.[89]

Mitterand did establish a definite pattern of intervention, however, in that, in future, it would take place only where requested explicitly by an African leader, and only then in cooperation with African forces. France would also try to avoid intervention in internal disputes, although what was considered to be purely internal remains unclear. Mitterand supported Senegalese intervention in the Gambia in July 1982, an external intervention by most accounts. As already mentioned, he refrained from intervening when CAR's David Dacko was overthrown by General André Kolingba in September 1981, although as Clayton indicates,[90] some logistical or intelligence support may well have been offered.[91]

Mitterand's 1986 Togo intervention in West Africa was a model of efficiency. Two hundred French parachutists were sent from the bases in CAR and Gabon just before the Lomé Franco-African summit meeting (excellent political timing), in order to quell what President Eyadema described as a Ghana-inspired opposition uprising (providing a useful anglophone foil). The Togo intervention demonstrated exactly what Mitterand had promised, and in fact what other French presidents would have hoped for in their interventions: French reliability and loyalty to its African partners, a successful demonstration of the potential speed and power of French force projection, and the ability to carry off a successful intervention with a small number of French troops in a brief time frame. There was some surprise internationally that Togo was still among the countries which could command an immediate French response but this, perhaps, made the demonstration all the stronger as to what France would do *even* if an otherwise loyal country did *not* go so far as to maintain French bases on its soil. There was also the requisite inter-African collaboration: President Mobutu sent a Zaïrian army detachment to Togo with the French troops and aircraft to protect his fellow francophone President Eyadema.[92]

Mitterand's adherence to his own constraints on African intervention became most difficult to uphold during France's continuing series of interventions in Chad. From 1983 on, Mitterand found that he needed to keep an active military presence in Chad, both to deter Libya (thereby preserving a Soviet containment credential without directly confronting the USSR), and to preserve Chad's always problematic territorial integrity. The continuing presence in Chad posed real political problems for the Mitterand government at home because high casualty levels were possible there and because France showed an apparent inability to leave Chad completely.[93] The following brief case study of Chad will illustrate this in more depth.

Chad

Of all of the interventions during the 1970s and 1980s, the multiple interventions in Chad represented perhaps the greatest test of the credibility and effectiveness of France's military cooperation with a former colony. In point of fact, these interventions went well beyond what was acceptable according to Chad's cooperation agreements, particularly in the mid-1980s, given that the agreement prohibited French military personnel in Chad from participating directly in war operations or in operations maintaining or re-establishing "order or legality."[94] In its central location, Chad was regarded from the colonial period as the "vital hinge" (Clayton's term) connecting the French territories of North, West, and Central Africa. Its political identity has always been problematic, as a country created somewhat artificially out of largely Moslem North African groups and generally non-Muslim southern populations, creating a noncohesive mixture of Arab-influenced Northern Chadians, nomadic Saharans, and sedentary sub-Saharans. The first period of unrest was under President Tombalbaye, the southerner who became president at independence. French troops were needed to contain disorder in 1962 and 1963. Further unrest occurred in 1965 in central and eastern Chad. By 1967, Tombalbaye's administration and military had lost the ability to govern effectively and maintain order. The year 1968 was to signal the beginning of France's need to give Chad more constant military attention than any of the other francophone states in the region. The Chadian army had become divided and government troops were engaged in serious and arbitrary repression. In 1968, Toubou Guard irregulars spread the revolt northward, massacring the Chadian government troops garrisoning the Aouzou region, which contained strategic mineral resources. The loosely federated revolt was drawn together organizationally as FROLINAT (the Front de Libération National Tchadien) by Ibrahim Abatcha, who had received his military training in North Korea. He was killed by the Chadian army in 1968. At this point, the roughly 3,000 FROLINAT insurgents not only overwhelmed the capacity of the Chadian government to respond but began to receive significant assistance from Libya.[95]

De Gaulle responded initially by flying in *both* an administrative team charged with the hopeless task of reforming Chad's civil government (which had been a loyal, if occasionally embarrassing, supporter of French policy), and a company of Foreign Legion *parachutistes*. The armed contingent was followed by a large training group commanded by General Arnaud, two more companies of Legionnaires, and part of a Marine infantry regiment with helicopters. General Cortadellas was appointed overall commander of an effort that was defined "selective pacification." In 1971, after considerable fighting during which 50 Frenchmen (including Cortadellas' son) were killed, FROLINAT was at least contained, if not removed. The solution had not been the tidy engagement that France had projected, and the ongoing commitment to Chad remained.[96]

France's enthusiasm for intervention was considerably dampened by the difficulties encountered in Chad. In addition, France began to negotiate various agreements with Libya which were to complicate further involvement in the region. A total of 3,000 French troops were withdrawn from Chad by 1972, leaving a single French Marine regiment and 600 other French Army advisers, who were deployed in Chadian uniforms. In 1974, FROLINAT captured the wife of an archaeologist, along with a German doctor (who was ransomed immediately by the German government). Madame Claustre, however, remained FROLINAT's hostage for three years, joined in captivity by her husband in 1975. In the meantime, President Tombalbaye had become mentally ill and was removed in 1975 by the head of Chad's army, General Félix Malloum. Malloum demanded a complete withdrawal of France's combat troops, but he signed a new cooperation agreement in 1976, receiving several hundred French advisers to help him contain FROLINAT. These advisers were not supposed to engage in combat, but this provision of the agreement was ignored.[97]

FROLINAT was also in some disarray, allowing Malloum and the French to contain its activities in the south and center of Chad, if not in the north, where Libyan-equipped and supported insurgents from FROLINAT took Faya-Largeau, the most important northern center of government. The Chadian army lost 2,000 troops defending the north, threatening its ability to hold the capital, N'Djamena. France prevented the loss of N'Djamena by sending strike aircraft and 1,500 troops, but incurred significant enough casualties in this assault that the Chadian effort became politically quite unpopular in France. To discourage further French domestic opposition, Paris tried to increase the capacity of the Chadian government to solve its own problems by encouraging Malloum to share his government with the leader of one of FROLINAT's more moderate branches, Hissène Habré. Habré became prime minister, with Malloum as head of state, in 1978. The majority tendencies within FROLINAT, however, continued to fight under Goukouni Oueddai, and they remained in control of the north. At this point, Libya annexed the Aouzou strip in the northwest of Chad. A new era in the Chadian saga began, as France tried simultaneously to (1) maintain a stable Chadian government with cooperative links to France, (2) contain Libyan expansionism (without losing its options to deal politically and economically with Libya in the future), and (3) limit French engagement to what was considered politically acceptable in Paris.[98]

As the political alliance between Malloum and Habré began to disintegrate, France managed to maintain a low French casualty rate, relative to the early 1970s, and based Foreign Legion and Marine parachute infantry and artillery regiments in Chad, supported by *Jaguar* strike aircraft. FROLINAT and Libya obliged France unintentionally by engaging in factional disputes among themselves. France was able, temporarily, to enforce military order in the south, but could not prevent Habré and Malloum from disagreeing with one another. The situation collapsed when a southern Malloum supporter, Colonel Kamougué, fought Habré for control of N'Djamena and lost. Oueddai and FROLINAT moved southward, and Habré had to retake N'Djamena from him. All the while, the French remained in their barracks.

Between 1978 and 1980, after numerous incidents of factional fighting and shifting alliances, diplomatic solutions were proposed, along with a first attempt at an all-African peacekeeping mediation effort. French and African diplomacy resulted in a new Chadian coalition which appointed Oueddai and Kamougué as president and vice president, respectively, with Habré as a minister. Other African countries (Congo-Brazzaville, Benin, and Guinea) were to supply peacekeeping troops whose presence in Chad would allow for a French military withdrawal. The 2,000 French troops based in Chad were halved to 1,000 and one African country (Congo-Brazzaville) provided 600 soldiers, which arrived at the point at which the political alliance in N'Djamena collapsed. Oueddai was unable, as he had thought, to remove the Libyans, which was to be the rationale for France's pull-back. Habré was removed from the coalition government and took his loyalists to the east. Kamougué consolidated his forces in the south, and Oueddai returned north to work again with Qaddafi. Chad was again officially at war.[99]

Habré retained French support and training assistance and came to terms with Kamougué. Oueddai continued with Qaddafi, but the relationship deteriorated due to Qaddafi's desire for complete Libyan hegemony over northern Chad. In 1982, Habré regained what was left of the capital and declared a government of national unity. France withdrew the last portion of its combat troops.[100]

In 1983, Libyan support was given to Oueddai and Kamougué for further insurgent efforts. An alternative government was established by this newly reconstituted movement in Bardai. Habré, whose Chadian resources were small and badly trained, and whose only external help came from Zaïrean army troops and some limited U.S. air support (contributed because of Qaddafi's participation with Soviet-trained troops), again found it necessary to call for French assistance. Operation Manta (Stingray) was the response from Mitterand, who was France's fourth president in succession to deal with the Chadian problem. *Manta* sent 4,000 French troops, mostly Legionnaires and Marines, including parachutists, infantry cavalry, and marine artillery units. Manta also brought, for the first time, some of France's newest antiaircraft and antitank weapons, and electronic equipment. Faced with this display of support for Habré, Qaddafi and Oueddai withdrew, and Qaddafi made an agreement with Mitterand that both French and Libyan forces would be withdrawn from Chad, except for a few advisers from each, and replaced by international supervision. Mitterand did not forcefully contest Libyan annexation of Aouzou at this time, and he withdrew as promised.[101]

Libya did not completely withdraw, and supported further insurgency by Oueddai in early 1986. Habré was able to counter the first attacks, but appealed yet again for French military support. At this point, however, Mitterand was managing political problems at home in the context of parliamentary elections. His response to Habré, Operation Épervier (which is translatable as either Sparrowhawk or Sweep-net), featured a French air force attack on the new Libyan air field in northern Chad, with some limited ground defense of Chadian airstrips. A force of 1,000 men was then stationed in Chad to provide daily northern patrol flights in the north, and effectively partitioning the country along the 16th parallel.[102] Épervier was politically risky in that it was apparently open-ended, but the risks of French casualties incurred by the previous operations in Chad were minimized. There was a greater risk in leaving Chad to disintegrate on its own, because this would have caused every other francophone African nation to question the value of its French cooperation agreements, with the subsequent loss to France's credibility as their security guarantor. It would also have caused France's fellow European powers to question its commitment to constraining Libyan (and proxy Soviet) aggression. France's strategic and economic power in Africa would be compromised seriously, therefore, if it abandoned Chad.

Épervier demonstrated, however, that France's airlift capacity needed enhancement if it were to remain effective in the African region by air force interventions rather than with massive ground troop actions. Algeria criticized overflight by the French to Chad, and Libya was actively hostile to overflight. Supply flights generally came from Senegal's Dakar base and Cameroon, and commandeering civilian aircraft for some of these flights caused additional controversy.[103]

In 1987, Habré received significant support not only from France but also from the United States in the form of arms, ammunition, and equipment. French garrison troops secured Habré's supply routes and bases, without having to participate much beyond this work. Eventually, Habré inflicted a series of losses on Libya and FROLINAT, while the French remained visibly ensconced on the 16th parallel, known as the Red Line.[104]

As Foltz demonstrates, external intervention of various kinds contributed to internationalizing, if not escalating, the internal conflicts in Chad. Contested and weakly defended borders, acute poverty and dependence on French aid,[105] and the constant solicitation of outside help by all parties in Chad's factional conflicts produced a situation of long-term regional insecurity. Libya, Nigeria, and Sudan each defended various factions, and Morocco, Zaïre, Egypt, Algeria, Congo-Brazzaville, Benin, Burkina-Faso, and Gabon all contributed various forms of direct or indirect aid to the Chadian groups, depending upon their alliances with, and external patronage from, larger external powers or interest groups: France, the United States, the USSR, and the Arab states. Saudi Arabia and Iraq even offered arms and made diplomatic initiatives, and some Arab states had provided FROLINAT with operational bases from which to launch attacks. Aid from the Arab states to Chad was made easier by Chad's break with Israel in 1972.[106] Nigeria's interest in the conflict came not only from its wish to play a powerful role in the West African region but from a history of border clashes in the Lake Chad area, centering around disputed islands, in the early 1980s.[107] It was, finally, France's presence in central and southern Chad that prevented Libya's air power preponderance over the Chadians from making inroads beyond the northern section that contained most of Qaddafi's factional allies. Qaddafi's only partial hold on the territory, his diplomatic mistakes, and his frequent lack of trust both in his own military and in his Chadian allies cost him the Aouzou strip and eventually most of his influence in northern Chad.[108]

In such a context, France's ability to hold on as the major external influence that eventually won the field should probably allow us to call the Chad interventions a "success" for France, even though the protracted conflict was costly and demonstrated a number of the weaknesses in France's intervention capacity. France not only managed to bring Hissene Habré, its chosen candidate, to power, but Paris also managed to retain enough influence to continue its role as a major military and economic backer for the military regime of Idriss Deby that ousted Habré by force of arms in 1990. Habré lost power because, in spite of his strong nationalism, his considerable negotiating skills and adaptability, and his military skills, he allowed his own relationship with the Chadian military to decay once he became president. He also allowed an unmanageably large degree of corruption and egregious violations of the human rights of his citizens, both of which were criticized abroad and embarrassed France. When Mitterand announced at the La Baule summit that future foreign aid would begin to take more account of democratization, Habré's reaction was less than diplomatic, and French aid slowed down. The French military garrison remaining in Chad began to take a neutral stance between Habré's regime and Deby's rebel faction, allowing Deby both a military and a diplomatic advantage. France was well acquainted with all parties in the dispute, and maintained its contacts with Deby during his rebellion. France's in-depth, long-term relationship with the Chadian military, combined with Chad's continuing military and economic dependence on France, were the major factors that led to President Deby's continued use of France as an influential patron in the 1990s.[109]

Chad was a notable example of one place where one nation (Libya) attempted to replace the colonial legacies implanted by France with its own *mission civilisatrice*, including people's revolutionary committees, compulsory use of Arabic, and ideological tutoring from Qaddafi's own *Green Book*. That Libya was ultimately unsuccessful after nearly fifteen years of intervention reflects not only the incompetence with which Qaddafi used his enormous military power but the historically entrenched power of France. France's power was supported not only in by military and diplomatic efforts but by Chadian economic and cultural habits as well. Qaddafi attempted to draw on Libya's historic relationships with its southern neighbor, but his reasoning resonated solely with inhabitants of the northern two-fifths of the country that shared a measure of "Arab" history with Libya.[110]

France's Ability to Conduct Humanitarian and Peacekeeping Operations

This section assesses whether France possessed the military capabilities (1) to offer humanitarian assistance in the event of a natural or man-made disaster, or (2) to offering "peacekeeping" assistance in the form of a barrier between warring parties or groups. In both of these cases, the French preference has been for preventive policies which forestall the need to intervene in the first place. If intervention becomes necessary, the French have had the capacity to intervene, but their *forte* (as with interventions described in the previous section) has been short-term intervention using base troops and the professional forces, rather than long-term, larger-scale operations which would require extensive airlift capacity (always problematic), more troops, and the need for parliamentary permission to employ conscripts overseas. The need for the latter type of intervention has increased, however, as African militaries have grown in technical capacity and troop strength, and as regional hegemonic hopefuls like Nigeria, Libya, and Angola have grown in strength and become more willing to intervene in their neighbors' affairs. The consequences are notable in terms of casualties, internally and externally displaced refugees, and the kind of general economic disruption that brings extensive misery, destitution, and disease. Even civil wars in Africa in the 1990s have increased in their magnitude and severity.

Disaster Assistance

Since these former French colonies were offered the continuing economic support of the Franc Zone and were provided with some disaster cushioning in the form of infrastructural and administrative support under the terms of the cooperation agreements, large-scale humanitarian crisis aid in the *chasse gardée* was largely unnecessary. The countries remained poor, and several were subject to frequent agricultural crisis due to drought, but none of them had an ongoing crisis of the strength and severity of, for example, Ethiopia's repeated humanitarian disasters of the past decades. As Zartman indicates, intervention in the case of a major collapse "must restore security, provide massive technical assistance and budgetary aid, and maintain a low profile." These measures are mutually contradictory, further inhibiting the desire to intervene, and increasing the incentive for the French to maintain preventive policies wherever possible in the *chasse gardée*. Indeed, Zartman emphasizes that economic intervention in the 1980s returned to a level that was more characteristic of the preindependence years, a level that the French had hoped would be unnecessary. This economic intervention, along with debt-rescheduling and other economic measures, largely forestalled the need for major humanitarian projects involving the French military, projects which would have been logistically and politically more risky if they had required long-term military contributions.[111]

"Peacekeeping" Missions

"Peacekeeping" is a problematic term, as it is presently used to refer to situations in which a neighboring state or great power might intervene between two warring parties in order to prevent their engagement. France used the term "selective pacification" to refer to some of its interventions, but these were still mostly shows of force which were billed as "peacekeeping." France continued during this period to conduct operations which *it* defined as peacekeeping, including most of the operations described above which involved riot suppression and the containment of civil disturbances. However, these were not peacekeeping missions in the 1990s sense of military "operations other than war." It remains difficult to know if these policing activities qualify as humanitarian. They continued to appear to be military actions preserving French power in the region rather than humanitarian missions.

"Peacekeeping" was the expressed intent of 1994's Operation Turquoise in Rwanda, which the French presented publically as a humanitarian act, namely, a *cordon sanitaire* to save lives during a genocidal civil war. However, one unanticipated result of Turquoise was more war, not less, because France protected a large portion of the command and control capability of the *génocidaire* Rwandan government which fled into eastern Zaïre. This group remains an insurgent military force to this day, although far less coherent, and has assisted President Kabila and various other parties during the ongoing devastating war in the Democratic Republic of Congo. Turquoise was, quite possibly, the first time France offered its troops for a short-term "peacekeeping" mission in the current sense of the term, but its effect was temporary, and the lives it saved were largely those of members of the particular political group who had been France's allies before the Rwandan conflict came to a head in 1994. France's supportive relationship with a genocidal government was given far more public scrutiny than it could withstand. It was not a political or public relations success, nor a humanitarian coup for the French military. The care with which France has approached its most recent peacekeeping intervention in 2003 Côte d'Ivoire may demonstrate some lessons learned in 1994 Rwanda.

Part Two: Other Resources and Constraints That Affected French Power in Late-Twentieth-Century Francophone Central Africa

The Gaullist military legacy is thought to have associated the glory of France as a great power with military force projection. This has become less useful in recent years. The French themselves occasionally question its legitimacy and wonder if "*grandeur*" cannot be obtained in economic and political terms rather than by military threat. It should be remembered that de Gaulle himself wished France to recover economic and political glory as well as independent military security. In contrast to his successors, he de-emphasized the military budget, except for the portion devoted to the *force de frappe*, and the French nuclear force was paid for by troop cutbacks in Africa and elsewhere.[112] Other means of support were called for, if France was to remain powerful in Africa. This next section details the economic and political means by which France maintained its power in the former Afrique Équatoriale Française.

France's Nonmilitary Power Resources

French influence had three nonmilitary tools which were critical to its success in continuing its influence in the Central African region:

- *Financial support leverage* (control of the Franc Zone and financial aid to African governments),
- *French government and private investment* in African industries (particularly the oil industry), which supported both the economies of various states and their leadership elites, linking political support to economic leverage,
- *French political penetration of African governments* via other (noneconomic) public and private channels.

Even though the aid levels fluctuated over time due to the vicissitudes of changing regimes in France and in Africa, the consistency over time of these three interwoven types of support is remarkable, even in states like Congo-Brazzaville which had avowedly socialist regimes ostensibly open to political and economic support from the Soviet bloc nations.

The African Franc Zone, established well before the political independence of these countries, was possibly the most consistent and penetrative legacy of transitional colonialism. It continued to provide the structure and financial security that allowed French companies, and companies from other nations, to invest in francophone Africa. The zone offered a common convertible currency, less possibility of the hyperinflation common to developing countries, opportunities for bilateral aid, and a predictable investment environment. It also perpetuated African dependence on France, but did so in a way that offered a real incentive to remain dependent, given the poverty and unreliable economies of many of the zone's less fortunate neighbors.[113]

French support and penetration of the African banking systems and commercial investments were crucial to maintaining this relatively secure investment climate, as the CFAF continued to be pegged to the French franc. Countries like Côte d'Ivoire, which had started independence relatively healthy financially (at least compared to its neighbors), were enabled to remain so. Countries that were comparatively resource-poor, or dependent on a small number of exports, were given a boost above destitution by having a subsidized currency. Countries with natural resources useful to France (like the uranium in the Central African Republic and Niger) found that access to banking assistance in the Franc Zone allowed them to subsidize an unreliable agricultural base and even out the boom and bust cycles of the uranium market. The oil countries (Congo-Brazzaville, Benin, and Gabon) were able to cushion themselves somewhat against the pricing fluctuations and resultant shocks of the oil market. Membership in the Franc Zone did not preclude a need for assistance from the World Bank or the International Monetary Fund. However, it simplified some of the negotiations. The "Communauté Financière Africaine (CFA)" had replaced the "Colonies Françaises d'Afrique (CFA)", in a very neat acronymic transition.

Stanley Hoffmann identifies three long-term nonmilitary trends that nonetheless had frequent effects on the sovereignty, and susceptibility to intervention, of post–World War II states: economic interdependence, ideological polarization, and the delegitimization of colonialism.[114] France's need to remain a part of the economic and cultural climate in each of its former colonies often militated against its use of force and supported a choice for economic support in the form of further aid or capacity building, as did the increasing need for restraint if France was not to be seen any longer as an imperialist power. France was also extremely flexible during this period with those countries who chose (at least nominally) either of the two poles in the Cold War. Its own Socialist and Communist parties were active enough in maintaining their ties with similar parties in African countries that this may have preserved French influence from disappearing altogether in most of the new nations that veered to the far left. As Decalo notes, even "full-fledged Marxist states" like Burkina Faso and the People's Republics of Benin and Congo-Brazzaville remained not only dependent on French aid but solicitous of it. Burkina Faso was, if anything, more in need of French aid during its revolutionary phase than before its revolution. Congolese rhetoric about expanding state control over industry was actually combined with an increase in expatriate capital investments.[115]

Zartman gives a number of West and Central African examples of the types of French economic support that forestalled the need for military intervention. In the Central African Republic, low per capita income and low economic growth have frequently threatened political stability, and France has made frequent and effective economic interventions there. As is characteristic of many francophone nations receiving such support, the CAR has a large group of French expatriates, occupies a strategic position with respect to other francophone nations, has products useful to the French economy, maintains a French school system which perpetuates French as the language of government and trade (not so incidentally maintaining a sense of shared history and mutual political loyalty between the CAR and France), and, until quite recently, hosted a large contingent of French base troops. Economic support could be used (as has been suggested earlier) as either a carrot or a stick. Aid was withdrawn from President Bokassa in 1979, after continuing scandals over his use of French aid for his coronation as emperor, his gift of diamonds to President Giscard, and the beating deaths of Central African students. However, a sum roughly equal to a third of the state budget (over $40 million) was provided to the new Dacko government which replaced Bokassa a year later. The CAR's continuing willingness to maintain a close relationship with France on all fronts, military, economic, and political, combined with its neediness, also insured that France remained the preeminent partner in every type of agreement made with this country until the most recent military coup in 2003. France enlisted the assistance of other nations toward the economic support of nations like the CAR, but Paris remained the dominant partner even when other great powers joined in the effort.[116]

Gabon offers another example of how France's economic power and political leverage could be intertwined.[117] French business interests in Gabon were powerful during the postwar colonial period. In addition to extensive French investment in the Gabonese oil industry, the forestry lobby emerged historically as a particularly salient political force in Gabon, lobbying for concessions and even funding political parties. A French businessman, Roland Bru, led the foresters from the late 1940s onward, starting with price negotiations between the Syndicat Forestier du Gabon and the colonial Office de Bois in Paris. Bru became a "kingmaker" in Gabon because of the power and success of the forestry lobby, supporting sympathetic political party candidates even during the colonial period. The support of Bru and other business interests in Gabon, helped Léon Mba to found the Bloc Démocratique Gabonais in 1954 and later become president of Gabon in 1964, whereupon Mba dissolved the Gabonese assembly and called for elections in what was now a single-party state. When Bongo came to power in 1964, Bru and the foresters began to receive serious political competition from French oil interests in the political realm, partly because Bru apparently no longer had the power to control the more radical elements of his party.[118] French business interests continue to be a powerful force in Gabonese politics, as the story of the oil industry strikes told below indicates.

French political penetration continued to be both deep and personalized. Military governments with economic constraints continued to offer opportunities to France, streamlining the delivery of military aid and positioning French military *coopérants* within African political hierarchies.[119] Cabinet shuffles in francophone Africa often occurred as a result of French intervention, or with French consultation. France did not hesitate to intervene to influence the choice (or firing) of particular African government ministers when someone either suited French interests or got in their way. Charges of corruption were not always necessary in such cases, but they provided a convenient and omnipresent excuse. Although some level of governmental corruption was occasionally helpful in maintaining French influence, too much diversion of French aid (or its diversion into unintended hands), was sometimes a reason to intervene.[120]

In the early 1970s, a number of states requested the renegotiation of their cooperation agreements, the removal of some of the more restrictive clauses, and a greater "Africanization" of economic institutions. Although France responded to this readily, by renegotiating many of the agreements and by moving the two regional banks of Central and West Africa to Yaoundé (Cameroon) and Dakar (Senegal), France remained in effective charge of a number of African economic institutions. Since it remained the preponderant partner in the cooperation agreements, its flexibility of response was essentially preserved even if the language of the contracts appeared to offer it less room to maneuver. Since that time, however, it has become evident that the increasingly independent policies of African presidents make it more difficult for France to influence bilateral relationships as it once did.[121]

France's Freedom of Action, Given Domestic Political Constraints
France's freedom of action in Africa is linked integrally to the political freedom of action of the French presidents who have directed its Africa policy since 1960. The French Assemblée Nationale had relatively little to do with the direction and execution of this policy, and the political strength of de Gaulle and his ideological legacy were such that successive French presidents had remarkable freedom of choice as to which African leaders they supported and how they chose to support them. The domestic political constraints of the French presidency, even in as vocal a parliamentary democracy as that of France, were relatively small compared to those of the U.S. president or the U.K. prime minister. The military constraints were more salient, but these have already been discussed. Probably the biggest single domestic political constraint on the military was the requirement that French conscripts not be sent off of French soil without the approval of the Assemblée, a political constraint which made the interventionary forces largely a professional army.

Since de Gaulle's manner of leadership had, apparently, prevented France from losing its remaining colonies as violently as it had lost Algeria and Indochina, his Africa policy was transferred to later presidencies largely unaltered during the time of his successor, Georges Pompidou. Valéry Giscard d'Estaing intended his presidency to be an answer to the cognitive constraints of Gaullism, a new ideological position, but he found himself falling back into Gaullist patterns and policies in Africa when it became clear that those patterns constituted a working arrangement that worked as well for

African leaders as they did for the French. Since the system was set up through the cooperation agreements to require constant presence and vigilance, lapses in maintaining the *chasse gardée* in the careful centralized, watchful Gaullist manner would cause costly maintenance problems, as Giscard discovered in the Central African Republic, which became an empire during his presidency with the inadvertent help of French foreign aid. Finally, François Mitterand, in spite of his party differences from both the Gaullists and Giscard, found himself promoting Gaullist policies. This was not so much out of inertia, but because his own political past contained ties with African leaders that were much like de Gaulle's own, and these ties constituted a convenience and an advantage in dealing with African governments that proved impossible to give up completely.

Finally, all of these presidents benefited from the single biggest constraint that Gaullism placed on the *rest* of the French political system: the centralized, independent, autonomous strength of the French presidency. Non-Gaullist presidents acted like autonomous independent Gaullists because de Gaulle had left them with this personal autonomy as a tactical advantage built into the structure of the French political system.

Any examination of France's freedom of action during this century must take account of the structure of the French state, its centralizing tendencies, and the strength of the Gaullist presidency. It is well to realize, however, that these structural components are supported and shaped by a set of beliefs that can be treated as the constraining assumptions guiding the development and intentions of the twentieth-century French state in all its paradoxical duality, as both democracy and empire. While this set of beliefs is often called Gaullism, they are neither inflexibly static nor historically modern. Nor, in spite of the myth of French exceptionalism, do they solely pertain to France, which is not the only democracy ever to act imperially only to find that its founding principles are in contrast to its actions.

It is arguable that de Gaulle's postindependence Africa policy is a case of empire by other means, but the historical sections of these case studies should also have demonstrated that France's history in Africa, and the uses it has made of the continent, show a persistent pattern of assumptions concerning French imperial destiny that predates de Gaulle's entry on the French political scene by nearly a hundred years. This chapter opens in the year of the death of *l'Homme de Brazzaville*, and examines the Central African military legacy of Charles de Gaulle. It may be well at this point to take a closer examination of what, exactly, Gaullism is. As a static set of not always carefully articulated assumptions and beliefs, Gaullism should be distinguished from de Gaulle himself, who adapted his policies and actions to several quite different historical phases in French history, while remaining flexible and aware that France's political survival (and his own) would require occasional compromises with stated ideals. He never lost sight of those ideals, but, as Philip Gordon explains,

> Take, for example, de Gaulle's position on French overseas colonies— "the Empire." Never in the General's long life did he change his view on the importance of French grandeur and the destiny of France's global role. But he was not blind to the fact that World War II released forces in the colonies that could not be contained, even with all the political will he might muster among his compatriots. For this nationalist soldier to preside over the transformation of the empire and become the sponsor of Algerian independence was an extraordinary homage to his willingness to adapt.[122]

The ideal of the independent nation-state, and the legitimacy and the autonomy of its institutions, were deeply important to de Gaulle (for France, if not for the African countries). De Gaulle claimed occasionally to support the idea of a united Europe as well, but not at the cost of France. Even if France's independence had to be achieved at the cost of its alliances, as was true of its relationship with NATO, it was in the interest of France to retain its independence of action. Although de Gaulle supported a federated Europe if France remained the first among equals (much like the French Community plan for Africa in 1958), he opposed vehemently the idea of any federation wherein France would lose its priority and autonomy. De Gaulle was not only convinced that France was entitled to be a world power but also that it was entitled to global dominance because it was France. He admitted that his view of France was often more sentimental than reasonable, but he remained adamant that France offered the world an exceptional yet universalizable form of enlightenment that was expressed in its culture, language, and power, and further, that France had a global responsibility to perpetuate its enlightened values and organizing principles by whatever means possible at the time. This vision is of course a version of the colonial *mission civilisatrice*, and not unique to de Gaulle.[123] It needs to be considered both an impetus and a constraint to France's actions in Africa because the loyalty of various French politicians to what they perceived as Gaullist truisms directed much of the Africa policy immediately following de Gaulle's resignation and death. De Gaulle's legacy was also perpetuated in a less exalted form in the expedient and pragmatic, and sometimes downright dishonorable, tactics followed by de Gaulle's secretary for African and Malagasy affairs, Jacques Foccart.

Georges Pompidou was close to de Gaulle, and may properly be called the first Gaullist president, but he was nonetheless required to make a number of adaptations to the military expressions of Gaullism due to the increasing bipolarity of the global situation. The most surprisingly persistent Gaullism where Africa was concerned came from the next president, Valéry Giscard d'Estaing, an avowed parliamentary democrat and political liberal who promised France a less independent and more consultative and conciliatory presidency. It was during Giscard's "post-Gaullist" presidency that the contradictions inherent in Gaullist military policies became evident. After three years of reform, including a national security outlook that professed to be nonnuclear, more flexible, and more committed to Europe, Giscard returned to more orthodox Gaullist security patterns during his final four years in office. The acquisition of tactical nuclear weapons in 1972 was a part of this new conception of French flexibility.[124]

Whoever occupied the French presidency from de Gaulle onward, African intervention decisions were made almost entirely according to each president's personal commitment to the continent. France's speed of response and flexibility remained high so long as the decision-making capacity for African intervention remained closely tied to the French president and the Elysée's Office for African and Malagasy Affairs. Throughout the Gaullist period, this office was headed by Jacques Foccart, in "direct competition with the Ministry of Cooperation" as well as the Ministry of Foreign Affairs. Foccart's place at the center of an intelligence network with operatives in all of the African capitals made this office the first point of contact for anything of importance to France's Africa policy. The Ministry of Cooperation, which managed the Assistance Militaire Technique (AMT) agreements, was also intentionally kept separate from the Ministry of Foreign Affairs and the Ministry of Defense, and this streamlined the decision-making process considerably. Also, since sub-Saharan presidents effectively had their own Paris Ministry, African presidents were able to maintain a direct line to the Elysée and a more direct voice, consequently, in France's Africa policy.[125] The French Assembly generally dealt with most intervention decisions after the fact. The French press is lively and critical, but it played a role largely in rallying public outcry against (or defending) decisions that had already been made with respect to Africa. Certainly, in the case of a particularly outrageous ruler, the French press was able to have a considerable influence on public opinion as in the publication of the story of emperor Bokassa's gifts of diamonds to President Giscard, and the scathing press coverage of the emperor's coronation and human rights record. The subsequent criticism of Giscard may well have led to his orders for Operation Barracuda.

Operation Barracuda (1979) in the Central African Empire used French Marine parachute troops to seize the capital, Bangui, and depose President-for-Life and Emperor Jean-Bédel Bokassa, who was no longer an asset to French influence in the region. He had crowned himself emperor (using French aid for a lavish ceremony) and given enormous political embarrassment to his French *patron*, Giscard.[126] Giscard's refusal of continued protection for Bokassa was understandable, given inconvenient revelations in the French press that the emperor had given him personal gifts of diamonds. Bokassa's use of French aid for his coronation à la Napoléon,[128] and the Bokassa regime's horrifying human rights abuses which escalated in 1979 with the beating deaths of school-aged protesters in Ngaragba Prison (some possibly at the emperor's own hand), de-legitimized the Emperor as a candidate for further French aid. He could no longer be considered a reliable political partner. Another leader needed to be provided for *Centrafrique* if French protection were to be continued under the cooperation agreement. France sent in the *paras*, and David Dacko, who had been removed in Bokassa's coup d'état in 1965, was restored to the presidency and promptly nicknamed on the street and in the press *"le président parachuté."*[127]

The French public largely supported deposing Bokassa, but it was concerned by France's continued expanded troop presence after the fact. Dacko's government was swiftly overthrown in yet another coup, but France continued its relationship with the CAR by working with the new president, General André Kolingba. The intervention was certainly timely, but it was not limited sufficiently in terms of how long the externally based troops needed to be deployed in the CAR before returning to France. Even after the intervention forces eventually returned home, France's base troops in the CAR continued to provide a reassuring source of power for President Kolingba.

Another constraint on the French intervention capacity was evident during the Zaïrean intervention of 1977–1978 which supported President Mobutu against Lunda insurgency in Shaba province. France's airlift capacity was seriously questioned by the French parliament during this operation. This operation initially featured logistics assistance from France, combined with military air transport of Moroccan troops to Shaba in 1977. This was followed by a more extensive commitment in 1978 when French citizens were killed in Kolwezi. Operation Léopard (1978) dropped Foreign Legion parachutists from French and Zaïrean aircraft to seize Kolwezi. The Legionnaires were withdrawn later and replaced by an all-African force with continued logistical support from France.[129] The Front de Libération Nationale Congolaise (FLNC) invaded Shaba twice. Giscard had visited Zaïre in 1975 and improved French relations with the continent's largest francophone nation, not coincidentally improving as well French access to Zaïre's considerable cobalt, copper, and diamond resources. Zaïre participated in Franco-African summit meetings, and also—it was later discovered—signed a military cooperation agreement with France. The May 1978 intervention included initially 600 Legionnaires and 100 parachutists, followed in a few weeks by three further companies of troops. A total of 1,750 Belgian troops also participated. The U.S. military's airlift command provided transport, using French bases to refuel at Dakar in Senegal, and at Libreville in Gabon. The Giscard government justified the intervention publicly on the basis of keeping Africa free from great power rivalry, which the Gaullists contested because U.S. participation had been necessary for transporting French troops. Protecting and evacuating French citizens and other Europeans in Kolwezi was an important immediate factor in the decision, as was France's promise to protect Mobutu's government according to its agreement.[130]

Jacques Foccart was fired by Giscard for being *too* Gaullist, but his network and methodology survived nonetheless. Foccart became something of an *éminence grise* for the subsequent network of personal emissaries to Africa established by President Mitterand, and he was rehired by Prime Minister Chirac as *his* personal Africa adviser during the "cohabitation" period between 1986 and 1988. The Mitterand emissaries included the president's own son, Jean-Christophe Mitterand, a former Agence France Press journalist who had worked in Africa,[131] and whose derisive nickname among francophone Africans is *"Papa m'a dit."*[132]

Mitterand, whose military and political career was marked by the ability to adapt his actions and rhetoric to a variety of circumstances, was able to adapt as well to the challenge of the Atlantic Alliance. His leftist "third worldism" was maintained as needed in the context of his dealings with the United States (e.g., his opposition to SDI) and he was not accused as frequently at home as his predecessor Giscard of *"Atlanticisme."* He was all the more able to deflect domestic criticism and work with Washington when he needed to.[133] The advent of his presidency was initially hailed by African governments and ordinary Africans, who appeared to believe, first, that Mitterand was a pro-African politician with deep ties to African leaders dating from World War II and the last part of the colonial period, and, second, that a socialist presidency would be sympathetic to a greater degree of freedom for African political and economic growth. The former proved to be true, if not the latter. Mitterand's ties to the most loyal African leaders were maintained and nurtured with de Gaulle-like care, if not with overtly Gaullist ideological language. In spite of rhetoric designed to make Africa, the French public, and the rest of the world believe that France's neocolonialist support of dictatorships had come to an end, the Mitterand years were not so different from previous presidencies. Indeed, the Mitterand government both cultivated and supported repressive authoritarian governments in the Central African Republic, Rwanda, Burundi, Zaïre, Congo-Brazzaville, Cameroon, Gabon, and Chad.

Mitterand's decisions in Africa mirrored a trend visible in his administration of France's overall security policy, which had become almost definitively Gaullist fairly early in his presidency. The Socialist government adapted its defense policy to the Gaullist model, which it had previously criticized as unrealistic. By 1981, Mitterand had also adapted the Gaullist model to the changing security situation, increasing France's defense contribution to Europe considerably without giving up any of its autonomy. Part of the reason for this lingering and pervasive Gaullism was that, by the 1970s, the basic premises on which de Gaulle had based French military policy were firmly anchored in public opinion and within the military itself, which had no desire to abandon nuclear power status or to return to basing foreign (NATO) troops on French soil. The Socialists, whose rhetoric was previously in favor of becoming non-nuclear and more Europe-oriented, became de facto Gaullists once in power. Like his predecessors, Mitterand also discovered that the independent, personalized policymaking of the Gaullist presidential style was useful to him as well because it rendered domestic parliamentary constraints and public opinion into occasional political nuisances but never a straitjacket.[134]

International Regimes and Institutions That Either Supported or Worked against France's Objectives

An increasing number of regional and international regimes and institutions offered either opportunities or threats to French interests in the African region. The Organization of African Unity (OAU) and the United Nations were a little more influential during the period of this case study than the last, although not much more. The OAU and the regional francophone summit conferences remained the most salient arenas in which the African countries raised concerns about their relationships with France. The OAU was largely ineffective in countering France's influence, however, and also somewhat ineffective when it agreed to intervene in *support* of French objectives. The international institution with the most clout, where African (not only francophone) security was concerned, was not a political organization but an economic one almost entirely controlled by the West: the International Monetary Fund (IMF).

The UN's international human rights conventions and norms continued to be more honored in the breach, although human rights questions were raised far more frequently than in the 1960s in African politics, both nationally and internationally. While intergovernmental (IGO) and nongovernmental (NGO) organizations continued to provide fora for discussions of more democratic governance in francophone Africa, French policy continued to place France's interests paramount. The democratic development of the *chasse gardée* remained only a secondary concern.

International arms control agreements, as in most places, are not yet a salient factor in regulating the African continent's regional security climate, although the recent land mine, child soldier, and small arms conventions may have much more of an effect on African security when these instruments have been fully ratified and may even, perhaps, be taken seriously at some point by nations at war.[135,136]

The issue of military intervention became the biggest current issue facing the Organization of African Unity. Ironically (given Gabon's history of French intervention), this was particularly emphasized at the 1977 OAU summit in Libreville.[137] The issue was used opportunistically, most notably at the Lagos conference in 1979, when Libya succeeded in getting a resolution passed by the other nations that the presence of French troops in Chad was "an obstacle to peace." France left in 1980 upon receiving the promise that the other African nations would step into the breach, and Libya was attacking N'Djamena eight months later.[138]

Another related problem has been to determine the theoretical and practical distinctions between an intervention and an invasion. The OAU's charter mandates nonintervention in the affairs of member states, a mandate broken a number of times by Africans participating in multinational United Nations forces, by Uganda and Rwanda in the ongoing war in eastern Zaïre, by Liberia in Sierra Leone (and vice versa), by the ECOMOG force members in Liberia, by Zaïre in Angola, by Libya in Chad, and in more minor militarized interstate conflicts such as the ongoing Bakassi territorial dispute between Nigeria and Cameroon. As of 1989, no collective security measures had been taken by the OAU. Its supposed role in conflict resolution via its Mediation, Conciliation and Arbitration Commission was nonexistent.[139]

The fairly recent disappearance of superpower rivalry may have an effect on the effectiveness of regional institutions. However, Ayoob suggests that the removal of superpower restraints on regional systems may encourage the appearance of "regionally-preeminent powers interested in translating their preeminence into hegemony or at least into a managerial role within their respective regions."[140] Nigeria's intervention in Liberia, mentioned in the previous chapter, is an illustration of this.[141] Since it is becoming more difficult every year for France to act as Africa's "gendarme," there is an opening in regional policing and peacekeeping work which can be filled by the regional organizations. Failing this, the opening could also be filled by the United States. If it behaves as France has in the past, however, the United States is also likely to be accused of neocolonialism and imperialism.

The Organization of African Unity has largely supported France's larger peacekeeping objectives, particularly the intervention in Chad. In return, France has acted as a stabilizing force, and it has generally backed the OAU's attempts at mediation. France knew that giving political backing to the efforts of the OAU improved the apparent legitimacy of France's own interventions, particularly when OAU members contributed troops to France's missions.[142]

The attempts by the OAU to make peace in Chad and end the need for external interventions by France and Libya faced many of the same difficulties, however, that the UN has faced in its multilateral interventions in Africa (e.g., in Shaba). The OAU made three different attempts in Chad, with Nigeria acting somewhat on its own parallel to these efforts. First, Nigeria (which shares a frontier with Chad), summoned conferences in Kano and Lagos in 1979, and it sent a military force of 1,600 to Chad to uphold the Kano agreement. This force was ineffective, criticized by the Chadian factions for misbehavior by the Nigerian soldiers, and seen in Chad as an attempt to install Nigeria's own candidate, Chona Lol, in the Chadian presidency. Second, when the transitional Government of National Union of Chad (GUNT) was formed in 1979, a multinational OAU force was to be sent to preserve the peace agreements, composed of troops from Congo-Brazzaville, Benin, and Guinea. Only Congo sent a unit, which stayed for only a week, remaining in its barracks. Only $600,000 of the promised $6 million to support this force was actually paid by member states. Third, during the temporary political and military defeat of Habré in 1981, and the gradual withdrawal of French and Libyan troops, the OAU put together another intra-African force to be composed of six country contingents under a Nigerian commander. Guinea, Benin, and Togo did not send their troops, Nigeria sent 2,000, Zaïre sent 800 to 2,000, and Senegal about 500. This force achieved little and was withdrawn by June 1981. The force was dependent on Nigeria and the United States for financial and logistical support, and it was weakened by political divisions. The Chad efforts were very discouraging to proponents of an all-Africa intervention force within the Organization of African Unity.[143]

There were attempts to create an OAU pan-African defense force, but the more salient defense agreements were regional in nature like ECOWAS, and of limited effectiveness. The French interventions in Chad have highlighted the continuing possibility of neocolonial interference if African countries remain unable to interact in such a way as to make such extra-continental interference unnecessary or unprofitable. The OAU's intervention failures had many causes: the essential weakness of the OAU's nonintervention principle and consequent variance in its application, Africa's multiple regional connections and mutual issues, the militarized strategic culture of many states, shifting alliances among African states and leaders, and the ever-present problem of funding intra-African expeditions when promised contributions do not arrive. Promises of supplying weapons from states that had very little in the way of surplus weaponry and equipment were another frequent problem. A number of interventions were fueled by fear of a common enemy by several states within the OAU, resulting in varying levels of support from those nations that were less concerned with a particular opponent. The best example of common enemy intervention here is the fear of Libyan expansionism in Chad, which led to OAU-sponsored intervention by Senegal, Nigeria, and Zaïre,[144] and also fear of Libyan expansionism via proxy in Liberia, which led to the ECOMOG intervention.

The regular summit conferences by francophone heads of state continue to be a significant regional institution, so popular that they now include some non-francophone heads of state. They remain a forum for discussions and disputes, but ultimately a means by which francophone African governments impress France with their still-viable ability to unify as a bloc when deemed necessary. Although France instituted these summit meetings, French leaders do not receive a show of unquestioning loyalty there any more; indeed, loyal pro-French rhetoric no longer plays well with many African citizens in the home audiences. However, France is able to use the summit meetings to announce new initiatives and cement old ties. In addition, many of the heads of state and their entourages know one another well, and they have dealt with one another for some time now independently of their relationship with France. As Bayart describes Franco-African political culture:

> Franco-African links are reproduced by the social relations formed in universities, the military, brotherhoods and also in matrimonial exchanges, the importance of which must not be disregarded. This reproduction also occurs in political life: from the daily flow of information, visits, telephone conversations, and requests that make sub-Saharan diplomacy in the Elysée, the Quai d'Orsay and the Rue Monsieur resemble a clientelist system. It is symbolically strengthened by the Franco-African summits, started by Georges Pompidou.[145]

Lest one think that dynastic stabilization of alliances is a thing of the past, one of the matrimonial exchanges referred to here was the marriage of the daughter of Congo-Brazzaville's socialist president Sassou-Nguesso to President Bongo of Gabon.

It would be a mistake, however, to regard the histories of the francophone African states as in any way uniform other than a certain level of shared experience with the force and cultural hegemony imposed by French colonialism, as the disputes at the francophone summits demonstrate amply. Their nationalist histories differ distinguishably, and they must be seen against a salient background of African cultural influences that are particular to each country's combination of peoples, natural resources, geography, and history. This is why the histories of Guinea, Mali, and Cameroon differ so broadly from those of Senegal, Côte d'Ivoire, and Gabon, and why the existence of the francophone summit meetings in no way insures France of a continuing political, ideological, cultural, or military alignment by its African partners.[146]

Finally, one international institution which strongly influences security conditions in the region is the International Monetary Fund. Nearly three-quarters of African debt is owed to bilateral or multilateral creditors rather than to individual banks.[147] IMF structural adjustment programs have gained the reputation, fair or not, of contributing to economic hardships and consequent social unrest in some of the sub-Saharan states which have accepted these programs. If so, then this is an institution which must be considered a constraint on France's attempts to be an internal security guarantor for its cooperating allies. The role of the IMF structural adjustment program in the oil strikes in Gabon is treated below. The United States, furthermore, often backs the international funding institutions' decisions as to how and where aid conditionality is to be applied in cases of lagging political or economic reforms. France is also beginning to condition aid to its African allies on their adherence to reforms deemed necessary by the IMF and the World Bank. At the 1990 Franco-African summit of heads of state in La Baule, France, stated that it would pay increased attention to political and economic reforms and make its aid decisions accordingly, although exactly how the military cooperation agreements constrain these promises is not clear.[148,149]

Other Great Powers Capable of Intervening, or Active in the Region
Other great powers, primarily the United States and USSR, were capable of intervening in francophone Central Africa, although they did so relatively infrequently compared to France. Belgium and the United States intervened in Zaïre during the Shaba rebellion, and the United States CIA presence in Zaïre was aimed at holding back the ideological influence of the Soviets. The United States and USSR shared with France the capability for direct military

intervention in the region (and both had a better airlift capacity), but both of the great Cold War powers tended to prefer other forms of intervention (e.g., military and economic aid, technical assistance, teachers and technicians) which could be combined with what France was already doing in the *chasse gardée*, opening avenues of influence although not pushing France aside as the primary influence.

Between 1974 and 1978, twenty-two sub-Saharan states and African liberation movements received USSR and other communist country arms and equipment. Of these, the only Central African francophone recipients were Congo-Brazzaville and Chad.[150] In neither of these countries was the USSR a major strategic factor or a director of regional policy by the end of the 1980s. The USSR was active and capable of intervening; however, its influence in francophone Africa remained marginal.

The Soviet Union and Other Communist States

Although lacking historical ties to Africa, Soviet (and allied Cuban) influence and intervention in Africa has been a significant source of concern to France. Soviet policy was primarily pragmatic, supporting anticolonial groups where there was a reasonable expectation of political loyalty and the acquisition of hard currency from large-scale arms transfers to grateful new African nations. The USSR also offered training facilities for Portuguese (lusophone) and South African liberation movements. Clayton suggests that France's limited return to NATO may even have been a reaction to increased Soviet activity in the francophone African sphere of influence.[151]

Soviet policy in Africa was reinvigorated by the various anticolonial movements of the 1960s, and by the USSR's development of an oceangoing fleet of large warships posing an extra-European threat with a potentially global reach. Africa's three strategic seaways, Suez, the Horn of Africa, and the southern Cape, therefore required renewed attentiveness from the Atlantic allies. African governments noted these changes in the global environment, and they found ways to exploit the ensuing great power rivalries for their own benefit in terms of domestic and external security. The Soviets tended to prefer funding proxy interventions by Cuba in a number of francophone African countries, including Congo-Brazzaville (where Cubans had an air staging post for their Angola forces), and also Benin.[152] Soviet objectives continued to include securing logistical rights, encouraging the removal of as much French and other Western influence as possible, establishing friendly alliances by supporting various liberation movements, and discouraging Chinese influence.[153]

Data from 1979–1980 for the Communist "military adviser" presence (which does include troops) show that at least 7,000 Soviet and East

German "technicians" were placed in North and sub-Saharan Africa, with about 3,000 of these in Algeria and Libya, and the rest concentrated largely in Angola, Ethiopia, and Mozambique. While French presence remained fairly constant in its client countries throughout the region over the decades, waxing and waning according to policy decision made in Paris, Soviet presence was more opportunistic and tended to oscillate widely according to which African countries went Marxist or acquired an insurgent liberation movement. It is therefore more difficult to find a "representative year" from which to offer data on the presence of Soviet troops and technical advisers. Congo-Brazzaville was the only francophone host of Soviet advisers in Central Africa.[154] Cuban "technicians" (mostly soldiers) numbered roughly 30,000 in sub-Saharan Africa, of which 50 were in Guinea, and the remainder in Angola and Ethiopia.

Chinese military personnel in sub-Saharan Africa in 1979 numbered only 305, largely concentrated in non-francophone Equatorial Guinea.[155] The Chinese also sent a number of other technical (often agricultural) advisers, but these were not as significant a presence in the francophone countries, and their numbers often fluctuated according to whether a particular leader decided (usually because of renewed alliances with the West) to ask them to leave, as Bokassa did in the Central African Republic in 1966.

China participated in some of the African independence movements with some enthusiasm in the 1960s, largely in the former Portuguese colonies (often in competition with the USSR). In francophone Africa, China assisted southern Cameroonian insurgents in 1960. Recognition of the People's Republic of China was a factor in David Dacko's loss of the presidency of the CAR in Bokassa's 1965 coup d'état.[156] China lost its momentum in Africa later in the decade due to the need to concentrate on its own domestic political problems. China returned to Africa in the 1970s, however, largely contributing development projects and military education, either in China or by visiting Chinese training teams. Francophone countries receiving Chinese military training included Cameroon, Congo-Brazzaville, Guinea, Mali, Togo, and Zaïre. North Korea provided similar military training teams to Togo and possibly Madagascar, as well as to several anglophone African nations. China, Bulgaria, East Germany, North Korea, and Yugoslavia also offered training facilities for lusophone and South African liberation movements.[157]

The United States of America

The United States influence has generally been far more ad hoc, compared to its other interests in the developing world, although U.S. interest in

Africa has grown significantly since the 1970s as a way of countering the considerable Soviet influence in Angola, Mozambique, Libya, and Guinea. Covert assistance during the Reagan administration went to insurgent forces in Angola, Chad, and Libya.[158] U.S. resources have been invested in Sudan and Zaïre to counterbalance Libya and Cuban-supported Angola, respectively, and Clayton underlines the relative importance of the Rapid Deployment Joint Task Force formed in 1980, based in Kenya and Somalia. U.S. aid was given to Cameroon in return for overflight rights and access facilities on a possible route for rapid deployment forces. U.S. influence was important in southern Africa as a counterweight to the Cuban support for Angola, and the United States supported France's interventions in Chad.

In spite of the prominence of the U.S. Central Intelligence Agency (CIA) in African demonology, there has been only occasional *evidence* of its operations in Africa (a possible indication of either inactivity or success), most of it in Zaïre. Clayton gives credence to the following examples of U.S. CIA intervention, taken from the work of René Lemarchand: the CIA interest in overthrowing Mba in Gabon in 1964 and Tsiranana in Madagascar in 1971 (both of which were fended off by the French because these two presidents had been long-time allies since the colonial period),[159] CIA help toward the successful, if brief, accession to power of Colonel Ratsimandrava in Madagascar in 1975, and Zaïre-based CIA activities aimed at staving off Chinese influence in Burundi and Rwanda in the mid-1960s. Finally, there is the notorious history of CIA penetration of former Belgian administrative structures in Congo-Léopoldville at independence, allowing the CIA to help President Kasavubu in Congo-Léopoldville (later Zaïre) to dismiss Prime Minister Patrice Lumumba in 1960, and possibly to murder Lumumba in 1961, to hire mercenaries and aircraft to defeat the Simba uprising in 1964, to hijack Tshombe's movement in 1967, and to provide numerous but vague security-related services to President Mobutu Sese Seko throughout the following decades.[160] Decalo also mentions that the Chad-Libya merger announcement of 1981 triggered CIA support for future Chadian president Hissene Habré's faction.[161]

Bratton and van de Walle note that the end of the Cold War had a significant effect on U.S. policies in Africa, at least temporarily. The United States found less reason to intervene in Africa when the USSR was no longer a factor, failing to protect Samuel Doe in Liberia (although it did send financial support to ECOMOG), and sending missions to Somalia and Rwanda only when the humanitarian dimensions of these conflicts became large enough to provoke international outcry. The U.S. government took advantage of the choices made possible by the no-longer bipolar security climate by cutting back on overall aid to Africa and concentrating aid only on those places where it perceived openings for democratic governance, free markets, and political liberties (although market reform took precedence).[162] U.S. influence in Africa returned to help France with Chad, and it became quite important in southern Africa with the need to counterbalance Soviet influence in Angola.

Other States Active in the Region

Other Western nations intervening in Africa, if not so recently, have included Great Britain, which, although it left no permanent military garrisons at independence, has offered training aid to African countries, largely to its former possessions and the Commonwealth countries, and particularly to Nigeria during its civil war (which was probably an additional impetus to French aid to Biafra). Like the United States, Britain has also aided the Portuguese-speaking nations since independence in various ways. Portugal's intelligence activities have been more evident than its military: it gave covert aid to Biafra during the Nigerian Civil War, and it may have helped to assassinate the Mozambican leader of FRELIMO in 1969. Belgium has intervened twice in its former colony of Zaïre, and it has provided that country with training aid. Belgium is a small power, but Brussels is a frequent contributor to multinational forces, and it maintained a connection with President Mobutu (as part of Mobutu's supportive "Troika," the other two partners being France and the United States) in what had been the Belgian Congo. West Germany has given training aid to Gabon and Guinea, as well as to Nigeria. A number of other European countries have offered such aid, but largely to non-francophone states because of France's priority in its former colonies.[163]

Israel has found a number of allies in Africa, although this alliance is generally broken whenever an African nation finds the need for assistance from the Arab countries. In addition to large-scale aid to imperial Ethiopia, Uganda, and Tanzania, Israeli military and security training was particularly important in Zaïre.[164] In addition, Israel was an important buyer for the Central African Empire's diamonds, and Emperor Bokassa maintained ties with Israel in spite of his publicly expressed sympathy with the Arab League and what Kalck describes as an "ephemeral conversion to Islam." President Dacko of the CAR used Israeli aid to set up rural agricultural projects, industrial shops, and the National Young Pioneers.[165]

Arms Transfers to Francophone Africa by France and Other Nations

Here are some data (which can be compared with the figures from 1960–1969 in this same section of the previous chapter) on the types and sources of arms transfers to francophone African nations during the two decades following the death of de Gaulle. Note particularly that infantry weapons have been joined by much more heavy weaponry in the French section than was evident during the 1960s. *Mirage* counterinsurgency aircraft also start appearing in the totals for countries with French bases (Gabon and Côte d'Ivoire). However, the 1970s and 1980s also saw significant transfers by the USSR of MIG17, MIG19, and MIG21 combat aircraft to a few francophone countries (Guinea, Mali, Madagascar, and Congo-Brazzaville), although most of the Soviet attention (with MIGs) went to Angola, Ethiopia, Somalia, and Mozambique. In 1979, the USSR supplied about $4,635 million of the $5,400 million in arms that went to its allies in sub-Saharan Africa. China was not even a close second: in 1964–1978, China provided only $191 million in weapons to sub-Saharan Africa, although that figure jumped to $400 million in 1979.[166] France began to experience far more competition from other nations in its francophone African arms markets during this period.

Table 6.4. **Arms Transfers to Francophone African Countries, 1970–1989**

France, to	
Burkina Faso (Upper Volta)	15 armored cars, 13 armored personnel carriers, a few field guns, mortars, infantry weapons, and rocket launchers
Burundi	27 armored cars
Chad	Infantry weapons, mortars, antitank guided weapons
Djibouti	10 armored cars, infantry and artillery mortars, antitank guns
Gabon	15 armored cars, 12 armored personnel carriers and Mirage COIN (counterinsurgency) aircraft
Côte d'Ivoire	5 light tanks, 23 armored cars, 22 armored vehicles, 4 howitzers, large mortars, light antiaircraft guns, and 5 COIN aircraft
Mauritania	65 armored cars, some armored personnel carriers, mortars, and antitank rocket launchers
Niger	46 armored cars and 14 armored personnel carriers
Rwanda	27 armored cars, a few light artillery pieces and mortars to.
Senegal	54 armored cars, armored personnel carriers, mortars, and antitank guided weapons
Togo	10 armored cars, 5 armored personnel carriers
Zaïre	140 armored cars, 80 armored personnel carriers, and light field guns
	(France also sold weapons to Kenya and Nigeria during this period, largely armored cars and armored personnel carriers, and 50 Franco-German-designed ground-to-air missile units were also sold to Nigeria.)

(continued)

Table 6.4. (*continued*)

Belgium, to
Cameroon — Field howitzers and antitank guided weapons

Brazil, to
Gabon — 16 armored cars and two maritime reconnaissance aircraft
Togo — One COIN (counter-insurgency) aircraft

West Germany, to
Benin — 30 scout cars and 6 load carriers
Togo — 50 armored personnel carriers and a COIN aircraft

Sweden, to
Cameroon — Light antiaircraft guns

Switzerland, to
Cameroon — Light antiaircraft guns

Israel, to
Central African Republic — Automatic weapons

Soviet Union, to*
Benin — 8 BRDM 1 armored vehicles, 10 PT 76 armored vehicles, infantry weapons including mortars, grenade launchers
Burundi — A few mortars and light antiaircraft guns
Central African Republic — Light mortars and antitank rocket launchers, and possibly 20 light armored vehicles
Congo-Brazzaville — MIG15 and MIG17 combat aircraft, armored personnel carriers, and artillery rocket launchers
Djibouti — Some armored personnel carriers (possible origin Libyan)
Guinea — MIG21 and MIG17 combat aircraft, also tanks and armored personnel carriers
Madagascar — A few armored vehicles (which may not be Soviet in origin), as well as antiaircraft weapons, tanks, and MIG17 and MIG21 combat aircraft
Mali — 20 armored vehicles, surface-to-air missiles, 8 armored personnel carriers, tanks, and MIG21, MIG19 and MIG17 combat aircraft
Mauritania — A few anti-aircraft guns
Togo — 2 medium tanks (probably Libyan)
Zaïre — Small numbers of armored personnel carriers and artillery pieces, possibly of Chinese origin

China, to
Congo-Brazzaville — 15 medium tanks and 14 light tanks
Gabon — Automatic weapons
Madagascar — A few light tanks (unconfirmed)
Mali — 10 light tanks
Zaïre — Perhaps 50 light tanks and Shanghai-class naval craft
Guinea — Shanghai-class naval craft

Cuba, to	
Congo-Brazzaville	35 medium tanks, 37 armored vehicles, 68 armored personnel carriers, artillery weapons, artillery rocket launchers, light antiaircraft guns (precise source of some weapons uncertain; may be Soviet or Cuban)
United States, to	
Cameroon	26 light armored vehicles
Gabon	6 armored vehicles
Senegal	6 field guns
Togo	6 field guns
Zaïre	10 medium tanks and a number of armored personnel carriers

Sources: Adapted from Clayton in Baynham (1986: 228–249), also Laurance and Yu in Arlinghaus (1983: 46–47, 110) and IISS (1981–1982).[167]
* Some arms[85] went to Chad, but most likely to the opposition and not in concert with France's goals there.

One noticeable trend is that most African governments, with a few exceptions, still resisted buying large numbers of expensive fighter aircraft or tanks without good reason, although they continued to buy or request some of these in order to modernize their forces. Although symbolic of military independence, these weapons platforms require a high level of technical expertise for maintenance, expertise which is often locally unavailable except from expatriate trainers. Spare parts for repairs are equally expensive. In 1970, the only tanks found in sub-Saharan Africa were 5 French tanks in Côte d'Ivoire, 12 Soviet tanks in Guinea, 50 U.S. tanks in Ethiopia, 150 Soviet tanks in Somalia, and 10 Soviet tanks in Mali. Jet fighters in Africa in 1970 were: 8 Soviet planes in Guinea, 6 Soviet planes in Mali, 15 Soviet planes in Nigeria, 26 U.S./U.K. planes in Ethiopia, 18 Soviet planes in Somalia, and 7 Soviet planes in Uganda. Many of these items were undeployable in a short time after acquisition because of maintenance problems, or unused due to the lack of trained military personnel. Since 1970, tank and aircraft levels have increased, even in francophone Africa, but mostly in those countries which continued to be supplied at high levels by the Soviet Union: Ethiopia, Somalia, Angola and Zambia. The North African states were also very well armed by comparison, as befitted their status as a strategic zone of greater interest to NATO, as well as their oil-enhanced economies. Of these, Libya has demonstrated the most significant increases in hardware.[168]

From the 1960s through the early 1980s, the entire sub-Saharan African region acquired only 5 percent of its imported arms from the United States, and never accounted for more than 3 percent of U.S. military transfers during this time. The principal recipients of U.S. military transfers to Africa between 1950 and 1980 were in North Africa. Libya received a surprising $36.6 million worth of arms from the United States between 1971 and 1975, which had dropped rapidly to $1 million between 1976 and 1980. Of the francophone sub-Saharans during this thirty-year period, Cameroon received $15.5 million in military transfers from the United States, and Zaïre $102.6 million. These were not the only francophone recipients, as the list above indicates, but they were the only two to receive amounts showing that they were of strategic importance to the United States during this time. Zaïre's importance to the United States as a centrally located anticommunist bulwark has been indicated elsewhere. Cameroon's importance to the United States was less obvious; however, it granted the U.S. military overflight and landing rights, it was in a strategic position for reaching much of the region of immediate interest to Libya, and the U.S. Navy made its first port call there in 1980. The United States transferred arms to a number of other sub-Saharan nations, but Washington assumed that France would be the main Western presence and anti-Soviet guarantee in its former colonies. In the 1990s, of course, the United States has increased its presence considerably, and U.S. arms transfers to Africa in general since the 1980s have accelerated upward.[169]

Francophone African armies received most of their equipment from France, hence were almost completely dependent on France for repairs, training, and spare parts. The "second generation" of military cooperation agreements broadened their ability to seek arms elsewhere, but interoperability problems slowed this somewhat, although non-French sources are sought now more frequently. French arms transfers, up until the Chad interventions, demonstrated a need for modern weaponry in order to fight Libya, have emphasized less expensive, less complex arms that are appropriate to African conditions and easy to repair and maintain. Dual-use (civilian and military) technology is favored, hence the emphasis on cooperative operations which build civilian capacity, like roads and airstrips, and on transfers of communications equipment.

In 1980,[170] France provided the following percentages of these Central African countries' armaments: Gabon (52.7 percent), Cameroon (34.5 percent), Central African Republic (98.1 percent), Chad (98.4 percent), Congo-Brazzaville (24.7 percent), Rwanda (71.6 percent), and Zaïre (68 percent). Overall, France contributed more than 50 percent of the arms acquired by its former colonies in 1980, in addition to the technical and logistical support donated under the cooperation agreements. Of the remaining arms, 30 percent came from NATO countries, 13 percent from the USSR, and 7 percent from other sources.[171]

Note also that, by 1980 (before the death of President Touré), Guinea was again using French arms. Soviet arms transfers to Guinea dropped significantly in the early 1980s, as the Guinean president became disillusioned with the USSR for failing in its expected commitments to develop the Guinean armed forces. Soviet training of African pilots often took longer than the USSR had anticipated, and Soviet pilots often flew African planes as a stopgap measure. It was apparent that Guinea was useful to the USSR only as a base for Soviet operations in southern Africa. Indeed, except for its southern African clients, Soviet arms transfers to sub-Saharan Africa "slowed to a trickle" by the mid-1980s.[172]

Sub-Saharan Africa has not been, until recently, a primary market for France's more sophisticated arms products. The larger part of France's arms market remains North Africa and the Middle East. *Mirage* and *Alpha-Jet* fighters were occasionally sold to the richer states, but France remained in control of the military balance among its sub-Saharan allies throughout the 1980s by refusing some requests for the pricier arms. Interoperability has remained high, as the African troops were equipped and trained by France. The arms transfer policy has been another means by which France has encouraged these states (not always successfully) to develop at least some commonality of security interests, if not a common or entirely consistent security policy.[173] However, most African governments sought to modernize their armies as much as possible, and they continued to request more state-of-the-art equipment from France, or to seek it from elsewhere.[174]

Africa's own arms manufacturing remained limited during this period, with the notable exception of South Africa, which had become a major across-the-board manufacturer and supplier of arms, including aircraft, armored vehicles, missiles, and naval vessels. In 1980, the only three francophone African nations manufacturing any type of major armament were Gabon, Senegal, and Côte d'Ivoire, all of which were able to manufacture naval vessels. In addition to these three, out of all of the other francophone African nations, the only ones with any domestic arms production capability were Burkina Faso, Cameroon, Congo-Brazzaville, and Guinea, all of which could produce small arms and/or ammunition.[175]

The political economy of foreign aid cannot be examined without considering the balance between military aid (including arms contracts of various preferential kinds) and nonmilitary (economic, capacity building) aid. Both bilateral aid, such as that from one country to another, and multilateral aid, such as that from institutions like the World Bank or other international development banks, are ways in which the great powers have real effects on the peacetime security of developing countries. In 1983, the major economic aid donors to Africa were the leading capitalist countries: the United States, France, Japan, and West Germany. The Soviet Union continued to give more military aid than economic aid; however, economic aid makes it easier in some ways to shift budgets and spend more money on arms.[176]

Arms sales were the primary form of non-French military influence, but both the United States and the USSR also contributed development aid to the Central African countries. There were Peace Corps volunteers in both CAR and Zaïre at various times during the 1970s and 1980s, mostly serving as English teachers, fish-farming instructors, health workers, and latrine builders. While the author of this chapter was a U.S. Peace Corps "*coopérant*" stationed in the small town of Bérbérati in the Central African Empire in 1978–1979, she taught English language classes at a *lycée* which included three other Americans, three Russian science and mathematics teachers, and two Frenchmen (teaching French language and literature) on its faculty. The other faculty members were Central Africans. The school was structured and administered according to the French system of secondary education, even so far as the calculation of examination grades. This combination of contributing nations was mirrored in the faculties of secondary schools all over the country. We were also made aware (by Peace Corps fish farming instructors in the same town) that there was a Chinese agricultural cooperative just up the road. A Belgian diamond broker, a French monastery and school, and a Portuguese restaurant rounded out the local foreign presence in this town, which was a regional *préfecture*. While this anecdotal evidence hardly proves "intervention" in the traditional sense, it gives an interesting picture of some of the windows of opportunity granted by both France and Emperor Bokassa to outside cultural and political influences during this period.

Commercial interests occasionally dovetailed with military necessity in ways which allowed openings to smaller states. Some smaller powers sold arms to this region, and a few offered specialized security training. Some of these states have been quite effective, particularly starting in the 1990s, in exploiting regional conflicts as openings for commerce. Several private agencies from smaller powers (employing former government military personnel) provided security training to African governments, including the South African firm Executive Outcomes, and Israel's Levdan. The latter firm, which maintains ties to the Israeli government, was engaged by Congo-Brazzaville to train President Lissouba's private militia as well as his official guard. Third-party government-connected arms and security firms *do* impact via commerce and war on African states' capacities to maintain internal and external security, so they are relevant variables in this context. Also a problem was what Ross calls "multiple source acquisition" on the part of governments like Congo-Brazzaville and Zaïre, which cultivated ties to the USSR and United States, respectively. This refers to the collecting of various arms technologies from different sources which did not mesh well, leading to logistical problems and working against France's strategic goal of military standardization.[177]

Attempts for influence by the USSR were unsuccessful in francophone Africa, but the U.S. influence has grown since the end of the Cold War, and has been spread over more countries than before, most recently in response to a need for strategic bases from which to counter threats from the Middle East and Islamic terrorism. U.S. involvement had become substantial during the late 1990s. The Friends Committee on National Legislation's *Washington Newsletter* of May 1998 shows thirty-three African countries which participated in joint combat exercises with the United States during the years 1995–1998, five of which were Chad, CAR, Cameroon, Gabon, and Congo-Brazzaville. Also according to FCNL's research, between 1991 and 1995, 50 out of the 53 African countries received some form of U.S. military assistance, 42 African countries received military training from the United States, and the United States transferred $249 million worth of weapons to Africa, mostly small arms. Uganda became a major military presence in the East African region that borders on Rwanda, Burundi, and Zaïre, and received significant military aid from the United States, as did Rwanda. Turning to the United States could become a primary diplomatic bargaining chip for francophone African governments to use if they need concessions from France. Given the preponderance of U.S. power and intervention capacity over France, this may well prove to be France's most significant foreign policy challenge in future in the *chasse gardée*.

Regional States' Options to Put Pressure on France

What African influence existed continued to be exercised through long-term personal relationships at the highest levels of government. The most influential African presidents were those whose special relationship had existed over the course of decades of loyalty, like President Bongo of Gabon. However, the cooperation agreements provided a continuing arena for renegotiation with France. African partners in these cooperation agreements occasionally asked for significant economic and military help from other states, too much of which would threatened the special relationship which France was trying to maintain. Emperor Bokassa's flirtations with Libya and China are interesting examples of this; notably, he and the CAR always came back to France. France's continuing desire to be both the dominant partner and the primary external partner in any cooperation agreement could be used as a limited form of influence over France in order to leverage an occasional concession.

Presidents like Omar Bongo, whose loyalty was certain and who owed France their positions, could be counted on in large part to support France's preferences most of the time. Bongo, however, had an additional advantage. Gabon is not only a loyal part of the *chasse gardée* housing a large contingent of base troops, it is a key strategic location with a large oil industry under joint French-Gabonese control (Elf-Gabon), profitable timber interests, port facilities, and a relatively sophisticated infrastructure in which France has invested significant resources. Those francophone countries with fewer resources important to France than Gabon were in less of a position to push France for economic concessions, investment projects, and swift protective action.

Other francophone African governments have maintained themselves in power by using France's aid in a number of ways, some becoming adept in manipulating their most faithful donor's need to continue the relationship. Zartman emphasizes that one result of France's extended presence is an increasing susceptibility to African pressure:

> The more the Western presence spreads in Africa, the more its effects are diluted by the need to talk and listen to a larger number of African voices, often raised in concert to increase the volume. As the decolonization process became multilateral in Namibia through the inclusion of the Front-Line States and Nigeria and in the Franco-African summits through the inclusion of non-French-speaking states, greater French and Western activity in Africa brought greater African influence on the Western states. In the 1979 Franco-African summit a discussion of military cooperation could have taken place, as the French wanted, had it not been for the presence and opposition of a group of leftist states (Benin, Burundi, Congo, Mali).[178]

Bayart suggests that the threat of a quarrel among the francophone nations, and the consequent loss to France of its unified support, is occasionally enough to win further concessions from France, a point which underlines the importance of the annual francophone summit meetings. Bayart explains (in the context of Gabon):

> It would be insulting to infer from these admissions that political power in Gabon was mere puppetry, masking a false independence. Far from being the victims of their very real vulnerability, African governments exploit, occasionally skillfully, the resources of a dependence which is, it cannot ever be sufficiently stressed, astutely fabricated as much as predetermined. Both on their political stage and within the world system, they pursue their own objectives, within the margins of failure and success that the implementation of any strategy entails.[179]

When Cameroon and Niger refused to support Biafra during the Nigerian Civil War along with Côte d'Ivoire, it may have been a successful attempt to get a renegotiation of their cooperation agreements and diversify their economic relations. Bayart also refers to the 1981–1986 African exploitation of the "dependantist" assumptions of the French left wing during the Mitterand period as "blackmail diplomacy." Mitterand did make a large number of promises at the beginning of his presidency concerning aid to Africa, and the francophone nations were not slow to remind him of these upon occasion. President Mobutu of Zaïre became particularly fond of pulling France's strings by maintaining close relationships with rival powers (Belgium and the United States) and calling France to account for what had been promised.[180]

Strategic natural resources in the quantity owned by Gabon are a significant source of leverage, particularly when combined with their vulnerability to politically generated disruption. Another interesting facet of the power of France's long-term allies to pressure France is offered by examining the case of Gabon in more detail. The Gabonese president is not the only member of his government or citizen of his country with a firm grasp of what it might take to put pressure on France. Popular political organizations have far less of an influence on the Gabonese government than French economic concerns do, and using those economic concerns as pressure points is a tactic of various strands in Gabonese politics. An interesting series of events occurred in Gabon in the early 1990s which featured an ultimately failed attempt by labor organizations and employees in Gabon to influence the government by putting pressure on the French oil interests. An IMF austerity plan was put in place by President Bongo in order to alleviate the effects of falling oil prices. Bongo's political opponents from the MORENA party, based in Paris and hitherto cooptable by Bongo, profited from civil unrest caused by the economic hardships of the IMF structural adjustment plan. After a failed assassination attempt and coup in 1989, followed by another attempt later in the same year, Bongo entered into negotiations with MORENA's leaders toward a process of political liberalization. After Bongo announced to the country that he would tolerate no further disorder, teachers, students, and hospital workers went on strike in January 1990, demanding pay raises. They were followed by other workers in a general strike, accompanied by riots and the burning of public buildings. Gabonese policemen joined the strikers. The only major group not to join the general strike was the offshore oil workers. The offshore oil enclaves remained in operation, while those onshore came to a full halt.

In response to this internally generated pressure, Bongo announced that he would hold a conference of democratic reform, possibly including multiparty elections, which had not occurred in Gabon since Mba's rise to power.

Further strikes occurred by the banking and insurance company employees, university teachers, doctors at a Libreville teaching hospital, and at the country's only flour mill (which threatened a bread shortage in the capital). In March 1990, there was further serious unrest at the onshore oil facilities. Workers at Gabon's only refinery threatened a plant shutdown unless they received a wage increase from Elf-Gabon (their wages had been frozen under the IMF plan). The goals of these tactics included destabilizing Bongo's government, inducing some form of democratization process, and using France's frustration with the oil slowdowns and the danger to French expatriates to shift French support from Bongo to the opposition.

Bongo met a number of the workers' demands. (Oil workers in Gabon are government employees.) However, he was faced with riots again in May 1990 when an opposition leader, who was to have run in the April elections, was assassinated in his hotel room with what the protesters assumed was French complicity. The French became much more publicly involved at this point. The French consulate in Port-Gentil was burned down. A total of 500 Legionnaires arrived shortly thereafter, stationed throughout Libreville and Port-Gentil. Elf-Gabon evacuated all but 50 of its 600 French staff, 10 executives were taken hostage, and military cargo jets stood ready to evacuate the 1,800 French expatriates working in Gabon. For the first time in Gabon's history, the French oil company was forced to halt production. Gabon was losing $50 million a day in revenues, and France even more, as 65 percent of Elf-Gabon was controlled by the French state by either direct ownership or through state-owned companies. Elf-Gabon was responsible for almost a quarter of Elf's 1989 oil production worldwide.

At this point, Bongo went on French television demanding the return of Elf's French employees to Gabon, saying that his country would drop its services if production did not begin again soon. He called the French airlift "completely unjustified," and insisted that security could be maintained. In addition to Bongo's threat to drop Elf, the presence of French soldiers was a factor in Elf's subsequent decision to return its employees. French tanks took down the opposition barricades, fought with protesters, and crushed all antigovernment resistance in Port-Gentil. French troops withdrew and left security in the hands of the Gabonese troops and the Presidential Guard, which was reported to have fired indiscriminately on protesters. 500 French troops were kept in place to protect the oil facilities in Port-Gentil. "Multiparty" elections were rescheduled for September of 1990. They were characterized by intimidation and voting fraud and won by the president's party. The first multiparty presidential election was not until 1993. It was considered flawed but not completely fraudulent by international observers.[181]

The lessons of this case are twofold. First, every political tendency in Gabon was aware that France's protection and French interests remain salient sources of political power leverage and as such, were worth competing for by any means. If the Gabonese opposition had managed to get France to put real pressure on Bongo to hold fair multiparty elections, those elections might well have taken place. However, the second lesson reiterates a point made in a number of places in both of these chapters: a loyal African president, however undemocratic, was still given precedence over a problematic opposition, however democratically inclined. France may have hedged its bets on Gabon by giving MORENA members sanctuary in Paris, but the French did ultimately intervene to make certain that Bongo would stay on as president. His threat to drop Elf only strengthened his position.

Unity between France and its African partners involves more, then, than just preservation of markets, the extension of culture, the establishment of a strategic presence, and a promise to vote France's way in the United Nations. The strategic mineral and petroleum stocks are important enough to both Gabon and France to allow their owners (both French and Gabonese, and both private and state owners) some degree of leverage. Whether Bongo's successors will have the same kind of power is debatable because of the way Bongo has been able to make use of his historical relationships with successive French presidents. Gabon has been an extension of France itself, at first, and then of the French sphere of influence. France also needs Gabon now because of the pressure which Elf and the other French oil companies are able to put on the French government in their own domestic arena.

Some recent changes are evident in the Gabon case. French power can now be manipulated through its economic interests *both* by African presidents and also by France's own African employees. Also, having finally authorized ostensibly "democratic" elections, President Bongo's power must now depend as much on his political ability to manipulate the election process as on his ability to call for help from France. Bongo lost a major friend at the Elysée when Jacques Foccart was removed from office by Mitterand. However, President Chirac brought Foccart back briefly before his death, and has a continued respect for the presidential friendships and other personal ties that were built and cultivated by the Foccart network.

Common Objectives Shared By the Regional States and France

According to French rhetoric during this period, francophone African states and France still do share a number of common objectives. However, by the 1990s there were attacks on French citizens in francophone Africa countries that indicated a growing willingness on the part of ordinary African citizens to get rid of French influence in spite of the economic and security risks. There were also many indications that the interests shared by African and French leaders were not necessarily shared by ordinary African citizens, or by particular ethnic or social groups.

The Gabon case just cited provides an example of Gabonese employees of a French enterprise (Elf-Gabon) threatening French interests even if this action threatened their own livelihood. In the Central African Republic, regarded as one of the countries most loyal to France, the French Cultural Center in Bangui was attacked for the first time during a series of army mutinies in the late 1990s. There has also been an increase in attacks on French citizens in central African countries since Operation Turquoise in Rwanda. Even if their leaders maintain a high level of loyalty to France in return for the guarantee of continuing power, many ordinary francophone Africans are showing a high level of resentment against continuing French influence. Many of their leaders are also beginning to demonstrate greater independence. France's ability to roll with these punches is already being tested.

The francophone leadership summits are one place where common objectives between France and African nations can be articulated and supported. However, since these meetings have been used so frequently as a place where new French policy is announced, only to fall back on the same practices and assumptions later on, some cynicism on the part of African leaders is understandable as to whether France's goals are indeed in concert with theirs. For example, at the 1975 Francophone Summit in Bangui (CAR), Giscard told the assembled leaders that "the only competition which is in accordance with Africa's interests is that which promotes economic, social, and cultural development."[182] By the Dakar summit in 1977, Giscard had returned to an earlier formula, warning that prosperity and development could occur only if there was peace and stability, and a willingness on the part of those assembled to avoid the inducements of both poles of the Cold War in favor of alignment with French policies.[183] The priority, therefore, continued to be security as the condition of development and self-sufficiency (which could only be achieved with French help), rather than development as a condition of security (leading to greater African self-sufficiency and less loyalty to France).

Prestige, sovereignty, independence, and autonomy are as important to leaders in Africa as they were to de Gaulle and the French in Europe. (It is arguable that, since francophone African governments were supposed to accept French culture as a priority import, and take France as their model in all things, these preferences are inevitable.) However, the ongoing relationship that many countries have maintained with France has involved a sacrifice of all of these qualities to some degree or another. This sort of ambiguity has provided a continuing element of tension in the relationships between African governments and their French *patron*. In order to continue receiving French aid, the leaders of African states needed to maintain the stability of their country (or risk losing their presidency), and guarantee France access to their territory for military purposes and economic investment. Accomplishing these goals has often appeared to require repressive or at least undemocratic forms of government, a certain sacrifice of national autonomy, and the loss of any opportunity for the sort of prestige that France itself claims as one of the philosophical birthplaces of popular sovereignty. Elected French leaders can claim with some justification to lead in the name of the French people. While, for example, President Houphouët-Boigny claimed this also, largely on the basis of his political leadership during the preindependence phase of Côte d'Ivoire's existence, his perennial presidency postindependence was guaranteed by France and the loyalty of his own elites rather than by democratic election.

Only in the past decade has France begun to encourage the appearance, at least, of democratic government in the former French colonies. Having sacrificed autonomy in favor of security, the grandeur and trappings of public office became all the more important to African presidents, and France often colluded in providing these trappings in order to sweeten the deal. Presidential jets, limousines, and elegant uniforms were the most outward forms of solidarity with African governments shown by France, along with compliance with the use of aid money to purchase French villas, or to sustain foreign embassies—and ambassadors—at the requisite level of ostentation. The most extreme evidence of this collusion was probably the Napoleon-inspired coronation, complete with a golden eagle throne and ermine robes, of Bokassa the First of the Central African Empire, paid for in large part with French aid, derided in the French and international press, and merely winked at by the Giscard government. Thomas O'Toole[184] states that when President-for-Life Bokassa crowned himself emperor in 1977, the lavish ceremony also "made a number of French people very rich." The United States reacted by suspending its aid in 1977, although not the Peace Corps program. France did not suspend aid, but it made gradual arrangements for transferring the regime's leadership to a less peculiar political partner.[185]

Part Three: France's Ability to Shape the Peacetime Environment according to its Preferences in Its Former Central African Colonies during the Decades Following the Death of Charles De Gaulle

France's Objectives for the *Chasse Gardée*

Chapters 5 and 6 have illustrated that France's administration of the West and Central African regions of its sphere of influence must be understood in the context of the French leadership's perception of France as a major global player as the twentieth century drew to a close. French leaders used the sub-Saharan African colonies in order to regain and solidify the political, economic, and military strength that made France once again a great power after its demoralizing defeat at the hands of Germany, its need to regroup with the help of the Atlantic Alliance, and its loss of major colonies in Indochina and North Africa. In spite of leadership changes (from de Gaulle through the post-Gaullists to the Socialists), France's postwar Africa policy was coherent, consistent, carefully managed, and largely bipartisan. France retained much of its African preserve as a source of strategic resources, investment opportunities, economic and military cooperation, political influence, and as an illustration of the export strength of French culture.

The three main challenges for France in achieving its goals during this last quarter of the twentieth century remained: *first*, preserving and extending French power and influence against anglophone (and particularly U.S.) encroachments; *second*, preventing economic and military inroads in the French sphere by the USSR and its allies; and *third*, keeping its former colonies in some degree of continuing dependency on France in order to maintain its position as the dominant partner in the cooperation agreements.

As outlined earlier, there were to be five conditions under which France would intervene, using military force: to guarantee the safety of French citizens overseas, to protect the territorial integrity of overseas territories, to defend energy and strategic materials supplies and commercial transport routes, to fulfill France's obligations under its military cooperation agreements with allied nations, and to participate in international peacekeeping missions. These goals were clarified under the Mitterand government, but they did not differ from the intentions of previous French governments since the independence of the African colonies in 1960. France's ability to intervene with its forces of *intervention* and *présence* remained good in most of the purely domestic cases, but the results were not always as predictable as before, and more political damage control was necessary than during the 1960s.

It has become clear in this chapter that, while France succeeded to a remarkable degree in *shaping* the peacetime environment in its former colonies according to its preferences, France's *policing* duties as the "gendarme of Africa" in this environment showed some significant limitations as France entered the last quarter of the twentieth century.

France's Ability to Deter Unwanted Conflict in the Region
As a part of the prestige-conscious and politically independent policy formulated by Charles de Gaulle just prior to the African colonies' independence in 1960, and perpetuated by later French presidents, France successfully

shaped the peacetime environment to a remarkable degree in Central Africa in order to deter much of the unwanted conflict. Chad, Congo-Brazzaville, and the three formerly Belgian parts of the *chasse gardée* were the major exceptions, experiencing severe conflicts during the time period of this case. For the most part, however, France continued to fulfill its preferences for obtaining the desired resources, strategic flexibility, and global prestige and power in the region. The legal and structural components of this policy were provided by the military cooperation agreements signed with France by most of the newly independent francophone African nations in 1960, and revised throughout the following three decades. This work has focused mainly on the military factors—troop presence and intervention forces, intelligence capacity, and arms—which France used in the context of these cooperation agreements to control the postcolonial environment, but economic and political factors were significant as well as a means to reinforce the thorough French penetration of the region. Zartman also notes that French diplomatic efforts aimed at conflict management were "less distinctive" than its military responses to internal conflict or external insurgency, and they included several procedural facets: repeated offers of diplomatic "good offices" and often "good places" as venues for peace conferences, calls for restraint and respect for established boundaries and borders, and a concern with francophone prestige as a criterion for involvement.[186]

As a result of this "cooperative" shaping process, which can also be characterized as a deeply rooted, flexible, and well-integrated military, economic, political, and cultural penetration of the African region, France was able to respond to, and manage, *most* threats to its position as the dominant great power in the francophone sphere of influence. In spite of its predominance, however, France was *unable to completely control* or eliminate the larger-scale, more regionalized conflicts that occurred in the francophone African region after the 1960s. In other words, France was well prepared for the smaller scale policing duties, for example, predicting, assisting, preventing or otherwise managing the various military coups d'état like those in the Central African Republic. France's leaders found that long-term insurgent warfare (like the war in Chad), involving external interference on the part of regional neighbors (like Libya), was much more of a challenge to its military and political capabilities, and also challenged the political tolerance of French citizens.

France's intervention capacities as described here were clearly inadequate for making France a full participant in any full-scale regional or interstate war involving large armies, operations in which she clearly could not use the FAR, as it was constituted purely as an intervention force. France would intervene with the FAR only if it appeared that a smaller intervention could head off a larger problem, as she did in Chad with Operations Manta and Épervier, but as she signally failed to do in Rwanda with Operation Turquoise.[187]

In spite of France's continued military superiority in the Central and West African regions, a number of serious conflicts took place during this period of study. Sivard records 110,000 civilian and military casualties in the Burundian government's anti-Hutu campaign of 1972, with a further 170,000 dead during similar massacres between 1988 and 1995. The Chad wars of 1980–1987 and then again during 1990–1994 resulted in 7,000 and 6,000 civilian and military deaths, respectively. Violence in Congo-Brazzaville in 1993 claimed a further 2,000 lives, as did Rwanda's ethnic violence in 1992. Rwanda's total of at least 750,000 civilian and military deaths, during the 1994 genocide and its aftermath, represents perhaps the strongest indication that France's policy of assisting governments on the basis of their loyalty and usefulness to France in spite of demonstrably bad human rights records may need considerable revision in the future. France's participation in these conflicts was limited by the cooperation agreements within the African Community, but it seems in the case of Rwanda to have exacerbated rather than mitigated the insecurity of some developing nations.[188]

France's Ability to Control the Outcome of Regional Conflicts
France's ability to control the outcome of regional conflicts was somewhat mixed. Some of the conflicts that occurred remained within the boundaries of the countries concerned, as in the cases of Gabon and CAR, and they were largely matters of purely internal security affecting friendly governments. France was able to contain these using the base troops and a timely, short-term display of force in order to obtain the desired outcome. However, ongoing conflicts in several countries in the Central African region highlighted some clear limitations in France's ability to control the outcomes of regional conflicts, particularly those involving the chronic political targeting of particular ethnic or regional minority groups, as in Chad, Rwanda, and Burundi. The magnitude of these conflicts was severe enough in terms of the loss of human lives to warrant some rethinking of France's role in Africa during the 1980s and 1990s. Some of these revisions were evident in France's more restrained and subtle strategic aid during the recent Congo-Brazzaville civil war, with possibly better results in terms of the maintenance of French economic influence, although predictions at this point remain somewhat speculative.

France's interventions in the Chadian conflict could be considered a success if defined in terms of containment, although a series of different interventions were required which signally failed to solve the essential problems there over the long term. There is ongoing armed conflict with political opposition groups in southern Chad to this day. The operations in Chad pinpointed some problematic aspects of France's intervention capacity, and also the occasionally unpredictable vicissitudes of France's relationship with the largest regional power, Muammar Qaddafi's Libya. These successive interventions showed the results of France's more streamlined and more restrained approach to peacekeeping, and also demonstrated many of its limitations. On balance, France did manage to hold off Libyan expansionism and prevent any large-scale Soviet influence. It also began to make some use of regional institutions like the OAU in order to bolster and legitimate its efforts. Libya was probably the largest source of competition for France in Chad (and southward in the CAR) during this period. French presence: (1) prevented too many Soviet military and diplomatic initiatives in the Central African countries, though there were some, and (2) allowed the United States to concentrate its anti-Soviet attentions elsewhere (e.g., Angola).

France's major failure in controlling the outcome of a regional conflict was, of course, its outing in Rwanda. As Prunier shows, the horrifying results of France's loyalty to the Habyarimana regime, and particularly to the northern anti-Tutsi extremist Coalition for the Defense of the Republic (CDR) that planned the 1994 genocide, were a major setback to France's relations with most of the countries in East and Central Africa. France was supplying weapons and training to the groups which eventually planned and executed the genocide, and it is difficult to understand, given the very public nature of the Rwandan government's preparations for murdering a sizable portion of its minority population, how France could have been unaware of the use to which their military aid was being put.[189] The Habyarimana dictatorship was on shaky ground politically, and it was under attack by the Rwandan Patriotic Front, largely composed of Rwandan refugee Tutsis who had grown up in Uganda and received their military training in the Ugandan armies. Prunier suggests that France was desperate to hold on to Habyarimana in Rwanda because the alternative was an RPF victory, an English-speaking regime, and the loss of a piece of the *chasse gardée*.[190]

When it became clear that the Northern Hutu regime had lost the war, leaving hundreds of thousands of traumatized and murdered Rwandans spilling over the borders and down the rivers of East Africa, and that legitimate and effective UN and OAU intervention had become an impossibility, France launched two of its most controversial interventions. These were Operation Amaryllis, a small-scale intervention during the week of the April plane crash which merely evacuated all French nationals and provided no protection whatever to any of France's Tutsi and moderate Hutu employees, and Operation Turquoise, which set up a *cordon sanitaire* between June and August 1994 in the south of the country after the fall of Kigali. The safe zone saved the lives of a number of refugees, but also provided immediate protection to many of the CDR *génocidaires*, allowing them to escape into eastern Zaïre and regroup for further action against the new RPF government. While France claimed that Turquoise was in response to the humanitarian outcry in the wake of the carnage, it was also a convenient means by which to contain some of the damage done by its own military policies in Rwanda, placing many of its former allies in hiding and allowing numerous members of the CDR to escape capture and live in other countries in the region, including the Democratic Republic of Congo, CAR and Congo-Brazzaville.[191]

France's major miscalculations were: first, its assumption that it could continue to aid repressive regimes without containable diplomatic embarrassment and, second, assuming that further intervention would be accepted at face value without scrutiny of who exactly it was that France had rescued. The damage done by these actions had major repercussions in France's Africa policy of the late 1990s, and further interventions and military aid to the *chasse gardée* is being handled very carefully, as seen by the CAR, where France has now withdrawn its garrisons, and, in 2003, Côte d'Ivoire, where the current intervention force has a comparatively limited mandate as a backer for the African intervention forces.

France has also had no success in controlling interethnic warfare in Burundi over the decades of its presence there. However, it was able, by standing back and using the influence of its oil interests instead of its military specialists, to help its ally Sassou-Nguesso return to power in Congo-Brazzaville. ELF-Congo, the French oil company, backed Sassou during the recent civil war during which Sassou's militias, with Angolan assistance, ousted the (putatively fairly) elected government of Pascal Lissouba. France also allowed Sassou's partisans in exile to function as adjuncts to his movement in Congo, and maintained deniability and military restraint throughout. One of the ways that France has intervened in these countries has been by the seemingly passive method of providing a safe haven in France to francophone African dissidents in exile. France's limited and more subtle intervention in Congo-Brazzaville may represent one of France's preferred tactics in the future, now that Turquoise has definitively destroyed the illusion that France's military missions are in any way disinterested or humanitarian *missions civilisatrices*.

France's Ability to Reassure Aligned States in the Region
As seen above, France no longer moves as quickly, if at all, to protect loyal authoritarians who head African governments.[192] When it does so, its ac-

tions are more limited than they were in the previous three decades. Its ability to reassure its allies remains good, however, given that a large amount of French military and economic support remains to this day in Africa. France's record of support is a consistent one throughout the decades covered by this case, although its main advantage now is that African governments have become aware that France needs them for a number of reasons. Although France has made it clear that not all *leaders* will receive unqualified complete support, the *countries* themselves are still of importance to France and will remain so. French support has a reputation of returning to all of these places eventually, even if the French do not necessarily approve of who has taken charge.

France has intervened so frequently in the past in nonmilitary ways that it has appeared excessive to some, but the economic and development assistance remains a necessity to most francophone African nations. Where French citizens and economic interests are threatened, France will need to intervene, and these citizens and economic interests may well be used as bargaining chips by future African governments. The economic support is so woven into the fabric of French-speaking Africa that the French and African economies are thoroughly linked. Although France is commonly criticized throughout francophone Africa and elsewhere for its continuing paternalism regarding its former colonies, the leaders of these nations appear to believe that, even if France might be temporarily distressed by a change in government, a coup, or civil war, it will be back to protect its interests (and theirs) eventually.

Agreements covering internal security and French garrisons may well be revised, as they have been in the CAR. However, although France has not always provided the most high-tech of weaponry, it has come through with some form of military assistance in most cases, and the continuing need for spare parts, new weapons, and training on the part of African allies will probably insure a continuing Assistance Militaire Technique presence in many cases. Francophone Africans are by no means entirely comfortable with their great power overlord, but they recognize the fact that France and francophone Africa have forged integrated ties over the past century and a half that would be difficult to break without immense costs to both parties.

France's Ability to Protect Its Economic Interests in the Region

France's ability to protect its economic interests remained consistently excellent, more so than its ability to protect its military interests. A centrally directed, coordinated, and pervasive presence provided on-the-ground insurance and intelligence for preserving key French investments (e.g., Elf-Congo, Elf-Gabon) and the safety of expatriate business and banking personnel, and also offered some early warning capacity for predicting impending disturbances. The former colonies continued to be almost as dependent as they had been during the 1960s. Francophone Africa continued to offer France the most favorable access to raw materials and strategic resources. Development of an African industrial base continued to be slow, perpetuating dependence on French imports for arms, manufactured products, luxury goods, and even food and clothing. African cultural assimilation of French consumer preferences remained strong.

The integration of the Franc Zone into the commercial and lending structures in the region was deeply rooted, and it may still help to make these countries a relatively good macroeconomic market environment for investors. Since so many French interests were tied to the zone, however, any changes in the rate at which the CFAF was pegged to the FF affected both Africa and France in a significant fashion. The greatest congruence of shared interests among France and the francophone African countries was probably in the area of economic stability, largely because changes in the zone affected even its largest member.[193-195]

France's Ability to Ensure That Regional States Pursued Foreign Policies Desired by France

France was successful most of the time in manipulating the foreign policies of its francophone African allies during the 1970 and 1980s. They continued in large part to mirror France's own independence and nonalignment during the Cold War. They might collect what aid they could from other great powers and regional allies, the United States, USSR, China, and Libya, but their willingness to follow France's global or regional goals continued to be strong.

For the most part during the 1970s and 1980s, France was able to ensure a reasonable amount of diplomatic and foreign policy cooperation and coordination in the region, as shown by the numerous occasions on which African governments offered at least token troop or logistical support for French operations in their region. However, this friendly climate has changed significantly during the 1990s because of the level and number of military interventions necessary and the growing strength of African democratization efforts, which complicate France's enduring relationships with friendly government leaders. Many of the African and French leaders who worked well together from the colonial period onward (e.g., Senghor, Houphouët-Boigny, Bokassa, Mobutu, de Gaulle, Pompidou, Mitterrand, and Foccart) are now dead and those who remain, like Bongo in Gabon, face serious challenges to their continuing leadership. Military governments still exist in the region, but they are more independent from France than their predecessors (like those in Chad, Burundi, and once again, CAR). Even perennial ideologues with French sympathies like Sassou-Nguesso in Congo are finding a need to present a more independent attitude in order to attract allies other than France and retain the loyalty of their political constituencies at home. In addition, and strikingly in the cases of Sassou-Nguesso's return to Congo's presidency and General Bozize's successful recent coup in CAR, more powerful African states like Angola, Nigeria, Uganda, South Africa, and even Chad (in CAR) are beginning to have real effects as powerbrokers in the region.

During the 1990s, the U.S. foreign policy presence in Central Africa began to loom larger, and this may well become a constraint on France's ability to make its African allies pursue French policies. The losses of friendly authoritarian governments in Rwanda, and then Zaïre, were tremendous blows to French prestige and power in the Central African region. The "great power" gap in Rwanda was immediately filled by the United States with the help of its regional ally, Uganda. However, in the original *French* colonies (Rwanda and Zaïre were Belgian), France has been able to retain a significant ability to influence their foreign policies. With the loss of Soviet competition, however, the United States has become the viable alternative to France, and a much more congenial economic presence to many of the francophone governments than the Soviets were. Indeed, at the start of the new century, U.S. corporate interests in developing inland and offshore oil production in Chad, Cameroon, and Congo-Brazzaville have given the U.S. government a newfound stake in this region's political stability, and France is no longer their only potential source of great power support.

France's Ability to Further Domestic Developments Consistent with Its Values and Preferences (Democratic Development, Economic Development and Capitalist Policies, Continuing Support for French Interventions Elsewhere, Preserving the *Chasse Gardée*).
The French can still be considered quite successful, during this period, in developing the political, economic, and military capacities of the *chasse gardée* insofar as such development was consistent with French values and preferences. William Zartman describes the nature of the French commitment to African security as having four aspects, relating to culture, morality, economic interests, and power:

> There are at least four elements in this commitment: a cultural element that emphasizes the common heritage of French-speaking societies; a moral element that translates the experience gained during the colonial years into a

sense of ongoing responsibility; an economic element that seeks sure sources for crucial raw materials and growing markets for goods and investments; and a power element that recognizes that a large following within the Third World makes France a more important state. All but the economic element are absent from the attitudes of other European countries, including Great Britain, which might have been expected to hold similar views. The French view is perhaps most closely approximated by the attitudes of communist countries toward the Afro-Marxist regimes in Ethiopia, Angola and Mozambique.[196]

African military, political, and economic development occurred in a controlled fashion, along these aspects, that allowed France itself to stay well ahead of its clients militarily, politically, and economically, and to preserve its status as the dominant partner in its "cooperative" relationships.

France's overall goal during the period was to maintain French power in Africa in such a way as to encourage African states to remain as military and economic extensions of France itself. France's allies' relationships to the metropole during this period were still framed by the cooperation agreements, although these were modified considerably during the 1970s and 1980s, and the agreements continued to offer consistent and extensive military and economic benefits in return for economic, diplomatic, and military loyalty to France. Economic cooperation insured continuing dependency and cemented relationships between France and Africa elite leaderships. However, the continuing military relationships showed that sovereignty and security in Africa were still subject to France's interests and manipulation.

French preferences continued, during this period, to show evidence of the duality that has marked French political engagement in Africa from the beginning of the colonial period. Democratic France largely refrained from encouraging any semblance of democracy and complete freedom in political expression in its allies, leaving ample room for the rest of the world (and its African allies) to level occasional accusations of neocolonialism against France whenever this charge was politically convenient.

France's commitment to free market policies was far more evident. France introduced conditionality issues when Mitterand announced at the 1990 La Baule Franco-African summit that "heading toward more freedom," would be a condition for French aid. In spite of this announcement, regime stability and economic and military cooperation have continued to take precedence over political liberty as conditions for French aid. Mitterand's support for conditionality had become more lukewarm by the following year's francophone African leadership summit in Paris. Indeed, Benin became democratic following La Baule, and actually experienced a decline in French aid, while

Togo, Cameroon, and Zaïre (all of which continued to be authoritarian) received increases in French aid.[197]

Two countries discussed in depth here that followed French preferences particularly closely were the Central African Republic (or Empire), and Gabon. The CAR and Gabon are also exemplary of two different kinds of peacetime invention involving military means. They were also quite supportive of French intervention elsewhere using the troops based on their soil. Gabon had more peacetime stability in terms of regime changes. It has had only two heads of state since independence, and France's protection of Gabon's heads of state was been handled in a highly personal fashion through both official military protection and unofficial intermediaries whose ties to the French and Gabonese presidents were forged during World War II.[198] Gabon is a relatively wealthy state (oil) and CAR is not (although it has uranium and diamonds), and the relative economic pressures on the two formed an interesting contrast. Both countries housed French military bases, soldiers, and *coopérants* during the period. As discussed earlier, Gabon's domestic violence was controllable with the French base troops, with less frequent need for additional airborne intervention forces than were required for CAR.

The CAR case is a continuing illustration of French choices to intervene (or not) in support of presidents who were deemed more or less cooperative with French preferences and interests. Intervention was successful in each instance, and probably smoothed over some potential violence that would have occurred if Bokassa (and then Dacko) had needed to be overthrown entirely by indigenous forces at home. France maintained its connections by replacing Bokassa with Dacko, a choice it knew it could work with. When it was clear that Dacko would not be able to hold on to power, France assisted quietly in the Kolingba coup and maintained a fairly smoothly functioning relationship with that regime until the mid-1990s, when it became clear that *Centrafricain* democratization impulses needed to be recognized and responded to.

In both Gabon and CAR, it was evident during the 1990s that a greater desire for economic, political, and military independence from France in these two quite loyal allies would be a factor in France's future Africa policy. In 1993, students from the University of Bangui in CAR protested in the streets and were tear-gassed by Kolingba's security forces. Conflicts within the army arose from the country's economic constraints, and troops remained unpaid for months, at which point the army began a series of mutinies which resulted in the withdrawal of the most important French official in the CAR government, Colonel Jean-Claude Mansion, the resident French diplomatic adviser since Kolingba's coup in 1979. The first presidential elections were set up for August 1993 but took place with such factional acrimony that the winner, Bokassa's former prime minister Ange Patassé, was unable to control revolts on the part of the armed forces. French troops played a logistical role in the elections, but the violence sparked a major reformulation of French policy in this key strategic area of the *chasse gardée*. An African regional force of 800 troops was brought in for the official peacekeeping duty in CAR, followed by a UN peacekeeping force. The French closed its two military bases in CAR in March 1998.[199] After successfully maintaining power through diplomatic, military, and economic means in CAR for decades, France finally decided to remove its overt military presence and rely on less obvious military, economic, and diplomatic initiatives in the future. France's restraint during the most recent military coup in CAR in 2003 has been a striking change from its previous tactics, but not perhaps a change from its "wait and see" strategy of emphasizing shared interests and trying to work with the winners. In the case of General Bozize and his appointment of CAR's perennial opposition leader Abel Goumba, the most recent winners were not those whom France would have chosen to uphold its interests. France publicly deplored the coup, but Paris has maintained continued contact with the new leaders of this key member of *la Francophonie*.

Conclusion

The rapid technological and political changes of the past three decades have required France to continually reexamine its priorities in Africa. Its approach was still characterized by the consistency and clarity of the original Gaullist vision of the French Community, in which France and African nations would interact as independent states, but in which France continued to be the first among equals, and guarantor of the others' sovereignty. Under these conditions, France was able to intervene militarily to protect French citizens and economic interests, to protect the territorial integrity of its cooperating allies, to defend strategic natural resources and transport routes, to fulfill France's contracted obligations under its military cooperation agreements, and to participate in missions which it continued to define as "peacekeeping," even if they occasionally led to further war, as occurred after Turquoise in Rwanda. These goals were clarified and restated under the Mitterand government, but they did not differ from the intentions of previous French governments. However, these goals may be revised during the new century, as a new phase is apparent in the French relationship with its former colonies.

Nonetheless, France's goals of retaining its great power status, and its strategic and economic preponderance in the region, were largely met during the period covered by this chapter (1970–1995). It maintained its military presence, its ability to intervene effectively, and its economic strength. The military cost was considerable, as were the costs of supporting the Franc Zone, but, as in the first case, the costs were spread out over decades, and balanced somewhat by economic gains. The forces of *Présence* and *Intervention* were used frequently enough to demonstrate that their power was effective for limited operations, but the very frequency of their use has caused their ultimate utility to be questioned both internationally and domestically. France tarnished its prestige in Rwanda, CAR, and Gabon. Chad was a long drawn-out series of operations that raised serious questions concerning the potential benefits of remaining Africa's *gendarme*. Elements of the original *chasse gardée* may persist for a time but its structural integrity is slipping, and its rangers are fewer and less effective at controlling the inhabitants. The costs to France's budget and reputation of maintaining its sphere of influence in the classic Gaullist configuration may have become too high.

Notes

1. G. Wesley Johnson, in *Double Impact: France and Africa in the Age of Imperialism*, ed. G. Wesley Johnson (Westport, Conn.: Greenwood Press, 1985), 31.

2. As reported, among many other places, in the *Manchester Guardian Weekly* of December 15, 1996.

3. Francophone African military culture also offered the advantage of shared outlooks and contact opportunities among military leaderships. Claude Welch's example of "contagion" relates the shared strategic culture of francophone African leaders to their coup propensity and also to their international environment: "Three weeks after the assassination of President Olympio, Colonel David Thompson, commanding officer of Liberia's National Guard, was arrested on suspicion of plotting a *coup d'état*. 'If only 250 Togolese soldiers could overthrow their government, a Liberian Army of 5,000 could seize power easily,' Colonel Thompson is alleged to have argued. Successful seizure of control in one state may touch off a series of coups. The Zanzibar uprising may have helped trigger the East African mutinies; similarly, the intervention of Soglo in December 1965 may have helped touch off coups in the Central African Republic, Upper Volta, Nigeria, and Ghana. Contagion must be considered on two levels: the personal links among African officers in different countries, and the increasing extent of interstate ties. Shared experiences in the French army provided the leaders of intervention in the Central African Republic, Dahomey, Togo, and Upper Volta (respectively Bokassa, Soglo, Eyadema, and Lamizana) with potentially significant individual ties. All four served in Indochina. It is quite likely that the success of one in winning political control prompted the others to consider intervention—though no conclusive evidence can be adduced." Contagion cannot always be demonstrated clearly as a cause for military intervention either within

states or among states, and it remains a fuzzy concept when applied to social learning and development processes. However, since independence, African leaders have steadily improved their ability to communicate and cooperate with one another in alliances and regional accords. Africa has become a genuine geopolitical subsystem once again, as interstate relations in Africa become increasingly reciprocal and often present opportunities for joint military interventionism. It is in this subsystemic context that we need to examine postcolonial French intervention in Africa. See Claude E. Welch, Jr., ed., *Soldier and State in Africa: A Comparative Analysis of Military Intervention and Political Change* (Evanston, Ill.: Northwestern University Press, 1970), 26–27.

4. Gérard Prunier, *The Rwanda Crisis: History of a Genocide* (New York: Columbia University Press, 1995), 105.

5. Commander in chief in Algeria, quoted in John Chipman, *French Power in Africa* (Oxford, U.K.: Basil Blackwell Ltd., 1989), 78.

6. John Chipman, Veme *République et défense de l'Afrique* (Paris: Éditions Bosquet, 1986), 125.

7. International Institute for Strategic Studies (IISS), *The Military Balance 1979–1980* (London: Brassey's Publishers), 24, and *The Military Balance 1987–88*, 60.

8. IISS, *The Military Balance 1994–1995*, 45.

9. Ruth Leger Sivard, *World Military and Social Expenditures*, 16th ed. (Washington, D.C.: World Priorities, 1996), 28, 45–47. Also IISS, *The Military Balance 1994–1995*, 22, 111.

10. Philip H. Gordon, *A Certain Idea of France: French Security Policy and the Gaullist Legacy* (Princeton, N.J.: Princeton University Press, 1993), 69.

11. Gordon, *A Certain Idea of France*, 101–4.

12. Chipman, Veme *République*, 127.

13. Simon Baynham, in *Military Power and Politics in Black Africa*, ed. Simon Baynham (New York: St. Martin's Press, 1986), 22.

14. Chipman, *French Power in Africa*, 147.

15. Pascal Chaigneau, *La Politique militaire de la France en Afrique* (Paris: Le Centre des Hautes Études sur l'Afrique et l'Asie Modernes—CHEAM, 1984) 45.

16. Chipman, *French Power in Africa*, 147.

17. Bruce E. Arlinghaus, *Military Development in Africa: The Political and Economic Risks of Arms Transfers* (Boulder, Colo.: Westview Press, 1984), 37.

18. Anthony Clayton, *France, Soldiers and Africa* (London: Brassey's Defence Publishers Ltd., 1988), 389. See also Chipman *French Power in Africa*, 132. Chaigneau's citation for his data is Robin Luckham, "Le militarisme français en Afrique," *Politique Africaine* 5 (February 1982).

19. Abbott A. Brayton, "Arms Control in Africa," in Baynham, *Military Power and Politics*, 272, using IISS figures.

20. Charles P. Snyder's francophone West African data compares as follows: "Guinea's land army of 8,500 was well-regarded for discipline and training, and demonstrated the ability, as early as 1979 (in Liberia, as later in the 1990s) to inter-

vene in neighboring countries. Senegal, a light mobile infantry force of 8,500, benefitted from a large number of officers who had been NCOs and officers in the French colonial army. It intervened in Gambia in 1981, and was apparently capable of defending its borders. Mauritania lacked manpower and resources, and suffered from a racial divide between its Arab/Berber officers and largely black enlisted corps. Côte d'Ivoire's forces were small, but well-trained to provide enough internal security in a crisis until French help arrived. Benin, Mali, Togo, Niger, and Upper Volta (Burkina Faso) were also small light infantry forces. In the cases of Mali and Niger, this made them under-powered for protecting their large desert territories." Charles P. Snyder, "African Ground Forces," in *African Armies: Evolution and Capabilities*, ed. Bruce E. Arlinghaus and Pauline H. Baker (Boulder, Colo.: Westview Press, 1986), 128–32.

21. Sivard, *World Military and Social Expenditure*, 28, 45–47. Also IISS, *The Military Balance 1994–1995*, 22, 111.

22. Sivard, *World Military and Social Expenditures*, 47.

23. William J. Foltz, "Libya's Military Power," in *The Green and the Black: Qadhafi's Policies in Africa*, ed. René Lemarchand (Bloomington: Indiana University Press, 1988), 53–59.

24. What Jean-François Bayart calls the "horizontal structuring of space in Africa" occurred in this period around the regional poles of Nigeria and Côte d'Ivoire in West Africa, Algeria, South Africa, and, in the center, Zaïre (although Angola too became a preponderant regional military power in Central Africa during the early 1990s). Demographic size, economic strength, or military might are all factors in these polar attractions, some of which were discouraged by the French as challenges to their regional military (and linguistic) hegemony. The French tried to deflect the rise to power of any leadership in Niger that might be too friendly to fellow Hausas in the government of anglophone Nigeria. Côte d'Ivoire and Ghana vied for influence in Togo and Burkina Faso, while Mobutu's Zaïre was influential on the governments (and opposition factions) in Central African Republic, Rwanda, Burundi, Chad, and Angola. See Jean-François Bayart, *The State in Africa: The Politics of the Belly*, published in French as *L'État en Afrique: La Politique du Ventre*, trans. Mary Harper, Christopher Harrison, and Elizabeth Harrison (New York: Addison Wesley Longman Publishing, 1993), 202. Another recent "pole" was being created in the mid-1990s in Museveni's Uganda, with the help of regional allies (like his former comrade-in-arms, Paul Kagame in Rwanda) and the United States.

25. Harry E. Colestock III, "African Air Forces," in *African Armies*, ed. Arlinghaus and Baker, 141–47. Also in IISS, *The Military Balance 1983–1984*.

26. Larry D. Harrison, "African Sea Forces," in *African Armies*, ed. Arlinghaus and Baker, 168–73.

27. Arnold Hughes and Roy May, "Armies on Loan: Toward an Explanation of Transnational Intervention among Black African States: 1960–85," in *Military Power and Politics*, ed. Baynham, 191.

28. Hughes and May, "Armies on Loan," in Baynham, *Military Power and Politics*, 178–82, 194.

29. Hughes and May, "Armies on Loan," in Baynham, *Military Power and Politics*, 183–84.

30. Hughes and May, "Armies on Loan," in Baynham, *Military Power and Politics*, 183–84.

31. Hughes and May, "Armies on Loan," in Baynham, *Military Power and Politics*, 187–89.

32. Both the United States and the USSR maintained ties to African governments. The United States did so wherever it appeared that U.S. aid would balance forces supplied and aided by the USSR (e.g., by helping Zaïre to support UNITA's insurgency in Angola). The USSR was a major factor in countries that were ideologically sympathetic to socialism or lacking in French support, as in Guinea. During the two decades following the death of de Gaulle, however, in those countries that maintained cooperation agreements with France, the United States and the USSR were prevented from establishing more than a foothold, and that largely via arms sales. De Gaulle's desire to return post-Vichy France to its former "grandeur" has been well served by the French arms industry. Under the Gaullists and Giscard, and later under the Socialists, France built an extensive arms industry with independent research and development, capable of producing a complete line of modern weapons, with sea, land and air platforms, small arms, a variety of heavy artillery, and electronic communications systems. See Lawrence Freedman and Martin Navias, on the acquisition of Phillips by Thomson-CSF and the Space, Defense & Telecom Division of ACEL of Belgium by Alcatel in "Western Europe," in *Cascade of Arms: Managing Conventional Weapons Proliferation*, ed. Andrew J. Pierre (Cambridge, Mass.: Brookings/World Peace Foundation, 1997), 155.

33. A key concern, and the major concern, was to preserve and enhance France's ability to defend itself in Europe, independently of NATO. The rapid return to economic strength of France's ancient rival, Germany, was another focus in French strategic policy, as was the felt need to act as the "balancer" between the United States and the USSR.

34. As of 1996, France was one of the principal arms manufacturing and exporting countries in the world, and although there was regulatory control in the executive branch of government, there was almost no parliamentary control by the French Assemblée Nationale. Nearly 80 percent of the industry was partially state-owned, and export decisions were made by the French prime minister, advised by an inter-ministry committee, and implemented by the Defense Ministry. See Pierre, *Cascade of Arms*, 393. When French arms were used by Iraq against French troops in the first Gulf War, the Assemblée attempted to force the government to disclose its arms sales policies and contracts, but this has not occurred consistently.

35. Gordon, *A Certain Idea of France*, 127, 171.

36. Gordon, *A Certain Idea of France*, 180–81.

37. Chipman, *French Power in Africa*, 165, and Chaigneau, *La Politique militaire*, 85.

38. Gordon, *A Certain Idea of France*, 89.

39. Chipman, *French Power in Africa*, 118.

40. The French military base at Dakar was turned over to the Senegalese government, although there remained French troops stationed there. Even without a full-scale agreement, substantial military assistance continued to Senegal, including service in the Senegalese army by French officers.

41. Chipman, *French Power in Africa*, 128.

42. The defense accords, for example, signed between France and Gabon, continued to show the military administrative structures mentioned in chapter 5. At the individual state level, defense matters are referred to a "mixed Committee" assisted by the Bureau of Defense. The committee contains the French ambassador assigned to the country, the French commander of that particular overseas zone, and the African head of state. The Defense Bureau contains a French superior officer, the African country's superior military officer, and one or more *fonctionnaires* (bureaucrats) from the French embassy. At the regional level, if multiparty defense agreements are to be considered, there is another defense council, including once again the relevant African heads of state, the prime minister of France (or his representative), and a general of the French army delegated for this purpose in each African state. The francophone summit meetings are now an institutionalized routine that include not only the French-speaking countries of Africa, but non-French speakers as well. This is the continental dimension of the French diplomatic presence. According to Pascal Chaigneau, France had a twofold objective in maintaining its presence in African armies: to preserve the free maneuverability and ready networks indispensable to the conduct of military operations and to guarantee the internal security of each participating state. Chaigneau, *La Politique militaire*, 29.

43. The agreement with Dahomey (Benin) lapsed altogether, leaving (as happened earlier with Mali) an opening for Soviet influence. Nonetheless, France maintained some contacts with both Mali and Benin over the years, as a small number of military *coopérants* continued to be based there. The defense and technical military cooperation agreements now vary much more from state to state than they did in the early 1960s. Some of the lapsed or less controlling agreements left small openings for Soviet influence. The fall of the Youlou government in Congo-Brazzaville in 1963 and the subsequent rise to power of leaders whose ideological and political orientation was sympathetic to (although not subservient to, or even completely controllable by) the USSR, weakened the military cooperation link for some years, although Congo's socialist governments remained amenable to various continuing contacts with Paris. The government of Denis Sassou-Nguesso has remained quite open to French investment on the Congolese oil industry and other economic support from France. For a good account of Congo-Brazzaville, see John F. Clark, "Congo: Transition and the Struggle to Consolidate," in *Political Reform in Francophone Africa*, ed. John F. Clark and David E. Gardinier (Boulder, Colo.: Westview Press, 1997), 62–85.

44. Clayton, *France, Soldiers and Africa*, 389.

45. Clayton, *France, Soldiers and Africa*, 389–90.

46. Chipman, *French Power in Africa*, 119.

47. Anthony Clayton, "Foreign Intervention in Africa," in Baynham, *Military Power and Politics*, 213–14.

48. Clayton, *France, Soldiers and Africa*, 390.

49. Clayton, "Foreign Intervention in Africa," in Baynham, *Military Power and Politics*, 213.

50. Bayart, *The State in Africa*, 25.

51. Douglas A. Yates, *The Rentier State in Africa: Oil Rent Dependency and Neocolonialism in the Republic of Gabon* (Trenton, N.J.: Africa World Press Inc., 1996), 114–16.

52. Jacques Foccart's network (*"le réseau Foccart"*), in those formulations that have dubbed Gabon "Foccartland," was said to be composed of Foccart himself, President Omar Bongo, Bongo's influential assistant Georges Rawiri, the longtime French ambassador Maurice Robert, the former ambassador and French Elf-Gabon oil company chief Maurice Delauney, French mercenaries trained by Pierre Debizet, a security specialist, and a shadowy group of spies and ex-soldiers, some of whom had served in the French Resistance. Foccart himself joined the Resistance in 1940, working with the Bureau Central de Renseignement et d'Action (BCRA), the French Nazi-removal network based in London. His wartime paracommando unit became the basis of the French CIA equivalent, the SDECE. He drew contacts, operatives, and possible assassins from his wartime contacts, and formed the Service d'Action Civique as a special branch of the SDECE to perform the more covert, and often illegal or politically dodgy, operations necessary in the course of Foccart's lifelong service to numerous French presidents. (Yates, *The Rentier State*, 107–8, 110–11.) Foccart's private import-export company, SAFIEX, was a cover for information gathering for the French intelligence services. In addition to Mba and Bongo in Gabon, Foccart befriended Houphouët-Boigny of Côte d'Ivoire early in the Ivorian president's political career and maintained this friendship until both died in the mid-1990s. He was introduced to President Mba by President Houphouët. Like many of the later francophone African presidents, Mba and Houphouët could call Foccart at any time on the telephone without an intermediary, and he could do so with them. Foccart was appointed de Gaulle's technical adviser on African affairs in 1958, and was also his liaison between the Elysée and the SDECE. The foreign affairs ministry should have been the main architect of France's Africa policy but that responsibility fell early to Foccart, who also organized all visits to Paris by African heads of state, and all visits to Africa by the French president. Colonel Bob Denard, the French mercenary who was later responsible for a coup in the Comoros in 1975, was a member of the Foccart network in Gabon for many years, and he helped President Bongo to set up the paramilitary forces which are assigned to guard the buildings and installations of the French Elf-Gabon oil company. (Yates, *The Rentier State*, 108–9, 120.) The activities of Jacques Foccart in Gabon are frequently offered as the most egregious illustrations of France's "neocolonialism." Douglas Yates suggests indeed, that "unlike other French colonies that had to struggle for their freedom (e.g., Indochine, Algérie), it was the good fortune of Gabon to have been made free without

having to become so." However, in spite of the undoubted influence in Gabon of Foccart's network, and free or not as one cares to define freedom, Bongo was and is no total puppet, and he arguably gained as much power over his country from the French as they gained from him (Yates, *The Rentier State*, 86–87, 96).

53. Clayton, *France, Soldiers and Africa*, 438.

54. Other French intelligence activities in Chad produced even more startling results. In the early 1970s, Jacques Foccart himself was accused by Tombalbaye of conspiring with the Chadian opposition to overthrow his regime, which may have been true given that Tombalbaye was becoming increasingly irrational and difficult for France to deal with. Tombalbaye accused Foccart of being the sworn enemy of Chad, and he induced the Chadian National Assembly to pass a resolution denouncing him. Attacking Foccart personally was almost certainly a safer move than attacking the French president or France's public support of Chad, but risky nonetheless. See Samuel Decalo, *Historical Dictionary of Chad*, 2nd ed. African Historical Dictionaries No. 13 (Metuchen, N.J.: Scarecrow Press, 1987), 132.

55. Clayton, *France, Soldiers and Africa*, 389.

56. Article 2 of Gabon's defense agreement states that the "Gabonese Republic, in consideration of the help granted it by the French Republic, and in order to assure the standardization of armaments, engages itself to call exclusively on the French Republic for the maintenance and renewal of its materials" (Quoted in Chipman, *French Power in Africa*, 119). This provision is occasionally ignored by all defense agreement signatories (e.g., Gabon's purchase of tanks from Brazil) but the French have largely retained their status through these agreements as francophone Africa's primary armorer. Chipman, *French Power in Africa*, 119, from SIPRI.

57. Michel L. Martin, *Warriors to Managers: The French Military Establishment since 1945* (Chapel Hill: University of North Carolina Press, 1981), 331–32.

58. Cited in Chipman, *French Power in Africa*, 137.

59. Chipman, *French Power in Africa*, 136–37.

60. From Chipman, *French Power in Africa*, 138–39; and IISS, *The Military Balance 1988–1989*.

61. It will be interesting to see whether the 1998 decision to move the administration of cooperative Assistance Militaire Technique to the Ministry of Defense has had any effect on the near autonomy exercised by French presidents in military intervention decisions. (Personal communication from Douglas Yates.)

62. Chipman, *French Power in Africa*, 140.

63. Chaigneau, *La Politique militaire*, 22, 111.

64. Chaigneau, *La Politique militaire*, 25–27.

65. Chaigneau, *La Politique militaire*, 113–14.

66. Although many of the agreements of the early 1960s have been revised or terminated because of internal domestic factors, or credit problems with some of the poorer states, France managed to maintain a number of agreements with provisions specifically tailored to each nation. What France agreed to in each case is sometimes

not an indication as to how useful each of its options proved to be in responding to a particular case. Having detailed the nature of the technological superiority of which France is capable, one must also consider whether, and in what ways, technological superiority was an asset to France in Africa, where a French troop presence backed by a few airplanes was often all that was needed in order to make an impression. Chad, as will be demonstrated in the next section, required several larger-scale interventions which had less to do with the terms of the agreement than with the knowledge of what would happen if any agreements, even the informal ones which were made between France and the various Chadian insurgents and factional leaders, were seen to have failed. Clayton, *France, Soldiers and Africa*, 389.

67. Chaigneau, *La Politique militaire*, 79.

68. Chipman, *French Power in Africa*, 140–41. In addition to transport, air and ground equipment used in the 1980s included *Puma, Gazelle,* and *Alouette* helicopters, AMX 30 tanks, lighter armored vehicles (e.g., AMLPanhard, ERC 90 Sagaie and AMX 10s), mobile antitank vehicles, and the *Jaguar* bombers. Chaigneau, *La Politique militaire*, 80.

69. Chipman, *French Power in Africa*, 141–42. Replacement of the *Clemenceau* with a nuclear-powered aircraft carrier, the *Richelieu*, was also authorized in the Program Law.

70. Chipman, *French Power in Africa*, 141–43.

71. Chipman, *French Power in Africa*, 142–43.

72. This was the same Rwandan government that planned the 1994 genocide (Prunier, *The Rwanda Crisis*, 221). Prunier speculates, however, that it could not have been a short-range *Milan* which brought down President Habyarimana's plane in April 1994, but rather an antiaircraft missile, probably either a U.S.-built Stinger or more likely (and more available on the international market) a Russian SAM-7 or SAM-16, which would have required outside training for use.

73. Lemarchand, in *The Green and the Black*, ed. Lemarchand, 113.

74. Chipman, *French Power in Africa*, 144.

75. Chipman, *French Power in Africa*, 144–45.

76. Martin, *Warriors to Managers*, 350–51. The overseas-based missions had the following goals: "safeguarding the security and integrity of overseas departments and territories, participating in assisting (technically or militarily) friendly nations, and guaranteeing French influence and the safety of French citizens overseas. They were deployed into six interservice commands, and two independent commands. The interservice commands were in Antilles-Guyana, Cape Verde, Djibouti, South Indian Ocean, New Caledonia, and Polynesia. Of these, the Djibouti command was the most likely to be used to support sub-Saharan operations. The independent commands were based in Port Bouet (Côte d'Ivoire) and Libreville (Gabon). There were a total of 16,933 men under these commands, of whom only 2,828 were conscripts.

77. Arlinghaus, *Military Development in Africa*, 37.

78. Chipman, *French Power in Africa*, 145–46.

79. For example, Chipman cites the 1987 joint Gabonese-French exercise which combined the 6th BIMa with Gabon's security forces to produce and practice a de-

fense of the uranium and manganese mines near Franceville. Chipman, *French Power in Africa*, 149. Also Chaigneau, *La Politique militaire*, 76–79.

80. Chaigneau, *La Politique militaire*, 92.

81. Chipman, *French Power in Africa*, 149, 150.

82. Chipman, *French Power in Africa*, 133–34.

83. Samuel Decalo, "Military Rule in Africa: Etiology and Morphology," in Baynham, *Military Power and Politics*, 51.

84. It does include cases in which only the threat of force, if not its exercise, was used in order to make changes in government personnel, as in Mauritania in 1979 and 1980, and Upper Volta in May 1983. Claude E. Welch, Jr., "Military Disengagement from Politics: Incentives and Obstacles in Political Change," in Baynham, *Military Power and Politics*, 89–90.

85. David Goldsworthy, "Armies and Politics in Civilian Regimes," in Baynham, *Military Power and Politics*, 98.

86. Chipman, *French Power in Africa*, 124.

87. The unpopular Mauritanian intervention in 1977, one of the fewer (comparatively) in West Africa during this period, did not use French ground troops; but assisted the Moroccan forces employed against Polisario insurgents with *Jaguar* strike aircraft in 1977, 1978, and 1979, Clayton, *France, Soldiers and Africa*, 383–84. The Mauritanian military expanded from 3,000 to 15,000 in order to defend Mauritania's claim to the Western Sahara, but they got the worst of most engagements, and French participation was questioned at home. The July 1978 coup in Mauritania was encouraged by France as a means by which the country could be withdrawn from this war, and France also encouraged OAU mediation efforts between Algeria, Morocco, Mauritania, and the Polisario front. George E. Moose, "French Military Policy in Africa," in *Arms and the African*, ed. William J. Foltz and Henry S. Bienen (New Haven, Conn.: Yale University Press, 1985), 78–79.

88. Clayton, *France, Soldiers and Africa*, 135.

89. Moose, "French Military Policy," in Foltz and Bienen, *Arms and the African*, 87.

90. Clayton, *France, Soldiers and Africa*, 390.

91. Chipman, *French Power in Africa*, 135.

92. Chipman, *French Power in Africa*, 136. Also Clayton, *France, Soldiers and Africa*, 383–84, and Samuel Decalo, *Coups and Army Rule in Africa: Motivations and Constraints*, 2nd ed. (New Haven, Conn.: Yale University Press, 1990), 236, 238.

93. Chipman, *French Power in Africa*, 136.

94. Chipman, *French Power in Africa*, 158.

95. Clayton, *France, Soldiers and Africa*, 383–84, 437.

96. Clayton, *France, Soldiers and Africa*, 384–85, 437. Chaigneau, *La Politique militaire*, 96.

97. Chaigneau, *La Politique militaire*, 97. Also Clayton, *France, Soldiers and Africa*, 385, and Lemarchand, *The Green and the Black*, 112–13.

98. Clayton, *France, Soldiers and Africa*, 385.

99. Clayton, *France, Soldiers and Africa*, 386. Hughes and May, "Armies on Loan," in Baynham, *Military Power and Politics*, 189.

100. Clayton, *France, Soldiers and Africa*, 386–87. Lemarchand, *The Green and the Black*, 113.

101. Chaigneau, *La Politique militaire*, 97. Lemarchand, *The Green and the Black*, 119–20.

102. Foltz, "Libya's Military Power," in Lemarchand, *The Green and the Black*, 65.

103. Clayton, *France, Soldiers and Africa*, 387–88.

104. Decalo, *Historical Dictionary of Chad*, 274.

105. Decalo, *Historical Dictionary of Chad*, 12.

106. Decalo, *Historical Dictionary of Chad*, 12, 137.

107. Decalo, *Historical Dictionary of Chad*, 234–35.

108. William J. Foltz, "Reconstructing the State of Chad," in *Collapsed States: The Disintegration and Restoration of Legitimate Authority*, ed. I. William Zartman (Boulder, Colo.: Lynne Rienner Publishers, 1995), 18–27.

109. Foltz, "Reconstructing the State of Chad," in Zartman, *Collapsed States*, 28–31.

110. Lemarchand, *The Green and the Black*, 106, 108. Lemarchand's contributions, and those of others, to his edited volume on Libya are a very good source for military information on postindependence Chad.

111. I. William Zartman, "Africa and the West: The French Connection," in *African Security Issues: Sovereignty, Stability, and Solidarity*, ed. Bruce E. Arlinghaus (Boulder, Colo.: Westview Press, 1984), 48–49.

112. Gordon, *A Certain Idea of France*, 194–95.

113. Clark and Gardinier, *Political Reform*, 15–16.

114. Stanley Hoffmann, *The Ethics and Politics of Humanitarian Intervention* (Notre Dame, Ind.: University of Notre Dame Press, 1996), 14–15.

115. Decalo, *Coups and Army Rule*, 27–28, 39.

116. Zartman, "Africa and the West" in Arlinghaus, *African Security Issues*, 49.

117. Chipman, Veme *République*, 130. France's economic power and political leverage were inextricably intertwined during the period due to the interests of members of the African political elite as well as the government-owned nature of many African companies, parastatals, and resource extraction sectors. France's strong links with the African members of its economic and military sphere of influence, and the relative steadiness of the Franc Zone economies, made the zone itself a strong inducement to good relations with France, even on the part of countries which had initially rejected its help. In 1986, the new government of President Lansana Conté turned to Paris for aid to regenerate the Guinean economy, which France saw as an opportunity to reforge a relationship with one of its weakest francophone links. France proposed a program of economic cooperation with Guinea, which had not been part of the French sphere for a quarter of a century. On January 6, 1986, the Guinean syli was replaced by the Guinean franc, and Guinea joined the Franc Zone.

118. Yates, *The Rentier State*, 99, 114.

119. The intelligence capacity and personal services rendered to African governments by various members of Foccart's networks remained useful tools of government to both French and African leaders. Gabon has had a nominally civilian government for a long time, but the French intelligence presence in Gabon, although it is "informal," continues to partake of the character, methods, and personnel of the military relationships developed during the Free French period in Africa, and a number of the economic and political advisers are connected with it.

120. Decalo, *Coups and Army Rule*, 230. For example, international pressure from banks and the French government, which were tired of dealing with embezzlement of aid and loans by Togolese ministries, led to the firing in 1982 of one of the president's closest associates. France's ultimatum stated that it would have no economic dealings at all with any Togolese government that employed Minister Dogo, a minister of planning who had served in the Togolese cabinet since 1967.

121. Chipman, *French Power in Africa*, 254–55.

122. Gordon, *A Certain Idea of France*, 7–8.

123. Gordon, *A Certain Idea of France*, 12, 15–16.

124. Gordon, *A Certain Idea of France*, 83. Also Martin, *Warriors to Managers*, 26–27.

125. Chipman, *French Power in Africa*, 192, 232–33.

126. Clayton, *France, Soldiers and Africa*, 383–84. Also Chaigneau, *La Politique militaire*, 94.

127. Personal communication to the author from a fellow CAE Peace Corps Volunteer.

128. Decalo, "Military Rule in Africa," in Baynham, *Military Power and Politics*, 55.

129. Clayton, *France, Soldiers and Africa*, 383–84.

130. Chipman, *French Power in Africa*, 133.

131. Chipman, *French Power in Africa*, 155, 243, 249.

132. The name means "Daddy told me." It appeared frequently in Zaïrian emigré correspondence over the Internet whenever Jean-Christophe's presence was noted in Kinshasa for a visit to President Mobutu.

133. Gordon, *A Certain Idea of France*, 122.

134. Gordon, *A Certain Idea of France*, 106, 108, 113.

135. Joseph Smaldone has done the most recent research on local arms control initiatives in Africa, particularly Mali's West African regional arms control initiative.

136. Arms and military assistance have only recently been seriously considered as a source of instability rather than as a means of assuring stability. Arms sales can enhance a nation's internal security but exacerbate regional tensions, they can either redress a power imbalance or create one, and they can be used to repress citizens as well as protect them from harm. In addition, arms aid can result in either increased influence or embarrassment for the donor, and the costs of arms purchases and/or maintenance can be a hindrance to the economic development of the recipient, which may also have to make considerable concessions of its national sovereignty in order to receive military aid. Arlinghaus, *Military Development in Africa*, 24–25.

137. Francis M. Deng, "Security Problems: An African Predicament," and also D. Katete Orwa, "National Security: An African Perspective," in Arlinghaus, *African Security Issues*, 8, 206–7.

138. Lemarchand, *The Green and the Black*, 113.

139. Chipman, *French Power in Africa*, 173.

140. Mohammed Ayoob, "The Security Problematic of the Third World," *World Politics* 43 (January 1991): 282.

141. Nigeria's leadership in the combined-African ECOMOG forces that "policed" the Liberian civil war had the effect of regionalizing the conflict, made it effectively an interstate war, and offered Nigeria as a candidate for regional hegemony. This was made possible by the refusal of the United States to intervene on behalf of the Doe government, and a timely lack of support from the Soviet Union which might have channeled some aid to the preeminent Liberian warlord, Charles Taylor, through his sometime ally, Libya.

142. Chipman, Veme *République*, 132, 159.

143. Hughes and May, "Armies on Loan," in Baynham, *Military Power and Politics*, 188–90. Also Edward J. Laurance, "Soviet Arms Transfers in the 1980s: Declining Influence in Sub-Saharan Africa," in *Arms for Africa: Military Assistance and Foreign Policy in the Developing World*, ed. Bruce W. Arlinghaus (Lexington, Mass.: D.C. Heath and Company, 1983), 62–63.

144. Hughes and May, "Armies on Loan," in Baynham, *Military Power and Politics*, 191–92.

145. Bayart, *The State in Africa*, 197.

146. Bayart, *The State in Africa*, 199.

147. Michael Chege, "Sub-Saharan Africa: Underdevelopment's Last Stand," in *Global Change, Regional Response: The New International Context of Development*, ed. Barbara Stallings (Cambridge: Cambridge University Press, 1995), 332.

148. Stephan Haggard, *Developing Nations and the Politics of Global Integration* (Washington, D.C.: Brookings Institution, 1995), 24.

149. Actions by the IMF occasionally presented France with opportunities to strengthen ties with countries whose military and political cooperation had been less than it would have wished. When Benin's economically incompetent Marxist regime experienced several natural disasters on top of the man-made ones caused by waste of public resources, the Beninois government announced in 1987 that it could no longer balance budgets and remain independent of France (at least compared to previous governments). Dealings at this point with the IMF were sweetened by renewed French assistance, and the return in an advisory capacity of Jacques Foccart. Foccart arrived with much fanfare, having been persona non grata in Benin for ten years since the attempted mercenary coup in 1977 (led by the most infamous member of *le réseau Foccart*, Bob Denard), an incident over which France tried to maintain deniability with little success. In 1989, France and the IMF bailed out the Beninois government, which had apparently decided to value its economic security over its national autonomy. Decalo, *Coups and Army Rule*, 123, 128, 130.

150. David E. Albright, "Overview of Communist Arms Transfers to Sub-Saharan Africa," in Arlinghaus, *Arms for Africa*, 30. The West African francophone recipients were Guinea, Benin (Dahomey), and Mali.

151. Baynham, *Military Power and Politics*, 22–23. Also Clayton, "Foreign Intervention in Africa," in Baynham, *Military Power and Politics*, 216, 226.

152. Clayton, "Foreign Intervention in Africa," in Baynham, *Military Power and Politics*, 203, 220.

153. Arthur Jay Klinghoffer, "The Soviet Union and Superpower Rivalry in Africa," in Arlinghaus, *African Security Issues*, 27–29.

154. Guinea, Mali, Benin (Dahomey), and Madagascar also hosted a number of Soviet advisers.

155. Roger E. Kanet, "Military Relations between Eastern Europe and Africa," in Arlinghaus, *Arms for Africa*, 88, and also George T. Yu, "Chinese Arms Transfers to Africa," in Arlinghaus, *Arms for Africa*, 111.

156. Pierre Kalck, *Historical Dictionary of the Central Africa Republic*, 2nd ed., trans. Thomas O'Toole. African Historical Dictionaries No. 51 (Metuchen, N.J.: Scarecrow Press, 1992), 47.

157. Clayton, "Foreign Intervention in Africa," in Baynham, *Military Power and Politics*, 225, 226.

158. Michael T. Klare, "The Subterranean Arms Trade: Black-Market Sales, Covert Operations and Ethnic Warfare," in Pierre, *Cascade of Arms*, 55.

159. Yates, *The Rentier State*, 101.

160. René Lemarchand, "The CIA in Africa," *Journal of Modern African Studies* 14 (September 1976): 401–26. Also Clayton, "Foreign Intervention in Africa," in Baynham, *Military Power and Politics*, 220–22.

161. Decalo, *Historical Dictionary of Chad*, xxi.

162. Clark and Gardinier, *Political Reform*, 3. Also Michael Bratton and Nicolas van de Walle, *Democratic Experiments in Africa: Regime Transitions in Comparative Perspective* (Cambridge: Cambridge University Press, 1997), 135, 241.

163. Clayton, "Foreign Intervention in Africa," in Baynham, *Military Power and Politics*, 222–26.

164. Clayton, "Foreign Intervention in Africa," in Baynham, *Military Power and Politics*, 225–26.

165. Kalck, *Historical Dictionary of the Central Africa Republic*, 85.

166. Albright, "Overview of Communist Arms Transfers," in Arlinghaus, *Arms for Africa*, 21–22.

167. Data taken from Clayton, "Foreign Intervention in Africa," in Baynham, *Military Power and Politics*, 228–49. See also Laurance, "Soviet Arms Transfers," and Yu, "Chinese Arms Transfers," in Arlinghaus, *Arms for Africa*, 46–47 and 110. Also in IISS, *The Military Balance 1981–1982*.

168. Brayton, "Arms Control in Africa," in Baynham, *Military Power and Politics*, 282. See also Bruce E. Arlinghaus, "Linkage and Leverage in African Arms Transfers," and Laurance, "Soviet Arms Transfers," in Arlinghaus, *Arms for Africa*,

8–9 and 43–45, for values of arms transfers by country and supplier during the 1970s.

169. Joseph P. Smaldone, "U.S. Arms Transfers and Security-Assistance Programs in Africa: A Review and Policy Perspective," in Arlinghaus, *Arms for Africa*, 179, 191, 193.

170. Chaigneau, *La Politique militaire*, 37, using figures from Luckham, "Le militarisme français en Afrique," 99 and SIPRI.

171. Chaigneau, *La Politique militaire*, 37–38.

172. Laurance, "Soviet Arms Transfers," in Arlinghaus *Arms for Africa*, 48, 59. Also Arlinghaus, *Military Development in Africa*, 34.

173. Chipman, *French Power in Africa*, 148–49.

174. Arlinghaus, *Arms for Africa*, 11.

175. Andrew L. Ross, "Developing Countries," in Pierre, *Cascade of Arms*, 94–95.

176. Stephen Gill and David Law, *The Global Political Economy: Perspectives, Problems and Policies* (Baltimore: The Johns Hopkins University Press), 1988, 294–95.

177. Andrew L. Ross, "Arms Acquisition and National Security: The Irony of Military Strength," in *National Security in the Third World: The Management of Internal and External Threats*, ed. Edward E. Azar and Chung-In Moon (Aldershot, U.K.: Edward Elgar Publishing Limited, 1988), 166.

178. Zartman, "Africa and the West" in Arlinghaus, *African Security Issues*, 41.

179. Bayart, *The State in Africa*, 26.

180. Bayart, *The State in Africa*, 26.

181. This story is told more fully in Yates, *The Rentier State*, 125–34.

182. From *Le Monde*, May 11, 1976, 1, quoted by Moose, in "French Military Policy," in Foltz and Bienen, *Arms and the African*, 66.

183. Moose, "French Military Policy," in Foltz and Bienen, *Arms and the African*, 67.

184. Thomas O'Toole, "The Central African Republic: Political Reform and Social Malaise," in Clark and Gardinier, *Political Reform*, 114.

185. Kalck, *Historical Dictionary of the Central Africa Republic*, xxxiv.

186. Zartman, "Africa and the West" in Arlinghaus, *African Security Issues*, 56.

187. Turquoise did save some Rwandan lives, but it also succeeded in offering France's protection to a group of leaders who had used French aid and training in order to destroy the security of their own citizens, threatening the territorial integrity of Rwanda, and striking a serious blow to France's continuing efforts to show itself as a regime modernizer and preserver in Africa. France rationalized aid to the Habyarimana regime by saying that it was "democratic" to support majority (i.e., Hutu) rule in Rwanda, even though that regime held no elections and repressed its Tutsi minority as a matter of policy. These leaders, more importantly to French interests, lost control of their country to the RPF invaders, who were allied with anglophone Uganda and—through Uganda—the United States. Operation Turquoise, and France's earlier aid to the Habyarimana regime (which included the president's downed plane itself, a four-year-old Falcon 50 flown by a 3-man French crew), may

prove to have been a turning point in France's relations with its African allies—Rwandan loyalty to France in return for aid proved to be very damaging to French interests in the region and may no longer be reason enough to support a particular leader. Prunier, *The Rwanda Crisis*, 110–13, 211.

188. Sivard, *World Military and Social Expenditure*, 19.

189. Evidence of intent to murder large numbers of Tutsis was not only coming from the independent human rights organizations. For a particularly ironic example, given the initial U.S. refusal to call what was happening in Rwanda "genocide," see the 1993 U.S. State Department Human Rights Report for Rwanda, published two months before the tragedy began in April 1994, which describes militia trainings and killings in the north of Rwanda.

190. Prunier, *The Rwanda Crisis*, 99–103, 147–49, 164.

191. Prunier, *The Rwanda Crisis*, 110–13, 211, 281–312.

192. Chege, "Sub-Saharan Africa," 328.

193. The future of France's economic security in the region is less certain, due to recent developments in Europe and changes in policy by the Bretton Woods institutions. It has yet to be seen what the advent of the euro will mean for the value of the Franc Zone's currency. Also, although it was intended as an engine of regional financial stability, the IMF has become a less predictable influence in sub-Saharan Africa since the 1980s. IMF lending was $1 billion there in 1988, but only $527 million in 1992, and its structural adjustment programs are no longer looked upon by African states as an automatic guarantee of eventual prosperity via temporary retrenchment. The experience of Gabon and other IMF loan recipients indicates that IMF-ordered government cutbacks can cause enough impoverishment in the general population to translate into internal instability. The 1989 World Bank study attempted to win back some of the damaged reputation of the Bretton Woods institutions but it remains to be seen how France's African security interests will be affected by these developments. Chege, "Sub-Saharan Africa," 326.

194. The World Bank also concluded that most African countries lack sound economic policies and that macroeconomic stability in the region would require a change in the currency. France and the francophone economic community devalued the CFA franc in 1994. While the resulting inflation was not as high as was anticipated, this was an additional shock to a region where economic difficulties often do real political damage, with security implications for France and its African clients. As one means of softening these financial blows, France created a "conversion fund" whereby West African creditors can exchange nearly $1 billion of their debt into infrastructural development, and environmental improvement projects. Chege, "Sub-Saharan Africa," 327, 333.

195. France is reassessing its aid policies, taking note of the current security climate and the revised policies of the Bretton Woods institutions. As Bernard Conte notes, unlike the other OECD countries, France increased its overseas development aid in recent years, but Paris is revising its aid policies with an eye to both political and economic cost effectiveness. Conte states: "In future, French overseas aid will be

redeployed towards selected 'emerging countries' with a view to expanding trade relations; aid to Africa will be reduced and concentrated on a few countries, notably Côte d'Ivoire, Cameroun, Congo, Gabon, Senegal and South Africa. Both bilateral conditionality and commitments to non-project aid will be reduced in favour of greater coordination with other 'donors (including the Bretton Woods institutions). These changes in strategy will be accompanied by reforms in the French aid machinery, designed to 'modernise' and streamline administration." The aid policy will continue to place importance on France's sub-Saharan commitments as part of the historic relationship between France and its former colonies. However, the revisions are intended to move away from a relatively inflexible political client-based system and toward more efficient less "patrimonial" relationships with recipient countries. It is worth noting that of the six "notable" continuing aid recipients listed by Conte above, five of them are easily the most well-endowed francophone African nations in terms of natural resources, political stability and francophone loyalty, economic stability, and strategic military importance to France. Bernard Conte, "France's African Aid Policy: The End of an Era?" *Review of African Political Economy* 71 (1997): 139–40.

196. Zartman, "Africa and the West," in Arlinghaus, *African Security Issues*, 40.

197. Clark and Gardinier, *Political Reform*, 3. Also Bratton and van de Walle, *Democratic Experiments in Africa*, 135, 241.

198. Yates, *The Rentier State*, 85–136.

199. "French Troops Die in an African Clash, and Some Question Why," *New York Times*, January 9, 1997.

CHAPTER SEVEN

Conclusions

Edward Rhodes

In the wake of the terrorist attacks of September 11, 2001, the subsequent U.S. invasion of Afghanistan, and the U.S. occupation of Iraq, the question of how, when, where, and under what conditions military might can be employed to create a stable, peaceful, well-ordered world has become, both for U.S. policymakers and for the American public, a pressing one. Our concern in this study has been with understanding the ability of great powers to use their military presence in regions around the world to help shape political order and institutions in those regions, that is, with understanding great powers' ability to use their military predominance to shape regional peacetime political environments in ways consistent with their desires. We have focused both on what kinds of "shaping" have historically proved possible and on what attributes of military power appear to have been useful to great powers in their "shaping" efforts. Given the emphasis that post–Cold War American national security and military strategy has placed on proactive efforts to use peacetime military presence and engagement activities to support American goals, these questions take on enormous practical significance. With American forces deployed not only in Western Europe and Northeastern Asia but in Central Asia, the Middle East, and the Balkans, and potentially in troubled spots in Africa and Latin America, understanding what military force structures and deployments do or do not yield peacetime political influence is critically important.

Our approach has been inductive and empirical. Rather than beginning with some prior theoretical model, we have approached our historical material as naive investigators, asking a standardized set of questions about military power and political outcomes, and then looking for patterns in the answers we find to these questions. We have examined six very different cases in which democratic great powers attempted to shape political realities in regions in which they enjoyed military predominance. In each case, we asked the same nineteen questions about the great power's military capacity, the other resources available to it and constraints on its actions, and outcomes achieved. Clearly, such a study cannot offer conclusive answers. It can, however, begin to uncover general patterns and suggest propositions about the peacetime impact of military presence, and the ability to prevent and persuade, that deserve further analysis.

Case Summaries

Three of our cases are drawn from the British experience—two in a region geographically key to Britain, the eastern Mediterranean, and one in a region of economic significance but of only peripheral political importance, South America. In the first of the eastern Mediterranean cases, British presence in the region was largely military, with little political entanglement; in the second, Britain was deeply enmeshed in the domestic affairs of several of the key countries in the region, enjoying the benefits and experiencing the discomforts growing from a history of imperial involvement. In this second eastern Mediterranean case Great Britain was a declining power, facing increasing challenges from other great powers. Our fourth case is drawn from the American experience. We look at American efforts at the beginning of the twentieth century to influence political developments in the Caribbean basin, aimed at stabilizing the region and promoting democratic government. Perhaps most striking about this case is the extraordinary power that the United States could bring to bear. Our fifth and sixth cases examine the French experience in francophone Africa. What is perhaps unique about these cases is the extent of France's postcolonial penetration of the states of the region and the degree to which sovereignty was blurred, giving France enormous leverage in shaping political outcomes.

Taken together, these six very different cases suggest some general but controversial lessons about the problem of political shaping.

Great Britain in the Eastern Mediterranean, 1816–1852
Between 1816 and 1852, Britain aimed to stabilize the eastern Mediterranean region, prevent the collapse of the Ottoman Empire and the expan-

sion of other great powers' influence in the area, protect British commerce and communication routes, and encourage free trade and "progress." Though "peripheral" to the European theater, the eastern Mediterranean was geographically critical to Britain.

British naval power played the central role in implementing British policy in the region. British naval forces maintained a consistent presence in the eastern Mediterranean, facilitated by forward bases at Malta and in the Ionian Islands. In its dealings with regional actors, the qualitative edge enjoyed by Royal Navy forces over regional actors—an edge that proved critical at various points during the period—rested not on better technology but rather on the superior training and professionalism of its sailors and officers.

Given the weakness of the British army, the Royal Navy represented the only effective military tool at British disposal. Nonmilitary sources of power or influence were also quite limited—British trade and financial ties offered little leverage, and British political penetration of regional actors was minimal. (In Egypt, for example, British political penetration was less than France's; even in Constantinople, British counsels went frequently unheeded.)

The immediate use of British naval power was not significantly constrained by domestic opinion: foreign secretaries were typically able to manipulate public opinion rather than compelled to tailor their actions to it or to parliamentary pressure. Public and parliamentary opinion did, however, constrain British defense spending, thus resulting in serious overall limitations on British policy, and at the extreme it may have kept foreign secretaries from pursuing policies that would have precipitated great power war.

While not unchallenged—France and Russia both possessed the ability to intervene in the region—Britain clearly dominated the eastern Mediterranean, thanks to its naval power. Although great power interests, particularly with regard to the Straits question, frequently collided, in general British objectives were consistent with international regimes—the Concert of Europe which in broad terms endorsed the status quo and the antislavery regime that reflected British notions of "progress." British interest in preserving the Ottoman Empire meant that its goals and the Porte's were frequently (though not always) congruent; by the same token, however, it meant that British and Egyptian goals would often be in direct conflict.

Britain's ability to shape outcomes in the region appears to have been principally based on its ability to use its naval power to foreclose options to Egypt and, to a lesser extent, France and Russia. British naval power gave it a range of options, but few that extended further inland than the reach of its warships' guns. In general, speed of British reaction seems to have been important, in deterring adversaries and reassuring friends, in preventing undesired faits accomplis, and in achieving the goals of British policies.

While the British seem to have been generally successful in shaping outcomes in the eastern Mediterranean (with a few notable exceptions, such as the Ottoman turn to Russia in 1833), it is important to recognize the distinctly limited nature of British goals in the region. These goals were limited in two regards. First (again with a few notable exceptions, such as eventual British support for Greek independence), the British generally sought to prevent or defeat challenges to the status quo, not to transform that status quo or alter the objectives of challengers. That is, British policy was essentially a holding action, aimed at foiling the efforts of those who sought change. Second, the British did not seek to transform the domestic politics or domestic conditions of actors in the region. Given British liberal ideology and interest in "progress," this is perhaps surprising, but Britain seems to have consistently viewed "progress" in foreign policy terms, not in terms of domestic transformation. Thus the British sought to stem the slave trade and to encourage freer international trading, but London did not actively pursue the spread of constitutional government in the region.

In sum, within the clear and definite limits set by successive governments, British policy was largely effective in stabilizing the eastern Mediterranean. In general, the British were successful in using a consistent naval presence with better-trained naval forces to foreclose the military and diplomatic options open to regional actors and other great powers. By doing so, they deterred, limited, or ensured satisfactory outcomes in regional conflicts; limited political penetration by other great powers; protected British trade and commerce; and encouraged the emergence of a "progressive" international order based on free trade and antislavery norms. Though the evidence is less than definitive, it appears that the achievement of these goals depended on the presence of forces able actually to prevent or defeat challenges: given the existence of anti–status quo powers (at varying times, Egypt, Russia, and France), the Royal Navy's role was more than symbolic, and these powers were at least at times highly sensitive to the actual capabilities of forward-operating Royal Navy forces.

Great Britain in the Eastern Mediterranean, 1919–1937

Between 1919 and 1937, as during the period of the Concert of Europe, Britain sought to stabilize the eastern Mediterranean region, maintain the status quo, preserve British primacy, and deter conflict. The region remained a key one for British foreign policy, both because of its strategic position on the route to India and because of oil reserves in Iraq. British policy in the eastern Mediterranean was both facilitated and complicated by the British colonial role in the region and by British presence and influence in the postcolonial states. Unlike in the earlier period, British ability to stabilize the region was thus intimately linked to its ability to assure domestic order as well as to shape the international environment. The demands placed on Britain were thus substantially greater than in the preceding century. British policy demanded that Britain: deter great power aggression in the region; limit the spread of great power influence; limit the economic in-roads being made by other powers, particularly in key sectors like oil; and maintain order and prevent an anti-British political backlash in the Arab world that would jeopardize continued British control or influence.

British military resources were clearly overextended, both on land and at sea. British garrisons in its Arab protectorates and mandates were modest, even for the limited task of maintaining local order. They did, however, ensure a consistent presence ashore in the southern and eastern parts of the region, although this presence was only with difficulty projected into sparsely populated areas. As the Chanak crisis with Turkey illustrated, Britain was also hampered by the fact that, while its forces in the region might be sufficient to deter temporarily, a major war would require mobilization, which would be time-consuming and probably politically unacceptable. Though stretched globally, British naval power was regionally dominant. The Mediterranean represented the center of gravity for the Royal Navy, and roughly half the British fleet was deployed here during the interwar period, with major bases at Malta and Alexandria.

British technological superiority played an important role in solving at least one of the many problems facing British policymakers: how to police sparsely populated areas, maintaining order and preventing the coalescence of anti-British political movements. For this purpose, air power proved effective. The Trenchard system of air policing appears in general to have been a success. Two important observations need be noted, however. First, the system did not rest on a bluff or involve a hesitation to use violence; rather, it appears the coercive effectiveness of aircraft was predicated on a history of actual air bombardment. Second, the effectiveness of the system reflected the unusual geographic and sociopolitical conditions of the Arab hinterland. In urban areas, maintenance of order required some combination of boots-on-the-ground and political penetration, especially the mastery of divide-and-conquer approaches to political manipulation.

While British economic leverage vis-à-vis regional actors was, as in the earlier period, limited, in the interwar years British policy relied heavily on formal and informal British political penetration, especially in the Arab areas of the region. The presence of British advisers and administrators as much as of British soldiers was key to ensuring that foreign and domestic policies of the Arab states remained consistent with British aims and objectives. This political penetration, however, was something of a waning asset across the period and presented British policymakers with a no-win dilemma: continued British political presence tended to promote Arab nationalist opposition, while British political retrenchment in the region weakened British ability to control the anti-British tendencies and developments that were pushing for further withdrawal. British military presence in general remained able to cope with violent expressions of nationalism or anti-British sentiment, but only at increasing cost.

At home, antiwar sentiment, domestic preoccupations, and budgetary concerns all constrained British policy in the eastern Mediterranean as elsewhere in the world. Again, however, these domestic constraints tended to set overall bounds on British involvement rather than to sharply limit freedom of action in particular crises. These constraints were probably reinforced by the international naval arms control regime, although it is difficult to know how much more Britain—or its rivals—would have spent in the absence of the regime. British goals tended to be consistent with League of Nations aspirations (indeed, Britain was the essential power within the League); had League norms been more effective, this would probably have assisted British policy—especially vis-à-vis Italy.

The Italian invasion of Abyssinia represented a direct challenge to—and defeat for—British policy. Other challenges tended to be more chronic, however. The rise of Arab nationalism, the increasing ability of regional players like Turkey to play off the great powers, and the increasing economic penetration of the region by firms from other nations all posed long-run dilemmas for which the British had no long-run solution.

The overall picture that emerges is thus mixed. Using a combination of extensive political penetration (the legacy of British occupation and colonial or mandatory control) and forward military presence both in the waters of the region and in dispersed garrisons ashore, the British were able to retain their dominant position in the region and, with one notable exception (Abyssinia), were generally able to shape regional developments in ways roughly consistent with their preferences. This said, however, British ability to control or influence the more independent states of the region, Turkey and Greece, was limited, as demonstrated by Turkey's successful opposition to Anglo-Greek policies in the 1920s, the Greek turn away from Britain, and worrisome Turkish engagement with both Germany and the USSR.

Perhaps even more significantly, though British policies were carefully tailored to try to achieve economies, Britain's ability to shape regional developments was clearly waning and unsustainable. Three contributory factors can be identified. First, Britain's relative decline, coupled with ideological and domestic political constraints that made it unwilling to act preventively against emerging challengers like Italy, meant that it was increasingly unable to deter great power involvement or intervention in the region. Second, long-run economic developments were bringing other powers, most obviously America, into the region. Third, Britain was unable to control nationalist political development in the region. While British co-optation of elites and manipulation of domestic politics in the Arab world was at times masterful, British political and military presence does not appear to have contributed to the development of institutions and norms that would have sustained a long-term continued British presence.

In the short and medium term, British successes seem to have reflected the presence of well-tailored military forces (a dominant Navy at sea, garrisons of lightly armed soldiers ashore, and RAF aircraft to police the hinterland) closely tied to and informed by a network of colonial or postcolonial British administrators. This politicomilitary presence seems to have been designed with an eye to deterring or defeating the particular challenges the British faced. With this military and political establishment, the British attempted to walk the fine line between looking weak and thus inviting attack, on the one hand, and provoking nationalist outbursts through excessive displays of power, on the other hand.

In its own terms, British military presence should probably be regarded as successful. British goals, as enunciated, were modest. So too, though, was British success. And time was not working in Britain's favor.

Great Britain in South America, 1850–1900

If one of the themes of the first two cases is that a great power that sets its sights low enough is likely to achieve its goals, the case of British peacetime military presence in South America in the second half of the nineteenth century offers further supporting evidence. While Britain deliberately sought to influence the South American political environment, its aims, though clear and consistently pursued, were very modest. The objective of British policy was simply to ensure a free trade regime in the region. Since the nations of the region embraced the free trade norm, the only real threat to free trade was the reestablishment of European empires in South America. Thus, the implicit corollary to British support for free trade was that although Britain would not attempt to exclude other great powers from the region, it would look unfavorably on efforts to recolonize South America. While Britain assumed that free trade would ultimately lead to peace and "progress," in general it did not actively attempt to shape the peacetime environment in other ways, to prevent regional conflict, or to influence domestic political developments. Britain rarely involved itself in the region's quarrels, even when British property and investment were threatened. Not surprisingly, British policy has been described as one of "perfect indifference" and "masterly inactivity." Since the British objectives of free trade and preservation of South American sovereignty were broadly shared by political elites in states across the region, indifference and inactivity—coupled with symbolic reassurance that Britain would not permit the norms of sovereignty and free trade to be violated—were effective in achieving British goals.

Although the period marked the height of British naval mastery, Royal Navy presence in the region, though continuous, was negligible—a handful of generally obsolescent warships, operating out of facilities controlled by host states. In number and technology, these warships were typically inferior to the fleets of regional actors (though superior British training may have at least to some degree offset these inferiorities, as the engagement between Peruvian and British forces in 1877 suggested). The importance of the naval presence seems to have been largely symbolic—a reminder of the British naval might that was not present. It is probably important to note, however, that the limited nature of British political objectives meant that Britain was unlikely to seek to join in regional squabbles, intervene on one side or another in domestic fighting, or step in to protect British investments. As a practical matter, therefore, Britain's minimal naval presence probably did not deny it capabilities in the region it realistically might want.

The British state lacked not only military instruments in South America but economic and diplomatic ones as well. Given British commitment to free trade, it had little economic leverage. And British diplomatic presence in the region was maintained only at the lowest levels. This said, Britain did possess two important, if intangible, resources in its efforts to shape South America. The first was the respect for Britain and, particularly, for the Royal Navy that dated back to British support for Latin American independence. (This may help explain why the distinctly second-rate quality of Royal Navy forces in the region did not undermine British prestige.) The second, and more critical, was the intellectual commitment of South American elites to British-style economic liberalism. In this regard, Britain can be described as exerting something like Gramscian hegemony, having convinced ruling elites in the region that their interests and Britain's were at least generally consistent.

As in the two preceding cases, it is possible that parliamentary and public opinion restricted the broad outlines of British policy even if they did not constrain immediate responses to crises. It seems doubtful that there would have been political support had a British government wanted to increase British presence in the region, much less to intervene. The limited British policy in South America, by contrast, seems to have been broadly popular.

Several important observations derive from this case. First, when the interests of regional states and a great power are perceived by regional states as being shared, purely symbolic forces may be sufficient to reassure those regional states. Large deployments, or deployments by operationally effective units, may be unnecessary.

Second—and most interesting—in such a situation, increased military presence may be not only unnecessary but distinctly undesirable: as one British diplomat observed, "consuls without cannons had little impact, yet the use of warships had often inflamed local feelings and been counter productive." The logic at work here is not difficult to discern. More than token British presence would have manifestly given Britain the ability to intervene at those times and on those issues on which its interests diverged from those of particular South American states. While eliminating the Royal Navy presence might have left South American states feeling vulnerable to pressures from other European powers, increasing the Royal Navy presence would have created or exacerbated fears that Britain intended to intervene on behalf of its nationals, to support one faction or another in a civil conflict, or to weigh in on one side or another in a regional dispute. In this case, while presence was necessary, less was more. Indeed, this lesson that less was more may have been driven home by the unsuccessful and unpopular British effort in the 1840s to topple Argentina's Rosas regime by blockading the River Plate.

Third, while British policy was vastly successful in its own narrow terms—Britain was able to ensure free markets across South America—it was a failure in broader terms. An essential assumption underlying British policy, at least when it was being pursued by Liberal governments, was that free trade would result in peace, prosperity, and political progress. This proved simply wrong. The positive consequences (other than markets for British manufactured goods) that Britain expected from its support for free trade simply did not develop.

The United States in the Caribbean, 1903–1920

In a number of significant ways, the case of U.S. efforts to shape the Caribbean in the first decades of the twentieth century represents the reverse of the British involvement in Latin America in the late nineteenth century. Where British objectives were narrowly defined, American ones were sweeping; where Britain employed only limited forces, America made a major commitment of resources—military, economic, and political; where Britain avoided domestic involvement, America plunged in.

The United States had two principal goals in the Caribbean. The first, driven by realpolitik, was to prevent another great power from gaining influence in the region, which with the decision to construct an isthmian canal became critical to American security. This security concern with great-power presence had an important corollary implication for American involvement in the region's internal affairs, however. Because instability and an inability to repay European debts would justify and invite European intervention in the region (as the Venezuelan debt crisis of 1902–1903 and the subsequent Hague Court decision underscored), this realpolitik objective logically dictated the Roosevelt Corollary to the Monroe Doctrine—that the United States would intervene to prevent misgovernment in the minor states of the region. The second goal, which led to the same conclusion as the first, reflected the internal logic and moral imperative of American Progressive ideology: by Progressive reckoning, America had both a self-interest and a duty to use its power to establish stable, liberal, eventually democratic government in the region.

The U.S. naval construction program begun in 1890, the realities of geography that placed the Caribbean in close proximity to U.S. bases and far from Europe, and the balance of power in Europe that dictated European rivals keep their fleets close to home, combined to give the United States an ability to deploy decisive naval power in the region. Bases at Guantánamo, San Juan, and Culebra facilitated the maintenance of continuous naval presence by the Caribbean Squadron and by major units conducting training exercises. The United States possessed essentially all the naval power it could imagine using: examining the entire seventeen years included in this case, it has not been possible to identify any instance in which the United States did not have a warship to dispatch to a trouble spot identified by the State Department. Equally important, in the Marine Corps, which was dramatically expanded during this period, the United States possessed a professional, disciplined force that could intervene ashore with what by local standards represented overwhelming force.

In sum, the ability of any regional state to resist American military power, either at sea or ashore, was negligible. As was repeatedly demonstrated, American military power was sufficient to intervene, restore order, prevent the overthrow of governments, ensure the success of antigovernment movements, impose truces on warring parties or bring them to the peace table, and even undertake major civic construction projects.

Both at sea and ashore, U.S. military forces possessed a huge technological advantage over regional forces. Coupled with abundant forward-deployed forces, state-of-the-art communication technology permitted the United States to respond in a timely fashion to developing situations. At least as relevant, however, was the superior professionalism and discipline of American forces, which permitted small numbers of American troops to restore order or decisively influence events in the face of much larger numbers of opposing forces.

American power was not purely military, of course. In contrast to the three British cases discussed above, American business and financial institutions generally worked hand-in-glove with the American government and dominated the economies of the region. And, of course, in several important instances, the United States itself took over the public finances of Caribbean states. Beyond this indirect or direct control over Caribbean economies, the United States also enjoyed considerable political penetration of regional elites, which in some cases identified closely with the United States.

America's military freedom of action in the Caribbean during this period was essentially unlimited. In the wake of the Venezuelan crisis of 1902 the two great powers that might conceivably have disputed American hegemony, Great Britain (which had the naval power but not the interest) and Germany (which found itself diplomatically at odds with the United States but was otherwise engaged in Europe) effectively conceded the region. In American domestic politics, both conservatives and liberals, though for different reasons, supported the Progressive policy of intervention. No significant voices opposed involvement. And the day's international regimes provided the United States with, at minimum, a carte blanche and, more plausibly, strong encouragement for intervention. In short, options up to and including prolonged military occupation were entirely feasible.

Despite this overwhelming power and the absence of constraints on its use, U.S. policy must be judged as at best only partially successful. While the United States succeeded in deterring the involvement of other powers in the region, largely prevented interstate clashes between regional players, and protected American property and investments, it failed in its efforts to transform domestic societies in the region and to create stable internal order. The region remained marked by domestic instability and violence. While the United States was able to determine the political victors in internal struggles across the region, this did not result in the political progress the United States sought.

This is a striking finding worth underscoring. Despite the fact that the United States possessed overwhelming military, economic, and political capabilities, including the capacity to respond essentially immediately and decisively with naval power; despite little international opposition and strong domestic support; and despite the comic military and political weakness of regional states, the United States was unable to reshape domestic order in the region.

This case also implicitly suggests a second worrisome point: in the end, American intervention proved domestically unsustainable. After 1920, as part of a general rejection of U.S. interventionism, American public and elite opinion turned against the Caribbean policy, and efforts to politically reshape the region were largely abandoned.

France in West Africa, 1945–1970

There are important parallels between American involvement in the Caribbean in the early decades of the twentieth century and French involvement in francophone West and Central Africa in the post–World War II period. Both great powers sought to shape domestic as well as international conditions, using a mix of military, economic, and political tools. In both cases, the great power's economic and political penetration of the region was extraordinary. In both cases the great power had a relatively free hand—while suspicious of other great powers and determined to prevent encroachment in an area they saw of vital interest, both the United States and France actually enjoyed a widely, if only implicitly, recognized sphere of influence, and both American and French governments were able to act with only the most general domestic political constraints on their actions.

French and American objectives, however, differed substantially. For France, the goal of preserving a "*chasse gardée*" (literally a managed, feudal hunting preserve) in Africa stemmed from France's perceived need to restore its political prestige and retain effective control over the region's raw materials, manpower, and markets. This dictated "shaping" the region's politics in such a way that none of the three threats France perceived to the *chasse gardée*—political and cultural encroachment by the anglophone powers, ideological and diplomatic interference by the Soviet Union and its clients, and anti-neocolonial African nationalist sentiment—endangered the continued special politicoeconomic relationship between francophone Africa and France or the continued dominance of francophone culture. Thus where the underlying aim of American involvement in the Caribbean was ensuring stability and progress, the underlying aim of French involvement in Africa was protecting French hegemony and the French special relationship.

This difference in goals is noted not to claim some moral superiority for America, but to point out two factors that may plausibly help explain differences in success. First, in conception if not always in practice, American policy ultimately sought a profound transformation of political institutions and social relationships; French policy accepted a continuation of existing ones. Second, whatever pragmatic compromises it from time to time embraced, American policy during the Progressive period regarded disorder and the violent overthrow of governments as per se undesirable; French policy, by contrast, was willing to tolerate political violence and embrace undemocratic political transitions so long as they yielded leaders who continued to maintain the French relationship.

French efforts also displayed a greater continuity of purpose over time and a higher level of involvement: French politico-economic-military penetration of the region dated from the period of colonial expansion in the nineteenth century, followed a clear and consistent policy at least from the Brazzaville conference of 1944 onward, and, perhaps most important, was managed directly by a succession of French presidents, remarkably free not only from parliamentary scrutiny but from the red tape of bureaucratic management.

Finally, it should be noted that the level of French penetration of the region was a product of colonial history. It is difficult to imagine this level of penetration in any but a postcolonial context.

French military presence in the region took three simultaneous forms: the presence of French troops and bases; the existence of a network of French military and intelligence advisers and agents in key posts; and an ongoing pattern of military aid and transfers. Defense and military cooperation agreements signed at the time of independence not only provided the basis for French intervention but also served as the foundation for extensive political and politicomilitary penetration: French military advisers in Africa ranged between one and three thousand in the 1960–1980 period, expatriate French officers occupied key positions in most francophone African militaries, and substantial numbers of African officers were trained in French schools. France also provided the "visual trappings" of power—uniforms, jets, military ceremonies—that conveyed legitimacy for African rulers.

The relative superiority of French forces over possible regional adversaries during this period was large and unquestioned. The armies of francophone African states remained small and poorly trained. French technology provided French forces with airpower and superior mobility, though the logistics to support long-term actions were always problematic. French forces based in Africa were backed up by the metropolitan-based division-strength intervention force, a substantial portion of which was air-mobile and which enjoyed access to an extensive network of bases. Consequently, French military capacity in the region was neither theoretic nor limited to intervening in interstate conflicts: French forces possessed and frequently exercised the ability—and, under the terms of defense agreements, in many cases the legal right—to intervene in domestic politics, providing "internal security" within African states and for particular African leaders.

The depth of French penetration into African societies and political institutions was remarkable, and this had obvious implications for how the French "shaping" effort proceeded. While most of the francophone African states became independent in 1960, the French left in place the institutions and individuals necessary for extensive Franco-African "cooperation" on military, political, and economic matters. Economically, francophone Africa was completely dependent on France: France controlled currencies and dominated investment and trade. Equally important, French cultural dominance continued to pervade the region; in important cases, African rulers had long-term personal relationships with a succession of French presidents. In many ways, the borders of sovereignty were, and have remained, profoundly blurred.

Constraints on French actions were limited. Power to set and implement African policy was concentrated in the president's hands. Domestically, the only significant military constraint was the legal one against deploying conscripts abroad, necessitating the creation of nonconscript units. Competition from and complications caused by other great powers were also limited. Even when the Soviet Union and its allies provided significant aid, and even when African states declared themselves "Marxist," this occurred within the context of lingering French dominance.

Perhaps not surprisingly, given the resources at France's disposal, France was successful nearly everywhere in francophone West Africa in maintaining its hegemony during the 1945–1970 period: only one of its former colonies, Guinea, completely split with France during this period. Both anglophone and Soviet influence were largely excluded.

This said, it is also useful to note that managing the region required constant French attention, and the frequent use of French troops both in shows of force and to restore order. The *chasse gardée* did not maintain itself, nor was it a little piece of paradise. Although the situation in francophone West Africa was generally better than in Central Africa (more than 30,000 casualties in Cameroon, vice over 100,000 dead in interethnic conflict in Rwanda in the 1950s and 1960s and a similar number in Zaïre), it would obviously be an overstatement to describe the region as peaceful or politically stable—although, again, it is important to recognize that, thanks to careful French management, neither the periodic violence nor the endemic instability threatened France's position and, in places like Côte d'Ivoire, partnership with capable francophile leaders like Houphouët-Boigny actually yielded long-term internal stability. Francophone African rulers with close ties to French presidents knew they could count on French intervention on their behalf; francophone African rulers who thumbed their noses at France knew that without French backing they were vulnerable to their own domestic opponents.

Also interesting is that French influence and leverage does not appear to have extended into neighboring states where there was no French military presence or political penetration. France's indirect support for Biafra during the 1967–1970 Nigerian civil war was a failure, for example, as were its efforts to limit or reduce anglophone Nigeria's growing involvement in regional politics.

Finally, it is worth observing that France's success stemmed at least in part from the extraordinary weakness of its potential adversaries in the region. Typically, even very small numbers of French troops, if deployed in a timely fashion, could have a decisive impact. On those occasions, however, when France found itself facing an adversary of even limited capability and staying power—for example, when France confronted Libyan-backed forces during the protracted Chadian civil war—it found its military's ability stretched and was unable to impose solutions it found fully satisfactory.

France in Central Africa, 1970–1995

This case represents a sequel to the preceding one, and it illustrates the difficulties of continuing to shape a region over time. French goals in Central Africa in the 1970–1995 period were essentially identical to their goals in West Africa in the preceding period. As in the preceding period, too, French ability to shape political outcomes reflected an extraordinary and carefully maintained penetration of the region. This penetration involved not only military forces, advisers, and aid, but French "*cooperants*" placed throughout the state apparatus and French education for African officers and bureaucrats. Gradually but increasingly, however, the difficulties of preserving postcolonial influence grew across these decades. While to a remarkable degree France succeeded in preserving its African *chasse gardée*, this hunting preserve increasingly showed signs of decay and by the mid-1990s the prospects for its continued maintenance looked questionable.

The most spectacular French failures were in those parts of francophone Central Africa where French political penetration was historically most weakly rooted—in the former Belgian colonies of Zaïre and Rwanda. In Zaïre, French failure to shape the post-Mobutu years resulted in the effective collapse of the Zaïrean state, civil war, and intervention by non-francophone neighbors. In Rwanda, the victory of Ugandan- (i.e., anglophone-) supported Tutsi rebels, international condemnation of tacit French support for Hutu genocide, and international opposition to unilateral French military intervention (the widely reviled Operation Turquoise) all marked substantial setbacks for France.

These debacles need to be understood as the consequence of a number of long-term trends that increased the difficulty of controlling events and political outcomes in francophone Africa. (Indeed, although the trends are not identical, there are some parallels between this case and that of the British in the Eastern Mediterranean in the interwar years.) For the French in Africa, these trends included the passing of a generation of leaders in France and Africa for whom "*la francophonie*" was a powerful cognitive factor and for whom personal ties were deep and profound; it included the increasing globalization of economic forces; and it included the growth of African sentiment that transcended the historic division between anglophone and francophone, permitting anglophone Nigeria to play a growing role in West Africa and anglophone Uganda and South Africa to play a similarly threatening (from the French perspective) part in Central Africa. It also included the gradually increasing capacity of a few African states to challenge France's African presence militarily: substantial long-term French involvement in Chad, necessitated in part by Libyan military meddling, was a major drain throughout this period.

As in the earlier case, France retained a substantial land-based military presence in the region, backed up with France-based interventionary forces. Both Giscard and Mitterand invested in and expanded this interventionary capacity, though logistical support for large, prolonged operations remained problematic. Although technological sophistication grew in importance as France faced Libyan-backed forces in Chad, superior training and specialized capabilities, such as those for airborne assault, remained critical. Also as in the earlier case, French forces intervened frequently in domestic politics, restoring order, protecting French-supported governments (and, by implication, allowing the overthrow of governments that no longer enjoyed French support), and, in unusual cases like that of Emperor Bokassa of the Central African Empire, stepping in to topple governments that had become an embarrassment. More generally, however, French political penetration was sufficient to force changes in government composition or policy without more dramatic action.

While the overall appraisal must thus be that France was able to use its overwhelming political, economic, and military influence to shape the region into a French preserve, this case raises interesting cautionary notes. The failure of French policy to promote substantial political, social, or economic development has meant that French capacity to dominate the region has continued, but it has also resulted in instability that the French have found increasingly difficult to control, as Zaïre, Chad, and Rwanda have demonstrated.

Patterns

As this discussion suggests, certain patterns begin to emerge from these cases. In the interest of promoting spirited debate and expressing our findings in a format that may best trigger additional study, we present these observed patterns in the form of a series of propositions about "shaping." Obviously, as we noted at the outset, any propositions we formulate about the relationship between presence and prevention and persuasion that are based on a focused comparison of only six cases must be regarded as highly tentative. Two reasons for caution must be emphasized. First, there is the danger that our cases are in some way atypical, and that a larger selection of cases would have suggested another pattern of outcomes. Second, there is the danger that we have asked the wrong questions—that we have "focussed" on the wrong variables—in our case studies, and that an investigation that was theoretically better informed would have highlighted other, more general, or more useful lessons about the attributes of military power that matter. But it is necessary to start somewhere. So long as we are modest in our confidence about the propositions we derive and recognize that our conclusions must be subject to further testing, these six very different cases offer a good place to begin to think about the question of the peacetime political utility of regionally deployed military power.

Based on our research, we suggest ten basic propositions about "shaping."

Proposition 1: "Being There" Matters

That military presence in a region matters is at once the most obvious and most problematic of our conclusions—obvious because it seems from our examination that military presence has indeed clearly served as the necessary basis for effective political "shaping"; problematic because our cases offer little by way of counterfactual. Because one of our concerns in selecting cases was to find cases in which the great power clearly possessed military predominance in the region being examined, military presence was very much the norm in all our cases. Plainly, to demonstrate conclusively the importance of presence it is necessary to review cases in which great powers attempted to influence political developments in a region *without* maintaining a military presence and observe failure. This additional empirical work deserves to be done. Nonetheless, we are quite convinced from our detailed review of the record that military presence was a prerequisite for the peacetime political goals each of the great powers sought to accomplish. The variance we have observed in our cases supports what process-tracing within the cases also suggests: that presence makes a difference. In the Eastern Mediterranean during the Concert of Europe period, for example, on the occasions when British naval forces were not present, Britain's success in gaining the outcomes it sought declined sharply. During the interwar years, as British forces were withdrawn from the Arab world British ability to control domestic political outcomes declined sharply, and British influence along the northern littoral, where it generally lacked forces ashore, was always less than along the southern and eastern littorals. Similarly, in West and Central Africa, French influence was largely limited to those countries with which it had a postcolonial relationship and maintained a military presence. Our conclusion that presence matters is plainly consistent with the view of decision-makers involved at the time. Even in the South American case, where presence was most limited, British consuls clearly felt continued presence made a difference.

Proposition 2: Presence Must Be Tailored to Foreclose Specific Military Options

In general, "being there" does not seem to have some sort of existential impact. Rather, it appears to matter because it forecloses to regional actors and other great powers particular options they might otherwise be interested in (or makes available to them particular options that would otherwise not have been feasible). "Being there" may deter (or reassure), but what it deters (or reassures about) is quite specific. That is, when "being there" makes a difference it does so because it effectively blocks specific actions, or reassures friends in the region that specific actions desired by the great power will be safe.

For example, British naval presence in the Eastern Mediterranean mattered in the early years of the nineteenth century because that naval presence effectively foreclosed Egypt's option of attacking the Ottoman Empire. By contrast, in the early interwar years, British naval presence in the Mediterranean did not stop Turkey from pushing ahead with its demands for a revision of the regional settlement, largely because British military power, however superior to Turkey's, was not able to block Turkish actions directly—it did not foreclose Turkey's military options. In a very different context, the effectiveness of French presence in Africa seems linked to

French forces' ability to respond to the internal threats and domestic dangers that most clearly threatened local rulers.

Significantly, the cases suggest that regional actors, if sufficiently motivated, will try to "design around" the great power's presence. Because "being there" does not foreclose all hostile activities by regional actors—only those for which the forces that are there are militarily relevant—opponents will try to develop new political and military options that circumvent these capabilities. For example, British presence did not stop all Egyptian efforts to undermine the status quo during the Concert years, or change Egypt into a satisfied power. It only prevented those challenges to the status quo which required a mastery of the littoral. British military presence ashore in the Arab areas of the Eastern Mediterranean during the interwar years did not stop Arab nationalism, but it did foreclose particular expressions of it that would have been most damaging to British interests; similarly, British naval mastery of the Eastern Mediterranean did not prevent Turkey from pressing its terrestrial territorial ambitions.

On first blush, the case of Britain in South America during the height of the *Pax Britannica* would seem to offer a counterexample: after all, Britain was able to achieve its goals even though the forces deployed in region were trivial and possessed extremely limited capacity to intervene. On more careful examination, though, this case underscores rather than undercuts the proposition. In this case there were no military threats in the region to British objectives. The threat was political (that either regional states or other great powers would come to doubt British commitment to free trade and sovereignty), and token military forces were sufficient to make the political point that Britain remained committed. British global naval superiority may have mattered—no great power could establish South American colonies over British objections, given British ability to close sea lanes between metropole and colony—but this global naval mastery meant that Britain did not need significant forces in the region.

Our cases thus suggest that for military presence to be effective in "shaping" the environment, it must be tailored both to the political objectives of great power and to the nature of challenges from regional actors and other great powers. "Being there" implies a clear set of objectives and designing and deploying forces able to achieve those specific objectives. "Being there" is not just hanging around. Specifically, we would argue that the tailoring of military forces for presence must reflect three things:

- the nature of the great power's goals;
- the nature of the adversary;
- and the adversary's degree of commitment.

Here it is worth noting that "adversaries" are not necessarily states, either in the region or rival great powers from outside of it. Indeed, in many situations the key adversaries whose behavior and outlook must be affected will be nonstate ones. For example, they may also be insurgent movements or local political leaders (as was frequently the case in the Caribbean), nationalist movements or tribal actors (as in the Eastern Mediterranean in the interwar years), or feuding political elites or dissatisfied military officers (as in Africa). Different adversaries have vastly different goals and tools at their disposal, and their level of commitment to particular objectives will also vary significantly. As a consequence, the types of options these adversaries might find attractive will range widely, and the military or other measures the great power will need to take to ensure the outcomes it desires will vary as well. Forces that were appropriate or sufficient to shape one environment successfully may well be inappropriate or insufficient in another, *even if the great power's goals are the same in both.*

Five conclusions follow. First and most important, no generalizable picture emerges about precisely what kinds of military forces will be useful in efforts to shape peacetime political environments. It is impossible to determine in the abstract what forces are needed for effective presence—for example, air power, missile defense, precision strike, ground forces—precisely because there is no generalizable account of the nature of the great power's goals, the nature of the adversary, or the adversary's degree of commitment and therefore no generalizable account of what options need to be foreclosed or created.

Second, "one size" does *not* fit all: when used for peacetime presence, military forces need to be tailored to the particular scenario. "Standardizing" the forces that are forward deployed in peacetime for presence purposes is likely to be a suboptimal or even counterproductive approach.

Third, given the ability of adversaries to "design around" great-power commitments and threats, great powers find it useful to have presence forces that yield a range of capabilities and therefore the ability to tailor or retailor responses to adapt to particular events or challenges, or to solve the particular problem of a particular ally. Flexibility complicates adversaries' planning.

Fourth, speed of reaction is important. Foreclosing options and preventing faits accomplis clearly seems to have mattered in most of the cases we studied, the possible exception being the South American case. (A warning here is in order, however. The cases we examined offered little variance, and without exploring cases in which the great power lacked the capacity to respond quickly it is difficult to know exactly what difference speed made.)

Fifth, an understanding of regional actors and politics, and an ability to update assessments and to learn from and adapt quickly to changing conditions, is important. Situational awareness, resting on carefully established and consistently maintained intelligence networks, is key to responding flexibly and appropriately.

Caveat to Proposition 2: A Token or Symbolic Presence May Be Sufficient to Deter Weakly Motivated Adversaries
Although our cases underscore the point that forward-deployed forces are usually important because they offer specific military options, our cases raise the possibility that there may be some situations in which forward forces are important because they serve a symbolic or communicative function, that is, because they represent a credible token of the great power's commitment, or because they threaten to act as a "trigger" for a major intervention by the great power. This suggests that there may well be a direct relationship between degree of commitment, or strength of motivation, on the part of adversaries and the degree to which the great power must tailor its forces to foreclose specific threats. While the particular capabilities of the great power's forces in the region will matter when dealing with highly motivated adversaries that seek to "design around" the specific attributes of the great power's presence, the risk of escalation created by simply having any forces present may be sufficient to deter weakly motivated adversaries. Perhaps the clearest example of this comes from South America, on those rare occasions when Britain became involved in regional affairs, where the mere presence of British warships was sufficient to deter. In these cases, the challenger does not seem to be deeply committed to the particular objective, and a small risk that events might spiral out of control may be enough to deter.

Proposition 3: More (Presence) Is Not Always Better than Less (Presence)
The clearest illustration of this proposition comes from the British experience in South America, where it was widely recognized that a heightened British presence would have inflamed Latin American public opinion and frightened local elites with specters of British intervention, weakening rather than strengthening Britain's ability to shape the region. Other cases, however, possibly offer even more compelling evidence in support of this proposition. Certainly the British experience in the Eastern Mediterranean in the interwar years reveals the difficulties of walking the fine line between enough presence to deter and shape and an overbearing presence that heightens nationalist opposition. Increasingly, the French have faced the same problem in Africa; the case of Niger in the early 1960s may offer a useful example. Military presence

risks generating countervailing political or military pressures, and the danger probably grows as presence grows.

Interestingly, there is some indication that this proposition that "less is more" may be true in the long run as well as in the short or medium run. The mechanism here is different, though. Both the French cases and the case of American involvement in the Caribbean suggest the possibility that in addition to generating offsetting opposition, at least in some situations greater presence may create long-term structural obstacles that reduce the great power's ability to achieve its goals. It is precisely in those Caribbean nations in which American presence was greatest that the long-term development of democracy and stable government institutions has been most problematic. In the case of French involvement in Africa, the evidence is a little less clear (and we have less historical perspective), but again it seems that, at least in some nations, French military presence has been an alternative to, rather than aid to, the development of the stable domestic institutions that would facilitate low-cost maintenance of French influence. The point here is that optimizing military presence for "shaping" outcomes in the short run may result in an evolution—or atrophy—of political structures, and this in turn makes presence untenable in the long run or undercuts the long-term goals that prompted great-power involvement in the first place.

Proposition 4: Depending on Circumstances and on the Great Power's Objectives, Military Presence May Have to Be Ashore

This proposition is no more than a logical corollary to proposition 2, but one that is worth highlighting. In some cases it may be possible to deter interstate conflict or ensure a favorable outcome in wars from a position on the international commons (as Britain did in the Eastern Mediterranean in the Concert years and, with more limited objectives, in Latin America). Depending on geography and on the goals of adversaries, though, deterring or ensuring a favorable outcome in regional conflict may demand a presence ashore. For the British, this point was driven home by the Chanak Crisis with Turkey.

More important, though, when "stabilizing" a region or gaining the desired outcome requires changing domestic political institutions or influencing domestic actors rather than simply blocking particular foreign policy actions, typically this will require boots on the ground, either as routine presence or during crises or conflicts. In the Caribbean, to ensure "responsible" government that would deny European powers a pretext for intervening, American marines had to go ashore. In the Arab world in the interwar years, whether to prevent the rise of an uncontrolled Arab nationalism or to force particular policy changes by the Egyptian government, British forces had to be either permanently stationed or available to make demonstrations, as they did in Alexandria. To prevent (or at least limit) a humanitarian disaster when the Turks occupied Smyrna, British forces had to be ashore as well as at sea. Perhaps most strikingly, French efforts to control the composition and policies of African governments, and to reassure pro-French leaders, required forces in country or the manifest ability to get them there in a timely fashion.

The logical corollary to proposition 3 also holds here, however: forces ashore appear more likely to generate a countervailing reaction than forces at sea or forces outside the area. Certainly this seems to have been the British experience in the Arab world.

Especially given this last point, it is comforting to speculate that the range of tasks that can be accomplished by projecting military power from the sea or from the sky, that is the range of activities that can be deterred or the kinds of reassurance that can be provided by sea-based forces or with long-range airpower, is growing. And, obviously, a study like ours that looks to the past provides little or no guidance about what options technology will make possible in the future. What the historical record does underscore, however, is the tremendous diversity of challenges and threats that great powers confront in their efforts to impose their desired regional order and institutions. To the extent that great powers have perceived the need to ensure internal order, to support particular leaders, or (most problematically) to promote some sort of domestic transformation, this has in the past created a need to be ashore. Thus while this study cannot indicate what will be technologically possible in the future, it does offer some reason for caution about assuming that the shaping of a stable regional order and desired regional institutions can necessarily be accomplished from the sea or with long-range airpower. A sea-based ballistic missile shield may be critical in reassuring American allies that they will be protected from a rogue neighbor, and a sea-based arsenal of cruise missiles or long-range bombers with precision-guided weaponry may convince a would-be aggressor that its political and military command-and-control would not survive a conflict. It is less clear, however, how these capabilities, or the ability to deny access to the global common, would reassure a pro-American leader that an antidemocratic military coup is impossible, that revolutionaries or rebel forces will not be able to seize control of the hinterland, or that the demands of religious fundamentalist movements can safely be ignored.

Proposition 5: Technology Does Not Offer Magic Bullets
Again, to the extent that we are currently experiencing a "revolution" in military affairs, the past may not provide guidance to the future. But to whatever

extent the past continues to be relevant, it may be useful to note how limited the impact of technology has been. In several cases we examined, technology clearly served as a force multiplier. For the United States in the Caribbean, communication technology permitted the rapid dispatch of warships to trouble spots, reducing the number of vessels necessary for timely response to developing events. For the British in the interwar years, air power facilitated the policing of lightly populated parts of the Arab countryside, eliminating the need for larger garrisons. For the French in Africa, air mobility permitted rapid intervention with either forward forces or France based troops.

Four points seem worth highlighting, however. First, in two of the cases (in the case of the Eastern Mediterranean during the Concert and of South America), the great power was successful in achieving its peacetime goals using essentially the same technology that was available to regional actors. Second, in several cases regional military presence was principally the duty of the great power's older, less technologically advanced forces (the South American case, the French African cases, and, to some degree, the Eastern Mediterranean Concert case). Third, in most of the cases where technology does seem to have mattered, it involved the tailoring of particular technologies (air power; air mobility) to meet the particular military threats of the region (disrespect for British authority in distant areas; rapidly developing but lightly armed domestic instability or insurgency).

Fourth and perhaps most interesting, in these cases where technology made a difference it was the possession of *particular technologies* rather than the possession of technological *superiority* that mattered. Certain technologies—for example, radio communication or air bombardment capabilities—were useful to the great power given the nature of its goals and the nature of its opponents. It was not the relative level of technology possessed by the players or the development of advanced-state-of-the-art forces that figured prominently in the story but the intelligent employment of existing technology to solve particular problems. In other words, the key feature was not that the great power had access to technologies that could not conceivably have been available to regional players or to great power competitors, or that the great power was pushing the technological envelope to new limits, but rather that the great power creatively used available technologies to make the problem of peacetime presence easier to manage.

Proposition 6: Training, Discipline, and Professionalism Matter

Repeatedly, a critical force multiplier was the superior training, discipline, and professionalism of the great power's forces. This was a common theme in every case examined. Better training, discipline, and professionalism not only permitted relatively small forces to deal with numerically superior adversaries, but provided great power forces with flexibility and the ability to adapt to rapidly changing conditions. It thus played an important role in foreclosing options to potential adversaries.

Obviously, technology and training go hand in hand: the first demands the second, and the second permits effective use of the first. Nonetheless, to the extent that there is a budgetary trade-off between technological improvement and increased training, education, and morale, the cases suggest the importance of not neglecting the latter. Less clear, and worth further investigation, is the appropriate balance between focused, mission-specific training, designed to maximize capability to meet particular threats, and training aimed at maximizing ability to respond to a range of challenges. Overall, however, the importance of investing in human capital is clear.

Proposition 7: Staying Power Matters

This is really two propositions packaged together. First, great powers interested in imposing order and institutions on a region need "staying power," defined in terms of ability to support ongoing major military operations. Under some circumstances, the military forces needed to shape events may have to stay awhile, and to stay in large numbers. Limited French logistical ability to support forces in the field, for example, constrained their options in Chad and Rwanda, undercutting French ability to shape outcomes there. This proposition thus underscores the importance both of investing in appropriate logistical "tail" and of developing a base infrastructure in the region. Again to return to the French experience for illustration, the network of bases and airstrips available to French forces was critical to France's ability to respond quickly and forcefully to emerging political and military events.

Second and more important, great powers need "staying power" defined in terms of being able to remain in the region for the long haul. "Shaping" doesn't happen quickly. Indeed, it may be an open-ended commitment. This seems to be how the British regarded their South American commitment, and how the French regard their African ones. Thus effective "shaping" is likely to demand a basic political consensus within the great power on the wisdom or necessity of remaining engaged in the region and of paying the price of that engagement.

This proposition is logically connected to earlier ones. If peacetime military presence is aimed at deterring particular actions by revisionist players, it will require constant vigilance (as illustrated in the Eastern Mediterranean cases). If the goal is preserving particular governments or ensuring that whoever governs is favorably disposed (as, for example, in the French cases), this too represents an open-ended commitment. And if the overall objective requires transforming domestic social, economic, or political conditions (as with the United States in the Caribbean), it is likely to take a long, long time.

Obviously, in this context "staying power" involves picking objectives that will be sustainable in the long haul and creating the domestic political mechanisms or consensus that will permit long-term engagement. In other words, if economic and political resources are not sufficient for the long haul, this means reducing political goals. Declining economic power, as Britain experienced in the interwar years, or failure to maintain political support, as occurred in the United States at the close of the Progressive period, can force a retrenchment or abandonment of "shaping" efforts.

Proposition 8: In Democracies, Public and Legislative Opinion Is Likely to Set Overall Policy Parameters

Our cases suggested two very interesting historical lessons about the impact of public and legislative opinion on the ability of a democratic great power to use peacetime forward presence and engagement to shape regional developments. First, in the cases we examined there was little evidence that public or legislative opinion typically acted as a significant direct or immediate limit on great power action. Although in a few situations governments found or felt themselves constrained, in general they seem to have had a free hand to implement peacetime presence policies.

Second, however, in several of the cases we examined, public and legislative opinion set critical parameters on overall policy—by dictating national goals, by limiting budgets, or by prohibiting certain actions on ideological grounds. British policymakers during the interwar years, for example, found themselves constrained by a public and parliament that viewed war as an unacceptable political tool and that placed severe constraints on military expenditures—both of which necessarily constrained British regional efforts. Similarly, while French presidents had an impressively free hand in setting African policy, the overall scope of what was possible was limited by laws that effectively prohibited the deployment of conscripts overseas, thus limiting the logistical infrastructure that French leaders could draw upon and the scale of any African intervention. The case of American involvement in the Caribbean is perhaps even more interesting: while American public opinion through the teens was broadly supportive and the executive branch faced little opposition in the implementation of its interventionist policies, the "return to normalcy," that is to isolationism, in the 1920s dictated a fundamentally changed policy toward the region.

The lesson here seems to be that great power governments need to be sensitive to the need to maintain public support for their "shaping" efforts, at least if they wish to pursue these policies consistently in the long run.

Proposition 9: In the Long Run, "Winning Minds" Is Key

Ultimately, the success of efforts to shape regional order and institutions depends on influencing how foreign leaders or masses view their situation. In the simplest situations and in the shortest time frames, this may simply mean convincing a would-be adversary that it cannot achieve its foreign policy goal through military means and that it makes no sense to try. More generally and in the longer run, however, "shaping" is likely to involve a more fundamental change in how leaders and peoples in a region think about who they are, what their goals are, and how they can best go about trying to achieve those goals. It involves getting regional players to conclude they share the aspirations of the great power. Our cases suggest that to be successful in the long run, military presence must be viewed as an integrated part of overall "shaping" efforts, not as something separate.

Perhaps the clearest examples can be found in the French cases. The success of French efforts hinged on convincing African leaders that their interests were served by remaining within the French *chasse gardée*. In part, this meant making sure it *was* in their interest—making sure that African leaders who followed the French lead were protected from domestic threats and were able to reward supporters or demonstrate domestic economic or political successes. In part, though, it meant making sure they understood themselves as sharing some common purpose with France, or saw themselves as being part of a common cultural or personal community. To use the terminology now popular in the social sciences, French "shaping" efforts aimed at "constructing" a distinctive francophone African identity that left France in a parental role.

Similarly, consider the case of the British in South America. The key to British success was that Latin American elites had come to share British presumptions that free trade would be beneficial. Given this shared identification with free trade, British military efforts could largely be simply symbolic.

By contrast, despite America's overwhelming military power and its consequent ability essentially to determine who would rule various Caribbean nations, the United States was unable to reshape the Caribbean into a Progressive bastion. The failure to create either an elite or mass public with commitment to progressive goals doomed American policy to failure. (Here it may be useful to remember proposition 7: "staying power" matters.)

"Winning minds"—constructing regional identities in ways that encourage cooperation with the great power and convincing regional players that they share the great power's goals—is obviously difficult. It is not in any sense a classical military task. Nonetheless, military presence is clearly a factor, for better or worse. A military presence that underscores or exacerbates cultural, "civilizational," or ideological clashes is likely in the long run to prove unsustainable or counterproductive.

Proposition 10: "Shaping" Domestic Politics Is Very Difficult
Perhaps the most important finding of this study, though, is that when the great power's objectives involve more than deterring particular external actions, this can prove very difficult. Concern is thus warranted, given the expansive scope of post–Cold War American goals. The cases suggest that even overwhelming military predominance may be insufficient to shape a region when the great power's objectives involve domestic transformation. The clearest illustration is the American experience in the Caribbean: continuous American intervention provided a certain amount of surface stability, but failed to result in the construction of effective democratic political institutions. In Africa, the French began with a much higher level of political and intellectual penetration, based on the colonial legacy, and they pursued much more limited goals (the preservation of French influence versus the American goal of building stable government) while tolerating a higher level of political instability and violence. Even so, they, like the British during the interwar years in the Arab world, found their influence gradually declining and their ability to shape events decreasing.

Implications

Assuming for a moment that these propositions are correct, what does this suggest about post–Cold War U.S. efforts to use U.S. military power to encourage the development of a safer, more prosperous, and more democratic world, and, more specifically, about post–September 11 U.S. efforts to create a global environment hostile to terrorism?

It suggests the value of forward presence, with carefully tailored forces capable of speedy reaction, foreclosing options to the adversary, and designed with an eye to particular American goals in the region and good intelligence concerning the specific threats to those goals. In some cases, it may be desirable to reduce presence to low levels, while in other cases it may be necessary not only to be present offshore but in country. While technology may be useful, technological improvements at the margin are not likely to be cost effective. On the other hand, well-trained and highly professional forces may be critically important. Ultimately, peacetime "shaping" is about changing (or reinforcing) how foreign leaders and ordinary citizens think about politics—how they view themselves, their world, and the problems they face. Military activities may affect how individuals view these, not only by foreclosing options but by forcing individuals to rethink their basic premises, but this may take a long time and some military activities may be counterproductive. In its peacetime military policies, the United States thus needs to think about the long haul, recognizing there are no quick solutions and that its policies will need to be politically and economically sustainable across a period of decades. This may mean scaling back political goals to levels consistent with the means at America's disposal. The United States also needs to recognize that many of the domestic transformations it implicitly envisions are very difficult to accomplish.

The September 11, 2001, terrorist attacks drove home to American policymakers and the American public the need to use American power to shape a safer, more secure world order. The practical puzzle of how to use military forces to achieve peacetime political influence—of how to use peacetime military presence to prevent unwanted developments and to persuade friends and potential adversaries to join in the order and institutions sought by the United States—remains. American military victories in Afghanistan and Iraq have underscored the importance of solving this puzzle: the defeat of the Taliban and overthrow of Saddam Hussein may have been a necessary precondition for "reshaping" Central Asia and the Middle East, but the difficult task of winning the peace—of building a stable, liberal, democratic order—still remains. In the end, there are unlikely to be easy answers. As this study suggests, however, careful comparative study of the great powers' historical experience can yield important insights.

Appendix

Summary of Cases

Chapter 1: Britain in the Eastern Mediterranean, 1816–1852

Naval power played a key role in Britain's ability to shape the regional political environment in the eastern Mediterranean and the Levant in the three and a half decades following the Napoleonic Wars. British leaders pursued three goals in the region: peace with honor, prosperity, and progress, and for the most part achieved all three. Success depended in large measure on *military capabilities and presence*:

- Britain achieved its goals in the eastern Mediterranean despite a weak and debilitated army. The British army was scattered across the globe for home and imperial defense and was unavailable for deployment in the region; available forces were inferior to regional upstart Egypt's army.
- The British Royal Navy was the cornerstone of British influence over political developments in the region. Regional powers' navies were far weaker in overall capabilities, and they could not maintain as consistent a presence in the region.
- The Royal Navy was an effective instrument of policy despite its relative stagnancy in terms of technological advances, and its failure to maintain technological superiority over other regional powers. Britain's

comparative advantage centered on training and seamanship rather than a technological edge.
- Consistent, operationally capable forward presence and access to local bases facilitated rapid response to problems and crises, and minimized the occurrence of such events by deterring possible challengers to the status quo, with the important exception of inland military faits accomplis.

Britain's ability to achieve its goals in the eastern Mediterranean was also facilitated, conditioned, and constrained by a number of *nonmilitary factors*. Consider:

- The Britons led the way in terms of international trade and finance, though this distinction did not supplant the need for military forces in the region. Limited financial ties and mutually beneficial trade relations between Britain and local powers that left neither particularly vulnerable made these avenues of political influence only mildly effective.
- With rare exceptions, British political penetration of regional powers was quite limited and played very little role in the achievement of British objectives in the region. Diplomacy in conjunction with military demonstrations was more efficacious than the minimal political influence exercised from within regional states.
- While British defense spending was constrained for much of this period by political leaders' and citizens' concerns about the economy, domestic political factors played a minimal role in constraining British actions abroad. Foreign secretaries were occasionally mindful of public opinion, but more often led or even manipulated it to their advantage.
- International regimes and institutions did have an impact on great power interactions during this period and went a long way toward preserving peace and the status quo. However, their immediate effect on Britain's ability to achieve its regional aims was quite modest:
    - The Concert of Europe neither dictated British foreign policy nor prevented Britain from using force in the region. Its encouragement of status quopreservation was consonant with British aims.
    - Britain's call for an international antislavery regime was widely accepted and narrowly implemented. As the only state willing to implement the regime, Britain's ability to stop and search suspicious vessels provided an advantage in the Mediterranean, but one surely counteracted by the need to deploy antislave cruisers worldwide.

- Other great powers had the ability to use force in the region, with France and Russia the most likely, and most capable, candidates. Russia's ability to project force abroad in massive concentrations was suspect, however, and France really only became militarily competitive with Britain toward the end of the period.
- Though the Ottoman Empire's aims were often consonant with British objectives, revisionist Egypt posed a continual challenge. However, the Egyptians were forced to rely upon the military fait accompli, conducted sufficiently inland so as to be out of the Royal Navy's reach. Rapid inland military action was the only viable option for pressuring the Britons, aside from the tricky diplomacy of playing them off the French and Russians.

Britain achieved its overarching *goals in the region*—peace with honor, prosperity, and progress—with varying degrees of success:

- Achievement of peace (with honor) is reflected in the characterization of this period as part of the *Pax Britannica*. Britain at least temporarily deterred revisionist Egypt from taking aggressive action on several occasions, and Britain's complicity in some multilateral actions promoted peace or the rapid conclusion of ongoing conflicts. In addition, Britain reassured the leaders of the crumbling Ottoman Empire, prolonging the life span of that state (and perhaps forestalling the violence that accompanied its ultimate demise).
- Promotion of prosperity is evident in Britain's effective protection of its economic interests abroad, from both default and piracy. More important, Britain successfully protected its communications with, and its future short trading route with, India. British cruisers also helped to keep sea lanes open for increasingly freer trade.
- Britain's actions in the region resulted in some progress, as well. "Progress" here refers to a nineteenth century British sense of enlightenment, which comprises rejection of slavery, embracement of liberalism, and the navigation of the seas. British success in these areas is evident.
- While promoting the causes mentioned above, Britain did not encourage the peoples in the eastern Mediterranean and Levant to adopt constitutional democracy; thus, we can say very little about Britain's capacity to evoke domestic political change.

Chapter 2: Great Britain in the Eastern Mediterranean, 1919–1937

During the relatively peaceful period between World Wars I and II, Britain enjoyed regional prominence in the eastern Mediterranean and Levant, but was experiencing relative global decline. To maintain the status quo established after World War I, maintain peace, and preserve British primacy in this crucial region, British leaders used their overextended military resources in a number of ways, sometimes successfully, other times failing. Region-specific British *military capabilities* included:

- Garrisons and army personnel located on site in the Levant, though in modest complements, since the lion's share of British land forces were committed to imperial defense and administration elsewhere. These troops were more important for maintaining internal order in British dependencies than for deployment as a concentrated force abroad.
- The Royal Air Force (RAF), which reflected a new military dimension inaccessible to the peoples of the region. Coercive bombing techniques using aging RAF planes became a cheap, effective method of policing large expanses of sparsely populated land without costly, massive troop commitments.
- The Royal Navy, which emerged from World War I quite strong but was reduced time and again due to cost cutting and compliance with international naval arms limitation agreements. By the second decade of the interwar years, British naval preeminence was at best regional, and even there quite questionable indeed.
- The British did not consistently employ the latest military technology, and when they did it cut both ways. Neglect of the navy contributed to the Royal Navy's relative decline, but naval capacity still clearly exceeded that of small regional powers, and it could make a remarkable visual impact according to some. The RAF proved an invaluable asset for maintaining internal order in British dependencies, but not in urban settings, where the presence of lightly armed troops and the creation of networks of bribed informants were critical, though not always effective.
- Local presence and the ability to respond rapidly to problems or crises were mainstays of the British military configuration in the region. However, occasional lapses (often due to worldwide commitments) and the difficulty projecting into rugged inland areas proved costly at times for Britain.
- The active presence of British soldiers and administrators, in combination, within regional states was integral in the (re)direction of regional states' policies to minimize friction with British aims, though possibly provoking nationalist sentiment in response. Withdrawal of the capability to intervene in domestic affairs is associated with a diminution of British political influence in the region.

Britain's ability to achieve its goals in the eastern Mediterranean was also facilitated, conditioned, and constrained by a number of *nonmilitary factors*. Consider:

- Britain's economic slumps and relative decline globally were not reflected in a degradation of economic leverage in the region. Mild sensitivity to changes in trade took little away from British influence exercised through subsidies to local leaders, though these were reduced from wartime levels. Oil was an important strategic resource, but Britain's supply at the time came primarily from Persia.
- British political penetration of regional states and dependencies varied widely, but in the most dramatic cases gave British leadership control over these actors' foreign and defense policies. British administrators were typically inclined to allow local leaders to address domestic issues if they did not impinge upon Britain's strategic interests.
- Domestic political factors constrained British action abroad to a much greater degree than in earlier periods, owing much to the dramatic expansion of the franchise to voters pushing for peace and inward-looking governance, but also to the institutionalized drive for parsimony, reflected in the influence of the Treasury over defense spending. In any case, these factors tended to have a general impact rather than creating immediate constraints on British action in crisis situations.
- International regimes and institutions played integral roles in the history of the interwar period, yet their effect on British policy and action in the region was uneven. Consider the two most prominent examples:
- The League of Nations, though involved in arbitration of some regional disputes, put few real constraints on British ability to use force. It also tended to reinforce the status quo, much to the satisfaction of the Britons.
  - The naval armament limitations regime, the most prominent example of which is the Washington Conference and resulting treaties of 1921–1922, had an impact on British relative capacity, though that impact is sometimes difficult to separate from the impetus of parsimony in defense spending. For much of the period the cornerstone of the scattered Royal Navy's peacetime forces—cruisers—were unregulated, leaving the British a great deal of freedom.
- Other great powers, particularly France and, later, Italy were competitors of the British in the Mediterranean. France and Britain's policies were more accommodative than combative, but Italy's aggression against Abyssinia was not deterred by British presence in the eastern

Mediterranean, nor was it reversed in response to Britain's expressed disapproval of the act.
- Regional states—and especially dependencies—though often interested in pursuing goals at odds with British aims, had few options for pressuring the British. British military presence and/or internal dissension within these states often stood in the way of a concerted nationalist attempt to expel British agents. Independent states like Turkey with modest military means and the diplomatic ability to appeal to other great powers were capable of pressuring the British on occasion.

British leaders concerned with the *regional goals* of preserving the regional status quo, maintaining peace, and promoting British primacy in the region had a record of early successes but that become increasingly spotty over time. Consider:

- In the effort to maintain peace, Britain sought to deter potential aggressors and curtail regional conflicts at an early stage. Clear examples of deterrence success are hard to come by and perhaps not so meaningful, since Britain's control of its dependencies' foreign policies from within would presumably preclude some conflicts. However, we cannot dismiss the British failure to deter Italy from attacking Abyssinia as being at odds with British aims.
- In the interest of preserving the status quo, Britain sought to maintain internal order within dependencies and to prolong direct British influence on policy. Several bloody uprisings show that British presence was insufficient to deter internal conflict in urban settings, though British armed forces were usually capable of controlling such conflicts quickly and effectively once they broke out. The pressure brought upon Britain within these dependencies sometimes precipitated early withdrawal of British agents, and allowed for these dependencies to become independent states, thus disrupting the carefully constructed post–World War I status quo.
- Britain's stake in remaining the primary great power in the region was a substantial one. For strategic reasons, including access to the Suez Canal for passage to India and Singapore and access to oil to fill future energy needs, keeping other great powers out of the region was a priority. Britain retained a great deal of influence in the region and retained access to the Suez, but by the end of the period, American and Italian economic interests were making inroads into the oil-producing areas, and challenges to British primacy appeared on the horizon.

Chapter 3 Summary: The Royal Navy in South America, 1850–1900
British Interests and Goals in the Region: Promoting Free Trade

British interests in South America in the second half of the nineteenth century were very modest. With neither imperial nor strategic interests, South America remained peripheral to the study of British foreign policy. Britain's overarching interest was to promote free trade policies throughout the region. Since the British economy was the most efficient in the nineteenth century, a free trade policy in South America would naturally favor British trade. From the earliest South American independence movements Britain encouraged the emergence of independent, free-trading states throughout the region. Britain did not directly seek to shape the peacetime environment in any other way. Instead, the Foreign Office maintained a firm policy of neutrality and nonintervention. Even in times of domestic crises and wars in the region, British foreign policy has been aptly described as one of "perfect indifference" and "masterly inactivity." So long as the regional states professed policies of free trade and did not specifically threaten the interests of British merchants, Britain largely maintained its neutrality and nonintervention. While free trade was Britain's primary objective, there were two distant but related objectives: curbing any resurgent great power imperialism and paving the way to progress and civilization through the benefits of international trade.

The Nature of British Influence in the Region

Although the years from 1850 to 1900 were considered the heyday for British gunboat diplomacy, there was a marked decline in naval deployments and activities in South American waters during this period. While Britain was widely acknowledged as the foremost global power, British forces committed to the region were quite small. Many of the regional navies were better equipped than the Royal Navy's South American Squadron. At times, there were only four British warships in South American waters and military personnel serving the region fell to five hundred. These small naval forces, however, were emblematic of a larger British military force. The Royal Navy's global force cast a long shadow and appeared germane to regional actors, even from a great distance. As one historian concluded, even though British naval forces were relatively small in the region, "To a Latin American minister . . . the [British] consuls' power to summon cannons appeared a reality." It was this perception of a distant force that contributed to British influence in the region, not the token forces that composed the Royal Navy's South American Squadron. The South American Squadron was a symbolic reminder of the Royal Navy's capabilities, not a reflection of these capabilities.

There were other sources of influence that facilitated British influence. First, the Royal Navy enjoyed a special status for the role it played in assisting many independence movements in the early years of the century. Second, there was an ideological affinity that many South American elites had for British liberalism. Third, with London serving as the center of international finance, good relations with Great Britain were valued by both governments and merchants in South America.

The British Success in Promoting Free Trade in South America

The British were successful in promoting free trade in the region. But given the fact that regional actors stood to benefit from policies of free trade, this can hardly be considered a surprising foreign policy success. In the end, the British devoted very little to achieve these limited objectives. And in the end, they achieved them.

These goals were achieved with a very small and obsolete naval force in the South American Squadron. By keeping the most threatening forces at a distance, like a trump card that is never played, the Royal Navy's larger forces may have, somewhat ironically, contributed to British success in shaping the peacetime environment. If a major battle fleet had been deployed, regional opposition to British interests may have hardened. One British diplomat in South America depicted the complex relationship between influence and force: "consuls without cannons had little impact, yet the use of warships had often inflamed local feelings and been counter productive." In South America, British consuls had cannon, and even from a distance, these cannon appeared salient to the regional actors in South America.

The liberal goal of bringing peace and progress by free trade was not fully achieved. Many free traders in the Victorian Era like Cobden and Bright argued that "free trade was the panacea for all ills: it brought prosperity to all, it ensured international goodwill, it prevented war." Clearly free trade failed to bring about these benefits in South America. Instead, the period from 1850 to 1900 was one full of conflict and war in South America. Throughout these conflicts Britain maintained its "perfect indifference" and refused to intervene. British efforts to shape the peacetime environment within the domestic realm of South American states were minimal and unsuccessful.

Chapter Four: The United States Navy in the Caribbean, 1903–1920

American Interests: Strategic Control of the Region and Shaping Its Political Environment in Peacetime

U.S. naval presence in the Caribbean in the early years of the twentieth century constitutes the first sustained American attempt to shape a peacetime political environment. Naval presence throughout the region sought to achieve two interdependent objectives, one military in nature and the other political in nature. American foreign policy in the Caribbean was the first time that American national security interests were directly linked to economic and political stability in other states.

Military Goals

Once the United States committed to the unilateral construction of the Panama Canal, naval preeminence in the Caribbean became a vital national interest. The prime concern was to prevent another great power from gaining influence in the region. Naval interventions by Britain, Germany, and Italy during the Venezuelan debt crisis of 1902–1903 pointed out how indebtedness and domestic instability within Caribbean states might come to justify European intervention in the region.

Political and Economic Goals

One way of denying European powers the justification for intervention was to accept responsibility for the political and economic stability in the region. This was largely the point of the Roosevelt Corollary to the Monroe Doctrine. If the European powers were to be kept out of the Caribbean, the United States must promote a certain level of political and economic stability within the factious republics of the Caribbean. To help achieve these goals, the United States turned to its military, especially its naval forces.

American Power: The Sources of American Influence in the Region

Three factors contributed to American ability to shape the peacetime environment in the Caribbean.

Military Power

Military power was overwhelmingly in favor of the United States in the region. In any measure of material capabilities—especially in naval force levels—no regional power could approach the United States. In terms of other great powers, all had withdrawn any appreciable forces from the region. This left the United States as the only regional naval power.

Domestic Support

In addition to military preeminence, intervention in the Caribbean was encouraged by domestic reformers who embraced a liberal internationalist foreign policy. The interventionism in the Caribbean fit nicely with the "activism" that was the hallmark for the Progressive Era. American foreign policy in the

Caribbean can be seen as a logical extension of Progressivism and therefore received a fair degree of support from American Progressives. There was a marriage of convenience between the military strategists who envisioned a strong naval presence in the Caribbean as a vital national interest and the liberal internationalists who envisioned a strong naval presence as a way to impose order and foster reform in the troubled Caribbean states.

International Law and Norms

The third factor encouraging successful American intervention in the Caribbean rested on international law and norms. In its decision in the case of the Venezuelan debt crisis, The Hague reiterated the right of states to intervene to protect property and nationals. The United States interpreted this as a right to intervene to bring stability and avoid damage to property. No other powers challenged this right for the United States to intervene in the Caribbean.

American Success and Failure in Shaping the Peacetime Environment in the Caribbean

While the United States succeeded in protecting entrance to the Panama Canal and successfully deterred the encroachment of any other major powers into the region, its efforts to bring democracy, political stability, and economic development to the region failed. The American experience in the Caribbean during the Progressive Era should serve as a reminder of the difficulties inherent to a policy of fostering democracy and economic growth and stability abroad. Even when the United States possessed overwhelming material capabilities, near constant naval presence in the region, little international opposition, overwhelming economic leverage, and strong domestic support, it was still unable to transform the political institutions of nearby neighboring states.

Chapter 5: *La Chasse Gardée*: Post–World War II French West Africa (c. 1945–1970) and
Chapter 6: *Toujours la Chasse Gardée?*: French Power and Influence in Late Twentieth Century Francophone Central Africa (c. 1970–1995)

France's manipulation of events in its former African colonies is integrally linked to the French leadership's perception of France as a major global player during the second half of the twentieth century. French leaders used the sub-Saharan African colonies in order to regain, and then preserve, the political prestige, economic strength, and military capability that had distinguished France on the world stage before World War II. In spite of changes in leadership over time (from the Fourth Republic to the Fifth, from President de Gaulle through the post-Gaullists to the Socialists), postwar French interaction in sub-Saharan Africa reflected, for the most part, a coherent, consistent, carefully managed and largely bipartisan policy designed to retain and shape these countries as sources of strategically important materials, manpower, economic and military cooperation, political influence, and the export and perpetuation of French culture.

The three main challenges for France in achieving its goals during the second half of the twentieth century were: *first*, the traditional and ancient challenge of preserving and extending French power and influence against the encroachments of the English-speaking world, often broadly termed "*les Anglo-Saxons*" but personified in members of the Atlantic Alliance, particularly the United States; *second*, staving off determined attempts at influence in the developing world on the part of the Soviet Union and its allies; and *third*, the need to offer a form of "independence" to its former colonies which maintained their dependency within the French sphere of influence. This last might be considered a policy of deflecting revolution in favor of cooperative evolution.

France's behavior as a great power in West and Central Africa is examined in these chapters along dimensions which include France's military capability and security policy, other resources and constraints which have affected France's influence in Africa over time, and France's consequent capacity to shape a stable peacetime political and economic environment in its former colonies. Two main focal points are evident from the historical research so far: (1) France succeeded to a remarkable degree in *shaping* the peacetime environment in its former colonies according to its preferences, but (2) France's *policing* duties as the "gendarme of Africa" in this environment showed some significant limitations as France entered the last quarter of the twentieth century.

As a part of the prestige-conscious and politically independent policy formulated by Charles de Gaulle just prior to the African colonies' independence in 1960, and perpetuated by later French presidents, France successfully *shaped* the peacetime environment to a remarkable degree in West and Central Africa in order to obtain the desired resources, strategic flexibility, and global prestige and power in the region. The shape that this policy took has often been given the nickname of "*chasse gardée*," as in the title of these two chapters. The legal and structural components of this policy were provided by the military cooperation agreements signed with France by most of the newly independent francophone African nations in 1960. The chapters focus mainly, but not entirely, on military factors: troop presence and intervention forces, intelligence capacity, and arms transfers, which France used in the context of these cooperation agreements to control the postcolonial environment. However, economic and political factors were as important as the military dimension in establishing and maintaining French influence.

Key factors in maintaining military dominance were:

(1) The French command structure was centralized ("Cartesian"). The military command structure and intelligence networks were well integrated. Over the past four decades, France's Africa policy has been controlled centrally by the president's office with very little parliamentary interference and (counterintuitively) *infrequent* policy input from the French Ministry of Defense.

(2) The French had a preponderant military presence within the region. Land-based troop contingents were maintained in at least four key countries throughout the two case-study periods. This capacity was combined with a France-based rapid intervention force.

(3) French officers and trainers were kept in charge of African army units well after the independence of the colonies in 1960. In addition, French presidents and intelligence operatives made continued use of ties forged with African military and political elites who had served in France's colonial wars and with the Free French in World War II. France's "situational awareness," the information flow, and consequent flexibility of response was maintained at a very high level.

(4) France dominated the arms sales, military aid, repairs, maintenance, and military training of francophone African militaries.

(5) Adding to the flexibility of its long-term alliances, France had a high tolerance for: (a) socialism, which lessened Soviet influence considerably, and (b) authoritarian dictatorships and military regimes, even though it prided itself on being a cradle of democracy. The reasons for this included ease of control because of a continuity of leadership, loyalties, and personal ties to long-term rulers, and also the fact that military leadership increased both military and political "interoperability." The political loyalty of various African leaders was much more important than any commitment they might display toward a democratic ideology. A coup d'état would be tolerated or even approved if the resulting leader appeared to be loyal to France or at least pragmatically aware of France's dominant power.

(6) France had extensive economic control of the African economies through the Franc Zone.

As a result of this "cooperative" shaping process, which can also be characterized as a deeply rooted, flexible, and well-integrated military, economic, political, and cultural penetration of the African region, France was able to respond to, and manage, most of threats to its position as the dominant great power in the francophone sphere of influence. In spite of its predominance, however, France was unable to *completely* control or eliminate the larger-scale, more regionalized conflicts that occurred in the francophone African region after the 1960s. In other words, France was well prepared for the smaller scale policing duties, for example, predicting, assisting, preventing, or otherwise managing the various military coups d'état like those in the Central African Republic. However, there were some significant transport problems, and the base troops and rapid intervention forces had to be composed of professional enlisted men because French conscript forces (the majority of French troops) could not be sent overseas without parliamentary approval. France's leaders found that long-term insurgent warfare (like the war in Chad), involving external interference on the part of regional neighbors (like Libya), and its uncritical support of dictatorial regimes (like that of Juvenal Habyarimana in Rwanda) were much more of a challenge to its military and political capabilities, and presented more severe challenges to the political tolerance of French citizens.

Bibliography

Primary Sources

Caperton, William B. "History of U.S. Naval Operations Under Command of Rear Admiral W. B. Caperton, January 1915 to March 1919," 400 Pages of the Naval Records Collection of the Office of Naval Records and Library, Subject File ZN (Personnel) 1911–1927, Record Group 45, National Archives, Washington D.C.

Ship Log Books of the United States Navy. Record Group 41, General Records, 1798–1910. National Archives, Washington D.C.

Translations of Messages Sent in Cipher (Ten Volumes) Record Group 45, General Records, 1798–1910. National Archives, Washington D.C. These records consist of loosely bound collection of messages sent from Washington to various naval vessels. The majority of the ten volumes represent the years from 1895 to 1910.

Translations of Messages Received in Cipher (Six Volumes) Record Group 45, General Records, 1798–1910. National Archives, Washington D.C. These consist of the messages sent to the Navy Department in Washington primarily from ships on missions abroad.

Secondary Sources

Adelson, Roger. *London and the Invention of the Middle East: Money, Power, and War, 1902–1922.* New Haven, Conn.: Yale University Press, 1995.

Anderson, M. S. *The Ascendancy of Europe, 1815–1914.* New York: Longman, 1985.

———. *The Eastern Question, 1774–1923: A Study in International Relations.* New York: St. Martin's Press, 1966.

Anderson, R. C. *Naval Wars in the Levant 1559–1853*. Princeton, N.J.: Princeton University Press, 1952.

Arlinghaus, Bruce E., ed. *Arms for Africa: Military Assistance and Foreign Policy in the Developing World.* Lexington, Mass.: D.C. Heath and Company, 1983.

———. *Military Development in Africa: The Political and Economic Risks of Arms Transfers*. Boulder, Colo.: Westview Press, 1984.

———, ed. *African Security Issues: Sovereignty, Stability, and Solidarity*. Boulder, Colo.: Westview Press, 1984.

———, and Pauline H. Baker, eds. *African Armies: Evolution and Capabilities*. Boulder, Colo.: Westview Press, 1986.

Atkins, Pope. *Latin America in the International System*. Cambridge, Mass.: Harvard University Press, 1977.

Ayoob, Mohammed, "The Security Problematic of the Third World." *World Politics* 43 (January 1991): 257–83.

Azar, Edward E., and Chung-In Moon, eds. *National Security in the Third World: The Management of Internal and External Threats*. Aldershot, U.K.: Edward Elgar Publishing Limited, 1988.

Bach, John. "The Maintenance of Royal Navy Vessels in the Pacific Ocean, 1825–1875." *Mariner's Mirror* (August 1970): 259–73.

Baer, George. *One Hundred Years of Sea Power: The U.S. Navy, 1890–1990*. Stanford, Calif.: Stanford University Press, 1994.

Bailey, Frank Edgar. *British Policy and the Turkish Reform Movement: A Study in Anglo-Turkish Relations, 1826–1853*. New York: Howard Fertig, 1970 [1942].

Bailey, Norman. *Latin America in World Politics*. New York: Walker and Company, 1967.

Barnett, Correlli. *Britain and Her Army, 1509–1970*. New York: William Morrow and Co., 1970.

———. *The Collapse of British Power*. Phoenix Mill, U.K.: Alan Sutton, 1972.

Barros, James. *The League of Nations and the Great Powers: The Greek-Bulgarian Incident, 1925*. Oxford: Oxford University Press, 1970.

Bartlett, C. J. *Great Britain and Sea Power, 1815–1853*. Oxford: Clarendon, 1963.

———. "The Mid-Victorian Re-appraisal of Naval Policy." Pp. 189–208 in *Studies in International History: Essays Presented to W. Norton Medlicott*, edited by K. Bourne and D. C. Watts. London: Longmans, 1967.

———. "Statecraft, Power and Influence." In C.J. Bartlett, ed. *Britain Pre-eminent: Studies of British World Influence in the Nineteenth Century*. New York: St. Martin's Press, 1969.

Bayart, Jean-François. *The State in Africa: The Politics of the Belly*, published in French as *L'État en Afrique: La Politique du Ventre*, translated by Mary Harper, Christopher Harrison, and Elizabeth Harrison. New York: Addison Wesley Longman Publishing, 1993.

Baynham, Simon, ed. *Military Power and Politics in Black Africa*. New York: St. Martin's Press, 1986.

Beales, Derek. *From Castlereagh to Gladstone, 1815–1885*. London: Thomas Nelson and Sons, 1969.
Beeler, John F. *British Naval Policy in the Gladstone-Disraeli Era, 1866–1890*. Stanford, Calif.: Stanford University Press, 1997.
Behrman, Cynthia F. *Victorian Myths of the Sea*. Athens: Ohio University Press, 1977.
Bethel, Leslie. "Britain and Latin America in Historical Perspective." In *Britain and Latin America: A Changing Relationship*, edited by Victor Bulmer-Thomas. Cambridge: Cambridge University Press, 1989.
Bigelow, Robert. "The Wireless in Warfare, 1885–1914." *United States Naval Institute Proceedings* 77, no. 2 (February 1952): 112–34.
Blanco, Richard L. "Reform and Wellington's Post Waterloo Army, 1815–1854." *Military Affairs* 24, no. 3 (fall 1965): 123–31.
Blassingame, John. "The Press and American Intervention in Haiti and the Dominican Republic, 1904–1920." *Caribbean Studies* 9 (July 1969): 27–43.
Blechman, Barry. "The Intervention Dilemma." Pp. 147–58 in *Order and Disorder after the Cold War*, edited by Brad Roberts. Cambridge, Mass.: MIT Press, 1995.
Bond, Brian. *British Military Policy between the Two World Wars*. New York: Oxford University Press, 1980.
———, and Williamson Murray. "The British Armed Forces, 1918–39." Pp. 98–130 in *Military Effectiveness, Volume II: The Interwar Period*, edited by Allan R. Millett and Williamson Murray. Boston: Unwin Hyman, 1988.
Boot, Max. *The Savage Wars of Peace: Small Wars and the Rise of American Power*. New York: Basic Books, 2002.
Booth, Ken. "The Ten-Year Rule—An Unfinished Debate." *Journal of the Royal United Services Institute* 116, no. 663 (1971): 58–63.
Bourne, Kenneth. *The Foreign Policy of Victorian England, 1830–1902*. London: Oxford University Press, 1970.
Brands, H. W. *What America Owes the World: The Struggle for the Soul of Foreign Policy*. New York: Cambridge University Press, 1998.
Brassey, Thomas. *Brassey's Naval Annual/ Brassey's Naval and Shipping Annual*, various years. Portsmouth: J. Griffin and Company.
———. *Papers and Addresses: Naval and Maritime, 1872–1893*. Edited by S. Eardley Wilmot. London: Longmans, Green, and Company, 1894.
Bratton, Michael, and Nicolas van de Walle. *Democratic Experiments in Africa: Regime Transitions in Comparative Perspective*. Cambridge: Cambridge University Press, 1997.
Brecher, Michael, and Jonathan Wilkenfeld. *A Study of Crisis*. Ann Arbor: University of Michigan Press, 1997.
Brodie, Bernard. *Sea Power in the Machine Age*. Princeton, N.J.: Princeton University Press, 1941.
Brown, D. K. *Before the Ironclad: Development of Ship Design, Propulsion and Armament in the Royal Navy, 1815–60*. London: Conway Maritime Press, 1990.

Bryson, Thomas A. *Tars, Turks, and Tankers: The Role of the United States Navy in the Middle East, 1800–1979*. Metuchen, N.J.: Scarecrow Press, 1980.

Bullard, Reader, Sir. *Britain and the Middle East: From the Earliest Times to 1950*. London: Hutchinson's University Library, 1951.

Burr, Robert. *By Reason or Force: Chile and the Balance of Power in South America, 1830–1905*. Berkeley: University of California Press, 1967.

Bush, George W. "Remarks by the President at 2002 Graduation Exercise of the United States Military Academy, West Point, New York." <http://www.whitehouse.gov/news/releases/2002/06/20020601-3.html> (13 May 2003).

Bywater, Hector Charles. *Navies and Nations: A Review of Naval Developments since the Great War*. New York: Houghton, 1927.

Cable, James. *Gunboat Diplomacy: Political Applications of Limited Naval Force*. New York: Praeger, 1971.

Cady, John F. *Foreign Intervention in the Rio de la Plata 1838–1850*. New York: AMS Press, 1969.

Cain, P. J., and A. G. Hopkins. "The Political Economy of British Expansion Overseas, 1750–1914." *The Economic History Review*, second series, 33, no. 4 (November 1980): 463–90.

Calder, Bruce. *The Impact of Intervention: The Dominican Republic during the U.S. Occupation of 1916–1924*. Austin: University of Texas Press, 1984.

Callcott, Wilfred Hardy. *The Caribbean Policy of the United States, 1890–1920*. New York: Octagon Books, 1966.

Carver, Lord. *The Seven Ages of the British Army*. New York: Beaufort Books, 1984.

Chaigneau, Pascal. *La Politique militaire de la France en Afrique*. Paris: Le Centre des Hautes Études sur l'Afrique et l'Asie Modernes (CHEAM), 1984.

Challener, Richard D. *The French Theory of the Nation in Arms 1866–1939*. New York: Russell & Russell, 1965.

Chege, Michael. "Sub-Saharan Africa: Underdevelopment's Last Stand." In *Global Change, Regional Response: The New International Context of Development*, edited by Barbara Stallings, Cambridge: Cambridge University Press, 1995.

Chipman, John. *Veme République et défense de l'Afrique*, translated by R. Manicacci. Paris: Éditions Bosquet, 1986. Originally published in English as *French Military Policy and African Security*, International Institute for Strategic Studies, 1985.

———. *French Power in Africa*. Oxford: Basil Blackwell Ltd., 1989.

Clapham, Christopher. *Third World Politics*. Madison: University of Wisconsin Press, 1985.

Clark, John F., and David E. Gardinier, eds. *Political Reform in Francophone Africa*. Boulder, Colo.: Westview Press, 1997.

Claude, Inis L., Jr. *Swords into Plowshares: The Problems and Progress of International Organization*. 4th ed. New York: Random House, 1984.

Clayton, Anthony. *The British Empire as a Superpower, 1919–1939*. London: Macmillan, 1986.

———. *France, Soldiers and Africa*. London: Brassey's Defence Publishers, 1988.

Clayton, G. D. *Britain and the Eastern Question: Missolonghi to Gallipoli*. London: University of London Press, 1971.

Clodfelter, Michael. *Warfare and Armed Conflicts: A Statistical Reference to Casualty and Other Figures, 1618–1991*, Vol. I. Jefferson, N.C.: McFarland and Company, 1992.

Clogg, Richard. *A Concise History of Greece*. Cambridge: Cambridge University Press, 1992.

Clowes, William Laird. *The Royal Navy: A History from the Earliest Times to the Present* (six volumes). London: Low Marsten and Company, 1913.

———. *The Royal Navy: A History from the Earliest Times to the Present, Volume VI*. London: Chatham Publishing, 1997 [1901].

Cole, D. H., and E. C. Priestley. *An Outline of British Military History, 1660–1937*. London: Sifton Praed, 1937.

Conte, Bernard. "France's African Aid Policy: The End of an Era?" *Review of African Political Economy* 71 (1997): 139–56.

Cooper, John Milton. *The Warrior and the Priest: Woodrow Wilson and Theodore Roosevelt*. Cambridge, Mass.: Harvard University Press, 1983.

Correlates of War Project, Material Capabilities Data Vol. 2.1. <http://cow2.la.psu.edu/>.

Cosmas, Graham. "Cacos and Caudillos: Marines and Counterinsurgency in Hispaniola, 1915–1924." In *New Interpretations in Naval History*, edited by William Roberts and Jack Sweetman. Annapolis, Md.: Naval Institute Press, 1991.

Courtemanche, Regis. *No Need of Glory: The British Navy in American Waters, 1860–1864*. Annapolis, Md.: Naval Institute Press, 1977.

Craig, Gordon A., and Alexander L. George. *Force and Statecraft: Diplomatic Problems of Our Time*. 3rd ed. New York: Oxford University Press, 1995.

Crawley, C.W. "International Relations, 1815–1830." Pp. 668–90 in *The New Cambridge Modern History, Vol. IX*, edited by C.W. Crawley. Cambridge: Cambridge University Press, 1965.

Crimmin, Patricia. "The Royal Navy and the Levant Trade, c.1795–c.1805." In *The British Navy and the Use of Naval Power in the Eighteenth Century*, edited by Jeremy Black and Philip Woodfine. Leicester, U.K.: Leicester University Press, 1988.

Cunningham, Allan. *Eastern Questions in the Nineteenth Century: Collected Essays by Allan Cunningham, Volume Two*. Edited by Edward Ingram. London: Frank Cass, 1993.

Dakin, Douglas. *The Greek Struggle for Independence, 1821–1833*. Berkeley: University of California Press, 1973.

Dallett, Francis James. "The Creation of the Venezuelan Naval Squadron, 1848–1860." *American Neptune* 30, no. 4 (1970): 260–78.

Darwin, John. "Imperialism in Decline? Tendencies in British Imperial Policy between the Wars." *The Historical Journal* 23, no. 3 (September 1980): 657–79.

———. *Britain, Egypt and the Middle East: Imperial Policy in the Aftermath of War, 1918–1922*. London: Macmillan, 1981.

Davis, H. E., J. Finan, and F. T. Peck. *Latin American Diplomatic History: An Introduction*. Baton Rouge: Louisiana State University Press, 1977.

Davis, William Columbus. *The Last Conquistadores: The Spanish Intervention in Peru and Chile, 1863–1866*. Athens: University of Georgia Press, 1950.

Decalo, Samuel. *Historical Dictionary of Chad*. 2nd ed. African Historical Dictionaries No. 13. Metuchen, N.J.: Scarecrow Press, 1987.

———. *Historical Dictionary of Niger*. 2nd ed. African Historical Dictionaries No. 20. Metuchen, N.J.: Scarecrow Press, 1989.

———. *Coups and Army Rule in Africa: Motivations and Constraints*. 2nd ed. New Haven, Conn.: Yale University Press, 1990.

Doughty, Robert A. "The French Armed Forces, 1918–1940." Pp. 39–69 in *Military Effectiveness, Volume II: The Interwar Period*, edited by Allan R. Millett and Williamson Murray. Boston: Unwin Hyman, 1988.

Dupuy, Trevor N. *The Evolution of Weapons and Warfare*. Fairfax, Va.: Hero Books, 1984.

Dupuy, R. Ernest, and William H. Baumer. *The Little Wars of the United States*. New York: Hawthorne Publishers, 1968.

———, and Trevor N. Dupuy. *The Encyclopedia of Military History from 3500 B.C. to the Present*. 2nd. revised edition. New York: Harper and Row, 1986.

Echenberg, Myron. *Colonial Conscripts: The Tirailleurs Sénégalais in French West Africa, 1857–1960*. Portsmouth, N.H.: Heinemann Educational Books, 1991.

Eichengreen, Barry. *Golden Fetters: The Gold Standard and the Great Depression, 1919–1939*. New York: Oxford University Press, 1992.

Eisenach, Eldon. "Progressive Internationalism." Pp. 226–58 in *Progressivism and the New Democracy*, edited by Sidney Milkis and Jerome Mileur. Amherst, Mass.: University of Massachusetts Press, 1999.

Ellis, Stephen. "Liberia 1989–1994. A Study of Ethnic and Spiritual Violence." *African Affairs* 94 (1995): 165–97.

Elrod, Richard B. "The Concert of Europe: A Fresh Look at an International System." *World Politics* 28, no. 2 (January 1976): 159–74.

Fanning, Richard W. *Peace and Disarmament: Naval Rivalry and Arms Control 1922–1933*. Lexington: University Press of Kentucky, 1995.

Farwell, Byron. *Queen Victoria's Little Wars*. New York: Harper and Row, 1972.

Fermandois, Joaquin. "Chile and the Great Powers." Pp. 71–96 in *Great Power Relations in Argentina, Chile, and Antartica*, edited by Michael Morris. New York: St. Martin's Press, 1990.

Ferns, Henry S. *Britain and Argentina in the Nineteenth Century*. New York: Arno Press, 1977.

Ferrell, Robert. *American Diplomacy: A History*. New York: W.W. Norton and Company, 1975.

Ferris, John Robert. "Treasury Control, the Ten Year Rule and British Service Policies, 1919–1924." *The Historical Journal* 30, no. 4 (1987): 859–83.

———. *Men, Money and Diplomacy: The Evolution of British Strategic Policy, 1919–1926*. Ithaca, N.Y.: Cornell University Press, 1989.

Fiske, Bradley. *From Midshipmen to Rear Admiral.* New York: The Century Company, 1919.

Foltz, William J. *From French West Africa to the Mali Federation.* New Haven, Conn.: Yale University Press, 1965.

———, and Henry S. Bienen, eds. *Arms and the African.* New Haven, Conn.: Yale University Press, 1985.

Fortescue, John. "The Army." In *Early Victorian England, 1830–1865.* New York: Oxford University Press, 1934.

Friends Committee on National Legislation. *Washington Newsletter,* May 1998.

Fromkin, David. *A Peace to End All Peace: Creating the Modern Middle East 1914–1922.* New York: Henry Holt and Company, 1989.

Fuller, J. F. C. *Armament and History: A Study of the Influence of Armament on History from the Dawn of Classical Warfare to the Second World War.* New York: Charles Scribner's Sons, 1945.

Gallagher, John. "The Decline, Revival and Fall of the British Empire." Pp. 73–152 in *The Decline, Revival and Fall of the British Empire: The Ford Lectures and Other Essays,* edited by Anil Seal. Cambridge: Cambridge University Press, 1982.

———, and Ronald Robinson. "The Imperialism of Free Trade." *The Economic History Review,* second series, 6, no. 1 (1953): 1–15.

Gershoni, Israel. "Rejecting the West: The Image of the West in the Teachings of the Muslim Brotherhood, 1928–1939." Pp. 370–90 in *The Great Powers in the Middle East, 1919–1939,* edited by Uriel Dann, New York: Holmes and Meier, 1988.

Gill, Stephen, and David Law. *The Global Political Economy: Perspectives, Problems and Policies.* Baltimore: The Johns Hopkins University Press, 1988.

Glete, Jan. *Navies and Nations: Warships, Navies, and State-Building in Europe and America, 1500–1860,* 2 vols. Stockholm: Almqvist and Wiksell International, 1993.

Goldberg, Mitchell. "Naval Operations of the United States Pacific Squadron in 1861." *American Neptune* 33, no. 1 (January 1973): 41–47.

Goldstein, Erik. "Great Britain and Greater Greece, 1917–1920." *The Historical Journal* 32, no. 2 (June 1989): 339–56.

Gordon, G. A. H. *British Seapower and Procurement between the Wars: A Reappraisal of Rearmament.* London: Macmillan, 1988.

———. "The British Navy, 1918–1945." Pp. 161–80 in *Navies and Global Defense: Theories and Strategy,* edited by Keith Neilson and Elizabeth Jane Errington. Westport, Conn.: Praeger, 1995.

Gordon, Philip H. *A Certain Idea of France: French Security Policy and the Gaullist Legacy.* Princeton, N.J.: Princeton University Press, 1993.

Graham, Gerald S. *The Politics of Naval Supremacy.* Cambridge: Cambridge University Press, 1965.

———, and R. A. Humphreys. *The Navy and South America, 1807–1823.* London: Naval Records Society, 1962.

Graham, Richard. "Robinson and Gallagher in Latin America: The Meaning of Informal Empire." Pp. 217–21 in *Imperialism: The Robinson and Gallagher Controversy*, edited by W. R. Lewis. New York: Franklin Watts, 1976.

Grainger, John D. *The Royal Navy in the River Plate, 1806–1807*. Aldershot, U.K.: Scholar Press (for the Naval Records Society), 1996.

Griffin, Donald. "The American Navy at Work on the Brazil Station, 1827–1960." *American Neptune* 19, no. 2 (March 1959): 39–59.

Gruening, Ernest. "Conquest of Haiti and Santo Domingo." *Current History*, 1922.

Hackmann, Willem. *Seek and Strike: Sonar, Anti-submarine Warfare and the Royal Navy, 1914–54*. London: Her Majesty's Stationery Office, 1984.

Hagan, Kenneth J. *American Gunboat Diplomacy and the Old Navy, 1877–1889*. Westport, Conn.: Greenwood Press, 1973.

Haggard, Stephan. *Developing Nations and the Politics of Global Integration*. Washington, D.C.: Brookings Institution, 1995.

Hamilton, C. I. *Anglo-French Naval Rivalry 1840–1870*. New York: Oxford University Press, 1993.

Hannah, Ian C. *A History of British Foreign Policy*. London: Nicholson and Watson, 1938.

Hattendorf, John B., R. J. B. Knight, A. W. H. Pearsall, N. A. M. Rodger, and Geoffrey Till, eds. *British Naval Documents, 1204–1960*. Brookfield, Vt.: Scholar Press (for the Navy Records Society), 1993.

Haythornwaite, Philip J. *The Colonial Wars Sourcebook*. New York: Arms and Armour, 1995.

Headrick, Daniel R. *The Tools of Empire: Technology and European Imperialism in the Nineteenth Century*. New York: Oxford University Press, 1981.

Healy, David. *Gunboat Diplomacy in the Wilson Era: The U.S. Navy in Haiti, 1915–1916*. Madison: University of Wisconsin Press, 1976.

———. *Drive to Hegemony: The United States in the Caribbean, 1989–1917*. Madison: University of Wisconsin Press, 1988.

Herwig, Holger. *The Politics of Frustration: The United States in German Naval Planning, 1889–1941*. Boston: Little, Brown, 1976.

Higham, Robin. *Armed Forces in Peacetime: Britain, 1918–1940, a Case Study*. Hamden, Conn.: Archon Books, 1962.

Hilton, Stanley. *Brazil and the Great Powers*. Austin: University of Texas Press, 1975.

Hoffmann, Stanley. *The Ethics and Politics of Humanitarian Intervention*. Notre Dame, Ind: University of Notre Dame Press, 1996.

Hofstadter, Richard. *The Progressive Movement, 1900–1915*. Englewood Cliffs, N.J.: Prentice Hall, 1963.

Holbo, Paul S. "Perilous Obscurity: Public Opinion and the Press in the Venezuelan Crisis, 1902–1903." *Historian* 33, no. 3 (1970): 428–48.

Holbraad, Carsten. *The Concert of Europe: A Study in German and British International Theory, 1815–1914*. New York: Barnes and Noble, 1970.

Holsti, Kalevi J. *Peace and War: Armed Conflicts and International Order, 1648–1989*. New York: Cambridge University Press, 1991.

Hood, Miriam. *Gunboat Diplomacy, 1895–1905: Great Power Pressure in Venezuela*. London: Allen and Unwin, 1983.

Hough, Richard. *Dreadnought: A History of the Modern Battleship*. New York: MacMillan, 1964.

Hythe, Viscount. *The Naval Annual, 1913* (reprinted edition). New York: Arco Publications, 1970.

Inman, Samuel. *Inter-American Conferences 1826–1954: History and Problems*. Washington, D.C.: University Press, 1965.

International Institute for Strategic Studies (IISS). *The Military Balance 1970–1971, 1975–1976, 1979–1980, 1981–1982, 1983–1984, 1987–1988, 1988–1989, 1994–1995*. London: Brassey's Publishers.

Irwin, Douglas A. *Against the Tide: An Intellectual History of Free Trade*. Princeton, N.J.: Princeton University Press, 1996.

Jane, Fred T. *The British Battle-Fleet: Its Inception and Growth throughout the Centuries*. London: Conway Maritime Press, 1997 [1912].

Jenks, Leland Hamilton. *The Migration of British Capital to 1875*. New York: Alfred A. Knopf, 1927.

Johnson, G. Wesley, ed. *Double Impact: France and Africa in the Age of Imperialism*. Westport, Conn.: Greenwood Press, 1985.

Johnson, Robert David. *The Peace Progressives and American Foreign Relations*. Cambridge, Mass.: Harvard University Press, 1995.

Joint Chiefs of Staff. "Shape, Respond, Prepare Now: A Military Strategy for a New Era" (National Military Strategy of the United States of America), 1997.

Jones, C. G. Pitcairn, ed. *Piracy in the Levant, 1827–28*. Volume 72. London: Navy Records Society, 1934.

Jones, Chester Lloyd. *Caribbean Interests of the United States*. New York: D. Appleton and Company, 1916.

Joshua, Wynfred, and Stephen P. Gibert. *Arms for the Third World: Soviet Military Aid Diplomacy*. Baltimore: The Johns Hopkins University Press, 1969.

Kagan, Korina. "The Myth of the European Concert: The Realist-Institutionalist Debate and Great Power Behavior in the Eastern Question, 1821–41." *Security Studies* 7, no. 2 (winter 1997/98.): 1–57.

Kalck, Pierre. *Historical Dictionary of the Central Africa Republic*. 2nd ed., translated by Thomas O'Toole. African Historical Dictionaries No. 51. Metuchen, N.J.: Scarecrow Press, 1992.

Keegan, John. *The Price of Admiralty: The Evolution of Naval Warfare*. New York: Penguin Books, 1988.

Kelsey, Carl. "The American Intervention in Haiti and the Dominican Republic." *Annals of the American Academy of Political and Social Science* 100 (March 1922): 110–99.

Kennedy, Paul M. *The Realities Behind Diplomacy: Background Influences on British External Policy, 1865–1980*. London: George Allen and Unwin, 1981.

———. *The Rise and Fall of British Naval Mastery*. Atlantic Highlands, N.J.: Ashfield Press, 1983 [1976].

Kissinger, Henry. *A World Restored: Metternich, Castlereagh, and the Problems of Peace, 1812–1822*. Boston: Houghton Mifflin, 1973 [1957].

———. *Diplomacy*. New York: Simon and Schuster, 1994.

Kostiner, Joseph. "Britain and the Northern Frontier of the Saudi State, 1922–1925." Pp. 29–48 in *The Great Powers in the Middle East, 1919–1939*, edited by Uriel Dann. New York: Holmes and Meier, 1988.

Laing, E. A. M. "The Royal Navy on the River Parana during the Allied Intervention, 1845–1846." *American Neptune* 36, no. 2 (April 1976): 23–39.

Lambert, Andrew. *The Last Sailing Battlefleet: Maintaining Naval Mastery 1815–1850*. London: Conway Maritime Press, 1991.

———. "The Shield of Empire, 1815–1895." Pp. 161–99 in *The Oxford Illustrated History of the Royal Navy*, edited by J. R. Hill and Bryan Ranft. New York: Oxford University Press, 1995.

Laybourn, Keith. *Britain on the Breadline: A Social and Political History of Britain between the Wars*. Gloucester, U.K.: Alan Sutton, 1990.

Lea, Homer. *The Valor of Ignorance*. New York: Harper, 1909.

Lee, J. M. *African Armies and Civil Order*. New York: Frederick A. Praeger, 1969.

LeFeber, Walter. *The American Age: United States Foreign Policy at Home and Abroad since 1750*. New York: W. W. Norton, 1989.

Lemarchand, René. "The CIA in Africa." *Journal of Modern African Studies* 14 (September 1976): 401–26.

———, ed. *The Green and the Black: Qadhafi's Policies in Africa*. Bloomington: Indiana University Press, 1988.

Levy, Jack S. *War in the Modern Great Power System, 1495–1975*. Lexington: University Press of Kentucky, 1983.

———. "Domestic Politics and War." *Journal of Interdisciplinary History* 18, no. 3 (1988): 653–73.

Lewis, Michael A. *The History of the British Navy*. London: Penguin, 1957.

Livermore, Seward. "Battleship Diplomacy in South America, 1905–1925." *Journal of Modern History* 16, no. 1 (March 1944): 31–48.

———. "The American Navy as a Factor in World Politics, 1903–1913." *American Historical Review* 63, no. 4 (July 1958): 863–79.

Lloyd, C. C. "Navies." Pp. 76–90 in *The New Cambridge Modern History, Vol. IX*, edited by C. W. Crawley. Cambridge: Cambridge University Press, 1965.

Lord, Walter Frewen. *England and France in the Mediterranean 1660–1830*. Port Washington, N.Y.: Kennikat Press, 1970 [1901].

Luckham, Robin. "Le militarisme français en Afrique." *Politique Africaine* 5 (February 1982).

Lythe, S. G. E. "Britain, the Financial Capital of the World." In *Britain Pre-eminent: Studies of British World Influence in the Nineteenth Century*, edited by C. J. Bartlett. New York: St. Martin's Press, 1969.

Mamdani, Mahmood. *Citizen and Subject: Contemporary Africa and the Legacy of Late Colonialism*. Princeton, N.J.: Princeton University Press, 1996.

Manchester, Alan K. *British Pre-eminence in Brazil: Its Rise and Decline*. Chapel Hill: University of North Carolina Press, 1933.

Mansfield, Peter. *A History of the Middle East*. New York: Penguin Books, 1991.

Marder, Arthur. *From Dreadnought to Scapa Flow, Volume I*. London: Oxford University Press, 1961.

———. *From the Dreadnought to Scapa Flow: The Royal Navy in the Fisher Era, 1904–1919, Volume V: Victory and Aftermath (January 1918–June 1919)*. New York: Oxford University Press, 1970.

———. *From the Dardanelles to Oran: Studies of the Royal Navy in War and Peace, 1915–1940*. New York: Oxford University Press, 1974.

Marlowe, John. *Perfidious Albion: The Origins of the Anglo-French Rivalry in the Levant*. London: Elek Books, 1971.

Martin, Michel L. *Warriors to Managers: The French Military Establishment since 1945*. Chapel Hill: University of North Carolina Press, 1981.

Mathieson, William Law. *Great Britain and the Slave Trade, 1839–1865*. New York: Octagon Books, 1967 [1929].

McCleary, John William. "Anglo-French Naval Rivalry, 1815–1848." Ph.D. diss. Baltimore, The Johns Hopkins University, 1947.

Meinertzhagen, Richard. *Middle East Diary, 1917–1956*. London: The Cresset Press, 1959.

Miller, Rory. "The Decline of British Interests in Latin America." *History Today* 41, no. 12 (December 1991): 42–49.

———. *Britain and Latin America in the Nineteenth and Twentieth Centuries*. New York: Longman, 1993.

Millett, Allan, and Peter Maslowski. *For the Common Defense: A Military History of the United States of America* (revised edition). New York: The Free Press, 1994.

Mitchell, Brian R. *British Historical Statistics*. Cambridge: Cambridge University Press, 1988.

Mockaitis, Thomas R. *British Counterinsurgency, 1919–60*. New York: St. Martin's Press, 1990.

Modelski, George, and William R. Thompson. *Seapower in Global Politics, 1494–1993*. Seattle: University of Washington Press, 1988.

Monroe, Elizabeth. *Britain's Moment in the Middle East, 1914–1971*. 2nd ed. Baltimore: The Johns Hopkins University Press, 1981 [1963].

Mowat, Charles Loch. *Britain between the Wars, 1918–1940*. Chicago: University of Chicago Press, 1955.

Munro, Dana. *Intervention and Dollar Diplomacy in the Caribbean, 1900–1921*. Princeton N.J.: Princeton University Press, 1964.

———. *The United States and the Caribbean Republics, 1921–1933*. Princeton, N.J.: Princeton University Press, 1974.

Neidpath, James. *The Singapore Naval Base and the Defence of Britain's Eastern Empire, 1919–1941*. New York: Oxford University Press, 1981.

Newman, E. W. Polson. *The Mediterranean and Its Problems.* London: George Allen and Unwin, 1927.

Nye, Joseph. *Bound to Lead: The Changing Nature of American Power.* New York: Basic Books, 1990.

Offutt, Milton. "The Protection of Citizens Abroad by the Armed Forces of the United States." *Johns Hopkins University Studies in Historical and Political Science* 46, no. 4 (1928): 78–143.

Oliver, F. L. "Havana Episode." *United States Naval Institute Proceedings* (October 1952).

Ovendale, Ritchie. *The Middle East since 1914.* New York: Longman, 1992.

Pakenham, Thomas. *The Scramble for Africa: White Man's Conquest of the Dark Continent from 1876 to 1912.* New York: Avon Books, 1991.

Palmer, Alan. *Kemal Atatürk.* London: Macdonald and Company, 1991.

Paullin, Charles. *Paullin's History of Naval Administration, 1775–1911.* Annapolis Md.: United States Naval Institute, 1968.

Peden, G. C. *British Rearmament and the Treasury: 1932–1939.* Edinburgh: Scottish Academic Press, 1979.

Perkins, Bradford. *The Great Rapprochement: England and the United States, 1895–1914.* New York: Atheneum, 1968.

Perkins, Dexter. *A History of the Monroe Doctrine.* Boston: Little, Brown, 1963.

Pierre, Andrew J., ed. *Cascade of Arms: Managing Conventional Weapons Proliferation.* Cambridge, Mass.: Brookings/World Peace Foundation, 1997.

Platt, D. C. M. *Finance, Trade, and Politics in British Foreign Policy, 1815–1914.* New York: Oxford University Press, 1968.

———. "Further Objections to an 'Imperialism of Free Trade,' 1830–1860." Pp. 153–61 in *Imperialism: The Robinson and Gallagher Controversy,* edited by William Roger Louis. New York: Franklin Watts, 1976.

Polanyi, Karl. *The Great Transformation: The Political and Economic Origins of Our Time.* Boston: Beacon Press, 1957 [1944].

Pratt, Lawrence. "The Strategic Context: British Policy in the Mediterranean and the Middle East, 1936–1939." Pp. 12–26 in *The Great Powers in the Middle East, 1919–1939,* edited by Uriel Dann. New York: Holmes and Meier, 1988.

Preston, Anthony, and John Major. *Send a Gunboat! A Study of the Gunboat and Its Role in British Foreign Policy, 1854–1904.* London: Longmans, 1967.

Prunier, Gérard. *The Rwanda Crisis: History of a Genocide.* New York: Columbia University Press, 1995.

Pugh, Martin. *State and Society: British Political and Social History, 1870–1992.* London: Edward Arnold, 1994.

Pugh, Michael. "Pacifism and Politics in Britain, 1931–1935." *The Historical Journal* 23, no. 3 (September 1980): 641–56.

Puryear, Vernon John. *France and the Levant: From the Bourbon Restoration to the Peace of Kutiah.* Hamden, Conn.: Archon Books, 1968 [1941].

———. *International Economics and Diplomacy in the Near East: A Study of British Commercial Policy in the Levant, 1834–1853.* Hamden, Conn.: Archon Books, 1969 [1935].

Ralston, David B. *Importing the European Army: The Introduction of European Military Techniques and Institutions into the Extra-European World, 1600–1914.* Chicago: University of Chicago Press, 1990.

Ranson, Edward. *British Defence Policy and Appeasement between the Wars, 1919–1939.* London: The Historical Association, 1993.

Rasler, Karen A., and William R. Thompson. *The Great Powers and the Global Struggle, 1490–1990.* Lexington: The University Press of Kentucky, 1994.

Reynolds, Clark G. *Command of the Sea: The History and Strategy of Maritime Empires.* New York: William Morrow and Co., 1974.

Rhodes, Edward. "The Imperial Logic of Bush's Liberal Agenda." *Survival* 45, no. 1 (Spring 2003): 131–54.

Richardson, James L. *Crisis Diplomacy: The Great Powers since the Mid-Nineteenth Century.* New York: Cambridge University Press, 1994.

Ridings, Eugene. *Business Interest Groups in Nineteenth Century Brazil.* New York: Cambridge University Press, 1994.

Rippy, J. Fred. *The Caribbean Danger Zone.* New York: Putnam, 1940.

———. *British Investments in Latin America, 1822–1949.* Minneapolis: University of Minnesota Press, 1959.

———. *Rivalry of the United States and Great Britain over Latin America, 1808–1830.* New York: Octagon Books, 1964.

Riviere, Peter. *Absent-Minded Imperialism: Britain and the Expansion of Empire in Nineteenth Century Brazil.* New York: Tauris Academic Studies, 1995.

Rosen, Stephen Peter. *Winning the Next War: Innovation and the Modern Military.* Ithaca, N.Y.: Cornell University Press, 1991.

Roskill, Stephen. *Naval Policy between the Wars, Volume I: The Period of Anglo-American Antagonism, 1919–1929.* London: William Collins Sons and Company, 1968.

———. "The Ten Year Rule—The Historical Facts." *Journal of the Royal United Services Institution*, 117 (March 1972): 69–71.

———. *Naval Policy between the Wars, Volume II: The Period of Reluctant Rearmament, 1930–1939.* London: William Collins Sons and Company, 1976.

Ross, Andrew L. "Arms Acquisition and National Security: The Irony of Military Strength." Pp. 152–87 in *National Security in the Third World: The Management of Internal and External Threats*, edited by Edward E. Azar and Chung-In Moon. Aldershot, U.K.: Edward Elgar Publishing Limited, 1988.

Sachar, Howard M. *The Emergence of the Modern Middle East: 1914–1924.* New York: Alfred A. Knopf, 1969.

Sahni, Varun. "Not Quite British: A Study of External Influences on the Argentine Navy." *Journal of Latin American Studies* 25, no. 4 (1993): 489–513.

Schmidt, Hans. *The United States Occupation of Haiti, 1915–1934.* New Brunswick, N.J.: Rutgers University Press, 1995.

Schroeder, Paul W. "The 19th Century International System: Changes in the Structure." *World Politics* 39, no. 1 (October 1986): 1–26.

———. *The Transformation of European Politics, 1763–1848.* New York: Oxford University Press, 1994.

Schurman, D. M. *The Education of a Navy: The Development of British Naval Strategic Thought, 1867–1914*. Chicago: University of Chicago Press, 1965.

Scott, George. *The Rise and Fall of the League of Nations*. New York: Macmillan, 1973.

Semmel, Bernard. *Liberalism and Naval Strategy: Ideology, Interest, and Sea Power during the Pax Britannica*. Boston: Unwin Allen, 1986.

Shaw, Stanford J., and Ezel Kural Shaw. *History of the Ottoman Empire and Modern Turkey, Volume II: Reform, Revolution, and Republic: The Rise of Modern Turkey, 1808–1975*. New York: Cambridge University Press, 1977.

Sheppard, Eric William. *A Short History of the British Army*. 4th ed. London: Constable and Company, 1950 [1926].

Shipstead, Henrik. "Dollar Diplomacy in Latin America" *Current History* (1927).

Shmuelevitz, Aryeh. "Atatürk's Policy toward the Great Powers: Principles and Guidelines." Pp. 311–16 in *The Great Powers in the Middle East, 1919–1939*, edited by Uriel Dann. New York: Holmes and Meier, 1988.

Silverfarb, Daniel. *Britain's Informal Empire in the Middle East: A Case Study of Iraq, 1929–1941*. New York: Oxford University Press, 1986.

Silverman, Peter. "The Ten Year Rule." *Journal of the Royal United Services Institution*, 661 (1971): 42–45.

Singer, J. David, and Melvin Small. *The Wages of War 1816–1965: A Statistical Handbook*. New York: John Wiley and Sons, 1972.

———. *Resort to Arms*. Beverly Hills, Calif.: Sage, 1982.

Sivard, Ruth Leger. *World Military and Social Expenditures*. 16th ed. Washington, D.C.: World Priorities, 1996.

Smith, Goldwyn. *A History of England*. 2nd ed. New York: Charles Scribner's Sons, 1957 [1949].

Smith, Joseph. *Illusions of Conflict: The Anglo-American Diplomacy toward Latin America, 1865–1896*. Pittsburgh: University of Pittsburgh Press, 1979.

Snyder, Jack L. *Myths of Empire: Domestic Politics and International Ambition*. Ithaca, N.Y.: Cornell University Press, 1991.

Sontag, Raymond. *A Broken World, 1919–1939*. New York: Harper and Row, 1971.

Spector, Ronald. *Admiral of the New Empire*. Baton Rouge: Louisiana State University Press, 1974.

Spiers, Edward M. *The Army and Society, 1815–1914*. New York: Longman, 1980.

Sprout, Harold, and Margaret Sprout. *Toward a New Order of Sea Power: American Naval Policy and the World Scene, 1918–1922*. Princeton, N.J.: Princeton University Press, 1940.

———. *Foundations of National Power*. 2d ed. New York: D. Van Nostrand and Company, 1951 [1945].

Stockholm International Peace Research Institute (SIPRI). *World Armaments and Disarmament Yearbooks for 1982, 1985, and 1995*. New York: International Publications Service.

Stokesbury, James L. *Navy and Empire*. New York: William Morrow and Co., 1983.

Strachan, Hew. *Wellington's Legacy: The Reform of the British Army, 1830–54*. Manchester, U.K.: Manchester University Press, 1984.

———. "The British Army and 'Modern War': The Experience of the Peninsula and the Crimea." In *Tools of War: Instruments, Ideas, and Institutions of Warfare, 1445–1871*, edited by John A. Lynn. Urbana: University of Illinois Press, 1990.

Stuyt, A. M. *Survey of International Arbitrations, 1794–1970*. Dobbs Ferry, N.Y.: Oceana Publications, 1972.

Sullivan, Brian R. "The Italian Armed Forces, 1918–40." Pp. 169–217 in *Military Effectiveness, Volume II: The Interwar Period*, edited by Allan R. Millett and Williamson Murray. Boston: Unwin Hyman, 1988.

Temperley, Harold W. V. *England and the Near East: The Crimea*. New York: Longmans, Green and Co., 1936.

Thomson, David. *England in the Nineteenth Century (1815–1914)*. Baltimore, Md.: Penguin Books, 1959 [1950].

Till, Geoffrey. "Retrenchment, Rethinking, Revival." Pp. 319–47 in *The Oxford Illustrated History of the Royal Navy*, edited by J. R. Hill and Bryan Ranft. New York: Oxford University Press, 1995.

Tunstall, W. C. B. "Imperial Defence, 1815–1870." Pp. 806–41 in *The Cambridge History of the British Empire, Vol. II: The Growth of the New Empire, 1783–1870*. Cambridge: Cambridge University Press, 1961.

Vagts, Alfred. "Hopes and Fears of an American-German War, 1870–1915 I." *Political Science Quarterly* 54, no. 4 (December 1939): 514–35.

Vagts, Alfred. "Hopes and Fears of an American-German War, 1870–1915 II." *Political Science Quarterly* 55, no. 1 (March 1940): 53–76.

Vale, Brian. "Creation of the Imperial Brazilian Navy, 1822–23." *Mariner's Mirror* 57, no. 1 (January 1971): 63–88.

van Creveld, Martin. *Supplying War: Logistics from Wallenstein to Patton*. New York: Cambridge University Press, 1977.

von Albertini, Rudolf, with Albert Wirz. *European Colonial Rule, 1880–1940: The Impact of the West on India, Southeast Asia, and Africa*, translated by John G. Williamson. Westport, Conn.: Greenwood Press, 1992.

Walker, Thomas G. *Nicaragua: The Land of Sandino*. Boulder, Colo.: Westview Press, 1981.

Ward, A. W., and G. P. Gooch. *The Cambridge History of Foreign Policy* (three volumes). New York: MacMillan, 1923.

Webster, Charles. *The Foreign Policy of Palmerston, 1830–1841: Britain, the Liberal Movement and the Eastern Question*, 2 vols. New York: Humanities Press, 1969.

Weinberg, Albert. *Manifest Destiny: A Study of Nationalist Expansion in American History*. Chicago: Quadrangle Books, 1963.

Welch, Claude E., Jr., ed. *Soldier and State in Africa: A Comparative Analysis of Military Intervention and Political Change*. Evanston, Ill.: Northwestern University Press, 1970.

———. *No Farewell to Arms? Military Disengagement from Politics in Africa and Latin America*. Boulder, Colo.: Westview Press, 1987.

Weller, M., ed. *Regional Peace-Keeping and International Enforcement: The Liberian Crisis*. Cambridge International Documents Series, Vol. 6. Cambridge: Cambridge University Press, 1994.

Wells, Sumner. *Naboth's Vinyard: The Dominican Republic, 1844–1924*. New York: Arno Press, 1972.

The White House. "A National Security Strategy for a New Century" (National Security Strategy of the United States), October 1998.

The White House. "The National Security Strategy of the United States of America, September 2002." <http://www.whitehouse.gov/nsc/nss.html> (13 May 2003).

Williams, Ann. *Britain and France in the Middle East and North Africa, 1914–1967*. New York: St. Martin's Press, 1968.

Williams, John A. "U.S. Navy Missions and Force Structure: A Critical Appraisal." *Armed Forces and Society* 7, no. 4 (1981): 499–528.

Williams, Judith Blow. *British Commercial Policy and Trade Expansion, 1750–1850*. London: Oxford University Press, 1972.

Willock, Roger. *Bulwark of Empire: Bermuda's Fortified Naval Base 1860–1920*. Princeton, N.J.: Princeton University Press, 1962.

Winn, Peter. "British Informal Empire in Uruguay in the Nineteenth Century." *Past and Present* no. 73 (November 1976): 100–26.

Woodhouse, C. M. *The Battle of Navarino*. London: Hodder and Stoughton, 1965.

Worcester, Donald E. *Sea Power and Chilean Independence*. Gainesville: University of Florida Press, 1962.

Wyckoff, Don. "The Chilean Civil War, 1891." *United States Naval Institute Proceedings* 88, no. 10 (1962): 58–63.

Yapp, M. E. *The Near East since the First World War*. New York: Longman, 1991.

Yates, Douglas A. *The Rentier State in Africa: Oil Rent Dependency and Neocolonialism in the Republic of Gabon*. Trenton, N.J.: Africa World Press, 1996.

Yerxa, Donald. "The United States and the Caribbean, 1914–1941." *Naval History: The Sixth Symposium of the U.S. Naval Academy*, edited by Daniel Masterson. Wilmington, Del.: Scholarly Resources, 1987.

———. *Admirals and Empire: The United States Navy and the Caribbean, 1898–1945*. Columbia: University of South Carolina Press, 1991.

Young, Crawford. *The African Colonial State in Comparative Perspective*. New Haven, Conn.: Yale University Press, 1994.

Young, John W. *Britain and the World in the Twentieth Century*. New York: Arnold, 1997.

Zartman, I. William. "Internationalization of Communal Strife: Temptations and Opportunities of Triangulation." Pp. 27–42 in *The Internationalization of Communal Strife*, edited by Manus I. Midlarsky. New York: Routledge, 1993.

———, ed. *Collapsed States: The Disintegration and Restoration of Legitimate Authority*. Boulder, Colo.: Lynne Rienner Publishers, 1995.

Zolberg, Aristide R. "The Structure of Political Conflict in the New States of Tropical Africa." *American Political Science Review* 62, no. 1 (March 1968).

Index

Abbas II, 78
Abdullah, Emir, 82, 102
Aberdeen, Lord, 30
Abyssinia, 99, 107, 382, 411–12. See also Ethiopia
Afghanistan, 1, 377
Africa, 123–24, 137–38, 140, 144, 154, 388–93, 394–95, 396, 397, 398, 399, 400, 402, 403, 404, 416–19; arms transfers to, 204, 210, 212, 216, 219, 223, 232, 236, 246, 249–52, 250, 283, 292n32, 292n34, 292–94, 297, 302, 304–5, 315, 329n136, 336–42, 337–39, 353, 417–18; economic aid to Africa, 225, 229, 233–34, 266–67, 269, 271, 302, 304, 317, 319–22, 333, 341, 349, 351, 355, 356n195, 358, 418; See also Franc Zone and International Monetary Fund (IMF) French operations in, See Operations by French troops; military aid to Africa, 204, 212–13, 215, 219–29, 248–52, 267, 269, 287, 329n136, 336–43, 349, 353–54, 418; See also arms transfers, cooperation agreements, and military training sub-Saharan, 197–376, 416–19
African militaries, 200, 205–7, 210, 216–17, 224, 229, 284-86, 288, 289, 288–91, 288n20, 295. See also *Tirailleurs Sénégalais*
air forces and transport, French and African, 210, 213–15, 220, 241, 290–93, 299–300, 303n68, 303–6, 312–16, 326–27, 333, 337–41
air policing, 76, 80, 83, 105, 109, 113n26; see also Trenchard system
air power, 68, 71, 76,108; see also Royal Air Force (RAF), Trenchard system
Alexandria, 19, 21, 43, 72, 74, 75, 76, 99, 102, 120n128, 381, 399
Algeria, 208–9, 213–14, 218–19, 225, 230, 233, 237, 255–56, 261–62, 271–72, 290n24, 296, 297n52, 304, 314–15, 322, 324, 334

438 ~ Index

Algiers, French capture of (1830), 37
Al Qaeda, 1
Anglo-French naval race, 38
Anglo-Iraqi Treaty (1930), 87, 96, 121n139
Anglo-Persian Oil Company, 101
Anglo-Turkish Treaty (1809), 39
Angola, 247, 249, 285, 288–89, 292, 317, 329, 333–39, 353–54, 357–58
anti-slave patrols, 26, 36–37, 49
Arab world, 311, 315–16, 336, 381–83, 394, 395, 398–99, 400, 405. See also Middle East
Arab-Jew dispute, 79, 114n40
Argentina, 124, 127, 133–44, 160, 385
Armée Coloniale, 205, 207, 218. See also Troupes de Marine
army size, 37, 61n115, 110n3
asdic (sonar), 112n23
Asia, 74, 98, 138, 144
Asquith, Herbert, 84
Assemblée Nationale, 236, 238, 292n34, 298, 301, 322, 325
Assistance Militaire Technique (AMT), 220, 224, 226, 236, 239, 268, 300n61, 302–3, 305, 325, 355. See also cooperation agreements, military, and training, military
Assyrians, 78, 96
Atatürk (Mustafa Kemal), 78, 82–83, 97, 99, 100, 103, 115n55
Athens, 24, 33–34
Austria, 15, 34, 37, 40, 44, 49, 89, 108

Baez, Buenaventura, 174
balance of power, principle of, 34, 42
Balfour, Arthur, 178
Baltic Sea, 39
Baring Brothers and Company, 27–28, 133
Batraville, Benoit, 161
Belgium, 35, 177, 391; in Africa, 198, 210, 212, 245, 248, 250, 264, 281, 283, 291, 327, 332, 335–36, 338, 342, 345, 351
Benin (Dahomey), 198, 201, 210, 212, 214, 216n53, 219, 224–25, 228, 230, 245, 248, 250, 256, 259, 269, 291–92, 295n43, 308, 313, 319–20, 330, 332n149, 333, 338, 344, 358
Bermuda, 130
Beveridge, Albert, 168
Biafra, 210, 232, 246, 264–65, 268, 296, 336, 345, 391
Black Sea, 20, 39, 66, 93
blockade, 24, 26, 33, 45, 76, 109, 114n44; of Algiers (1824), 24; of Athens, 24, 34; of the Morea, 24; of the River Plate (1847), 126, 132, 134
Bokassa, Jean-Bédèl, 215n51, 230, 239, 258–59, 269n178, 282n3, 291, 296, 320–21, 325–26, 334, 336, 342–43, 349, 356, 359, 392
Bolivar, Simone, 134, 144, 148
Bongo, Omar, 222, 239–40, 242, 296–97, 297n52, 304, 307, 309, 321, 332, 343–47, 356
Bosphorus, 39, 41, 63n139
Brassey, Lord, 133, 141
Brazil, 124, 127, 160
Brazzaville Conference (1944), 202, 281, 284, 389
Bright, John, 147
Britain, 13–121 passim, 157, 172, 177, 178, 180–81, 183, 184, 378, 386, 387, 392, 394, 395, 399, 415; Admiralty of, 22, 52n20, 70, 74, 80, 90, 99; army of, 15–16, 21, 51n4, 67, 68, 110n3, 111n9; debt burden of, 81, 116n64; dispute with France over spheres of influence, 91; domestic politics in, 15–16, 31–34, 84–85; and eastern Mediterranean (1816–1852), 378–80, 394, 395, 398, 400, 407–9; and eastern Mediterranean

(1919–1937), 380–83, 395, 397, 400, 402, 409–12; electorate in, 31, 48, 84, 86; Foreign Office of, 31, 123–24, 131, 137–38, 140, 141, 148–49; foreign policy goals of, 14, 42, 47–49; military capabilities of, in Mediterranean (1816–1852), 14–27; military capabilities of, in Mediterranean (1919–1937), 66–80; military capabilities of, in South America (1850–1900), 125–36; naval parity with United States, 70, 93; nonmilitary sources of influence of, in Mediterranean (1816–1852), 27–31; nonmilitary sources of influence of, in Mediterranean (1919–1937), 80–83; nonmilitary sources of influence of, in South America (1850–1900), 136–46; Parliament in, 22, 31, 33, 50, 96, 104; political parties in, 31, 46, 84–85; press in, 84, 85; public opinion in, 31, 48, 86, 87; Royal Armed Services, *See* Royal Air Force, Royal Marines, and Royal Navy; and South America (1850–1900), 146–50, 383–85, 395, 397, 398 400, 401, 403, 413–14; in sub-Saharan Africa, 199, 209, 226, 246, 250, 263, 282, 322, 336, 339, 358; Treasury in, 84, 90, 106
British Empire, 66, 85, 97
Buenos Aires, 139
Bulgaria, 89
Burkina Faso (Upper Volta), 198, 201, 210, 212, 214, 215n51, 216n53, 219, 228, 230, 243–44, 248, 250, 256, 269, 282n3, 308, 320, 337, 341
Burundi, 198, 210, 212, 228, 230, 248, 250, 281, 283, 287–89, 291, 294–95, 303, 308, 328, 335, 337–38, 343–44, 352, 354, 357
Bush, George W., 2–3

Cairo, 71, 72
Callao, Peru 130–31, 144
Cameroon, 198–99, 202, 210, 212, 216, 219–21, 227–28, 248, 250, 263–64, 281, 287–90, 294–95, 302–4, 309–10, 314, 322, 328–29, 332, 334, 338–41, 343, 345, 357–59, 390
Campbell, Rear-Admiral Patrick, 36
Canning, George, 13, 32, 46, 137, 140, 145, 146, 147, 149
Canning, Stratford, 30, 45, 82
Cape of Good Hope, 29, 42
Caperton, William B., 162, 166, 170–72, 174, 183, 184
Caribbean Sea, and environs, 93, 385–88, 396, 398, 400, 403, 414–16
Castlereagh, Viscount, 17, 27, 32, 34, 46
Central African Empire, 392. *See also* Central African Republic (CAR)
Central African Republic (CAR, also Central African Empire and Oubangui-Chari), 199, 202, 210, 212, 216–17, 219–20, 227–28, 230, 232, 239, 250, 258–59, 264, 269n178, 281, 287–89, 291, 294–96, 298, 302–3, 306–10, 319–21, 323, 325–26, 328, 334, 338, 340, 342–43, 348–49, 351–61, 419
Central American Treaty Convention (1907), 168, 186
centralized "Cartesian" government, 205, 240–41, 286, 298, 323, 418. *See also* presidentialism
Chad, 199, 202, 210, 212, 216–17, 219, 221, 227, 231–32, 234, 242, 250, 257, 264, 281, 287, 292, 294–95, 297n54, 297–98, 301–2, 304–5, 307–16, 328–31, 333, 340, 343, 351–53, 357, 361, 391, 392, 393, 401, 419
Chanak Crisis, 85, 88, 95, 103, 381, 398
chasse gardée, 198–99, 201, 203, 208, 211, 213, 217, 222, 248–49, 256–57,

260, 262–63, 266–72, 281, 283–84, 286, 317, 323, 329, 333, 343–44, 349, 351, 353–54, 357, 360–61, 388, 391, 403, 416–17
Chile, 124, 127, 128, 129
China, 159; in Africa, 204, 230, 248–52, 268, 284, 333–35, 337–38, 342–43, 356
Chirac, Jacques, 281, 327, 347
civil war, 210, 230–31, 244, 246, 262–65, 268, 289, 317–18, 329n141, 336, 345, 351–55; in South America, 147; in United States, 143
Clarendon, Lord, 124
Clayton-Bulwer Treaty (1850), 125
Clowes, William Laird, 129, 134
Cobden, Richard, 33, 147
Codrington, Admiral, 23, 26, 45
Cold War, 5, 208, 245, 268, 286, 335, 348, 356
Colombia, 160, 170, 185
Concert of Europe, 34–35, 47, 48, 55n47, 59n96, 60n104, 76, 379, 394, 395, 408
Congo-Brazzaville (Republic of Congo), 198–99, 202, 202n11, 208, 210, 212, 216, 219, 221–22, 227–28, 247–51, 253, 264, 266, 269, 281, 287–90, 292, 294, 295n43, 296, 302–4, 308, 313, 319–20, 328, 330, 332–34, 337–44, 351–52, 354, 357
Congo-Kinshasa. *See* Zaïre
Congress at Aix-la-Chapelle, 28
Congress at Paris, 28
Congress of Vienna, 13, 22
conscripts and conscription, 16, 91, 200; restrictions on use outside France, 205, 241, 285, 293, 298, 300–301, 306n76, 316, 322, 417, 418
Constantinople, 21, 23, 44, 45, 46, 95, 100
coopérants, 211, 211n46, 214, 223, 226, 235–36, 257, 260, 267, 285, 287, 295, 301–2, 321, 342, 359. *See also* aid to Africa, military and aid to Africa, economic
cooperation agreements, including Franco-African defense agreements, 208, 210–11, 218–27, 233, 236, 246, 253, 259, 263–65, 271, 282, 284, 291, 294–96, 300–303, 306–7, 309, 312, 322–23, 327, 343, 350–52, 358–60, 418. *See also* Assistance Militaire Technique and Africa, military aid to
Corfu Crisis, 92
Corn Laws, 33, 140
Costa Rica, 164
Côte d'Ivoire, 198, 201–2, 210, 212, 216–20, 224–25, 229–30, 232, 236–37, 239–40, 243–46, 248, 250, 254–55, 259, 263, 266–67, 269, 290, 290n24, 292, 294, 295n43, 296, 303–4, 306–9, 318–19, 332, 337–39, 341, 345, 349, 354, 390–91
Council of the League of Nations, 87, 103
coups d'état, 215n51, 222, 227–30, 259, 269, 282n3, 297n52, 296–98, 301, 308–10, 309n87, 321, 326, 332n149, 334, 345, 351, 355, 357, 359–60, 418–19
Crimean War, 15, 50, 140
Croly, Herbert, 168
Cromer, Lord, 104
Cuba, 160, 386; in Africa, 251–52, 268, 285, 287, 333–35, 339
Culebra (Puerto Rico), 159, 386
culture, 203, 225, 237–38, 246, 253, 258, 261–62, 266, 270, 284, 309, 316, 324, 332, 342, 348–50, 356–58, 417
Curzon, Lord, 66, 94
Czechoslovakia, 247, 250

Dacko, David, 230, 296, 310, 321, 326, 334, 336, 359

Dahomey. *See* Benin
Dardanelles, 39, 95, 100, 103
de Brazza, Pierre Savorgnan, 200, 258
de Gaulle, Charles, 197, 201–3, 206, 208, 229–32, 239–40, 247, 253, 255–56, 261–62, 264–65, 271–72, 281, 283, 285, 296, 298, 311, 322–25, 328, 348, 350, 356, 417. *See also* Gaullism
de Madariaga, Salvador, 89
de Rigny, Admiral, 45
de Robeck, Admiral Sir John, 100
Declaration of Paris (1856), 142
democracy, and democratization, 226, 261–62, 269–70, 301, 323, 325, 328–29, 345–49, 352n187, 356, 358–59
Democratic Republic of Congo (DRC). *See* Zaïre
dependency, 198, 202, 209, 216, 224, 237, 239, 245, 253–54, 258, 260, 262, 266, 282, 284, 319, 344–45, 348, 350, 355–56, 358, 417
deterrence, 43, 44, 50, 71, 99, 107, 109
Dewey, George, 180
diamonds, 321, 325–26, 336, 359
Dillingham, A. C., 167, 169, 171–72, 184
Djibouti, 216–17, 271, 294, 306n76, 337–38
dollar diplomacy, 172–3
Dominican Republic, 160–64, 166–68, 170, 173–74, 184–85, 188–89
Don Pacifico Affair (1850), 24, 33

East India Company, 28, 35
Eastern Question, 14, 40, 108
ECOMOG (ECOWAS Monitoring Group), 243–46, 291, 329, 329n141, 331, 335
ECOWAS (Economic Community of West African States), 232, 242–45, 290, 330

Ecuador, 138, 160
education, 207, 211–12, 214–16, 215n51, 216n53, 223–25, 234, 238, 240, 242, 260, 320, 342. *See also* military training
Egypt, 13, 16, 30, 41, 46, 49, 66, 67, 68, 74, 75, 76, 78, 81, 82, 94, 96, 102, 379, 394, 395, 398, 409; army of, 21, 52n12, 67, 72; independence of, 82, 96, 108; navy of, 19–20; Egypt-Red Sea Station, 80
El Salvador, 187
empire. *See* imperialism
Ethiopia, 247–49, 260, 317, 334, 336–39, 358; *See also* Abyssinia

Fashoda syndrome, 198n1, 283. *See also* prestige
Feisal, Emir, 77, 81, 91
Fisher, John, 178
Fiske, Bradley, 164
Foccart, Jacques, 222, 239, 265, 267, 296–97, 297n52, 297n54, 306, 321n119, 324–25, 327, 332n149, 347, 356. *See also* intelligence
Forces de Présence. *See* French base troops
Forces d'Intervention. *See* French rapid reaction forces
Franc Zone (*Communauté Financière Africaine*, CFA), 223, 225–26, 233–35, 266–67, 270, 272, 301, 317, 319–20, 321n117, 356, 356n193, 356n194, 361, 418
France, 4, 13, 19, 25, 36, 37, 41, 49, 65, 69, 91, 94, 98, 103, 106, 107, 108, 131, 144, 166, 378, 379, 380, 394–95, 397, 398, 399, 400, 401, 403, 404, 409, 411; army of, 38; and Central Africa (1970–1995), 281–376, 391, 416–19; and West Africa (1945–1970), 197–280, 388–91, 416–19; navy of, 37–38, 91

Franco-African summit meetings, 223, 242, 295n42, 302, 310, 316, 326, 328, 331–32, 344, 348, 358
Free French, 201n9, 202, 206, 209, 240, 306, 321n119, 418. *See also* World War II
free trade, 85, 104, 123, 136–8, 140, 142, 145, 147
French base troops (*Forces de Présence*), 204–5, 209, 213, 217–18, 223, 227, 259, 263–64, 282–83, 287, 294–95, 294n40, 298, 302–3, 305–8, 306n76, 315, 320, 326, 344, 350, 352, 354–55, 359–61, 417–19
French Community (1958), 198, 255–56, 271, 324
French Foreign Legion. *See Légion Étrangère*
French rapid reaction forces (*Forces d'Intervention* and *Force d'Action Rapide*), 205, 209, 213, 217–18, 220–21, 223, 226–27, 231, 263, 285–86, 289, 292–94, 298–300, 302–7, 306n76, 309, 350–52, 354, 359–61, 417–19. *See also Légion Étrangère* and *Troupes de Marine*
French Revolutionary Wars, 17, 20. *See also* French Wars
French Wars, 18, 34

Gabon, 199, 202, 210, 212, 216–17, 219–20, 222, 227–28, 232, 239–40, 242, 250, 255, 259, 263–65, 281, 287–90, 292, 294–97, 295n42, 297n52, 297n56, 302–4, 306–10, 319, 321, 321n119, 327–29, 332, 335–41, 343–48, 352, 359, 361
Gallipoli, 85
Gaullism, and Gaullists, 197, 202, 283, 285–86, 292n32, 297–98, 301, 318, 322–25, 327–28, 350, 361
Geddes Committee, and "Geddes Axe," 86, 118n93

Germany, 89, 97, 157, 158, 177, 178–81, 183, 382, 387, 415; in Africa, 198, 204, 248, 251, 263, 283, 292n33, 312, 334, 336–38, 342, 350; in eastern Mediterranean, 93, 96, 103, 104; as threat to France, 92, 94
Gibraltar, 22, 24, 33, 99
Giscard d'Éstaing, Valéry, 285–86, 292n32, 293, 298–99, 305, 308, 321–23, 325–27, 348–49, 392
Gladstone, William, 33
Gough-Calthorpe, Admiral, 101
Granville, Lord, 140, 147, 150
Great Depression, 80
Greece, 14, 66, 67, 73, 76, 77, 78, 79, 88, 89, 100, 108, 380, 382; navy of, 26, 76; as revisionist power, 103
Greek War of Independence (1821–1829), 24, 26, 28, 39, 44–47
Grey, Edward, 178
Guantanamo, 159, 164, 386
Guatemala, 161
guerre de course, 38, 62n119
guerrilla war, 30, 75
Guinea, 198, 201, 208, 210, 224–25, 243, 245, 247–50, 256, 259, 269, 288n20, 290–91, 309, 313, 321n117, 330, 332, 334–39, 341, 390
gunboat diplomacy, 87, 89, 124, 177

Habyarima, Juvénal, 292, 305n72, 352n187, 353, 419
Hague International Court of Arbitration, 158, 172, 177, 386, 416
Haiti, 160–63, 166–67, 169–71, 174, 179, 181, 183–85, 187–89
Halifax, Nova Scotia, 131
Harding, Warren, 176
Hitler, Adolf, 66, 93
Holy Alliance, 28, 34, 57n65
Honduras, 164–65, 170, 181, 187
Horse Guards, 16

Houphouët-Boigny, Félix, 229–30, 236–40, 244–45, 253–55, 263, 297n52, 304, 309, 349, 356, 391
House of Lords, 141
human rights, 242, 259, 316, 325–26, 328, 352, 353n189
humanitarian intervention, in eastern Mediterranean, 26–27, 57n61, 78–79
Hussein, Saddam, 405
Hutu, 352–53, 352n187, 392

imperialism, 201, 203, 225, 238, 261, 323–24, 330
India, 68, 94, 107, 108, 380, 409, 412; British colonial garrisons in, 15; trade routes to, 29
Indian Ocean, 17, 98
'Indian Navy,' 35–36
Indochina, 202, 206, 209, 213, 233, 239, 261, 271–72, 282n3, 297n52, 322, 350
Industrial Revolution, 71
intelligence, operations in Africa, 204, 207, 210–11, 220, 222–24, 226, 235, 239, 245–46, 260, 265, 267, 269, 283, 286, 293, 295–97, 297n52, 297n54, 302, 305–7, 310, 321n119, 325, 332, 335, 355, 417–18
International Monetary Fund (IMF), 320, 328, 332, 332n149, 345–46, 356n193
international regimes, 34–37, 49, 87–91, 106
Invergordon Mutiny, 70, 86
Ionian Islands, 22, 24, 55n41, 379
Iran. *See* Persia
Iraq, 2, 4, 66, 67, 68, 74, 75, 76, 86, 87, 89, 94, 95, 98, 99, 101, 103, 104, 292n34, 293, 298, 315, 377, 380
Iraq Petroleum Company, 101
Israel, 211, 315, 336, 338, 342
Italo-Abyssinian crisis, 76, 92, 99

Italy, 73, 91, 92, 94, 96, 99, 107, 157, 167, 177, 183, 382, 411–12, 415
Ivory Coast. *See* Côte d'Ivoire

Japan, 69, 71, 90, 98, 181
Jimenez, Juan Isidro, 168

Kaffir War (1851–1852), 21
Kemal, Mustafa. *See* Atatürk
Kingcome, Rear Admiral, 138, 148
Kingston, Jamaica, 130
Kolingba, André, 259, 296, 310, 326, 359
Kuwait, 103

La Francophonie, 215, 253, 258, 282, 360
la mission civilizatrice, 140
Lampson, Sir Miles, 78
Latin America, 249. *See also* South America
League of Nations, 75, 83–84, 86, 87, 89, 94, 97, 99, 106, 382, 411
Lebanon, 14, 30, 66, 91, 93
Légion Étrangère (French Foreign Legion), 218, 220, 241, 299–300, 312–14, 326–27, 346–47
Levant Company, 28, 57n70
liberalism, 42, 46, 50, 104, 123, 125, 136, 138–39, 141–42, 145–46, 151
Liberia, 242–46, 282n3, 291, 329, 331, 335
Libya, 99, 204, 231, 242–45, 248, 257, 265, 268, 269n178, 283, 288–90, 294, 305, 310–17, 329n141, 329–31, 334–35, 340, 343, 351, 353, 356, 391, 392, 419
Lloyd George, David, 84
Loi Cadre, 237, 254–55, 262
London, 23, 38, 123, 124–25, 132, 134, 137, 151
London Treaty (1840), 40
London Treaty (1930), 119n103
López War (1865–1870), 147
Loraine, Sir Percy, 82

Madagascar, 216–17, 219, 250, 253, 255–56, 334–35, 337–38
Madriz, Jose, 169, 132
Mali Federation, 219, 227–28, 256, 263
Mali, 198, 201, 210, 212, 214, 216n53, 219, 224, 228, 245, 247–50, 256, 259, 295n43, 329n135, 332, 334, 337–39, 344
Malta, 22, 24, 44, 45, 55n40, 68, 72, 73, 74, 76, 120n128, 379, 381
Marconi, Guglielmo, 165
marines, 24–25, 76
Mauritania, 198, 201, 210, 212, 216, 219, 221, 224, 227, 253, 264, 269, 298, 308, 309n87, 337–38
Mba, Léon, 222, 227–28, 240, 265, 297, 297n52, 309, 321, 335, 345
McCrea, Henry, 170, 185
Mediterranean Sea, 13–64 *passim*, 65–110 *passim*, 203, 208, 284; bases in, 17, 22, 24, 48; British fleet in, 74, 91, 99; military balance in (1816–1852), 14–20; military balance in (1919–1937), 66–70
Mehemet Ali. *See* Muhammad Ali
'men-on-the-spot,' 80
Metternich, Prince Clemens von, 27, 34–35, 45, 59n87
Mexico, 131, 137, 142
Middle East, 15, 31, 66, 74, 81, 94, 98, 108, 206, 244, 249, 270, 298, 341, 343. *See also* Arab world
Military Program Laws, 241, 298–99, 303
military training, in Africa, 207, 210–12, 212, 214–19, 215n51, 216n53, 223–24, 247–48, 251, 284, 287–88, 291–92, 294, 302, 307, 342–43, 353, 355, 418
Milne, Sir Alexander, 131
Minié rifle, 21
mission civilisatrice, 200, 238–39, 316, 324, 354

Mitterand, François, 203n19, 211, 237, 240, 271, 292–93, 298–99, 310–11, 314, 316, 323, 327n132, 327–28, 345, 347, 350, 356, 358, 360, 392
Mobutu Sese Seko, Joseph-Désire, 248, 285, 291–92, 310, 326–28, 327n132, 335–36, 345, 356, 391
Monagos, Jose, 135
Monroe Doctrine (1823), 142–43, 145, 177, 179–80, 187, 386, 415
Moody, Roscoe, 166–67
Morocco, 22, 160, 208–9, 291–92, 309n87, 315, 326
Mosul, 81, 87, 88, 96, 98, 101, 103, 113n26
Muhammad (Mehemet) Ali, 13, 16, 19–21, 30, 37, 41, 43–44, 46, 67
Mussolini, Benito, 99

Naples, revolt in (1820), 34
Napoleon, 15
Napoleonic Wars, 15, 17, 20, 27, 31, 34, 35, 37, 47, 50. *See also* French Wars
National Military Strategy of the United States, 3–4, 5
National Security Strategy of the United States, 3, 5
nationalism, 198, 247, 253–54, 261–62, 282, 315, 324, 332
NATO. *See* North Atlantic Treaty Organization
Nauplia, 23, 26
naval disarmament or limitation, 81, 89–91, 98, 106
naval forces and transport, French and African, 205, 210, 213, 218, 241, 270, 290–91, 303–5, 304n69, 338, 340–41
Navarino Bay, 20, 23, 26, 39, 46
neocolonialism, 211, 253, 272, 282, 297n52, 307, 327, 330, 358
Netherlands, 159

Nicaragua, 161, 163–67, 169, 181–82, 186–88
Niger, 198, 201, 210, 212, 216, 216n53, 219, 221, 224–25, 227, 229, 231–32, 248, 250, 265–66, 308, 319, 337, 345, 397
Nigeria, 204, 210, 231–32, 242–47, 260, 264–65, 268, 288–91, 290n24, 315, 317, 329–31, 336–37, 339, 345, 357, 391, 392
North Africa, 202, 205–9, 217, 272, 311, 334, 339–41, 350
North Atlantic Treaty Organization (NATO), 208–9, 272, 292n33, 299–300, 324, 328, 333, 339–40
nuclear arms (*force de frappe*), 204, 214, 219, 241, 272, 285–86, 318, 325, 328

offshore bombardment, 19, 25
oil, or petroleum, 65, 81, 95, 106, 232, 235, 266, 268, 270, 272, 284, 290, 295n43, 297, 297n52, 304–5, 319–21, 332, 339, 344–47, 354, 357, 359–80, 381, 411, 412
Olney, Richard, 168
Olympio, Sylvanus, 222, 265, 282n3
Operations by French troops:
Operation Barracuda, 296, 309, 325–26; *Operation Épervier*, 314, 352; *Operation Léopard*, 326; *Operation Manta*, 301, 314, 352; *Operation Turquoise* (including *Operation Amaryllis*), 232, 318, 348, 352n187, 352–54, 360, 392
ordinary, ships in, 18, 32, 52n20
Organization of African Unity (OAU), 241–42, 245, 268, 291–92, 307, 309, 328–31, 353
Ottoman Empire, 26, 37, 40, 41, 43, 47, 49, 50, 66, 378, 379, 380, 394, 409; army of, 17; commercial ties of, with Britain, 30, 41; navy of, 19, 20; decline of, 14, 22, 42, 44, 46, 49, 108. *See also* Eastern Question, Turkey

Pacific Ocean, 17, 40, 93
Page, Walter Hines, 176
Palestine, 66, 68, 71, 72, 74, 75, 79, 80, 81, 93, 94, 96, 97, 102, 104
Palmerston, Lord, 13, 31–34, 42, 44–47, 134, 140
Panama, 144, 181, 183, 187
Panama Canal, 93, 157–8, 165, 415
Pasha, Ibrahim, 20, 45
Pax Britannica, 13, 16, 17, 49
Peace Ballot, 86, 118n92
Peace of Paris, 100
peacekeeping, in eastern Mediterranean, 25–26, 78–80, 115n55
Permanent Court of International Justice, 87
Persia (Iran), 81, 82, 95, 98, 102, 106, 411
Persian Gulf, 17, 36, 77, 98
Peru, 129–30, 138
Plate River, Anglo-French blockade of (1847), 126, 132, 134, 385
Pompidou, Georges, 242, 253, 285, 322, 324, 331, 356
Port Mahon, 41
Portugal, 25, 26, 28, 36, 146, 142 and Africa, 247, 333–34, 336, 342
presidentialism, in French and African presidencies, 239–41, 261, 298, 300–301, 322–24, 347–48, 418
prestige, 14, 42, 197, 202, 262, 272, 283–84, 348–49, 351, 357, 417
Progressive movement in the United States, 158, 172, 174–76, 177, 184, 189
Prussia, 15, 27, 34, 37, 40, 49
Puerto Rico, 386
Purchase System, 16

Qaddafi, Moammar, 244–45, 269n178, 290, 305, 313–16, 353
Quintuple Treaty (1841), 36

Red Sea, 29, 80, 92
Regia Aeronautica (Italian air force), 92
Republic of Congo. *See* Congo-Brazzaville
Richelieu, Duc de, 27
Rio de Janeiro, 130
Roman Empire, 33
Roosevelt, Theodore, 172, 176–77, 187
Roosevelt Corollary, 386, 415
Rosas, Juan Manuel de, 134, 385
Rothschilds, 27–28
routes to India, 29, 35, 42, 45, 50
Royal Air Force (British), 67, 68, 69, 71, 74, 75, 76, 80, 83, 86, 95, 100, 105, 381, 383, 410
Royal Marines (British), 72, 76
Royal Navy (British), 13, 14, 15, 23, 36, 38, 39, 43, 44, 45, 46, 47, 69, 70, 72, 73, 74, 78, 85, 89, 90, 93, 95, 99, 100, 104, 105, 106, 109, 111n17, 379, 380, 381, 383, 384, 385, 394, 397, 407–8, 409, 410, 411, 413–14; in the Caribbean Sea (1903–1920), 157, 178, 180, 181; speed of response in Mediterranean Sea, 23–24, 74–76; in South America (1850–1900), 124–32; two-navy standard of, 135. *See also* two-power standard
Russia, 13, 14, 15, 17, 18, 19, 32, 34, 37, 39–40, 41, 49, 50, 108, 379, 380, 409. *See also* Soviet Union
Russo-Turkish War (1827–29), 32, 39, 47
Rwanda, 198, 199n3, 210, 212, 232, 250, 264, 281, 283, 287–89, 292, 294–95, 303, 305, 305n72, 308, 318, 328–29, 335, 337, 340, 343, 348,

352n187, 353n189, 352–54, 357, 360–61, 390, 391–92, 393, 401, 419

Salisbury, Lord, 147
Sam, Guillame, 163, 166
San Juan, 159, 386
Sassou-Nguesso, Dénis, 252, 332, 354, 357
Scapa Flow, 69, 93
Schlieffen Plan, 180
sea lanes, 33, 50, 109
seamanship, 20–21, 48, 54n32
Second Lima Conference (1864), 145
Senegal, 198, 201, 210, 212, 214, 216–20, 224–25, 227–28, 236–37, 243, 245, 248, 250, 252–55, 259, 263–65, 267, 291–92, 294, 294n40, 303–4, 306–10, 314, 322, 327, 330–32, 337, 339, 341
Senghor, Léopold, 227–28, 236–38, 240, 252–55, 263–65, 309, 356
Seppings, Sir Robert, 53n31
Service d'Action Civique, 286, 296. *See also* intelligence, and Foccart, Jacques
Service de Documentation Extérieure Contre Espionage (SDECE), 286, 296, 297n52. *See also* intelligence
shipbuilding, 19, 39, 69, 70, 81, 91, 93
shipping, British, 29, 33, 81
showing the flag, 24–25, 76
Sidqi, General Bakr, 78
Sigsbee, Charles, 180
Sinai Peninsula, 14, 29
Singapore, 68, 91, 98, 107, 119n104, 412
situational awareness, 199, 207, 418
slavery, 379, 380, 408
Smyrna, 23, 45, 78, 79, 88, 115n57, 116n58, 399
socialism and socialists,197, 203, 203n19, 208, 237, 247–48, 251, 266–70, 292n32, 295n43, 298, 310,

319–20, 327–28, 332, 334, 350, 417–18
Society of the Muslim Brothers, 96
Somalia, 248–49, 335, 337–39
Somaliland, 92, 99. See also Somalia
sonar. See asdic
South Africa, Republic of, 283, 290n24, 333–34, 341–42, 357, 392
South America, 383–85, 395, 396, 397, 400, 403, 413–14. See also Latin America
Soviet Union (USSR), 5, 93, 94, 97, 104382, 388, 390, 417; in Africa, 198, 203–4, 208, 245, 246–52, 256, 260, 268–70, 272, 282, 284–87, 289–90, 292, 292n32, 295n43, 296, 299, 305, 309–10, 315, 319, 332–43, 350, 353, 356–57, 417
Spain, 28, 36, 135–36, 142–44, 146, 149, 177, 247
Spanish Revolution, 34
St. Helena, 130
St. Petersburg Protocol (1826), 32
Stack, Sir Lee, 72, 102
Standard Oil, 101
status quo, 34–35, 42, 48, 49–50, 66, 87, 97, 98, 103, 104, 106, 107
steam-powered ships, 20, 51n4, 54n32
strategic adjustment, 68, 82
Sublime Porte, 41, 45, 49
submarines, 69, 70, 74, 91, 111–12n17, 112n23
Sudan, 265, 315, 335
Suez Canal, 65, 82, 98, 107, 333, 412
Sweden, 159
Syria, 14, 17, 20, 21, 40, 44, 66, 81, 91, 93
Syrian Crisis, 23, 30, 35, 38, 40, 44, 61n106, 109

Taft, William Howard, 173, 176, 182
Tagus River, 25, 26
Taliban, 1, 4

Tanzania, 244, 267, 291–92, 336
Taylor, Charles, 243–46, 329n141
TEEC. See Treasury Emergency Expenditure Committee
Teller Amendment, 175
Ten Year Rule, 84, 117n80
terrorism, 1–2, 405
Tirailleurs Sénégalais, 201n9, 205–7, 216–17, 270, 295
Tirpitz, Alfred von, 179, 181
Titchfield, Marquis de, 50
Togo, 198, 201, 210, 212, 219, 224, 228, 231, 243, 248, 250, 259, 265–66, 292, 294, 298, 307, 310, 322n120, 330, 337–39, 359
Toulon, French naval base at, 37
Touré, Sekou, 198, 247–48, 253–56, 261, 309, 341
Trafalgar, 17
Transjordan, 66, 75, 81, 82, 102
Treasury Emergency Expenditure Committee (TEEC), in Britain, 118n96
Treaty of Friendship, Commerce, and Navigation (1825), 145–46
Treaty of Lausanne, 74, 93, 100
Treaty of London (1827), 23
Treaty of Sèvres, 96, 100
Treaty of Unkiar-Skelessi (1833), 39, 63n139
Trenchard system, 71, 74, 76, 80, 105, 114n42, 381, 400, 410
Troppau, conference at, 34
Troupes de Marine, 205, 207, 218, 292, 295, 299–300, 303, 306–7, 312–14, 325
Trucial System, 35–36
Tunisia, 202, 209
Turkey, 14, 29, 32, 43, 46–47, 49, 67, 73–74, 76–79, 83, 87, 93–94, 97, 100, 103–4, 106, 108, 159, 381, 382, 394, 395, 398, 399, 412. See also Ottoman Empire

Turkish Petroleum Company, 95, 101
Turkish Straits, 39, 41, 44, 66, 93, 379. *See also* Bosphorus, Dardanelles
Turkish-Soviet Treaty of Friendship, 95
Turko-Egyptian fleet, 19, 20, 26, 44, 46, 53n25
Tutsi, 352n187, 353, 392
two-power standard, 18, 47

Uganda, 244, 283, 290n24, 292, 329, 336, 339, 343, 352n187, 353, 357, 392
United Kingdom. *See* Britain
United Nations (UN), 223–24, 226, 241, 243, 257, 268, 302, 328, 330, 353, 360
United States of America, 36, 40, 65, 69, 70, 73, 80, 89, 93, 94, 98, 135, 142–45, 149–50; and Africa, 198, 204, 208–9, 241, 244–45, 246, 248–51, 260, 268–69, 282–86, 289, 292, 292n32, 296, 303, 315, 322, 327, 330, 332, 334–36, 339–40, 342–43, 345, 349–50, 352n187, 353, 353n189, 356–57, 417, 383, 388, 389, 412, 417; and Caribbean, 173, 186–87, 378, 385–88, 398, 400, 402, 403, 404, 414–16; Marine Corps, 386, 398; and Mediterranean, 90, 93; military capabilities of, in the Caribbean, 159–172; navy of, 40–41, 93, 386; nonmilitary sources of influence of, in the Caribbean, 172–183; Progressive movement in, 158, 172, 174–76, 177, 184, 189, 386, 389, 402, 403, 415–16; security strategy of, 1–8, 377–78, 404–5; shaping ability of, in the Caribbean, 183–190
Upper Volta. *See* Burkina Faso
uranium, 232, 256, 265–66, 272, 284, 307n79, 319, 359
Urquhart, Brian, 47

Valparaiso, 130; Spanish bombardment of (1866), 135–36, 143–44, 149
Venezuelan Debt Crisis (1902–1903), 157–58, 159, 172–73, 177, 180, 183, 188, 386, 387, 415, 416
Venizelos, Eleutherios, 78, 100, 103
Vera Cruz, 131
Vichy, 201n9, 202–3, 206
Victorian thought, 139–40, 146, 147, 150–51

Wafd, in Egypt, 78, 94, 96, 104
War of 1812, 40, 62n128
War of the Pacific, 129, 148
Washington Conference, 89, 90, 93, 106, 411
Washington Naval Arms Limitation Treaties, 67, 89
Waterloo, 15
Welles, Sumner, 168, 174
Wellington, Duke of, 15, 16
Wilhelm II, Kaiser, 179–80
World Bank, 320, 332, 341, 356n193, 356n194, 356n195
World War I, 65, 66, 68, 69, 70, 74, 77, 80, 81, 83, 86, 91, 93, 97, 98, 103, 104, 107, 108
World War II, 7, 65, 104, 105, 197–98, 202–7, 209, 213, 229, 234, 261, 263, 270–71, 295, 324, 327, 359, 416, 418

Yugoslavia, 92

Zaïre (also Congo-Leopoldville, Congo-Kinshasa, Democratic Republic of Congo, DRC), 198–99, 210, 212, 228, 230, 245, 248, 250, 264, 281–83, 285, 287–92, 294–96, 298, 290n24, 303, 306, 308–10, 314, 318, 326–32, 327n132, 334–40, 342–43, 345, 354, 357, 359, 390, 391–92, 393
Zeyala, Jose Santos, 164–65, 169, 181–82, 184, 187

About the Authors

Edward Rhodes is Dean for Social and Behavioral Sciences at Rutgers University. The author of *Power and MADness: The Logic of Nuclear Coercion* (Columbia, 1989) and co-editor of *The Politics of Strategic Adjustment: Ideas, Institutions, and Interest* (Columbia, 1998), Rhodes has published extensively on U.S. national security policy, U.S. naval strategy and force posture, and problems of deterrence.

Jonathan M. DiCicco is a Ph.D. candidate in international relations at Rutgers University; he has served the Center for Global Security and Democracy both as a research associate and associate director. DiCicco's research focuses primarily on the dynamics of long-term international conflict. He is completing a dissertation investigating the impact of war on international rivalries and has coauthored an article in the *Journal of Conflict Resolution*.

Sarah S. Milburn is a research associate at the Center for Global Security and Democracy. She is a Ph.D. candidate in comparative politics at Rutgers University, working on francophone African political economy and security issues. She is a country specialist for Amnesty International, specializing in francophone Central Africa and human rights concerns during armed conflict, including child soldiers, military intervention, and the arms trade.

Thomas C. Walker is Assistant Professor of Political Science at the State University of New York–Albany. He received his Ph.D. in 2000 from Rutgers University. Walker's research interests include interstate alliances, militarization, and international conflict, as well as the application of political philosophy to international relations theory. Among Walker's recent publications is an article in *International Studies Quarterly*.